JESUS

Peace be with him
Through Shi'ite Narrations

Selected by
Mahdi Muntazir Qa'im

JESUS

Peace be with him
Through Shi'ite Narrations

Selected by
Mahdi Muntazir Qa'im

Translated by
Muhammad Leganhausen

بسم الله الرحمن الرحيم

Published by
Tahrike Tarsile Qur'an, Inc.
Publishers & Distributors of Holy Qur'an
80-08 51st Avenue
Elmhurst, New York 11373

بسم الله الرحمن الرحيم

Published by
Tahrike Tarsile Qur'an, Inc.
Publishers & Distributors of Holy Qur'an
80-08 51st Avenue
Elmhurst, New York 11373
E-mail: read@koranusa.org
http://www.koranusa.org

First U.S. Edition 2005

Library of Congress Catalog Number:

British Library Cataloguing in Publication Data

ISBN: 1-879402-14-9

بسم الله الرحمن الرحيم

In the name of Allah,
the Beneficent, the Merciful

ALHODA
Publishers & Distributors
55 – 57 Banner street
London EC1y 8PX
Tel: 020 74904321
Fax: 020 74904849

عيسى عليه السلام

فى القرآن وروايات الشيعة

المؤلّف

مهدى منتظرقائم

المترجم

الدكتور محمّد لِكَنهاوسِن

بالتعاون مع المؤلّف

TABLE OF CONTENTS

الفهرس

PREFACE

What is offered here is a fairly comprehensive selection of the Āyāt (signs) of Holly Qur'ān and narrations pertaining to Jesus(a) said to have been reported by the Shī'ī Imams, peace be with them. It is generally admitted that not everything reported in this literature is correct, and the science of hadith has been developed by Muslim scholars precisely for the purpose of sorting through the narrations and evaluating their strength. No attempt has been made in what follows to select only hadiths considered reliable. The narrations selected provide an overview of what various reporters of hadiths have claimed that the Imams have said about Jesus(a). At the same time, we cannot claim that our selection exhausts all such narrations. Sometimes we have found several reports that differ only in some insignificant details, in which case we have generally selected the most complete form of the report. Also omitted are reports in which Jesus is mentioned only incidentally, although where such incidental mention seemed interesting to us, we have provided the excerpt from the hadith. The *isnād*, or chains of transmission that accompany the reports, have been omitted from the English translations since they would only be of use to those who have fluency in Arabic.

It is rather disheartening to find that so much misunderstanding remains between Christians and Muslims in the world today. Hopefully the collection presented here will be seen by Christians as a gift from the Shī'ah to show the reverence they have for Jesus(a). The vision of Jesus(a) to be found here is different from that of Christianity, and the difference is bound to lead some to respond negatively, "No. The Christ we know is not like that." We are not concerned to argue here for the veracity of the vision of Christ presented. Of course Christians will deny what conflicts with their beliefs. However, it is hoped that the reader will be able to bracket the question of what reports about Jesus ﷺ are best considered factual, because this question depends on the standards used for such evaluations, whether doctrinal, historical or otherwise. According to our faith, as Shī'ah, the overall picture of Christ presented below is true, although questions may be raised about particular narrations or details thereof. This is how we think of Christ ﷺ. It is a different way of thinking about him from what is familiar to Christians. However, it is by no means disrespectful, and it offers a way to understand the more general religious vision of Islam, particularly Shī'i Islam. It is up to our readers to chose to respond by focusing on differences and rejecting what is contrary to their beliefs, or to find how much we have in common and on this basis to search for what is of value in the Muslim's view, even where it differs from what one is prepared to accept.

We expect that our readers will include English speaking Muslims, both Sunni and Shī'i, as well as Christians. To them we offer this collection as an opportunity to reacquaint themselves with Islamic teachings about Jesus, and hope that it will inspire better relations between Muslims and Christians. Even as we stand fast in our own faith, we should be prepared to deepen our appreciation of the commitment of Christians to follow the teachings of one held in such high esteem in the Qur'ān and hadith.

In the glorious Qur'ān, in a passage describing the annunciation to the Blessed Virgin Mary, Jesus ﷺ is described as a Word from God: ﴾*O Mary! Verily Allah gives you the glad tidings of a Word from Him; his name is the Messiah, Jesus son of Mary, prominent in this world and in the Hereafter of those near [to God].*﴿ (3:44)

The context in which this *āyah* was revealed was one of interreligious encounter. It is said that the Christians of Najran sent a delegation to the Prophet of Islam ﷺ at Mecca to question him about the teachings of Islam concerning Jesus ﷺ, and that God revealed the above and other *āyāt* of *Sūrah Āl-i 'Imrān* in response. The response is not merely a denial of Christian teachings, although the divinity of Christ is clearly rejected, but an affirmation of much believed by Christians, as well, even the designation of Christ as *logos:* ﴾*O People of the Book! Do not transgress in your religion, and do not say of Allah but the Truth. Verily, the Messiah, Jesus the son of Mary, is only an apostle of Allah and His Word which He conveyed unto Mary, and a Spirit from Him.*﴿ (4:171) So, in addition to being called the Word of God, Jesus ﷺ is also called the Spirit of God, and in some of the narrations reported in the Shī'ī tradition, this title is used.

Of course, the interpretation of the *logos* in Christian theology differs markedly from the interpretation of the *kalimah* by Muslim scholars. For the Christian, according to the Gospel of John, the Word was God and the Word became flesh. For the Muslim, on the other hand, the Word is creature, even while it is the creative principle, for it is in God's utterance of the word "Be!" that creation takes place. To call Christ the Word of Allah is not to deify him, but to verify his status as prophet. Because of his high status as prophet, Jesus ﷺ becomes a complete manifestation of God, one who conveys the message of God, one who can speak on behalf of God, and thus, the Word of God. Jesus ﷺ becomes the Word of God not because of an incarnation whereby his flesh becomes divine, but because his spirit is refined to such an extent that it becomes a mirror whereby divinity comes to be known. The temple is holy not because of any inherent sanctity in the structure, but because it is the place of the worship of God.

The differences between Islamic and Christian thinking about Jesus ﷺ are as important as they are subtle. Both accept the virgin birth, although it is ironic that a growing number of liberal Christians have come to have doubts about this miracle while Muslims remain steadfast! Among the other miracles attributed to

Jesus ﷺ in the Glorious Qur'ān are the revival of the dead and the creation of a bird from clay, but all of the miracles performed by Jesus ﷺ are expressly *by the permission of Allah.* Just as in the miracle of his birth, Jesus ﷺ came into the world by a human mother and divine spirit, so too, his miracles are performed as human actions with divine permission. In this regard the error of the Christians is explained by the great Sūfī theoretician, Ibn al-'Arabī, as follows:

This matter has led certain people to speak of incarnation and to say that, in reviving the dead, he is God. Therefore, since they conceal God, Who in reality revives the dead, in the human form of Jesus, He has said, ﴿*They are concealers [unbelievers] who say that God is the Messiah, son of Mary.*﴾ (5:72)[(1)]

The point is that Muslims can find God in Jesus ﷺ without deifying him, and furthermore that deifying Jesus ﷺ is really an obstacle to their finding God in Jesus ﷺ, for deification is an obstacle to searching in Jesus ﷺ for anything beyond him.

One of the central questions of Christian theology is: "Who was Jesus Christ?" The formulation of answers to this question is called *Christology.* In this area of theology, Christians have debated the significance of the historical Jesus as opposed to the picture of Jesus presented in the traditions of the Christian Churches and the Biblical understanding of Jesus. The time has come for Muslims to begin work in this area, as well. Through the development of an Islamic Christology we can come to a better understanding of Islam as contrasted with Christianity, and Islam in consonance with Christianity, too. Indeed, the first steps in this direction are laid out for us in the Qur'ān itself, in the verses mentioned above and others.

Contemporary work toward an Islamic Christology is scarce.

---

[1] Ibn al-'Arabī, *The Bezels of Wisdom (Fuṣūṣ al-Ḥikam),* tr. R. W. J. Austin (Lahore: Suhail, 1988), p. 177.

Christian authors have tended to stress the salvific function of Jesus(عليه السلام) which seems to have no place in Islam, which leads to questions of religious pluralism when Christians ask one another whether Christ(عليه السلام) can be the savior of Muslims and others who are not Christians. Christians should be reminded that Muslims accept Jesus(عليه السلام) as savior, along with all the other prophets, for the prophetic function is to save humanity from the scourge of sin by conveying the message of guidance revealed by God. The important difference between Islam and Christianity here is not over the issue of whether Jesus(عليه السلام) saves, but how he saves. Islam denies that salvation is through redemption resulting from the crucifixion, and instead turns its attention to the instruction provided in the life of the prophets(عليهم السلام). Christian scholarship on Jesus as presented in Islam tends to ignore *ḥadīth* and focus on the Qur'ān. Often the research is polemical as authors attempt to support an interpretation of the Qur'ān that is more in keeping with Christian than Islamic doctrine. A general review and introduction to this work may be found in Neal Robinson's *Christ in Islam and Christianity.*[1]

Muslims, on the other hand, have tended to produce their own polemical works showing how much of what is in the Bible is consistent with the Islamic view of Christ(عليه السلام) as prophet rather than as a person of the Trinity.[2] Aḥmad Deedat's work along these lines has attracted much attention. More profound insights into the differences between Islam and other faiths, including Christianity, may be found in the writings of Frithjof Schuon, Shaykh 'Īsā Nūr al-Dīn Aḥmad, who presents the beginnings of a genuine Christology

---

(1) Neal Robinson, *Christ in Islam and Christianity* (Albany: SUNY, 1991), ch. 2. This work also contains an excellent survey of how Muslim historians and apologists have approached issues pertaining to Christ and Christianity, and an examination of various exegeses of the Qur'ān on the verses about Jesus.

(2) For example, see Ahmed Deedat, *Was Jesus Crucified?* (Chicago: Kazi, 1992).

from a Sufi perspective in his *Islam and the Perennial Philosophy.*(1) In his *The Muslim Jesus : Sayings and Stories in Islamic Literature*, Tarif Khalidi has collected Islamic references to Jesus from the eighth to the 18th centuries, including mystical works, historical texts about prophets and saints and selections from the *hadīth* and Qur'ān.(2) As Khalidi notes, these writings, form the largest body of texts relating to Jesus in any non-Christian literature.

These days there is much discussion of dialogue between different faith communities. Conferences have been held for this purpose in the Islamic Republic of Iran as well as in Africa, Europe and the United States. Perhaps one of the best ways Christians can find common ground for discussion with Muslims is to become familiar with the portrait of Jesus(a) presented in Islamic sources, the most important of which are the Qur'ān and *aḥādīth*, and for the latter, no matter what one's religious orientation, it must be admitted that the narrations handed down through the Household of the Prophet(s) deserve careful attention. For those of us who have the honor of being counted among the Shī'ah, the importance of what has been related by the *Ahl al-Bayt* weighs especially heavily, as it should, according to the famous *ḥadīth al-thaqalayn*, in which the Prophet(s), in the last year of his life, is reported to have said:

Verily, I am leaving with you two weighty things *(thaqalayn)*: the Book of Allah and my kindred, my household, for indeed, the two of them will never separate until they return to me by the Pond [of *Kauthar* on the Last Day].

Perhaps some Christians will be dismissive of what is said of Jesus(a) in the Islamic narrations because the main debate about contemporary Christology among Christians is whether research

(1) Frithjof Schuon, *Islam and the Perennial Philosophy* (Lahore: Suhail, 1985).

(2) Tarif Khalidi, *The Muslim Jesus : Sayings and Stories in Islamic Literature* (Cambridge: Harvard University Press, 2003).

about the historical Jesus(a) is relevant to religion, or whether knowledge of Jesus(a) requires attention to the role he plays in the Church and in theology. The Islamic narrations, coming centuries after the life of Christ(a) (and in some cases more than a century after the life of Muḥammad(s)) will likely be dismissed by liberal Christians in pursuit of a portrait of Jesus(a) based on the standards of historical research currently accepted in the West. The neo-orthodox Christian claims that the Savior is not to be found in history, but in the Church, so it will not be surprising if he displays no interest in what Islam has to say about Christ(a). However, the Christian may find that the Islamic perspective illuminates a middle ground between the historian's emphasis on the natural and the ecclesiastical emphasis on the supernatural. The humanity of Jesus(a) is evident in the narrations of the Shī'ah, but it is a humanity transformed, a perfected humanity, and as such there is no denying its supernatural dimension.

The Muslim always seems to appear as a stranger to the Christian, but perhaps it is from the stranger that the Christian can best come to know his savior. The crucifix has hung in the Church for so long that it becomes difficult for the Christian to find significance there. The attraction of the quest for the historical Jesus is that it provides a fresh look at the subject, even if that quest is marred by naturalistic presumptions inimical to the religious outlook. By trying to see Jesus(a) as the Muslim sees him, the Christian may find his savior come to life, lifted up to God in his own inner life rather than crucified.(1)

If we have given reason for Christians to study the narrations of the Shī'ah about Jesus(a), the question of the value of such study for Muslims remains. Some might wonder why, when we have the Qur'ān and *sunnah*, we should be especially interested in Jesus(a).

---

(1) We are reminded by the glorious Qur'ān: "Recall when God said: 'O Jesus, I will take you away and lift you up to Me.'". (3:54)

Preface

To begin with, Jesus, along with the prophets Noah, Abraham, Moses, Peace be with them, and Muḥammad has a special status in Islam as one of the greatest prophets, the *ūlū' al-'azm,* the prophets who brought the divine law. What was revealed to the last of them is a confirmation of what was revealed to the others. The truth of the revelation is not to be found in its particularity but in its universality, and we come to understand this best when we understand the teachings of all the prophets. Is this not why so much attention is given to the previous prophets in the Qur'ān?

All of the prophets have brought a gospel of love, love of God and love of neighbor and love even for the meanest of His creatures. So, in the reports narrated below we find Jesus giving some of his food to the creatures of the sea. At the same time, however, this love is not to be confused with a sentimentalism which would prevent the execution of the divine law. Jesus found fault with the Pharisees not because of their regard for the exterior forms of religion, but because of their disregard for its interior forms, that is, because of their hypocrisy.(1)

The Words of the Spirit of Allah reported in the selections that follow are primarily concerned with morals. These are Christian morals and at the same time Islamic morals. Today Christendom is in a state of moral upheaval. Peculiarly modern ideas of what is right and wrong have found their way into the theologians' understandings of ethics. Significant areas of agreement are difficult to find. The simple morality taught by Jesus and which continues to be emphasized in Islam resonates in the narrations of the Shī'ah. While excessive asceticism is forbidden, we are to turn, like Jesus, away from the world to find refuge in God.

From the following narrations we not only become reacquainted with the moral teachings of Jesus and with his character, but we also

---

(1) Cf. Matt. 23:25.

discover what the dear friends of Allah, the Household of the Prophet ﷺ found it important to transmit about him, and thereby we get a glimpse into their moral teachings and characters, too.

SOURCES

Biḥār al-Anwār is a collection of hadiths in Arabic written by Mawlā Muḥammad Bāqir ibn Muḥammad Taqī, known as Majlīsī the Second, or simply 'Allāmah Majlīsī (A.H. 1037-1110). He is one of the most prolific Shī'ī writers, and was Shaykh al-Islām during the Safavid period. He authored thirteen books in Arabic and fifty-three in Farsi. His largest and most important work is *Biḥār al-Anwār al-Jāmi'ah li-Durar Akhbār al-A'immah al-Aṭhār.* This is the most comprehensive of all collections of Shī'ī hadiths, and it includes almost all hadiths attributed to the Prophet ﷺ through Shī'ī chains of transmission, almost all of the *aḥādīth qudsī* (narrations of the words of God revealed to the Prophet ﷺ not included in the Qur'ān) and other narrations attributed to the Imams ؑ. One of the features of this work is that 'Allāmah Majlīsī went to great pains to separate his own views from the transmission of the *aḥādith.* It took him thirty-six years to compile the work, from A.H. 1070 to A.H. 1106, with the cooperation of other scholars of the day and students. In the first volume, he identifies his sources, and later in the same volume he evaluates their reliability. His sources include close to four hundred titles, among which are sixteen works of Shaykh Ṣadūq, sixteen works of Shaykh Ṭūsī, eighteen works of Shaykh Mufīd, twelve works of Sayyid Murtaḍā, twelve works of Shaḥīd Awwal, twenty-one works of Sayyid ibn Ṭāwūs, twenty-three works of 'Allāmah Ḥillī and twelve works of Shahīd Thānī. He also made use of ninety works by Sunnī authors for correcting the words of the narrations or determining their meanings, and he mentions each of these sources by name in his introduction. There are three extant editions that have been published of *Biḥār*, one is a lithograph print in twenty-five volumes, known as the old edition. The second is that of *Dar al-*

Kutub al-Islāmiyyah, Tehran, Bazār Sulṭāni, in one hundred ten volumes (no date), known as the new edition. In the Terhan edition, volumes 54, 55 and 56 contain a table of contents. The third edition is really just a reprint of the Tehran edition published by Mu'assasah al-Wafā' of Beirut. In the Beirut edition, the contents have been moved to volumes 108, 109 and 110, and a volume 0 was added in which there is an introduction to the author and the authors of his sources.(1) We have used the new edition published in Tehran.

Tuḥaf al-'Uqūl fī Mā Jā'a min al-Ḥikam wa al-Mawā'iẓ 'an Āl al-Rasūl by Abū Muḥammad Ḥasan ibn 'Alī ibn Ḥusayn ibn Shu'bah Ḥarrānī Ḥalabī is one of the most well known collections of Shī'ī narrations. The author was a contemporary of Shaykh Ṣadūq and died in A.H. 381. Shaykh Mufīd reports narrations from him, and he, in turn, reports traditions from Shaykh Abū 'Alī Muḥammad ibn Hammām, who died in A.H. 336. The book contains narrations from the Prophetﷺ followed by narrations of the first eleven Imamsعليه السلام in order. After this, there are four more parts to the book: (1) the whispered counsel (*munājāt*) of God to Mosesعليه السلام; (2) the whispered counsel of God to Jesusعليه السلام; (3) the advice of the Messiahعليه السلام in the gospel and other places; and (4) advice of Mufaḍḍal ibn 'Umar, one of the companions of Imam Ṣādiqعليه السلام to the Shī'ah. In the introduction to this work, Ibn Shu'bah writes:

I did not mention the chains of transmission in order to reduce the volume of the book and keep it short. Most of the narrations in this book are ones I have heard. Most of them pertain to manners and wisdom which testify to their own validity and the correctness of their attribution.

Scholars in this field consider the work to be reliable and refer to it in support of their opinions about hadiths and fiqh. The book was

---

(1) This infomation is given in the article "*Biḥār al-Anwār*" by Bahā' al-Dīn Khoramshāhī in *Dayirah al-Ma'ārif Tashshayyu',* Vol. 3, (Tehran: *Mu'assasah Dayirah al-Ma'ārif Tashshayyu',* 1371/1992), p. 91-98.

first published in A.H. 1303 in Iran, and later in Iraq, Lebanon and Iran.[1] The edition we have used is that of Qom: Mu'assasah al-Nashr al-Islāmī, A.H. 1416.

The narrations we have translated from *Tuḥaf al-'Uqūl* are given without mention of a chain of transmission, although there is an indication in this work that they are reported by Imam Mūsā ibn Ja'far al-Kāẓim ﷺ.[2] Part of the narration may also be found in *al-Kāfī*, Vol. 2, p. 319, attributed to Imam Ṣadiq ﷺ.

Al-Kāfī is one of the four most authoritative sources of Shī'i narrations. It was written by Muḥammad ibn Ya'qūb ibn Isḥāq al-Kulaynī al-Rāzī (d. A.H. 328) and contains six thousand narrations divided into thirty-four sections. It took twenty years to write during the minor occultation of the twelfth Imam ﷺ. It has been published in eight volumes in Tehran by *Dār al-Kutub al-Islāmiyyah.* We have used the 1362/1983 edition. The whispered counsel of God to Jesus ﷺ translated below from *al-Kāfī,* Vol. 8, 131-141, may also be found in *Tuḥaf al-'Uqūl,* p. 496, without mention of the name of the Imam from whom it was narrated, and in *Al-Amālī* of Shaykh Ṣadūq it is narrated from Imam Ṣādiq ﷺ.

Another of the "four books" of Shī'i narrations containing reports about Jesus ﷺ is *Tahdhīb al-Aḥkām* by Shaykh al-Ṭā'ifah Abū Ja'far Muḥammad ibn al-Ḥasan ibn 'Alī al-Ṭūsī (b. A.H. 385, d. A.H. 460). There are said to have been four hundred small books of Shī'i narrations extant during the author's lifetime, known as *Uṣūl al-Arba'ah Mi'ah,* and the author claims to have compiled this collection from these. This book is a commentary on *Al-Muqni'ah* of Shaykh Mufīd, a work of jurisprudence containing references to hadiths. The edition of the *Tahdhīb al-Aḥkām* we have used is that of

---

[1] See the article "Tuḥaf al-'Uqūl" by Sayyid Mahdī Ḥā'irī in *Dayirah al-Ma'ārif Tashshayyu',* Vol. 4, (Tehran: *Mu'assasah Dayirah al-Ma'ārif Tashshayyu',* 1373/1994), p. 169.

[2] *Tuḥaf al-'Uqūl,* p. 392.

Tehran: *Dār al-Kutub al-Islāmiyyah*, no date.

Mustadrak al-Wasā'il wa Mustanbaṭ al-Masā'il by Hājj Mīrzā Ḥusayn Nūrī al-Ṭabarsī ibn Muḥammad Taqī (A.H. 1254-1320) contains more than twenty-three thousand narrations and has been published in Qom by *Mu'assasah Āl al-Bayt*ﷺ *li Iḥyā' al-Turāth,* first edition published in A.H. 1408. This is considered one of the four most important collections of Shī'ī hadiths of the modern period, that is, after the eleventh/seventeenth century, the others being *Al-Wāfī* by Fayḍ Kāshānī, *Biḥār al-Anwār* by 'Allāmah Majlisī and *Wasā'il al-Shī'ah* by Shaykh Ḥurr al-'Āmilī. It was written in order to complete the narrations not included in the *Wasā'il al-Shī'ah.*(1)

Muḥammad Legenhausen
The Imam Khomeini Education and Research Institute, Qom
Rajab 1426/August 2005

---

(1) I would like to express my gratitude to 'Abbās Ḥusaynī for assistance in the translation of some of the Ḥadīths and to Muntaẓir Qā'im for his guidance in the translation of all of them. Thanks also are due to Prof. Tofighi for his suggestions. We are also grateful to the Imam Khomeini Education and Research Institute for providing the opportunity for this work.

INTRODUCTION

In the Name of Him the Exalted

Jesus the son of Mary has always been revered and held in high esteem among Christians and Muslims, but there are differences as well as common points. Those who are familiar with the character of Christ, whether Muslim or Christian, will find many such points by reading this book.

Prior to the publication of this collection, the valuable book of Tarif Khalidi, The Muslim Jesus, Sayings and Stories in Islamic Literature, has introduced Jesus as understood mostly through narrations found in the collections of Sunni Muslims. Today, the present book, Jesus through The Qur'ān and Shi'ite Narrations, introduces Jesus from the perspective of The Qur'ān and the Imams of the Household of the Prophet, peace be with them.

According to Shi'ite narrations, 'Imrān and Ḥannah were the parents of Mary; and Allah revealed to Imrān: "I will grant you a boy, blessed, who will cure the blind and the leper and who will raise the dead by My permission." When Mary was born Ḥannah said: "O my Lord! Verily I have delivered a female," and when Mary grew up, the angels said to her, ❮*O Mary! Verily Allah has chosen you and purified you and chosen you above the women of the worlds.*❯ (3:42)

Then the Sure Spirit (*al-Rūḥ al-Amīn*) came down at noon on a Friday and said to her: ❮*I am but a messenger come from your Lord, to give you a boy most pure.*❯ (19:19) Then he blew into her breast and she became pregnant with Jesus. When Jesus, the spirit of Allah and His word, was born, on the night of the twenty-fifth of the twelfth lunar month, Dhū al-Qa'dah, Mary said: ❮*Oh! Would that I had died before this, and had been forgotten in oblivion*❯ (19:23).

المقدّمة

بسمه تعالي

لقد كان عيسى بن مريم عليه السلام ولازال موضع احترام النصارى والمسلمين وتقديرهم، وبينهما فيه نقاط التقاء وافتراق؛ وسيقف المطّلعون على ملامح المسيح عليه السلام، مسيحيّين كانوا أم مسلمين، بقراءتهم لهذا الكتاب، على كثير من تلك الوجوه المختلفة.

قبل هذا قام الكتاب القيّم "عيسى لدى المسلمين"[١] للسيّد طريف الخالدى، بتعريف عيسى عليه السلام انطلاقاً من أحاديث أهل السنّة بالخصوص, وقد جاء هذا الكتاب اليوم: "عيسي في القرآن وروايات الشيعة" محاولاً استجلاء صورته من خلال القرآن وما ورد عن أئمّة أهل البيت عليهم السلام.

إنّ والدَىّ مريم –وفق النصوص الشيعيّة– هما عمران وحنّة؛ وإنّ الله أوحي إلي عمران: ﴿إنّى واهِبٌ لكَ ذكَراً مباركاً يُبرِئُ الأكمهَ والأبرَصَ ويُحيى الموتَي بإذْنِي.﴾ ولمّا ولدت مريم، قالت حنّة: ﴿رَبِّ إنّى وَضَعْتُها أنثَي!﴾ ولمّا كبرت مريم، قالت الملائكة:﴿يا مَرْيَمُ، إنّ اللهَ اصطفاكِ وطَهّرَكِ واصطفاكِ عَلَي نِساءِ العالَمينَ.﴾

ثمّ هبط الروح الأمين في ظهر جمعة قائلاً لها: ﴿إنّما أنا رَسُولُ رَبِّكِ لِأهَبَ لكِ غُلاماً زَكِيّاً.﴾ فتفل في جيبها فحملت بعيسي عليه السلام, فولد عيسي، روح الله وكلمته، سحر ليلة الخامس والعشرين من ذى القعدة, وقالت مريم: ﴿يا لَيْتَنِى مِتُّ قَبْلَ هَذا وَكُنْتُ نَسْياً مَنْسِيّاً.﴾

---

[1]. Tarif Khalidi, The Muslim Jesus, Sayings and Stories in Islamic Literature, Harvard University Press, 2001.

Then Allah opened the tongue of Jesus and he said: ﴾*Verily, I am a servant of Allah. He has given me the Book, and has made me a prophet, and has made me blessed wherever I may be. And He has enjoined on me prayer and charity (zakāh) as long as I live.*﴿ (19:30-31) Allah made his speech as an exoneration of his mother.

That night Iblīs (the devil) went to the East and West in search of him. Then he found him in a room of a convent, with the angels surrounding him. He tried to get close to him. The angels shouted, "Get away!" He said to them, "Who is his father?" They answered, "His case is like that of Adam." Iblīs said, "Verily, I will mislead four fifths of the people by him." Allah, the mighty and magnificent, only wanted to make his affair as a sign and mark for it to be known by this that He has power over all things.

Jesus stood as an authority (*ḥujjah*) when he was three years old. When he reached seven years he spoke as a prophet and messenger, while he received revelation from Allah, the Exalted. When Allah commissioned him, He bestowed upon him light, knowledge and wisdom, and the knowledge of all the prophets before him, and He added to this the Gospel. He commissioned him to Jerusalem (*Bayt al-Maqdis*) for the children of Israel to invite them to His book and wisdom and to faith in Allah and His prophet. According to Shi'ite belief, if one denies Jesus the son of Mary عليه السلام, but confesses to all the other prophets, he is still not considered a believer.

Jesus was noble, a worshipper, an ascetic, an itinerant, possessor of splendor, was loving to all the believers and excellent in his conduct with others. His ring was engraved with two sayings he took from the Gospel, "Blessed is the servant because of whom Allah is remembered, and woe unto the servant because of whom Allah is forgotten."

His *shariah* (law) included *tawḥīd* (divine unity), *ikhlāṣ* (purity), the dismissal of peers [for Allah], and the liberal uprightness of human nature. He made lawful what is pure in it, and prohibited what is filthy, and He removes from them their burdens and the shackles that

فأطلق الله لسان عيسي عليه السلام، فقال: ﴿إنِّي عَبْدُ اللهِ آتانِيَ الكِتابَ، وَجَعَلَنِي نَبِيّاً، وَجَعَلَنِي مُبارَكاً أيْنَ ما كُنْتُ، وأوْصانِي بالصلاةِ والزَّكاةِ مادُمتُ حَيّاً.﴾ فجعل الله، منطقه عذراً لأمّه.

أتي إبليس تلك الليلة المشرق والمغرب يطلبه, فوجده في بيت دير قد حقّت به الملائكة, فذهب يدنو, فصاحت الملائكة: «تَنَحَّ» فقال لهم: «مَنْ أبُوهُ؟» فأجابت الملائكة: «مَثَلُهُ كَمَثَلِ آدَمَ» فقال إبليس: «لأضِلَّنَّ بِهِ أرْبَعَةَ أخْماسِ الناسِ.» وإنّما أراد الله، عزّ وجلّ، أن يجعل أمره عليه السلام آية وعلامة, ليعلم بذلك أنّه علي كلّ شيء قدير.

نعم, قام عيسي عليه السلام بالحجّة وهو ابن ثلاث سنين, فلمّا بلغ سبع سنين تكلّم بالنبوة والرسالة حين أوحي الله، تعالي، اليه. ولمّا بعثه الله استودعه النور والعلم والحكمة وعلوم الأنبياء قبله جميعها، وزاده الإنجيل، وبعثه إلي بيت المقدس إلي بني إسرائيل، يدعوهم إلي كتابه وحكمته, وإلي الإيمان بالله وبرسوله.

إنّ اعتقاد الشيعة, أنّ من انكر عيسي بن مريم عليه السلام وأقرّ بمن سواه من الرسل لم يؤمن.

كان عيسي عليه السلام، رجلاً, كريماً, عابداً, زاهداً, سائحاً, ذا بهاء, محبّاً لكل مؤمن, حسن المعاشرة, وكان نقش خاتمه حرفين اشتقّهما من الإنجيل: «طُوبَي لِعَبْدٍ ذُكِرَ اللهُ مِنْ أجْلِهِ وَوَيْلٌ لِعَبْدٍ نُسِيَ اللهُ مِنْ أجْلِهِ.»

كان من شريعته التّوحيد, والإخلاص, وخلع الأنداد, والفطرة الحنيفيّة السّمحة. أحلّ فيها الطيّبات, وحرّم فيها الخبيثات, ووضع عنهم إصرهم والأغلال التي كانت عليهم.

were upon them.[1] His law included the prayer, alms, and also restricting marriage to one woman, for the sake of women's affairs.

Admonitions and parables were sent down to him in the *Injīl,* but there was no law of retaliation (*qiṣāṣ*) in it nor precepts of retribution (*aḥkām al-ḥudūd*), and no obligations for inheritance. What was sent down to him was a mitigation of what was sent down to Moses in the Torah. Jesus commanded those with him who were believers and followed him that they believe in the law of the Torah, the laws of all prophets and the *Injīl.*"

The Christians differed among themselves about Jesus ﷺ. Some of them said, the Eternal, the Mighty and Magnificent, is united with Christ, His son. But the Eternal does not become non-eternal by this creature who is Jesus, and Jesus does not become eternal by the Eternal who is Allah.

His people split into three sects: a sect of believers, and they were the disciples, a sect of his enemies, and they were the Jews, and a sect that exaggerated about him, and they left the faith.

The apostles were twelve men and they were his followers and helpers. When Jesus ﷺ asked, "Who are my helpers for Allah?" The disciples said, "We will be the helpers of Allah."[2] So, they were called *Naṣārā* because of their help to the religion of Allah.

Jesus lived for thirty-three years; he was not killed nor crucified, but it was made to appear so to the Christians. On the night of the twenty-first of Ramaḍān he was raised while there were nine thousands three hundred thirteen angles with him. He was raised from the earth alive and his soul was taken between heaven and earth, then he was raised to heaven and his soul was returned to him. He will come down to the world before the Resurrection day with the twelfth Imam of the Household of the Prophet, and invite the people to Allah. In the resurrection will come a man in a group and the angels will be around him with wings outspread and the light will be in front of them. Then the people of the Garden will crane their

---

(1) See (7:157).

(2) See (61:14).

وكان من شريعته الصلاة, والزكاة, والدية, وعدم جواز تزويج الرجال سوي الواحدة؛ مراعاة لمصلحة النساء.

لقد أنزل عليه في الإنجيل مواعظ وأمثال، وليس فيها قصاص, ولا أحكام حدود, ولا فرض مواريث. كما أنزل عليه تخفيف ما كان نزّل علي موسيعليه السلام فى التوراة. وأمر عيسيعليه السلام من معه ممّن تبعه من المؤمنين أن يؤمنوا بشريعة التوراة, وشرائع النبيّين جميعاً, والإنجيل أيضاً.

أمّا النصاري فقد اختلفت فيهعليه السلام, فبعضهم قال: «إنَّ القَدِيمَ، عَزَّ وَجَلَّ، اتَّحَدَ بِالمَسِيحِ ابنهِ», ولكنّ القديم لا يصير محدثاً لوجود هذا المحدث الذى هو عيسي، كما أنّ عيسي لا يصير قديماً لوجود القديم الذى هو الله.

وقد افترق قوم عيسيعليه السلام ثلاث فرق: فرقة مؤمنون، وهم الحواريون؛ وفرقة عادوه، وهم اليهود؛ وفرقة غلوا فيه فخرجوا عن الإيمان.

وكان الحواريون اثني عشر، وكانوا شيعته وأنصاره، وإذ سأل عيسيعليه السلام: ﴿مَنْ أنْصارى إلي الله؟﴾ قالوا: ﴿نَحْنُ أنْصارُ اللهِ﴾ فسمّوا النصاري؛ لنصرة دين الله.

لقد عمّر عيسيعليه السلام في الدنيا ثلاثة وثلاثين سنة، وما قتل وما صلب, ولكن شبّه للنصاري, بل رفع ليلة إحدي وعشرين من رمضان ومعه تسعة آلاف وثلاث مائة وثلاث عشر ملكاً، رفع من الأرض حيّاً، وقبضت روحه بين السماء والأرض، ثمّ رفع إلي السماء وردّت عليه روحه، وينزل قبل يوم القيامة إلي الدنيا, مع الإمام الثانى عشر من أئمّة أهل البيت, ويدعو الناس إلي الله، وفى القيامة, يخرج رجل فى موكب حوله الملائكة قد صفّت أجنحتها، والنور أمامهم،

necks toward him and say, 'Who is this who is thus allowed by Allah?' The angels will say, 'This is the spirit of Allah and His word! This is Jesus the son of Mary!'

Jesus once said about himself, "I sleep while I have nothing and I rise while I have nothing, and yet there is no one on earth more wealthy than I," and he said another time, "I began the morning with my Lord, the Blessed and Supreme, above me and the fire (of hell) before me and death in pursuit of me. I have not obtained that for which I wished and I cannot keep away the things I hate. So who of the poor is poorer than I?"

Jesus عليه السلام passed by a man who was blind, leprous and paralytic, and Jesus heard him giving thanks and saying, "Praise be to Allah Who has protected me from the trials with which He afflicts the majority of men." Jesus عليه السلام said, "What trial remains which has not been visited upon you?" He said, "He protected me from a trial which is the greatest of trials, and that is disbelief." Then Jesus عليه السلام touched him, and Allah cured him from his illnesses and beautified his face. Then he became a companion of Jesus عليه السلام and worshipped with him.

These two stories about him suffice to show his humility. He served a meal to the Apostles, and when they had eaten it, he himself washed them, and another time he stood up and washed their feet. They said, "It would have been more proper for us to have done this, O Spirit of Allah." He said, "Verily, it is more fitting for one with knowledge to serve the people. Indeed, I humbled myself only so that you may humble yourselves among the people after me even as I have humbled myself among you."

The conversations of Jesus عليه السلام with the Disciples are very interesting. They asked him, "O spirit of Allah, so with whom should we keep company?" He said, "He the sight of whom reminds you of Allah, his speech increases your knowledge and his action makes you desirous of the other world." And a man asked Jesus the son of Mary عليه السلام, "Which people is the best?" He took two handfuls of earth and said, "Which of these is the best? The people are created from earth, so the most honorable of them is the most God-wary."

فيمدّ إليه أهل الجنّة أعناقهم، فيقولون:«مَنْ هَذا الذى قَدْ أُذِنَ لَهُ عَلَي اللهِ؟» فتقول الملائكة:«هَذا رُوحُ اللهِ وَكَلِمَتُهُ، هَذا عِيسَي بْنُ مَرْيَمَ.»

لقد قال عيسي عليه السلام مرّة في وصف نفسه: «أبيتُ وَلَيْسَ لِى شَىْء، وأصبَحُ وَلَيْسَ لِى شَىْء، وَلَيْسَ عَلي وَجْهِ الأرْضِ أحَدٌ أغْنَي مِنِّى.» قال مرّةً أخري: «أصْبَحْتُ وَرَبِّى، تَبارَكَ وَتَعالَي، مِنْ فَوْقِى، والنارُ أمامى، والمَوْتُ فِى طَلَبى، لا أمْلِكُ ما أرْجُو، وَلا أُطِيقُ دَفْعَ ما أكْرَهُ، فأىُّ فَقِيرٍ أفْقَرُ مِنِّى؟!»

وفى الموروث الدينى أنّ عيسي عليه السلام مرّ علي رجل أعمي مجذوم مبروص مفلوج، فسمعه يشكر ويقول: «الحَمْدُ لِلّهِ الذى عافانِى مِن بَلاءٍ ابْتَلي بِهِ أكْثَرَ الخَلْق», فقال عليه السلام: «ما بَقِىَ مِنْ بَلاءٍ لَمْ يُصِبْكَ؟!» قال: «عافانى مِنْ بَلاءٍ هُوَ أعْظَمُ البَلايا، وَهُوَ الكُفْرُ» فمسّه، فشفاه الله من تلك الأمراض وحسن وجهه، فصاحبه وهو يعبد معه.

ويكفى في تواضعه عليه السلام ذكر هاتين الواقعتين: إنّه صنع مرّةً للحواريين طعاماً، فلمّا أكلوا، وضّأهم بنفسه. ومرّة أخري قام فغسل أقدامهم. فقالوا: «كُنّا نَحْنُ أحَقَّ بِهذا، يا رُوحَ اللهِ!» فَقالَ: «إنَّ أحَقَّ الناسِ بِالخِدْمَةِ، العالِمُ, إنَّما تَواضَعْتُ هَكَذا، لِكَيْما تَتَواضَعُوا بَعْدِى فِى الناسِ، كَتَواضُعِى لَكُمْ.»

أمّا محادثة عيسي عليه السلام للحواريين فجذّابة جدّا، لقد سألوه: «مَنْ نُجالِسُ؟ يا رُوحَ اللهِ!» فقالَ: «مَنْ يُذَكِّرُكُم اللهَ رُؤْيَتُهُ، وَيَزِيدُ فِى عِلْمِكُمْ مَنْطِقُهُ، وَيُرَغِّبُكُمْ فِى الآخِرَةِ عَمَلُهُ.» ورجل سأله: «أىُّ الناسِ أفْضَلُ؟» فأخذ قبضتين من تراب، فقال: «أى هاتَيْنِ أفْضَلُ؟ الناسُ خُلِقُوا مِن تُرابٍ، فأكْرَمُهُمْ أتْقاهُمْ.»

God also introduced Himself to Jesus, He described His endless mercy to him, and He gave him necessary instructions. Once He said to him, "O Jesus! I do not forget those who forget Me, so how could I forget those who remember Me! I am not stingy with those who disobey Me, so how could I be stingy with those who obey Me." And he said another time, "Be to the people like the earth below in meekness, like the flowing water in generosity, and like the sun and the moon in mercy, which shine on the good and sinner alike."

The advice attributed to Jesus in Shi'ite narrations is full of wisdom, guidance and direction. Among the advice he gives in order to improve relations among people is: "That which is not loved by you for someone to do to you, do not do that to others, and if someone strikes you on the right cheek, turn to him your left cheek also."

The Shi'ah believe that the Bible as it exists today has been distorted, but that despite this, much of what it contains is consistent with the spirit of the teachings of Jesus عليه السلام, and this is confirmed by many of the narrations attributed to the Imams, peace be with them. An example of this is that Jesus عليه السلام said: "In truth I say to you, whoever looks at a snake that intends to strike his brother and does not warn him until it kills him, he will not be secure from partnership in his murder. Likewise, whoever looks at his brother doing something wrong, and does not warn him of its consequences until it encompasses him, he will not be secure from partnership in his sin."

The narrations presented here have been selected from many books of Shi'ite narrations. It has been arranged into nine parts. In the first part, about the life of Jesus عليه السلام, we find a few narrations that conflict with each other. Some of the chains of narration through which the narrations are reported are weak. At the end of the eighth part there are four narrations reported to be from the Gospel, but we do not know from which Gospel they have been reported. The last narration in this book is about the respect given to Jesus by the Christians of one thousand three hundred sixty-four years ago. This narration has several ambiguities. On the other hand, the contents of parts two through eight are considered firm and are beautiful. Mostly, the Muslim and Christian beliefs are consistent with each other here.

لقد عرّف الله نفسه لعيسي عليه السلام ووصف له رحمته الواسعة, وأمره بأوامره, وقال له ذات مرّة: «يا عِيسَي، إنِّي لا أنْسَي مَنْ يَنْسانِي، فَكَيْفَ أنْسَي مَنْ يَذْكُرُنِي! أنا لا أبْخَلُ عَلَي مَنْ عَصانِي، فَكَيْفَ أبْخَلُ عَلَي مَنْ يُطِيعُنِي!» ومرّة أخري: «كُنْ لِلنّاسِ فِي الحِلْمِ كالأرْضِ تَحْتَهُمْ, وَفِي السَخاءِ كالماءِ الجارِي, وَفِي الرحْمَةِ كالشمْسِ والقَمَرِ, فانَّهُما يَطْلُعانِ عَلَي البَرِّ والفاجِرِ.»

إنّ وصايا عيسي عليه السلام التى جاءت في روايات الشيعة حكيمة وهادية ومرشدة. فمن وصاياه لحسن معاشرة الناس قولُه: «ما لا تُحِبُّ أنْ يُفْعَلَ بِكَ, فَلا تَفْعَلْهُ بِأحَدٍ؛ وإنْ لَطَمَ أحَدٌ خَدَّكَ الأيْمَنَ, فأعْطِ الأيْسَرَ.»

ومع اعتقاد الشيعة بتحريف الكتاب المقدّس الموجود حالياً, إلّا أنّهم يرون الكثير من مفاهيمه منسجماً مع روح تعاليم عيسي عليه السلام, ويؤيّدها العديد من أحاديث أئمّة أهل البيت عليهم السلام. فمن نماذج ذلك قول عيسي عليه السلام: «بِحَقٍّ أقُولُ لَكُمْ, مَنْ نَظَرَ إلَي الحَيَّةِ, تَؤُمُّ أخاهُ لِتَلْدِغَهُ, ولَمْ يُحَذِّرْهُ حَتَّي قَتَلَتْهُ, فَلا يأمَنُ أنْ يَكُونَ قَدْ شَرِكَ فِي دَمِهِ. وكَذلِكَ, مَنْ نَظَرَ إلَي أخِيهِ يَعْمَلُ الخَطِيئَةَ, ولَمْ يُحَذِّرْهُ عاقِبَتَها حَتَّي أحاطَتْ بِهِ, فَلا يأمَنُ أنْ يَكُونَ قَدْ شَرِكَ فِي اثْمِهِ.»

لقد اختيرت أخبار هذا الكتاب من كثير من كتب أحاديث الشيعة, ودوّنت فى تسعة فصول: ففى الفصل الأوّل سردت الروايات الحاكية عن حياة عيسي عليه السلام حيث لا نواجه أخباراً متعارضة إلّا نادراً, نعم أسانيد بعضها ضعيفة. وفى آخر الفصل الثامن نري أربعة أخبار منقولة عن الإنجيل, ولا ندرى عن أيّ الأناجيل. وفى الخبر الأخير، فى قصّة علاقة النصاري منذ أكثر من ألف وثلاثمائة وأربعة وستين عاماً, نواجه نقاطاً مبهمة.

أمّا مضمون الأخبار فى الفصل الثانى حتّي الثامن فهو متقن وجميل جدّا، وغالباً مايشكّل أحد محاور الالتقاء بين النصاري والمسلمين.

Introduction

We do not believe in the divinity of Jesus(A), but we do believe that he was inseparable from God. They have an attraction in such a way that they have an effect on the hearts of those ready to receive them, and increase love for Jesus(A).

This collection of hadiths was published in Qom, Iran by Ansariyan Publications in 2004. The verses of the Qur'an pertaining to Jesus, peace be with him, are now being added, with the translation of Ali Quli Qara'i, from his recently published exquisite translation of the entire Qur'an. *The Qur'an: With a Phrase-by-Phrase English Translation,* (London: Islamic College for Advanced Studies Press, 2004), so that the reader might have in a single volume the verses of the Qur'an and Shi'ite narrations about Jesus.

We should express our gratitude for the trouble taken by our brother Ali Asgari Yazdi to arrange for the publication of this volume by Aunali Khalfan, who has worked so diligently over the years for the sake of Islam.

We would like to thank our readers and solicit their assistance if they find any errors in the text or its translation. [1]

Mahdī Muntaẓir Qā'im
Rajab 1426/August 2005

---

[1] The work of collecting, sorting, editing and translating these narrations into English, began ten years ago. It has been completed with the help of some of my teachers and friends. Prof. Muḥammad Hādī Yūsufī Gharavī reviewed the Arabic text of the narrations. Ḥājj Muḥammad Legenhausen was the main translator of the narrations into English. Sayyid Muḥammad Naṣīḥatkon helped with the Arabic vocalization marks and Badr Shāhīn with the typesetting. Likewise, my wife also showed much patience with this work. I thank all of them. I would especially like to thank the Center for Shi'ite Studies, in whose library a portion of this work was carried out.

I hope it may be accepted by Allah, and I offer the blessings for it to those who have a right over us, especially my parents and brothers. *Wa salām.*

نحن لانعتقد بألوهيّة عيسي عليه السلام, ولكنّه ليس منفكّاً عن الله، ونري أقواله وأفعاله إلهيّة، وفيها جاذبيّة خاصّة, بحيث تؤثّر كثيراً فی القلوب المستعدّة, وتزيد فی ودّهم وحبّهم لعيسي عليه السلام.

هذه المجموعة الحديثية قامت بطبعها مؤسسة أنصاريان في مدينة قم – ايران للمرّة الأولى في عام ٢٠٠٤ م. ١٤٢٥ ق. و قد تمت في هذه الطبعة إضافة الآيات القرآنية المتعلقة بعيسي مع ترجمتها المأخوذة من ترجمة الرائعة للسيد علي قلي قرائي للقرآن التی تم نشرها مؤخراً, ترجمة عبارات القرآن للغة الإنجليزية (المطبوعة في لندن, مطبعة الكلية الإسلامية للدراسات العليا، ٢٠٠٤)، لكی يكون لدي القاريء الكريم مجلد يحوی النصوص القرآنية والأحاديث الشيعية المتعلقة بالسيد المسيح.

كما أعبّر عن خالص امتنانی للجهود التی قام بها الأخ علی عسكری يزدی الذی رتّب إعادة طبع هذا السفر عن طريق السيد عونعلی خلفان الذی عمل جاهداً لأعوام من أجل خدمة الإسلام.

وأخيراً نتقدّم من الإخوة القرّاء الأعزّاء بالشكر علي تتبّعهم للنصوص, وترجمتها فی هذا الكتاب، متمنّين عليهم إتحافنا بملاحظاتهم عليها.[1]

مهدی منتظرقائم

مرداد ١٣٨٤هـ. ش، رجب ١٤٢٦هـ. ق

---

[1]. بدأ العمل فی جمع هذه الأخبار وتبويبها وتصحيحها وترجمتها إلي اللغة الإنجليزيّة منذ عشرة أعوام, وتمّ اليوم بمساعدة بعض أساتذتی وأصدقائی, فالأستاذ محمّد هادی اليوسفیّ الغرویّ تعهّد بمراجعة نصوص الأحاديث, وكان للأستاذ محمّد لِكِنهاوسِن الدور الأساس فی ترجمتها إلي الإنجليزيّة. كما ساعدنی فی إعرابها السيد محمّد نصيحت كن, وفی الإخراج الفنیّ السيد بدر شاهين, وكان لمثابرة زوجتی معی دور فی هذا العمل. فأنا أشكرهم جميعاً وأخصّ (مؤسّسه شيعه شناسي: مؤسّسةٌ تُعنَي برَصد الشيعة وأوضاعهم فی العالم) حيث كتبتُ شطراً من هذا الكتاب فی مكتبتها. أرجو من الله القبول, وأهدی ثوابه إلي ذوی الحقوق علیَّ لاسيّما والدَیَّ و إخوانی. والسّلام.

CHAPTER ONE
JESUS ﷺ THROUGH THE QUR'ĀN

SŪRAT AL-BAQARAH

Certainly We gave Moses the Book, and followed him with the apostles, and We gave Jesus, the son of Mary, manifest proofs, and confirmed him with the Holy Spirit. Is it not that whenever an apostle brought you that which was not to your liking, you would act arrogantly; so you would impugn a part [of them], and slay a[nother] part? (2:87)

Say, 'We have faith in Allah, and that which has been sent down to us, and that which was sent down to Abraham, Ishmael, Isaac, Jacob and the Tribes, and that which Moses and Jesus were given, and that which the prophets were given from their Lord; we make no distinction between any of them, and to Him do we submit,' (2:136)

These are the apostles, some of whom We gave an advantage over others: of them are those to whom Allah spoke, and some of them He raised in rank, and We gave Jesus, son of Mary, manifest proofs and strengthened him with the Holy Spirit. Had Allah wished, those who succeeded them would not have fought each other afterthe manifest proofs had come to them. But they differed. So there were among them those who had faith and there were among them those who were faithless, and had Allah wished, they would not have fought one another; but Allah does whatever He desires. (2:253)

القسم الأوّل

عيسى عليه السلام فى القرآن

سورة البقرة:

وَلَقَدْ ءَاتَيْنَا مُوسَى ٱلْكِتَـٰبَ وَقَفَّيْنَا مِنۢ بَعْدِهِۦ بِٱلرُّسُلِ ۖ وَءَاتَيْنَا عِيسَى
ٱبْنَ مَرْيَمَ ٱلْبَيِّنَـٰتِ وَأَيَّدْنَـٰهُ بِرُوحِ ٱلْقُدُسِ ۗ أَفَكُلَّمَا جَآءَكُمْ رَسُولٌۢ بِمَا لَا تَهْوَىٰٓ
أَنفُسُكُمُ ٱسْتَكْبَرْتُمْ فَفَرِيقًا كَذَّبْتُمْ وَفَرِيقًا تَقْتُلُونَ ﴿٨٧﴾

قُولُوٓا۟ ءَامَنَّا بِٱللَّهِ وَمَآ أُنزِلَ إِلَيْنَا وَمَآ أُنزِلَ إِلَىٰٓ إِبْرَٰهِـۧمَ وَإِسْمَـٰعِيلَ وَإِسْحَـٰقَ
وَيَعْقُوبَ وَٱلْأَسْبَاطِ وَمَآ أُوتِىَ مُوسَىٰ وَعِيسَىٰ وَمَآ أُوتِىَ ٱلنَّبِيُّونَ مِن رَّبِّهِمْ لَا
نُفَرِّقُ بَيْنَ أَحَدٍ مِّنْهُمْ وَنَحْنُ لَهُۥ مُسْلِمُونَ ﴿١٣٦﴾

تِلْكَ ٱلرُّسُلُ فَضَّلْنَا بَعْضَهُمْ عَلَىٰ بَعْضٍ ۘ مِّنْهُم مَّن كَلَّمَ ٱللَّهُ ۖ وَرَفَعَ بَعْضَهُمْ
دَرَجَـٰتٍ ۚ وَءَاتَيْنَا عِيسَى ٱبْنَ مَرْيَمَ ٱلْبَيِّنَـٰتِ وَأَيَّدْنَـٰهُ بِرُوحِ ٱلْقُدُسِ ۗ وَلَوْ شَآءَ ٱللَّهُ مَا
ٱقْتَتَلَ ٱلَّذِينَ مِنۢ بَعْدِهِم مِّنۢ بَعْدِ مَا جَآءَتْهُمُ ٱلْبَيِّنَـٰتُ وَلَـٰكِنِ ٱخْتَلَفُوا۟ فَمِنْهُم مَّنْ
ءَامَنَ وَمِنْهُم مَّن كَفَرَ ۚ وَلَوْ شَآءَ ٱللَّهُ مَا ٱقْتَتَلُوا۟ وَلَـٰكِنَّ ٱللَّهَ يَفْعَلُ مَا يُرِيدُ ﴿٢٥٣﴾

SŪEAT ĀI-I 'IMRĀN

When the angels said, 'O Mary, Allah gives you the good news of a Word from Him whose name is Messiah, Jesus, son of Mary, distinguished in the world and the Hereafter, and one of those brought near [to Allah]. (3:45)

And when Jesus sensed their faithlessness, he said, 'Who will be my helpers toward Allah?' The disciples said, 'We will be helpers of Allah. We have faith in Allah, and bear witness that we are *muslims*. (3:52)

When Allah said, 'O Jesus, I shall take your [soul], and I shall raise you up toward Myself, and I shall clear you of [the calumnies of] the faithless, and I shall set those who follow you above the faithless until the Day of Resurrection. Then to Me will be your return, whereat I will judge between you concerning that about which you used to differ. (3:55)

Indeed the case of Jesus with Allah is like the case of Adam: He created him from dust, then said to him, 'Be,' and he was. (3:59)

Say, 'We have faith in Allah, and in what has been sent down to us, and what was sent down to Abraham, Ishmael, Isaac, Jacob and the Tribes, and that which Moses and Jesus were given, and the prophets, from their Lord. We make no distinction between any of them, and to Him do we submit.' (3:84)

سورة آل عمران:

إِذْ قَالَتِ ٱلْمَلَٰٓئِكَةُ يَٰمَرْيَمُ إِنَّ ٱللَّهَ يُبَشِّرُكِ بِكَلِمَةٍ مِّنْهُ ٱسْمُهُ ٱلْمَسِيحُ عِيسَى ٱبْنُ مَرْيَمَ وَجِيهًا فِي ٱلدُّنْيَا وَٱلْءَاخِرَةِ وَمِنَ ٱلْمُقَرَّبِينَ ﴿٤٥﴾

فَلَمَّآ أَحَسَّ عِيسَىٰ مِنْهُمُ ٱلْكُفْرَ قَالَ مَنْ أَنصَارِىٓ إِلَى ٱللَّهِ ۖ قَالَ ٱلْحَوَارِيُّونَ نَحْنُ أَنصَارُ ٱللَّهِ ءَامَنَّا بِٱللَّهِ وَٱشْهَدْ بِأَنَّا مُسْلِمُونَ ﴿٥٢﴾

إِذْ قَالَ ٱللَّهُ يَٰعِيسَىٰٓ إِنِّى مُتَوَفِّيكَ وَرَافِعُكَ إِلَىَّ وَمُطَهِّرُكَ مِنَ ٱلَّذِينَ كَفَرُواْ وَجَاعِلُ ٱلَّذِينَ ٱتَّبَعُوكَ فَوْقَ ٱلَّذِينَ كَفَرُوٓاْ إِلَىٰ يَوْمِ ٱلْقِيَٰمَةِ ۖ ثُمَّ إِلَىَّ مَرْجِعُكُمْ فَأَحْكُمُ بَيْنَكُمْ فِيمَا كُنتُمْ فِيهِ تَخْتَلِفُونَ ﴿٥٥﴾

إِنَّ مَثَلَ عِيسَىٰ عِندَ ٱللَّهِ كَمَثَلِ ءَادَمَ ۖ خَلَقَهُۥ مِن تُرَابٍ ثُمَّ قَالَ لَهُۥ كُن فَيَكُونُ ﴿٥٩﴾

قُلْ ءَامَنَّا بِٱللَّهِ وَمَآ أُنزِلَ عَلَيْنَا وَمَآ أُنزِلَ عَلَىٰٓ إِبْرَٰهِيمَ وَإِسْمَٰعِيلَ وَإِسْحَٰقَ وَيَعْقُوبَ وَٱلْأَسْبَاطِ وَمَآ أُوتِىَ مُوسَىٰ وَعِيسَىٰ وَٱلنَّبِيُّونَ مِن رَّبِّهِمْ لَا نُفَرِّقُ بَيْنَ أَحَدٍ مِّنْهُمْ وَنَحْنُ لَهُۥ مُسْلِمُونَ ﴿٨٤﴾

SŪEAT AL-NISĀ'

Then because of their breaking their covenant, their defiance of Allah's signs, their killing of the prophets unjustly and for their saying, 'Our hearts are uncircumcised.' Rather Allah has set a seal on them for their unfaith, so they do not have faith except a few. (4:155)

And for their faithlessness, and their uttering a monstrous calumny against Mary, (4:156)

And for their saying, 'We killed the Messiah, Jesus son of Mary, the apostle of Allah' though they did not kill him, but so it was made to appear to them. Indeed those who differ concerning him are surely in doubt about him: they do not have any knowledge of that beyond following conjectures, and certainly they did not kill him. (4:157)

Rather Allah raised him up toward Himself, and Allah is all-mighty, all-wise. (4:158)

There is none among the People of the Book but will surely believe in him before his death; and on the day of Resurrection he will be a witness against them. (4:159)

We have indeed revealed to you as We revealed to Noah and the prophets after him, and [as] We revealed to Abraham and Ishmael, Isaac, Jacob, and the Tribes, Jesus and Job, Jonah, Aaron, and Solomon, and We gave David the Psalms. (4:163)

O People of the Book! Do not exceed the bounds in your religion, and do not attribute anything to Allah except the truth. The Messiah, Jesus son of Mary, was only an apostle of Allah, and His Word that He cast toward Mary and a spirit from Him. So have faith in Allah and His apostles, and do not say, '[God is] a trinity.' Relinquish [such a creed]! That is better for you. Allah is but the One God. He is far too immaculate to have any son. To Him belongs whatever is in the heavens and whatever is on the earth,

سورة النساء:

فَبِمَا نَقْضِهِم مِّيثَٰقَهُمْ وَكُفْرِهِم بِـَٔايَٰتِ ٱللَّهِ وَقَتْلِهِمُ ٱلْأَنۢبِيَآءَ بِغَيْرِ حَقٍّ وَقَوْلِهِمْ قُلُوبُنَا غُلْفٌۢ ۚ بَلْ طَبَعَ ٱللَّهُ عَلَيْهَا بِكُفْرِهِمْ فَلَا يُؤْمِنُونَ إِلَّا قَلِيلًا ﴿١٥٥﴾

وَبِكُفْرِهِمْ وَقَوْلِهِمْ عَلَىٰ مَرْيَمَ بُهْتَٰنًا عَظِيمًا ﴿١٥٦﴾

وَقَوْلِهِمْ إِنَّا قَتَلْنَا ٱلْمَسِيحَ عِيسَى ٱبْنَ مَرْيَمَ رَسُولَ ٱللَّهِ وَمَا قَتَلُوهُ وَمَا صَلَبُوهُ وَلَٰكِن شُبِّهَ لَهُمْ ۚ وَإِنَّ ٱلَّذِينَ ٱخْتَلَفُوا۟ فِيهِ لَفِى شَكٍّ مِّنْهُ ۚ مَا لَهُم بِهِۦ مِنْ عِلْمٍ إِلَّا ٱتِّبَاعَ ٱلظَّنِّ ۚ وَمَا قَتَلُوهُ يَقِينًۢا ﴿١٥٧﴾

بَل رَّفَعَهُ ٱللَّهُ إِلَيْهِ ۚ وَكَانَ ٱللَّهُ عَزِيزًا حَكِيمًا ﴿١٥٨﴾

وَإِن مِّنْ أَهْلِ ٱلْكِتَٰبِ إِلَّا لَيُؤْمِنَنَّ بِهِۦ قَبْلَ مَوْتِهِۦ ۖ وَيَوْمَ ٱلْقِيَٰمَةِ يَكُونُ عَلَيْهِمْ شَهِيدًا ﴿١٥٩﴾

إِنَّآ أَوْحَيْنَآ إِلَيْكَ كَمَآ أَوْحَيْنَآ إِلَىٰ نُوحٍ وَٱلنَّبِيِّـۧنَ مِنۢ بَعْدِهِۦ ۚ وَأَوْحَيْنَآ إِلَىٰٓ إِبْرَٰهِيمَ وَإِسْمَٰعِيلَ وَإِسْحَٰقَ وَيَعْقُوبَ وَٱلْأَسْبَاطِ وَعِيسَىٰ وَأَيُّوبَ وَيُونُسَ وَهَٰرُونَ وَسُلَيْمَٰنَ ۚ وَءَاتَيْنَا دَاوُۥدَ زَبُورًا ﴿١٦٣﴾

يَٰٓأَهْلَ ٱلْكِتَٰبِ لَا تَغْلُوا۟ فِى دِينِكُمْ وَلَا تَقُولُوا۟ عَلَى ٱللَّهِ إِلَّا ٱلْحَقَّ ۚ إِنَّمَا ٱلْمَسِيحُ عِيسَى ٱبْنُ مَرْيَمَ رَسُولُ ٱللَّهِ وَكَلِمَتُهُۥٓ أَلْقَىٰهَآ إِلَىٰ مَرْيَمَ وَرُوحٌ مِّنْهُ ۖ فَـَٔامِنُوا۟ بِٱللَّهِ وَرُسُلِهِۦ ۖ وَلَا تَقُولُوا۟ ثَلَٰثَةٌ ۚ ٱنتَهُوا۟ خَيْرًا لَّكُمْ ۚ إِنَّمَا ٱللَّهُ إِلَٰهٌ وَٰحِدٌ سُبْحَٰنَهُۥٓ أَن يَكُونَ لَهُۥ وَلَدٌ ۘ لَّهُۥ مَا فِى ٱلسَّمَٰوَٰتِ وَمَا فِى ٱلْأَرْضِ ۗ

and Allah suffices as trustee. (4:171)

The Messiah would never disdain being a servant of Allah, nor would the angels brought near [to Him]. And whoever disdains His worship and is arrogant, He will gather them all toward Him. (4:172)

SŪRAT AL-MĀ'IDAH

They are certainly faithless who say, 'Allah is the Messiah, son of Mary.' Say, 'Who can avail anything against Allah should He wish to destroy the Messiah, son of Mary, and his mother, and everyone upon the earth?' To Allah belongs the kingdom of the heavens and the earth, and whatever is between them. He creates whatever He wishes, and Allah has power over all things. (5:17)

The Jews and the Christians say, 'We are Allah's children and His beloved ones.' Say. 'Then why does He punish you for your sins?' Rather you are humans from among His creatures. He forgives whomever He wishes, and punishes whomever He wishes, and to Allah belongs the kingdom of the heavens and the earth, and whatever is between them, and toward Him is the return. (5:18)

And We followed them with Jesus son of Mary, to confirm that which was before him of the Torah, and We gave him the Evangel containing guidance and light, confirming what was before it of the Torah, and as guidance and advice for the Godwary. (5:46)

Let the people of the Evangel judge by what Allah has sent down in it. Those who do not judge by what Allah has sent down, it is they who are the transgressors. (5:47)

وَكَفَىٰ بِٱللَّهِ وَكِيلًا ﴿١٧١﴾

لَّن يَسْتَنكِفَ ٱلْمَسِيحُ أَن يَكُونَ عَبْدًا لِّلَّهِ وَلَا ٱلْمَلَٰٓئِكَةُ ٱلْمُقَرَّبُونَ ۚ وَمَن يَسْتَنكِفْ عَنْ عِبَادَتِهِۦ وَيَسْتَكْبِرْ فَسَيَحْشُرُهُمْ إِلَيْهِ جَمِيعًا ﴿١٧٢﴾

سورة المائدة:

لَّقَدْ كَفَرَ ٱلَّذِينَ قَالُوٓا۟ إِنَّ ٱللَّهَ هُوَ ٱلْمَسِيحُ ٱبْنُ مَرْيَمَ ۚ قُلْ فَمَن يَمْلِكُ مِنَ ٱللَّهِ شَيْـًٔا إِنْ أَرَادَ أَن يُهْلِكَ ٱلْمَسِيحَ ٱبْنَ مَرْيَمَ وَأُمَّهُۥ وَمَن فِى ٱلْأَرْضِ جَمِيعًا ۗ وَلِلَّهِ مُلْكُ ٱلسَّمَٰوَٰتِ وَٱلْأَرْضِ وَمَا بَيْنَهُمَا ۚ يَخْلُقُ مَا يَشَآءُ ۚ وَٱللَّهُ عَلَىٰ كُلِّ شَىْءٍ قَدِيرٌ ﴿١٧﴾

وَقَالَتِ ٱلْيَهُودُ وَٱلنَّصَٰرَىٰ نَحْنُ أَبْنَٰٓؤُا۟ ٱللَّهِ وَأَحِبَّٰٓؤُهُۥ ۚ قُلْ فَلِمَ يُعَذِّبُكُم بِذُنُوبِكُم ۖ بَلْ أَنتُم بَشَرٌ مِّمَّنْ خَلَقَ ۚ يَغْفِرُ لِمَن يَشَآءُ وَيُعَذِّبُ مَن يَشَآءُ ۚ وَلِلَّهِ مُلْكُ ٱلسَّمَٰوَٰتِ وَٱلْأَرْضِ وَمَا بَيْنَهُمَا ۖ وَإِلَيْهِ ٱلْمَصِيرُ ﴿١٨﴾

وَقَفَّيْنَا عَلَىٰٓ ءَاثَٰرِهِم بِعِيسَى ٱبْنِ مَرْيَمَ مُصَدِّقًا لِّمَا بَيْنَ يَدَيْهِ مِنَ ٱلتَّوْرَىٰةِ ۖ وَءَاتَيْنَٰهُ ٱلْإِنجِيلَ فِيهِ هُدًى وَنُورٌ وَمُصَدِّقًا لِّمَا بَيْنَ يَدَيْهِ مِنَ ٱلتَّوْرَىٰةِ وَهُدًى وَمَوْعِظَةً لِّلْمُتَّقِينَ ﴿٤٦﴾

وَلْيَحْكُمْ أَهْلُ ٱلْإِنجِيلِ بِمَآ أَنزَلَ ٱللَّهُ فِيهِ ۚ وَمَن لَّمْ يَحْكُم بِمَآ أَنزَلَ ٱللَّهُ فَأُو۟لَٰٓئِكَ هُمُ ٱلْفَٰسِقُونَ ﴿٤٧﴾

They are certainly faithless who say, 'Allah is the Messiah, son of Mary.' But the Messiah had said, 'O Children of Israel! Worship Allah, my Lord and your Lord. Indeed whoever ascribes partners to Allah, Allah shall forbid him [entry into] paradise, and his refuge shall be the Fire, and the wrongdoers will not have any helpers.' (5:72)

They are certainly faithless who say, 'Allah is the third [person] of a trinity,' While there is no god except the One God. If they do not relinquish what they say, there shall befall the faithless among them a painful punishment. (5:73)

Will they not repent to Allah and plead with Him for forgiveness? Yet Allah is all-forgiving, all-merciful. (5:74)

The Messiah, son of Mary, is but an apostle. Certainly [other] apostles have passed before him, and his mother was a truthful one. Both of them would eat food. *Look* how We clarify the signs for them, and yet, *look*, how they go astray! (5:75)

Say, 'Do you worship, besides Allah, what has no power to bring you any benefit or harm, while Allah----He is the All-hearing, the All-knowing?!' (5:76)

Say, 'O people of the Book! Do not unduly exceed the bounds in your religion and do not follow the fancies of a people who went astray in the past, and led many astray, and [themselves] strayed from the right path.' (5:77)

The faithless among the Children of Israel were cursed on the tongue of David and Jesus son of Mary. That, because they would disobey and used to commit transgression. (5:78)

They would not forbid one another from the wrongs that they committed. Surely, evil is what they had been doing. (5:79)

When Allah will say, "O Jesus son of Mary, remember My blessing upon you and upon your mother, when I strengthened you with the Holy Spirit, so you would speak to the people in the cradle and in adulthood, and when I taught you the Book

لَّقَدْ كَفَرَ ٱلَّذِينَ قَالُوٓاْ إِنَّ ٱللَّهَ ثَالِثُ ثَلَٰثَةٍۘ وَمَا مِنْ إِلَٰهٍ إِلَّآ إِلَٰهٌ وَٰحِدٌۚ وَإِن لَّمْ يَنتَهُواْ عَمَّا يَقُولُونَ لَيَمَسَّنَّ ٱلَّذِينَ كَفَرُواْ مِنْهُمْ عَذَابٌ أَلِيمٌ ﴿٧٣﴾

أَفَلَا يَتُوبُونَ إِلَى ٱللَّهِ وَيَسْتَغْفِرُونَهُۥۚ وَٱللَّهُ غَفُورٌ رَّحِيمٌ ﴿٧٤﴾

مَّا ٱلْمَسِيحُ ٱبْنُ مَرْيَمَ إِلَّا رَسُولٌ قَدْ خَلَتْ مِن قَبْلِهِ ٱلرُّسُلُ وَأُمُّهُۥ صِدِّيقَةٌۖ كَانَا يَأْكُلَانِ ٱلطَّعَامَۗ ٱنظُرْ كَيْفَ نُبَيِّنُ لَهُمُ ٱلْأَيَٰتِ ثُمَّ ٱنظُرْ أَنَّىٰ يُؤْفَكُونَ ﴿٧٥﴾

قُلْ أَتَعْبُدُونَ مِن دُونِ ٱللَّهِ مَا لَا يَمْلِكُ لَكُمْ ضَرًّا وَلَا نَفْعًاۚ وَٱللَّهُ هُوَ ٱلسَّمِيعُ ٱلْعَلِيمُ ﴿٧٦﴾

قُلْ يَٰٓأَهْلَ ٱلْكِتَٰبِ لَا تَغْلُواْ فِي دِينِكُمْ غَيْرَ ٱلْحَقِّ وَلَا تَتَّبِعُوٓاْ أَهْوَآءَ قَوْمٍ قَدْ ضَلُّواْ مِن قَبْلُ وَأَضَلُّواْ كَثِيرًا وَضَلُّواْ عَن سَوَآءِ ٱلسَّبِيلِ ﴿٧٧﴾

لُعِنَ ٱلَّذِينَ كَفَرُواْ مِنۢ بَنِيٓ إِسْرَٰٓءِيلَ عَلَىٰ لِسَانِ دَاوُۥدَ وَعِيسَى ٱبْنِ مَرْيَمَۚ ذَٰلِكَ بِمَا عَصَواْ وَّكَانُواْ يَعْتَدُونَ ﴿٧٨﴾

كَانُواْ لَا يَتَنَاهَوْنَ عَن مُّنكَرٍ فَعَلُوهُۚ لَبِئْسَ مَا كَانُواْ يَفْعَلُونَ ﴿٧٩﴾

إِذْ قَالَ ٱللَّهُ يَٰعِيسَى ٱبْنَ مَرْيَمَ ٱذْكُرْ نِعْمَتِي عَلَيْكَ وَعَلَىٰ وَٰلِدَتِكَ إِذْ أَيَّدتُّكَ بِرُوحِ ٱلْقُدُسِ تُكَلِّمُ ٱلنَّاسَ فِي ٱلْمَهْدِ وَكَهْلًاۖ وَإِذْ عَلَّمْتُكَ ٱلْكِتَٰبَ

and wisdom, the Torah and the Evangel, and when you would create from clay the form of a bird, with My leave, and you would breathe into it and it would become a bird, with My leave; and you would heal the blind and the leper, with My leave, and you would raise the dead, with My leave; and when I held off [the evil of] the Children of Israel from you when you brought them manifest proofs, whereat the faithless among them said, 'This is nothing but plain magic.'" (5:110)

And When I inspired the disciples, [saying], 'Have faith in Me and My apostle,' they said, 'We have faith. Bear witness that we are *muslims.*' (5:111)

When the disciples said, 'O Jesus son of Mary! Can your Lord send down to us a table from the sky?' Said he, 'Be wary of Allah, should you be faithful.' (5:112)

They said, 'We desire to eat from it, and our hearts will be at rest: we shall know that you have told us the truth, and we shall be among the witnesses to it.' (5:113)

Said Jesus son of Mary, 'O Allah! Our Lord! Send down to us a table from the sky, to be a festival for us, for the first ones and the last ones among us and as a sign from You, and provide for us; for You are the best of providers.' (5:114)

Allah said, 'I will indeed send it down to you. But should any of you disbelieves after this, I will indeed punish him with a punishment such as I do not punish anyone in all creation.' (5:115)

And when Allah will say, 'O Jesus son of Mary! Was it you who said to the people, "Take me and my mother for gods besides Allah"?' He will say, 'Immaculate are You! It does not behoove me to say what I have no right to [say]. Had I said it, You would certainly have known it: You know whatever is in my self, and I do not know what is in Your Self, Indeed You are knower of al that is Unseen. (5:116)

وَٱلْحِكْمَةَ وَٱلتَّوْرَىٰةَ وَٱلْإِنجِيلَ ۖ وَإِذْ تَخْلُقُ مِنَ ٱلطِّينِ كَهَيْـَٔةِ ٱلطَّيْرِ بِإِذْنِى فَتَنفُخُ فِيهَا
فَتَكُونُ طَيْرًۢا بِإِذْنِى ۖ وَتُبْرِئُ ٱلْأَكْمَهَ وَٱلْأَبْرَصَ بِإِذْنِى ۖ وَإِذْ تُخْرِجُ ٱلْمَوْتَىٰ
بِإِذْنِى ۖ وَإِذْ كَفَفْتُ بَنِىٓ إِسْرَٰٓءِيلَ عَنكَ إِذْ جِئْتَهُم بِٱلْبَيِّنَٰتِ فَقَالَ ٱلَّذِينَ كَفَرُوا۟
مِنْهُمْ إِنْ هَٰذَآ إِلَّا سِحْرٌ مُّبِينٌ ﴿١١٠﴾

وَإِذْ أَوْحَيْتُ إِلَى ٱلْحَوَارِيِّـۧنَ أَنْ ءَامِنُوا۟ بِى وَبِرَسُولِى قَالُوٓا۟ ءَامَنَّا وَٱشْهَدْ بِأَنَّنَا
مُسْلِمُونَ ﴿١١١﴾

إِذْ قَالَ ٱلْحَوَارِيُّونَ يَٰعِيسَى ٱبْنَ مَرْيَمَ هَلْ يَسْتَطِيعُ رَبُّكَ أَن يُنَزِّلَ عَلَيْنَا
مَآئِدَةً مِّنَ ٱلسَّمَآءِ ۖ قَالَ ٱتَّقُوا۟ ٱللَّهَ إِن كُنتُم مُّؤْمِنِينَ ﴿١١٢﴾

قَالُوا۟ نُرِيدُ أَن نَّأْكُلَ مِنْهَا وَتَطْمَئِنَّ قُلُوبُنَا وَنَعْلَمَ أَن قَدْ صَدَقْتَنَا وَنَكُونَ عَلَيْهَا
مِنَ ٱلشَّٰهِدِينَ ﴿١١٣﴾

قَالَ عِيسَى ٱبْنُ مَرْيَمَ ٱللَّهُمَّ رَبَّنَآ أَنزِلْ عَلَيْنَا مَآئِدَةً مِّنَ ٱلسَّمَآءِ تَكُونُ لَنَا عِيدًا
لِّأَوَّلِنَا وَءَاخِرِنَا وَءَايَةً مِّنكَ ۖ وَٱرْزُقْنَا وَأَنتَ خَيْرُ ٱلرَّٰزِقِينَ ﴿١١٤﴾

قَالَ ٱللَّهُ إِنِّى مُنَزِّلُهَا عَلَيْكُمْ ۖ فَمَن يَكْفُرْ بَعْدُ مِنكُمْ فَإِنِّىٓ أُعَذِّبُهُۥ عَذَابًا لَّآ
أُعَذِّبُهُۥٓ أَحَدًا مِّنَ ٱلْعَٰلَمِينَ ﴿١١٥﴾

وَإِذْ قَالَ ٱللَّهُ يَٰعِيسَى ٱبْنَ مَرْيَمَ ءَأَنتَ قُلْتَ لِلنَّاسِ ٱتَّخِذُونِى وَأُمِّىَ إِلَٰهَيْنِ مِن دُونِ
ٱللَّهِ ۖ قَالَ سُبْحَٰنَكَ مَا يَكُونُ لِىٓ أَنْ أَقُولَ مَا لَيْسَ لِى بِحَقٍّ ۚ إِن كُنتُ قُلْتُهُۥ فَقَدْ
عَلِمْتَهُۥ ۚ تَعْلَمُ مَا فِى نَفْسِى وَلَآ أَعْلَمُ مَا فِى نَفْسِكَ ۚ إِنَّكَ أَنتَ عَلَّٰمُ ٱلْغُيُوبِ
﴿١١٦﴾

I did not say to them [anything] except what You had commanded me [to say]: "Worship Allah, my Lord and your Lord," And I was a witness to them so long as I was among them. But when You had taken me away, You Yourself were watchful over them, and You are witness to al things. (5:117)

If You punish them, they are indeed Your creatures; but if You forgive them, you are indeed the All-mighty, the All-wise.' (5:118)

Allah will say, 'This day truthfulness shall benefit the truthful. For them there will be gardens with streams running in them, to remain in them forever. Allah is pleased with them and they are pleased with Him. That is the great success.' (5:119)

To Allah belongs the kingdom of the heavens and the earth and whatever there is in them, and He has power over all things. (5:120)

SŪRAT AL-AN'ĀM

And Zechariah, John, Jesus and Ilyās – each of them among the righteous – (6:85)

SŪRAT AL-TAWBAH

The Jews say, 'Ezra is the son of Allah,' and the Christians say, 'Christ is the son of Allah.' That is an opinion that they mouth, imitating the opinions of the faithless of former times. May Allah assail them, where do they stray?! (9:30)

They have taken their scribes and their monks as Lords besides Allah, and also Christ, Mary's son; though they were commanded to worship only the One God, there is no god except Him; He is far too immaculate to have any partners that they ascribe [to Him]. (9:31)

مَا قُلْتُ لَهُمْ إِلَّا مَآ أَمَرْتَنِى بِهِۦٓ أَنِ ٱعْبُدُوا۟ ٱللَّهَ رَبِّى وَرَبَّكُمْ ۚ وَكُنتُ عَلَيْهِمْ شَهِيدًا مَّا دُمْتُ فِيهِمْ ۖ فَلَمَّا تَوَفَّيْتَنِى كُنتَ أَنتَ ٱلرَّقِيبَ عَلَيْهِمْ ۚ وَأَنتَ عَلَىٰ كُلِّ شَىْءٍ شَهِيدٌ ﴿١١٧﴾

إِن تُعَذِّبْهُمْ فَإِنَّهُمْ عِبَادُكَ ۖ وَإِن تَغْفِرْ لَهُمْ فَإِنَّكَ أَنتَ ٱلْعَزِيزُ ٱلْحَكِيمُ ﴿١١٨﴾

قَالَ ٱللَّهُ هَٰذَا يَوْمُ يَنفَعُ ٱلصَّٰدِقِينَ صِدْقُهُمْ ۚ لَهُمْ جَنَّٰتٌ تَجْرِى مِن تَحْتِهَا ٱلْأَنْهَٰرُ خَٰلِدِينَ فِيهَآ أَبَدًا ۚ رَّضِىَ ٱللَّهُ عَنْهُمْ وَرَضُوا۟ عَنْهُ ۚ ذَٰلِكَ ٱلْفَوْزُ ٱلْعَظِيمُ ﴿١١٩﴾

لِلَّهِ مُلْكُ ٱلسَّمَٰوَٰتِ وَٱلْأَرْضِ وَمَا فِيهِنَّ ۚ وَهُوَ عَلَىٰ كُلِّ شَىْءٍ قَدِيرٌۢ ﴿١٢٠﴾

سورة الأنعام:

وَزَكَرِيَّا وَيَحْيَىٰ وَعِيسَىٰ وَإِلْيَاسَ ۖ كُلٌّ مِّنَ ٱلصَّٰلِحِينَ ﴿٨٥﴾

سورة التوبة:

وَقَالَتِ ٱلْيَهُودُ عُزَيْرٌ ٱبْنُ ٱللَّهِ وَقَالَتِ ٱلنَّصَٰرَى ٱلْمَسِيحُ ٱبْنُ ٱللَّهِ ۖ ذَٰلِكَ قَوْلُهُم بِأَفْوَٰهِهِمْ ۖ يُضَٰهِـُٔونَ قَوْلَ ٱلَّذِينَ كَفَرُوا۟ مِن قَبْلُ ۚ قَٰتَلَهُمُ ٱللَّهُ ۚ أَنَّىٰ يُؤْفَكُونَ ﴿٣٠﴾

ٱتَّخَذُوٓا۟ أَحْبَارَهُمْ وَرُهْبَٰنَهُمْ أَرْبَابًا مِّن دُونِ ٱللَّهِ وَٱلْمَسِيحَ ٱبْنَ مَرْيَمَ وَمَآ أُمِرُوٓا۟ إِلَّا لِيَعْبُدُوٓا۟ إِلَٰهًا وَٰحِدًا ۖ لَّآ إِلَٰهَ إِلَّا هُوَ ۚ سُبْحَٰنَهُۥ عَمَّا يُشْرِكُونَ

They desire to put out the light of Allah with their mouths, but Allah is intent on perfecting His light though the faithless should be averse. (9:32)

SŪRAT MARYAM

And *mention* in the Book Mary, when she withdrew from her family to an easterly place. (19:16)

Thus did she seclude herself from them, whereupon We sent to her Our Spirit and he became incarnate for her as a well-proportioned human. (19:17)

She said, 'I seek the protection of the All-beneficent from you, should you be Godwary!' (19:18)

He Said, 'I am only a messenger of your Lord that I may give you a pure son.' (19:19)

She said, 'How shall I have a child seeing that no man has ever touched me, nor have I been unchaste?, (19:20)

He said, 'So shall it be. Your Lord says. "It is simple for Me." And so that We may make him a sign for mankind and a mercy from Us, and it is a matter [already] decided.' (19:21)

Thus she conceived him, then withdrew with him to a distant place. (19:22)

The birth pangs brought her to the trunk of a date palm. She said, 'I wish I had died before this and become a forgotten thing, beyond recall.' (19:23)

Thereupon he called her from below her [saying,] 'Do not grieve! Your Lord has made a spring to flow at your feet. (19:24)

Shake the trunk of the palm tree, freshly picked dates will drop upon you. (19:25)

يُرِيدُونَ أَن يُطْفِـُٔواْ نُورَ ٱللَّهِ بِأَفْوَٰهِهِمْ وَيَأْبَى ٱللَّهُ إِلَّآ أَن يُتِمَّ نُورَهُۥ وَلَوْ كَرِهَ
ٱلْكَٰفِرُونَ ﴿٣٢﴾

سورة مريم:

وَٱذْكُرْ فِى ٱلْكِتَٰبِ مَرْيَمَ إِذِ ٱنتَبَذَتْ مِنْ أَهْلِهَا مَكَانًا شَرْقِيًّا ﴿١٦﴾

فَٱتَّخَذَتْ مِن دُونِهِمْ حِجَابًا فَأَرْسَلْنَآ إِلَيْهَا رُوحَنَا فَتَمَثَّلَ لَهَا بَشَرًا سَوِيًّا ﴿١٧﴾

قَالَتْ إِنِّىٓ أَعُوذُ بِٱلرَّحْمَٰنِ مِنكَ إِن كُنتَ تَقِيًّا ﴿١٨﴾

قَالَ إِنَّمَآ أَنَا۠ رَسُولُ رَبِّكِ لِأَهَبَ لَكِ غُلَٰمًا زَكِيًّا ﴿١٩﴾

قَالَتْ أَنَّىٰ يَكُونُ لِى غُلَٰمٌ وَلَمْ يَمْسَسْنِى بَشَرٌ وَلَمْ أَكُ بَغِيًّا ﴿٢٠﴾

قَالَ كَذَٰلِكِ قَالَ رَبُّكِ هُوَ عَلَىَّ هَيِّنٌ ۖ وَلِنَجْعَلَهُۥٓ ءَايَةً لِّلنَّاسِ وَرَحْمَةً مِّنَّا ۚ وَكَانَ
أَمْرًا مَّقْضِيًّا ﴿٢١﴾

۞ فَحَمَلَتْهُ فَٱنتَبَذَتْ بِهِۦ مَكَانًا قَصِيًّا ﴿٢٢﴾

فَأَجَآءَهَا ٱلْمَخَاضُ إِلَىٰ جِذْعِ ٱلنَّخْلَةِ قَالَتْ يَٰلَيْتَنِى مِتُّ قَبْلَ هَٰذَا وَكُنتُ
نَسْيًا مَّنسِيًّا ﴿٢٣﴾

فَنَادَىٰهَا مِن تَحْتِهَآ أَلَّا تَحْزَنِى قَدْ جَعَلَ رَبُّكِ تَحْتَكِ سَرِيًّا ﴿٢٤﴾

وَهُزِّىٓ إِلَيْكِ بِجِذْعِ ٱلنَّخْلَةِ تُسَٰقِطْ عَلَيْكِ رُطَبًا جَنِيًّا ﴿٢٥﴾

Eat, drink, and be comforted. Then if you see any man, say, "Indeed I have vowed a fast to the All-beneficent, so I will not speak to any human today." ' (19:26)

Then carrying him she brought him to her people. They said, 'O Mary, you have certainly come up with an odd thing! (19:27)

O sister of Aaron ['s lineage]! Your father was not an evil man, nor was your mother unchaste.' (19:28)

Thereat she pointed to him. They said, 'How can we speak to one who is yet a baby in the cradle?' (19:29)

He said, 'Indeed I am a servant of Allah! He has given me the Book and made me a prophet. (19:30)

He has made me blessed, wherever I may be, and He has enjoined me to [maintain] the prayer and to [pay] the *zakāt* as long as I live, (19:31)

And to be good to my mother, and He has not made me self-willed and wretched. (19:32)

Peace to me the day I was born, and the day I die, and the day I am raised alive.' (19:33)

That is Jesus, son of Mary, a word of the Real concerning whom they are in doubt. (19:34)

It is not for Allah to take a son. Immaculate is He! When He decides on a matter, He just says to it, 'Be!' and it is. (19:35)

'Indeed Allah is my Lord and your Lord. So worship Him. This is a straight path.' (19:36)

But the factions differed among themselves. So woe to the faithless at the scene of a tremendous day. (19:37)

How well they will hear and how well they will see on the day when they come to Us! But today the wrongdoers are in manifest error. (19:38)

فَكُلِى وَٱشْرَبِى وَقَرِّى عَيْنًا ۖ فَإِمَّا تَرَيِنَّ مِنَ ٱلْبَشَرِ أَحَدًا فَقُولِىٓ إِنِّى نَذَرْتُ لِلرَّحْمَٰنِ
صَوْمًا فَلَنْ أُكَلِّمَ ٱلْيَوْمَ إِنسِيًّا ﴿٢٦﴾

فَأَتَتْ بِهِۦ قَوْمَهَا تَحْمِلُهُۥ ۖ قَالُوا۟ يَٰمَرْيَمُ لَقَدْ جِئْتِ شَيْـًٔا فَرِيًّا ﴿٢٧﴾

يَٰٓأُخْتَ هَٰرُونَ مَا كَانَ أَبُوكِ ٱمْرَأَ سَوْءٍ وَمَا كَانَتْ أُمُّكِ بَغِيًّا ﴿٢٨﴾

فَأَشَارَتْ إِلَيْهِ ۖ قَالُوا۟ كَيْفَ نُكَلِّمُ مَن كَانَ فِى ٱلْمَهْدِ صَبِيًّا ﴿٢٩﴾

قَالَ إِنِّى عَبْدُ ٱللَّهِ ءَاتَىٰنِىَ ٱلْكِتَٰبَ وَجَعَلَنِى نَبِيًّا ﴿٣٠﴾

وَجَعَلَنِى مُبَارَكًا أَيْنَ مَا كُنتُ وَأَوْصَٰنِى بِٱلصَّلَوٰةِ وَٱلزَّكَوٰةِ مَا دُمْتُ حَيًّا ﴿٣١﴾

وَبَرًّۢا بِوَٰلِدَتِى وَلَمْ يَجْعَلْنِى جَبَّارًا شَقِيًّا ﴿٣٢﴾

وَٱلسَّلَٰمُ عَلَىَّ يَوْمَ وُلِدتُّ وَيَوْمَ أَمُوتُ وَيَوْمَ أُبْعَثُ حَيًّا ﴿٣٣﴾

ذَٰلِكَ عِيسَى ٱبْنُ مَرْيَمَ ۚ قَوْلَ ٱلْحَقِّ ٱلَّذِى فِيهِ يَمْتَرُونَ ﴿٣٤﴾

مَا كَانَ لِلَّهِ أَن يَتَّخِذَ مِن وَلَدٍ ۖ سُبْحَٰنَهُۥٓ ۚ إِذَا قَضَىٰٓ أَمْرًا فَإِنَّمَا يَقُولُ لَهُۥ كُن
فَيَكُونُ ﴿٣٥﴾

وَإِنَّ ٱللَّهَ رَبِّى وَرَبُّكُمْ فَٱعْبُدُوهُ ۚ هَٰذَا صِرَٰطٌ مُّسْتَقِيمٌ ﴿٣٦﴾

فَٱخْتَلَفَ ٱلْأَحْزَابُ مِنۢ بَيْنِهِمْ ۖ فَوَيْلٌ لِّلَّذِينَ كَفَرُوا۟ مِن مَّشْهَدِ يَوْمٍ عَظِيمٍ ﴿٣٧﴾

أَسْمِعْ بِهِمْ وَأَبْصِرْ يَوْمَ يَأْتُونَنَا ۖ لَٰكِنِ ٱلظَّٰلِمُونَ ٱلْيَوْمَ فِى ضَلَٰلٍ مُّبِينٍ ﴿٣٨﴾

وَأَنذِرْهُمْ يَوْمَ ٱلْحَسْرَةِ إِذْ قُضِىَ ٱلْأَمْرُ وَهُمْ فِى غَفْلَةٍ وَهُمْ لَا يُؤْمِنُونَ ﴿٣٩﴾

Warn them of the Day of Regret, when the matter will be decided, while they are [yet] heedless and do not have faith. (19:39)

Indeed We shall inherit the earth and whoever there is on it, and to Us they shall be brought back. (19:40)

SŪRAT AL-MU'MINŪN

And We made the son of Mary and his mother a sign, and sheltered them in a highland, level and watered by a stream. (23:50)

SŪRAT AL-AḤZĀB

[*Recall*] when We took a pledge from the prophets, and from you and from Noah and Abraham and Moses and Jesus son of Mary, and We took from them a solemn pledge, (33:7)

So that He may question the truthful concerning their truthfulness. And He has prepared for the faithless a painful punishment. (33:8)

SŪRAT AL-SHŪRĀ

He has prescribed for you the religion which He had enjoined upon Noah and which We have [also] revealed to you, and which We had enjoined upon Abraham, Moses and Jesus, declaring, 'Maintain the religion, and do not be divided in it.' Hard on the polytheists is that to which you summon them. Allah chooses for it whomever He wishes and He guides to it whomever returns penitently. (42:13)

وَأَنذِرْهُمْ يَوْمَ ٱلْحَسْرَةِ إِذْ قُضِىَ ٱلْأَمْرُ وَهُمْ فِى غَفْلَةٍ وَهُمْ لَا يُؤْمِنُونَ ﴿٣٩﴾

إِنَّا نَحْنُ نَرِثُ ٱلْأَرْضَ وَمَنْ عَلَيْهَا وَإِلَيْنَا يُرْجَعُونَ ﴿٤٠﴾

سورة المؤمنون:

وَجَعَلْنَا ٱبْنَ مَرْيَمَ وَأُمَّهُۥٓ ءَايَةً وَءَاوَيْنَٰهُمَآ إِلَىٰ رَبْوَةٍ ذَاتِ قَرَارٍ وَمَعِينٍ ﴿٥٠﴾

سورة الأحزاب:

وَإِذْ أَخَذْنَا مِنَ ٱلنَّبِيِّـۧنَ مِيثَٰقَهُمْ وَمِنكَ وَمِن نُّوحٍ وَإِبْرَٰهِيمَ وَمُوسَىٰ وَعِيسَى ٱبْنِ مَرْيَمَ ۖ وَأَخَذْنَا مِنْهُم مِّيثَٰقًا غَلِيظًا ﴿٧﴾

لِّيَسْـَٔلَ ٱلصَّٰدِقِينَ عَن صِدْقِهِمْ ۚ وَأَعَدَّ لِلْكَٰفِرِينَ عَذَابًا أَلِيمًا ﴿٨﴾

سورة الشورى:

شَرَعَ لَكُم مِّنَ ٱلدِّينِ مَا وَصَّىٰ بِهِۦ نُوحًا وَٱلَّذِىٓ أَوْحَيْنَآ إِلَيْكَ وَمَا وَصَّيْنَا بِهِۦٓ إِبْرَٰهِيمَ وَمُوسَىٰ وَعِيسَىٰٓ ۖ أَنْ أَقِيمُوا۟ ٱلدِّينَ وَلَا تَتَفَرَّقُوا۟ فِيهِ ۚ كَبُرَ عَلَى ٱلْمُشْرِكِينَ مَا تَدْعُوهُمْ إِلَيْهِ ۚ ٱللَّهُ يَجْتَبِىٓ إِلَيْهِ مَن يَشَآءُ وَيَهْدِىٓ إِلَيْهِ مَن يُنِيبُ ﴿١٣﴾

They did not divide [into sects] except after the knowledge had come to them, out of envy among themselves; and were it not for a prior decree of your Lord [granting them reprieve] until a specified time, decision would have been made between them. Indeed those who were made heirs to the Book after them are surely in grave doubt concerning it. (42:14)

So *summon* to this [unity of religion], and be steadfast, just as you have been commanded, and *do not follow* their desires, and *say*, 'I believe in whatever Book Allah has sent down. I have been commanded to be do justice among you. Allah is our Lord and your Lord. Our deeds belong to us and your deeds belong to you. There is no argument between us and you. Allah will bring us together and toward Him is the destination.' (42:15)

SŪRAT AL-ZUKHRUF

When the Son of Mary was cited as an example, behold, your people raise an outcry. (43:57)

They say. 'Are our gods better or he?' They only cite him to you for the sake of contention. Rather they are a contentious lot. (43:58)

He was just a servant whom We had blessed and made an exemplar for the Children of Israel. (43:59)

Had We wished We would have set in your stead angels to be [your] successors on the earth. (43:60)

Indeed he is a portent of the Hour; so do not doubt it and follow Me. This is a straight path. (43:61)

Do not let Satan bar you [from the way of Allah]. Indeed he is your manifest enemy. (43:62)

When Jesus brought the manifest proofs, he said, 'I have certainly brought you wisdom, and [I have come] to make clear to you some of the things that you differ about. So be wary of Allah and obey me.' (43:63)

وَمَا تَفَرَّقُوٓاْ إِلَّا مِنۢ بَعۡدِ مَا جَآءَهُمُ ٱلۡعِلۡمُ بَغۡيَۢا بَيۡنَهُمۡۚ وَلَوۡلَا كَلِمَةٞ سَبَقَتۡ مِن رَّبِّكَ إِلَىٰٓ أَجَلٖ مُّسَمّٗى لَّقُضِيَ بَيۡنَهُمۡۚ وَإِنَّ ٱلَّذِينَ أُورِثُواْ ٱلۡكِتَٰبَ مِنۢ بَعۡدِهِمۡ لَفِي شَكّٖ مِّنۡهُ مُرِيبٖ ﴿١٤﴾

فَلِذَٰلِكَ فَٱدۡعُۖ وَٱسۡتَقِمۡ كَمَآ أُمِرۡتَۖ وَلَا تَتَّبِعۡ أَهۡوَآءَهُمۡۖ وَقُلۡ ءَامَنتُ بِمَآ أَنزَلَ ٱللَّهُ مِن كِتَٰبٖۖ وَأُمِرۡتُ لِأَعۡدِلَ بَيۡنَكُمُۖ ٱللَّهُ رَبُّنَا وَرَبُّكُمۡۖ لَنَآ أَعۡمَٰلُنَا وَلَكُمۡ أَعۡمَٰلُكُمۡۖ لَا حُجَّةَ بَيۡنَنَا وَبَيۡنَكُمُۖ ٱللَّهُ يَجۡمَعُ بَيۡنَنَاۖ وَإِلَيۡهِ ٱلۡمَصِيرُ ﴿١٥﴾

سورة الزخرف:

۞ وَلَمَّا ضُرِبَ ٱبۡنُ مَرۡيَمَ مَثَلًا إِذَا قَوۡمُكَ مِنۡهُ يَصِدُّونَ ﴿٥٧﴾

وَقَالُوٓاْ ءَأَٰلِهَتُنَا خَيۡرٌ أَمۡ هُوَۚ مَا ضَرَبُوهُ لَكَ إِلَّا جَدَلَۢاۚ بَلۡ هُمۡ قَوۡمٌ خَصِمُونَ ﴿٥٨﴾

إِنۡ هُوَ إِلَّا عَبۡدٌ أَنۡعَمۡنَا عَلَيۡهِ وَجَعَلۡنَٰهُ مَثَلٗا لِّبَنِيٓ إِسۡرَٰٓءِيلَ ﴿٥٩﴾

وَلَوۡ نَشَآءُ لَجَعَلۡنَا مِنكُم مَّلَٰٓئِكَةٗ فِي ٱلۡأَرۡضِ يَخۡلُفُونَ ﴿٦٠﴾

وَإِنَّهُۥ لَعِلۡمٞ لِّلسَّاعَةِ فَلَا تَمۡتَرُنَّ بِهَا وَٱتَّبِعُونِۚ هَٰذَا صِرَٰطٞ مُّسۡتَقِيمٞ ﴿٦١﴾

وَلَا يَصُدَّنَّكُمُ ٱلشَّيۡطَٰنُۖ إِنَّهُۥ لَكُمۡ عَدُوّٞ مُّبِينٞ ﴿٦٢﴾

وَلَمَّا جَآءَ عِيسَىٰ بِٱلۡبَيِّنَٰتِ قَالَ قَدۡ جِئۡتُكُم بِٱلۡحِكۡمَةِ وَلِأُبَيِّنَ لَكُم بَعۡضَ ٱلَّذِي تَخۡتَلِفُونَ فِيهِۖ فَٱتَّقُواْ ٱللَّهَ وَأَطِيعُونِ ﴿٦٣﴾

Indeed Allah is my Lord and your Lord; so worship him. This is a straight path.' (43:64)

SŪRAT AL-ḤADĪD

Then We followed them up with Our apostles and We followed [them] with Jesus son of Mary, and We gave him the Evangel, and We put in the hearts of those who followed him kindness and mercy. But as for monasticism, they innovated it – We had not prescribed it for them – only for seeking Allah's pleasure. Yet they did not observe it with due observance. So We gave to the faithful among them their [due] reward, but many of them are transgressors. (57:27)

SŪRAT AL-ṢAFF

And when Jesus son of Mary said, 'O Children of Israel! Indeed I am the apostle of Allah to you, to confirm what is before me of the Torah, and to give the good news of an apostle who will come after me, whose name is Ahmad.' Yet when he brought them manifest proofs, they said, 'This is plain magic.' (61:6)

And who is a greater wrongdoer than him who fabricates falsehoods against Allah, while he is being summoned to Islam? And Allah does not guide the wrongdoing lot. (61:7)

They desire to put out the light of Allah with their mouths, but Allah shall perfect His light though the faithless should be averse. (61:8)

إِنَّ ٱللَّهَ هُوَ رَبِّى وَرَبُّكُمْ فَٱعْبُدُوهُ ۚ هَـٰذَا صِرَٰطٌ مُّسْتَقِيمٌ ﴿٦٤﴾

سورة الحديد:

ثُمَّ قَفَّيْنَا عَلَىٰٓ ءَاثَـٰرِهِم بِرُسُلِنَا وَقَفَّيْنَا بِعِيسَى ٱبْنِ مَرْيَمَ وَءَاتَيْنَـٰهُ ٱلْإِنجِيلَ وَجَعَلْنَا فِى قُلُوبِ ٱلَّذِينَ ٱتَّبَعُوهُ رَأْفَةً وَرَحْمَةً وَرَهْبَانِيَّةً ٱبْتَدَعُوهَا مَا كَتَبْنَـٰهَا عَلَيْهِمْ إِلَّا ٱبْتِغَآءَ رِضْوَٰنِ ٱللَّهِ فَمَا رَعَوْهَا حَقَّ رِعَايَتِهَا ۖ فَـَٔاتَيْنَا ٱلَّذِينَ ءَامَنُوا۟ مِنْهُمْ أَجْرَهُمْ ۖ وَكَثِيرٌ مِّنْهُمْ فَـٰسِقُونَ ﴿٢٧﴾

سورة الصف:

وَإِذْ قَالَ عِيسَى ٱبْنُ مَرْيَمَ يَـٰبَنِىٓ إِسْرَٰٓءِيلَ إِنِّى رَسُولُ ٱللَّهِ إِلَيْكُم مُّصَدِّقًا لِّمَا بَيْنَ يَدَىَّ مِنَ ٱلتَّوْرَىٰةِ وَمُبَشِّرًۢا بِرَسُولٍ يَأْتِى مِنۢ بَعْدِى ٱسْمُهُۥٓ أَحْمَدُ ۖ فَلَمَّا جَآءَهُم بِٱلْبَيِّنَـٰتِ قَالُوا۟ هَـٰذَا سِحْرٌ مُّبِينٌ ﴿٦﴾

وَمَنْ أَظْلَمُ مِمَّنِ ٱفْتَرَىٰ عَلَى ٱللَّهِ ٱلْكَذِبَ وَهُوَ يُدْعَىٰٓ إِلَى ٱلْإِسْلَـٰمِ ۚ وَٱللَّهُ لَا يَهْدِى ٱلْقَوْمَ ٱلظَّـٰلِمِينَ ﴿٧﴾

يُرِيدُونَ لِيُطْفِـُٔوا۟ نُورَ ٱللَّهِ بِأَفْوَٰهِهِمْ وَٱللَّهُ مُتِمُّ نُورِهِۦ وَلَوْ كَرِهَ ٱلْكَـٰفِرُونَ ﴿٨﴾

It is He who has sent His Apostle with the guidance and the religion of truth that He may made it prevail over all religions though the polytheists should be averse. (61:9)

O you who have faith! Be Allah's helpers, just as Jesus son of Mary said to the disciples, 'Who will be my helpers for Allah's sake?' The disciples said, 'We will be Allah's helpers!' So a group of the Children of Israel believed, and a group disbelieved. Then We strengthened the faithful against their enemies, and they became the dominant ones. (61:14)

هُوَ ٱلَّذِىٓ أَرۡسَلَ رَسُولَهُۥ بِٱلۡهُدَىٰ وَدِينِ ٱلۡحَقِّ لِيُظۡهِرَهُۥ عَلَى ٱلدِّينِ كُلِّهِۦ وَلَوۡ كَرِهَ ٱلۡمُشۡرِكُونَ ﴿٩﴾

يَٰٓأَيُّهَا ٱلَّذِينَ ءَامَنُواْ كُونُوٓاْ أَنصَارَ ٱللَّهِ كَمَا قَالَ عِيسَى ٱبۡنُ مَرۡيَمَ لِلۡحَوَارِيِّـۧنَ مَنۡ أَنصَارِىٓ إِلَى ٱللَّهِۖ قَالَ ٱلۡحَوَارِيُّونَ نَحۡنُ أَنصَارُ ٱللَّهِۖ فَـَٔامَنَت طَّآئِفَةٞ مِّنۢ بَنِىٓ إِسۡرَٰٓءِيلَ وَكَفَرَت طَّآئِفَةٞۖ فَأَيَّدۡنَا ٱلَّذِينَ ءَامَنُواْ عَلَىٰ عَدُوِّهِمۡ فَأَصۡبَحُواْ ظَٰهِرِينَ ﴿١٤﴾

CHAPTER TWO

JESUS ﷺ THROUGH SHI'ITE NARRATIONS

1

THE LIFE OF JESUS ﷺ

1.1. HIS BIRTH

1.1.1. It is reported that Abū Baṣīr said, "I asked Abū Ja'far ﷺ about 'Imrān, whether he was a prophet. He said, 'Yes. He was a prophet and an apostle to his people. And Ḥannah, the wife of 'Imrān and Ḥanānah, the wife of Zachariah were sisters. Mary was born to 'Imrān from Ḥannah, and John ﷺ was born to Zachariah from Ḥananah. Mary gave birth to Jesus ﷺ and Jesus ﷺ was the son of the daughter of John's aunt. John ﷺ was the son of the aunt of Mary. And the aunt of one's mother is like one's aunt."

(*Biḥār*, 14, 202, 14)

1.1.2. It is reported that Ya'qūb ibn Ja'far ibn Ibrāhīm said, "I was close to Abū al-Ḥasan Mūsā ﷺ when a Christian came to him. We were at 'Uraiḍ. The Christian said to him, 'I came to you from a far land and have had a difficult journey. I have been asking my Lord for thirty years to guide me to the best religion and the best servants and the most knowledgeable of them. In a dream someone came to me and described a man for me who was in the upper regions of Damascus. I went until I reached him. Then I spoke with him. He

القسم الثاني

عيسى عليه السلام في روايات الشيعة

١

حياة عيسى عليه السلام

١-١- ولادته

١-١-١- بالإسنادِ إلي الصدُوق, عَنْ ابن المُتَوكِّل, عَنْ الحِمْيَري, عَنْ ابن عِيسَي, عَنْ ابن مَحْبُوبٍ, عَنْ ابن رئابٍ, عَنْ أبي بَصِيرٍ, قالَ: «سألْتُ أبا جَعْفَرٍ عليه السلام عَنْ عِمْرانَ, أكانَ نَبيّاً؟ فَقالَ: 'نَعم كانَ نَبيّاً مُرْسَلاً إلي قَوْمِهِ؛ وكانَتْ حَنّةُ امْرأةُ عِمْرانَ وحَنّانَةُ امْرأةُ زكَرِيّا أخْتَيْنِ. فَوُلِدَ لِعِمْرانَ مِنْ حَنّة مَرْيَمُ، ووُلِدَ لِزكَرِيّا مِن حَنّانَة يَحْيَي عليه السلام، وَوَلَدَتْ مَرْيَمُ عِيسَي عليه السلام، وكانَ عِيسَي عليه السلام ابن بِنْتِ خالَتِهِ، وكانَ يَحْيَي عليه السلام ابن خالةِ مَرْيَمَ؛ وَخالَةُ الأمِّ بِمَنْزِلَةِ الخالَةِ.'»

(بحار الأنوار، ١٤، ٢٠٢، ١٤)

١-١-٢- أحْمَدُ بْنُ مِهْرانَ وَعَليُّ بْنُ إبْراهِيمَ جَمِيعاً عَنْ مُحَمَّدِ بْنِ عَليٍّ، عَنْ الحَسَنِ بْنِ راشِدٍ، عَنْ يَعْقُوبَ بْنِ جَعْفَرِ بْنِ إبْراهِيمَ، قالَ: «كُنْتُ عِنْدَ أبِي الحَسَنِ مُوسَي عليه السلام إذْ أتاهُ رَجُلٌ نَصْرانِيٌّ وَنَحْنُ مَعَهُ بالعُرَيْضِ. فَقال لَهُ النَصْرانِيُّ: 'أتَيْتُكَ مِنْ بَلَدٍ بَعِيدٍ وَسَفَرٍ شاقٍّ، وَسألْتُ رَبِّي مُنْذُ ثَلاثِينَ سَنَةً أنْ يُرْشِدَنِي إلي خَيْرِ الأدْيانِ وإلَي خَيْرِ العِبادِ وأعْلَمِهِمْ. وأتانِي آتٍ فِي النَوْمِ، فَوَصَفَ لِي رَجُلاً بِعُلْيا دِمَشْقَ. فانْطَلَقْتُ حَتَّي أتَيْتُهُ

said, "I am the most knowledgeable among the people of my religion, but there is one who is more knowledgeable than I." I said, "Guide me to the one who is more knowledgeable than you. I do not care how long the journey; a long distance is not too far for me. I have read the Gospels, all of them, the Psalms of David, and I have read four books of the Torah, and I have read the Qur'an outwardly, until I learned all of it."
Then the scholar said to me, "If you want to study about Christianity, I am the most knowledgeable person among the Arabs and non-Arabs. If you want to study about Judaism, Bāṭī ibn Shuraḥbīl al-Sāmirī is the most knowledgable of men today. If you want knowledge of Islam, knowledge of the Torah and knowledge of the Gospel and the Psalms, and the book of Hūd, and all of what has been sent down to every prophet in your time and the times of others... I will guide you to him, so go to him, even if you have to walk..."

Abū Ibrāhīm [Imam Mūsā Kāẓim] said to him, "I will inform you of something that only a few people know who have read the books. Tell me what is the name of the mother of Mary, and the day on which Mary was breathed into, and what hour of the day, and on what day Mary gave birth to Jesus and what hour of the day?" The Christian said, "I do not know."

Abū Ibrāhīm said, "As for the mother of Mary, her name was Mirtha, in Arabic, Wahibah (gift). As for the day on which Mary conceived, it was Friday at noon, and that was the day that the *Rūḥ al-Amīn* (the trustworthy spirit) came down, and there is no festival better than this for Muslims. Allah, the Blessed and Almighty, magnified it, and Muḥammad magnified it and He ordered that it should be a holiday, and it was Friday. As for the day on which Mary was born, it was Tuesday, at four thirty in the afternoon. And do you know what was the river beside which Mary gave birth to Jesus?" He said, "No." He said, "It was the Euphrates, and beside it were date palms and grape vines. There is nothing like the grapes and date palms near the Euphrates..."

(*Kāfī*, 1, 478, 4)

فكَلَّمْتُهُ. فقالَ: 'أنا أعْلَمُ أهْلِ دِينِي، وَغَيْرِى أعْلَمُ مِنِّى.' فقُلْتُ: 'أرْشِدْنِي إلَي مَنْ هُوَ أعْلَمُ مِنْكَ، فإنِّى لا أسْتَعْظِمُ السفَرَ وَلا تَبْعُدُ عَلَيَّ الشُقَّةُ. وَلَقَدْ قَراْتُ الإنجيلَ كُلَّها وَمَزاميرَ داوُدَ، وَقَراْتُ أرْبَعَةَ أسْفارٍ مِنَ التوْراةِ، وَقَراْتُ ظاهِرَ القُرْآنِ حَتَّي اسْتَوْعَبْتُهُ كُلَّهُ.

فَقالَ لِى العالِمُ: 'إنْ كُنْتَ تُرِيدُ عِلْمَ النصْرانيَّةِ، فأنا أعْلَمُ العَرَبِ والعَجَمِ بِها؛ وإنْ كُنْتَ تُرِيدُ عِلْمَ اليَهُودِ، فَباطِي بْنُ شُرَحْبِيلَ السامِرِىُّ أعْلَمُ الناسِ بِها اليَوْمَ؛ وإنْ كُنْتَ تُرِيدُ عِلْمَ الإسْلامِ وَعِلْمَ التَوْراةِ وَعِلْمَ الإنجيلِ وَعِلْمَ الزبُورِ وكِتابَ هُودٍ وكُلَّ ما أُنْزِلَ عَلي نَبِيٍّ مِنَ الأنبياءِ فِى دَهْرِكَ وَدَهْرِ غَيْرِكَ...، فأرْشِدُكَ إليهِ فَأتهِ وَلَوْ مَشْياً عَلَى رِجْلَيْكَ...''

فقالَ لَهُ أبُو إبْراهِيمَ عليه السلام: ' أُعَجِّلُكَ أيْضاً خَبَراً لا يَعْرِفُهُ إلّا قَلِيلٌ مِمَّنْ قَرأ الكُتُبَ. أخْبِرْنِى ما اسْمُ أُمِّ مَرْيَمَ، وأيُّ يَوْمٍ نُفِخَتْ فِيهِ مَرْيَمُ، وَلِكَمْ مِنْ ساعَةٍ مِنَ النَهارِ وأيُّ يَوْمٍ وَضَعَتْ مَرْيَمُ فِيهِ عِيسَي عليه السلام، وَلِكَمْ مِنْ ساعَةٍ مِنَ النَهارِ؟' فَقالَ النَصْرانِيُّ، 'لا أدْرِى.'

فَقالَ أبُو إبْراهِيمَ عليه السلام: 'أمّا أمُّ مَرْيَمَ فاسْمُها مَرْثا، وَهِيَ وَهِيبَةُ بالعَرَبِيَّةِ، وأمّا اليَوْمُ الذى حَمَلَتْ فِيهِ مَرْيَمُ فَهُوَ يَوْمُ الجُمُعَةِ لِلزَّوالِ، وَهُوَ اليَوْمُ الذى هَبَطَ فِيهِ الروحُ الأمِينُ؛ وَلَيْسَ لِلْمُسْلِمِينَ عِيدٌ كانَ أوْلَي مِنْهُ. عَظَّمَهُ الله، تَبارَكَ وَتَعالي، وَعَظَّمَهُ مُحَمَّدٌ صلى الله عليه وآله وسلم، فأمَرَ أنْ يَجْعَلَهُ عِيداً، فَهُوَ يَوْمُ الجُمُعَةِ. وأمّا اليَوْمُ الذى وَلَدَتْ فِيهِ مَرْيَمُ، فَهُوَ يَوْمُ الثَلاثاءِ لأرْبَعِ ساعاتٍ وَنِصْفٍ مِنَ النَهارِ؛ والنَهرُ الذى وَلَدَتْ عَلَيْهِ مَرْيَمُ عِيسَي عليه السلام هَلْ تَعْرِفُهُ؟' قالَ: 'لا.' قالَ: 'هُوَ الفُراتُ، وَعَلَيْهِ شَجَرُ النَخْلِ والكَرْمِ، وَلَيْسَ يُساوِى بالفُراتِ شَىْءٌ لِلْكُرُومِ والنَخِيلِ... .'»

(الكافى، ١، ٤٧٨، ٤)

1.1.3. It is reported that Abū 'Abd Allah said, "If we tell you something about one of us, but you do not find it so, but it is so of his child or grandchild, then do not deny what we said. Verily, Allah revealed to Imrān, 'I will grant you a boy, blessed, who will cure the blind and the leper and who will raise the dead by My permission. And I will set him as an Apostle to the Children of Israel.' Then he related this to his wife Ḥannah, the mother of Mary. When she became pregnant with Mary, she thought that her burden was a boy. When she delivered a female, she said, 'O my Lord! Verily I have delivered a female, and the male is not like the female, for a girl will not be a prophet.' Allah said, ❮*And Allah knows better what has been delivered.*❯ (3:36) When Allah granted Jesus to Mary, it was he of whom Allah had given glad tidings to Imrān and had promised him.

So, if we tell you something about one of us, but it is in his child or grandchild, do not deny it. When Mary became grown, she went into the cloister (*miḥrāb*) and put a covering over herself so no one saw her. Zachariah came to her in the cloister, and found that she had summer fruit in the winter and winter fruit in the summer. He said to her, 'Whence to you is this?' She said, 'It is from Allah. Verily Allah provides for whomsoever He wants without measure.' When the angels said, ❮*O Mary! Verily Allah has chosen you and purified you and chosen you above the women of the worlds.*❯ (3:42) He said that Mary was twice chosen. The first choosing was her selection [with glad tidings given to Imrān], but the second was that she became pregnant without a man. So, she was chosen over all the women of the world."

(*Biḥār*, 14, 199, 8)

١-١-٣- عَنْ الحَسَن بن مَحْبُوبٍ, عَنْ عَليٍّ بن رئابٍ, عَنْ أبي بَصِيرٍ, عَنْ أبي عبدِ اللهِ عليه السلام، قالَ: «إن قُلنا لَكُمْ فِي الرجُلِ مِنّا قولاً، فَلَمْ يَكُنْ فِيهِ وكانَ فِي وَلَدِهِ أو وَلَدِ وَلَدِهِ، فَلا تُنكِرُوا ذَلِكَ. إنّ الله أوحَي إلَي عِمرانَ: 'إنّي واهِبٌ لكَ ذكَراً مُباركاً يُبرِئُ الأكْمَهَ والأبرصَ ويُحيِي الموتَي بِإذْنِي، وجاعِلُهُ رَسُولاً إلَي بَنِي إسرائيلَ.' فَحدَّثَ امرأتَهُ حنّةَ بذَلِكَ، وَهِيَ أمُّ مَرْيَمَ. فَلمّا حَمَلَتْ بِها كانَ حَمْلُها عِنْدَ نَفْسِها غُلاماً. فَلمّا وَضَعَتْها أنثَي ﴿قالَتْ: 'رَبِّ إنّي وَضَعْتُها أنثَي.'﴾ ﴿'وَلَيْسَ الذّكَرُ كالأنْثَي.'﴾ لأنّ البِنْتَ لا تَكُونُ رَسُولاً. يَقُولُ اللهُ: ﴿واللهُ أعْلَمُ بِما وَضَعَتْ.﴾ فَلمّا وَهَبَ اللهُ لِمَرْيَمَ عِيسَي عليه السلام، كانَ هُوَ الذي بَشّرَ اللهُ بِهِ عِمرانَ وَوَعَدَهُ إيّاهُ. فإذا قُلنا لَكُم فِي الرجلِ مِنّا شَيئًا، وكانَ فِي وَلَدِهِ أو وَلَدِ وَلَدِهِ، فَلا تُنكِروا ذَلِكَ.

فَلمّا بَلَغَت مَرْيَمُ صارَت فِي المِحرابِ وأرْخَت عَلَي نَفْسِها سِتراً؛ وكانَ لا يَراها أحدٌ، وكانَ يَدخلُ عَلَيْها زَكَرِيّا المحرابَ، فَيَجِدُ عِنْدَها فاكهةَ الصَيف فِي الشِتاءِ وفاكهةَ الشِتاءِ فِي الصَيفِ، فَكانَ يَقُولُ لها: ﴿أنَّي لكِ هذا؟﴾ فَتَقُولُ: ﴿هُوَ مِنْ عِنْدِ اللهِ، إنّ اللهَ يَرْزُقُ مَنْ يَشاءُ بِغَير حِسابٍ.﴾ ﴿وإذْ قالَتْ الملائكَةُ: 'يا مَرْيَمُ، إنّ اللهَ اصْطَفاكِ وَطَهَّرَكِ واصْطَفاكِ عَلَي نِساءِ العالمَينَ.'﴾» قالَ: «اصْطَفاها مَرّتَين: أمّا الأولَي فاصْطَفاها أي اخْتارَها؛ وأمّا الثانيةُ فانّها حَمَلَتْ مِنْ غَير فَحْلٍ، فاصْطَفاها بِذَلِكَ عَلَي نِساءِ العالمَينَ.»

(بحار الأنوار، ١٤، ١٩٩، ٨)

1.1.4. It is reported that Ismā'īl al-Ju'fī said that Abū Ja'far said, "When the wife of 'Imrān vowed that what was in her womb would be dedicated, [and what was meant was that he would be]) dedicated to the mosque, when he was delivered he would enter the mosque and never leave,(then when Mary was born, [her mother] said, ﴾*My Lord! I have delivered a female. And Allah knows best what she delivered. And the male is not like the female, and I have name her Mary, and I commend her to Your protection from the cast off Satan and also her offspring.*﴿ (3:36)

Then the prophets cast lots and the lot fell to Zachariah, and he was the husband of her sister and her custodian, and she was brought to the mosque. When she matured to when a woman menstruates, she was the most beautiful of women, and when she prayed, the cloister became bright by her light. Then Zachariah entered and found that before her there was winter fruit in the summer and summer fruit in the winter. Then he said, ﴾*From whence is this?' She said, 'It is from Allah.*﴿ (3:37) Because of this, Zachariah prayed to his Lord, ﴾*And verily I fear my kindred after me, and my wife is barren.*﴿ (19:5), and so on with what Allah mentioned of the story of Zachariah and John."

(*Biḥār*, 14, 204, 18)

1.1.5. Layth ibn Sa'd said, "I said to Ka'b, who was with Mu'awīyah, 'How would you describe the birth of the Prophet ﷺ? Do you see any excellence in his progeny?' Then Ka'b turned to Mu'awīyah, to see what he wanted. Allah, the Mighty and Magnificent, put [these words] on his tongue, 'O Abū Isḥāq, may Allah have mercy on you, say whatever you know!' Ka'b said, 'I have read seventy-two books all of which were sent from heaven, and I have read the entire scripture of Daniel. In all of them I have

١-١-٤- أبُو خالِدٍ القمّاطُ, عَنْ إسْماعِيلَ الجُعْفِيِّ, عَنْ أبِي جَعْفَرٍ عليه السلام، قالَ: «إنَّ امْراةَ عِمْرانَ لَمّا نَذرَتْ ما فِي بَطْنِها مُحَرَّراً،» قال: «والمُحَرَّرُ لِلْمَسْجِدِ، إذا وَضَعَتْهُ، دَخلَ المَسْجِدَ فلَمْ يَخرُجْ مِنَ المَسْجِدِ أبَداً. فلَمّا وُلِدَتْ مَرْيَمُ، قالَتْ:﴿رَبِّ إنِّي وَضَعْتُها أُنْثَي! واللهُ أعْلَمُ بِما وَضَعَتْ ولَيْسَ الذَّكَرُ كالأُنْثَي، وإنِّي سَمَّيْتُها مَرْيَمَ، وانِّي أُعِيذُها بِكَ وَذُرِّيَّتَها مِنَ الشيْطانِ الرجِيمِ.﴾

فساهَمَ علَيْها النَبِيُّونَ؛ فأصابَ القُرْعَةُ زكَرِيّا، وَهُوَ زَوْجُ أُخْتِها، وكَفّلَها وأدْخَلَها المَسْجِدَ. فلَمّا بلَغَتْ ما تَبْلُغُ النساءَ مِنَ الطَّمْثِ، وكانَتْ أجْملَ النساءِ، وكانَتْ تُصلّي فتُضِيءُ المِحْرابَ لِنُورها، فَدخَلَ علَيْها زكَرِيّا، فإذا عنْدَها فاكِهَةُ الشِتاءِ فِي الصيْفِ وفاكِهَةُ الصيْفِ فِي الشِتاءِ. فَقالَ:﴿أنَّي لَكِ هَذا؟ قالَتْ: 'هوَ مِنْ عِنْدِ اللهِ.'﴾ فَهُنالِكَ دَعا زكَرِيّا رَبَّهُ، قالَ:﴿إنِّي خِفْتُ المَوالِيَ مِنْ وَرائِي.﴾ إلَي ما ذكَرَ اللهُ مِنْ قِصَّةِ زكَرِيّا وَيَحْيَي.»

(بحار الأنوار، ١٤، ٢٠٤، ١٨)

١-١-٥- ابن المُتَوكِّلِ، عَنْ عَلِيٍّ، عَنْ أبِيهِ، عَنْ مُحَمَّدِ بْنِ سِنانَ، عَنْ زِيادِ بْنِ المُنْذِرِ، عَنْ لَيْثِ بْنِ سَعْدٍ، قالَ: «قُلْتُ لِكَعْبٍ, وَهُوَ عِنْدَ مُعاوِيَةَ,'كَيْفَ تَجِدُونَ صِفَةَ مَوْلِدِ النَبِيِّ صلى الله عليه وآله وسلم، وَهَلْ تَجِدُونَ لِعِتْرَتِهِ فَضْلاً؟' فالتَفَتَ كَعْبٌ إلَي مُعاوِيَةَ لِيَنْظُرَ كَيْفَ هَواهُ، فأجْرَي اللهُ، عَزَّ وَجلَّ، علَي لِسانِهِ، فَقالَ: 'هاتِ يا أبا إسْحاقَ, رَحِمَكَ اللهُ, ما عِنْدَكَ.' فَقال كَعْبٌ: 'إنِّي قَدْ قَرأتُ اثْنَيْنِ وَسَبْعِينَ كِتاباً, كُلُّها أُنْزِلَتْ مِنَ السَماءِ, وَقَرأتُ صُحُفَ دانْيالَ كُلَّها، وَوَجَدْتُ فِي كُلِّها ذِكْرَ مَوْلِدِهِ وَمَوْلِدِ عِتْرَتِهِ،

found mention of the birth of the Prophet and his progeny. The name of the Prophet is also known there. No prophet was born with angels being sent down, except Jesus and Aḥmad, may the blessings of Allah be with them both. The covering of heaven was not drawn for any woman except Mary and Āminah, the mother of Aḥmad. Angels guarded no pregnant women except Mary, the mother of the Messiah, and Āminah, the mother of Aḥmad....'"

(*Biḥār*, 15, 261, 12)

1.1.6. It is reported that Imām Riḍā said to al-Mukārī, "...Do you not know that, verily, Allah, the Blessed and Exalted, revealed to 'Imrān, 'I will grant you a boy,' but He granted him Mary and He granted Jesus to Mary. So, Jesus is from Mary and Mary is from Jesus. Jesus and Mary are a single thing. I am from my father and my father from me. I and my father are a single thing."

(*Faqīh*, 3, 155, 3564)

1.1.7. It is reported that Abū 'Abdullah said, "By Allah! In the Qur'ān Allah related Jesus the son of Mary to Abraham from his mother's side." Then he recited this verse, ﴾*and of his [Abraham's] descendants David and Solomon and Job and Joseph and Aaron, and thus do We reward those who do good./ And Zachariah and John and Jesus and Elias, every one was of the good.*﴿ (6:84-85)

(*Biḥār*, 93, 243, 8)

1.1.8. Abū Bāṣir said, "I said to Abū 'Abd Allah, 'Why did Allah create Jesus without any father and created the other people by fathers and mothers?' He said, 'So that the people would know all of His power and its perfection, and so that they would know that He has power to create a creature without a male. Likewise, He has power to create one without a male or female, and He, the Mighty and Magnificent, did that so it would be known that He has power over all things."

(*Biḥār*, 14, 218, 23)

وإنَّ اسْمَهُ لَمَعْرُوفٌ، وإنَّهُ لَمْ يُولَدْ نَبِيٌّ قَطُّ فَنَزَلَتْ عَلَيْهِ المَلائِكَةُ ما خَلا عِيسَي وأحْمَدُ صلى الله عليه وسلم، وَما ضَرَبَ عَلَي آدَمِيَّةٍ حُجُبَ الجَنَّةِ غَيْرَ مَرْيَمَ وآمِنَةَ، اُمِّ أحْمَدَ صلى الله عليه وسلم، وَما وُكِّلَتِ المَلائِكَةُ بِاُنْثَى حَمَلَتْ غَيْرَ مَرْيَمَ اُمِّ المَسِيحِ عليه السلام وآمِنَةَ اُمِّ أحْمَدَ صلى الله عليه وسلم... .'»

(بحار الأنوار، ١٥، ٢٦١، ١٢)

١-١-٦- دَخَلَ ابن أبِى سَعِيدٍ المُكارى عَلَي الرضا عليه السلام فقالَ لَه: «... أما عَلِمْتَ أنَّ اللهَ، تَبارَكَ وَتَعالَي، أوْحَي إلَي عِمْرانَ: 'إنِّى واهِبٌ لَكَ ذَكَراً' فَوَهَبَ لَهُ مَرْيَمَ، وَوَهَبَ لِمَرْيَمَ عِيسَي؟ فَعِيسَي مِنْ مَرْيَمَ، وَمَرْيَمُ مِنْ عِيسَي، وَعِيسَي وَمَرْيَمُ شَيْءٌ واحِدٌ؛ وانا مِنْ أبي، وأبِى مِنِّى، وأنا وأبِى شَيْءٌ واحِدٌ.»

(كتاب من لا يحضره الفقيه، ٣، ١٥٥، ٣٥٦٤)

١-١-٧- عَنْ بَشِيرِ الدهانِ، عَنْ أبِى عَبْدِ اللهِ عليه السلام، قالَ: «واللهِ لَقَدْ نَسَبَ اللهُ عيسَي بن مَرِيَمَ فِى القُرْآنِ إلَي إبْراهِيمَ عليه السلام مِنْ قِبَلِ النِساءِ.» ثُمَّ تَلا: ﴿وَمِنْ ذُرِّيَّتِهِ داوُدَ وَسُلَيْمانَ﴾ إلَي آخِرِ الآيَتَيْنِ وَذَكَرَ عِيسَي.

(بحار الأنوار، ٩٣، ٢٤٣، ٨)

١-١-٨- الدقاقُ، عَنْ الأسدِيِّ، عَنْ النَخَعِي، عَنْ النَوْفِلِي، عَنْ عَلِيِّ بْن سالِمٍ، عَنْ أبِيهِ، عَنْ أبِى بَصِيرٍ، قالَ: «قُلْتُ لأبِى عَبْدِ اللهِ عليه السلام : 'لِمَ خَلَقَ اللهُ عِيسَي مِنْ غَيْرِ أبٍ، وَخَلَقَ سائِرَ الناسِ مِنَ الآباءِ والأمَّهاتِ؟' فَقالَ: 'لِيَعْلَمَ الناسُ تَمامَ قُدْرَتِهِ وكَمالَها وَيَعْلَمُوا أنَّهُ قادِرٌ عَلَي أنْ يَخْلُقَ خَلْقاً مِنْ أُنْثَي مِنْ غَيْرِ ذَكَرٍ، كَما هُوَ قادِرٌ عَلَي أنْ يَخْلُقَهُ مِنْ غَيْرِ ذَكَرٍ وَلا أُنْثَي؛ وانَّهُ، عَزَّ وَجَلَّ، فَعَلَ ذَلِكَ لِيُعْلَمَ أنَّهُ عَلَي كُلِّ شَيءٍ قَدِيرٌ.'»

(بحار الأنوار، ١٤، ٢١٨، ٢٣)

1.1.9. Salmān al-Fārsī reported that when the Prophet died, the catholicos came... He said to 'Alī the son of Abū Ṭālib, "This is true. Inform me about what your prophet said about the Christ and his being a creature. How did he confirm the creation for him and reject the divinity from him and made necessary imperfection for him?" The Commander of the Faithful said, "He confirmed the creation for him by his destiny and shape, that is necessary for him, chainging from one state to another, increase and decrease that are not separated from him. He did not reject his prophethood, infallibility, perfection and confirmation. It is revealed from Allah that Jesus is like Adam whom Allah created him from clay, then said to him, 'Be.' So he was.'..."

(*Kharā'ij Wa al-Jarā'iḥ*, 2, 554)

1.1.10. Al-Aḥwal said, "I asked Abu 'Abd Allah about the spirit that was in Adam [mentioned in the *āyah*] in which Allah says, ❴*When I straightened him and blew in him from My sprit.* Qur'ān (15:29 and 38:72)❵ He answered, 'This is a created sprit and the sprit that was in Jesus was created.'"

(*Kāfī*, 1, 133, 1)

1.1.11. Hamrān ibn A'yan said, "I asked Abū Ja'far about what Allah, the Mighty and Magnificent, said, and about the spirit from Him. He said: 'It is something created that Allah created with His wisdom in Adam and Jesus."

(*Biḥār,* 4, 12, 4)

1.1.12. It is reported that Abū 'Abd Allah said, "Verily, Mary bore Jesus for nine hours, each hour of which was a month."

(*Kāfī* 8, 332, 516).

١-١-٩- رُوِىَ عَنْ سَلْمانِ الفارْسِيِّ: «لَمّا قُبِضَ النَبِىُّ صلى الله عليه وآله وسلم، قَدِمَ جاثَليقُ... قال الجاثَليقُ: 'هَذا هُوَ الحَقُّ. خَبِّرَنِى ما قالَهُ نَبِيُّكُمْ فِى المَسِيحِ، وأنَّهُ مَخْلُوقٌ؛ مِنْ أيْنَ أثْبَتَ لَهُ الخَلْقَ، وَنَفَي عَنْهُ الإلِهِيَّةَ، وأوْجَبَ فِيهِ النَقْصَ؟' فَقالَ أمِيرُ المُؤْمِنِينَ عليه السلام: 'أثْبَتَ لَهُ الخَلْقَ، بِالتَقْدِيرِ الذى لَزِمَهُ، والتَصْوِيرِ والتَغْيِيرِ مِنْ حالٍ إلِي حالٍ، والزِّيادَةِ الَتِى لَمْ يَنْفَكَّ مِنْها والنقْصانِ. وَلَمْ أنْفِ عَنْهُ النبُوَّةَ، وَلا أخْرَجْتُهُ عَنِ العِصْمَةِ والكَمالِ والتَأيِيدِ. وَقَدْ جاءَنا عَنِ اللهِ بِأنَّهُ مِثْلُ آدَمَ، خَلَقَهُ اللهُ مِنْ تُرابٍ، ثُمَّ قالَ لَهُ: 'كُنْ،' فَيَكُونُ...'»

(الخرائج والجرائح، ٢ ،٥٥٤)

١-١-١٠- عِدَّةٌ مِنْ أصْحابِنا، عَنْ أحْمَدَ بْنِ مُحَمَّدِ بْنِ عِيْسَي، عَنْ ابن أبِى عُمَيْرٍ، عَنْ ابن أذَيْنَة، عَنْ الأحْوَلِ، قالَ: «سألتُ أبا عَبْدِ اللهِ عليه السلام عَنْ الروحِ الَتِى فِى آدمَ عليه السلام قَوْلَهُ: ﴿فإذا سَوَّيْتُهُ وَنَفَخْتُ فِيْهِ مِنْ رُوحِى...﴾ قالَ: 'هَذِهِ رُوحٌ مَخْلُوقَةٌ، والروحُ الَتِى فِى عِيْسَي مَخْلُوقَةٌ.'»

(الكافى، ١، ١، ١٣٣)

١-١-١١- حَمْرانُ بْنُ أعْيَنَ قالَ: سألْتُ أبا جَعْفَرٍ عليه السلام, عَنْ قَوْلِ اللهِ، عَزَّ وَجَلَّ، ﴿وَرُوحٌ مِنْهُ﴾ قالَ: 'هِىَ مَخْلُوقَةٌ خَلَقَها اللهُ بِحِكْمَتِهِ فِى آدم وَفِى عِيسَي عليه السلام.'»

(بحار الأنوار، ٤، ١٢، ٤)

١-١-١٢- أبانٌ، عَنْ رَجُلٍ، عَنْ أبِى عَبْدِ اللهِ عليه السلام، قالَ: «إنَّ مَرْيَمَ عليها السلام حَمَلَتْ بِعِيسَي عليه السلام تِسْعَ ساعاتٍ، كُلُّ ساعَةٍ شَهْراً.»

(الكافى، ٨، ٣٣٢، ٥١٦)

1.1.13. Abū Muḥammad al-Ḥasan ibn-'Alī al-Thānī (the second) said, "Al-Ḥusayn was born in al-Madinah Tuesday, five days before Jamādī al-'Ūlā, three years after al-Hijrah. His mother became pregnant with al-Ḥusayn fifteen nights after his birthday and she was pregnant during six monthes and then she bore him. And no baby was born in six months exept him and Jesus the son of Mary.

(*Dalā'il al-Imāma*, 71)

1.1.14. Shāmī asked the Commander of the Faithful about the six creatures that were never in a womb. He said, "Adam and Eve, the ram of Abraham, the snake of Moses, the she-camel of Ṣāliḥ and the bat that Jesus the son of Mary made and then it flew by the permission of Allah."

(*Biḥār*, 11, 385, 9)

1.1.15. It is reported that al-Ṣādiq said, "When Christ was born, Allah kept his birth secret, and hid him, for Mary, when she bore him, she withdrew to a remote place. (19:22) Then Zachariah and her aunt came searching for her, until they came upon her when she put down what was in her belly and said, ﴾*Oh! Would that I had died before this, and had been forgotten in oblivion*﴿ (19:23). Then Allah, may his remembrance be exalted, opened the tongue of Jesus to excuse his mother and to manifest her authority. When he appeared calamities and persecution had become intense against the children of Israel, and the tyrants and oppressors fell upon them, until the affair of Christ as reported by Allah took place..."

(*Biḥār*, 14, 213, 10)

1.1.16. It is reported that Wahab al-Yamānī said: "A Jew asked the Prophet this question: 'O Muḥammad! Were you, according to the Mother of the Book, a prophet before you were created?' He answered, 'Yes.' He said, 'And were these, your faithful companions,

١-١-١٣- قَالَ أَبُو مُحَمَّدٍ الحَسَنُ بْنُ عَلِيٍّ الثَّانِى: «وُلِدَ الحُسَيْنُ بالمَدِينَةِ يَوْمَ الثَّلَاثَاء لِخَمْسٍ خَلَوْنَ مِنْ جُمَادَي الأُولَي، سَنَة ثَلَاثٍ مِنَ الهِجْرَةِ. وَعَلَقَتْ بالحُسَيْنِ أُمُّهُ بَعْدَ وِلادَةِ الحَسَنِ بِخَمْسِينَ لَيْلَةٍ، سَنَة ثَلَاثٍ مِنَ الهِجْرَةِ، وَحَمَلَتْ بِهِ سِتَّة أَشْهُرٍ، فَوَلَدَتْهُ. وَلَمْ يُولَدْ مَوْلُودٌ سِوَاهُ لِسِتَّةِ أَشْهُرٍ سِوَي عِيسَي بْنِ مَرْيَمَ.»

(دلائل الإمامة، ٧١)

١-١-١٤- سَألَ الشامِيُّ أميرَ المُؤْمِنينَ ﷵ, عَنْ سِتَّةٍ لَمْ يَرْكِضُوا فِى رَحِمٍ فقَالَ: «آدَمُ وَحَوَّاءُ وَكَبْشُ إِبْرَاهِيمَ وَعصا مُوسَي وناقةُ صالِحَ والخُقاشُ الذى عَمَلَهُ عِيسَي بْنُ مَرْيَمَ فطارَ بإِذْنِ اللهِ، عَزَّ وَجَلَّ.»

(بحار الأنوار، ١١، ٣٨٥، ٩)

١-١-١٥- القَطَّانُ، عَنِ السُّكَّرِيِّ, عَنِ الجَوْهَرِيِّ, عَنِ ابن عُمارَةٍ, عَنْ أبِيهِ, عَنِ الصادِقِ، قَالَ: «لمّا وُلِدَ المَسِيحُ أخْفَي اللهُ وِلادَتَهُ وَغَيَّبَ شَخْصَهُ, لأنَّ مَرْيَمَ لَمّا حَمَلَتْهُ انْتَبَذَتْ بِهِ مَكاناً قصِيّاً. ثُمَّ إِنَّ زَكَرِيّا وَخالَتها أَقْبَلا يَقُصّانِ أثَرَها، حَتَّي هَجَما عَلَيها وَقَدْ وَضَعَتْ ما فِى بَطْنِها, وَهِىَ تَقُولُ:﴿يا لَيْتَنِى مِتُّ قَبْلَ هَذا وَكُنْتُ نَسْياً مَنْسِيّاً.﴾ فأطلقَ اللهُ، تعالي ذِكرُهُ, لِسانَهُ بعُذْرِها وإظهار حُجَّتِها. فلمّا ظَهَرَ، اشْتَدَّتِ البَلْوَي والطَّلَبُ عَلَي بَنِى إِسْرائِيلَ وأكَبَّ الجَبابِرَةُ والطَّواغِيتُ عَلَيْهِم, حَتَّي كانَ مِنَ أمْرِ المَسِيحِ ﷵ ما قَدْ أخْبَرَ اللهُ بِهِ... .»

(بحار الأنوار، ١٤، ٢١٣، ١٠)

١-١-١٦- عَنْ وَهَبٍ اليَمانِيِّ، قَالَ: «إِنَّ يَهُودِياً سَألَ النَّبِيَ، فقَالَ: 'يا مُحَمَّدُ أكُنْتَ فِى أُمِّ الكِتابِ نَبِيّاً قَبْلَ أنْ تُخْلَقَ؟' قَالَ: 'نَعَمْ.' قَالَ: 'وَهَؤُلَاءِ

with you before they were created?' He answered, 'Yes.' He said, 'What was the matter with you that you did not speak wisdom when you came out of your mother's belly, like Jesus the son of Mary spoke, as you claim, while you were a prophet before that?'

The Prophet answered, 'Verily, my affair was not like the affair of Jesus. Allah, the Mighty and Magnificent, created Jesus the son of Mary of a mother without any father, just as He created Adam without a father or mother. And if Jesus did not speak wisdom when he came out of his mother's belly, there would not have been any excuse for his mother before the people, because she had brought him without a father, and the people would take her as they do those women who had married [outside the law]. So, Allah, the Mighty and Magnificent, made his speech as an excuse for his mother.'"

(*Biḥār,* 14, 215, 16)

1.1.17. Al-Shāmī asked the Commander of the Faithful, "Which of the prophets were created by Allah circumcised?" He said, "Allah created Adam circumcised, and Seth was born circumcised, and Idrīs, Noah, Sām ibn Nūḥ, Abraham, David, Solomon, Lot, Ismael, Moses, Jesus and Muḥammad, may the blessings of Allah be with all of them."

(*Biḥār*, 15, 296, 32)

1.1.18. It is reported that Ḥasan ibn 'Alī al-Washshā' said, "I was with my father and I was a youth, and we spent the night with Imam Riḍā. It was the night of the twenty-fifth of Dhū al-Qa'dah and he said to my father, 'On the night of the twenty-fifth of Dhū al-Qa'dah Abraham was born and on it Jesus the son of Mary was born, and on it the earth beneath the Ka'bah became broadened. Whoever fasts of that day, it is as if he were to fast for sixty months."

(*Faqīh*, 2, 89, 1814)

أصْحابُكَ المُؤمِنُونَ مُثيثُونَ معَكَ قَبْلَ أنْ يَخْلُقوا؟' قالَ: 'نعَمْ.' قالَ: 'فما شأنُكَ لَمْ تَتَكَلَّمْ بِالحِكْمَةِ حِينَ خَرَجْتَ مِنْ بَطْنِ أُمِّكَ, كَما تَكَلَّمَ عِيسَي بْنُ مَرْيَمَ عَلَي زَعْمِكَ, وَقَدْ كُنْتَ قَبْلَ ذَلِكَ نَبِيّاً؟'

فقالَ النَبِيُّ صلى الله عليه وآله وسلم: 'إنَّهُ لَيْسَ أمْرَى كأمْرِ عِيسَي بْنِ مَرْيَمَ عليه السلام. إنَّ عِيسَي بْنَ مَرْيَمَ خَلَقَهُ اللهُ، عَزَّ وَجَلَّ، مِنْ أُمٍّ لَيْسَ لَهُ أبٌ كَما خَلَقَ آدَمَ مِنْ غَيْرِ أبٍ وَلا أُمٍّ. وَلَوْ أنَّ عِيسَي عليه السلام حِينَ خَرَجَ مِنْ بَطْنِ أُمِّهِ لَمْ يَنْطِقْ بِالحِكْمَةِ, لَمْ يَكُنْ لِأُمِّهِ عُذْرٌ عِنْدَ الناسِ, وَقَدْ أتَتْ بِهِ مِنْ غَيْرِ أبٍ, وَكانُوا يأخُذُونَها كَما يأخُذُونَ بِهِ مِنَ المُحْصِناتِ. فَجَعَلَ اللهُ، عَزَّ وَجَلَّ، مَنْطِقَهُ عُذْراً لِأُمِّهِ.'»

(بحار الأنوار،١٤، ٢١٥، ١٦)

١-١-١٧- فِي خَبَرِ الشامِيِّ, أنَّهُ سألَ أمِيرَ المُؤْمِنِينَ عليه السلام: «مَنْ خَلَقَ اللهُ مِنَ الأنبياءِ مَخْتُوناً؟» قالَ: «خَلَقَ اللهُ، عَزَّ وَجَلَّ، آدمَ عليه السلام مَخْتُوناً, وَوُلِدَ شِيْثُ عليه السلام مَخْتُوناً, وإدْرِيسُ وَنُوحٌ وَسامُ بْنُ نُوحٍ وإبْراهِيمُ وَداوُدُ وَسُلَيْمانُ وَلُوطُ وإسْماعِيلُ وَمُوسَي وعِيسَي ومُحَمَّدٌ صلى الله عليه وآله وسلم.»

(بحار الأنوار، ١٥، ٢٩٦، ٣٢)

١-١-١٨- رُوِيَ عَنْ الحَسَنِ بْنِ عَلِيٍّ الوَشّاءِ، قالَ: «كُنْتُ مَعَ أبِي وأنا غُلامٌ، فَتَعَشَّيْنا عِنْدَ الرضا عليه السلام لَيْلَةَ خَمْسَةٍ وَعِشْرِينَ مِنْ ذِي القَعْدَةِ. فَقالَ لَه: 'لَيْلَةُ خَمْسَةٍ وَعِشْرِينَ مِنْ ذِي القَعْدَةِ وُلِدَ فِيها إبْراهِيمُ عليه السلام، وَوُلِدَ فِيها عيسَي بن مَريَمَ عليه السلام، وَفِيها دُحِيَتِ الأرض مِنْ تَحْتِ الكَعْبَةِ. فَمَنْ صامَ ذَلِكَ اليَوْمَ كانَ كَمَنْ صامَ سِتِّينَ شَهْراً.'»

(كتاب من لا يحضره الفقيه، ٢، ٨٩، ١٨١٤)

1.1.19. It is reported that Imam Bāqir ﷺ said, "When the Commander of the Faithful was returning from battle with the Kharajites he came upon a monk in a monestary. He said, 'O monk! May I come down?' The monk said to him, 'Do not come down here with your troops.' He said, 'Why not?' He said, 'Because no one should come down here except a prophet or the successor of a prophet along with his troops who fight in the way of Allah. We have read this in our books...'

He continued, 'I have found your characteristics in the Gospel, and that you will come down in the land of Burāthā, the house of Mary, the place of Jesus.' The Commander of the Faithful said, 'Stop! Do not say anything to us.' Then he went to a spot and he said, 'Stamp your feet here.' And he himself did this. A spring gushed up from there. He said, 'This is the fountain of Mary, to where she was led. Dig here seventeen cubits.' A white rock was discovered. He ﷺ said, 'Mary put Jesus down from her shoulder onto this rock, and there she prayed.' Then the Commander of the Faithful placed the rock somewhere and prayed beside it. He stayed there for four days and said his prayers there in their complete form. The tents of the troops were placed around it within earshot. Then he said, 'The land of Burāthā is here, the house of Mary. This is a holy place at which the prophets prayed.'"

(*Biḥār*, 33, 438, 645)

1.1.20. Mufaḍḍal reported in a lengthy narration from al-Ṣādiq ﷺ, "Then Abū 'Abd Allah ﷺ took a breath and said, 'O Mufaḍḍal! The places on the earth boasted among themselves,...

١-١-١٩- المُفِيدُ, عَنْ عَلِيٍّ بْنِ بَلالٍ, عَنْ إسْماعِيلِ بْنِ عَلِيٍّ الخَزاعِي, عَنْ أبيهِ, عَنْ عِيسَي بْنِ حَمِيدٍ الطّائِيِّ, عَنْ أبيهِ, عَنْ عَلِيِّ بْنِ الحُسَيْنِ بْنِ عَلِيٍّ بْنِ الحُسَيْنِ, عَنْ أبِيهِ, قالَ: «سَمِعْتُ أبا جَعْفَرٍ عليه السلام يَقُولُ: 'إنَّ أمِيرَ المُؤْمِنِينَ عليه السلام لَمّا رَجَعَ مِنْ وَقْعَةِ الخَوارِج ....، إذا هُوَ بِراهِبٍ فِي صَومَعَةٍ. فَقالَ لَهُ: 'يا راهِبُ أنْزِلُ هاهُنا؟' فَقالَ لَهُ الراهِبُ: 'لا تَنْزِلْ هَذِهِ الأرضَ بِجَيْشِكَ.' قالَ: 'وَلِمَ؟' قالَ: 'لِأنَّهُ لا يَنْزِلُها إلّا نَبِيٌّ أوْ وَصِيُّ نَبِيٍّ بِجَيْشِهِ, يُقاتِلُ فِي سَبِيلِ اللهِ, عَزَّ وَجَلَّ. هَكَذا نَجِدُ فِي كُتُبِنا...
إنِّي وَجَدْتُ فِي الإنجيلِ نَعْتَكَ وأنَّكَ تَنْزِلُ أرضَ بُراثا, بَيْتَ مَرْيَمَ وأرْضَ عِيسَي عليه السلام.' فَقالَ أمِيرُ المُؤْمِنِينَ عليه السلام: 'قِفْ وَلا تُخْبِرْنا بِشَيءٍ.' ثُمَّ أتَي مَوْضِعاً فَقالَ: 'الكِزُوا هَذا.' فَلَكَزَهُ بِرِجْلِهِ عليه السلام. فانْبَجَسَتْ عَيْنُ خَرارَةٍ. فَقالَ: 'هَذِهِ عَيْنُ مَرْيَمَ الَّتِي انْبَعَثَ لَها.' ثُمَّ قالَ: 'إكْشِفُوا هاهُنا عَلَي سَبْعَةَ عَشَرَ ذِراعاً.' فَكَشَفَ فإذا بِصَخْرَةٍ بَيْضاءَ. فَقالَ(ع): 'عَلَي هَذِهِ وَضَعَتْ مَرْيَمُ عِيسَي مِنْ عاتِقِها وَصَلَّتْ هاهُنا.' فَنَصَبَ أمِيرُ المُؤْمِنِينَ عليه السلام الصَخْرَةَ وَصَلَّي إلَيها, وأقامَ هُناكَ أرْبَعَةَ أيّامٍ يَتِمُّ الصَلاةَ, وَجَعَلَ الحَرَمَ فِي خَيْمَةٍ مِنَ المَوْضِعِ عَلَي دَعْوَةٍ. ثُمّ قالَ: 'أرْضُ بُراثا, هذا, بَيْتُ مَرْيَمَ عليها السلام. هَذا المَوْضِعُ المُقَدَّسُ صَلَّي فِيهِ الأنبياء.'.»
(بحار الأنوار، ٣٣، ٤٣٨، ٦٤٥)

١-١-٢٠- رُوِيَ فِي بَعْضِ مُؤَلَّفاتِ أصْحابِنا, عَنْ الحُسَيْنِ بْنِ حَمْدانَ, عَنْ مُحَمَّدِ بْنِ إسْماعِيلَ وَعَلِيِّ بْنِ عَبْدِ اللهِ الحَسَنِيِّ, عَنْ أبِي شُعَيْبٍ وَمُحَمَّدِ بْنِ نصيرٍ, عَنْ عَمْرِو بْنِ الفُراتِ, عَنْ مُحَمَّدِ بْنِ المُفَضَّلِ، عَنْ المُفَضَّلِ بْنِ عُمَرَ, قالَ: «...ثُمَّ تَنَفَّسَ أبُو عَبْدِ اللهِ عليه السلام وَقالَ: 'يا مُفَضَّلُ إنَّ بُقاعَ الأرضِ تَفاخَرَتْ... فَأوحَي اللهُ:

Allah revealed, "... It [Karbala] is a blessed place from which Moses was called from a bush, it is a hill where Mary and Christ found refuge, at which there is a river where the head of Ḥusayn was washed and where Mary washed Jesus, and where Mary washed herself after giving birth to Jesus. It is the best place from which the Apostle of Allah ascended when he was absent, and for our *Shī'ah* there are blessings until the appearance of the *Qā'im*.'"

(*Biḥār*, 53, 1-11)

1.1.21. The Prophet said, "When a woman gives birth, the first thing she should eat is a sweet fresh half-ripe date (*ruṭab*) or a ripe date (*tamr*). If there were anything better than this, Allah, the Exalted, would have given it to Mary when Jesus was born."

(*Biḥār*, 59, 295)

1.1.22. It is reported that (for hardship with labor) al-Sādiq said, "After the *bismillāh* it should be written, 'Mary bore Jesus. ﴾*He it is Who created you from dust, then from a life-germ, then from a clot, then He brings you forth as a babe, then that you may reach your full strenght, then that you may be old*﴿ (40:67); ﴾*Verily, with difficulty is ease/ Verily with difficulty is ease*﴿ (94:5-6); and may the blessings of Allah be with Muhammad and his progeny and may He offer him greetings of peace.

(*Miṣbāḥ*, 159)

1.1.23. Al-Bāqir said, "Verily, it was announced to Mary [that she would bear] Jesus. She was in the sanctuary when the Sure Spirit (*al-Rūḥ al-Amīn*) became like a sound human. She said, 'I take refuge in the Merciful from you, if you are God-wary.' He said, 'I am but a messenger come from your Lord, to give you a boy most pure.' Then he blew into her breast and she became pregnant with Jesus. But he did not stay until she bore [the child]...

'... فإنَّها [كَرْبَلاء] البُقعَةُ المُبارَكَةُ الّتِى نُودِىَ مُوسَي مِنْها مِنَ الشجَرَةِ وإنَّها الربْوَةُ الّتِى أوَتْ إلَيْها مَرْيَمُ والمَسِيحُ وإنَّها الدالِيَةُ الّتِى غُسِلَ فِيها رأسُ الحُسَيْنِ عليه السلام وَفِيها غَسَلَتْ مَرْيَمُ عِيسَي عليه السلام واغْتَسَلَتْ مِنْ وِلادَتِها وإنَّها خَيْرُ بُقعَةٍ عَرَجَ رَسُولُ اللهِ صلى الله عليه وآله مِنْها وَقتَ غَيْبَتِهِ ولَيَكُونَنَّ لِشِيعَتِنا فِيْها خِيَرَةٌ إلَي ظُهُورِ قائِمِنا عليه السلام.'»

(بحار الأنوار، ٥٣، ١- ١١)

١-١-٢١- قالَ النَبِىُّ صلى الله عليه وآله: «إذا وَلَدَتْ امْرأةٌ, فَلْيَكُنْ أوّلُ ما تأكُلُ الرطَبَ الحُلْوَ أوِ التَمْرَ. فانَّهُ لَوْ كانَ شَيءٌ أفْضَلَ مِنْهُ أطْعَمَهُ اللهُ تَعالَي مَرْيَمَ حِينَ وَلَدَتْ عِيسَي عليه السلام.»

(بحار الأنوار، ٥٩، ٢٩٥)

١-١-٢٢- عَنِ الصادِقِ عليه السلام (لِتَعَسُّرِ الوِلادَةِ) «تُكْتَبُ بَعْدَ البَسْمَلَةِ: مَرْيَمُ وَلَدَتْ عِيسَي. ﴿هُوَ الذى خَلَقَكُمْ مِنْ تُرابٍ ثُمَّ مِنْ نُطْفَةٍ ثُمَّ مِنْ عَلَقَةٍ ثُمَّ يُخْرِجُكُمْ طِفْلاً ثُمَّ لِتَبْلُغُوا أشُدَّكُمْ ثُمَّ لِتَكُونُوا شُيُوخاً.﴾ ﴿فإنَّ مَعَ العُسْرِ يُسْراً. إنَّ مَعَ العُسْرِ يُسْراً.﴾ وَصَلَّي اللهُ عَلَي مُحَمَّدٍ وآلِ مُحَمَّدٍ وَسَلَّمَ تَسْلِيماً.»

(المصباح، ١٥٩)

١-١-٢٣- قالَ الباقِرُ عليه السلام: « إنَّ مَرْيَمَ بُشِّرَتْ بِعِيسَي فَبَيْنا هِيَ فِى المِحْرابِ إذْ تَمَثَّلَ لَها الروحُ الأمِينُ بَشَراً سَوِيّاً. ﴿قالَتْ: إنِّى أعُوذُ بِالرحْمَنِ مِنْكَ إنْ كُنْتَ تَقِيّاً. قالَ: 'إنَّما أنا رَسُولُ رَبِّكِ لأهَبَ لَكِ غُلاماً زَكِيّاً.'﴾ فَتَفَلَ فِى جَيْبِها فَحَمَلَتْ بعِيسَي, فَلَمْ يَلْبَثْ أنْ وَلَدَتْ...

Iblīs came that night and it was said to him that a child had been born that night, and that there was no idol on the earth that did not fall on its face. Iblīs went to the East and West in search of him. Then he found him in a room of a convent. The angels surrounded him. He tried to get close to him. The angels shouted, "Get away!" He said to them, "Who is his father?" They said, "His case is like that of Adam." Iblīs said, "Verily, I will mislead four fifths of the people by him."

(*Biḥār,* 14, 215, 14)

1.1.24. It is reported that Abū 'Abd Allah al-Ṣādiq said, "The devil, may Allah curse him, used to pass through the seven heavens. When Jesus was born, he was barred from three heavens...."

(*Biḥār,* 15, 257, 9)

1.1.25. It is reported that Abū 'Abd Allah said, "The Prophet prohibited Muslims from having four names:[1] Abū 'Īsā (father of Jesus), Abū al-Ḥakam (father of the Governor), Abū Mālik (father of the King), and Abū al-Qāsim (father of Qāsim) if his first name is Muḥammad."[2]

(*Biḥār*, 16, 401)

1.1.26. It is reported that the Prophet said, "Between Moses and David there were five hundred years, and between David and Jesus, one thousand one hundred years."

(*Biḥār*, 13, 363, 1)

1.1.27. Abū al-Rabī' reported that Nāfi' said, "O Muḥammad ibn 'Alī! I have read the Torah, the Gospel and the Pslams and the Furqān, and I have learned what is permitted and forbidden in them. I have come to ask you a question that none can answer but a prophet, the successor of a prophet or the progeny of a prophet."

---

(1) The kind of name mentioned here is the *konyah*, which is used as a term of respect and takes the form 'father of...', 'son of...', 'mother of...', etc.

(2) No one is permitted to have the name Muḥammad Abū al-Qāsim because these are the first names and *qunya* of the Prophet.

وأتَي إبْلِيسُ تِلْكَ اللَيْلَة. فقِيلَ لَهُ: 'وُلِدَ الليْلَة وَلَدٌ لَمْ يَبْقَ عَلَي وَجْهِ الأرض صَنَمٌ إلّا خَرَّ لِوَجْهِهِ وأتَي المَشْرِق والمَغْرِبَ يَطْلُبُهُ فَوَجَدَهُ فِي بَيْتِ دَيْرٍ قَدْ حَفَّتْ بِهِ المَلائِكَةُ فَذَهَبَ يَدْنُو فصاحَتِ المَلائِكَةُ تَنَحَّ. فقالَ لَهُمْ: 'مَنْ أبُوهُ؟' فقالَتْ: 'فَمَثَلُهُ كَمَثَلِ آدَمَ.' فقالَ إبْلِيسُ: 'لأضِلَّنَّ بِهِ أرْبَعَةَ أخْماسِ الناسِ.'»

(بحار الأنوار، ١٤، ٢١٥، ١٤)

١-١-٢٤- ابن البَرْقِيِّ, عَنْ أبِيهِ, عَنْ جَدِّهِ, عَنْ البَزَنْطِيِّ, عَنْ أبانِ بْنِ عُثْمانَ, عَنْ أبِي عَبْدِ اللهِ الصادِقِ عليه السلام، قالَ: «كانَ إبْلِيسُ لَعَنَهُ اللهُ يَخْتَرِقُ السَماواتِ السَبْعَ. فلَمّا وُلِدَ عِيسَي عليه السلام حُجِبَ عَنْ ثَلاثِ سَماواتٍ... .»

(بحار الأنوار ١٥، ٢٥٧، ٩)

١-١-٢٥- رَوَي الكُلَيْنِيُّ والشَيْخُ, عَنْ عَلِيِّ بْنِ إبْراهِيمَ, عَنْ أبِيهِ, عَنْ النَوْفِلِيِّ, عَنْ السَكُونِيِّ, عَنْ أبِي عَبْدِ اللهِ عليه السلام: «أنَّ النَبِيَّ صلى الله عليه وآله وسلم نَهَي, عَنْ أرْبَعِ كُنَيً: عَنْ أبِي عِيسَي وَعَنْ أبِي الحَكَمِ وَعَنْ أبِي مالِكٍ وَعَنْ أبِي القاسِمِ، إذا كانَ الاسْمُ مُحَمَّداً.»

(بحار الأنوار، ١٦، ٤٠١)

١-١-٢٦- قالَ النَبِيُّ صلى الله عليه وآله وسلم: «وكانَ بَيْنَ مُوسَي وَبَيْنَ داوُدَ خَمْسُ مِائَةِ سَنَةٍ, وَبَيْنَ داوُدَ وَعِيسَي الفُ سَنَةٍ وَمِائة سَنَةٍ.»

(بحار الأنوار، ١٣، ٣٦٣، ١)

١-١-٢٧- عِدَّةٌ مِنْ أصْحابِنا، عَنْ أحْمَدَ بْنِ مُحَمَّدِ بْنِ خالِدٍ، عَنْ الحَسَنِ بْنِ مَحْبُوبٍ، عَنْ أبِي حَمْزَةَ ثابِتِ بْنِ دِينارِ الثُمالِيِّ؛ وابِي مَنْصُورٍ، عَنْ أبِي الربِيعِ، قالَ: «... فقالَ نافِعٌ: '... يا مُحَمَّدُ بْنُ عَلِيٍّ، إنِّي قَرأتُ التَوْراةَ والإنجيلَ والزَبُورَ والفُرْقانَ، وَقَدْ عَرَفْتُ حَلالَها وَحَرامَها، وَقَدْ جِئْتُ أسألُكَ عَنْ مَسائِلَ لا يُجِيبُ فِيها إلّا نَبِيٌّ أوْ وَصِيُّ نَبِيٍّ أو ابن

Then Abū Ja'far raised his head and said, "Ask whatever is on your mind." He said, "Inform me how many years were between Jesus and Muḥammad?" He said, "Should I inform you according to what I say, or according to what you say?" He said, "Inform me of both." He said, "According to what I say, there were five hundred years, but according to what you say, there were six hundred...."

(*Kāfī*, 8, 120, 93)

1.1.28. It is reported that Abū 'Abd Allah said, "Between Jesus and Muḥammad there were five hundred years, of which two hundred fifty were without any prophet or any manifest teacher (*'ālim ẓāhir*)." [The narrator said,] I said, "What were they?" He said, "They clung to the religion of Jesus." I said, "What were they?" He said, "Believers." Then he said, "The earth is never without a teacher (*'ālim*) in it."

(*Biḥār*, 23, 33, 54)

1.1.29. Ya'qūb ibn Shu'ayb said "I said to Abū-'Abd-Allah, 'What do you say about a group whose leader has died?" He said to me, "Do not you read the Book of Allah (Qur'ān) ﴾ *Why should not a company from every party of them go forth that they may acquire understanding in religion, and that they may warn their people when they return unto them so that they may be cautious?*﴿" (9:122) I said "May I be your sacrifice! Then what should those who are waiting do until the scholars come back?" He said to me, "Did you not know that there were two hundred fifty years beetween Muḥammad and Jesus (may Allah bless both of them)? During this time som groups died bleaving the religion of Jesus expecting the religion of Muḥammad, and Allah gave them their wages twice."

(*Biḥār*, 27, 298, 10)

1.1.30. It is reported that Abū al-Ḥasan al-Riḍā said: "...And all of the eleven Imams after the prophet were killed, some by the sword, the Commander of the Faithful and Ḥusayn, peace be with

نَبِيٌّ.' قالَ: 'فَرَفَعَ أَبُو جَعْفَرٍ عليه السلام رأسَهُ، فقالَ: 'سَلْ عَمّا بَدا لكَ.''
فقالَ: 'أخْبِرْنِي كَمْ بَيْنَ عِيسَي وَبَيْنَ مُحَمَّدٍ صلى الله عليه وآله وسلم مِنْ سَنَةٍ؟' قالَ: 'أُخْبِرُكَ بِقَوْلِي أوْ بِقَوْلِكَ؟' قالَ: 'أخْبِرْنِي بالقَوْلَيْنِ جَمِيعاً.' قالَ: 'أمّا فِي قَوْلِي فَخَمْسُ مِائة سَنَةٍ، وأمّا فِي قَوْلِكَ فَسِتُّ مِائة سَنَةٍ... .'»

(الكافي، ٨، ١٢٠، ٩٣)

١-١-٢٨- أبِي, عَنْ مُحَمَّدٍ العَطّار, عَنْ ابن يَزِيْدٍ, عَنْ ابن أبِي عُمَيْرٍ, عَنْ سَعْدِ بْنِ أبِي خَلَفٍ, عَنْ يَعْقُوبَ بْنِ شُعَيْبٍ, عَنْ أبِي عَبْدِ اللهِ عليه السلام, قالَ: «كانَ بَيْنَ عِيسَي وَبَيْنَ مُحَمَّدٍ صلى الله عليه وآله وسلم خَمْسُ مِائة عامٍ. مِنْها مِئَتانِ وَخَمْسُونَ عاماً لَيْسَ فِيها نَبِيٌّ وَلا عالِمٌ ظاهِرٌ.» قُلْتُ: «فَما كانُوا؟» قالَ: «كانُوا مُسْتَمْسِكِينَ بِدِينِ عِيسَي عليه السلام.» قُلْتُ: «فَما كانُوا؟» قالَ: «مُؤْمِنِينَ.» ثُمَّ قالَ(ع): «وَلا تَكُونُ الأرضُ إلّا وَفِيها عالِمٌ.»

(بحار الأنوار، ٢٣، ٣٣، ٥٤)

١-١-٢٩- عَنْ يَعْقُوبَ بْنِ شُعَيْبَ, عَنْ أبِي عَبْدِ اللهِ عليه السلام. قالَ: «قُلْتُ لَهُ: 'ما تَقُولُ فِي قَوْمٍ هَلَكَ إمامُهُمْ كَيْفَ يَصْنَعُونَ؟'» قالَ: «فَقالَ لِي: 'أما تَقْرَءُ كِتابَ اللهِ: ﴿فَلَوْ لا نَفَرَ مِنْ كُلِّ فِرْقَةٍ﴾ إلي قَوْلِهِ: ﴿يَحْذَرُونَ؟﴾' قُلْتُ: 'جُعِلْتُ فِداكَ، فَما حالُ المُنْتَظِرِينَ حَتَّي يَرْجِعَ المُتَفَقِّهُونَ؟'» قالَ: 'فَقالَ لِي: 'يَرْحَمُكَ اللهُ، أما عَلِمْتَ أنَّهُ كانَ بَيْنَ مُحَمَّدٍ وَعِيسَي, صَلَّي اللهُ عَلَيْهِما, خَمْسُونَ وَمِئَتا سَنَةٍ؟ فَماتَ قَوْمٌ عَلَي دِينِ عِيسَي، انْتِظاراً لِدِينِ مُحَمَّدٍ، فأتاهُمُ اللهُ أجْرَهُمْ مَرَّتَيْنِ؟'»

(بحار الأنوار، ٢٧، ٢٩٨، ١٠)

١-١-٣٠- قال أبُوالحَسَنِ الرِضا عليه السلام: «... وَجَمِيعُ الأئمَّةِ الأحَدَ عَشَرَ بَعَدَ النَبِيِّ صلى الله عليه وآله وسلم قُتِلُوا. مِنْهُمْ بِالسَيْفِ وَهُوَ أمِيرُ المُؤْمِنِينَ بَعَدَ النَبِيِّ صلى الله عليه وآله وسلم

them, and the rest by poison. The tyrants of their times killed every one of them, and indeed this was done to them, truly, not like anything the extremists (*ghulāh*) or the delegators (*mufawiḍah*), may Allah curse them. They say, 'They (the Imams) were not really killed, and it was only a likeness of their affair that appeared to them.' So, they lied, may the wrath of Allah be upon them. Indeed, the affair of none of the prophets of Allah and His authorities, peace be with them, appeared doubtful to the people, except the affair of Jesus the son of Mary alone, for he was raised from the earth alive and his soul was taken between heaven and earth, then he was raised to heaven and his soul was returned to him, and that is what the saying of Allah, the Mighty and Magnificent, is about: ﴾*When Allah said: "O Jesus! I will take you to Me, and I will raise you to Me*﴿ (3:55).

And Allah, the Mighty and Magnificent, said, narrating the speech of Jesus on the Resurrection Day, ﴾*And I was a witness over them, so long as I was among them, but when You took me to Yourself, You were Yourself the watcher over them. You Yourself are witness over everything.*﴿ (5:117)...

And since it is permitted that all of the prophets and His messengers and authorities after Adam were born of fathers and mothers, but among them Jesus was born without any father, it will be permitted that his affair appeared doubtful to the people, but not the affairs of the other prophets and authorities, peace be with them. Likewise, it was permitted for him to be born without a father, but not the others. Allah, the mighty and magnificent, only wanted to make his affair as a sign and mark for it to be known by this that He has power over all things.'"

(*Biḥār*, 25, 117)

والحُسَيْنُ عليه السلام, والباقُونَ قُتِلُوا بِالسَمِّ. قَتَلَ كُلَّ واحِدٍ مِنْهُمْ طاغُوتُ زَمانِهِ وَجَرَي ذَلِكَ عَلَيْهِمْ عَلَي الحَقِيقَةِ والصحَّةِ, لا كَما تَقُولُهُ الغُلاةُ والمُفَوِّضَةُ، لَعَنَهُمُ اللهُ. فإنَّهُمْ يَقُولُونَ: 'إنَّهُمْ عليهم السلام لَمْ يُقتَلُوا عَلَي الحَقِيقَةِ وإنَّهُ شُبِّهَ لِلنّاسِ أمْرُهُمْ. وكَذِبُوا، عَلَيْهِمْ غَضَبُ اللهِ، فانَّهُ ما شُبِّهَ أمْرُ أحَدٍ مِنَ أنْبِياءِ اللهِ وَحُجَجِهِ عَلَيْهِمُ السَلامُ لِلنّاسِ إلّا أمْرُ عِيسَي بْنِ مَرْيَمَ عليه السلام وَحْدَهُ. لِأنَّهُ رُفِعَ مِنَ الأرضِ حيّاً، وَقُبِضَ رُوحُهُ بَيْنَ السَماءِ والأرضِ، ثُمَّ رُفِعَ إلَي السَماءِ وَرُدَّ عَلَيْهِ رُوحُهُ. وَذَلِكَ قَوْلُ اللهِ، عَزَّ وَجَلَّ: ﴿إذ قالَ اللهُ: 'يا عِيسَي إنِّى مُتَوَفِّيْكَ وَرافِعُكَ إلَىّ.﴾

وَقالَ اللهُ، عَزَّ وَجَلَّ، حِكايَةً لِقَوْلِ عِيسَي يَوْمَ القِيامَةِ: ﴿وَكُنْتُ عَلَيْهِمْ شَهِيداً مادُمتُ فِيهِمْ. فَلَمّا تَوَفَّيْتَنِى كُنْتَ أنتَ الرقِيبَ عَلَيْهِمْ وأنْتَ عَلَي كُلِّ شَيءٍ شَهِيدٍ.﴾

وَيَقُولُ المُتَجاوِزُونَ لِلْحَدِّ فِى أمرِ الأئمَّةِ عليهم السلام: 'إنَّهُ إنْ جازَ أنْ يُشَبَّهَ أمْرُ عِيسَي لِلنّاسِ فَلِمَ لا يَجُوزُ أنْ يُشَبَّهَ أمْرُهُمْ أيْضاً؟' والَّذِى يَجِبُ أنْ يُقالَ لَهُمْ: 'إنَّ عِيسَي، عليه السلام، هُوَ مُوْلُودٌ مِنْ غَيْرِ أبٍ. فَلِمَ لا يَجُوزُ أنْ يَكُونُوا مَوْلُودِينَ مِنْ غَيْرِ آباءٍ؟' فإنَّهُمْ لا يَجْسُرُونَ عَلَي إظْهارِ مَذْهَبِهِمْ. لَعَنَهُمُ اللهُ فِى ذَلِكَ. وَمَتَي جازَ أنْ يَكُونَ جَمِيعُ أنْبِياءِ اللهِ وَرُسُلِهِ وَحُجَجِهِ بَعْدَ آدَمَ عليه السلام مَوْلُودِينَ مِنَ الآباءِ والأمَّهاتِ، وكانَ عِيسي مِنْ بَيْنِهِمْ مَوْلُوداً مِنْ غَيْرِ أبٍ، جازَ أنْ يُشَبَّهَ لِلنّاسِ أمْرُهُ دُونَ أمْرِ غَيْرِهِ مِنَ الأنبياءِ والحُجَجِ عليهم السلام، كَما جازَ أنْ يُولَدَ مِنْ غَيْرِ أبٍ دُونَهُمْ. وانَّما أرادَ اللهُ، عَزَّ وَجَلَّ، أنْ يَجْعَلَ أمْرَهُ عليه السلام آيَةً وَعَلامَةً لِيُعْلَمَ بِذَلِكَ أنَّهُ عَلَي كُلِّ شَىءٍ قَدِيرٌ.'»

(بحار الأنوار، ٢٥، ١١٧)

1.1.31. It is narrated that Yāsir al-Khādim said: "I heard [Imam] Riḍā say, 'The most terrifying events for creatures are three: the day one is born and comes out of his mother's belly and sees the world, the day he dies and sees the afterlife and its people, and the day he is raised and sees laws he did not see in this world, and Allah made John secure in these three events and protected him from fear, and He said, ﴾*Peace be with him the day he was born and the day he dies and the day he is raised to life*﴿ (19:15).

And Jesus the son of Mary made himself secure in these three events, and he said, ﴾*Peace be with me the day I was born and the day I die and the day I am raised to life*﴿ (19:33).'"

(*Biḥār*, 14, 246, 26)

1.2. HIS CHILDHOOD

1.2.1. It is reported that Abū Ja'far [Imam Baqir] said: "When Jesus the son of Mary was born, when he was one day old he was like a two month old boy. When he was seven months old, his mother took his hand and brought him to a school and sat him before a teacher. The teacher said to him, "Say: 'In the Name of Allah, the Merciful, the Compassionate.'" Jesus said, "In the Name of Allah, the Merciful, the Compassionate." The teacher said to him, "Say *abjad*."[1] Jesus raised his head and said, "Do you know what is *abjad*?" The teacher raised the lash to hit him. Jesus said, "O my teacher! Do not hit me if you know it, and if not, ask me so that I may explain it." He said, "Explain it to me." Jesus said, "As for the *alif*, it is a blessing (*ālā'*) of Allah, and the *bā* is the bliss (*bahjah*)

[1] An old Semitic sequence of letters, called *abjad*, is used in Hebrew and Arabic in which each letter is used to represent a number in addition to its vocal value.

١-١-٣١- ابن الوَلِيدِ, عَنْ سَعْدٍ, عَنْ أحْمَدَ بْنِ حَمْزَةَ الأشعَرِى, عَنْ ياسِرِ الخادِمِ, قالَ: «سَمِعْتُ الرضا عليه السلام يَقُولُ: 'إنَّ أوْحَشَ ما يَكُونُ هَذا الخَلْقُ فِى ثَلاثَةِ مَواطِنَ: يَوْمَ يَلِدُ فَيَخْرُجُ مِنْ بَطْنِ أُمِّهِ فَيَرَي الدنْيا, وَيَوْمَ يَمُوتُ فَيُعايِنُ الآخِرَةَ وأهْلَها, وَيَوْمَ يُبْعَثُ فَيَرَي أحْكاماً لَمْ يَرَها فِى دارِ الدنْيا. وَقَدْ سَلَّمَ اللهُ عَلَي يَحْيَي عليه السلام فِى هَذِهِ الثَّلاثَةِ المَواطِنَ وآمَنَ رَوْعَتَهُ. فَقالَ: ﴿وَسَلامٌ عَلَيْهِ يَوْمَ وُلِدَ وَيَوْمَ يَمُوتُ وَيَوْمَ يُبْعَثُ حَيّاً.﴾ وَقَدْ سَلَّمَ عِيسَي بْنُ مَرْيَمَ عَلَي نَفْسِهِ فِى هَذِهِ الثَّلاثَةِ المَواطِنِ. فَقالَ: ﴿والسَلامُ عَلَيَّ يَوْمَ وُلِدْتُ وَيَوْمَ أمُوتُ وَيَوْمَ أُبْعَثُ حَيّاً.﴾'»
(بحار الأنوار، ١٤، ٢٤٦، ٢٦)

١-٢- طُفُولِيَّتُه

١-٢-١- الطالِقانِىُّ, عَنْ أحْمَدَ الهَمْدانِىِّ, عَنْ جَعْفَرِ بْنِ عَبْدِ اللهِ بْنِ جَعْفَرِ العَلَوِىِّ, عَنْ كَثِيرِ بْنِ عَيّاشِ القَطّانِ, عَنْ أبِى الجارُودِ, عَنْ أبِى جَعْفَرٍ عليه السلام قالَ: «لَمّا وُلِدَ عِيسَي بْنُ مَرْيَمَ عليه السلام كانَ ابن يَوْمٍ كأنَّهُ ابن شَهْرَيْنِ. فَلَمّا كانَ ابن سَبْعَةِ أشْهُرٍ أخَذَتْ والِدَتُهُ بِيَدِهِ وَجاءَتْ بِهِ إلَي الكُتّابِ وأقْعَدَتْهُ بَيْنَ يَدَى المُؤَدِّبِ. فَقالَ لَهُ المُؤَدِّبُ: 'قُلْ: 'بِسْمِ اللهِ الرحْمَنِ الرحِيمِ.'' فَقالَ عِيسَي عليه السلام: 'بِسْمِ اللهِ الرحْمَنِ الرحِيمِ.' فَقالَ لَهُ المُؤَدِّبُ: 'قُلْ: 'أبْجَدْ.'' فَرَفَعَ عِيسَي راسَهُ فَقالَ: 'وَهَلْ تَدْرِى ما أبْجَدْ؟' فَعَلاهُ بِالدرَّةِ لِيَضْرِبَهُ. فَقالَ: 'يا مُؤَدِّبُ، لا تَضْرِبْنِى إنْ كُنْتَ تَدْرِى، وإلّا فاسْألْنِى حَتَّي أفَسِّرَ لَكَ.' فَقالَ: 'فَسِّرْ لِى.' فَقالَ عِيسَي: 'أمّا الألِفُ آلاءُ اللهِ, والباءُ بَهْجَةُ اللهِ, والجِيمُ جَمالُ اللهِ, والدالُ دِينُ اللهِ. هَوَّزْ: الهاءُ هَوْلُ

of Allah, and the *jīm* is the beauty (*jamāl*) of Allah, and the *dal* is the religion (*dīn*) of Allah. *Hawwaz:* the *hā* is the terror (*hawl*) of hell, and the *wāw* is 'Woe (*wayl*) to the people of the fire,' and the *zā* is the moaning (*zafīr*) of hell. *Ḥuṭṭī:* The sins are forgiven (*ḥuṭṭat*) of those who ask the forgiveness of Allah. *Kaliman*: The speech (*kalām*) of Allah, there is no one who can change His words. *Sa'afiṣ*: Measure for measure (*ṣā'*) and wages for wages. *Qarashat*: He will gather them (*qarashahum*) and resurrect them." Then the teacher said, "O woman! Take your son's hand, indeed he already knows, and he has no need of a teacher."

(*Biḥār*, 14, 286, 8)

1.2.2. Abū 'Abd Allah said, "Verily, Jesus the son of Mary, used to cry intensely, so that Mary was at wits end regarding his profuse crying. He said to her, 'Get some of the bark of that tree, make a tonic from it and feed me with it.' When he drank it, he cried intensely. Mary said, 'What sort of prescription did you give me?' He said, 'O my mother! Knowledge of prophethood and weakness of childhood.'"

(*Biḥār* 14, 254, 47)

1.3. HIS PROPHETHOOD

1.3.1. It is reported that Imam Ṣādiq said, "...Follow the Apostle of Allah, and confess to what has been sent down from Allah, and follow the signs of guidance, for they are the signs of trustworthiness and God-wariness; and know that if one denies Jesus the son of Mary, but confesses to all the prophets but him, he does not believe..."

(*Biḥār*, 23, 96, 3)

جَهَنَّمَ, والواوُ وَيْلٌ لِأهْلِ النارِ, والزّاءُ زَفِيرُ جَهَنَّمَ. حُطّى, حُطَّتِ الخَطايا, عَنِ المُسْتَغْفِرِينَ. كَلِمَنْ, كَلامُ اللهِ لا مُبَدِّلَ لِكَلِماتِهِ. سَعَفَصْ, صاعٌ بِصاعٍ والجَزاءُ بِالجَزاءِ. قَرَشَتْ, قَرَشَهُمْ فَحَشَرَهُمْ.' فَقالَ المُؤَدِّبُ: 'أيَّتُها المَرْأةُ، خُذِى بِيَدِ ابنكِ, فَقَدْ عَلِمَ وَلا حاجَةَ لَهُ فِى المُؤَدِّبِ.'»

(بحار الأنوار، ١٤، ٢٨٦، ٨)

١-٢-٢- فِى رِوايَةِ إسْماعِيلَ بْنِ جابِرٍ, قالَ أبُو عَبْدِ اللهِ عليه السلام: «إنَّ عِيسَي بْنَ مَرْيَمَ عليه السلام كانَ يَبْكِى بُكاءً شَدِيداً. فَلَمّا أعْيَتْ مَرْيَمَ كَثْرَةُ بُكائِهِ, قالَ لَها: 'خُذِى مِنْ لِحا هَذِهِ الشجَرَةِ, فاجْعَلِى وُجُوراً, ثُمَّ اسْقِينِيهِ.' فإذا سُقِيَ, بَكَي بُكاءً شَدِيداً. فَتَقُولُ مَرْيَمُ: 'ما ذا أمَرْتَنِي؟' فَيَقُولُ: 'يا أمّاه، عِلْمَ النبُوَةِ وَضَعْفَ الصبَا.'»

(بحار الأنوار، ١٤، ٢٥٤، ٤٧)

١-٣- نُبُوَّتُه

١-٣-١- أبِى عَنْ سَعْدٍ, عَنْ البَرْقِيِّ, عَنْ أبِيهِ، عَنْ ابن أبِى عُمَيْرٍ, عَنْ مُحَمَّدِ بْنِ عَبْدِ الرحْمَنِ بْنِ أبِى لِيْلَي, عَنْ أبِى عَبْدِ اللهِ الصادِقِ عليه السلام, فِى حَدِيثٍ طَوِيلٍ يَقُولُ فِى آخِرِهِ: «...إتَّبِعُوا قَوْلَ رَسُولِ اللهِ صلى الله عليه وآله وسلم وأقِرُّوا بِما نُزِّلَ مِنْ عِنْدِ اللهِ, عَزَّ وَجَلَّ. إتَّبِعُوا آثارَ الهُدَي, فإنَّها عَلاماتُ الأمانَةِ والتقي, واعْلَمُوا أنَّهُ لَوْ أنْكَرَ رَجُلٌ عِيسَي بْنَ مَرْيَمَ وأقَرَّ بِمَنْ سِواهُ مِنَ الرسُلِ لَمْ يُؤْمِنْ... .»

(بحار الأنوار، ٢٣، ٩٦، ٣)

1.3.2. The Apostle of Allah said, "Verily, Gabriel brought down a book to me in which there was information about the kings before me, and information about the prophets and apostles who were

commissioned before I was:... Ashbakh ibn Ashjān was a king called *al-Kays* who ruled for two hundred sixty-six years. In the fifty-first year of his rule Allah commissioned Jesus the son of Mary and bestowed upon him light, knowledge and wisdom, and the knowledge of all the prophets before him, and He added to this the Gospel. He commissioned him to Jerusalem (*Bayt al-Maqdis*) for the children of Israel to invite them to the divine book and wisdom and to faith in Allah and the prophet. Most of them turned away from him rebelliously and disbelieving.

When they failed to believe, Jesus called his Lord and was adamant, and some of them were transformed into devils to show them a sign from which they could take a lesson; but this did not increase in them anything but rebellion and disbelief. So, Jesus came to Jerusalem, invited them and encouraged them to what is near to Allah for thirty-three years, until the Jews sought him and (afterward) claimed to have punished him and buried him alive. Some of them claimed to have killed him and to have crucified him. Allah did not let them gain sovereignty over him, but it was a mistake they made.

They were not able to chastise him or bury him, and they could not kill him or crucify him, because of the saying of Allah, the mighty and magnificent, ﴾*I am going to take you away and lift you up unto Me and purify you of those who disbelieve*﴿ (3:55). So, they were not able to kill him or crucify him, for if they had been able to do so, this would belie His saying, ﴾*Allah raised him up unto Himself*﴿ (4:158), after Allah took him. When Allah wanted to raise him, He revealed to him to entrust the light of Allah, His wisdom and the knowledge of His book to Simon ibn Ḥamūn al-Ṣafā, his successor among the believers. So, he did this...."

(*Biḥār*, 14, 515, 4)

١-٣-٢- أبِي وابْنُ الولِيدِ مَعاً, عَنْ سَعْدٍ, عَنْ ابن عِيسَي, عَنْ ابن مَعْرُوفٍ, عَنْ ابن مَهْزِيارٍ, عَنْ الحَسَنِ بْنِ سَعِيدٍ, عَنْ مُحَمَّدِ بْنِ إسْماعِيلَ القُرَشِيِّ عمَّنْ حَدَّثَهُ, عَنْ إسْماعِيلَ بْنِ أبِي رافِعٍ, عَنْ أبيهِ, قالَ: «قالَ رَسُولُ اللهِ (صلى الله عليه وآله وسلم): 'إنَّ جَبْرَئِيلَ نَزلَ عَلَيَّ بِكِتابٍ فِيهِ خَبَرُ المُلُوكِ, مُلُوكِ الأرضِ قَبْلِي, وَخَبَرُ مَنْ بُعِثَ قَبْلِي مِنَ الأنبياءِ والرسُلِ... لَمّا مَلِكَ أشْبَخُ بْنُ أشْجانَ, وكانَ يُسَمَّي الكَيْسُ, وَمَلِكَ مِئَتَيْنِ وَسِتاً وَسِتِّينَ سَنَةٍ, فَفِي سَنَةِ إحْدَي وَخَمْسِينَ مِنْ مُلْكِهِ بَعَثَ اللهُ عِيسَي بْنَ مَرْيَمَ(عليه السلام), واسْتَوْدَعَهُ النورَ والعِلْمَ والحِكْمَةَ وَجَمِيعَ عُلُومِ الأنبياءِ قَبْلَهُ, وَزادَهُ الإنجيلَ. وَبَعَثَهُ إلَي بَيتِ المَقْدِسِ إلَي بَنِي إسْرائِيلَ , يَدْعُوهُمْ إلَي كِتابِهِ وَحِكْمَتِهِ وإلَي الإيمانِ بِاللهِ وَبِرَسُولِهِ. فابَي أكْثَرُهُمْ إلّا طُغْياناً وكُفْراً.

فَلمّا لَمْ يُؤْمِنُوا بِهِ, دَعا رَبَّهُ وَعَزمَ عَلَيْهِ, فَمَسَخَ مِنْهُمْ شَياطِينَ لِيُرِيَهُمْ آيَةً فَيعْتَبِرُوا. فَلَمْ يَزِدْهُمْ ذَلِكَ إلّا طُغْياناً وكُفْراً. فأتَي بَيْتَ المَقْدِسِ يَدْعُوهُمْ وَيَرْغَبُهُمْ فِي ما عِنْدَ اللهِ ثَلاثاً وَثَلاثِينَ سَنَةٍ, حَتَّي طَلَبَتْهُ اليَهُودُ, وادَّعَتْ أنَّها عَذَّبَتْهُ وَدَفَنَتْهُ فِي الأرضِ حَيّاً, وادَّعَي بَعْضُهُمْ أنَّهُمْ قَتَلُوهُ وَصَلَبُوهُ. وَما كانَ اللهُ لِيَجْعَلَ لَهُمْ عَلَيْهِ سُلْطاناً, وإنَّما شُبِّهَ لَهُمْ.

وَما قَدَرُوا عَلَي عَذابِهِ وَدَفْنِهِ وَلا عَلَي قَتْلِهِ وَصَلْبِهِ. قَوْلُهُ, عَزَّ وَجَلَّ: ﴿إنِّي مُتَوَفِّيكَ وَرافِعُكَ إلَيَّ وَمُطَهِّرُكَ مِنَ الذينَ كَفَرُوا.﴾ فَلَمْ يَقْتَدِرُوا عَلَي قَتْلِهِ وَصَلْبِهِ. لأنَّهُمْ لَوْ قَدَرُوا عَلَي ذَلِكَ كانَ تَكْذِيباً لِقَوْلِهِ. بَلْ رَفَعَهُ اللهُ إلَيهِ بَعْدَ أنْ تَوَفّاهُ(عليه السلام). فَلَمّا أرادَ اللهُ أنْ يَرْفَعَهُ, أوْحَي إلَيهِ أنْ يَسْتَوْدِعَ نُورَ اللهِ وَحِكْمَتَهُ وَعِلْمَ كِتابِهِ شَمْعُونَ بْنَ حَمُّونَ الصفا, خَلِيفَتَهُ عَلَي المُؤْمِنِينَ؛ فَفَعَلَ ذَلِكَ... .'»

(بحار الأنوار، ١٤، ٥١٥، ٤)

1.3.3. Ṣafwān ibn Yaḥyā said, "I said to Imam Riḍā, 'We used to ask you [about the Imam after you], before Allah had granted you Abū Ja'far, and you used to say, "Allah will grant me a son." Now, Allah has given him to you. Our eyes have been brightened! May Allah never show us the day [of your sorrow]! But if it should happen, whom should we follow?' He pointed with his hand toward Abū Ja'far, who was standing before him. Then I said, 'May I be your sacrifice! This boy is only three years old.' He said, 'That does not matter. Jesus stood as an authority (*ḥujjah*) when he was three years old."

(*Kāfī,* 1, 321, 10)

1.3.4. Before his son (Muḥammad al-Taqī) was born, al-Riḍā said, "By Allah, He will make from me something by which the truth and its followers are proven, and He will destroy by it what is wrong and its followers," then al-Taqi was born after a year. Then he said, "This is Abū Ja'far. I put him in my seat, and I set him in my place. We are the Folk of the Household whose children inherit from their elders exactly." It was said to him, "This son is only three years old." He said, "It does not harm him. Jesus stood as an authority (*ḥujjah*) when he was less than three years old."

(*Kharā'ij Wa al-Jarā'iḥ*, 2, 899)

1.3.5. It is reported that [Imam] Riḍā said, "Verily Allah, the Exalted, authorized Jesus when he was two years old."

(*Biḥār*, 14, 257, 54)

1.3.6. Abū al-Ḥasan said, "...On the Resurrection day there will be four people from among the first ones and four people from among the last ones on the Throne of Allah, the Mighty and Magnificent. As for the four of the first, they are Noah, Abraham, Moses and Jesus and the last are Muḥammad, 'Alī, al-Ḥasan and al-Ḥusayn, peace be with them."

(*Tahdhib*, 6, 84, 3)

١-٣-٣- مُحَمَّدُ بْنُ يَحْيَي، عَنْ أحْمَدَ بْنِ مُحَمَّدٍ، عَنْ صَفْوانَ بْنِ يَحْيَي قالَ: «قُلْتُ لِلرِّضاعليه السلام: 'قَدْ كُنّا نَسْألُكَ قَبْلَ أنْ يَهَبَ اللهُ لَكَ أبا جَعْفَرٍعليه السلام، فَكُنْتَ تَقُولُ: 'يَهَبُ اللهُ لِي غُلاماً.' فَقَدْ وَهَبَهُ اللهُ لَكَ فاقَرَّ عُيُونَنا. فَلا أرانا اللهُ يَوْمَكَ. فانْ كانَ كَوْنٌ، فإلَي مَنْ؟' فأشارَ بِيَدِهِ إلَي أبِي جَعْفَرٍعليه السلام وَهُوَ قائِمٌ بَيْنَ يَدَيْهِ. فَقُلْتُ: 'جُعِلْتُ فِداكَ، هَذا ابن ثَلاثِ سِنِينَ!' فَقالَ: 'وَما يَضُرُّهُ مِنْ ذَلِكَ. فَقَدْ قامَ عِيسَيعليه السلام بِالحُجَّةِ وَهُوَ ابن ثَلاثِ سِنِينَ.'»

الكافي، ١، ٣٢١، ١٠)

١-٣-٤- قالَ الرضاعليه السلام قَبْلَ وِلادَتِهِ [مُحَمَّدِ بْنِ عَلِيٍّ التَقِيِّ]: «واللهِ لَيَجْعَلَنَّ اللهُ مِنِّي ما يَثْبُتُ بِهِ الحَقَّ وأهْلَهُ وَيَمْحَقُ بِهِ الباطِلَ وأهْلَهُ.» فَوُلِدَ التَقِيُّعليه السلام بَعْدَ سَنَةٍ. فَقالَ: «هَذا أبُو جَعْفَرٍ. قَدْ أجْلَسْتُهُ مَجْلِسِي وَصَيَّرْتُهُ مَكانِي. إنّا أهْلُ بَيْتٍ يَتَوارَثُ أصاغِرُنا أكابِرَنا, القُذَّةُ بِالقُذَّةِ.» قِيلَ: «هَذا ابن ثَلاثِ سِنِينَ.» فَقالَ: «ما يَضُرُّ مِنْ ذَلِكَ, وَقَدْ قامَ عِيسَي بِالحُجَّةِ وَهُوَ ابن أقَلَّ مِنْ ثَلاثِ سِنِينَ.»

(الخرائج والجرائح، ٢، ٨٩٩)

١-٣-٥- عَلِيُّ بْنُ مُحَمَّدٍ, عَنْ مُحَمَّدِ بْنِ الحَسَنِ, عَنْ عَبْدِ اللهِ بْنِ جَعْفَرٍ الحِمْيَرِيّ, عَنْ الرضاعليه السلام، قالَ: «إنَّ اللهَ تَعالَي احْتَجَّ بِعِيسَيعليه السلام وَهُوَ ابن سَنَتَيْنِ.»

(بحار الأنوار، ١٤، ٢٥٧، ٥٤)

١-٣-٦- قالَ أبُو الحَسَنِ مُوسَيعليه السلام: «... إذا كانَ يَوْمُ القِيامَةِ كانَ عَلَي عَرْشِ اللهِ، عَزَّ وَجَلَّ، أرْبَعَةٌ مِنَ الأوَّلِينَ وأرْبَعَةٌ مِنَ الآخِرِينَ. فأمّا الأرْبَعَةُ الذينَ هُمْ مِنَ الأوَّلِينَ فَنُوحٌ وإبْراهِيمُ وَمُوسَي وَعِيسَيعليه السلام واما الآخِرُونَ فَمُحَمَّدٌ وَعَلِيٌّ والحَسَنُ والحُسَيْنُعليه السلام.»

(التهذيب، ٦، ٨٤، ٣)

1.3.7. Abū Dhar, may Allah have mercy upon him, said, "The Apostle of Allah was sitting in the mosque alone when I entered it. So I took advantage of his solitude and said, "... O Apostle of Allah! How many prophets were there?" He said, "One hundred twenty-four thousand." I said, "How many apostles were there?" "Three hundred and thirteen all together." I said, "Who was the first prophet?" He said, "Adam." I said, "Was he an apostle among the prophets?" He replied, "Yes, Allah created him by His hand and blew into him from His spirit." Then he continued, "O Abū Dhar these four prophets among the prophets are Siryānī: Adam, Seth, Ukhnūkh, that is, Idrīs, who was the first person to write with a pen, and Noah, peace be with them. And four of them are Arab: Hūd, Ṣāliḥ, Shu'ayb and your prophet Muḥammad. The first prophet from the children of Isreal was Moses and the last of them was Jesus, and six hundred prophets were between them." I said, "O the Apostle of Allah! How many books did Allah send?" He replied "One hundred and four books. He sent fifty scrolls to Seth, thirty scrolls to Idrīs, and twenty scrolls to Abraham. And He sent the Torah, Bible, Psalms and Furqān."

(*Khiṣāl*, 2, 524)

1.3.8. Ja'far ibn Muḥammad said, "Gabriel remained forty days and did not descend to the Prophet. He said, "O my Lord my yearning for your Prophet has become intense, alow me." Allah the Exalted revealed to him, "O Gabriel descend to My friend and My Prophet, then give him My greetings of peace, and inform him that I have distinguished him with prophethood and made him surpass all the prophets, and give my greetings of peace to his successor and inform him that I have distinguished him with succession and made him surpass all the successors." Gabriel descended to the Prophet and said, "...O Muḥammad! Whoever followed Seth would be saved by Seth, Seth was saved by Adam and Adam was saved by Allah.

١-٣-٧- عَنْ أبي ذَرٍ, رَحْمَةُ اللهِ عَلَيْهِ, قالَ: «دَخَلْتُ عَلَي رَسُولِ اللهِ صلى الله عليه وآله وسلم, وَهُوَ جالِسٌ فِي المَسْجِدِ وَحْدَهُ, فاغْتَنَمْتُ خَلْوَتَهُ ... قُلْتُ: 'يا رَسُولَ اللهِ، كَمِ النَبِيُّونَ؟' قالَ: 'مِائَة الفٍ وأربعَةٌ وَعِشْرُونَ الفَ نَبِيٍّ.' قُلْتُ: 'كَمِ المُرْسَلُونَ مِنْهُمْ؟' قالَ: 'ثَلاثُ مِائَة وَثَلاثَةٌ عَشَرَ, جَمّاءَ, غَفِيراءَ.' قُلْتُ: 'مَنْ كانَ أوَّلُ الأنبياءِ؟' قالَ: 'آدَمُ.' قُلْتُ: 'وَكانَ مِنَ الأنبياءِ مُرْسَلاً؟' قالَ: 'نَعَم. خَلَقَهُ اللهُ بِيَدِهِ وَنَفَخَ فِيهِ مِنْ رُوحِهِ.' ثُمَّ قالَ صلى الله عليه وآله وسلم: 'يا أبا ذَرٍ، أربعَةٌ مِنَ الأنبياءِ سِرْيانِيُّونَ: آدَمُ وَشِيْثُ وأخْنُوخُ, وَهُوَ إدْرِيسُ عليه السلام وَهُوَ أوَّلُ مَنْ خَطَّ بِالقَلَمِ وَنُوحٌ عليه السلام. وأربَعَةٌ مِنَ الأنبياءِ مِنَ العَرَبِ: هُودٌ وَصالِحٌ وَشُعَيْبٌ وَنَبِيُّكَ مُحَمَّدٌ. وأوَّلُ نَبِيٍّ مِنْ بَنِي إسْرائِيلَ مُوسَي وآخِرُهُمْ عِيسَي وَ[بَيْنَهُما] سِتُّ مِائَة نَبِيٍّ.' قُلْتُ: 'يا رَسُولَ اللهِ، كَمْ أنْزَلَ اللهُ مِنْ كِتابٍ؟' قالَ: 'مِائَة كِتابٍ وأربَعَة كُتُبٍ. أنْزَلَ اللهُ عَلَي شِيْثَ خَمْسِينَ صَحِيفَةً وَعَلَي إدْرِيسَ ثَلاثِينَ صَحِيفَةً وَعَلَي إبْراهِيمَ عِشْرِينَ صَحِيفَةً, وأنْزَلَ التَوْراةَ والإنجيلَ والزبُورَ والفُرْقانَ.'»

(الخصال،٢، ٥٢٤)

١-٣-٨- حَدَّثَنِي [ثنا] عَلِيُّ بْنُ الحُسَيْنِ مُعَنْعَناً, عَنْ جَعْفَرِ بْنِ مُحَمَّدٍ عليه السلام, قالَ: «مَكَثَ جَبْرَئِيلُ أربعِينَ يَوْماً لَمْ يَنْزِلْ عَلَي النَبِيِّ صلى الله عليه وآله وسلم. فَقالَ: 'يا رَبِّ، قَدِ اشْتَدَّ شَوْقِي إلَي نَبِيِّكَ, فاذَنْ لِي.' فأوْحَي اللهُ تَعالَي إلَيْهِ: 'يا جَبْرَئِيلُ، اهْبِطْ إلَي حَبِيبِي وَنَبِيِّي فاقْرِئْهُ مِنِّي السَلامَ, وأخْبِرْهُ أنِّي [قَدْ] خَصَصْتُهُ بِالنبُوَّةِ وَفَضَّلْتُهُ عَلَي جَمِيعِ الأنبياءِ, واقْرَءْ وَصِيَّهُ مِنِّي [مِنّا] السَلامَ, وأخْبِرْهُ أنِّي خَصَصْتُهُ بِالوَصِيَّةِ وَفَضَّلْتُهُ عَلَي جَمِيعِ الأوْصِياءِ.'» قالَ: «فَهَبَطَ جَبْرَئِيلُ [ع] عَلَي النَبِيِّ صلى الله عليه وآله وسلم ... فَقالَ جَبْرَئِيلُ: 'يا مُحَمَّدُ، نَجا مَنْ تَوَلّي شَيْئاً بِشِيْثٍ وَنَجا شِيْثُ بِآدَمَ وَنَجا آدَمُ بِاللهِ,

Whoever followed Shem would been saved by Shem, Shem was saved by Noah and Noah wad saved by Allah. Whoever followed Āṣif would be saved by Āṣif, and Āṣif was saved by Solomon. Whoever followed Yūsha' would be saved by Yūsha', and Yūsha' would be saved by Moses, and Moses was saved by Allah. Whoever followed Simon would be saved by Simon, and Simon would be saved by Jesus, and Jesus was saved by Allah. Whoever followed 'Alī would be saved by 'Alī and 'Alī would be saved by you, and you are saved by Allah. Verily, all things are by Allah. Verily, the angels and guardians are honored among all the angels for being in the company of 'Alī." He said, "Then 'Alī sat down while hearing the speech of Gabriel, although he did not see him.

(*Tafsīr Furāt al-Kūfī*, 378).

1.3.9. It is reported that Ibn Abū Ya'fūr said, "I heard Abu 'Abd Allah say, 'The chiefs of the prophets and apostles are five and they are the possessors of constancy among the apostles, and they are the axis about which [the other prophets] turn: Noah, Abraham, Moses, Jesus and Muḥammad, peace be with him and his descendants and all of the prophets.

(*Kāfī*, 1, 175, 3)

1.3.10. Among the questions of Shāmī is that he asked the Commander of the Faithful about the six prophets who had [special] names. He said, "Yūsha' ibn Nūn was Dhū al-Kifl, Ya'qūb ibn Isḥāq was Isrā'īl, Khiḍr was Ḥilqiyā, Yūnus was Dhū al-Nūn, Jesus was the Messiah and Muḥammad was Aḥmad, may the blessings of Allah be with all of them."

(*Biḥār,* 16, 90, 22)

1.3.11. It is reported that [Imam] Bāqir said, "Allah sent Jesus especially to the children of Israel, and his prophecy was in Jerusalem, and after him there were twelve apostles."

(*Biḥār*, 14, 250)

وَنَجا مَنْ تَوَلَّي ساماً بِسامٍ وَنَجا سامٌ بِنُوحٍ وَنَجا نُوحٌ بِاللهِ, وَنَجا مَنْ تَوَلَّي آصِفَ بِآصِفَ وَنَجا آصِفُ بِسُلَيْمانَ وَنَجا سُلَيْمانُ بِاللهِ, وَنَجا مَنْ تَوَلَّي يُوشَعَ بِيُوشَعَ وَنَجا يُوشَعُ بِمُوسَي وَنَجا مُوسَي بِاللهِ, وَنَجا مَنْ تَوَلَّي شَمْعُونَ بِشَمْعُونَ وَنَجا شَمْعُونُ بِعِيسَي وَنَجا عِيسَي بِاللهِ, وَنَجا مَنْ تَوَلَّي عَلِيّاً بِعَلِيٍّ وَنَجا عَلِيٌّ بِكَ وَنَجَوْتَ أنتَ بِاللهِ. وانَّما كُلُّ شَيءٍ بِاللهِ. وانَّ المَلائِكَةَ والحَفَظَةَ لَيَفْخَرُونَ عَلَي جَمِيعِ المَلائِكَةِ لِصُحْبَتِها إيّاهُ.'» قالَ: «فَجَلَسَ عَلِيٌّ عليه السلام يَسْمَعُ كَلامَ جَبْرَئِيلَ [ع] وَلا يَرَي شَخْصَهُ.»

(تفسير فُرات الكوفيّ، ٣٧٨)

١-٣-٩- عِدَّةٌ مِنْ أصْحابِنا، عَنْ أحْمَدَ بْنِ مُحَمَّدٍ، عَنْ مُحَمَّدِ بْنِ يَحْيَي الخَثْعَمِيِّ، عَنْ هِشامٍ، عَنْ ابنِ أبِي يَعْفُورٍ، قالَ: «سَمِعْتُ أبا عَبْدِ اللهِ عليه السلام يَقُولُ: 'سادَةُ النَبِيينَ والمُرْسَلِينَ خَمْسَةٌ، وَهُمْ أُولُو العَزْمِ مِنَ الرسُلِ وَعَلَيْهِمْ دارَتِ الرحَي: نُوحٌ وإبْراهِيمُ وَمُوسَي وَعِيسَي وَمُحَمَّدٌ، صَلَّي اللهُ عَلَيْهِ وآلِهِ وَعَلَي جَمِيعِ الأنبياءِ.»

(الكافى، ١، ١٧٥، ٣)

١-٣-١٠- فِي أسْئِلَةِ الشامِي, سأَلَ أمِيرَ المُؤْمِنِينَ عليه السلام عَنْ سِتَّةٍ مِنَ الأنبياءِ لَهُمْ إسْمانِ. فَقالَ: «يُوشَعُ بْنُ نُونَ, وَهُوَ ذُو الكِفْلِ, وَيَعْقُوبُ بْنُ إسْحاقَ عليه السلام, وَهُوَ إسْرائِيلُ, والخِضْرُ عليه السلام, وَهُوَ حِلْقِيا, وَيُونُسُ عليه السلام, وَهُوَ ذُو النونِ, وَعِيسَي عليه السلام, وَهُوَ المَسِيحُ, وَمُحَمَّدٌ صلى الله عليه وآله وسلم, وَهُوَ أحْمَدُ, صَلَواتُ اللهِ عَلَيْهِمْ.»

(بحار الأنوار، ١٦، ٩٠، ٢٢)

١-٣-١١- الطالِقانِيُّ عَنِ ابنِ عُقْدَةٍ, عَنْ عَلِيِّ بْنِ الحَسَنِ بْنِ فَضّالٍ, عَنْ أبِيهِ, عَنْ مُحَمَّدِ بْنِ الفُضَيْلِ, عَنْ الثُمالِيِّ, عَنْ الباقِرِ عليه السلام قالَ: «إنَّ اللهَ أرْسَلَ عِيسَي إلَي بَنِي إسْرائِيلَ خاصَّةً, وَكانَتْ نُبُوَّتُهُ بِبَيْتِ المَقْدِسِ,

1.3.12 Sufyān ibn ‘Uyaynah reported that Mujāhid narrated this saying of the Prophet, “There are four antecedents [who are the first followers of the prophets.] Yūsha‘ to Moses, Sāḥib Yāsīn to Jesus and ‘Ali to the Prophet.”

(*Ṣirāṭ al-Mustaqīm*, 3, 158)

1.3.13. Al-Ḥusayn ibn al-Khālid narated that Abū al-Ḥasan al-Riḍā said, “It was engraved on the ring of Adam, ‘There is no god but Allah. Muhammad is the Apostle of Allah.’” He continued until he said, “Then Noah engraved on his ring, ‘There is no god but Allah, one thousand times. O my Lord! Reform me.’”

He continued until he said, “And Allah sent a ring to Abraham on which there were these six letters, ‘There is no god but Allah. Muhammad is the Apostle of Allah. There is no power and no strength save in God. I entrust my work to Allah. I lean on Allah.

Allah is sufficient for me.’ Then Allah, may His Magnificence be magnified, revealed to him ‘Wear this ring. I will change the fire into coldness and peace.’ And the ring of Moses was engraved with these two letters, that he took them from Torah, ‘Have patience, you will be given wages. Tell the truth, you will be saved.’ The ring of Solomon was engraved with two letters he took, ‘Glory is to Him Who put the bridle on the Jinn by His words.’ The ring of Jesus was engraved with two letters he took from the Gospel, ‘Blessed is the servant because of whom Allah is remembered, and woe unto the servant because of whom Allah is forgotten.’ The ring of Muhammad was engraved with ‘There is no god but Allah. Muhammad is the Apostle of Allah.’”

(Wasā’il al-Shī‘ah, 5, 101, 6041.)

وكانَ مِنْ بَعْدِهِ مِنَ الحَوارِيِّين اثنَي عَشَرَ.»

(بحار الأنوار، ١٤، ٢٥٠)

١-٣-١٢- سُفْيانُ بْنُ عُيَيْنَةٍ رَوَي عَنْ مُجاهِدٍ قَوْلَ النَبِيِّ صلى الله عليه وآله وسلم: «السبّاقُ أرْبَعَةٌ: يُوشَعُ إلَي مُوسَي وَصاحِبُ يَس إلَي عِيسَي وَعَلِيٌّ إلَي النَبِي صلى الله عليه وآله وسلم.»

(الصراط المستقيم، ٣، ١٥٨)

١-٣-١٣- فِي المَجالِسِ وَعُيُونِ الأخْبارِ عَنْ أبِيهِ، عَنْ سَعْدِ بْنِ عَبْدِ الله، عَنْ أحْمَدَ بْنِ مُحَمَّدِ بْنِ خالِدٍ، عَنْ مُحَمَّدِ بْنِ عَلِيٍّ الكُوفِيِّ، عَنْ الحَسَنِ بْنِ أبِي العُقْبِ الصَيْرَفِيِّ، عَنْ الحُسَيْنِ بْنِ خالِدٍ، عَنْ أبِي الحَسَنِ الرضا عليه السلام، فِي حَدِيثٍ، قالَ: «كانَ نَقْشُ خاتَمِ آدَمَ، 'لا إلَهَ إلّا اللهُ مُحَمَّدٌ رَسُولُ اللهِ.'» إلَي أنْ قالَ: «فَنَقَشَ نُوحٌ فِي خاتَمِهِ: 'لا إلَهَ إلّا اللهُ الفَ مَرَّةٍ، يا رَبِّ، أصْلِحْنِي.'» إلَي أنْ قالَ: «وأهْبَطَ اللهُ عَلَي إبْراهِيمَ خاتَماً فِيهِ سِتَّةُ أحْرُفٍ: 'لا إلَهَ إلّا اللهُ، مُحَمَّدٌ رَسُولُ اللهِ، لا حَوْلَ وَلا قُوَّةَ إلّا بِاللهِ، فَوَّضْتُ أمْرِي إلَي اللهِ، أسْنَدْتُ ظَهْرِي إلَي اللهِ،

حَسْبِيَ اللهُ.' فأوْحَي اللهُ، جَلَّ جَلالُهُ، إلَيهِ: 'تَخَتَّمْ بِهَذا الخاتَمِ، فإنِّي أجْعَلُ النارَ عَلَيكَ بَرْداً وَسَلاماً.'» قالَ: «وَكانَ نَقْشُ خاتَمِ مُوسَي عليه السلام حَرْفَينِ اشْتَقَّهُما مِنَ التَوْراةِ: 'إصْبِرْ تُؤْجَرْ، أصْدُقْ تَنْجُ.'» قالَ: «وَكانَ نَقْشُ خاتَمِ سُلَيْمانَ عليه السلام حَرْفَينِ اشْتَقَّهُما: 'سُبْحانَ مَنْ الجَمَ الجِنَّ بِكَلِماتِهِ.' وَكانَ نَقْشُ خاتَمِ عِيسَي عليه السلام حَرْفَينِ اشْتَقَّهُما مِنَ الإنجِيلِ: 'طُوبَي لِعَبْدٍ ذُكِرَ اللهُ مِنْ أجْلِهِ وَوَيْلٌ لِعَبْدٍ نُسِيَ اللهُ مِنْ أجْلِهِ.' وكانَ نَقْشُ خاتَمِ مُحَمَّدٍ: 'لا إلَهَ إلّا اللهُ، مُحَمَّدٌ رَسُولُ اللهِ...'»

(وسائل الشيعة، ٥، ١٠١، ٦٠٤١)

1.4. HIS CHARACTERISTICS

1.4.1. The Apostle of Allah said, "I saw Abraham, Moses and Jesus. Moses was a tall man, and his hair was hanging down, like the men of the Zuṭ, and like the men of the Shanū'ah.[1] Jesus was a ruddy faced man with curly hair and medium height." Then he was silent. They said to him, "O Apostle of Allah! What about Abraham?" He said, "Look at your companion [me]."

(*Biḥār* 12, 10, 24)

1.4.2. Āminah [the mother of the Prophet] said, "When the birth of the Apostle of Allah became near I would hear a sound, 'Bring Muḥammad around the East and West and show him to the *jinn*, people, birds and wild animals and give him the clarity of Adam, the tenderness of Noah, the loveliness of Abraham, the tongue of Ismā'il, the perfection of Joseph, the good news of Ya'qūb, the voice of David, the asceticism of John and the nobility of Jesus.' Then he appeared [i.e., the Prophet was born]. So, I faced him...."

(*Biḥār,* 15, 272, 17)

1.4.3. The Apostle of Allah said, "Everyone who wants to look at Adam in his knowledge, Noah in his piety, Abraham in his perseverance (*ḥilm*), Moses in his awe and Jesus in his worship should look at 'Alī ibn Abī Ṭālib."

(*Biḥār,* 39, 39)

---

[1] The Zuṭ are a tribe from India, with wide faces with little facial hair, and the Shanwah are like the Qaḥṭaniyah of the Arabs. -Majlisī

١-٤- أوصافه

١-٤-١- عَنِ الصادِقِ عليه السلام، قالَ: «قالَ رَسُولُ اللهِ صلى الله عليه وآله وسلم: 'رأيْتُ إبْراهِيمَ وَمُوسَي وَعِيسَي عليهم السلام. فأمّا مُوسَي، فَرَجُلٌ طُوالٌ سَبْطٌ يُشْبِهُ رجالَ الزُّطِّ وَرجالَ أهْلِ شَنُوءَةِ؛ وأمّا عِيسَي، فَرَجُلٌ أحْمَرُ جَعِدٌ رَبِعَةٌ.'» قالَ: «ثُمَّ سَكَتَ. فَقِيلَ لَهُ: 'يا رَسُولَ اللهِ، فإبْراهِيمُ؟' قالَ: 'اُنْظُرُوا إلي صاحِبِكُم.' يعَنْي نَفْسَهُ.»

(بحار الأنوار، ١٢، ١٠، ٢٤)

١-٤-٢- أبانُ بْنُ عُثْمانَ رَفَعَهُ بإسْنادِهِ, قالَتْ آمِنَةُ، رَضِيَ اللهُ عَنْها،: «لَمّا قَرُبَتْ وِلادَةُ رَسُولِ اللهِ صلى الله عليه وآله وسلم ...، سَمِعْتُ نِداءَ: 'طُوفُوا بِمُحَمَّدٍ الشرْقَ والغَرْبَ، واعْرِضُوُه عَلَي رُوْحانِيِّ الجِنِّ والإنْسِ والطَّيرِ والسِّباعِ، وأعْطُوهُ صَفاءَ آدَمَ وَرِقَّةَ نُوحٍ وَخُلَّةَ إبْراهِيمَ وَلِسانَ إسْماعِيلَ وَكَمالَ يُوسُفَ وَبُشْرَيَ يَعْقُوبَ وَصَوْتَ داوُدَ وَزُهْدَ يَحْيَي وَكَرَمَ عِيسَي.' ثُمَّ انْكَشَفَ عَنْهُ، فإذا أنا بِهِ... .»

(بحار الأنوار، ١٥، ٢٧٢، ١٧)

١-٤-٣- قَدْ رَوَي البَيْهَقِيُّ بِسَنَدِهِ إلي رَسُولِ اللهِ صلى الله عليه وآله وسلم، أنَّهُ قالَ: «مَنْ أرادَ أنْ يَنْظُرَ إلي آدَمَ فِي عِلْمِهِ، وإلي نُوحٍ فِي تَقْواهُ، وإلي إبْراهِيمَ فِي حِلْمِهِ، وإلي مُوسَي فِي هَيْبَتِهِ، وإلي عِيسَي فِي عِبادَتِهِ، فَلْيَنْظُرْ إلي عَلِيٍّ بْنِ أبى طالِبٍ عليه السلام.»

(بحار الأنوار، ٣٩، ٣٩)

1.4.4. It is reported from Abū al-Ḥamrā' that the prophet said, "Everyone who wants to look at Adam in his dignity, Moses in the intensity of his grip,(1) and Jesus in his asceticism, should look at the one coming." Then 'Alī came.

(*Biḥār*, 40, 78)

1.4.5. It is reported that Abū Dhārr al-Ghifārī said, "One day we were before the Apostle of Allah when he stood, bowed, and prostrated in thanks to Allah, the Exalted. Then he said, 'O Jundab! Whoever wants to look at Adam in his knowledge, Noah in his understanding, Abraham in his friendship, Moses in his intimate prayers, and Jesus in his journeying, Job in his patience and calamity, look at the man coming who is like the sun and the moon in radiance, and stars shining bright, whose heart is bravest of all people, and whose hand is more generous, so that may the curse of Allah, the angels and the people be upon those who hate him.' He said, 'The people turned to see who was coming when 'Alī ibn Abī Ṭālib came."

(*Biḥār,* 39, 38, 9)

1.4.6. Ibn 'Abbās said, "Gabriel was near the Prophet at the right side of him, then the Commander of the Faithful came. Gabriel laughed and said, '... O Muhammad! If you yearn for the face of Jesus and his worship, the asceticism of John and his obedience, the inheritence of Solomon and his generosity, look at the face of 'Alī ibn Abū Ṭālib.' Then Allah the Exalted sent: ❴*And when the example of the son of Mary is given, they laughed and exclaimed their surprise*❵ (43:57), that is, the son of Mary is like 'Alī ibn Abū Ṭālib and 'Alī is like Jesus.

(*Biḥār*, 35, 47)

(1) Compare the language in (85:12).

١-٤-٤- عَنْ أبِى الحَمْراءَ: «عَنْهُ صلى الله عليه وآله وسلم: 'مَنْ أرادَ أنْ يَنْظُرَ إلَي آدَمَ فِي وَقارِهِ، وإلَي مُوسَي فِي شِدَّةِ بَطْشِهِ، وإلَي عِيسَي فِي زُهْدِهِ، فَلْيَنْظُرْ إلَي هذا المُقْبِلِ.' فأقبَلَ عَلِيٌّ عليه السلام.»

(بحار الأنوار، ٤٠، ٧٨)

١-٤-٥- أحْمَدُ بْنُ عَبْدِ الجَبّار, عَنْ زَيْدِ بْنِ الحارِثِ, عَنْ الأعْمَشِ, عَنْ إبْراهِيمَ التَمِيمِيِّ, عَنْ أبِيهِ, عَنْ أبِى ذَرِ الغِفارِيِّ, قالَ: «بَيْنَما ذاتَ يَوْمٍ مِنَ الأيّامِ بَيْنَ يَدَىْ رَسُولِ اللهِ صلى الله عليه وآله وسلم، إذْ قامَ وَرَكَعَ وَسَجَدَ شُكْراً للهِ تعالَي, ثُمَّ قالَ: 'يا جُنْدَبُ، مَنْ أرادَ أنْ يَنْظُرَ إلَي آدَمَ فِي عِلْمِهِ، وإلَي نُوحٍ فِي فَهْمِهِ، وإلَي إبْراهِيمَ فِي خُلَّتِهِ، وإلَي مُوسَي فِي مُناجاتِهِ، وإلَي عِيسَي فِي سِياحَتِهِ، والَي أيُّوبَ فِي صَبْرِهِ وَبلائِهِ، فَلْيَنْظُرْ إلَي هذا الرجُلِ المُقابِلِ الذى هُوَ كالشمْسِ والقَمَرِ السّارِىِّ والكَوْكَبِ الدرِّىِّ. أشْجَعُ الناسِ قَلْباً، وأسْخَي الناسِ كَفاً. فَعَلَي مُبْغِضِهِ لَعْنَةُ اللهِ والمَلائِكَةِ والناسِ أجْمَعِينَ.'» قالَ: «فالتَفَتَ الناسُ يَنْظُرُونَ مَنْ هَذا المُقْبِلُ. فإذا هُوَ عَلِيٌّ بْنُ أبِى طالِبٍ، عَلَيْهِ الصَلاةُ والسَلامُ.»

(بحار الأنوار، ٣٩، ٣٨، ٩)

١-٤-٦- الأعْمَشُ عَنْ أبِى صالِحٍ, عَنِ ابن عَبّاسٍ قالَ: «كانَ جَبْرَئِيلُ عليه السلام جالِساً عِنْدَ النَبِيِّ صلى الله عليه وآله وسلم, عَنْ يَمِينِهِ، إذْ أقبَلَ أمِيرُ المُؤْمِنِينَ عليه السلام. فَضَحِكَ جَبْرَئِيلُ فَقالَ: '... يا مُحَمَّدُ، إنْ اشْتَقْتَ إلَي وَجْهِ عِيسَي وَعِبادَتِهِ، وَزُهْدِ يَحْيَي وَطاعَتِهِ، وَمِيراثِ سُلَيْمانَ وَسَخاوَتِهِ، فانْظُرْ إلَي وَجْهِ عَلِيِّ بْنِ أبِى طالِبٍ.' وأنْزَلَ اللهُ، تعالَي، ﴿وَلَمّا ضُرِبَ ابن مَرْيَمَ مَثَلاً﴾ يَعْنِى شِبْهاً لِعَلِيِّ بْنِ أبِى طالِبٍ، وَعَلِيُّ بْنُ أبِى طالِبٍ شِبْهاً لِعِيسَي بْنِ مَرْيَمَ.»

(بحار الأنوار، ٣٥، ٤٧)

1.4.7. When a comparison was made before the Apostle of Allah, in his loudest voice he said, "O servants of Allah! Whoever wants to look at Adam in his majesty, to look at Seth in his wisdom, to look at Idrīs in his nobility and dignity, to look at Noah in his thanks to his Lord and his worship, to look at Abraham in his frendship and loyalty, to look at Moses in his hatred to every enemy of Allah and his opposing them, and to look at Jesus in his love of every believer and his good relations, look at 'Alī ibn Abū Ṭālib, here."

(*Tafsīr al-Imām al-'Askarī*, 498)

1.4.8. The Apostle of Allah ﷺ said, "He who wants to look at the asceticism of Jesus the son of Mary, look at Abū Dhar."

(*Biḥār*, 22, 343)

1.4.9. It is reported that the Apostle of Allah said, "The imams after me are twelve, the number of the months of the year, and from us is the Mahdī of this community who will have the awesomeness of Moses, the magnificence of Jesus, the judgment of David and the patience of Job."

(*Biḥār*, 36, 303, 141)

1.4.10. Zayd al-Kunāsī said, "I heard that Abū Ja'far would say, 'In the Sāḥib hādhā al-'amr [the twelfth Imām] there is an attribute (*sunnah*) of Joseph, an attribute of Moses, an attribute of Jesus and an attribute of Muḥammad. As though his likeness to Joseph is that his brothers acknowledge him as a leader and address him while they do not know him. His likeness to Moses is that he is fearful. His likeness to Jesus is journeying and his likeness to Muḥammad is the sword.'"[1]

(*Dalā'il al-Imāmah*, 291)

---

[1] The sword is used as a symbol of authority, not as a symbol of war or violence.

١-٤-٧- فَلَمّا مُثِّلَ بَيْنَ يَدَيْ رَسُولِ اللهِ ﷺ، قالَ رَسُولُ اللهِ ﷺ بِأَعْلَى صَوْتِهِ: «يا عِبادَ اللهِ، مَنْ أرادَ أنْ يَنْظُرَ وَمَهابَتِهِ إلى آدَمَ فِى جَلالَتِهِ، وَإلى شِيثٍ فِى حِكْمَتِهِ، وَإلى إدْرِيسَ فِى نَباهَتِهِ، وَإلى نُوحٍ فِى شُكْرِهِ لِرَبِّهِ وَعِبادَتِهِ، وَإلى إبْراهِيمَ فِى خُلَّتِهِ وَوَفائِهِ، وَإلى مُوسَى فِى بُغْضِ كُلِّ عَدُوٍّ للهِ وَمُنابَذَتِهِ، وَإلى عِيسَى فِى حُبِّ كُلِّ مُؤْمِنٍ وَحُسْنِ مُعاشَرَتِهِ، فَلْيَنْظُرْ إلى عَلِىِّ بْنِ أبِى طالِبٍ هَذا.»

(تفسير الإمام العسكريّ، ٤٩٨)

١-٤-٨- قالَ رَسُولُ اللهِ ﷺ: «مَنْ أرادَ أنْ يَنْظُرَ إلى زُهْدِ عِيسَى بْنِ مَرْيَمَ، فَلْيَنْظُرْ إلى أبِى ذَرٍّ.»

(بحار الأنوار، ٢٢، ٣٤٣)

١-٤-٩- أبُو عَبْدِ اللهِ الحُسَيْنُ بْنُ مُحَمَّدِ بْنِ سَعِيدِ بْنِ عَلِىٍّ الخُزاعِىٌّ،... عَنْ سَلْمانَ قالَ: «قالَ رَسُولُ اللهِ ﷺ: 'الأئِمَّةُ بَعْدِى اثْنا عَشَرَ، عَدَدَ شُهُورِ الحَوْلِ. وَمِنّا مَهْدِىُّ هَذِهِ الأُمَّةِ، لَهُ هَيْبَةُ مُوسَى وَبَهاءُ عِيسَى وَحُكْمُ داوُدَ وَصَبْرُ أيُّوبَ.»

(بحار الأنوار، ٣٦، ٣٠٣، ١٤١)

١-٤-١٠- حَدَّثَنِى أبُو المُفَضَّلِ مُحَمَّدُ بْنُ عَبْدِ اللهِ، قالَ: «حَدَّثَنا أبُو العَبّاسِ أحْمَدُ بْنُ مُحَمَّدِ بْنِ سَعِيدِ بْنِ عُقْدَةَ. قالَ: 'حَدَّثَنا يَحْيَى بْنُ زَكَرِيّا، عَنِ الحَسَنِ بْنِ مَحْبُوبٍ، عَنْ هِشامِ بْنِ سالِمٍ، عَنْ زَيْدٍ الكُناسِى. قالَ: 'سَمِعْتُ أبا جَعْفَرٍ يَقُولُ: 'صاحِبُ هَذا الأمْرِ فِيهِ سُنَّةٌ مِنْ يُوسُفَ وَسُنَّةٌ مِنْ مُوسَى وَسُنَّةٌ مِنْ عِيسَى وَسُنَّةٌ مِنْ مُحَمَّدٍ. وَأمّا شِبْهُهُ مِنْ يُوسُفَ، فَإنَّ إخْوَتَهُ يُبايِعُونَهُ وَيُخاطِبُونَهُ، وَهُمْ لا يَعْرِفُونَهُ وَأمّا شِبْهُهُ مِنْ مُوسَى، فَخائِفٌ،

1.4.11. Sa'id ibn Jubayr reported, "I heard the saying of 'Alī ibn al-Ḥusayn, 'There are many attributes (*sunnah*) of six prophets in our al-Qāim: Noah, Abraham, Moses, Jesus, Job and Muḥammad. As for the attribute from Noah, it is long life, from Abraham, it is having a hidden birth and being separated from the people, from Moses, it is fear and absence, from Jesus, it is the disagreement of people about him, from Job, it is release after suffering and from Muḥammad, it is going out with the sword.

(*Al-Ṣirāṭ al-Mustaqīm*, 2, 238)

1.4.12. Jābir reported that Abū Ja'far said, "Verily the Lord, the blessed and almighty, says, 'Enter into heaven by my mercy, save yourselves from the Fire by my pardon and devide the heaven according to your deeds. By My glory! I will send you down in the everlasting and noble dwelling.' When they enter it they will become like Adam with his height..., like Jesus, with the youth of thirty-three years, like Muḥammad with the Arabic language, like Joseph, with a beautiful figure shining with light, and like Job, with a heart of purity from hatred."

(*Biḥār*, 8, 218, 207)

1.4.13. Abū 'Abdullah said, "...Then Noah took the Ark (of the covenant) and buried it in al-Gharī, the part of the mountain on which Allah talked with Moses, on which He sanctified Jesus, on which He took Abraham as a friend, took Muḥammad as a beloved, and made it a dwelling for the prophets...."

(Jāmi' al-Akhbār, 21)

وأمّا شِبْهُهُ مِنْ عِيسَي فالسِّياحَةُ، وأمّا شِبْهُهُ مِنْ مُحَمَّدٍ فالسَّيْفُ.'»

(دلائل الإمامة، ٢٩١)

١-٤-١١- مِمّا جاءَ فِيهِ, عَنْ عَلِيِّ بْنِ الحُسَيْنِ عليه السلام ما رَواهُ حَمْزَةُ بْنُ حَمْرانَ, عَنْ أبِيهِ حَمْرانِ بْنِ أعْيَنَ, عَنْ سَعِيدِ بْنِ جُبَيْرٍ قالَ: «سَمِعْتُهُ يَقُولُ: 'فِي القائِمِ مِنّا سُنَنٌ مِنْ سِتَّةٍ مِنَ الأنبياءِ عليهم السلام: سُنَّةٌ مِنْ نُوحٍ وَسُنَّةٌ مِنْ إبْراهِيمَ وَسُنَّةٌ مِنْ مُوسَي وَسُنَّةٌ مِنْ عِيسَي وَسُنَّةٌ مِنْ أيُّوبَ وَسُنَّةٌ مِنْ مُحَمَّدٍ. فأمّا مِنْ نُوحٍ فَطُولُ العُمْرِ، وَمِنْ إبْراهِيمَ الخِفاءُ لِلْوِلادَةِ واعْتِزالُ الناسِ إيّاهُ، وَمِنْ مُوسَي الخَوْفُ والغَيْبَةُ، وَمِنْ عِيسَي اخْتِلافُ الناسِ فِيهِ، وَمِنْ أيُّوبَ الفَرَجُ بَعْدَ البَلْوَي، وَمِنْ مُحَمَّدٍ صلى الله عليه وآله وسلم الخُرُوجُ بِالسَّيْفِ.'»

(الصراط المستقيم، ٢، ٢٣٨)

١-٤-١٢- عَنْ عَوْفِ بْنِ عَبْدِ اللهِ, عَنْ جابِرٍ, عَنْ أبي جَعْفَرٍ عليه السلام، قالَ: «إنَّ الربَّ، تَبارَكَ وَتَعالَي، يَقُولُ: 'أدْخُلُوا الجَنَّةَ بِرَحْمَتِي، وانْجُوا مِنَ النارِ بِعَفْوِي، وَتَقَسِّمُوا الجَنَّةَ بِأعْمالِكُم، فَوَعِزَّتِي لأنْزِلَنَّكُمْ دارَ الخُلُودِ وَدارَ الكَرامَةِ.' فإذا دَخَلُوها صارُوا عَلَي طُولِ آدَمَ...؛ وَعَلَي مَلَدِ عِيسَي، ثَلاثاً وَثَلاثِينَ سَنَةٍ؛ وَعَلَي لِسانِ مُحَمَّدٍ، العَرَبِيَّةِ؛ وَعَلَي صُورَةِ يُوسُفَ، فِي الحُسْنِ، ثُمَّ يَعْلُو وُجُوهَهُمُ النورُ؛ وَعَلَي قَلْبِ أيُّوبَ، فِي السَلامَةِ مِنَ الغِلِّ.»

(بحار الأنوار، ٨، ٢١٨، ٢٠٧)

١-٤-١٣- قالَ أبُو عَبْدِ اللهِ عليه السلام: «... فأخَذَ نُوحٌ عليه السلام التابُوتَ، فَدَفَنَهُ فِي الغَرِيِّ، وَهُوَ قِطْعَةٌ مِنَ الجَبَلِ الذى كَلَّمَ اللهُ مُوسَي [عليه] تَكْلِيماً، وَقَدَّسَ عَلَيْهِ عِيسَي تَقْدِيساً، واتَّخَذَ إبْراهِيمَ خَلِيلاً، واتَّخَذَ مُحَمَّداً حَبِيباً، وَجَعَلَهُ لِلنَّبِيِّينَ مَسْكَناً... .»

(جامع الأخبار، ٢١)

1.4.14. Among the intimate conversations between Allah and Moses ibn Imrān is, "O Moses! I recommend to you as One Who is kind and compassionate to you Ibn Baṭūl, Jesus the son of Mary, who has a donkey and a burnoose, olive oil and olives and a prayer niche."

(Biḥār 13, 332, 13)

1.4.15. The Prophet said, "Whoever says the prayer of Tuesday night with thirty rak'a and in each rak'a he reads Sūra Ḥamd and the verse al-Kursī one time and Sūra Tawḥīd seven times, Allah will give him the reward of Job, the patient, John the son of Zachariah and Jesus the son of Mary...."

(*Mustadrak al-Wasā'il*, 6, 370, 7014)

1.5. HIS RELIGION

1.5.1. Al-Ṣādiq said about ﴾*...He has enjoined on me prayer and the poor-rate so long as I live.*﴿ (19:31) that by the "poor-rate" what is meant is *zakah al-ru'ūs*,[1] because not all people have wealth, but the *fiṭrah* is [to be paid] by the poor and the rich, the little and the big.

(*Tafsīr al-Qumī*, 2, 50)

1.5.2. It is reported that there was retaliation in the revealed law of Moses and blood money was necessary in the revealed law of Jesus. So the true and tolerant religion [Islam] came down permitting both of them.

(*'Awālī al-La'ālī*, 1, 387)

---

[1] There are two kinds of *zakah* or poor-rate. One is based upon a person's wealth, and is not imposed upon the poor. The other is given at the end of Ramaḍān by believers who are not so poor that they are elegible to receive alms, regardless of wealth.

١-٤-١٤- مُناجاةُ اللهِ، عَزَّ وَجَلَّ، لِمُوسَي بْنِ عِمْرانَ: «... يا مُوسَي، أوصيكَ وَصِيَّةَ الشفيقِ المُشْفِقِ، بِابْنِ البَتُولِ، عِيسَي بْنِ مَرْيَمَ، صاحِبِ الأتانِ والبُرْنُسِ والزيْتِ والزيْتُونِ والمِحْرابِ.»

(بحارالأنوار، ١٣، ٣٣٢، ١٣)

١-٤-١٥- عَنْهُ صلى الله عليه وآله وسلم أنَّهُ قالَ: «مَنْ صَلَّي لَيْلَةَ الأربَعاءِ ثَلاثِينَ رَكْعَةً، يَقرأ فِي كُلِّ رَكْعَةٍ الحَمْدَ مَرَّةً، وآيَةَ الكُرْسِيِّ مَرَّةً، وَسَبْعَ مَراتٍ قُلْ هُوَ اللهُ أحَدٌ، أعْطاهُ اللهُ تَعالَي يَوْمَ القِيامَةِ ثَوابَ أيُّوبَ الصابِرِ، وَثَوابَ يَحْيَي بْنِ زَكَرِيّا، وَثَوابَ عيسَي بن مَريَمَ...»

(مستدرك الوسائل، ٦، ٣٧٠، ٧٠١٤)

١-٥- دِيْنُهُ

١-٥-١- قالَ الصادِقُ عليه السلام فِي قَوْلِهِ [عِيسَي عليه السلام]: ﴿وأوْصانِي بِالصلاةِ والزَّكاةِ﴾ قالَ: «زَكاةُ الرؤوسِ، لأنَّ كُلَّ الناسِ لَيْسَ لَهُمْ أمْوالٌ، وانَّما الفِطْرَةُ عَلَي الفَقِيرِ والغَنِيِّ والصغِيرِ والكَبِيرِ.»

(تفسيرالقميّ، ٢، ٥٠)

١-٥-٢- رُوِيَ أنَّ القِصاصَ كانَ فِي شَرْعِ مُوسَي، والدِيَةَ حَتْماً كانَ فِي شَرْعِ عِيسَي، فَجاءَتِ الحَنِيفِيَّةُ السَمْحَةُ بِتَسْوِيغِ الأمْرَيْنِ.

(عوالى اللئالى، ١، ٣٨٧)

1.5.3. It is reported in true narrations that getting married without limit [to the number of wives] was permitted in the revealed law of Moses for the sake of men's affairs; and in the revealed law of Jesus only one was permitted for the sake of women's affairs. So this revealed law [of Islam] came for the sake of both.

(*'Awālī al-La'ālī*, 1, 446)

1.5.4. It is reported that Abū al-Ḥasan al-Riḍā ﷺ said, "Every prophet who was in the time of Moses ﷺ and after him had the revealed law of Moses and his rites and followed his Book until the time of Jesus ﷺ. And every prophet who was in the time of Jesus and after him had the rites of Jesus and his revealed law and followed his Book until the time of our Prophet Muḥammad ﷺ. Then these five prophets who possessed resolution (*ulū al-'azm*) are the most noble prophets and apostles, peace be upon them. And the revealed law of Muḥammad will not be abrogated until the Resurrection Day and there will be no prophet after him until the Resurrection Day.

(*'Ilal al-Sharā'I'*, 1, 122)

1.5.5. It is reported that Abū 'Abd-Allah narrated from his fathers, in order, until the Commander of the Faithful peace be upon all of them, that one day the people of five religions, the Jews, the Christians, the Naturalists (*dahriyah*), the Dualists and the 'Arab Idolaters gathered before the Apostle of Allah. The Jews said, "We say, 'Ezra is the son of Allah.' O Muḥammad! We came to you to see what you say. If you follow us, we were right prior to you and better than you, and if you oppose us, we will argue with you."

١-٥-٣- فِي الأحاديثِ الصَحِيحَةِ، رُوِيَ أنَّ التَزْوِيجَ كانَ فِي شَرْعِ مُوسَي جائِزاً بِغَيْرِ حَصْرٍ مُراعاةً لِمَصالِحِ الرجالِ، وَفِي شَرْعِ عِيسَي لا يَحِلُّ سِوَي الواحِدَةَ مُراعاةً لِمَصْلِحَةِ النساءِ، فَجاءَتْ هَذِهِ الشريعَةُ بِرِعايَةِ المَصْلَحَتَيْنِ.

(عوالى اللئالى، ١، ٤٤٦)

١-٥-٤- رُوِيَ, عَنْ أبِي الحَسَنِ الرضا عليه السلام: «كُلُّ نَبِيٍّ كانَ فِي زَمَنِ مُوسَي عليه السلام وَبَعْدَهُ كانَ عَلَي شَرِيعَةِ مُوسَي وَمِنْهاجِهِ وَتابِعاً لِكِتابِهِ إلَي أيّامِ عِيسَي عليه السلام، وَكُلُّ نَبِيٍّ كانَ فِي أيّامِ عِيسَي عليه السلام وَبَعْدَه كانَ عَلَي مِنْهاجِ عِيسَي وَشَرِيعَتِهِ وَتابِعاً لِكِتابِهِ إلَي زَمَنِ نَبِيِّنا مُحَمَّدٍ صلى الله عليه وآله وسلم. فَهؤُلاءِ الخَمْسَةُ هُمْ أولُو العَزْمِ وَهُمْ أفْضَلُ الأنبياءِ والرسُلِ عليهم السلام. وَشَرِيعَةُ مُحَمَّدٍ صلى الله عليه وآله وسلم لا تُنْسَخُ إلَي يَوْمِ القِيامَةِ، وَلا نَبِيَّ بَعْدَهُ إلَي يَوْمِ القِيامَةِ.»

(علل الشرائع، ١، ١٢٢)

١-٥-٥- لَقَدْ حَدَّثَنِي أبِي الباقِرُ عليه السلام, عَنْ جَدِّي عَلِيٍّ بْنِ الحُسَيْنِ زَيْنِ العابِدِينَ, عَنْ أبِيهِ الحُسَيْنِ بْنِ عَلِيٍّ سَيِّدِ الشهَداءِ, عَنْ أمِيرِ المُؤْمِنِينَ عَلِيِّ بْنِ أبِي طالِبٍ، صَلَواتُ اللهِ عَلَيْهِم أجْمَعِينَ، أنَّهُ اجْتَمَعَ يَوْماً عِنْدَ رَسُولِ اللهِ صلى الله عليه وآله وسلم أهْلُ خَمْسَةِ أدْيانٍ: اليَهُودُ والنَصارَي والدهْرِيَّةُ والثَنَوِيَّةُ وَمُشْرِكُو العَرَبِ. فَقالَتِ اليَهُودُ: «نَحْنُ نَقُولُ: 'عُزَيْرٌ ابن اللهِ.' وَقَدْ جِئْنَاكَ يا مُحَمَّدُ لِنَنْظُرَ ما تَقُولُ. فإنْ تَبِعْتَنا فَنَحْنُ أسْبَقُ إلَي الصوابِ مِنْكَ وأفْضَلُ، وإنْ خالَفْتَنا خَصَمْناكَ.»

The Christians said, "We say, 'Verily Jesus is the son of Allah who united with Him.' We came to you to see what you say. If you follow us, we were right prior to you and better than you, and if you oppose us we will argue with you." The Naturalists said, "We say, 'There is no begining of things and they are everlasting.' We came to you to see what you say. If you follow us, we were right prior to you and better than you, and if you oppose us we will argue with you." The Dualists said, "We say, 'Verily the light and the darkness are the administrators.' We came to you to see what you say. If you follow us, we were right prior to you and better than you, and if you oppose us we will argue with you." The 'Arab Idolaters said, "We say, 'Verily our idols are gods.' We came to you to see what you say. If you follow us, we were right prior to you and better than you, and if you oppose us we will argue with you."

The Apostle of Allah said, "I believe in God alone. There is no partner for Him, and I deny every god but Him." Then he said to them, "Verily Allah the Exalted raised me for all of the people as a bearer of good news, a warner and as an athority for the inhabitants of the world, and Allah will turn the deceptions of those who deceive in His religion back on them."...

Then he faced the Christians and said to them, "You said that the Eternal is united with Christ, His son. What do you mean by this saying? Do you want to say that the Eternal became non-eternal by this creature who is Jesus, or that the non-eternal, who is Jesus, became eternal by the Eternal who is Allah, or your saying, 'He united with him' means that 'He distinguished him by nobility while He did not ennoble anyone but him.' If you mean that the Eternal, the Exalted, became non-eternal, you are wrong. For it is impossible for the eternal to change and become non-eternal, and if you mean

وَقالَتِ النَصارَي: «نَحْنُ نَقولُ: 'إنَّ المَسيحَ ابن اللهِ، اتَّحَدَ بِهِ.' وَقَدْ جِئْناكَ لِنَنْظُرَ ما تَقولُ. فإنْ تَبِعْتَنا فَنَحْنُ أسْبَقُ إلَي الصَوابِ مِنْكَ وأفْضَلُ، وانْ خالَفْتَنا خَصَمْناكَ.» وَقالَتِ الدهْرِيَّةُ: «نَحْنُ نَقولُ: 'الأشياءُ لا بَدْءَ لَها وَهِيَ دائِمَةٌ،' وَقَدْ جِئْناكَ لِنَنْظُرَ ما تَقولُ. فإنْ تَبِعْتَنا فَنَحْنُ أسْبَقُ إلَي الصَوابِ مِنْكَ وأفْضَلُ، وإنْ خالَفْتَنا خَصَمْناكَ.» وَقالَتِ الثَنَوِيَّةُ: «نَحْنُ نَقولُ: 'إنَّ النورَ والظُلْمَةَ هُما المُدَبِّرانِ.' وَقَدْ جِئْناكَ لِنَنْظُرَ ما تَقولُ. فإنْ تَبِعْتَنا فَنَحْنُ أسْبَقُ إلَي الصَوابِ مِنْكَ وأفْضَلُ، وإنْ خالَفْتَنا خَصَمْناكَ.» وَقالَ مُشْرِكُو العَرَبِ: «نَحْنُ نَقولُ: 'إنَّ أوْثانَنا آلِهَةٌ.' وَقَدْ جِئْناكَ لِنَنْظُرَ ما تَقولُ. فإنْ تَبِعْتَنا فَنَحْنُ أسْبَقُ إلَي الصَوابِ مِنْكَ وأفْضَلُ، وإنْ خالَفْتَنا خَصَمْناكَ.»

فَقالَ رَسُولُ اللهِ صلى الله عليه وآله وسلم: «آمَنْتُ بِاللهِ وَحْدَهُ لا شَريكَ لَهُ، وَكَفَرْتُ بِكُلِّ مَعْبُودٍ سِواهُ.» ثُمَّ قالَ لَهُم: «إنَّ اللهَ تَعالَي بَعَثَنِي كافَّةً لِلنّاسِ بَشِيراً وَنَذِيراً، حُجَّةً عَلَي العالَمِينَ وَسَيَرُدُّ اللهُ كَيْدَ مَنْ يَكِيدُ دِينَهُ...»

ثُمَّ أقبَلَ صلى الله عليه وآله وسلم عَلَي النَصارَي فَقالَ لَهُم: «وأنتُم قُلْتُم: 'إنَّ القَدِيمَ، عَزَّ وَجَلَّ، اتَّحَدَ بِالمَسِيحِ ابنِهِ.' ما الذى أرَدْتُمُوهُ بِهَذا القَوْلِ؟ أرَدْتُم أنَّ القَدِيمَ صارَ مُحْدَثاً لِوُجُودِ هَذا المُحْدَثِ الذى هُوَ عِيسَي؟ أوِ المُحْدَثُ الذى هُوَ عِيسَي صارَ قَدِيماً لِوُجُودِ القَدِيمِ الذى هُوَ اللهُ؟ أوْ مَعْنَي قَوْلِكُم: 'إنَّهُ اتَّحَدَ بِهِ' أنَّهُ اخْتَصَّهُ بِكَرامَةٍ لَمْ يُكْرِمْ بِها أحَداً سِواهُ؟ فَإنْ أرَدْتُمْ أنَّ القَدِيمَ، تَعالَي، صارَ مُحْدَثاً، فَقَدْ أبْطَلْتُم؛ لأنَّ القَدِيمَ مُحالٌ أنْ يَنْقَلِبَ فَيَصِيرَ مُحْدَثاً. وإنْ أرَدْتُم أنَّ المُحْدَثَ صارَ قَدِيماً، فَقَدْ أحَلْتُمْ؛

that the non-eternal became eternal you are wrong for it is

impossible too for the non-eternal to change to the eternal, and if you mean that He united with him whereby He distinguished him and chose him among His other servants, you confess to the originality of Jesus and everything that is united with him for his own sake. Because if Jesus is non-created and Allah is united with him and changed him to the best creature before Him, Jesus and Him would have been non-eternal, and this is opposite to what you said in the begining."

The Cristians said, "O Muḥammad! Allah the Exalted manifested some strange things by the hand of Jesus, so He took him as His son for the sake of nobility." The Apostle of Allah said, "You heared what I said to the Jews about what you said." Then he repeated all of that. They said nothing except one of them who said, "O Muhammad! Do not you say, 'Abraham is *khalīl Allah* (the friend of Allah)?' So when you say this why do you reject our saying, 'Jesus is the son of Allah.'"

The Apostle of Allah said, "These are not alike for *khalīl Allah* is taken from *khallah* or *khullah* and the meaning of *khallah* is poverty and neediness. He was a friend of his Lord and needy of Him, chastely, abstemiously and independently separated from all but Him. Because when they wanted to throw him into the fire and to cast him with a catapult, Allah, the Exalted, raised Gabriel and said to him, 'Catch My servant!' Gabriel came to him, met him in the air, and said, 'Commission me for what happened to you, for Allah the Exalted rised me to help you.' He said, 'But Allah is sufficient for me and He is the best Trustee (*wakīl*). I ask no one but Him and there is no need for me unless of Him.'

لأنَّ المُحْدَثَ أيْضاً مُحالٌ أنْ يَصيرَ قَديماً. وإنْ أرَدْتُمْ أنَّهُ اتَّحَدَ بِهِ بِأن اخْتَصَّهُ واصْطَفاهُ عَلَي سائِرِ عِبادِهِ، فَقَدْ أقْرَرْتُمْ بِحُدُوثِ عِيسَي، وَبِحُدُوثِ المَعْنَي الذى اتَّحَدَ بِهِ مِنْ أجْلِهِ. لِأنَّهُ إذا كانَ عِيسَي مُحْدَثاً وَكانَ اللهُ اتَّحَدَ بِهِ، بِأنْ أحْدَثَ بِهِ مَعْنيً صارَ بِهِ أكْرَمَ الخلْقِ عِنْدَهُ، فَقَدْ صارَ عِيسَي وَذَلِكَ المَعْنَي مُحْدَثَينِ. وَهَذا خِلافُ ما بَدأتُم تَقُولُونَهُ.»

قالَ: «فَقالَتِ النَصارَي: 'يا مُحَمَّدُ، إنَّ اللهَ، تَعالَي، لَمّا أظْهَرَ عَلَي يَدِ عِيسَي مِنَ الأشياءِ العَجِيبَةِ ما أظْهَرَ، فَقَدْ اتَّخَذَهُ وَلَداً عَلَي جِهَةِ الكَرامَةِ.'» فَقالَ لَهُم رَسُولُ اللهِ صلى الله عليه وآله وسلم: «فَقَدْ سَمِعْتُمْ ما قُلْتُهُ لِلْيَهُودِ فِى هَذا المَعْنَي الذي ذَكَرْتُمُوهُ.» ثُمَّ أعادَ صلى الله عليه وآله وسلم ذَلِكَ كُلَّهُ، فَسَكَتُوا إلّا رَجُلاً واحِداً مِنْهُم، فَقالَ لَهُ: «يا مُحَمَّدُ، أوَلَسْتُمْ تَقُولُونَ إنَّ إبْراهِيمَ خَلِيلُ اللهِ؟» [قالَ: «قَدْ قُلْنا ذَلِكَ.» فَقالَ:] «فإذا قُلْتُمْ ذَلِكَ فَلِمَ مَنَعْتُمُونا مِنْ أنْ نَقُولَ: 'إنَّ عِيسَي ابن اللهِ.'»

فَقالَ رَسُولُ اللهِ صلى الله عليه وآله وسلم: «إنَّهُما لَمْ يَشْتَبِها، لِأنَّ قَوْلَنا: 'إنَّ إبْراهِيمَ خَلِيلُ اللهِ،' فإنَّما هُوَ مُشْتَقٌّ مِنَ الخلَّةِ والخُلَّةِ. فأمّا الخلَّةُ فانَّما مَعْناها الفقْرُ والفاقَةُ، فَقَدْ كانَ خَلِيلاً إلَي رَبِّهِ فَقِيراً، وإلَيْهِ مُنْقَطِعاً، وَعَنْ غَيْرِهِ مُتَعَفِّفاً، مُعْرِضاً، مُسْتَغْنِياً. وَذَلِكَ لِما أُرِيدَ قَذْفُهُ فِى النارِ، فَرُمِيَ بِهِ فِى المَنْجَنِيقِ. فَبَعَثَ اللهُ تعالَي جَبْرَئِيلَ عليه السلام وَقالَ لَهُ: 'أدْرِكْ عَبْدِى.' فَجاءَهُ فَلَقِيَهُ فِى الهَواءِ، فَقالَ: 'كَلِّفْنِى ما بَدا لَكَ، فَقَدْ بَعَثَنِى اللهُ لِنُصْرَتِكَ.' فَقالَ: 'بَلْ حَسْبِيَ اللهُ وَنِعْمَ الوَكِيلُ، إنِّى لا أسْألُ غَيْرَهُ وَلا حاجَةَ لِى إلّا إلَيهِ.'

Then He named him His friend (*khalīl*), that means His poor and needy, and who is separated from all but Him. When the meaning of *khalīl* is taken from need (*khullah*) and he is needy (*takhalal*) of Him and knows His secrets that no one else knows, it means that he knows Him and His affairs. And it does not cause the likeness of Allah to him. Do not you see that if he did not separate from all but Him, he would not have been His friend, and if he did not know His secrets he would not have been His friend. One's father is he of whom one is born, even if his father slanders him and sends him far away, for the meaning of being born of him remains. Then if it is necessary for you to compare Jesus with Abraham and say Jesus is His son for He said, 'Abraham is My friend,' it is necessary for you to say, 'Moses is His son,' For his miracles were no less than the miracles of Jesus. So you should say 'Moses is His son too.' And it is permitted for you to say, 'He is his shaykh, master, uncle, chief and commander,' in the meaning that I said it to the Jews." Then some of the Christians said, "According to the revealed books Jesus said, 'I go to my father.'" The Apostle of Allah said, "If you do according to that book, you should say, 'All of the people that He addressed were His sons as Jesus was his son.' For according to that book, Jesus said, 'I go to Him who is my father and yours.' Then something that is in that book makes invalid what you think, that only Jesus is His son because he was so distinguished. For you said, 'Jesus is His son because He, the Exalted, distinguished him by that which He did not distinguish the others.' But you know that Jesus was chosen for something that this group was not chosen for, and Jesus said to this group, 'I go to Him who is my father and yours.' So it is wrong that only Jesus is chosen. For this is proven for you [that Jesus is not distinguished as His son] by the saying of Jesus to those who were not so distinguished. You narrated the words of Jesus but you interpreted it wrongly. For when he said, 'my father and yours' he wanted to say something you do not say and impute. What do you know? Perhaps it was in his mind, 'I go to Adam and

فَسَمّاهُ خَلِيلَهُ، أيْ فَقِيرَهُ وَمُحْتَاجَهُ، والمُنْقَطعَ إلَيهِ عَمَّنْ سِواهُ. وإذا جُعِلَ مَعْنَي ذَلكَ مِنَ الخُلَّةِ وَهُوَ أنَّهُ قَدْ تَخَلَّلَ [بِهِ] مَعانِيهِ، وَوَقَفَ عَلَي أسْرارٍ لَمْ يَقِفْ عَلَيْها غَيْرُهُ، كانَ مَعْناهُ، العالِمُ بِهِ وَبِأمُورِهِ. وَلا يُوجِبُ ذَلِكَ تَشْبِيهَ اللهِ بِخَلْقِهِ. ألا تَرَوْنَ أنَّهُ إذا لَمْ يَنْقَطِعْ إلَيْهِ لَمْ يَكُنْ خَلِيلَهُ وإذا لَمْ يَعْلَمْ بِأسْرارِهِ لَمْ يَكُنْ خَلِيلَهُ وأنَّ مَنْ يَلِدُهُ الرجُلُ، وإنْ أهانَهُ وأقصاهُ، لَمْ يَخْرُجْ عَنْ أنْ يَكُونَ وَلَدَهُ، لِأنَّ مَعْنَي الوِلادَةِ قائِمٌ. ثُمَّ إنْ وَجَبَ لِأنَّهُ قالَ اللهُ: 'إبْراهِيمُ خَلِيلِي،' أنْ تَقِيسُوا أنتُم فَتَقُولُوا: 'إنَّ عِيسَي ابنهُ،' وَجَبَ أيْضاً كَذَلِكَ أنْ تَقُولُوا لِمُوسَي: 'إنَّهُ ابنهُ،' فإنَّ الذى مَعَهُ مِنَ المُعْجِزاتِ لَمْ يَكُنْ بِدُونِ ما كانَ مَعَ عِيسَي، فَقُولُوا: 'إنَّ مُوسَي أيْضاً ابنهُ،' وأنَّهُ يَجُوزُ أنْ تَقُولُوا عَلَي هَذا المَعْنَي: 'شَيْخُهُ وَسَيِّدُهُ وَعَمُّهُ وَرَئِيسُهُ وأمِيرُهُ،' كَما قَدْ ذَكَرْتُهُ لِلْيَهُودِ.» فَقالَ بَعْضُهُم: «وَفِي الكُتُبِ المُنْزَلَةِ أنَّ عِيسَي قالَ: 'أذْهَبُ إلَي أبِى.'» فَقالَ رَسُولُ اللهِ (صلى الله عليه وآله وسلم): «فإنْ كُنْتُمْ بِذَلِكَ الكتابِ تَعْمَلُونَ، فإنَّ فِيهِ «أذْهَبُ إلَي أبِى وأبِيكُم» فَقُولُوا: 'إنَّ جَمِيعَ الذينَ خاطَبَهُم كانُوا أبناءَ اللهِ، كَما كانَ عِيسَي ابنهُ مِنَ الوَجْهِ الذى كانَ عِيسَي ابنهُ. ثُمَّ إنَّ ما فِي هَذا الكِتابِ يُبْطِلُ عَلَيْكُم هَذا [المَعْنَي] الذى زَعَمْتُم أنَّ عِيسَي مِنْ جِهَةِ الاخْتِصاصِ كانَ ابناً لَهُ، لِأنَّكُم قُلْتُم: 'إنَّما قُلْنا: 'إنَّهُ ابنهُ.' لِأنَّهُ، تَعالَي، إخْتَصَّهُ بِما لَمْ يَخْتَصَّ بِهِ غَيْرَهُ.' وأنتُم تَعْلَمُونَ أنَّ الذى خُصَّ بِهِ عِيسَي لَمْ يُخَصَّ بِهِ هَؤُلاءِ القَوْمِ الذينَ قالَ لَهُمْ عِيسَي: 'أذْهَبُ إلَي أبِى وأبِيكُم.' فَبَطَلَ أنْ يَكُونَ الاخْتِصاصُ لِعِيسَي. لِأنَّهُ قَدْ ثَبَتَ عِنْدَكُمْ بِقَوْلِ عِيسَي لِمَنْ لَمْ يَكُنْ لَهُ مِثْلُ اخْتِصاصِ عِيسَي. وأنتُم إنَّما حَكَيْتُمْ لَفْظَةَ عِيسَي وَتَأوَّلْتُمُوها عَلَي غَيْرِ وَجْهِها. لِأنَّه إذا قالَ: 'أبِى وابِيكُم.' فَقَدْ أرادَ غَيْرَ ما ذَهَبْتُمْ إلَيهِ وَنَحَلْتُمُوهُ. وَما يُدْرِيكُمْ لَعَلَّهُ عَنَي: 'أذْهَبُ إلَي آدَمَ وإلَي نُوحٍ،' إنَّ اللهَ يَرْفَعُنِى

Noah. Allah raises me to them and gathers me with them. Adam is my father and your father, and Noah is likewise.' But he did not mean anything but this meaning." The Christians became silent; then they said, "We did not see a disputant or an opponent like what we saw today, and we will think about our affairs...."

(*Tafsīr al-Imām al-'Askarī*, 530-535, 323)

1.5.6. Imam al-'Askarī reported that about the verse, "*It is not righteousness that you turn your faces toward the East and the West, but righteousness is this, that one should believe in Allah, the Last Day, the angels, the Book and the prophets, give away wealth out of love for him to the near of kin, the orphans, the needy, the wayfarer, beggars and for the emancipation of captives, keep up the prayers and pay the poor-rate...*" (2:177) 'Ali Ibn al-Ḥusayn said, "The Apostle of Allah favored 'Alī and informed [his people] about his majesty before his Lord, the Mighty and Magnificent, and revealed the favor for his followers and the helpers of his calling and rebuked the Jews and Christians for their disblief and their concealing the mention of Muḥammad, 'Alī and their descendents, peace be with them, about their being favored and good deeds. Then the Jews and Christians became proud [thinking themselves better]. The Jews said, "We prayed to this our *qiblah* many prayers. There are some people among us who stay awake nights with praying to this *qiblah* which is the *qiblah* of Moses; and Allah commanded us about it." The Christians said, "We prayed to this our *qiblah* many prayers. There are some people among us who stay awake nights with praying to this *qiblah* which is the *qiblah* of Jesus; and Allah commanded us about it." Each of these two sects said, "Do you think that our Lord makes invalid our numerous works and our prayers to our *qiblah*, because we do not follow the desire of Muḥammad for himself and his brother?" Then Allah the Exalted, sent, "O Muḥammad! Say, 'Righteousness is not the obedience by which you reach heaven and merit forgiveness and sanctity. In your prayers you turn your faces to the East, O Christians! And to the West, O Jews! But you oppose the command of Allah and you are angry with the friend (*walī*) of Allah. But righteous is he who believes in Allah, in His being one, alone and unique, impermeable (*ṣamad*); Who makes whom He wants

إلَيْهِمْ وَيَجْمَعُنِى مَعَهُمْ، وآدَمُ أبِى وأبُوكُمْ. وَكَذَلِكَ نُوحٌ، بَلْ ما أرادَ غَيْرَ هَذا.» قالَ: «فَسَكَتَتْ النَصارَي، وَقالُوا: 'ما رأيْنا كاليَوْمِ مُجادِلاً وَلا مُخاصِماً وَسَنَنْظُرُ فِى أمُورِنا... .'»

(تفسير الإمام العسكرىّ، ٥٣٠- ٥٣٥، ٣٢٣)

١-٥-٦- قالَ الإمامُ [العَسْكَرِىّ] عليه السلام: «قالَ عَلِىُّ بْنُ الحُسَيْنِ عليه السلام: ﴿لَيْسَ البِرَّ أنْ تُوَلُّوا﴾ الآيَة. قالَ: 'إنَّ رَسُولَ اللهِ صلى الله عليه وآله وسلم لَمّا فَضَّلَ عَلِيّاً عليه السلام واخْبَرَ عَنْ جَلالَتِهِ عِنْدَ رَبِّهِ، عَزَّ وَجَلَّ، أبانَ عَنْ فَضائِلِ شِيعَتِهِ وأنْصارِ دَعْوَتِهِ، وَوَبَّخَ اليَهُودَ والنَصارَي عَلَي كُفْرِهِمْ، وَكِتْمانِهِمْ لِذِكْرِ مُحَمَّدٍ وَعَلِيٍّ وآلِهِما عليهم السلام فِى كُتُبِهِمْ بِفَضائِلِهِمْ وَمَحاسِنِهِمْ، فَخَرَّتِ اليَهُودُ والنَصارَي عَلَيْهِمْ. فقالَتْ اليَهُودُ: 'قَدْ صَلَّيْنا إلَي قِبْلَتِنا هَذِهِ، الصَلاةَ الكَثِيرَةَ، وَفِينا مَنْ يُحيى اللَيْلَ صَلاةً إلَيْها، وَهِىَ قِبْلَةُ مُوسَي الَّتِى أمَرَنا بِها.' وَقالَتْ النَصارَي: ' قَدْ صَلَّيْنا إلَي قِبْلَتِنا هَذِهِ، الصَلاةَ الكَثِيرَةَ، وَفِينا مَنْ يُحيى اللَيْلَ صَلاةً إلَيْها، وَهِىَ قِبْلَةُ عِيسَي الَّتِى أمَرْنا بِها.' وَقالَ كُلُّ واحِدٍ مِنَ الفَرِيقَيْنِ: 'أتَرَي رَبَّنا يُبْطِلُ أعْمالَنا هَذِهِ الكَثِيرَةَ، وَصَلَواتَنا إلَي قِبْلَتِنا, لأنّا لا نَتَّبِعُ مُحَمَّداً عَلَي هَواهُ فِى نَفْسِهِ وأخِيهِ؟' فأنْزَلَ اللهُ، تَعالَي: 'قُلْ يا مُحَمَّدُ صلى الله عليه وآله وسلم: ﴿لَيْسَ البِرَّ﴾ الطاعَةَ الَّتِى تَنالُونَ بِها الجِنانَ وَتَسْتَحِقُّونَ بِها الغُفْرانَ والرِضْوانَ، ﴿أنْ تُوَلُّوا وُجُوهَكُمْ﴾ بِصَلاتِكُمْ ﴿قِبَلَ المَشْرِقِ﴾ أيُّها النَصارَي، وَ﴿قِبَلَ المَغْرِبِ﴾ أيُّها اليَهُودُ، وأنتُم لأمْرِ اللهِ مُخالِفُونَ وَعَلَي وَلِىِّ اللهِ مُغْتاظُونَ. ﴿وَلَكِنَّ البِرَّ مَنْ آمَنَ بِاللهِ﴾ بِأنَّهُ الواحِدُ الأحَدُ، الفَرْدُ الصَمَدُ، يُعَظِّمُ مَنْ يَشاءُ وَيُكْرِمُ مَنْ يَشاءُ،

great, makes honor for whom He wants, makes despicable and humble whom He wants—no one can refute His order and none can reprove His judgement. Also righteous is he who believes in the Last Day, the Resurrection Day."

(*Tafsīr al-Imām al- 'Askarī*, 589)

1.5.7. It is reported that Abū 'Abd Allah said, "Verily, Allah, the blessed and exalted, gave to Muḥammad the laws of Noah, Abraham, Moses and Jesus: *tawḥīd* (divine unity), *ikhlāṣ* (purity), the dismissal of peers [for Allah], the liberal uprightness of human nature, there is no monasticism and no mendicancy, what is pure is made lawful and what is filthy is prohibited, and He removes from them their burdens and the shackles that were upon them.(1) So, He made known his excellence with this. Then He made obligatory for him the prayer, alms, fasting, the pilgrimage, enjoining the good, prohibiting evil, the allowable (*ḥalāl*) and the forbidden (*ḥarām*), the laws of inheritance, the penal laws, the obligations, jihad in the way of Allah, and He added the minor ablution, He made him excellent by the opening of the Book,(2) the closing part of *sūrah Baqarah*, and the detailed *suwar*,(3) He made lawful for him the spoils of war and booty, He aided him with fear [in the hearts of his enemies], He made the earth for prostration and made it purifying, He sent him universally, to the white and the black, the jinn and the humans, and He gave him the *jizyah* (poll tax for non-Muslims), and taking the pagans as captives and releasing them. Then He made it his duty what was not the duty of any of the other prophets, He sent him a sword from heaven without a scabbord, and it was said to him, ﴾*Fight in the way of Allah, and you are not obliged for anyone but yourself.*﴿." (4:84)

(*Biḥār,* 16, 330, 26)

---

(1) See (7:157).

(2) That is, the opening sūrah of the Qur'ān.

(3) The detailed suras, *mufaṣṣal*, are considered by some to be those from *surah Muḥammad* to the end, but there are other opinions among scholars as to which suras are to be included under this heading.

وَيُهينُ مَنْ يَشاءُ وَيُذِلُّهُ، لا رادَّ لِأَمْرِهِ، وَلا مُعَقِّبَ لِحُكْمِهِ, وآمَنَ بِالْيَوْمِ الآخِرِ يَوْمِ القِيامَةِ.'»

(تفسير الإمام العسكريّ، ٥٨٩)

١-٥-٧- أبُو إسْحاقِ الثَّقَفِيّ, عَنْ مُحَمَّدِ بْنِ مَرْوانَ, عَنْ أبانِ بْنِ عُثْمانَ عَمَّنْ ذَكَرَهُ, عَنْ أبِي عَبْدِ اللهِ عليه السلام, قالَ: «إنَّ اللهَ, تَبارَكَ وَتَعالَي, أعْطَي مُحَمَّداً شَرائِعَ نُوحٍ وإبْراهِيمَ وَمُوسَي وَعِيسَي عليه السلام، التَوحِيدَ والإخْلاصَ وَخَلْعَ الأنْدادِ والفِطْرَةَ الحَنِيفِيَّةَ السَمْحَةَ. لا رَهْبانِيَّةَ وَلا سِياحَةَ. أحَلَّ فِيها الطَّيِّباتِ, وَحَرَّمَ فِيها الخَبِيثاتِ, وَوَضَعَ عَنْهُمْ إصْرَهُمْ والأغْلالَ الَّتِي كانَتْ عَلَيْهِم. فَعُرِفَ فَضْلُهُ بذَلِكَ. ثُمَّ افْتَرَضَ عَلَيْهِ فِيها الصَلاةَ والزَّكاةَ والصيامَ والحَجَّ والأمْرَ بِالمَعْرُوفِ والنَهْيَ عَنِ المُنْكَرِ, والحَلالَ والحَرامَ, والمَوارِيثَ والحُدُودَ والفَرائِضَ والجِهادَ فِي سَبِيلِ اللهِ, وَزادَهُ الوُضُوءَ, وَفَضَّلَهُ بِفاتِحَةِ الكِتابِ وَبِخَواتِيمِ سُورَةِ البَقَرَةِ والمُفَصَّلِ, وأحَلَّ لَهُ المَغْنَمَ والفَيْءَ, وَنَصَرَهُ بِالرعْبِ, وَجَعَلَ لَهُ الأرضَ مَسْجِداً وَطَهُوراً, وأرْسَلَهُ كافَّةً إلَي الأبْيَضِ والأسوَدِ والجِنِّ والإنْسِ, وأعْطاهُ الجِزْيَةَ وأسْرَ المُشْرِكِينَ وَفِداهُمْ. ثُمَّ كُلِّفَ ما لَمْ يُكَلَّفْ أحَدٌ مِنَ الأنبياءِ، أنْزَلَ عَلَيْهِ سَيْفاً مِنَ السَماءِ فِي غَيْرِ غِمْدٍ، وَقِيلَ لَهُ: ﴿فَقاتِلْ فِي سَبِيلِ اللهِ لا تُكَلَّفُ إلّا نَفْسَكَ.﴾»

(بحار الأنوار، ١٦، ٣٣٠، ٢٦)

1.5.8. It is reported that Sama'ah ibn Mahran said that he asked Abū 'Abd Allah about the saying of Allah, the mighty and magnificent, 'So, bear with patience as did those who had resolution (*Ulu al-'azm*)' (46:35). He said, "Noah, Abraham, Moses, Jesus and Muḥammad." I said, "How did they become those who had resolution?" He said, "Because Noah was raised as a prophet with a book and a divine law, and all who came after Noah held to his book, law and his way until Abraham came with a scripture and resolution, and he was obliged to leave the book of Noah without disbelieving in it.

Then each of the prophets who came after Abraham held to the law of Abraham and his way and his scripture, until Moses came with the Torah and his law and way and resolution and he was obliged to leave the [previous] scripture. Then each of the prophets who came after Moses held to the Torah and his law and way, until the Messiah came with the Gospel and resolution, and he had to leave the law of Moses and his way. Then each of the prophets who came after the Messiah held to his law and way, until Muhammad came and brought the Qur'ān and his law and way, and his permissions (*ḥalāl*) are permitted until the Resurrection Day and his prohibitions (*ḥarām*) are prohibited until the Resurrection Day. So, it is they who are those who had resolution."

(*Kāfī,* 2, 17, 2)

1.5.9. It is reported that Abū 'Abd Allah said that when Christians of Najrān came to the Apostle of Allah, they arrived at the time of their prayer, so they started to sing with a bell and prayed. Their chiefs were al-Ahtam, al-'Aqib and al-Sayyid. The companions of the Apostle of Allah said, "O Apostle of Allah! This? In your mosque!?"

١-٥-٨- عِدَّةٌ مِنْ أصْحابِنا، عَنْ أحْمَدَ بْنِ مُحَمَّدِ بْنِ خالِدٍ، عَنْ عُثْمانَ بْنِ عِيسَي، عَنْ سَماعَةَ بْنِ مِهْرانَ، قالَ: «قُلْتُ لِأبِي عَبْدِ اللهِ عليه السلام قَوْلَ اللهِ، عَزَّ وَجَلَّ: ﴿فاصْبِرْ كَما صَبَرَ أولُوا العَزْمِ مِنَ الرسُلِ﴾ فقالَ: 'نوحٌ وابْراهِيمُ وَمُوسَي وَعِيسَي وَمُحَمَّدٌ صلى الله عليه وآله وسلم.' قُلْتُ: 'كَيْفَ صارُوا أولِي العَزْمِ؟' قالَ: 'لِأنَّ نُوحاً بُعِثَ بِكِتابٍ وَشَرِيعَةٍ، وَكُلُّ مَنْ جاءَ بَعْدَ نُوحٍ أخَذَ بِكِتابِ نُوحٍ وَشَرِيعَتِهِ وَمِنْهاجِهِ حَتَّي جاءَ إبْراهِيمُ عليه السلام بالصحُفِ وَبِعَزِيمَةِ تَرْكِ كِتابِ نُوحٍ لا كُفْراً بِهِ.

فكُلُّ نَبِيٍّ جاءَ بَعْدَ إبْراهِيمَ عليه السلام أخَذَ بِشَرِيعَةِ إبْراهِيمَ وَمِنْهاجِهِ وَبالصحُفِ، حَتَّي جاءَ مُوسَي بالتوْراةِ وَشَرِيعَتِهِ وَمِنْهاجِهِ وَبِعَزِيمَةِ تَرْكِ الصحُفِ. وَكُلُّ نَبِيٍّ جاءَ بَعْدَ مُوسَي عليه السلام أخَذَ بالتوْراةِ وَشَرِيعَتِهِ وَمِنْهاجِهِ، حَتَّي جاءَ المَسِيحُ عليه السلام بالإنجيلِ وَبِعَزِيمَةِ تَرْكِ شَرِيعَةِ مُوسَي وَمِنْهاجِهِ. فكُلُّ نَبِيٍّ جاءَ بَعْدَ المَسِيحِ أخَذَ بِشَرِيعَتِهِ وَمِنْهاجِهِ، حَتَّى جاءَ مُحَمَّدٌ صلى الله عليه وآله وسلم فَجاءَ بالقرآنِ وَبِشَرِيعَتِهِ وَمِنْهاجِهِ. فَحَلالُهُ حَلالٌ إلَي يَوْمِ القِيامَةِ وَحَرامُهُ حَرامٌ إلَي يَوْمِ القِيامَةِ. فَهؤُلاءِ أولُو العَزْمِ مِنَ الرسُلِ عليهم السلام.'»

(الكافى، ٢، ١٧، ٢)

١-٥-٩- أبِي عَنِ النَضْرِ, عَنِ ابن سَنانَ, عَنْ أبِي عَبْدِ اللهِ عليه السلام: «إنَّ نَصارَي نَجْرانَ لَمّا وَفَدُوا عَلَي رَسُولِ اللهِ, وَكانَ سَيِّدُهُمْ الأهْتَمَ والعاقِبَ والسَيِّدَ وَحَضَرَتْ صَلَواتُهم, فأقبَلوا يَضْرِبُونَ بِالناقُوسِ وَصَلُّوا. فَقالَ أصْحابُ رَسُولِ اللهِ: 'يا رَسُولَ اللهِ, هَذا فِي مَسْجِدِكَ!'

He said, "Leave them alone." When they finished they approached the Apostle of Allah and said, "To what do you invite us?" He said, "To bear witness that there is no god except Allah and that I am the Apostle of Allah and that Jesus is a created servant. He eats, drinks and deficates." They said, "So who is his father?" Then a revelation descended to the Apostle of Allah, and it said, "Ask them what they say about Adam. Was he a created servant who ate, drank, spoke and married." Then the Prophet asked them this. They answered, "Yes." He asked, "Then who is his father?" They were silent. Then Allah sent down, ﴾*Truly the likeness of Jesus in the sight of Allah is as Adam's likeness; He created him of dust, then He said to him, 'Be,' and he was. The Truth is from Your Lord, so do not be of the doubters. And whoever disputes with you after the knowledge that has come to you, say: 'Come now. Let us call our sons and your sons, our wives and your wives, our selves and your selves; then let us humbly pray and place the curse of Allah upon the liers.*﴿ (3:59-61) Then the Prophet said, "So let us curse one another. If I am truthful the curse will be sent down upon you and if I am lying the curse will be sent down upon me." They said, "You are fair."

Then they agreed upon the mutual cursing. When they returned to their homes, their chiefs, al-Sayyid, al-'Aqib and al-Ahtam, said, "If he would curse us with his people, then we will curse him, for he is not a prophet; but if he would curse us specifically with his household, then we will not curse him, for surely he would not stand up against his household unless he were sincere." When morning came, they came to the Apostle of Allah, and with him was the Commander of the Faithful, Fāṭimah, Ḥasan and Ḥusayn, peace be with them. The Christians said, "Who are they?" It was said to them, "That is his uncle's son, and his trustee, his son-in-law, 'Alī ibn Abī Ṭālib, and that is his daughter, Fāṭimah, and those are his grandsons, Ḥasan and Ḥusayn." Then they parted, and they said to the Apostle of Allah ﷺ "We are satisfied with you, so pardon us from the mutual cursing." Then the Apostle of Allah compromised with them for the *jizyah* and they left.

(*Biḥār*, 21, 340, 5)

فقالَ: 'دَعُوهُم.' فلمّا فرَغُوا دنَوا مِنْ رَسُولِ اللهِ فقالُوا: 'إلي ما تَدْعُو؟' فقالَ: 'إلي شَهادَةِ أنْ لا إلهَ إلّا اللهُ، وأنّي رَسُولُ اللهِ صلى الله عليه وآله وسلم، وأنَّ عِيسَي عَبْدٌ مَخْلُوقٌ يأكُلُ وَيَشْرَبُ وَيُحْدِثُ.' قالُوا: 'فَمَنْ أبُوهُ؟' فنُزِّلَ الوَحْيُ عَلي رَسُولِ اللهِ صلى الله عليه وآله وسلم. فقالَ: 'قُلْ لَهُمْ: ما يَقُولُونَ فِي آدَمَ؟ أكانَ عَبْداً مَخْلُوقاً يأكُلُ وَيَشْرِبُ وَيُحْدِثُ وينْكَحُ؟'' فسألَهُمُ النَبِيُّ صلى الله عليه وآله وسلم. فقالُوا: 'نَعَم.' فقالَ: 'فَمَنْ أبُوهُ؟' فبَقَوْا ساكِتِينَ. فأنْزَلَ اللهُ: ﴿إنَّ مَثَلَ عِيسَي عِنْدَ اللهِ كَمَثَلِ آدَمَ...﴾ الآية إلي قَوْلِهِ ﴿فَنَجْعَلْ لَعْنَتَ اللهِ عَلي الكاذِبِينَ.﴾ فقالَ رَسُولُ اللهِ صلى الله عليه وآله وسلم: 'فَباهِلُونِي. إنْ كُنْتُ صادِقا أنْزِلَتْ اللعْنَةُ عَلَيْكُمْ، وإنْ كُنْتُ كاذِباً أنْزِلَتْ عَلَيَّ.' فقالُوا: 'أنْصَفْتَ.'

فَتَواعَدُوا لِلْمُباهَلَةِ فلَمّا رَجَعُوا إلي مَنازِلِهِمْ قالَ رُؤَساؤُهُمْ, السَيِّدُ والعاقِبُ والأهْتَمُ: 'إنْ باهَلَنا بِقومِهِ، باهَلْناهُ فانَّهُ لَيْسَ بِنَبِيٍّ وإنْ باهَلَنا بِأهْلِ بَيْتِهِ خاصَّةً، فَلا نُباهِلُهُ. فإنَّهُ لا يَقْدِمُ عَلي أهْلِ بَيْتِهِ إلّا وَهُوَ صادِقٌ.' فَلَمّا أصْبَحُوا جاؤوا إلي رَسُولِ اللهِ صلى الله عليه وآله وسلم، وَمَعَهُ أمِيرُ المُؤْمِنِينَ وَفاطِمَةُ والحَسَنُ والحُسَيْنُ عليهم السلام. فَقالَ النَصارَي: 'مَنْ هؤُلاءِ؟' فَقِيلَ لَهُمْ: 'هذا اِبْنُ عَمِّهِ وَوَصِيُّهُ وَخَتَنُهُ عَلِيُّ بْنُ أبِي طالِبٍ، وَهَذِهِ ابنتُهُ فاطِمَةُ، وَهذانِ أبناهُ الحَسَنُ والحُسَيْنُ.' فَفَرَّقُوا وَقالُوا لِرَسُولِ اللهِ صلى الله عليه وآله وسلم: 'نُعْطِيكَ الرضا، فاعْفُنا عَنِ المُباهَلَةِ.' فَصالَحَهُم رَسُولُ اللهِ صلى الله عليه وآله وسلم عَلَي الجِزْيَةِ, وانْصَرَفُوا.»

(بحار الأنوار، ٢١، ٣٤٠، ٥)

1.5.10. It is reported that when a delegation from Najrān came, the Prophet ﷺ invited their chiefs, al-'Āqib and al-Ṭayyib, to Islām. They said, "We became Muslims before you." He said, "You lie. Love of the cross and drinking wine prevent you from it." Then he called them to curse one another. They promised him that they would come tomorrow morning. The Prophet ﷺ came the next morning while he took the hand of 'Alī, al-Ḥasan, al-Ḥusayn and Fāṭima. They said, "He came with his immediate family. They trust in their religion." So they refrained from cursing each other. The Prophet ﷺ said, "If they had done it, fire would have been showered on them in the desert."

(*Biḥār*, 21, 341, 6)

1.5.11. It is reported that Abū 'Abd Allah ﷺ said, "Between David and Jesus the son of Mary there were four hundred years. The religion of Jesus was *tawḥīd* (divine unity), *ikhlāṣ* (purity) and what Noah, Abraham and Moses, peace be with them, had bidden. The *Injīl* (gospel) was sent down to him. The pledge that was taken from the other prophets was also taken from Jesus, and it was made law for him in the book to establish prayer with religion, enjoining the good and prohibiting evil, forbidding what was forbidden, and allowing what was allowed. Admonitions and parables were sent down to him in the *Injīl,* but there was no law of retribution in it nor precepts of retribution (*aḥkām al-ḥudūd*), and no obligations for inheritance. What was sent down to him was an alleviation of what was sent down to Moses in the Torah. This is in the saying of Allah in which Jesus the son of Mary said to the Children of Israel, ﴾*and to make lawful to you certain things that before were forbidden to you*﴿ (3:50). Jesus commanded those with him who were believers and followed him that they believe in the law of the Torah and *Injīl.*"

(*Biḥār*, 14, 234, 4)

١-٥-١٠- رُوِىَ أَنَّهُ لَمّا قَدِمَ وَفْدُ نَجْرانَ، دَعا النَبِىُّ صلى الله عليه وآله وسلم العاقِبَ والطيِّبَ, رئِيسَيْهِمْ, إلَي الإسْلامِ. فقالا: «أسلَمْنا قبْلَكَ.» فقالَ: «كَذِبْتُما. يَمْنَعُكُما مِنْ ذلِكَ حُبُّ الصلِيبِ وَشُرْبُ الخمْرِ.» فدَعاهُما إلَي المُلاعَنَةِ. فواعَداهُ عَلَي أنْ يُغادِياهُ. فغَدا رَسُولُ اللهِ صلى الله عليه وآله وسلم، وَلَقَدْ أخذَ بِيَدِ عَلِيٍّ والحَسَنِ والحُسَيْنِ وَفاطِمَةَ. فقالا: «أتَي بِخَواصِّهِ، واثِقاً بِدِيانَتِهِمْ.» فأبَوْا المُلاعَنَةَ. فقالَ(ص): «لَوْ فعَلا، لأمْطَرَ الوادِى عَلَيْهِمْ ناراً.»

(بحار الأنوار، ٢١، ٣٤١، ٦)

١-٥-١١- عَنْ مُحَمَّدٍ الحَلَبِيِّ, عَنْ أبِى عَبْدِ اللهِ عليه السلام, قالَ: «كانَ بَيْنَ داوُدَ وَعِيسَي بْنِ مَرْيَمَ عليه السلام أرْبَعُ مِائة سَنَةٍ، وكانَ شَرِيعَةُ عِيسَي أنَّهُ بُعِثَ بِالتوْحِيدِ والإخْلاصِ وَبِما أوْصَي بِهِ نُوحٌ وإبْراهِيمُ وَمُوسَي عليه السلام, وأنْزلَ عَلَيْهِ الإنجيلُ, وأخِذ عَلَيْهِ المِيثاقُ الذى أُخِذ عَلَي النَبِيِّينَ, وَشُرِّعَ لَهُ فِى الكِتابِ إقامُ الصَلاةِ مَعَ الدينِ والأمْرُ بِالمَعْرُوفِ والنَهْىُ عَنِ المُنْكَرِ, وَتَحْرِيمُ الحَرامِ وَتَحْلِيلُ الحَلالِ, وأنْزلَ عَلَيْهِ فِى الإنجيلِ مَواعِظُ وأمْثالٌ. وَلَيْسَ فِيها قِصاصٌ وَلا أحْكامُ حُدُودٍ وَلا فرْضُ مَوارِيثَ, وأنْزلَ عَلَيْهِ تَخْفِيفُ ما كانَ نُزِّلَ عَلَي مُوسَي عليه السلام فِى التَوْراةِ, وَهُوَ قوْلُ اللهِ فِى الذى قالَ عِيسَي بْنُ مَرْيَمَ لِبَنِى إسْرائِيلَ: ﴿وَلِأُحِلَّ لَكُمْ بَعْضَ الذى حُرِّمَ عَلَيْكُمْ.﴾ وأمَرَ عِيسَي مَنْ مَعَهُ مِمَّنِ اتَّبَعَهُ مِنَ المُؤْمِنِينَ أنْ يُؤْمِنُوا بِشَرِيعَةِ التَوْراةِ والإنجيلِ.» .

(بحار الأنوار، ١٤، ٢٣٤، ٤)

1.5.12. It is reported that Abū Ja'far said, "...then Allah commissioned Jesus to witness that there is no god but Allah and to recite what was brought to him from Allah, and He made for him a law and a method. Then the Saturday, which they previously had been commanded to strictly observe, was abrogated, and generally the path and customs that had been practiced that were brought by Moses. Then, one who does not follow the path of Jesus, Allah will cast him into the fire, although what all the prophets brought is not to associate anything with Allah."

(*Kāfī,* 2, 29)

1.5.13. Ibn 'Abbās said, "A group of the scholars of Jews came to 'Umar when he was Caliph of the Muslims... Then 'Alī said to [the chief of them], 'Ask.' He said, 'Inform me about a group from early times who died and after three hundred-nine years Allah revived them. What was their story?' 'Alī started and wanted to read *Sūra al-Kahf.* The scholar said, 'How much we have heared of your Qur'ān! If you know them, inform us about their story, names, number, the name of their dog, cave, king and the name of their city.'

'Alī said, 'There is no power and no strength save in Allah, the High, the Great. O Jewish brother! Muḥammad reported to me that there was a city, named Aqsūs, on the territory of Rūm and it had a pure king. Their king died. So they differed in their words [among each other]. A king, from the kings of Persia, named Daqyānūs, heard of their differences and turned with one hundred thausand persons and entered the city of Aqsūs. Then he took it as a part of the realm of his country and made a palace in it, one parasang by one parasang. In the palace there was a hall that was a thousand cubits in length by a thousand in width in polished marble.

١-٥-١٢- رُوِىَ عَنْ أبى جَعْفَرٍ عليه السلام أنّه قالَ: «... ثُمَّ بَعَثَ الله عِيسَيَ عليه السلام بِشَهادَةِ أنْ لا إلَهَ إلّا اللهُ والإقرارِ بِما جاءَ بِهِ مِنْ عِنْدِ الله، وَجَعَلَ لَهُمْ شِرْعَةً وَمِنْهاجاً. فَهَدَمَتِ السَبْتَ الذى أُمِرُوا بِهِ أن يُعَظِّمُوهُ قَبْلَ ذَلِكَ، وَعامَّةَ ما كانُوا عَلَيْهِ مِنَ السَبِيلِ، والسُنَّةِ الّتِى جاءَ بِها مُوسَي. فَمَنْ لَمْ يَتَّبِعْ سَبِيلَ عِيسَي أدْخَلَهُ اللهُ النارَ، وإنْ كانَ الذى جاءَ بِهِ النَبِيونَ جَمِيعاً أنْ لا يُشْرِكُوا بِاللهِ شَيْئاً.»

(الكافى، ٢، ٢٩)

١-٥-١٣- ابن بابَوَيْهِ, ... عَنِ ابن عَبّاسٍ, قالَ: «لَمّا كانَ فِى عَهْدِ خِلافَةِ عُمَرَ، أتاهُ قَوْمٌ مِنْ أحْبارِ اليَهُودِ... فَقالَ عَلِىٌّ عليه السلام: 'سَلْ.' قالَ: 'أخْبِرْنِى, عَنْ قَوْمٍ كانُوا فِى أوّلِ الزَّمانِ، فَماتُوا ثَلاثَ مِائَة وَتِسْعَ سِنِينَ، ثُمَّ أحْياهُمُ الله. ما كانَ قِصَّتُهُمْ؟' فابْتَدا عَلِىٌّ عليه السلام وأرادَ أنْ يَقْرا سُورَةَ الكَهْفِ. فَقالَ الحِبْرُ: 'ما أكْثَرَ ما سَمِعْنا قُرْآنَكُم! فإنْ كُنْتَ عالِماً بِهِمْ أخْبِرْنا بِقِصَّةِ هَؤُلاءِ وَبِأسْمائِهِمْ وَعَدَدِهِمْ واسْمِ كَلْبِهِمْ واسْمِ كَهْفِهِمْ واسْمِ مَلِكِهِمْ واسْمِ مَدِينَتِهِمْ.'

فَقالَ عَلِىٌّ عليه السلام: 'لا حَوْلَ وَلا قُوَّةَ إلّا بِاللهِ العَلِىِّ العَظِيمِ. يا أخا اليَهُودِ، حَدَّثَنِى مُحَمَّدٌ صلى الله عليه وآله وسلم أنَّهُ كانَ بِأرْضِ الرومِ مَدِينَةٌ، يُقالُ لَها أقسُوسُ، وَكانَ لَها مَلِكٌ صالِحٌ، فَماتَ مَلِكُهُمْ فاخْتَلَفَتْ كَلِمَتُهُمْ. فَسَمِعَ بِهِمْ مَلِكٌ مِنْ مُلُوكِ فارِسَ، يُقالُ لَهُ دَقيانُوسُ، فأقبَلَ فِى مِائَة الفٍ حَتَّي دَخَلَ مَدِينَةَ أقسُوسَ. فاتَّخَذَها دارَ مَمْلَكَتِهِ, واتَّخَذَ فِيها قَصْراً طُولُهُ فَرْسَخٌ فِى عَرْضِ فَرْسَخٍ, واتَّخَذَ فِى ذَلِكَ القَصْرِ مَجْلِساً طُولُهُ الفُ ذِراعٍ فِى عَرْضِ مِثْلِ ذَلِكَ، مِنَ الرخامِ المُمَرَّدِ.

In that hall there were four thousand golden columns, one thousand golden chandeliers, for each of which was a chain of silver, and lit with scented oil. There were eighty windows in the Eastern wall, and in the Western wall it was the same. When the sun rose, in lit the hall, and there was sunlight in the hall wherever the sun went. In the hall was a golden throne that was forty by eighty cubits whose legs were silver studded with jewels, and on it were small cushions.

On the right of the throne there were eighty chairs of gold decorated with green chrysolite. There the Baṭāriqah sat. At the left there were eighty silver chairs decorated with red rubies, on which sat the Harāqilah. Then the king ascended the throne and placed the throne on his head.' The Jew started and said, 'What was his crown made of?' Imam 'Alī said, 'Golden mesh with seven pillars on each of which was a white pearl that shone like a light shining in a dark night. There were fifty youths of the Harāqilah with shirts of red brocade and skirts of green brocade. They wore crowns, bangles and anklets. They had golden scepters and stood at the head of the king. He took six young man as ministers and stood three of them at his right and three of them at his left.' The Jew said, 'What were their names?'

'Alī said, 'The names of those who were at his right were Tamlīkhā, Maksalmīnā and Mīshilīnā, and the names of those who were at his left were Mirnūs, Dīrnūs and Shādhariūs. He consulted them about all his affairs. Every day he held court in the yard of his house with the Baṭāriqah at his right and the Harāqilah at his left. Three boys were at the hand of one of them serving a golden goblet with powdered musk, and at the hand of another was a silver goblet full of rose water.

واتَّخَذَ فِي ذَلِكَ المَجْلِسِ أرْبَعَةَ آلافِ أسْطُوانَةٍ مِنْ ذَهَبٍ، واتَّخَذَ الفَ قَنْدِيلٍ مِنْ ذَهَبٍ لَها سَلاسِلَ مِنَ اللجَيْنِ تُسْرَجُ بِأطْيَبِ الأدْهانِ. واتَّخَذَ فِي شَرْقِيِّ المَجْلِسِ ثَمانِينَ كُوَّةً ولِغَرْبِيِّهِ كَذَلِكَ. وكانَتْ الشَمْسُ إذا طَلَعَتْ طَلَعَتْ فِي المَجْلِسِ كَيْفَما دارَتْ. واتَّخَذَ فِيهِ سَرِيراً مِنْ ذَهَبٍ, طُولُهُ ثَمانُونَ ذِراعاً فِي عَرْضِ أرْبَعِينَ ذِراعاً, لَهُ قَوائِمُ مِنْ فِضَّةٍ مُرَصَّعَةٍ بِالجَواهِرِ وَعَلاهُ بِالنَمارِقِ.

واتَّخَذَ مِنْ يَمِينِ السَرِيرِ ثَمانِينَ كُرْسِيّاً مِنَ الذَّهَبِ مُرَصَّعَةً بِالزَّبَرْجَدِ الأخْضَرِ, فأجْلَسَ عَلَيْها بَطارِقَتَهُ، واتَّخَذَ مِنْ يَسارِ السَرِيرِ ثَمانِينَ كُرْسِيّاً مِنَ الفِضَّةِ مُرَصَّعَةً بِالياقُوتِ الأحْمَرِ, فأجْلَسَ عَلَيْها هِراقِلَتَهُ. ثُمَّ عَلا السَرِيرَ فَوَضَعَ التَاجَ عَلي راسِهِ.' فَوَثَبَ اليَهُودِيُّ فَقالَ: 'مِمَّ كانَ تاجُهُ؟' قالَ: 'مِنَ الذَّهَبِ المُشَبَّكِ، لَهُ سَبْعَةُ أركانٍ عَلَي كُلِّ رُكْنٍ لُؤْلُؤَةٌ بَيْضاءُ تُضِيءُ كَضَوْءِ المِصْباحِ فِي اللَيْلَةِ الظَلْماءِ.

واتَّخَذَ خَمْسِينَ غُلاماً مِنْ أوْلادِ الهَراقِلَةِ فَقَرْطَقَهُمْ بِقَراطِقِ الدِيْباجِ الأحْمَرِ وَسَرْوَلَهُمْ بِسَراوِيلاتِ الحَرِيرِ الأخْضَرِ وَتَوَّجَهُمْ ودَمْلَجَهُمْ وَخَلْخَلَهُمْ، وأعْطاهُمْ أعْمِدَةً مِنَ الذَّهَبِ وَوَقَّفَهُمْ عَلَي راسِهِ. واتَّخَذَ سِتَّةَ غِلْمَةٍ وُزَراءَهُ، فأقامَ ثَلاثَةً عَنْ يَمِينِهِ وثَلاثَةً عَنْ يَسارِهِ.' فَقالَ اليَهُودِيُّ: 'ما كانَ أسْماءُ الثَلاثَةِ والثَلاثَةِ؟'

فَقالَ عَلِيٌّ (عليه السلام): 'الَّذِينَ عَنْ يَمِينِهِ أسْماؤُهُمْ: تَمْلِيخا وَمَكْسَلْمِينا وَمِيشِيلِينا، وأمّا الذينَ عَنْ يَسارِهِ فأسْماؤُهُمْ مِرْنُوسْ وَدِيْرْنُوسْ وَشاذَرِيُوسْ، وكانَ يَسْتَشِيرُهُمْ فِي جَمِيعِ أمُورِهِ. وكانَ يَجْلِسُ فِي كُلِّ يَوْمٍ فِي صَحْنِ دارِهِ والبَطارِقَةُ عَنْ يَمِينِه والهَراقِلَةُ عَنْ يَسارِهِ. وَيَدْخُلُ ثَلاثَةُ غِلْمَةٍ فِي يَدِ أحَدِهِمْ جامٌ مِنْ ذَهَبٍ مَمْلُوءٌ مِنَ المِسْكِ المَسْحُوقِ, وَفِي يَدِ الآخَرِ جامٌ مِنْ فِضَّةٍ مَمْلُوءٌ مِنْ ماءِ الوَرْدِ.

On the hand of another was a white bird with a red beak. Whenever the king looked at the bird, he would call it, and it would fly until it fell into the goblet of rose water, in which it drenched itself. Then it would fall into the goblet of musk, which would stick to its feathers and wings. Then the king would call it again, and it would fly onto the crown of the king, and what was on its feathers and wings would fall onto the head of the king. When the king saw this, he would exult and pride himself. Then he would claim Lordship for himself to the exclusion of Allah and call his people to it. So he gave, granted and clothed everyone who obeyed him in this. He killed everyone who did not swear allegiance to him.

So all of them answered him. He held a celebration for them every year. One day, at a feast, the people of Baṭāriqah were at his right and the people of Ḥarāqilah were at his left. Suddenly, a Biṭrīq came to him and informed him that an army from Persia had overcome him. So he became sad for it as his crown fell from his head. One of those three who were at his right was called Tamlīkhā and was a young man. He said to himself, 'If Daqyānūs is God, as he thinks, he should not become sad, should not fear, urinate, deficate or sleep.

These deeds are not the deeds of God. Those six young people were in the house of one of them every day and that day were in the house of Tamlīkhā. He prepared pure food for them. Then he said to them, 'O brothers! There is something in my heart that has kept me from eating, drinking and sleeping.' They said, 'What is that? O Tamlīkhā!' He said, 'I thought about this sky for a long time and said to myself, "Who raised its ceiling without any support and without any bond above it? Who placed the sun and the moon in it as two luminous signs? Who adorned it with stars?" Then I thought about the earth for a long timeand I said, "Who spread it over the back of the brimming sea? Who has kept down the earth with mountains so that it does not move all over?" Then I thought about myself for a long time: "Who brought me out as a fetus from the belly of my mother? Who fed me and who raised me? Verily, there is a creator and a director other than the king Daqyūs. He is not anyone but the King of kings and the Almighty of the heavens."'

وَفِى يَدِ الآخَرِ طَائِرٌ أَبْيَضُ لَهُ مِنْقَارٌ أَحْمَرُ. فَإِذا نَظَرَ المَلِكُ إلي ذَلِكَ الطَّائِرِ صَفَّرَ بِهِ، فَيَطِيرُ الطَّائِرُ حَتَّي يَقَعَ فِى جَام ماء الوَرْدِ، فَيَتَمَرَّغُ فِيهِ، ثُمَّ يَقَعُ عَلي جَام المِسْكِ، فَيَحْمِلُ ما فِى الجَام بِرِيشِهِ وَجِنَاحِهِ. ثُمَّ يُصَفِّرُ بِهِ الثَّانِيَةَ فَيَطِيرُ الطَّائِرُ عَلي تاج المَلِكِ فَيَنْقُدُ ما فِى رِيشِهِ وَجِنَاحِهِ عَلي رَأس المَلِكِ.

فَلَمّا نَظَرَ المَلِكُ إلي ذَلِكَ عَتا وَتَجَبَّرَ، فادَّعَي الرُّبُوبِيَّةَ مِنْ دُونِ اللهِ، وَدَعا إلي ذَلِكَ وُجُوهَ قَوْمِهِ. فَكُلُّ مَنْ أطاعَهُ عَلي ذَلِكَ أعْطاهُ وَحَبَاهُ وَكَسَاهُ، وَكُلُّ مَنْ لَمْ يُبايِعْهُ قَتَلَهُ. فاسْتَجابُوا لَهُ رَأسًا، واتَّخَذَ لَهُمْ عِيدًا فِى كُلِّ سَنَةٍ مَرَّةً. فَبَيْنا هُمْ ذاتَ يَوْمٍ فِى عِيدٍ والبَطارِقَةُ عَنْ يَمِينِهِ والهَراقِلَةُ عَنْ يَسارِهِ، إذْ أتاهُ بِطَرِيقٌ فَأخْبَرَهُ أنَّ عَساكِرَ الفُرْسِ قَدْ غَشِيَهُ. فاغْتَمَّ لِذَلِكَ حَتَّي سَقَطَ التَّاجُ عَنْ رَأسِهِ. فَنَظَرَ إلَيْهِ أحَدُ الثَّلاثَةِ الذِينَ كانُوا عَنْ يَمِينِهِ، يُقالُ لَهُ تَمْلِيخا، وكانَ غُلامًا. فَقالَ فِى نَفْسِهِ: 'لَوْ كانَ دَقْيانُوسُ إلهًا، كَما يَزْعَمُ، إذا ما كانَ يَغْتَمُّ وَلا يَفْزَعُ وَما كانَ يَبُولُ وَلا يَتَغَوَّطُ وَما كانَ يَنامُ.

وَلَيْسَ هَذِهِ مِنْ فِعْلِ الإلهِ.' قالَ: 'وكانَ الفِتْيَهُ السِّتَّةُ كُلَّ يَوْمٍ عِنْدَ أحَدِهِمْ، وكانُوا ذَلِكَ اليَوْمَ عِنْدَ تَمْلِيخا. فاتَّخَذَ لَهُمْ مِنْ طَيِّبِ الطَّعامِ، ثُمَّ قالَ لَهُمْ: 'يا إخْوَتاهُ، قَدْ وَقَعَ فِى قَلْبِى شَىءٌ مَنَعَنِى الطَّعامَ والشَّرابَ والمَنامَ.' قالُوا: 'وَما ذاكَ!' يا تَمْلِيخا! قالَ: 'أطَلْتُ فِكْرِى فِى هَذِهِ السَّماءِ، فَقُلْتُ: 'مَنْ رَفَعَ سَقْفَها مَحْفُوظَة بِلا عَمَدٍ وَلا عَلاقَةٍ مِنْ فَوْقِها؟ وَمَنْ أجْرَي فِيها شَمْسًا وَقَمَرًا آيَتانِ مُبْصِرَتانِ؟ وَمَنْ زَيَّنَها بِالنُّجُومِ؟' ثُمَّ أطَلْتُ الفِكْرَ فِى الأرضِ فَقُلْتُ: 'مَنْ سَطَحَها عَلي ظَهْرِ اليَمِّ الزَّاخِرِ؟ وَمَنْ حَبَسَها بِالجِبالِ أنْ تَمِيدَ عَلي كُلِّ شَىءٍ؟' وأطَلْتُ فِكْرِى فِى نَفْسِى: 'مَنْ أخْرَجَنِى جَنِينًا مِنْ بَطْنِ أُمِّى؟ وَمَنْ غَذَّانِى؟ وَمَنْ رَبَّانِى؟ إنَّ لَها صانِعًا وَمُدَبِّرًا غَيْرَ دَقْيُوسَ المَلِكِ، وَما هُوَ إلّا مَلِكُ المُلُوكِ وَجَبَّارُ السَّماواتِ.'' فانْكَبَّتُ الفِتْيَهُ

Then that group fell at his feet, kissed them and said, 'Allah guided us from going astray by your guidance, so show us the way.' Tamlīkhā jumped, sold some dates from his garden for three thousand dirhams and put them in his bag. They rode their horses and went out of the city. When they went three miles, Tamlīkhā said to them, 'O brothers! The dwelling of the other world came and the kingdom of this world went. Go down from your horses and walk by foot. Allah may put relief and escape for you.'

They went down from their horses and walked for seven farsangs that day, until their feet bled. A shepherd met them. They said, "O shepherd! Do you have any milk or water?" The shepherd said, "I have whatever you want, but I see that your faces are those of princes. I suspect that you have fled from King Daqyūs." They said, "O shepherd! It is not permitted for us to lie. If we tell you the truth, will we be safe from you?" Then they told him their story. The shepherd fell at their feet and kissed them, and he said, "O people! In my heart I realized what you realized in your hearts. Give me time to return these beasts to their owners and join you. They waited for him. He returned the beasts and hurried back. The dog followed.' The Jew stood and said, 'O 'Alī! What was the name of the dog, and what was its color?' 'Alī said, 'There is no power and no strength save in Allah, the High, the Great. The color of the dog was between white and black, more toward black. The name of the dog was Qiṭmīr. When the youths looked at the dog, some of them said, "We are afraid that the barking will reveal us." So they threw stones at it. Allah, the Exalted, magnificent is His remembrance, made the dog speak: 'Let me be, so I can protect you from your enemies.'

The shepherd constantly guided them until he brought them up a mountain. Then he brought them down to a cave called al-Waṣīd. At the entrance to the cave there were springs and fruit trees. They ate the fruit and drank the water, and the night covered them. They took refuge in the cave, and the dog lied down to sleep at the entrance of

عَلي رِجْلَيْهِ يُقَبِّلُونَها وقَالُوا: 'بِكَ هَدانا اللهُ مِنَ الضَّلالَةِ إلي الهُدَي، فأشِرْ عَلَيْنا.' قالَ: 'فَوَثَبَ تَمْلِيخا، فَباعَ تَمْراً مِنْ حائِطٍ لَهُ بِثَلاثَةِ آلافِ دِرْهَمٍ, وَصَرَّها فِي رِدْنِهِ، وَرَكِبُوا خُيُولَهُمْ وَخَرَجُوا مِنَ المَدِينَةِ. فَلَمّا سارُوا ثَلاثَةَ أمْيالٍ، قالَ لَهُم تَمْلِيخا: 'يا إخْوَتاهُ، جاءَتْ مَسْكَنَةُ الآخِرَةِ وَذَهَبَ مُلْكُ الدنْيا. انزِلُوا عَنْ خُيُولِكُمْ وامْشُوا عَلَي أرْجُلِكُمْ، لَعَلَّ اللهَ أنْ يَجْعَلَ لَكُمْ مِنْ أمْرِكُمْ فَرَجاً وَمَخْرَجاً.'

فَنَزَلُوا عَنْ خُيُولِهِمْ وَمَشَوْا عَلَي أرْجُلِهِمْ سَبْعَةَ فَراسِخَ فِي ذَلِكَ اليَوْمِ، فَجَعَلَتْ أرْجُلُهُمْ تَقْطُرُ دَماً. قالَ: 'فاسْتَقْبَلَهُمْ راعٍ فَقالُوا: 'يا أيُّها الراعِيَ، هَلْ مِنْ شَرْبَةِ لَبَنٍ أوْ ماءٍ؟' فَقالَ الراعِيَ: 'عِنْدِي ما تُحِبُّونَ، ولَكِنْ أرَي وُجوهَكُمْ وُجُوهَ المُلُوكِ، وَما أظُنُّكُمْ إلّا هُرّاباً مِنْ دَقْيُوسِ المَلِكِ.' قالُوا: 'يا أيُّها الراعِيَ، لا يَحِلُّ لَنا الكِذْبُ. أفَيُنَجِّيْنا مِنْكَ الصدْقُ؟' فاخْبَرُوهُ بِقِصَّتِهِمْ. فانْكَبَّ الراعِي عَلَي أرْجُلِهِمْ يُقَبِّلُها وَيَقُولُ: 'يا قَوْمُ، لَقَدْ وَقَعَ فِي قَلْبِي ما وَقَعَ فِي قُلُوبِكُمْ, ولَكِنْ أمْهِلُونِي حَتَّي أرُدَّ الأغنامَ عَلَي أرْبابِها وألحَقَ بِكُمْ.' فَتَوَقَّفُوا لَهُ، فَرَدَّ الأغْنامَ واقْبَلَ يَسْعَي يَتْبَعُهُ الكَلْبُ لَهُ.'»

قالَ: «فَوَثَبَ اليَهُودِيُّ, فَقالَ: 'يا عَلِيُّ ما كانَ اسْمُ الكَلْبِ وَما لَوْنُهُ؟' فَقالَ عَلِيٌّ عليه السلام: 'لا حَوْلَ وَلا قُوَّةَ إلّا بِاللهِ العَلِيِّ العَظِيمِ. أمّا لَوْنُ الكَلْبِ فَكانَ أبْلَقَ بِسَوادٍ، وامّا اسْمُ الكَلْبِ فَقِطْمِيرٌ. فَلَمّا نَظَرَ الفِتْيَةُ إلي الكَلْبِ قالَ بَعْضُهُمْ: 'إنّا نَخافُ أنْ يَفْضَحَنا بِنُباحِهِ.' فالَحُّوا عَلَيْهِ بِالحِجارَةِ. فانْطَقَ اللهُ، تَعالَي, جَلَّ ذِكْرُهُ، الكَلْبَ: 'ذَرُونِي حَتَّي أحْرُسَكُمْ مِنْ عَدُوِّكُمْ.'

فَلَمْ يَزَلْ الراعِي يَسِيرُ بِهِمْ حَتَّي عَلاهُمْ جَبَلاً, فانْحَطَّ بِهِمْ عَلَي كَهْفٍ يُقالُ لَهُ: 'الوَصِيدُ.' فإذا بِفِناءِ الكَهْفِ عُيُونٌ وأشْجارٌ مُثْمِرَةٌ. فأكَلُوا مِنَ الثَّمَرِ وَشَرِبُوا مِنَ الماءِ وَجَنَّهُمُ اللَيْلُ فأوَوْا إلي الكَهْفِ، وَرَبَضَ الكَلْبُ عَلَي بابِ الكَهْفِ وَمَدَّ يَدَيْهِ

the cave, and stretched out its paws. Then Allah, the Exalted, revealed to the angel of death to take their spirits, and for each of the men Allah appointed two angels to turn them from right to left and from left to right. The Allah, the Mighty and Exalted, revealed to the keepers of the sun so it inclined from their cave toward the right and passed them by on the left. [See Qur'ān (18:17)]

When Daqyūs, the king, came back from his celebration, he asked about them. He was informed that they had left the city out of fear. He mounted a horse with eighty thousand others, and they constantly searched for any trace of them, until they ascended and arrived at their cave. When they looked at them, they saw that they were asleep. The king said, 'If I had wanted to chastise them, I would not have chastised them more than they have chastised themselves. Bring the builders.' They dammed the entrance of the cave with lime and stone. The king said to his companions, 'Tell them to ask their God Who is in heaven to save them and to get them out of here.'

'Alī continued, "O Jewish brothers! They stayed there for three hundred nine years. When Allah wanted to revive them, he commanded the angel Isrāfīl to breathe the spirit into them. He breathed. Then they stood up from their sleep. When the sun rose, some of them said, we neglected our worship the God of heaven during the night. They stood and the water of the spring had sunken, and the trees had withered. Some of them said, 'How strange is our affair! Like this sunken spring that had been full, and these trees that have withered in a single night.' They were hungry. They said, ❴*Now send one of you with this coin of yours to the city. Then let him see which of them has purest food; so let him bring you provision from it, and let him behave with gentleness, and by no means make your case known to anyone.*❵ (18:19)

عَلَيْهِ. فأوْحَي اللهُ، تَعالَي, عَزَّ وَعَلا، إلَي مَلَكِ المَوْتِ بِقَبْضِ أرْواحِهِمْ، وَوَكَّلَ اللهُ بِكُلِّ رَجُلٍ مَلَكَيْنَ يُقَلِّبانِهِ مِنْ ذاتِ اليَمِينِ إلَي ذاتِ الشِمالِ وَمِنْ ذاتِ الشِمالِ إلَي اليَمِينِ. فأوْحَي اللهُ، تَعالَي, عَزَّ وَعَلا، إلَي خُزّانِ الشمْسِ، ﴿فكانَتْ تَزاوَرُ عَنْ كَهْفِهِمْ ذاتَ اليَمِينِ وتَقرِضُهُمْ ذاتَ الشمالِ.﴾

فلَمّا رَجَعَ دَقيُوسُ مِنْ عِيدِهِ سألَ عَنِ الفِتْيَةِ. فأخْبِرَ أنَّهُمْ خَرَجُوا هُرّاباً. فرَكِبَ فِي ثمانِينَ الفَ حِصانٍ. فلَمْ يَزَلْ يَقفُو أثرَهُمْ حَتَّي عَلا فانْحَطَّ إلَي كَهْفِهِمْ. فلَمّا نَظَرَ إلَيْهِمْ, إذا هُمْ نِيامٌ. فقالَ المَلِكُ: 'لَوْ أرَدْتُ أنْ أعاقِبَهُمْ بِشَيْءٍ، لَما عاقبْتُهُمْ بِأكْثَرَ مِمّا عاقبُوا بِهِ أنْفُسَهُمْ، وَلَكِنْ ايتُونِي بِالبَنّاءِيْنَ.' فسَدَّ بابَ الكَهْفِ بِالكِلْسِ والحِجارَةِ وَقالَ لأصحابِهِ: 'قُولُوا لَهُمْ: 'يَقولُوا لإلَهِهِمُ الذي فِي السَماءِ لِيُنَجِّيهِمْ وأنْ يُخْرِجَهُمْ مِنْ هذا المَوْضِعِ.''

قالَ عَلِيٌّ عليه السلام: 'يا أخا اليَهُودِ، فمَكَثُوا ثلاثَ مِائةِ سَنَةٍ وتِسْعَ سِنِينَ. فلَمّا أرادَ اللهُ أنْ يُحْيِيَهُمْ، أمَرَ إسْرافِيلَ المَلَكَ أنْ يَنْفخَ فِيهِمُ الروحَ، فنَفخَ، فقامُوا مِنْ رَقْدَتِهِمْ. فلَمّا أنْ بَزَغَتْ الشمْسُ, قالَ بَعْضُهُمْ: 'قَدْ غَفلْنا فِي هَذِهِ اللَيْلَةِ عَنْ عِبادَةِ إلَهِ السَماءِ.' فقامُوا، فإذا العَيْنُ قَدْ غارَتْ وإذا الأشجارُ قَدْ يَبِسَتْ. فقالَ بَعْضُهُمْ: 'إنَّ أمُورَنا لَعَجَبٌ, مِثْلُ تِلْكَ العَيْنِ الغَزِيرَةِ قَدْ غارَتَ, والأشجارُ قَدْ يَبِسَتْ فِي لَيْلَةٍ واحِدَةٍ.' وَمَسَّهُمُ الجُوعُ. فقالُوا: ﴿ابْعَثُوا بِوَرِقِكُمْ هَذِهِ إلَي المَدِينَةِ فلْيَنْظُرْ أيُّها أزْكَي طَعاماً, فلْيأتِكُمْ بِرِزْقٍ مِنْهُ وَلْيَتَلَطَّفْ وَلا يُشْعِرَنَّ بِكُمْ أحَداً.﴾

Tamlīkhā said, 'No one but I will go for your needs. O shepherd! Give me your clothes.' So the shepherd gave his clothes to him and he set out for the city. He saw places that he did not know and roads with which he was unfamiliar, until he reached the gate of the city, where there was a green flag on which was written, "There is no god but Allah, and Jesus is the Apostle of Allah." He looked at the flag and rubbed his eyes and said, "Am I dreaming?" Then he entered the city until he came to the market. He came to a baker and said, "O baker! What is the name of this city of yours?" He said, "Aqsūs." He said, "And what is the name of your king?" He said, "'Abd al-Raḥmān."

He said, "Give me food for this money." The baker started in surprise at the weight and size of the dirham.' The Jew stood up and said, 'O 'Alī! What was the weight of a dirham.' He said, 'The weight of every dirham was that of ten and two thirds dirhams.' 'Alī continued, "Then the baker said, 'O you! Have you found a treasure?' Tamlīkhā said, 'This is the money I made selling dates three days ago, and then I left this city to escape worshipping King Daqyūs.'

The baker took his hand and brought him to the king. The king said, 'What is the story of this youth?' The baker said, 'He is a man who found a treasure.' The king said, 'O youth! Do not be afraid, for our prophet, Jesus, commanded us only to take a fifth of what is found of treasure. So, give us a fifth of it and go in peace.' Tamlīkhā said, 'O king! Look at my affair. I did not find a treasure. I am a man of this city.' The king said, 'You are of its people?' He said, 'Yes.' He said, 'Does anyone here know you?' He said, 'Yes.' He said, 'What is your name?' He said, 'My name is Tamlīkhā.' He said, 'There is no such name among the names of our times.' The king said, 'Do you have a house in this city?' He said, 'Yes. O king! Mount and come with me.' The king mounted and so did his people with him. Tamlīkhā brought them to the highest building in the city. He said, 'This is my house.'

قالَ تَمْلِيخا: 'لا يَذْهَبُ فِي حَوائِجِكُمْ غَيْرِي، ولَكِنْ ادْفَعْ أيُّها الراعِي ثِيابَكَ إلَيَّ.'» قالَ: «فَدَفَعَ الراعِي ثِيابَهُ وَمَضي يؤُمُّ المَدِينَةَ، فَجَعَلَ يَرَي مَواضِعَ لا يَعْرِفُها وَطَرِيقاً هُوَ يُنْكِرُها، حَتَّي أتَي بابَ المَدِينَةِ، وإذا عَلَيْهِ عَلَمٌ أخْضَرُ مَكْتُوبٌ عَلَيْهِ: 'لا إلَهَ إلّا اللهُ، عِيسَي رَسُولُ اللهِ.'» قالَ: «فَجَعَلَ يَنْظُرُ إلَي العَلَمَ وَجَعَلَ يَمْسَحُ عَيْنَيْهِ وَيَقُولُ: 'أرانِي نائِماً.' ثُمَّ دَخَلَ المَدِينَةَ حَتَّي أتَي السُّوقَ فأتَي رَجُلاً خَبّازاً، فَقالَ: 'أيُّها الخَبّازُ! ما اسْمُ مَدِينَتِكُمْ هَذِهِ؟' قالَ: 'أقسُوسُ.' قالَ: 'وَما اسْمُ مَلِكِكُمْ؟' قالَ: 'عَبْدُ الرحْمَنِ.'

قالَ: 'ادْفَعْ إلَيَّ بِهَذِهِ الوَرَقِ طَعاماً.' فَجَعَلَ الخَبّازُ يَتَعَجَّبُ مِنْ ثِقْلِ الدراهِمِ وَمِنْ كِبَرِها.» قالَ: «فَوَثَبَ اليَهُودِيُّ وَقالَ: 'يا عَلِيُّ، وَما كانَ وَزْنُ كُلِّ دِرْهَمٍ مِنْها؟' قالَ: 'وَزْنُ كُلِّ دِرْهَمٍ عَشْرَةُ دَراهِمَ وَثُلُثَي دِرْهَمٍ. فَقالَ الخَبّازُ: 'يا هَذا أنتَ أصَبْتَ كَنْزاً!' فَقالَ تَمْلِيخا: 'ما هَذا إلّا ثَمَنُ تَمْرٍ بِعْتُها مُنْذُ ثَلاثٍ وَخَرَجْتُ مِنْ هَذِهِ المَدِينَةِ وَتَرَكْتُ الناسَ، يَعْبُدُونَ دَقْيُوسَ المَلِكَ'

قالَ: 'فَأخَذَ الخَبّازُ بِيَدِ تَمْلِيخا وأدْخَلَهُ عَلَي المَلِكِ.' فَقالَ: 'ما شانُ هَذا الفَتَي؟' قالَ الخَبّازُ: 'هَذا رَجُلٌ أصابَ كَنْزاً.' فَقالَ المَلِكُ: 'يا فَتَي ، لا تَخَفْ . فانَّ نَبِيَّنا، عِيسَي عليه السلام أمَرَنا أنْ لا نأخُذَ مِنَ الكَنْزِ إلّا خُمْسَها. فأعْطِنِي خُمْسَها وامْضِ سالِماً.' فَقالَ تَمْلِيخا: 'أنْظُرْ أيُّها المَلِكَ فِي أمْرِي، ما أصَبْتُ كَنْزاً. أنا رَجُلٌ مِنْ أهْلِ هَذِهِ المَدِينَةِ.' فَقالَ المَلِكُ: 'أنْتَ مِنْ أهْلِها؟' قالَ: 'نَعَم.' قالَ: 'فَهَلْ تَعْرِفُ بِها أحَداً؟' قالَ: 'نَعَم.' قالَ: 'ما اسْمُكَ؟' قالَ: 'اسْمِي تَمْلِيخا.' قالَ: 'وَما هَذِهِ الأسماءُ أسْماءُ أهْلِ زَمانِنا.' فَقالَ المَلِكُ: 'فَهَلْ لَكَ فِي هَذِهِ المَدِينَةِ دار"؟' قالَ: 'نَعَم. ارْكَبْ أيُّها المَلِكُ مَعِي.' قالَ: 'فَرَكِبَ المَلِكُ والناسُ مَعَهُ فأتَي بِهِمْ أرْفَعَ دارٍ فِي المَدِينَةِ.' قالَ تَمْلِيخا: 'هَذِهِ الدارُ لِي.

He knocked on the door. An elderly man came out, whose eyebrows covered his eyes because of his age, and said, 'What do you want?' The king said, "This young man brought us something strange. He thinks that this is his house." The old man said to him, "Who are you?" He said, "I am Tamlīkhā son of Qusṭikin." The old man fell at his feet and kissed them, and said, "He is my grandfather, by the Lord of the Ka'bah. O king! These six are those who escaped out of fear of King Daqyūs."

The king came down from his horse and carried Tamlīkhā on his shoulders, and the people started kissing his hands and feet. He said, "O Tamlīkhā! What have your companions done?" He informed him of the cave. In those days there was in the city a *muslim* king and a Jewish king. Both mounted with their companions. When they got close to the cave, Tamlīkhā said, "I am afraid that my companions will hear the sound of the hooves of the horses and suspect that King Daqyūs is coming after them. Give me time to go ahead and inform them." The people waited and Tamlīkhā went ahead until he entered the cave. When they looked at him and gathered around him and said, "Praise Allah Who delivered you from Daqyūs." Tamlīkhā said, "Leave off this talk of Daqyūs."

He said, ﴾*How long have you tarried? They said, We have tarried for a day or a part of a day.*﴿ (18:19). Tamlīkhā said, "You have tarried three hundred nine years, and Daqyūs has died, and centuries have passed. Allah raised a prophet called the Messiah, Jesus the son of Mary. Allah made him ascend. The king came to our side and the people with him." They said, "O Tamlīkhā! Do you want to make a trial by us for the people?" Tamlīkhā said, "So, what do you want?" They said, "Pray to Allah, Whose remembrance is glorious, and we will pray with you that our souls will be taken."

They raised their hands. Then Allah commanded that their souls be taken. Then Allah covered the door of the cave from the people. The two kings came and circled about the door of the cave for seven days

فقَرَعَ البابَ، فخَرَجَ إليْهِمْ شيْخٌ، وقَدْ وقَعَ حاجِباهُ علَي عَيْنَيْهِ مِنَ الكِبَرِ. فقالَ: 'ما شأنُكُمْ؟' فقالَ المَلِكُ: 'أتانا هَذا الغُلامُ بِالعَجائِبِ. يَزْعَمُ أنَّ هَذِهِ الدارَ دارُهُ.' فقالَ لهُ الشيْخُ: 'مَنْ أنْتَ؟' قالَ: 'أنا تَمْلِيخا بْنُ قُسْطِيكِينَ.' قالَ: 'فانْكَبَّ الشيْخُ علَي رِجْلَيْهِ يُقَبِّلُهُما ويَقُولُ: 'هُوَ جَدِّى ورَبِّ الكَعْبَةِ.' فقالَ: 'أيُّها المَلِكُ، هؤُلاءِ السِّتَّةُ الذينَ خرَجُوا هُرّاباً مِنْ دقْيُوسَ المَلِكِ.' قالَ: 'فنَزَلَ المَلِكُ, عَنْ فَرَسِهِ وَحمَلَهُ علَي عاتِقِهِ وَجعَلَ الناسُ يُقَبِّلُونَ يَدَيْهِ وَرِجْلَيْهِ.' فقالَ: 'يا تَمْلِيخا، ما فَعَلَ أصْحابُكَ؟' فأخْبَرَ أنَّهُمْ فِى الكَهْفِ. وكانَ يَوْمَئِذٍ بِالمَدِينَةِ مَلِكٌ مُسْلِمٌ وَمَلِكٌ يَهُودِىٌّ. فرَكِبُوا فِى أصْحابِهِمْ. فلَمّا صارُوا قَرِيباً مِنَ الكَهْفِ، قالَ لَهُمْ تَمْلِيخا: 'إنِّى أخافُ أنْ تَسْمَعَ أصْحابى أصْواتَ حَوافِرِ الخُيُولِ، فيَظُنُّونَ أنَّ دقْيُوسَ المَلِكَ قَدْ جاءَ فِى طَلَبِهِمْ. ولَكِنْ أمْهِلُونِى حَتَّي أتَقَدَّمَ فأخْبَرَهُمْ.' فوَقَفَ الناسُ. فأقبَلَ تَمْلِيخا حَتَّي دَخَلَ الكَهْفَ. فلَمّا نَظَرُوا إلَيْهِ، إعْتَنَقُوهُ وَقالُوا: 'الحَمْدُ للهِ الذى نَجّاكَ مِنْ دقْيُوسَ.' قالَ تَمْلِيخا: 'دَعُونِى عَنْكُمْ وَعَنْ دقْيُوسِكُمْ.'

﴿قالَ: 'كَمْ لَبِثْتُمْ؟' قالُوا: 'لَبِثْنا يَوْماً أوْ بَعْضَ يَوْمٍ.'﴾ قالَ تَمْلِيخا: 'بَلْ لَبِثْتُم ثَلاثَ مِائَةٍ وَتِسْعَ سِنِينَ، وَقَدْ ماتَ دقْيُوسُ، وانْقَرَضَ قَرْنٌ بَعْدَ قَرْنٍ، وَبَعَثَ اللهُ نَبِيّاً، يُقالُ لَهُ: 'المَسِيحُ، عِيسَي بْنُ مَرْيَمَ عليه السلام،' وَرَفَعَهُ اللهُ إلَيْهِ. وَقَدْ أقبَلَ إلَيْنا المَلِكُ والناسُ مَعَهُ.' قالُوا: 'يا تَمْلِيخا، أتُرِيدُ أنْ تَجْعَلَنا فِتْنَةً لِلعالَمِينَ؟' قالَ تَمْلِيخا: 'فَما تُرِيدُونَ؟' قالُوا: 'أدْعُ اللهَ، جَلَّ ذِكْرُهُ، وَنَدْعُوهُ مَعَكَ، حَتَّي يَقْبِضَ أرْواحَنا.' فرَفَعُوا أيْدِيَهُمْ. فأمَرَ اللهُ، تَعالَي، بِقَبْضِ أرْواحِهِمْ، وَطَمَسَ اللهُ بابَ الكَهْفِ علَي الناسِ. فأقبَلَ المَلِكانِ، يَطُوفانِ علَي بابِ الكَهْفِ سَبْعَةَ أيّامٍ، لا يَجِدانِ لِلْكَهْفِ باباً. فقالَ

without finding it. The *muslim* King said, "They died with our religion. I will build a mosque over the door of the cave." The Jew said, "No! Rather they died with my religion. I will build a synagogue over the door of the cave." Then they fought. The *muslim* won, and built a mosque over it.' O Jew! Does this agree with what is in your Torah?" The Jew said, "You have not added or subtracted a letter, and I bear witness that there is no god but Allah and that Muḥammad is His servant and His apostle."

(*Biḥār*, 14, 411- 419, 1)

1.5.14. It is reported that Ṣafwān the son of Yaḥyā, the companion of al-Sābirī said: "Abū Qurrah, the companion of al-Jāthilīq, asked me to bring him to al-Riḍā. Then I asked him for permission. He said, 'Bring him to me.' Then, when he came to him, Abū Qarah kissed the carpet and said, 'This is our duty, according to our religion, that we must do for the nobles of our time.'

Then Abū Qarah said to him, 'May Allah help you. What would you say about a sect that claimed something, and another sect bore witness that it was right?' He answered, 'The claim is in their favor.' He said, ' [What about] another sect that claims something but finds no witnesses for it but themselves?' He answered, 'There is nothing in their favor.' He said, 'So we, ourselves, claim that Jesus is the spirit of Allah and His word, and the Muslims agree with us about this. But the Muslims claim that Muḥammad is the prophet, while we do not follow them in this. That on which we agree is better than that about which we differ.' Al-Riḍā said to him, 'What is your name?' He answered, 'Yūḥannā.' He said, 'O Yūḥannā! We believe in Jesus, the spirit of Allah and His word, who believed in Muḥammad and gave tidings of him and acknowledged that he was His servant and subject. So, if Jesus, the spirit of Allah and His word, as you hold, is not one who believed in Muḥammad, and gave tiding

المَلِكُ المُسْلِمُ: 'ماتُوا عَلَي دِينِنا. أبنى عَلَي بابِ الكَهْفِ مَسْجِداً.' وَقالَ اليَهُودِيُّ: 'لا، بَلْ ماتُوا عَلَي دِينِي. أبنى عَلَي بابِ الكَهْفِ كَنِيسَةً.' فاقتَتَلا. فَغَلَبَ المُسْلِمُ وَبَنَي مَسْجِداً عَلَيْهِ. يا يَهُودِيُّ، أيُوافِقُ هَذا ما فِي تَوْراتِكُمْ؟ قالَ: 'ما زِدْتَ حَرْفاً وَلا نَقَصْتَ. وأنَا أشْهَدُ أنْ لا إلَهَ إلّا اللهُ، وأنَّ مُحَمَّداً عَبْدُهُ وَرَسُولُهُ.''»

(بحار الأنوار، ١٤، ٤١١-٤١٩، ١)

١-٥-١٤- الهَمْدانِيُّ والمُكَتِّبُ والوَرّاقُ, عَنْ أبِيهِ, عَنْ عَلِيٍّ, عَنْ صَفْوانَ بْنِ يَحْيَي صاحِبِ السّابُرِيِّ, قالَ: «سألَنِي أبُو قُرَّة، صاحِبُ الجاثَلِيق, أنْ أوصِلَهُ إلَي الرضا عليه السلام. فاستَأذَنْتُهُ فِي ذَلِكَ. فَقالَ: 'أدْخِلْهُ عَلَيَّ.' فَلَمّا دَخَلَ عَلَيْهِ، قَبَّلَ بِساطَهُ وَقالَ: 'هَكَذا عَلَيْنا فِي دِيْنِنا أنْ نَفْعَلَ بِأشْرافِ أهْلِ زَمانِنا.'

ثُمَّ قالَ لَهُ: 'أصْلَحَكَ اللهُ، ما تَقُولُ فِي فِرْقَةٍ ادَّعَتْ دَعْوَيً فَشَهِدَتْ لَهُمْ فِرْقَةٌ أُخْرَي مُعَدَّلُونَ؟' قالَ: 'الدعْوَي لَهُمْ.' قالَ: 'فادَّعَتْ فِرْقَةٌ أُخْرَي دَعْوَيً فَلَمْ يَجِدُوا شُهُوداً مِنْ غَيْرِهِمْ؟' قالَ: 'لا شَيْء لَهُمْ.' قالَ: 'فانّا نَحْنُ ادَّعَيْنا أنَّ عِيسَي رُوحُ اللهِ وَكَلِمَتُهُ، فَوافَقَنا عَلَي ذَلِكَ المُسْلِمُونَ. وادَّعَي المُسْلِمُونَ أنَّ مُحَمَّداً نَبِيٌّ، فَلَمْ نُتابِعْهُمْ عَلَيْهِ. وَما أجْمَعْنا عَلَيْهِ خَيْرٌ مِمّا افْتَرَقْنا فِيهِ.' فَقالَ لَهُ الرضا عليه السلام: 'ما اسْمُكَ؟' قالَ: 'يُوحَنّا.' قالَ: 'يا يُوحَنّا، إنّا آمَنّا بِعِيسَي, رُوحِ اللهِ وَكَلِمَتِهِ الذى كانَ يُؤْمِنُ بِمُحَمَّدٍ وَيُبَشِّرُ بِهِ وَيُقِرُّ عَلَي نَفْسِهِ أنَّهُ عَبْدٌ مَرْبُوبٌ. فإنْ كانَ عِيسَي الذى هُوَ عِنْدَكَ، رُوحَ اللهِ وَكَلِمَتَهُ، لَيْسَ هُوَ الذى آمَنَ بِمُحَمَّدٍ وَبَشَّرَ بِهِ, وَلا هُوَ

of him, and who acknowledged that he is the servant of Allah and that He is the Lord, then we are acquitted of him. So, on what do we agree?' Then he stood up and said to Safwān the son of Yaḥyā, 'Stand up! We did not get anything out of this meeting.'"

(*Biḥār,* 10, 30, 341)

1.5.15. Isḥāq ibn 'Ammār said: "I asked Abū 'Abd Allah about what Allah, the blessed and exalted, said, ﴾*and aforetime they used to pray for victory against those who disbelieved, but when there came to them (the Prophet) that which they did not recognize, they disbelieved in him,*﴿ (2:89). He answered, 'There was a group between Muḥammad ﷺ and Jesus that used to threaten disbelievers with a prophet and they used to say, "Verily a prophet will appear and will break your idols and will do with you this and that," but when the Prophet of Allah appeared, they disbelieved him.'"

(*Kāfī,* 8, 310, 482)

1.5.16. Ḥasan ibn Muḥammad al-Nūfalī said, "When 'Alī ibn Mūsā al-Riḍa came before Ma'mūn the later commanded Faḍl ibn Sahl to gather the scholars (*aṣḥāb al-maqālāt*) such as the Catholicos (*Jāthalīq*), the Exilarch (*Ra's al-Jalūt*), the chiefs of the Sabeans, Hirbidh al-Akbar, the Zoroastrians, Nasṭās al-Rūmī and the theologians so as to hear his words and their words. Faḍl ibn Sahl gathered them and informed Ma'mūn of their gathering.

Ma'mūn said, 'Bring them before me.' He did it. Ma'mūn welcomed them; then he said to them, 'I gathered you here for the good, and I would like you to debate with my cousin from Madīnah who has come before me. Come here early tomorrow morning, and let not one of you be remiss.' They said, 'We hear and we obey, O Commander of the Faithful! We will be here early tomorrow morning, God willing.'...

الّذِى أقرَّ لِلهِ بِالعُبُودِيَّةِ والربُوبِيَّةِ، فَنَحْنُ مِنْهُ بُرَآءٌ. فأيْنَ اجْتَمَعْنا؟' فقامَ، فقالَ لِصَفْوانَ بْنِ يَحْيَي: 'قمْ. فما كانَ أغْنانا, عَنْ هَذا المَجْلِسِ.»

(بحار الأنوار، ١٠، ٣٠،٣٤١)

١-٥-١٥- عَلِيُّ بْنُ إبْراهِيمَ، عَنْ أبِيهِ عَنْ صَفْوانَ بْنِ يَحْيَي، عَنْ إسْحاقَ بْنِ عَمّارٍ، قالَ: «سألْتُ أبا عَبْدِ اللهِ عليه السلام عَنْ قَوْلِ اللهِ، تَبارَكَ وَتَعالَي: ﴿وَكانُوا مِنْ قَبْلُ يَسْتَفْتِحُونَ عَلَي الذينَ كَفَرُوا. فَلَمّا جاءَهُمْ ما عَرَفُوا كَفَرُوا بِهِ.﴾ قالَ: 'كانَ قَوْمٌ فِي ما بَيْنَ مُحَمَّدٍ وَعِيسَي، صَلَّي اللهُ عَلَيْهِما. وَكانُوا يَتَوَعَّدُونَ أهْلَ الأصْنامِ بالنَبِي صلى الله عليه وآله وسلم وَيَقُولُونَ: 'لَيَخْرُجَنَّ نَبِيٌّ فَلَيُكَسِّرَنَّ أصْنامَكُمْ وَلَيَفْعَلَنَّ بِكُمْ [وَلَيَفْعَلَنَّ]' فَلَمّا خَرَجَ رَسُولُ اللهِ صلى الله عليه وآله وسلم كَفَرُوا بِهِ.»

(الكافى، ٨، ٣١٠، ٤٨٢)

١-٥-١٦- حَدَّثَنا أبُو مُحَمَّدٍ جَعْفَرُ بْنُ عَلِيِّ بْنِ أحْمَدَ الفَقِيهِ القُمِيِّ ثُمَّ الإيلاقِيِّ، رَضِيَ اللهُ عَنْهُ، قالَ: «أخْبَرَنا أبُو مُحَمَّدٍ، الحَسَنُ بُنُ مُحَمَّدِ بْنِ عَلِيِّ بْنِ صَدَقَةٍ القُمِيِّ. قالَ: 'حَدَّثَنِي أبُو عَمْرٍو مُحَمَّدُ بْنُ عُمَرَ بْنِ عَبْدِ العَزِيزِ الأنْصارِيِّ الكَجِيِّ. قالَ: 'حَدَّثَنِي مَنْ سَمِعَ الحَسَنَ بْنَ مُحَمَّدٍ النَوْفِلِيِّ ثُمَّ الهاشِمِيِّ يَقُولُ: 'لَمّا قَدِمَ عَلِيُّ بْنُ مُوسَي الرضا عليه السلام عَلي المأمُونِ، أمَرَ الفَضْلَ بْنَ سَهْلٍ أنْ يَجْمَعَ لَهُ أصْحابَ المَقالاتِ، مِثْلَ الجاثَلِيقِ وَرَاسِ الجالُوتِ وَرُؤَساءِ الصابِئِينَ والهِرْبَذِ الأكْبَرِ وأصْحابِ زَرْدَهَشْتَ وَنَسْطاسِ الرومِي والمُتَكَلِّمِينَ لِيَسمَعَ كَلامَهُ وكَلامَهُمْ. فَجَمَعَهُمُ الفَضْلُ بْنُ سَهْلٍ، ثُمَّ أعْلَمَ المامُونَ بِاجْتِماعِهِمْ.

فَقالَ المأمُونُ: 'أدْخِلْهُمْ عَلَيَّ.' فَفَعَلَ فَرَحَّبَ بِهِمُ المامُونُ، ثُمَّ قالَ لَهُمْ: 'إنِّي إنَّما جَمَعْتُكُمْ لِخَيْرٍ، وأحْبَبْتُ أنْ تُناظِرُوا ابن عَمِّي، هَذا المَدَنِيَّ القادِمَ عَلَيَّ. فإذا كانَ بُكْرَةً فاغْدُوا عَلَيَّ وَلا يَتَخَلَّفْ مِنْكُمْ أحَدٌ.' فَقالُوا: 'السمْعُ والطّاعَةُ يا أمِيرَ المُؤْمِنِينَ. نَحْنُ مُبْكِرُونَ إنْ شاءَ اللهُ...'

The next morning, Faḍl ibn Sahl came and said to Riḍā, 'May I be your sacrifice. Your cousin is waiting for you. The people have gathered. What is your view about coming before him?' Riḍā said to him, 'You precede me, and I will come to you, God willing.' Then he made ablutions (*wuḍū'*) as though for prayer, and he drank some barley water (*sharbah sawīq*) and we also drank some. Then he left, and we left with him, until we entered before Ma'mūn. All at once it was crowded, and Muḥammad ibn Ja'far was among the Ṭālibiyyin, the Hāshimiyyin and the Quwwād. When Riḍā entered, Ma'mūn stood up, and Muḥammad ibn Ja'far and all the Hāshimiyyin. They waited until Riḍā sat with Ma'mūn and ordered them to sit. Then they sat, and Ma'mūn faced him and spoke with him for an hour.

Then Ma'mūn turned toward the Catholicos and said, 'O Catholicos! This is my cousin, 'Alī ibn Mūsā ibn Ja'far, who is a descendent of Fāṭimah the daughter of our Prophet and 'Alī ibn Abī Ṭālib, may they both be blessed. So, I would like you to speak with him and debate fairly.' The Catholicos said, 'O Commander of the Faithful! How can I debate with someone who relies upon a book that I deny and a prophet in whom I have no faith?' Riḍā said to him, 'O Christian! If I debate against you by your Gospel, will you concede?' The Catholicos said, 'Can I reject what is spoken in the Gospel? Yes, by God, I will concede even if I do not like it.' Riḍā said to him, 'Ask whatever comes to your mind, and understand the answer.' The Catholicos said, 'What do you say about the prophethood of Jesus and his book? Do you deny them?'

Riḍā said, 'I confess the prophethood of Jesus and his book, and the glad tidings to his community to which the Apostles also confessed. And I disbelieve in the prophethood of any Jesus who did not confess the prophethood of Muḥammad and in his book and who did not give glad tidings of him to his community.' The Catholicos said, 'Is it not the case that you consider the judgment of

فلمّا أصبَحْنا، أتانا الفَضلُ بْنُ سَهلٍ. فقالَ لهُ: 'جُعِلتُ فِداكَ. ابن عمِّكَ يَنتَظِرُكَ، وقَدِ اجتَمَعَ القَوْمُ. فما رأيُكَ فِى إتيانِهِ؟' فقالَ لهُ الرضاعليه السلام: 'تَقدَّمْني، فانّى سائِرٌ إلي ناحِيَتِكُمْ، إنْ شاءَ اللهُ.' ثُمَّ تَوَضّأعليه السلام وُضُوءَهُ لِلصَّلاةِ وَشَرِبَ شَرْبَةَ سَويقٍ وَسَقانا مِنْهُ. ثُمَّ خَرَجَ وَخَرَجْنا مَعَهُ حَتّي دَخَلْنا عَلَي المامُونِ. فإذا المَجْلِسُ غاصَ بِأهْلِهِ، وَمُحَمَّدُ بْنُ جعْفَرٍ فِى جَماعَةِ الطّالِبِيِّينَ والهاشِمِيِّينَ، والقُوّادُ حُضُورٌ. فلَمّا دَخَلَ الرضاعليه السلام، قامَ المأمُونُ وَقامَ مُحَمَّدُ بْنُ جَعْفَرٍ وَجَمِيعُ بَنِى هاشِمٍ. فَما زالُوا وُقُوفاً، والرضاعليه السلام جالِسٌ مَعَ المامُونِ حَتّي أمَرَهُمْ بِالجُلُوسِ، فَجلَسُوا. فلَمْ يَزَلْ المأمُونُ مُقبِلاً عَلَيْهِ، يُحَدِّثُهُ ساعَةً.

ثُمَّ التَفَتَ إلي الجاثَليق، فقالَ: 'يا جاثَليقُ، هَذا ابن عَمّى، عَلِيُّ بْنُ مُوسَي بْنُ جَعْفَرٍ. وَهُوَ مِنْ وُلْدِ فاطِمَةَ بِنْتِ نَبِيِّنا، وابْنُ عَلِيٍّ بْنِ أبِى طالِبٍ، صَلَواتُ اللهِ عَلَيْهِما. فأحِبُّ أنْ تُكَلِّمَهُ وَتُحاجَّهُ وَتُنْصِفَهُ.' فقالَ الجاثَليقُ: 'يا أمِيرَ المُؤْمِنِينَ، كَيْفَ أحاجُّ رَجُلاً يَحْتَجُّ عَلَيَّ بِكِتابٍ أنا مُنْكِرُهُ وَنَبِيٍّ لا أومِنُ بِهِ؟' فقالَ لهُ الرضاعليه السلام: 'يا نَصْرانِيُّ، فإنْ احْتَجَجْتُ عَلَيْكَ بِإنْجيلِكَ، أتُقِرُّ بِهِ؟' قالَ الجاثَليق: 'وَهَلْ أقدِرُ عَلَي دَفْعِ ما نَطَقَ بِهِ الإنجيلُ! نَعَم واللهِ أقِرُّ بِهِ عَلَي رَغْمِ أنْفِى.' فقالَ لهُ الرضاعليه السلام: 'سَلْ عَمّا بَدا لَكَ وافْهَمْ الجَوابَ.' قالَ الجاثَليقُ: 'ما تَقولُ فِى نُبُوَّةِ عِيسَي وَكِتابِهِ؟ هَلْ تُنْكِرُ مِنْهُما شَيْئًا؟'

قالَ الرضاعليه السلام: 'أنا مُقِرٌّ بِنُبُوَّةِ عِيسَي وَكِتابِهِ وَما بَشَّرَ بِهِ أُمَّتَهُ وأقَرَّتْ بِهِ الحَوارِيُّونَ؛ وَكافِرٌ بِنُبُوَّةِ كُلِّ عِيسَي لَمْ يُقِرَّ بِنُبُوَّةِ مُحَمَّدٍصلى الله عليه وآله وسلم وَبِكِتابِهِ وَلَمْ يُبَشِّرْ بِهِ أُمَّتَهُ.' قالَ الجاثَليقُ: 'ألَيْسَ إنَّما تَقْطَعُ الأحْكامُ بِشاهِدَىْ عَدْلٍ؟'

two just witnesses decisive?' He said, 'Yes.' The Catholicos said, 'Then bring two witnesses for the prophethood of Muḥammad from a nation other than yours who are not denied by the Christians, and ask us for the like from other than our nation.' Riḍā said, 'Now you are being fair, O Christian! Do you not accept from me the earlier just ones who were with the Messiah, Jesus the son of Mary?'

The Catholicos said, 'Who is that just one? Tell me his name?' He said, 'What do you say about John Daylamī?' He said, 'Very well! You have mentioned the most beloved person to the Messiah.' He said, 'I swear to you, does the Gospel not say that John said, "The Messiah informed me of the religion of Muḥammad the Arab, and he gave me glad tidings of him, that he would come after him; then I gave glad tidings of him to the Apostles, so believe in him."?' The Catholicos said, 'John mentioned this from the Messiah and he gave glad tidings about the prophethood of a man and about his folk and his trustee. But he did not specify when this would be, and he did not name these people for us so that we could recognize them.'

Riḍā said, 'If we bring someone who reads the Gospel and he recites for you the mention of Muḥammad and his folk and his community, will you believe in him?' He said, 'Surely.' Riḍā said to Nasṭās al-Rūmī, 'How is your memory of the third scripture of the Gospel?' He said, 'I do not remember it.'Then he turned to the chief of al-Jālūt and said, 'Do you not read the Gospel?' He said, 'Yes, by my soul.' He said, 'Start the third scripture for me. If the mention of Muḥammad and his folk and his community is in it, bear witness to it for me, and if it is not there, then do not bear witness for me.' Then he recited the scripture until when he arrived at the mention of the Prophet he stopped.

Then he said, 'O Christian! I ask you by the right of the Messiah and his mother, did you know that I know the Gospel?' He said, 'Yes.' Then he recited for us the mention of Muḥammad, his folk and his community. Then he said, 'What do you say, O Christian? This is the speech of Jesus the son of Mary. If you belie what is said in the Gospel then you belie Moses and Jesus, peace be with them, and when you deny this mention, it is obligatory for you to be killed, because you would be a disbeliever in your Lord, your prophet and your book.'

قالَ: 'بلي.' قالَ: 'فأقِمْ شاهِدَيْنِ، مِنْ غيْرِ أهْلِ مِلَّتِكَ، علَي نُبُوَّةِ مُحَمَّدٍ، مِمَّنْ لا تُنْكِرُهُ النصْرانِيَّةُ. وَسَلْنا مِثْلَ ذلِكَ مِنْ غيْرِ أهْلِ مِلَّتِنا.' قالَ الرضاعليه السلام: 'ألآنَ جِئْتَ بِالنَصفَةِ، يا نَصْرانِيُّ. ألا تَقْبَلُ مِنِّى العَدْلَ المُقَدَّمَ عِنْدَ المَسيحِ، عِيسَي بْنِ مَرْيَمَ؟' قالَ الجاثَليقُ: 'مَنْ هذا العَدْلُ؟ سَمِّهْ لِي.' قالَ: 'ما تَقولُ فِى يُوحَنّا الديْلمِيِّ؟' قالَ: 'بَخٍّ بَخٍّ! ذَكَرْتَ أحَبَّ الناسِ إلِي المَسيحِ.' قالَ عليه السلام: 'فأقْسِمْتُ علَيْكَ، هَلْ نَطَقَ الإنجيلُ أنَّ يُوحَنّا قالَ: 'إنَّ المَسيحَ أخْبَرَنِى بِدِينِ مُحَمَّدٍ العَرَبِيِّ وَبَشَّرَنِى بِهِ أنَّهُ يَكُونُ مِنْ بَعْدِهِ. فَبَشَّرْتُ بِهِ الحَوارِيِّينَ، فآمَنُوا بِهِ.'' قالَ الجاثَليقُ: 'قَدْ ذَكَرَ ذلِكَ يُوحَنّا عَنْ المَسيحِ وَبَشَّرَ بِنُبُوَّةِ رَجُلٍ وَبِأهْلِ بَيْتِهِ وَوَصِيِّهِ، وَلَمْ يُلَخِّصْ مَتَي يَكُونُ ذلِكَ، وَلَمْ يُسَمِّ لَنا القَوْمَ فَنَعْرِفَهُمْ.'

قالَ الرضاعليه السلام: 'فإنْ جِئْناكَ بِمَنْ يُقِرُّ الإنجيلَ، فَتَلا علَيْكَ ذِكْرَ مُحَمَّدٍ وأهْلِ بَيْتِهِ وأمَّتِهِ أتُؤْمِنَ بِهِ؟' قالَ: 'شَدِيداً.' قالَ الرضاعليه السلام لِنَسْطاسِ الرومِيِّ: 'كَيْفَ حِفْظُكَ لِلسِّفْرِ الثالِثِ مِنَ الإنجيلِ؟' قالَ: 'ما أحْفَظَنِى لَهُ.' ثُمَّ التَفَتَ إلِي رأسِ الجالُوتِ، فَقالَ: 'ألَسْتَ تَقْرءُ الإنجيلَ قالَ: 'بلَي، لَعَمْرِى.' قالَ: 'فَخُذْ علَي السِّفْرِ الثالِثِ. فإنْ كانَ فِيهِ ذِكْرُ مُحَمَّدٍ وأهْلِ بَيْتِهِ وأمَّتِهِ، فاشْهَدُوا لِي؛ وانْ لَمْ يَكُنْ فِيهِ ذِكْرُهُ فَلا تَشْهَدُوا لِى .'ثُمَّ قَرءَعليه السلام السِّفْرَ الثالِثَ، حَتَّي إذا بَلَغَ ذِكْرَ النَبِىِّصلى الله عليه وآله وسلم وَقَفَ.

ثُمَّ قالَ: 'يا نَصْرانِيُّ، إنِّى أسْألُكَ، بِحَقِّ المَسيحِ وأمِّهِ، أتَعْلَمُ إنِّى عالِمٌ بِالإنجيلِ؟' قالَ: 'نَعَم.' ثُمَّ تَلا علَيْنا ذِكْرَ مُحَمَّدٍ وأهْلِ بَيْتِهِ وأمَّتِهِ. ثُمَّ قالَ: 'ما تَقُولُ؟ يا نَصْرانِيُّ، هَذا قَوْلُ عِيسَي بْنِ مَرْيَمَ. فإنْ كَذَّبْتَ ما يَنْطِقُ بِهِ الإنجيلُ، فَقَدْ كَذَّبْتَ مُوسَي وَعِيسَيعليه السلام؛ وَمَتَي أنْكَرْتَ هَذا الذِّكْرَ وَجَبَ علَيْكَ القَتْلُ. لِأنَّكَ تَكُونُ قَدْ كَفَرْتَ بِرَبِّكَ وَبِنَبِيِّكَ وَبِكِتابِكَ.'

The Catholicos said, ‘I will not deny what is clear for me in the Gospel. I will confess to it.’ Riḍā said, ‘Bear witness to what he has confessed.’ Then he said, ‘O Catholicos! Ask whatever comes to your mind.’

The Catholicos said, ‘Inform me about the Apostles of Jesus the son of Mary. How many were they? And how many were the scholars of the Gospel?’ Riḍā said, ‘You have come to one who is well informed. As for the Apostles, they were twelve men, and the most noble and knowledgeable of them was Luke. As for the Christian scholars, they were three men: John the Great of Ajj,(1) John of Qirqīsā and John Daylamī of Zijār, and it is he who mentions the Prophet, and mentions his folk and his community, and it is he who brought the glad tidings of him to the community of Jesus and to the Children of Israel.’

Then he said to him, ‘O Christian! Verily, we do indeed, by Allah, believe in Jesus who believed in Muḥammad and we do not resent anything about your Jesus except his weakness and the small amount that he fasted and prayed.’ The Catholicos said, ‘By Allah! You spoiled your knowledge and weakened your affair. I imagined nothing less than that you were the most knowledgeable of the folk of Islam.’ Riḍā said, ‘How is that?’ The Catholicos said, ‘Because of what you said about Jesus being weak and having little fasting and prayer, while Jesus never broke his fast and slept through not a single night; he was constantly fasting and holding vigals.’ Riḍā said, ‘So, for whom did he fast and pray?’

Then the Catholicos was dumbfounded and stopped speaking. Riḍā said, ‘O Christian! I want to ask you about a problem.’ He said, ‘Ask. If I know anything about it, I will answer you.’ Riḍā said, ‘Why did you deny that Jesus raised the dead by the permission of Allah, the Mighty and Magnificent?’ The Catholicos said, ‘I denied it because whoever raises the dead and cures the blind and the leper is the lord deserving to be worshipped.’

---

(1) Some say that what is meant here is Akh in Basra.

قالَ الجاثَليقُ: 'لا أُنْكِرُ ما قَدْ بانَ لِي فِي الإنجيلِ، وانِّي لَمُقِرٌّ بِهِ.' قالَ الرضا عليه السلام: 'اشْهَدُوا عَلَي إقرارِهِ.' ثُمَّ قالَ: 'يا جاثَليقُ، سَلْ عمّا بَدا لَكَ.' قالَ الجاثَليقُ: 'أخْبِرْنِي, حَوارِيٌّ عِيسَي بْنِ مَرْيَمَ كَمْ كانَ عِدَّتُهُمْ؟ وَعَنْ عُلَماءِ الإنجيلِ، كَمْ كانُوا؟' قالَ الرضا عليه السلام: 'عَلَي الخَبِيرِ سَقَطْتَ. أمّا الحَوارِيُّونَ، فكانُوا اثْنَي عَشَرَ رَجُلاً، وكانَ أفْضَلَهُمْ وأعْلَمُهُمْ، ألُوقا. وأمّا عُلَماءُ النَصارَي، فكانُوا ثَلاثَةَ رِجالٍ: يُوحَنّا الأكْبَرُ بِأَجٍ، وَيُوحَنّا بِقِرْقِيسا، وَيُوحَنّا الديْلَمِيّ بِزجارٍ، وَعِنْدَهُ كانَ ذِكْرُ النَبِيِّ صلى الله عليه وآله وسلم وَذِكْرُ أهْلِ بَيْتِهِ وأُمَّتِهِ؛ وَهُوَ الذى بَشَّرَ أُمَّةَ عِيسَي وَبَنِي إسْرائِيلَ بِهِ.'

ثُمَّ قال لَهُ: 'يا نَصْرانِيٌّ، واللهِ إنّا لَنُؤْمِنُ بعِيسَي الذى آمَنَ بِمُحَمَّدٍ صلى الله عليه وآله وسلم، وَما نَنْقِمُ عَلَي عِيساكُمْ شَيْئًا إلّا ضَعْفَهُ وَقِلَّةَ صِيامِهِ وَصَلاتِهِ.' قالَ الجاثَليقُ: 'أفْسَدْتَ واللهِ عِلْمَكَ وَضَعَّفْتَ أمْرَكَ، وَما كُنْتُ ظَنَنْتُ إلّا أنَّكَ أعْلَمُ أهْلِ الإسْلامِ.' قالَ الرضا عليه السلام: 'وَكَيْفَ ذاكَ؟' قالَ الجاثَليقُ: 'مِنْ قَوْلِكَ: 'إنَّ عِيسَي كانَ ضَعِيفاً، قَلِيلَ الصيامِ، قَلِيلَ الصَلاةِ.' وَما أفْطَرَ عِيسَي يَوْماً قَطُّ، وَلا نامَ بِلَيْلٍ قَطُّ، وَما زالَ صائِمَ الدهْرِ، قائِمَ الليْلِ.' قالَ الرضا عليه السلام: 'فَلِمَنْ كانَ يَصُومُ وَيُصَلّي؟'

قالَ: 'فَخَرَسَ الجاثَليقُ وانْقَطَعَ.' قالَ الرضا عليه السلام: 'يا نَصْرانِيٌّ، أسألُكَ, عَنْ مَسْألَةٍ.' قالَ: 'سَلْ. فانْ كانَ عِنْدي عِلْمُها، أجَبْتُكَ.' قالَ الرضا عليه السلام: 'ما أنْكَرْتَ أنَّ عِيسَي كانَ يُحيِى المَوْتَي بِإذْنِ اللهِ، عَزَّ وَجَلَّ.' قالَ الجاثَليقُ: 'أنْكَرْتُ ذلِكَ، مِن قبلِ أنَّ مَنْ أحْيا المَوْتَي وأبْرءِ الأكْمَهَ والأبرصَ فَهُوَ رَبٌّ مُسْتَحَقٌّ لأنْ يُعْبَدَ.'

Riḍā said, 'Elisha also did things like Jesus did: walked on the water, raised the dead and cured the blind and the leper, but his community did not take him to be the Lord, and not one of them worshipped him instead of Allah, the Mighty and Magnificent. And the prophet Ezekiel also did things like what Jesus the son of Mary did, for he raised thirty-five thousand men after they had been dead for sixty years.' Then he turned to the Exilarch and said to him, 'O Exilarch! Do you find in the Torah what there is about the youths of the Children of Israel who were exiled by Nebuchadnezzar when they revolted in Jerusalem and then he sent them to Babylon? Then Allah, the Exalted, sent one to them and Allah revived them. This is in the Torah. None of you deny this unless he is a disbeliever.'

The Exilarch said, 'We heard this and know about it.' He said, 'You spoke the truth.'Then he said, 'O Jew! Consider the scripture of the Torah.' Then he recited some verses of the Torah. The Jew started at his recitation and was surprised. Then he faced the Christian and said, 'O Christian! Did this take place before Jesus or was Jesus before that?' He said, 'No. They were before him.'

Riḍā said, 'Once the Quraysh gathered before the Apostle of Allah and asked him to raise their dead for them. He had 'Alī ibn Abī Ṭālib accompany them, then he said to him, 'Go to al-Jubbānah and call that clan by their names, those about whom they had asked, with your loudest voice: O so-and-so! O so-and-so! And O so-and-so! Muḥammad the Apostle of Allah says to you, "Rise, by the permission of Allah, the Mighty and Magnificent."'Then they rose and wiped the dust from their heads.

The Quraysh received them and asked how they were. Then they told them that Muḥammad had been raised as a prophet. They said, 'We would love to see him and to believe in him.' He cured the blind, the leper and the insane. The beasts, birds, genies and devils spoke to him, but we did not take him as a Lord instead of Allah, the Mighty and Magnificent. We do not deny the virtues of any of them.

قالَ الرضا عليه السلام: 'فإنَّ اليَسعَ قَدْ صنَعَ مِثْلَ ما صنَعَ عِيسَي: مَشَي عَلَي الماءِ وأحْيا المَوْتَي وأبْرء الأكْمَهَ والأبرصَ؛ فلَمْ تَتَّخِذْهُ أمَّتُهُ ربّاً ولَمْ يَعْبُدْهُ أحَدٌ مِنْ دُونِ اللهِ، عَزَّ وَجَلَّ. ولَقَدْ صنَعَ حِزْقِيلُ النَبِيُّ مِثْلَ ما صنَعَ عِيسَي بْنُ مَرْيَمَ: فأحْيا خَمْسَةَ وَثَلاثِينَ الفَ رَجُلٍ مَنْ بَعْدِ مَوْتِهِمْ بِسِتِّينِ سَنَةٍ.' ثُمَّ التَفَتَ إلي رأسِ الجالُوتِ، فقالَ لَهُ: 'يا رأسَ الجالُوتِ، أتَجِدُ هَؤُلاءِ فِي شَبابِ بَنِي إسْرائِيلَ فِي التَوْراةِ؟ اخْتارَهُمْ بُخْتُ نَصَّرَ مِنْ سَبْيِ بَنِي إسْرائِيلَ، حِينَ غَزا بَيْتَ المَقْدِسَ، ثُمَّ انْصرَفَ بِهِمْ إلي بابِلَ؛ فأرْسَلَهُ اللهُ، تَعالَي عَزَّ وَجَلَّ، إلَيْهِمْ، فأحْياهُمُ اللهُ. هَذا فِي التَوْراةِ، لا يَدْفَعُهُ إلّا كافِرٌ مِنْكُمْ.'

قالَ رأسُ الجالُوتِ: 'قَدْ سَمِعْنا بِهِ وَعَرَفْناهُ.' قالَ: 'صَدَقْتَ.' ثُمَّ قالَ: 'يا يَهُودِيُّ، خُذْ عَلَي هَذا السِفْرِ مِنَ التَوْراةِ.' فتَلا عليه السلام عَلَيْنا مِنَ التَوْراةِ آياتٍ. فأقْبَلَ اليَهُودِيُّ يَتَرَجَّحُ لِقِراءَتِهِ وَيَتَعَجَّبُ. ثُمَّ أقْبَلَ عَلَي النَصْرانِيِّ، فَقالَ: 'يا نَصْرانِيُّ، أفَهَؤُلاءِ كانُوا قَبْلَ عِيسَي أمْ عِيسَي كانَ قَبْلَهُمْ؟' قالَ: 'بَلْ كانُوا قَبْلَهُ.'

قالَ الرضا عليه السلام: 'لَقَدْ اجْتَمَعَتْ قُرَيْشُ إلي رَسُولِ اللهِ صلى الله عليه وآله وسلم، فَسألُوهُ أنْ يُحيِي لَهُمْ مَوْتاهُمْ. فَوَجَّهَ مَعَهُمْ عَلِيَّ بْنَ أبِي طالِبٍ عليه السلام، فقالَ لَهُ: 'اذْهَبْ إلي الجَبانَةِ، فَنادِ بأسْماءِ هَؤُلاءِ الرهْطِ الذيْنَ يَسْألُونَ عَنْهُمْ بِأعْلَي صَوْتِكَ: 'يا فُلانٌ وَيا فُلانٌ وَيا فُلانٌ، يَقُولُ لَكُمْ مُحَمَّدٌ رَسُولُ اللهِ: 'قُومُوا بِإذْنِ اللهِ، عَزَّ وَجَلَّ.' فَقامُوا، يَنْفُضُونَ التَرابَ, عَنْ رُؤُوسِهِمْ.

فأقْبَلَتْ قُرَيْشٌ، تَسْألُهُمْ, عَنْ أمُورِهِمْ. ثُمَّ أخْبَرُوُهُمْ أنَّ مُحَمَّداً صلى الله عليه وآله وسلم قَدْ بَعَثَ نَبِيّاً، وَقالُوا: 'وَدَدْنا أنّا أدْرَكْناهُ، فَنُؤْمِنُ بِهِ. ولَقَدْ أبْرء الأكْمَهَ والأبرصَ والمَجانِينَ، وَكَلَّمَهُ البَهائِمُ والطَّيْرُ والجِنُّ والشَياطِينُ، ولَمْ نَتَّخِذْهُ رَبّاً مِنْ دُونِ اللهِ، عَزَّ وَجَلَّ، ولَمْ نُنْكِرْ

So, when you take Jesus as Lord, it becomes allowable to take Elijah and Ezekiel as Lords, because both of them did things like what Jesus did, such as raising the dead, etc... Verily, there was a tribe of the Children of Israel who fled their town because of plague and fear of death, and they were thousands, but in a single hour Allah made them die.[1] The people from that town set up an enclosure for them, and they [the dead] were always in it, until their bones rotted and decayed. Then one of the prophets of the Children of Israel passed them, and wondered about them and the great quantity of their rotted bones. So, Allah, the Mighty and Magnificent, revealed to him, 'Would you like Me to revive them for you and warn them?' He said, 'Yes, O my Lord!' Allah, the Mighty and Magnificent, revealed to him that he should call them. He said, 'O you rotted bones! Rise, by the permission of Allah, the Mighty and Magnificent!' Then they rose living, all of them. They wiped the dust from their heads.

Then, Abraham, the friend of the Merciful, when he took the birds and cut them up, then put a portion of them on each mountain, then called them and they went toward him with effort.[2] Then there was Moses of 'Imrān and seventy of his chosen companions who went with him toward a mountain, and said to him, 'You have seen Allah, glory be to Him, so show Him to us as you saw Him.'[3]

He said to them, 'Verily, I did not see Him.' They said, 'We will not believe in you until we see Allah openly. Then they were struck by lightning. They burned, to the last of them, and Moses remained alone. He said, 'O my Lord! Verily, I chose seventy men of the Children of Israel. I brought them here, but return alone. So, how is my people to affirm what I report to them? If you wanted, you could have destroyed them before and me. Would You destroy us because of what the fools among us did?' Then Allah revived them after their

---

(1) See Qur'ān, (2:243).

(2) See Qur'ān (2:260).

(3) See Qur'ān, (7:155).

لِأحَدٍ مِنْ هَؤُلاءِ فَضْلُهُمْ. فَمَتَي اتَّخَذْتُمْ عِيسَي رَبّاً، جازَ لَكُمْ أنْ تَتَّخِذُوا اليَسَعَ والحِزْقِيلَ؛ لِأنَّهُما قَدْ صَنَعا مِثْلَ ما صَنَعَ عِيسَي مِنْ إحْياءِ المَوْتَي وَغَيْرِهِ. وإنَّ قَوْماً مِنْ بَنِي إسْرائِيلَ هَرَبُوا مِنْ بِلادِهِمْ مِنَ الطّاعُونِ، وَهُمْ أُلوفٌ، حَذَرَ المَوْتِ، فَأماتَهُمُ اللهُ فِي ساعَةٍ واحِدَةٍ. فَعَمَدَ أهْلُ تِلْكَ القَرْيَةِ، فَحَظَرُوا عَلَيْهِمْ حَظِيرَةً، فَلَمْ يَزالُوا فِيها حَتَّي نَخِرَتْ عِظامُهُمْ وَصارُوا رَمِيماً. فَمَرَّ بِهِمْ نَبِيٌّ مِنْ أنْبِياءِ بَنِي إسْرائِيلَ فَتَعَجَّبَ مِنْهُمْ وَمِنْ كَثْرَةِ العِظامِ البالِيَةِ. فَأوْحَي اللهُ، عَزَّ وَجَلَّ، إلَيْهِ: 'أتُحِبُّ أنْ أُحْيِيَهُمْ لَكَ، فَتُنْذِرَهُمْ؟' قالَ: 'نَعَم، يا رَبِّ.' فَأوْحَي اللهُ، عَزَّ وَجَلَّ، إلَيْهِ أنْ نادِهِمْ. فَقالَ: 'أيَّتُها العِظامُ البالِيَةُ، قُومِي بِإذْنِ اللهِ، عَزَّ وَجَلَّ. فَقامُوا أحْياءً أجْمَعُونَ، يَنْفُضُونَ التُرابَ, عَنْ رُؤُوسِهِمْ.

ثُمَّ إبْراهِيمُ خَلِيلُ الرحْمَنِ، حِينَ أخَذَ الطَّيْرَ، فَقَطَّعَهُنَّ قِطَعاً، ثُمَّ وَضَعَ عَلَي كُلِّ جَبَلٍ مِنْهُنَّ جُزْءًا، ثُمَّ ناداهُنَّ، فَأقْبَلْنَ سَعْياً إلَيْهِ. ثُمَّ مُوسَي بْنُ عِمْرانَ وأصْحابُهُ السَبْعُونَ الذِينَ اخْتارَهُمْ، صارُوا مَعَهُ إلَي الجَبَلِ، فَقالُوا لَهُ: 'إنَّكَ قَدْ رَأيْتَ اللهَ سُبْحانَهُ، فَأرِناهُ كَما رَأيْتَهُ.' فَقالَ لَهُمْ: 'إنِّي لَمْ أرَهُ.'

فَقالُوا: ﴿لَنْ نُؤْمِنَ لَكَ حَتَّي نَرَي اللهَ جَهْرَةً.﴾ فَأخَذَتْهُمُ الصاعِقَةُ، فاحْتَرَقُوا, عَنْ آخِرِهِمْ، وَبَقِيَ مُوسَي وَحِيداً. فَقالَ: 'يا رَبِّ، إنِّي اخْتَرْتُ سَبْعِينَ رَجُلاً مِنْ بَنِي إسْرائِيلَ، فَجِئْتُ بِهِمْ، وأرْجِعُ وَحْدِي. فَكَيْفَ يُصَدِّقُنِي قَوْمِي بِما أُخْبِرُهُمْ بِهِ! فَلَوْ شِئْتَ، أهْلَكْتَهُمْ مِنْ قَبْلُ وإيّايَ. أتُهْلِكُنا بِما فَعَلَ السُّفَهاءُ مِنّا!' فَأحْياهُمُ اللهُ، عَزَّ وَجَلَّ، مِنْ بَعْدِ مَوْتِهِمْ. وَكُلُّ شَيْءٍ ذَكَرْتُهُ لَكَ مِنْ هَذا، لا تَقْدِرُ عَلَي دَفْعِهِ.

death. Everything I have mentioned to you, you cannot deny, for the Torah, the Gospel, the Psalms, the Qur'ān have spoken of it. If everyone who raises the dead, cures the blind, the leper and the insane is to be taken as a Lord, instead of Allah, then take all of these as Lords. What do say, O Christian?' The Catholicos said, 'It is as you say, and there is no god but Allah.'

Then he turned to the Exilarch and said, "O Jew! Listen to me, for I want to ask you about ten verses which descended to Moses ibn 'Imrān. Do you find this written in the Torah about Muḥammad and his community: 'When the last community comes following the rider of the camel, and they glorify the Lord very earnestly with a new glorification in new synagogues. Then let the Children of Israel seek refuge with them and their king so that their hearts may be assured. Verily, there are swords in their hands by which they obtain revenge against the disbelieving communities in the regions of the earth.'?" Do you find anything like this written in the Torah?"

The Exilarch said, "Yes. We find the like of this." Then he said to the Catholicos, "O Christian! How is your knowledge of the book Sha'yā?" He said, "I know it word for word." Then he said to him, "Are you familiar with these words from it: 'O people! Verily I saw a figure riding a donkey clothed in a garb of light, and I saw the rider of a camel whose radiance is like the radiance of the moon.'?" They both said, "Certainly Sha'yā said this."

Riḍā said, "O Christian! Do you know the saying of Jesus in the Gospel: 'Verily, I am going to your Lord and my Lord, and the paraclete (*bārqalīṭā*) is coming, he who will testify for me truly, even as I testify for him. And he will interpret all things for you, and he is the one who will reveal the sins of the nations, and he will break the pillar of disbelief.'?" The Catholicos said, "You have not mentioned anything from the Gospel that we do not confess." He said, "Do you find this set in the Gospel, O Catholicos?" He said, "Yes." Riḍā said, "O Catholicos! Will you not inform me about

لأنَّ التوْراةَ والإنجيلَ والزَّبُورَ والفُرْقانَ قَدْ نَطقَتْ بِهِ. فإنْ كانَ كُلٌّ مَنْ أحْيا المَوْتَي وأبْرء الأكْمَهَ والأبرصَ والمَجانِينَ يَتَّخِذُ رَبّاً مِنْ دُونِ اللهِ، فاتَّخَذَ هَؤُلاءِ كُلُّهُمْ أرْباباً. ما تَقُولُ يا نَصرانِيٌّ؟' قالَ الجاثَليقُ: 'القَوْلُ قَوْلُكَ، وَلا إلَهَ إلّا اللهُ.'

ثُمَّ التَفَتَ عليه السلام إلي راسِ الجالُوتِ، فقالَ: 'يا يَهُودِيُّ، أقبِلْ عَلَيَّ، أسْألُكَ بِالعَشْرِ الآياتِ الَّتِى أُنْزِلَتْ عَلي مُوسَي بْنِ عِمْرانَ. هَلْ تَجِدُ فِى التَوْراةِ مَكْتُوباً نَبأ مُحَمَّدٍ وأُمَّتِهِ؟ إذا جاءَتِ الأُمَّةُ الآخِيرَةُ، أتْباعُ راكِبِ البَعِيرِ، يُسَبِّحُونَ الربَّ جِداً، جِداً، تَسْبِيحاً جَدِيداً فِى الكَنائِسِ الجُدَدِ، فَلْيَفْزَعْ بَنُو إسْرائِيلَ إلَيهِمْ وإلَي مَلِكِهِمْ، لِتَطْمَئِنَّ قُلُوبُهُمْ. فإنَّ بِأيْدِيهِمْ سُيُوفاً يَنْتَقِمُونَ بِها مِنَ الأُمَمِ الكافِرَةِ فِى أقطارِ الأرضِ. أهَكَذا هُوَ فِى التَوْراةِ مَكْتُوبٌ؟'

قالَ راسُ الجالُوتِ: 'نَعَم، إنّا لَنَجِدُهُ كَذَلِكَ.' ثُمَّ قالَ لِلْجاثَليقَ: 'يا نَصْرانِيٌّ، كَيْفَ عِلْمُكَ بِكِتابِ شَعْيا؟' قالَ: 'أعْرِفُهُ، حَرْفاً حَرْفاً.' قالَ لَهُما: 'أتَعْرِفانِ هَذا مِنْ كَلامِهِ؟: 'يا قَوْمُ إنِّى رأيْتُ صُورَةَ راكِبِ الحِمارِ، لابِساً جَلابِيبَ النورِ؛ وَرأيْتُ راكِبَ البَعِيرِ، ضَوْؤُهُ مِثْلُ ضَوْءِ القَمَرِ.'' فقالا: 'قَدْ قالَ ذَلِكَ شَعْيا.'

قالَ الرضا عليه السلام: 'يا نَصْرانِيٌّ، هَلْ تَعْرِفُ فِى الإنجيلِ قَوْلَ عِيسَي: 'إنِّى ذاهِبٌ إلي رَبِّكُمْ وَرَبِّى. والبارْقِلِيطا جاءَ، هُوَ الذى يَشْهَدُ لِى بِالحَقِّ، كَما شَهِدْتُ لَهُ. وَهُوَ الذى يُفَسِّرُ لَكُمْ كُلَّ شَيْءٍ، وَهُوَ الذى يُبْدِئُ فَضائِحَ الأُمَمِ، وَهُوَ الذى يَكْسِرُ عَمُودَ الكُفْرِ.'' فقالَ الجاثَليقُ: 'ما ذَكَرْتَ شَيْئًا فِى الإنجيلِ، إلّا وَنَحْنُ مُقِرُّونَ بِهِ.' قالَ: 'أتَجِدُ هَذا فِى الإنجيلِ ثابِتاً، يا جاثَليقُ؟' قالَ: 'نَعَم.' قالَ الرضا عليه السلام: 'يا جاثَليقُ، ألا تُخْبِرُنِى عَنْ الإنجيلِ الأوَّلِ، حِينَ افْتَقَدْتُمُوهُ عِنْدَ مَنْ وَجَدْتُمُوهُ، وَمَنْ وَضَعَ لَكُمْ

the first Gospel,when it was lost, with whom was it found? And who compiled this Gospel for you?" He said, "We did not lose it, except for one day, and when we found it, it was like new, and it was brought out by John and Matthew." Then Riḍā said to him, "How little is your knowledge of the mystery[1] of the Gospel and its scholars! If it is as you imagine, then why are there differences about the Gospel? And verily, there are differences about the Gospel that is in your hands today. If it were the original testament, you would not differ about it. But I will offer you knowledge about it. Know that when the original Gospel was lost, the Christians gathered around their scholars and said to them, 'Jesus the son of Mary was killed, the Gospel has been lost, and you are scholars, so what is in your possession?' Luke and Mark said to them, 'Verily, the Gospel is within our breasts, and we will bring it out scripture by scripture for everyone, so do not worry about it. Do not empty the synagogues. So, we will soon recite for every one of you scripture by scripture until it is all collected.' Luke, Mark, John and Matthew sat down and compiled this Gospel for you after you had lost the original Gospel. These four persons were students of the first students. Did you know this?"

The Catholicos said, "I did not know this, but now I know it. The extent of your knowledge of the Gospel has become clear to me. I heard something to the truth of which my heart testifies, so I want to increase my understanding."

Riḍā said to him, "What do you think about that to which they all testify?" He said, "It is allowed; they are the scholars of the Gospel. Everything to which they testify is true." Riḍā said to Ma'mūn and to his folk and others with him present, "Bear witness to this." They said, "We bear witness." Then he said to the Catholicos, "By the truth of the son and his mother, do you know that Matthew says, 'Verily the Messiah is the son of David son of Abraham son of Isaac son of Jacob son of Yahūdā son of Ḥaḍrūn,' and that Mark, regarding

---

[1] In another text, instead of *mystery (sirr)* there is *traditions (sunan).*

هَذا الإنجيلَ؟' قالَ لَهُ: 'ما افْتَقَدْنا الإنجيلَ، إلّا يَوْماً واحِداً، حَتَّي وَجَدْناهُ غَضّاً طَرِيّاً. فأخْرَجَهُ إلَينا يُوحَنّا ومَتَّي.' فقالَ لَهُ الرضاعليه السلام: 'ما أقَلَّ مَعْرِفَتَكَ بِسِرِّ الإنجيلِ وَعُلَمائِهِ! فإنْ كانَ هَذا كَما تَزْعَمُ، فَلِمَ اخْتَلَفْتُمْ فِي الإنجيلِ؟ وانَّما وَقَعَ الاخْتِلافُ فِي هَذا الإنجيلِ الذى فِي أيْدِيكُمْ اليَوْمَ. فَلَوْ كانَ عَلَي العَهْدِ الأوَّلِ لَمْ تَخْتَلِفُوا فِيهِ. ولَكِنِّي مُفِيدُكَ عِلْمَ ذَلِكَ. اعْلَمْ أنَّهُ لَمّا افْتُقِدَ الإنجيلُ الأوَّلُ، اجْتَمِعَتِ النَصارَي إلَي عُلَمائِهِمْ، فقالُوا لَهُمْ: 'قُتِلَ عِيسَي بْنُ مَرْيَمَ وافْتَقَدْنا الإنجيلَ وأنتُم العُلَماءُ. فَما عِنْدَكُمْ؟' فَقالَ لَهُمْ ألُوقا وَمِرْقابُوسُ: 'إنَّ الإنجيلَ فِي صُدُورِنا وَنَحْنُ نُخْرِجُهُ إلَيْكُمْ سِفْراً سِفْراً فِي كُلِّ أحَدٍ. فَلا تَحْزَنُوا عَلَيْهِ وَلا تَخْلُوا الكَنائِسَ، فإنّا سَنَتْلُوهُ عَلَيْكُمْ فِي كُلِّ أحَدٍ سِفْراً سِفْراً، حَتَّي نَجْمَعَهُ كُلَّهُ.' فَقَعَدَ ألُوقا وَمِرْقابُوسُ وَيُوحَنّا وَمَتَّي، فَوَضَعُوا لَكُمْ هَذا الإنجيلَ بَعْدَ ما افْتَقَدْتُمُ الإنجيلَ الأوَّلَ. وانَّما كانَ هَؤُلاءُ الأربَعَةُ تَلامِيذَ التَلامِيذِ الأوَّلِينَ. أعَلِمْتَ ذَلِكَ؟'

قالَ الجاثَلِيقُ: 'أمّا هَذا، فَلَمْ أعْلَمْهُ، وَقَدْ عَلِمْتُهُ الآنَ وَقَدْ بانَ لِي مِنْ فَضْلِ عِلْمِكَ بِالإنجيلِ، وَسَمِعْتُ أشْياءَ مِمّا عَلِمْتَهُ، شَهِدَ قَلْبِي أنَّها حَقٌّ، فاسْتَزَدْتُ كَثِيراً مِنَ الفَهْمِ.'

فَقالَ لَهُ الرضاعليه السلام: 'فَكَيْفَ شَهادَةُ هَؤُلاءِ عِنْدَكَ؟' قالَ: 'جائِزَةٌ، هَؤُلاءِ عُلَماءُ الإنجيلِ، وَكُلُّ ما شَهِدُوا بِهِ فَهُوَ حَقٌّ.' فَقالَ الرضاعليه السلام لِلْمأمُونِ: 'وَمَنْ حَضَرَهُ مِنْ أهْلِ بَيْتِهِ وَمِنْ غَيْرِهِمْ، اشْهَدُوا عَلَيْهِ.' قالُوا: 'قَدْ شَهِدْنا.' ثُمَّ قالَ لِلْجاثَلِيقَ: 'بِحَقِّ الابْنِ وأُمِّهِ، هَلْ تَعْلَمُ أنَّ مَتَّي قالَ: 'إنَّ المَسِيحَ هُوَ ابن داوُدَ بْنِ إبْراهِيمَ بْنِ إسْحاقَ بْنِ يَعْقُوبَ بْنِ يَهُودا بْنِ حَضْرُونَ.' وَقالَ مِرْقابُوسُ فِي نِسْبَةِ عِيسَي بْنِ مَرْيَمَ: 'أنَّهُ كَلِمَةُ اللهِ،

the lineage of Jesus the son of Mary says, 'Verily, he is the word of Allah, He made it incarnate in the body of a man; so it became man,' and that Luke says, 'Verily, Jesus the son of Mary and his mother were two persons of flesh and blood, and the holy spirit entered into them,' and then you say that Jesus testifies about himself, 'In truth I say to you, O company of disciples, verily, no one ascends to heaven unless he descends from it, except the rider of the camel, the seal of the prophets. Verily, he ascends to heaven and then descends from it.'? What do you say about this saying?"

The Catholicos said, "That is the saying of Jesus; we do not deny it." Riḍā said, "So, what do you say about the testimony of Luke, Mark and Matthew about Jesus and what they have attributed to him?" The Catholicos said, "They lied about Jesus." Riḍā said, "O people! Did he not just say that they were pure and testify that they were scholars of the Gospel, and that their word is the truth?" The Catholicos said, "O scholar of the Muslims! I would like you to pardon me for this about them." Riḍā said, "We have done it. Ask, O Christian, whatever comes to your mind!"

The Catholicos said, "Let someone other than me ask you. Nay! By the truth of the Messiah! I never imagined that a scholar like you was among the Muslims." Then Riḍā turned to the Exilarch and said to him, "Will you question me or shall I question you?" He said, "I would question you, and I will not accept any argument from you unless it is from the Torah, the Gospel, the Psalms of David or from what is in the scriptures of Abraham and Moses."

Riḍā said, "Do not accept any argument from me unless it is spoken of in the Torah by the tongue of Moses ibn 'Imrān, the Gospel by the tongue of Jesus the son of Mary or the Psalms by the tongue of David." the Exilarch said, "How do you prove that Muḥammad was a prophet?" Riḍā said, "Moses ibn 'Imrān, Jesus the son of Mary and David the Steward of Allah, the mighty and magnificent, on earth bore witness to it." So he said to him, "Prove the saying of Moses ibn 'Imrān."

أحلّها فِي الجَسَدِ الآدمِيِّ فصارَتْ إنْساناً.' وَقالَ ألوقا: 'إنَّ عِيسَي بْنَ مَرْيَمَ وأمَّهُ، كانا إنْسانَيْنِ مِنْ لَحْمٍ وَدَمٍ؛ فَدَخَلَ فِيهِما رُوحُ القُدُسِ.' ثُمَّ إنَّكَ تَقُولُ مِنْ شَهادَةِ عِيسَي عَلَي نَفْسِهِ: 'حَقاً أقُولُ لَكُمْ، يا مَعْشَرَ الحَوارِيِّينَ، إنَّهُ لا يَصْعَدُ إلَي السَماءِ إلّا مَنْ نَزَلَ مِنْها، إلّا راكِبَ البَعِيرِ، خاتَمَ الأنبياءِ؛ فإنَّهُ يَصْعَدُ إلَي السَماءِ وَيَنْزِلُ.' فَما تَقُولُ فِي هَذا القَوْلِ؟' قالَ الجاثَلِيقُ: 'هَذا قَوْلُ عِيسَي؛ لا نُنْكِرُهُ.' قالَ الرضاعليه السلام: 'فَما تَقُولُ فِي شَهادَةِ ألُوقا وَمِرْقابُوسَ وَمَتَّي عَلَي عِيسَي وَما نَسَبُوهُ إلَيْهِ؟' قالَ الجاثَلِيقُ: 'كَذَّبُوا عَلَي عِيسَي.' قالَ الرضاعليه السلام: 'يا قَوْمُ، ألَيْسَ قَدْ زَكّاهُمْ، وَشَهِدَ أنَّهُمْ عُلَماءُ الإنجيلِ، وَقَوْلُهُمْ حَقٌّ؟' فَقالَ الجاثَلِيقُ: 'يا عالِمَ المُسْلِمِينَ، أُحِبُّ أنْ تُعْفِيَنِي مِنْ أمْرِ هَؤُلاءِ.' قالَ الرضاعليه السلام: 'فإنّا قَدْ فَعَلْنا؛ سَلْ يا نَصْرانِيُّ، عَمّا بَدا لَكَ.'

قالَ الجاثَلِيقُ: 'لِيَسْألْكَ غَيْرِي. فَلا وَحَقِّ المَسِيحِ، ما ظَنَنْتُ أنَّ فِي عُلَماءِ المُسْلِمِينَ مِثْلَكَ.' فالتَفَتَ الرضاعليه السلام إلَي رأسِ الجالُوتِ، فَقالَ لَهُ: 'تَسألُنِي أوْ أسْألُكَ؟' فَقالَ: 'بَلْ أسْألُكَ، وَلَسْتُ أقْبَلُ مِنْكَ حُجَّةً، إلّا مِنَ التَوْراةِ أوْ مِنَ الإنجيلِ أوْ مِنْ زَبُورِ داوُدَ أوْ بِما فِي صُحُفِ إبْراهِيمَ وَمُوسَي.'

قالَ الرضاعليه السلام: 'لا تَقْبَلْ مِنِّي حُجَّةً، إلّا بِما تَنْطِقُ بِهِ التَوْراةُ عَلَي لِسانِ مُوسَي بْنِ عِمْرانَ والإنجيلُ عَلَي لِسانِ عِيسَي بْنِ مَرْيَمَ والزَّبُورُ عَلَي لِسانِ داوُدَ.' فَقالَ رأسُ الجالُوتِ: 'مِنْ أيْنَ تَثْبُتُ نُبُوَّةَ مُحَمَّدٍ؟' قالَ الرضاعليه السلام: 'شَهِدَ بِنُبُوَّتِهِ مُوسَي بْنُ عِمْرانَ وَعِيسَي بْنُ مَرْيَمَ وَداوُدُ، خَلِيفَةُ اللهِ، عَزَّ وَجَلَّ، فِي الأرضِ.' فَقالَ لَهُ: 'ثَبِّتْ قَوْلَ مُوسَي بْنَ عِمْرانَ.'

Riḍā said, "Do you know, O Jew, that Moses ibn 'Imrān left a will for the Children of Israel in which he said to them, 'Verily, there will soon come to you a prophet from among your brethren, so affirm him and listen to him.' Do you know any brethren of the Children of Israel other than the offspring of Ismā'īl, if you know of the kinship of Israel and Ismā'īl, and the relation between them from Abraham?" The Exilarch said, "That is the saying of Moses; we do not deny it." Riḍā said to him, "Has there come to you from the brethren of the Children of Israel any prophet other than Muḥammad?" He said, "No." Riḍā said, "Is this not correct according to you?"

He said, "Yes, but I would like you to show the correctness of this matter from the Torah." Riḍā said to him, "Do you deny that the Torah says to you, 'Light came from Mount Sinai, and that it radiates to us from Mount Sā'ir, and it has appeared to us from Mount Fārān.'?" The Exilarch said, "I know these words, but I do not know the interpretation of them."

Riḍā said, "I will inform you of it. As for its saying, 'Light came from Mount Sinai,' that is the revelation of Allah, the blessed and exalted, which He sent down to Moses at Mount Sinai; as for His saying, 'and that it radiates to us from Mount Sā'ir,' it is the mountain at which Allah, the mighty and magnificent, sent revelation to Jesus the son of Mary when he was on it; and as for His saying, 'and it has appeared to us from Mount Fārān,' this is one of the mountains of Mecca which is one day's journey from Mecca. The prophet Sha'yā says in the Torah, what your and your companions also say, 'I saw two riders for whom the earth became illuminated, one of them on a donkey and the other on a camel.' Who is the rider on the donkey and who is the rider of the camel?" The Exilarch said, "I do not know those two, so inform me of them." He said, "The rider of the donkey is Jesus, and the rider of the camel is Muḥammad. Do you deny that this is from the Torah?" He said, "No, I do not deny it."

قالَ الرضا عليه السلام: 'هَلْ تَعْلَمُ يا يَهُودِيُّ، أنَّ مُوسَي بْنَ عِمْرانَ أوْصَي بَنِى إسْرائِيلَ، فَقالَ لَهُمْ: 'إنَّهُ سَيأتِيكُم نَبِىٌّ مِنْ إخْوانِكُمْ؛ فَبِهِ فَصَدِّقُوا وَمِنْهُ فاسْمَعُوا.' فَهَلْ تَعْلَمُ أنَّ لِبَنِى إسْرائِيلَ إخْوَةٌ غَيْرُ وُلْدِ إسْماعِيلَ، إنْ كُنْتَ تَعْرِفُ قِرابَةَ إسْرائِيلَ مِنْ إسْماعِيلَ والنَسَبَ الذى بَيْنَهُما مِنْ قِبَلِ إبْراهِيمَ؟' فَقالَ رأسُ الجالُوتُ: 'هَذا قَوْلُ مُوسَي، لا نَدْفَعُهُ.'

فَقالَ لَهُ الرضا عليه السلام: 'هَلْ جاءَكُمْ مِنْ إخْوَةِ بَنِى إسْرائِيلَ نَبِىٌّ غَيْرُ مُحَمَّدٍ؟' قالَ: 'لا.' قالَ الرضا عليه السلام: 'أفَلَيْسَ قَدْ صَحَّ هَذا عِنْدَكُمْ؟' قالَ: 'نَعَم، ولَكِنِّى أُحِبُّ أنْ تُصَحِّحَهُ لِى مِنَ التَوْراةِ.' فَقالَ لَهُ الرضا عليه السلام: 'هَلْ تُنْكِرُ أنَّ التَوْراةَ تَقُولُ لَكُمْ: 'قَدْ جاءَ النورُ مِنْ جَبَلِ طُورِ سَيْناءَ وأضاءَ لَنا مِنْ جَبَلِ ساعِيرَ واسْتَعْلَنَ عَلينا مِنْ جَبَلِ فارانِ.'' قالَ رأسُ الجالُوتِ: 'أعْرِفُ هَذِهِ الكَلِماتِ، وَما أعْرِفُ تَفْسِيرَها.'

قالَ الرضا عليه السلام: 'أنا أُخْبِرُكَ بِهِ. أمّا قَوْلُهُ: 'جاءَ النورُ مِنْ قِبَلِ طُورِ سَيْناءِ.' فَذَلِكَ وَحْيُ اللهِ تَبارَكَ وَتَعالَي الذى أنْزَلَهُ عَلَي مُوسَي، عَلَي جَبَلِ طُورِ سَيْناءَ؛ وأمّا قَوْلُهُ: 'وأضاءَ الناسَ مِنْ جَبَلِ ساعِيرَ.' فَهُوَ الجَبَلُ الذى أوْحَي اللهُ، عَزَّ وَجَلَّ، إلَي عِيسَي بْنِ مَرْيَمَ، وَهُوَ عَلَيْهِ؛ وأمّا قَوْلُهُ: 'واسْتَعْلَنَ عَلَيْنا مِنْ جَبَلِ فارانَ.' فَذَلِكَ جَبَلٌ مِنْ جِبالِ مَكَّةَ، بَيْنَهُ وَبَيْنَها يَوْمٌ. وَقالَ شَعْيا النَبيُّ، فِى ما تَقُولُ أنتَ وأصحابُكَ فِى التَوْراةِ: 'رأيْتُ راكِبَينِ أضاءَ لَهُما الأرضُ: أحَدُهُما عَلَي حِمارٍ، والآخَرُ عَلَي جَمَلٍ. فَمَنْ راكِبُ الحِمارِ وَمَنْ راكِبُ الجَمَلِ؟' قالَ رأسُ الجالُوتِ: 'لا أعْرِفُهُما. فَخَبِّرْنِى بِهِما.' قالَ(ع): 'أمّا راكِبُ الحِمارِ، فَعِيسَي، وأمّا راكِبُ الجَمَلِ، فَمُحَمَّدٌ. أتُنْكِرُ هَذا مِنَ التَوْراةِ؟' قالَ: 'لا، ما أُنْكِرُهُ.'

Then Riḍā said, "Do you know the prophet Habakkuk?" He said, "Yes. I know of him." He said, "He said, and this is narrated in your book, 'Allah brought down speech on Mount Fārān, and the heavens were filled with the glorification of Muḥammad and his community. His horse carries him over water as it carries him over land. He will bring a new book to us after the ruin of the holy house [the temple in Jerusalem].' What is meant by this book is the Qur'ān. Do you know this and believe in it?" The Exilarch said, "Habakkuk the prophet has said this and we do not deny what he said." Riḍā said, "In his Psalms, David said, and you recite it, "O God! Send one to revive the tradition after it has languished.' Do you know a prophet other than Muḥammad who has revived the tradition after it languished?"

The Exilarch said, "This is the saying of David. We know it and do not deny it, however, what is meant by this is Jesus, and his day was the period of languishing." Riḍā said to him, "You are ignorant. Verily, Jesus did not oppose the tradition, but he was in agreement with the tradition of the Torah, until Allah raised him to Himself. It is written in the Gospel, 'Verily, the son of the good woman will leave, and the paraclete will come after him, and he will lighten the burden, and he will interpret everything for you, and he will bear witness for me as I bear witness for him. I have brought parables for you, and he will bring for you exegesis.' Do you believe in this from the Gospel?" He said, "Yes. I do not deny it."

Riḍā said to him, "O Exilarch (*Ra's al-Jālūt*)! I ask you about your prophet Moses ibn 'Imrān." He said, "Ask!" He said, "What proof do you have that Moses was a prophet?" The Jew said, "Verily, he brought that which had not been brought by any prophet before him." He said to him, "Like what?" He said, "Like the splitting of the sea, changing his staff into [a serpent] running, hitting the rock so that fountains sprung from the cleft, bringing out his hand white for the observers, and signs for the like of which people have no power."

ثُمَّ قالَ الرضا عليه السلام: 'هَلْ تَعْرِفُ حَيْقُوقَ النَبِيِّ؟' قالَ: 'نَعَم، إنِّي بِهِ لَعارِفٌ.' قالَ عليه السلام: 'فإنَّهُ قالَ، وكِتابُكُمْ يَنْطِقُ بِهِ: 'جاءَ اللهُ بِالبَيانِ مِنْ جَبَلِ فارانٍ، وامْتَلأتِ السَماواتُ مِنْ تَسْبِيحِ أحْمَدَ وامَّتِهِ. يُحْمَلُ خَيْلُهُ فِي البَحْرِ كَما يُحْمَلُ فِي البَرِّ. يأتِينا بِكِتابٍ جَدِيدٍ بَعْدَ خَرابِ بَيْتِ المَقْدِسِ. يَعْنِي بِالكِتابِ، القرآن. أتَعْرِفُ هَذا وتُؤمِنُ بِهِ؟' قالَ رأسُ الجالُوتِ: 'قَدْ قالَ ذَلِكَ حِيْقُوقُ النَبِيِّ، وَلا نُنْكِرُ قَوْلَهُ.' قالَ الرضا عليه السلام: 'فَقَدْ قالَ داوُد فِي زَبُورِهِ، وأنْتَ تَقْرَؤُهُ: 'اللهُمَّ ابْعَثْ مُقِيمَ السُنَّةِ بَعْدَ الفَتْرَةِ.' فَهَلْ تَعرِفُ نَبِيّاً أقامَ السُنَّةَ بَعْدَ الفَتْرَةِ غَيْرَ مُحَمَّدٍ؟'

قالَ رأسُ الجالُوتِ: 'هَذا قَوْلُ داوُدَ، نَعْرِفُهُ وَلا نُنْكِرُهُ، وَلَكِنْ عَنَي بِذَلِكَ عِيسَي، وأيّامُهُ هِيَ الفَتْرَةُ.' قالَ لَهُ الرضا عليه السلام: 'جَهِلْتَ. إنَّ عِيسَي لَمْ يُخالِفْ السُنَّةَ وكانَ مُوافِقاً لِسُنَّةِ التَوْراةِ، حَتَّي رَفَعَهُ اللهُ إلَيهِ. وَفِي الإنجيلِ مَكْتُوبٌ: 'إنَّ ابن البرَّةِ ذاهِبٌ، والبارْقِلِيطا جاءَ مِنْ بَعْدِهِ، وَهُوَ يُخَفِّفُ الآصارَ وَيُفَسِّرُ لَكُمْ كُلَّ شَيْء وَيَشْهَدُ لِي كَما شَهِدَتُ لَهُ. أنا جِئْتُكُمْ بِالأمْثالِ وَهُوَ يأتِيكُمْ بِالتأويلِ. أتُؤْمِنُ بِهَذا فِي الإنجيلِ؟' قالَ: 'نَعَم، لا أنْكِرُهُ.'

فقالَ لَهُ الرضا عليه السلام: 'يا رأسَ الجالُوتِ، أسألُكَ عَنْ نَبِيِّكَ مُوسَي بْنِ عِمْرانَ.' فَقالَ: 'سَلْ.' قالَ عليه السلام: 'ما الحُجَّةُ عَلَي أنَّ مُوسَي ثَبَتَتْ نُبُوَّتُهُ؟' قالَ اليَهُودِيُّ: 'إنَّهُ جاءَ بِما لَمْ يَجِئْ بِهِ أحَدٌ مِنَ الأنبياءِ قَبْلَهُ.' قالَ لَهُ: 'مِثْلُ ما ذا؟' قالَ: 'مِثْلُ فَلْقِ البَحْرِ، وَقَلْبِهِ العَصا حَيَّةً تَسْعَي، وَضَرْبِهِ الحَجَرَ فانْفَجَرَتْ مِنْهُ العُيُونُ، وإخْراجِهِ يَدَهُ بَيْضاءَ لِلنّاظِرِينَ، وَعَلاماتٍ لا يَقْدِرُ الخَلْقُ عَلَي مِثْلِها.'

Riḍā said to him, “You spoke truly that the proof of his being a prophet was that he brought that for the like of which people have no power. Is it not the case that it becomes obligatory for you to affirm whoever claims to be a prophet then brings the like of that for which people have no power?” He said, “No. Because there was no one like Moses in station before his Lord, and nearness to Him; and it is not obligatory for us to admit the prophethood of one who claims it unless he bring signs like what he brought.”

Riḍā said, “So, how do you admit that there were prophets prior to Moses, while they did not split the sea, and did not cleft the rock so that twelve fountains sprung from it, and they did not bring out their hands as Moses brought his hand out white, and they did not change staves into running serpants.” The Jew said to him, “I will indeed inform you that when one brings a sign the like of which people have no power to bring, even if they are not what Moses brought or are other than what he brought, it becomes obligatory to affirm him.”

Riḍā said, “O Exilarch (*Ra's al-Jālūt*)! So, what prevents you from admitting [to the prophethood of] Jesus the son of Mary, while he revived the dead, cured the blind and the leper, and created of clay what had the form of birds, then blew into them and they became birds by the permission of Allah?” The Exilarch said, “It is said that he did this, but we did not witness it.”

Riḍā said, “Tell me, did you witness the signs that Moses brought? Is it not the case that narrations from the trusted companions of Moses conveyed that he did these things?” He said, “Yes.” He said, “Then likewise, successively confirmed reports (*akhbār mutawāttir*) have come to you about what Jesus the son of Mary did. So how is it that you affirm Moses but you do not affirm Jesus?” He gave no answer.

قالَ لَهُ الرضا عليه السلام: 'صَدَقتَ فِي أنَّهُ كانَتْ حُجَّةً عَلي نُبُوَّتِهِ، إنَّهُ جاءَ بِما لا يَقدِرُ الخَلقُ عَلي مِثلِهِ. أفَلَيسَ كُلُّ مَنْ ادَّعَي أنَّهُ نَبيٌّ ثُمَّ جاءَ بِما لا يَقدِرُ الخَلقُ عَلي مِثلِهِ، وَجَبَ عَلَيْكُمْ تَصْدِيقُهُ؟' قالَ: 'لا. لأنَّ مُوسَي لَمْ يَكُنْ لَهُ نَظِيرٌ، لِمَكانِهِ مِنْ رَبِّهِ وَقُرْبِهِ مِنْهُ. وَلا يَجِبُ عَلَيْنا الإقرارُ بِنُبُوَّةِ مَنْ ادَّعاها، حَتَّي يَأتِيَ مِنَ الأعلامِ بِمِثلِ ما جاءَ بِهِ.'

قالَ الرضا عليه السلام: 'فَكَيْفَ أقرَرتُمْ بِالأنبياءِ الذينَ كانُوا قبْلَ مُوسَي، وَلَمْ يَفْلِقُوا البَحْرَ، وَلَمْ يَفْجُروا مِنَ الحَجَرِ اثنَتَيْ عَشْرَةَ عَيْناً، وَلَمْ يُخْرِجُوا بِأيْدِيهِمْ مِثْلَ إخْراجِ مُوسَي يَدَهُ بَيْضاءَ، وَلَمْ يَقْلِبُوا العَصا حَيَّةً تَسْعَي؟' قالَ لَهُ اليَهُودِيُّ: 'قَدْ خَبَرْتُكَ أنَّهُ مَتَي ما جاؤوا عَلي نُبُوَّتِهِمْ مِنَ الآياتِ بِما لا يَقدِرُ الخَلقُ عَلي مِثلِهِ، وَلَوْ جاءُوا بِما لَمْ يَجِئْ بِهِ مُوسَي، أوْ كانَ عَلي غَيْرِ ما جاءَ بِهِ مُوسَي، وَجَبَ تَصْدِيقُهُمْ.'

قالَ: 'قالَ الرضا عليه السلام: 'يا رأسَ الجالُوتِ، فَما يَمْنَعُكَ مِنَ الاقرارِ بِعِيسَي بْنِ مَرْيَمَ وَقَدْ كانَ يُحيي المَوْتَي وَيُبْرِئُ الأكْمَهَ والأبرَصَ وَيَخْلُقُ مِنَ الطِّينِ كَهَيْئَةِ الطَّيْرِ ثُمَّ يَنْفُخُ فِيهِ فَيَكُونُ طَيْراً بِإذْنِ اللهِ؟' قالَ رأسُ الجالُوتِ: 'يُقالُ: 'إنَّهُ فَعَلَ ذَلِكَ.' وَلَمْ نَشْهَدْهُ.''

قالَ الرضا عليه السلام: 'أرأيْتَ ما جاءَ بِهِ مُوسَي مِنَ الآياتِ شاهَدْتَهُ، ألَيْسَ إنَّما جاءَتْ الأخْبارُ مِنَ ثِقاتِ أصْحابِ مُوسَي، أنَّهُ فَعَلَ ذَلِكَ؟' قالَ: 'بَلَي.'

قالَ: 'فَكَذَلِكَ، أيْضاً، أتَتْكُمْ الأخْبارُ المُتَواتِرَةُ بِما فَعَلَ عِيسَي بْنُ مَرْيَمَ. فَكَيْفَ صَدَّقْتُمْ بِمُوسَي وَلَمْ تُصَدِّقُوا بِعِيسَي؟' فَلَمْ يَحِرْ جَواباً.

Riḍā said, "And likewise the affair of Muḥammad and what he brought, and the affair of every prophet commissioned by Allah. Among the signs Muḥammad had was that he was an orphan, poor, a shepherd and a wage laborer who did not study any book and who was not taught by any teacher, yet brought the Qur'ān in which there are the stories of the prophets and reports of them letter by letter, and reports of those who have gone before, and the peoples who will remain until the day of resurrection. He reported about their secrets and what they had done in their houses, and he brought unaccountably many signs." The Exilarch said, "According to us, neither the reports about Jesus nor the reports about Muḥammad are correct, and it is not permitted for us to affirm these two by what is incorrect."

Riḍā said, "So, the witnesses who testified for Jesus and Muḥammad, may the peace and blessings of Allah be with them both, are not valid?" He gave no answer.

(*Biḥār*, 10, 299-310, 1)

1.6. HIS SUCCESSOR

1.6.1. One of the companians of the Commander of the Faithful said that some of his companians said, "O Commander of the Faithful! The executor of Moses showed the signs to his companians after Moses and the executor of Jesus showed the signs to his companians after Jesus. So, will you not show us?" He said, 'You do not remain [in your belief.]' They insisted on it and said, 'O Commander of the Faithful!' Then he took the hands of nine persons among them and took them out toward the houses of *Hajars* until he overlooked a salt marsh. Then he spoke slowly and said to his hand, 'Disclose what you have covered.' Then every thing in the Heaven that has been described by Allah, was before their eyes with its gladness and beauty. Then four of them came back and said, 'Magic!

قالَ الرضا عليه السلام: 'وَكَذلِكَ أمرُ مُحمَّدٍ صلى الله عليه وآله وسلم وَما جاءَ بِهِ، وأمرُ كُلِّ نَبيٍّ بَعَثَهُ اللهُ. وَمِنْ آياتِهِ أنَّهُ كانَ يَتيماً، فقيراً، راعِياً، أجيراً، لَمْ يَتَعلَّمْ كِتاباً وَلَمْ يَختَلِفْ إلي مُعلِّمٍ؛ ثُمَّ جاءَ بِالقرآن الذى فِيهِ قِصَصُ الأنبياءِ وأخبارُهُمْ، حَرْفاً حَرْفاً؛ وأخْبارُ مَنْ مَضَي وَمَنْ بَقِيَ إلي يَوْمِ القِيامَةِ. ثُمَّ كانَ يُخْبِرُهُمْ بِأسْرارِهِمْ وَما يَعْمَلُونَ فِي بُيُوتِهِمْ وَجاءَ بِآياتٍ كَثِيرَةٍ لا تُحْصَي.'' قالَ: 'قالَ رأسُ الجالُوتِ: 'لَمْ يَصِحَّ عِنْدَنا خَبَرُ عِيسَي وَلا خَبَرُ مُحَمَّدٍ، وَلا يَجُوزُ لَنا أنْ نُقِرَّ لَهُما بِما لَمْ يَصِحَّ.''

قالَ الرضا عليه السلام: 'فالشاهِدُ الذى شَهِدَ لِعِيسَي وَلِمُحَمَّدٍ, صَلَّي اللهُ عَلَيْهِما، شاهِدُ زُورٍ.' فَلَمْ يَحِرْ جَواباً.''»

(بحار الأنوار، ١٠، ٢٩٩-٣١٠، ١)

١-٦- وَصِيُّه

١-٦-١- الحُسَيْنُ بْنُ الحَسَنِ بْنِ أبانٍ, قالَ: «حَدَّثَنِي الحُسَيْنُ بْنُ سَعِيدٍ وَكَتَبَهُ لِي بِخَطِّهِ بِحَضْرَةِ أبِي الحَسَنِ بْنِ أبانٍ, قالَ: 'حَدَّثَنِي مُحَمَّدٌ بْنُ سِنانٍ, عَنْ حَمّادٍ البَطْحِيِّ, عَنْ زَمِيلِهِ وَكانَ مِنْ أصْحابِ أمِيرِ المُؤْمِنِينَ عليه السلام قالَ: 'إنَّ نَفَراً مِنْ أصْحابِهِ قالُوا: 'يا أمِيرَ المُؤْمِنِينَ، إنَّ وَصِيَّ مُوسَي كانَ يُرِيهِمُ العَلاماتِ بَعْدَ مُوسَي، وإنَّ وَصِيَّ عِيسَي كانَ يُرِيهِمُ العَلاماتِ بَعْدَ عِيسَي، فَلَوْ أرَيْتَنا.' فَقالَ: 'لا تَقِرُّونَ.' فَألَحُّوا عَلَيْهِ وَقالُوا: 'يا أمِيرَ المُؤْمِنِينَ!' فأخَذَ بِيَدِ تِسْعَةٍ مِنْهُمْ وَخَرَجَ بِهِمْ قِبَلَ أبْياتِ الهَجَرِيِّينَ، حَتَّي أشْرَفَ عَلَي السَبْخَةِ، فَتَكَلَّمَ بِكَلامٍ خَفِيٍّ، ثُمَّ قالَ بِيَدِهِ: 'اكْشِفِي غِطاءَكِ.' فإذا كُلُّ ما وَصَفَ اللهُ فِي الجَنَّةِ نَصْبُ أعْيُنِهِمْ مَعَ

Magic!' One of them remained [in his belief], as Allah wills, and sat somewhere (in an assembly) and reported some of it. So the people gathered around him and brought him to the Commander of the Faithful."

(*Al-Ikhtiṣāṣ*, 326)

1.6.2. Al-Mufaḍḍal ibn 'Umar said, "Abū 'Abd Allah said to me, 'On the Resurrection Day four days hurry to Allah, the Mighty and Magnificent, like the bride who hurries to her quarters of the tent, *al-Fiṭr, al-'Aḍḥā, al-Jum'ah* (Friday) *and Ghadīr Khum. Ghadīr Khum* is between *al-Fiṭr* and *al-'Aḍḥā.* Friday is like the moon among the stars. Allah puts the cherubim, the prophets of Allah who are apostles, the chosen executors and the friends of Allah on *Ghadīr Khum.* On that day, the master of the angels is Gabriel, the master of the prophets is Muḥammad, the master of the executors is the Commander of the Faithful and the masters of the friends of Allah are Salmān, Abūdhar, al-Miqdād and 'Ammār. These days bring them into heaven just as the shepherd brings his sheep to the water and grassland.' I said to him, 'O my master! Do you order me to fast on it?' He answered, 'Yes, By Allah. Yes, By Allah. Yes, By Allah. Verily it is the day on which Allah accepted the repentance of Adam and he abstained on it to thank Allah. It is the day on which Allah, the Exalted, saved Abraham from the fire and he abstained on it to thank Allah, the Exalted. It is the day on which Moses established Hārūn like a flag, and he abstained on it to thank Allah, the Exalted. It is the day on which Jesus revealed his executor Simon al-Ṣafā and he abstained on it to thank Allah, the Mighty and Magnificent.

It is the day on which the Apostle of Allah established 'Alī like a flag for the people and revealed his favor and his being the executor, and he abstained on it to thank Allah, the Blessed and Exalted. It is the day of fasting, vigil, feeding [the poor], and visiting with the brothers, and in it there are the satisfaction of al-Raḥmān and the dislike of Satan.'"

(*Al-'Iqbāl*, 466)

رَوْحِها وَزَهْرَتِها. فَرَجَعَ مِنْهُمْ أرْبَعَةٌ، يَقُولُونَ: 'سِحْراً سِحْراً،' وَثَبَتَ رَجُلٌ مِنْهُمْ بِذلِكَ، ما شاءَ اللهُ. ثُمَّ جَلَسَ مَجْلِساً فَنَقَلَ مِنْهُ شَيْئًا مِنَ الكَلامِ فِى ذلِكَ، فَتَعَلَّقُوا بِهِ، فَجاؤوا بِهِ إلَي أميرِ المُؤْمِنِينَ.'»

(الاختصاص، ٣٢٦)

١-٦-٢- رَوَيَ مُحَمَّدُ بْنُ عَلِيٍّ بْنِ مُحَمَّدٍ الطَّرازِىّ فِى كِتابِهِ بِإسْنادِهِ المُتَّصِلِ إلَي المُفَضَّلِ بْنِ عُمَرَ، قالَ: «قالَ لِى أبُو عَبْدِ اللهِ عليه السلام: 'إذا كانَ يَوْمَ القِيامَةِ زُفَّتْ أرْبَعَةُ أيّامٍ إلَي اللهِ، عَزَّ وَجَلَّ، كَما تُزَفُّ العَرُوسُ إلَي خِدْرِها: يَوْمُ الفِطْرِ وَيَوْمُ الأضْحَي وَيَوْمُ الجُمُعَةِ وَيَوْمُ غَدِيرِ خُمٍّ. وَيَوْمُ غَدِيرِ خُمٍّ بَيْنَ الفِطْرِ والأضْحَي؛ وَيَوْمُ الجُمُعَةِ كالقَمَرِ بَيْنَ الكَواكِبِ. وإنَّ اللهَ لَيُوَكِّلُ بِغَدِيرِ خُمٍّ مَلائِكَتَهُ المُقَرَّبِينَ، وَسَيِّدُهُمْ يَوْمَئِذٍ جَبْرَئِيلُ عليه السلام؛ وأنْبِياءُ اللهِ المُرْسَلِينَ، وَسَيِّدُهُمْ يَوْمَئِذٍ مُحَمَّدٌ صلى الله عليه وآله وسلم؛ وأوْصِياءُ اللهِ المُنْتَجَبِينَ، وَسَيِّدُهُمْ يَوْمَئِذٍ أمِيرُ المُؤْمِنِينَ؛ وأوْلِياءُ اللهِ، وَساداتُهُمْ يَوْمَئِذٍ سَلْمانُ وابُوذَرُ والمِقْدادُ وَعَمّارُ، حَتَّي يُورِدَهُ الجِنانَ كَما يُورِدُ الراعِى بِغَنَمِهِ الماءَ والكِلاءَ.'» قالَ المُفَضَّلُ: «سَيِّدِى تامُرُنِى بِصِيامِهِ؟» قالَ لِى: «إىْ واللهِ، إىْ واللهِ، إىْ واللهِ. إنَّهُ اليَوْمُ الذى تابَ اللهُ فِيهِ عَلَي آدَمَ عليه السلام، فَصامَهُ [فَصام] شُكْراً لِلهِ؛ وإنَّهُ اليَوْمُ الذى نَجي اللهُ تَعالَي فِيهِ إبْراهِيمَ عليه السلام مِنَ النارِ، فَصامَ شُكْراً لِلهِ، تَعالَي، عَلَي ذلِكَ اليَوْمِ؛ وإنَّهُ اليَوْمُ الذى أقامَ مُوسَي هارُونَ عليه السلام عَلَماً، فَصامَ شُكْراً لِلهِ، تعالَي، ذلِكَ اليَوْمَ؛ وإنَّهُ اليَوْمُ الذى أظْهَرَ عِيسَي عليه السلام وَصِيَّهُ شَمْعُونَ الصَفا، فَصامَ شُكْراً لِلهِ، عَزَّ وَجَلَّ [عَلَي] ذلِكَ اليَوْمِ؛ وإنَّهُ اليَوْمُ الذى أقامَ رَسُولُ اللهِ صلى الله عليه وآله وسلم عَلِيّاً لِلنّاسِ عَلَماً، وأبانَ فِيهِ فَضْلَهُ وَوَصِيَّهُ، فَصامَ شُكْراً لِلهِ، تَبارَكَ وَتَعالَي، ذلِكَ اليَوْمَ؛ وانَّهُ لَيَوْمُ صِيامٍ وَقِيامٍ وإطْعامٍ وَصِلَةِ الإخْوانِ، وَفِيهِ مَرْضاتُ الرحْمنِ وَمَرْغَمَةُ الشَيْطانِ.'»

(الإقبال، ٤٦٦)

1.6.3. Ibn 'Abbās said, "When Allah, the Blessed and Exalted, sent the verse, '﴿*...And fullfill My covenant, so I will fullfill your covenant.*﴾' (2, 40) the Apostle of Allah said, 'By Allah, Adam made a covenant with his people concerning his son, Seth and went out from this world, but his people did not fulfill it. Noaḥ made a covenant with his people concerning his executor, Sām and went out from this world, but his people did not fulfill it. Abraham made a covenant with his people concerning his executor, Ismā'īl and went out from this world, but his people did not fulfill it.

Moses made a covenant with his people concerning his executor, Yūsha' ibn Nūn and went out from this world, but his people did not fulfill it. Jesus the son of Mary made a covenant with his people concerning his executor Simon ibn Ḥamūn al-Ṣafā and was raised to heaven, but his people did not fulfill it.

Also I will separate from you soon and will leave you. I have made a covenant with my community concerning 'Alī ibn Abū Ṭālib, but they will continue with the rites of the previous communities in opposing my executor and disobeying him....'"

(*Ma'ānī al-Akhbār*, 373)

1.6.4. It is reported that Qays, the servant of 'Alī ibn Abī Ṭālib said, "Once when 'Alī, the Commander of the Faithful, was near the mountain at Siffīn, the time for the evening prayers came. So, he went farther away and called for the prayers. When he finished the call to prayer, a man appeared from near the mountain with grey hair and beard, and a bright white face. He said, 'Peace be with you, O Commander of the Faithful, and mercy and blessings from Allah! Welcome to the successor of the last of the prophets, leader of the ones with bright, brilliant faces, magnanimous and protected, excellent and one who has the reward of the truthful, master of all the successors!'

So, the Commander of the Faithful said, 'And peace be with you. How are you?'

١-٦-٣- حَدَّثَنا أبِى رَضِىَ اللهُ عَنْهُ, قالَ: «حَدَّثَنا مُحَمَّدُ بْنُ أبِى القاسِمِ, عَنْ مُحَمَّدِ بْنِ عَلِيٍّ القُرَشِيِّ، قالَ: 'حَدَّثَنا أبُو الربيعِ الزَّهْرانِيِّ، قالَ: 'حَدَّثَنا حَرِيزٌ, عَنْ لَيْثِ بْنِ أبِى سَلِيمٍ, عَنْ مُجاهِدٍ, عَنْ ابن عَبّاسٍ، قالَ: 'قالَ رَسُولُ اللهِ صلى الله عليه وآله وسلم، لَمّا أنْزَلَ اللهُ، تَبارَكَ وتَعالَي، ﴿وأوْفُوا بِعَهْدِى أُوفِ بِعَهْدِكُمْ،﴾: 'واللهِ لَقَدْ خَرَجَ آدَمُ مِنَ الدنْيا، وَقَدْ عاهَدَ قَوْمَهُ عَلَي الوَفاءِ لِوَلَدِهِ شِيْثَ، فَما وَفَي [قومه] لَهُ؛ وَلَقَدْ خَرَجَ نُوحٌ مِنَ الدنْيا، وَعاهَدَ قَوْمَهُ عَلَي الوَفاءِ لِوَصِيِّهِ سامَ، فَما وَفَتْ أُمَّتُهُ؛ وَلَقَدْ خَرَجَ إبْراهِيمُ مِنَ الدنْيا، وَعاهَدَ قَوْمَهُ عَلَي الوَفاءِ لِوَصِيِّهِ إسْماعِيلَ، فَما وَفَتْ أُمَّتُهُ؛ وَلَقَدْ خَرَجَ مُوسَي مِنَ الدنْيا، وَعاهَدَ قَوْمَهُ عَلَي الوَفاءِ لِوَصِيِّهِ يُوشَعَ بْنِ نُونَ، فَما وَفَتْ أُمَّتُهُ؛ وَلَقَدْ رُفِعَ عِيسَي بْنُ مَرْيَمَ إلَي السَماءِ، وَقَدْ عاهَدَ قَوْمَهُ عَلَي الوَفاءِ لِوَصِيِّهِ شَمْعُونَ بْنِ حَمُّونَ الصَفا، فَما وَفَتْ أُمَّتُهُ؛ وإنِّى مُفارِقُكُمْ, عَنْ قَرِيبٍ، وَخارِجٌ مِنْ بَيْنِ أظْهُرِكُمْ، وَقَدْ عَهِدْتُ إلَي أُمَّتِى فِى عَلِيِّ بْنِ أبِى طالِبٍ، وانَّها الراكِبَةُ سُنَنَ مَنْ قَبْلَها مِنَ الأمَمِ فِى مُخالَفَةِ وَصِيِّى وَعِصْيانِهِ... .''''»

(معاني الأخبار، ٣٧٣)

١-٦-٤- عَنْ قَيْسٍ, مَوْلَي عَلِيِّ بْنِ أبِى طالِبٍ عليه السلام, قالَ: «إنَّ عَلِيّاً, أميرَ المُؤْمِنِينَ عليه السلام, كانَ قَرِيباً مِنَ الجَبَلِ بِصِفِّينِ, فَحَضَرَتْ صَلاةُ المَغْرِبِ, فأمْعَنَ بَعِيداً, ثُمَّ أذَّنَ. فَلَمّا فَرَغَ مِنْ أذانِهِ, إذا رَجُلٌ مُقْبِلٌ نَحْوَ الجَبَلِ, أبْيَضُ الرأسِ واللحْيَةِ والوَجْهِ. فَقالَ: 'السَلامُ عَلَيْكَ يا أمِيرَ المُؤْمِنِينَ وَرَحْمَةُ اللهِ وَبَرَكاتُهُ. مَرْحَباً بِوَصِيِّ خاتَمِ النَبِيِّينَ وَقائِدِ الغُرِّ المُحَجَّلِينَ والأغَرِّ المامُونِ والفاضِلِ الفائِزِ بِثَوابِ الصدِّيقِينَ وَسَيِّدِ الوَصِيِّينَ.'

فَقالَ لَهُ أمِيرُ المُؤْمِنِينَ عليه السلام: 'وَعَلَيْكَ السَلامُ. كَيْفَ حالُكَ؟'

He replied, 'I am well, waiting for the holy spirit. I do not know of any name that is greater in the estimation of Allah, His Name is Mighy and Magnificent, at the time of an ordeal than yours, nor of any who has earned more rewards than you, nor of anyone who has an eleveated place higherthan yours. Put up with all that your face, O my brother, until you meet the beloved. Verily, I have witnessed whatever happened to our companions in the past at the hands of the children of Israel. They cut them apart with the saw and carried them over the bier.' And then pointing towards the people of Syria, he said, 'And if these poor, ugly faces knew what chastisement and exemplary punishment awaited them for fighting against you, they would withdraw.; And then pointing to the people of Iraq, he said, 'And if these bright faces knew that award awaited them for having obeyed you, they would love to be cut by scissors. And peace and His mercy and blessings be with you.' Then he disappeared. At that time, Ammār ibn Yāsir, 'Abdul Haytham ibn al-Tīhan, Abū Ayyūb al-Anṣārī, 'Ubaydah ibn al-Ṣāmit, Khuzayma ibn Thābit and Hāshim al-Marqal, among a group of his followers, having heard what the man had said, stood up and said, 'O Commander of the Faithful! Who was that man?' The Commander of the Faithful said, 'He is Simon, the successor of Jesusعليه السلام. Allah sent him to me to give me solace for this confrontation with His enemies.' They said, 'May our parents be your ransom! By Allah! We will help you the way we helped the Apostle of Allahﷺ, and none from the *Muhājirīn* nor *Anṣār* shall desert you, except the unfortunate one.' Then the Commander of the Faithful said some kind words to them."

(*Amālī,* 1, 104-106, 5)

1.6.5. Imam Bāqirعليه السلام said, "Verily, Allah sent Muḥammadﷺ to the genies and the people, and after him He put twelve exectutors (*waṣīy*). Some of them have gone and some remain. Each executor put a way (*sunnah*) into practice, and the executors after Muḥammadﷺ followed the way of the executors of Jesus, who were also twelve, and the Commander of the Faithfulعليه السلام followed the way of the Messiahعليه السلام."

(*Kāfī,* 1, 532, 10)

فَقالَ: 'بِخَيْرٍ. أنا مُنْتَظِرُ رُوحِ القُدُسِ, وَلاَ أعْلَمُ أحَداً أعْظَمُ فِي اللهِ, عَزَّ وَجَلَّ اسْمُهُ, بَلاءً وَلا أحْسَنُ ثَواباً مِنْكَ, وَلا أرْفَعُ عِنْدَ اللهِ مَكاناً. إصْبِرْ, يا أخِي, عَلَي ما أنتَ فِيهِ, حَتَّي تَلْقَي الحَبِيبَ. فَقَدْ رأيْتُ أصْحابَنا ما لَقَوْا بِالأمْسِ مِنْ بَنِي إسْرائِيلَ, نَشَرُوهُمْ بِالمَناشِيرِ وَحَمَلُوهُمْ عَلَي الخَشَبِ. وَلَوْ يَعْلَمُ هَذِهِ الوُجُوهُ التَرِبَةُ الشائِهَةُ- وأوْمأ بِيَدِهِ إلَي أهْلِ الشامِ- ما أعَدَّ لَهُمْ فِي قِتالِكَ, مِنْ عَذابٍ وَسُوءِ نَكالٍ, لَأقصَرُوا. وَلَوْ تَعْلَمُ هَذِهِ الوُجُوهُ المُبْيَضَّةُ- وأوْمأ بِيَدِهِ إلَي أهْلِ العِراقِ- ماذا لَهُمْ مِنَ الثَّوابِ فِي طاعَتِكَ, لَوَدَّتْ أنَّها قُرِّضَتْ بِالمَقارِيضَ, والسَلامُ عَلَيْكَ وَرَحْمَةُ اللهِ وَبَرَكاتُهُ.' ثُمَّ غابَ مِنْ مَوْضِعِهِ. فَقامَ عَمّارٌ بْنُ ياسِرٍ وأبُو الهَيْثَمِ بْنُ التَيْهانِ وأبُو أيُّوبٍ الأنْصارِيِّ وَعُبادَةُ بْنُ الصامِتِ وَخُزَيْمَةُ بْنُ ثابِتٍ وَهاشِمُ المِرْقالَ فِي جَماعَةٍ مِنْ شِيعَةِ أمِيرِ المُؤْمِنِينَ عليه السلام, وَقَدْ كانُوا سَمِعُوا كَلامَ الرجُلِ, فَقالُوا: 'يا أمِيرَ المُؤْمِنِينَ! مَنْ هَذا الرجُلُ؟' فَقالَ لَهُمْ أمِيرُ المُؤْمِنِينَ عليه السلام: 'هَذا شَمْعُونُ, وَصِيُّ عِيسَي عليه السلام. بَعَثَهُ اللهُ يُصَبِّرُنِي عَلَي قِتالِ أعْدائِهِ.' فَقالُوا لَهُ: 'فِداكَ آباؤُنا وأمَّهاتُنا؛ واللهِ لَنَنْصُرَنَّكَ نَصْرَنا لِرَسُولِ اللهِ صلى الله عليه وآله وسلم, وَلا يَتَخَلَّفُ عَنْكَ مِنَ المُهاجِرِينَ والأنْصارِ إلّا شَقِيٌّ.' فَقالَ لَهُمْ أمِيرُ المُؤْمِنِينَ عليه السلام مَعْرُوفاً.»

(الأمالي، ١، ١٠٤ - ١٠٦، ٥)

١-٦-٥- عَلِيُّ بْنُ إبْراهِيمَ، عَنْ مُحَمَّدِ بْنِ عِيسَى بْنِ عُبَيْدٍ، عَنْ مُحَمَّدِ بْنِ الفُضَيْلِ، عَنْ أبِي حَمْزَةَ، عَنْ أبِي جَعْفَرٍ عليه السلام، قالَ: «إنَّ اللهَ أرْسَلَ مُحَمَّداً صلى الله عليه وآله وسلم إلَي الجِنِّ والانْسِ، وَجَعَلَ مِنْ بَعْدِهِ اثْنَي عَشَرَ وَصِيّاً؛ مِنْهُمْ مَنْ سَبَقَ وَمِنْهُمْ مَنْ بَقِيَ. وَكُلُّ وَصِيٍّ جَرَتْ بِهِ سُنَّةٌ والأوْصِياءُ الذِينَ مِنْ بَعْدِ مُحَمَّدٍ صلى الله عليه وآله وسلم، عَلَي سُنَّةِ أوْصِياءِ عِيسَي؛ وَكانُوا اثْنَي عَشَرَ، وَكانَ أمِيرُ المُؤْمِنِينَ عليه السلام عَلَي سُنَّةِ المَسِيحِ.»

(الكافي، ١، ٥٣٢، ١٠)

1.6.6. Mūsā ibn Ja'far narrated from his fathers, peace be with them, that 'Alī said to Salmān, "Will you not inform us about the beginning of your matter?" He said, "I am from Shīrāz and I was a dear boy to my father. I was with him in a cloister on one of their festival days. Then one in it called, 'I testify that there is no god but Allah, Jesus is the Spirit of Allah and Muḥammad is the beloved of Allah.' Then the loveliness of him entered into my flesh and blood. My father said, 'Why do not you prostrate for the rise of the sun?' I argued with him until he became silent. When I came back to my house I saw a book hung below the ceiling. I said to my mother, 'What is this book?' She said, 'O Rūzbih! When we returned from our festival, we saw this book that was hung. So do not approach that place. If not, your father will kill you.' I implored her until the darkness of night came and my father and mother went to sleep. Then I stood and took the book. Written in it was, 'In the name of Allah, the Compassionate, the Merciful. This is a covenant from Allah to Adam that He will create from his loins a prophet, who will be named 'Muḥammad.' He will command noble virtue and prohibit the worship of idols. O Rūzbih! Go to the executor of the executor of Jesus and be at his service. He will guide you to your aim.'Then I lost my consciousness. My parents understood and put me in a well and said, 'Do not come back, otherwise we will kill you.' I said, 'Do to me what you want. The love of Muḥammad will not go from my breast.'

I did not know Arabic, but Allah taught me on that day. They sent small loaves of bread to me. I spent a long time in the wll, and I raised my hands to the sky and said, 'O My Lord! You evoked the love of Muḥammad and his executor in me. By the right of his means, may You hasten my emergence.'

Then one who wore white clothes came to me and said, 'O Rūzbih! Stand up.' Then he took my hand and brought me to the cloister. I went up to it. The monk said, 'Are you Rūzbih?' I answered, 'Yes.' I

١-٦-٦- بالإسنادِ, عَنْ مُوسَي بْنِ جَعْفَرٍ, عَنْ آبائِهِ عليهم السلام، قالَ: «إنَّ عَلِيّاً عليه السلام قالَ لِسَلْمانَ: 'ألا تُخْبِرُنا بِبَدْءِ أمْرِكَ؟' قالَ: 'أنا كُنْتُ مِنْ أهْلِ شِيرازٍ، وكُنْتُ عَزِيزاً عَلَي والِدِي. بَيْنا أنا سائِرٌ مَعَهُ فِي عِيْدٍ لَهُمْ، إذا أنا بِصَوْمَعَةٍ، فإذا رَجُلٌ مِنْها يُنادِي: 'أشْهَدُ أنْ لا إلَهَ إلّا اللهُ، وانَّ عِيسَي رُوحُ اللهِ، وانَّ مُحَمَّداً حَبِيبُ اللهِ.' فوَقَعَ حُبُّ مُحَمَّدٍ فِي لَحْمِي ودَمِي.

فقالَ لِي أبِي: 'ما لكَ لا تَسْجُدُ لِمَطْلَعِ الشمْسِ؟' فكابَرْتُهُ حَتَّي سَكَتَ. فلَمّا انْصَرَفْتُ إلي مَنْزِلِي، إذا أنا بِكِتابٍ مُعَلَّقٍ فِي السقْفِ. فقُلْتُ لِأُمِّي: 'ما هَذا الكِتابُ؟' فقالَتْ: 'يا رُوزْبِهُ! إنَّ هَذا الكِتابُ لمّا رَجَعْنا مِنْ عِيدِنا رأيْناهُ مُعَلَّقاً. فلا تَقْرَبْ ذلِكَ المَكانَ. فإنَّكَ إنْ قَرَّبْتَهُ قَتَلَكَ أبُوكَ.' قالَ: 'فجاهَدْتُها، حَتَّي جُنَّ اللَيْلُ ونامَ أبِي وأمِّي. فقُمْتُ وأخَذْتُ الكِتابَ، فإذا فِيهِ مَكْتُوبٌ: 'بِسْمِ اللهِ الرحْمَنِ الرحيمِ. هَذا عَهْدٌ مِنَ اللهِ إلي آدَمَ، أنَّهُ خالِقٌ مِنْ صُلْبِهِ نَبِيّاً، يُقالُ لَهُ: 'مُحَمَّدٌ،' يأمُرُ بِمَكارِمِ الأخْلاقِ ويَنْهَي, عَنْ عِبادَةِ الأوْثانِ. يا رُوزْبِهُ! إئْتِ وَصِيَّ وَصِيِّ عِيسَي، فاخْدِمْهُ فَهُوَ يُرْشِدُكَ إلي مُرادِكَ.' فصَعِقْتُ صَعْقَةً. فعَلِمَ أبَوايَ بِذلِكَ، فجَعَلُونِي فِي بِئْرٍ وقالُوا: 'إنْ رَجَعْتَ، وإلّا قَتَلْناكَ.' فقُلْتُ: 'افْعَلُوا بِي ما شِئْتُمْ. حُبُّ مُحَمَّدٍ لا يَذْهَبُ مِنْ صَدْرِي.'

قالَ: 'وكُنْتُ لا أعْرِفُ العَرَبِيَّةَ، ولَقَدْ فَهَّمَنِي اللهُ العَرَبِيَّةَ فِي ذلِكَ اليَوْمِ. وكانُوا يَنْزِلُونَ عَلَيَّ قُرْصاً صِغاراً. فلمّا طالَ أمْرِي فِي البِئْرِ، رَفَعْتُ يَدِي إلي السَماءِ، وقُلْتُ: 'يا رَبِّ! إنَّكَ حَبَّبْتَ مُحَمَّداً ووَصِيَّهُ إلَيَّ، فبِحَقِّ وَسِيلَتِهِ عَجِّلْ فرَجِي.'

فأتانِي آتٍ، عَلَيْهِ ثِيابٌ بِيْضٌ، فقالَ: 'قُمْ يا رُوزْبِهُ!' فأخَذَ بِيَدِي وأتَي بِي إلي الصَوْمَعَةِ؛ وَصَعَدْتُها. فقالَ الدَيْرانِيُّ: 'أنْتَ رُوزْبِهْ!' قُلْتُ: 'نَعَم.'

stayed near him two years and served him. When he was in the throes of death, he directed me to a monk in Antioch and gave me a tablet on which the attributes of Muḥammad were written.When I came to the monk of Antioch and went up to his cloister, he said, 'Are you Rūzbih?' I answered, 'Yes.' He welcomed to me and I served him for two years, too. He informed me of the attributes of Muḥammad and his executor.

When he was in the throes of death, he said to me, 'O Rūzbih! The raising of Muḥammad is near.' After his death, I went out with a group to Ḥijāz and served them. Once they killed a sheep with a blow, roasted it, prepared wine and said to me, 'Eat and drink.' I refused. They wanted to kill me. I said, 'Do not kill me. I confess that I will be a servant to you.'

Then they bought me to a Jew. He asked me about my story. I told him the matter from the beginning to the end. He said, 'I hate you and Muḥammad.' and brought me out of his house. There was much sand near the door of his house. He said, 'If you do not transfer all of this sand from here to there, I will kill you.' I began to carry it during the night. When I became tired, although I had moved but a little of it, I would say, 'O My Lord! You evoked the love of Muḥammad and his executor in me. By the right of his means, give me rest from this.' So Allah raised a wind by which the sand moved from its place to the place that the Jew had said. In the morning the Jew said to me, 'You are a witch. I will bring you out of this village for you cannot destroy us.' He brought me out and sold me to a good woman. She loved me. She put me in a garden for her and said, 'Eat, grant and give alms from it.' One day when I was in the garden, I saw that seven groups were coming and a cloud was shading them and went with them. I said, 'Verily there is a prophet among them.'"

(*Al-Kharā'ij wa al-Jarā'iḥ*, 3, 1078, 1081)

وأقَمْتُ عِنْدَهُ وَخَدَمْتُهُ حَوْلَيْنِ. فَلمّا حَضَرَتْهُ الوَفاةُ، دلّني عَلَي راهِبٍ بِأنْطاكِيَّةَ، وَناوَلَنِي لَوْحاً فِيهِ صِفاتُ مُحَمَّدٍ ﷺ. فَلمّا أتَيْتُ راهِبَ أنْطاكِيَّةَ وَصَعَدْتُ صَوْمَعَتَهُ، قالَ: 'أنْتَ رُوزْبِهٌ!' قُلْتُ: 'نَعم.' فَرَحَّبَ بِي؛ وَخَدِمْتُهُ حَوْلَيْنَ أيْضاً. وَعَرَّفَنِي بِصِفاتِ مُحَمَّدٍ وَوَصِيِّهِ.

فَلمّا حَضَرَتْهُ الوَفاةُ، قالَ لِي: 'يا رُوزْبِهُ! إنَّ مُحَمَّدَ بْنَ عَبْدِ اللهِ قَدْ حانَ خُرُوجُهُ.' فَخَرَجْتُ بَعْدَ مَوْتِهِ مَعَ قَوْمٍ يَخْرُجُونَ إلَي الحِجازِ؛ فَصِرْتُ أخْدِمُهُمْ. فَقَتَلُوا شاةً بِالضَّرْبِ وَشَوَوْا واحْضَرُوا الخَمْرَ، وَقالُوا لِي: 'كُلْ واشْرِبْ.' فامْتَنَعْتُ. فأرادُوا قَتْلِي. فَقُلْتُ: 'لا تَقْتُلونِي، أقِرُّ لَكُمْ بِالعُبُودِيَّةِ.'

فَباعُونِي مِنْ يَهُودِيٍّ. فَسألنِي, عَنْ قِصَّتِي. فأخْبَرْتُهُ بِخَبَرِي مِنْ أوَّلِهِ إلَي آخِرِهِ. فَقالَ: 'إنِّي أبْغِضُكَ وأبْغِضُ مُحَمَّداً.' فأخْرَجَنِي إلَي خارِجِ دارِهِ، وإذا رَمْلٌ كَثِيرٌ عَلَي بابِهِ. فَقالَ: 'إنْ أصْبَحْتُ وَلَمْ تَنْقُلْ هَذا الرمْلَ، كُلَّهُ، مِنْ هَذا المَوْضِعِ إلَي هَذا المَوْضِعِ، لأقْتُلَنَّكَ.' فَجَعَلْتُ أحْمِلُ طُولَ لَيْلَتِي. فَلمّا تَعِبْتُ، وَلَمْ أنْقُلْ مِنْهُ إلّا القَلِيلَ، فَقُلْتُ: 'يا رَبِّ إنَّكَ حَبَّبْتَ مُحَمَّداً وَوَصِيَّهُ إلَيَّ، فَبِحَقِّ وَسِيلَتِهِ، أرِحْنِي مِمّا أنا فِيهِ.' فَبَعَثَ اللهُ رِيحاً قَلَعَتْ ذَلِكَ الرمْلَ مِنْ مَكانِهِ إلَي المَكانِ الذي قالَ اليَهُودِيُّ. فَلمّا أصْبَحَ، قالَ لِي: 'إنَّكَ ساحِرٌ. لأخْرِجَنَّكَ مِنْ هَذِهِ القَرْيَةِ، لِئَلاّ تُهْلِكَنا.' فأخْرَجَنِي، فَباعَنِي مِنْ امْرأةٍ سَلِيمَةٍ. فأحَبَّتْنِي؛ وَكانَ لَها حائِطٌ، فَجَعَلَتْنِي فِيهِ، فَقالَتْ: 'كُلْ مِنْهُ وَهَبْ وَتَصَدَّقْ.' فَبَيْنا أنا فِي الحائِطِ يَوْماً، إذا أنا بِسَبْعَةِ رَهْطٍ قَدْ أقْبَلُوا، تُظِلُّهُمْ غَمامَةٌ تَسِيرُ مَعَهُمْ. قُلْتُ: 'إنَّ فِيهِمْ نَبِيّاً.''»

(الخرائج والجرائح، ٣، ١٠٧٨-١٠٨١)

1.7. DISCIPLES

1.7.1. It is reported that al-Bāqir said, "Verily, Allah sent Jesus only to the Children of Israel and his prophecy was at the Sacred House [Jerusalem], and after him there were twelve apostles."

(*Biḥār,* 14, 250, 40)

1.7.2. It is reported that Ibn 'Abbās said, "I said, 'O Apostle of Allah! How many imams will there be after you?' He said, 'The number of the disciples of Jesus, the number of tribes of Moses, the number of the chieftans of the children of Israel.' I said, 'O Apostle of Allah! How many were they?' He said, 'They were twelve, and the imams after me will be twelve....'"

(*Biḥār*, 36, 285, 107)

1.7.3. It is reported that 'Alī ibn al-Ḥasan ibn Faḍāl reported that his father said, "I said to Riḍā, 'Why were the disciples (*ḥawāriyīn*) called *ḥawāriyīn?*' He said, 'According to the people, they were called *ḥawāriyīn* because they were bleachers who used to clean clothes from filth by washing, and this name is derived from *ḥawārī* (bleached) bread, but according to us they are called *ḥawāriyīn* because they were pure in themselves and purified others from the filth of sin by sermons and remembrance.' Then it was asked, 'Why were the Christians (*Naṣārā*) called *Naṣārā*?' He said, 'Because they were from a village named *Nāṣirah* among the towns of Syria. Mary and Jesus settled in it after they returned from Egypt.'"

(*Biḥār*, 14, 273, 2)

١-٧- الحَوارِيُّون

١-٧-١- الطالِقانِيُّ, عَنِ ابن عُقْدَةٍ, عَنْ عَلِيِّ بْنِ الحَسَنِ بْنِ فَضّال, عَنْ أبيهِ, عَنْ مُحَمَّدِ بْنِ الفُضَيْلِ, عَنْ الثُّمالِي, عَنِ الباقِرِ عليه السلام، قالَ: «إنَّ اللهَ أرْسَلَ عِيسَي إلَي بَنِي إسْرائِيلَ خاصَّةً، وَكانَتْ نُبُوَّتُهُ بِبَيْتِ المَقْدِسِ، وَكانَ مِنْ بَعْدِهِ مِنَ الحَوارِيِّينَ اثْنَي عَشَرَ.»

(بحار الأنوار، ١٤، ٢٥٠، ٤٠)

١-٧-٢- عَلِيُّ بْنُ الحُسَيْنِ, ... عَنْ طاوس اليَمانِيّ, عَنْ عَبْدِ اللهِ بْنِ العَبّاسِ، قالَ: «... قُلْتُ: 'يا رَسُولَ اللهِ، فَكَمْ الأئِمَةُ بَعْدَكَ؟' قالَ: 'بِعَدَدِ حَوارِيِّ عِيسَي وأسْباطِ مُوسَي وَنُقَباءِ بَنِي إسْرائِيلَ.' قُلْتُ: 'يا رَسُولَ اللهِ، فَكَمْ كانُوا؟' قالَ: 'كانُوا اثْنَي عَشَرَ، والأئِمَةُ بَعْدِي اثْنا عَشَرَ.'»

(بحار الأنوار، ٣٦، ٢٨٥، ١٠٧)

١-٧-٣- الطالِقانِيُّ, عَنْ أحْمَدَ الهَمْدانِيِّ, عَنْ عَلِيِّ بْنِ الحَسَنِ بْنِ فَضّال, عَنْ أبِيهِ، قالَ: «قُلْتُ لِلرِّضا عليه السلام: 'لِمَ سُمِّيَ الحَوارِيُّونَ، الحَوارِيِّينَ؟' قالَ: 'أمّا عِنْدَ الناسِ، فَإنَّهُمْ سُمُّوا حَوارِيِّينَ، لِأنَّهُمْ كانُوا قَصّارِينَ، يُخَلِّصُونَ الثِّيابَ مِنَ الوَسَخِ بِالغَسْلِ؛ وَهُوَ اسْمٌ مُشْتَقٌّ مِنَ الخُبْزِ الحَوارِيِّ. وأمّا عِنْدَنا، فَسُمِّيَ الحَوارِيُّونَ حَوارِيِّينَ، لِأنَّهُمْ كانُوا مُخْلِصِينَ فِي أنْفُسِهِمْ وَمُخَلِّصِينَ لِغَيْرِهِمْ مِنَ أوْساخِ الذُّنُوبِ بِالوَعْظِ والتذْكِيرِ.' قالَ: 'فَقُلْتُ لَهُ: 'فَلِمَ سُمِّيَ النَصارَي نَصارَي؟' قالَ: 'لِأنَّهُمْ مِنْ قَرْيَةٍ، اسْمُها ناصِرَةٌ، مِنْ بِلادِ الشامِ، نَزَلَتْها مَرْيَمُ وَعِيسَي عليه السلام بَعْدَ رُجُوعِهِما مِنْ مِصْرَ.'»

(بحار الأنوار، ١٤، ٢٧٣، ٢)

1.7.4. Abū 'Abd Allah said, "Verily the disciples of Jesus were his followers, and our followers are our disciples. The disciples of Jesus were not more obedient than our disciples are to us. Jesus said to the disciples, 'Who are my helpers for Allah?' The disciples said, 'We will be the helpers of Allah.'(1) By Allah, they did not help him from the Jews and they did not fight with them for him, but our followers, by Allah, always have helped us since Allah, may His remembrance be magnified, took [the soul of] the Apostle of Allah, and they have fought for us, have been burned and tormented and frightened away in the cities. May Allah give them the best reward for us."

(*Kāfī,* 8, 268, 396)

1.7.5. Anas ibn Mālik said, "I asked the Apostle of Allah about the disciples of Jesus. He said, 'They were those chosen by him as best, and they were twelve who were unmarried and quick to help Allah and His Apostle. There was neither pride in them nor weakness nor doubt. They helped him with vision, influence, seriousness and suffering.' I said, 'So, who are your disciples, O Apostle of Allah?' He said, 'The leaders (*imāms*) after me who are twelve from the loins of 'Alī and Fāṭimah. They are my disciples and the helpers of my religion, may peace be granted to them from Allah.'"

(*Biḥār*, 36, 310, 149)

1.7.6. Mufaḍḍal reported in a lengthy narration that he said to al-Ṣādiq, "O my guardian and master! Why are the people of Moses called *Yahūd* (Jews)?" He said, "Because of the saying of Allah, the mighty and magnificent, ❴*'Verily, we turn (hudnā) unto You'*❵ (7:156), that is, 'we seek Your guidance.'" He said, "What about the *Naṣārā* (Christians)?" He said, "Because of the saying of Jesus, ❴*'Who will be my helpers in the way of Allah?' The disciples said, 'We are the helpers (anṣār) of Allah. We believe in Allah and bear*

(1) See (61:14).

١-٧-٤- حدَّثَنا ابن مَحْبُوبٍ، عَنْ أبي يَحْيَي كَوْكَبِ الدمِ، عَنْ أبي عَبْدِ اللهِ عليه السلام، قالَ: «إنَّ حَوارِيَّ عِيسَي عليه السلام كانُوا شِيعَتَهُ، وإنَّ شِيعَتَنا حَوارِيُّونا. وَما كانَ حَوارِيُّ عِيسَي بِأطْوَعَ لَهُ مِنْ حَوارِيِّنا لَنا. وإنَّما قالَ عِيسَي عليه السلام لِلْحَوارِيِّينَ: 'مَنْ أنْصارِي إلَي اللهِ؟' قال الحَوارِيُّونَ: 'نَحْنُ أنْصارُ اللهِ.' فَلا واللهِ، ما نَصَرُوهُ مِنَ اليَهُودِ وَلا قاتَلُوهُمْ دُونَهُ؛ وَشِيعَتُنا واللهِ لَمْ يَزالُوا، مُنْذُ قَبَضَ اللهُ، عَزَّ ذِكْرُهُ، رَسُولَهُ صلى الله عليه وآله وسلم يَنْصُرُونا وَيُقاتِلُونَ دُونَنا وَيُحْرَقُونَ وَيُعَذَّبُونَ وَيُشَرَّدُونَ فِي البُلْدانِ. جَزاهُمُ اللهُ عَنّا خَيْراً.»

(الكافي، ٨، ٢٦٨، ٣٩٦)

١-٧-٥- أبُو المُفَضَّلِ، عَنْ رَجاءِ بْنِ يَحْيَي العَبَرتائِيِّ الكاتِبِ، عَنْ مُحَمَّدِ بْنِ خَلّادٍ الباهِلِيِّ، عَنْ مَعاذِ بْنِ مَعاذٍ، عَنِ ابن عَوْنٍ، عَنْ هِشامِ بْنِ زَيْدٍ، عَنْ أنَسِ بْنِ مالِكٍ، قالَ: «سألْتُ رَسُولَ اللهِ صلى الله عليه وآله وسلم، عَنْ حَوارِيِّ عِيسَي، فَقالَ: 'كانُوا مِنْ صَفْوَتِهِ وَخِيرَتِهِ، وكانُوا اثْنَي عَشَرَ، مُجَرَّدِينَ مُكْمِشِينَ فِي نُصْرَةِ اللهِ وَرَسُولِهِ. لا زَهْوَ فِيهِمْ وَلا ضَعْفَ وَلا شَكَّ. كانُوا يَنْصُرُونَهُ عَلَي بَصِيرَةٍ وَنَفاذٍ وَجِدٍّ وَعَناءٍ.' قُلْتُ: 'فَمَنْ حَوارِيُّكَ؟ يا رَسُولَ اللهِ.' فَقالَ: 'الأئِمَةُ بَعْدِي اثْنا عَشَرَ، مِنْ صُلْبِ عَلِيٍّ وَفاطِمَةَ. هُمْ حَوارِيِّي وأنْصارُ دِينِي. عَلَيْهِم مِنَ اللهِ التَحِيَّةُ والسَلامُ.'»

(بحار الأنوار، ٣٦، ٣١٠، ١٤٩)

١-٧-٦- قالَ المُفَضَّلُ: «يا مَوْلايَ وَسَيِّدِي، لِمَ سُمِّيَ قَوْمُ مُوسَي، اليَهُودُ؟» قالَ(ع): «لِقَوْلِ اللهِ، عَزَّ وَجَلَّ:﴿إنّا هُدْنا إلَيْكَ.﴾ أيْ، اهْتَدَيْنا إلَيْكَ.» قالَ: «فالنَصارَي؟» قالَ(ع): «لِقَوْلِ عِيسَي عليه السلام:﴿مَنْ أنْصارِي إلَي اللهِ؟﴾ » «وَتَلا الآيَة

witness that we are ones who submit.'❳ (3:52) So, they were called *Naṣārā* because of their help to the religion of Allah."

(*Biḥār*, 53, 5)

1.7.7. It was said to Abū 'Abd Allah, "Why is it that the companions of Jesus walked on water, while it was not this way with the companions of Muḥammad?" He said, "Verily, the companions of Jesus were saved the trouble of livelihood, but the latter were tested by livelihood."

(*Kāfī,* 5, 71, 3)

1.7.8. It is reported that Imam Ṣādiq said, "When Jesus wanted to wish farewell to his disciples, he called them together and order them to be for weak creatures and he prohibited them from despots. Then he sent two of them to Antioch. They arrived on the day of a festival. They found the people there had uncovered idols and were worshipping them. They hurried toward them violently. They were put in irons and thrown into prison. When Simon found out about this, he went to Antioch and visited them in the prison. He said, 'Did I not prohibit you from despots?'

Then he left them, and sat with the weak people. He began gradually to discuss matters with them. Then the weak spoke of these things with those who were stronger, while they kept it a most confidential secret. Their words kept ascending until they finally reached the king. He asked, 'Since when has this man been in my kingdom?' They said, 'For two months.' He said, 'Bring him to me.' They brought him.

When the king saw Simon, he felt love for him. He said, 'I will not sit, unless he is beside me.' Later after having had a frightening dream, he asked Simon about it. Simon gave a good answer that gladdened the king. Later he had another terrifying dream. Simon

إلي آخرِها.» «فسمُّوا النصارَي، لِنُصرَةِ دِينِ اللهِ.»

(بحار الأنوار، ٥٣، ٥)

١-٧-٧- عَلِيُّ بْنُ مُحَمَّدِ بْنِ بُنْدارَ، عَنْ أَحْمَدَ بْنِ أَبِي عَبْدِ الله، عَنْ إبْراهِيمَ بْنِ مُحَمَّدٍ الثَّقَفِيِّ، عَنْ عَلِيِّ بْنِ المُعَلَّي، عَنْ القاسِمِ بْنِ مُحَمَّدٍ، رَفَعَهُ إلَي أَبِي عَبْدِ اللهِ عليه السلام، قالَ: «قِيلَ لَهُ: 'ما بالُ أَصْحابِ عِيسَي عليه السلام، كانُوا يَمْشُونَ عَلَي الماءِ ولَيْسَ ذَلِكَ فِي أَصْحابِ مُحَمَّدٍ صلى الله عليه وآله وسلم؟' قالَ: «إنَّ أَصْحابَ عِيسَي عليه السلام كُفُوا المَعاشَ، وإنَّ هَؤُلاءِ ابْتُلُوا بِالمَعاشِ.»

(الكافي، ٥، ٧١، ٣)

١-٧-٨- بِالإسنادِ إلَي الصدُوقِ, عَنْ أبيهِ, عَنْ سَعْدٍ, عَنْ مُحَمَّدِ بْنِ الحُسَيْنِ, عَنْ مُحَمَّدِ بْنِ سِنانٍ, عَنْ إسْماعِيلَ بْنِ جابِرٍ, عَنِ الصادِقِ عليه السلام: «أنَّ عِيسَي عليه السلام، لَمّا أرادَ وداعَ أَصْحابِهِ، جَمَعَهُمْ وأمَرَهُمْ بِضُعَفاءِ الخَلْقِ ونَهاهُمْ, عَنِ الجَبابِرَةِ. فَوَجَّهَ اثْنَيْنِ إلَي أَنْطاكِيَّةَ. فَدَخَلا فِي يَوْمِ عِيدٍ لَهُمْ، فَوَجَداهُمْ قَدْ كَشَفُوا عَنِ الأصْنامِ وَهُمْ يَعْبُدُونَها. فَعَجَّلا عَلَيْهِمْ بِالتعْنِيفِ. فَشُدّا بِالحَدِيدِ وَطُرِحا فِي السِّجْنِ. فَلَمّا عَلِمَ شَمْعُونُ بِذَلِكَ، أتَي أَنْطاكِيَّةَ حَتَّي دَخَلَ عَلَيْهِما فِي السِّجْنِ، وقالَ: 'أَلَمْ أَنْهَكُما, عَنِ الجَبابِرَةِ؟'

ثُمَّ خَرَجَ مِنْ عِنْدِهِما وَجَلَسَ مَعَ الناسِ مَعَ الضُّعَفاءِ، فأقبَلَ يَطْرَحُ كَلامَهُ الشيْءَ بَعْدَ الشَيْءِ. فأقبَلَ الضَّعِيفُ يَدْفَعُ كَلامَهُ إلَي مَنْ هُوَ أقْوَي مِنْهُ. وأخْفَوْا كَلامَهُ إخْفاءاً شَدِيداً. فَلَمْ يَزَلْ يَتَراقِي الكَلامَ، حَتَّي انْتَهَي إلَي المَلِكِ. فقالَ: 'مُنْذُ مَتَي هَذا الرجُلُ فِي مَمْلِكَتِي؟' قالُوا: 'مُنْذُ شَهْرَيْنِ.' فقالَ: 'عَلَيَّ بِهِ.' فأتَوْهُ.

فَلَمّا نَظَرَ إلَيْهِ وَقَعَتْ عَلَيْهِ مَحبَّتُهُ، فَقالَ: 'لا أجْلِسُ إلّا وَهُوَ مَعِي.' فَرأي فِي مَنامِهِ شَيْئًا أفْزَعَهُ. فَسألَ شَمْعُونَ عَنْهُ، فأجابَ بِجَوابٍ حَسَنٍ فَرِحَ بِهِ.

interpreted it in such manner that the king's happiness increased. They conversed thus until Simon came to have influence over the king. Then he said, 'Verily, there are two men in your jail who insulted you.' The king said, 'Yes.' Simon said, 'Bring them to me.' When they were brought to Simon, he asked, 'What is the god you worship?' They said, 'Allah.' He said, 'When you ask Him for something, does He hear you, and does He answer you when you pray to Him?' They said, 'Yes.' Simon said, 'I want to ask you something to gain assurance from you about this.'

They said, 'Ask.' He said, 'Does He cure the leper?' They said, 'Yes.' He said, 'Bring a leper.' He said, 'Ask Him to cure this leper.' They laid hands upon him and he was cured. Simon said, 'I, also, can do the like of what you have done.' Then he said, 'Bring another.' Simon laid hands on the leper and he was cured. Another mark remains; if you answer this I will believe in your God.' They said, 'What is it?' He said, 'Can you revive the dead?' They said, 'Yes.' Then Simon faced the king and asked, 'Do you have a dead person who's passing has been hard for you?' He said, 'Yes. My son.'Simon said, 'Bring us to his grave.' Then he said, 'They have put themselves at risk for you.'

Then they turned to the grave and raised their hands [in prayer], as did Simon, then suddenly the grave cracked open and the youth stood up. He faced his father who said to him, 'How are you?' He said, 'I was dead, and terrified, when I understood there to be three persons standing before Allah with their hands raised in prayer to Him. They prayed that He revive me. They were those two and he.' Simon said, 'I am a believer in your God.' The king said, 'O Simon, I believe in Him in Whom you have come to believe.' The viziers of the king said, 'And we believe in Him in Whom our master has come to believe.' The weak always followed the strong. In Antioch none remained who did not believe."

(*Biḥār*, 14, 252)

ثُمَّ الْقي عَلَيْهِ فِى المَنامِ ما أهالَهُ. فأوَّلَها لَهُ بِما ازْدادَ بِهِ سُرُوراً. فَلَمْ يَزَلْ يُحادِثُهُ حَتَّي اسْتَوْلي عَلَيْهِ، ثُمَّ قالَ: 'إنَّ فِى حَبْسِكَ رَجُلَيْنِ، عابا عَلَيْكَ.' قالَ: 'نَعم.' قالَ: 'فَعَلَيَّ بِهِما.' فَلَمّا أتَي بِهِما، قالَ: 'ما إلهُكُما الذى تَعْبُدانِ؟' قالا: 'اللهُ.' قالَ: 'يَسْمَعُكُما إذا سألْتُماهُ، وَيُجيبُكُما إذا دَعَوْتُماهُ؟' قالا: 'نَعَم.' قالَ شَمْعُونُ: 'فأنا أُريدُ أنْ أسْتَبْرِئَ ذَلِكَ مِنْكُما.' قالا: 'قُلْ.' قالَ: 'هَلْ يَشْفِى لَكُما الأبرصَ؟' قالا: 'نَعَم.' قالَ، فأتَي بِأبْرَصَ. فقالَ: 'سَلاهُ أنْ يَشْفِى هَذا.'» قالَ: «فَمَسَحاهُ، فَبَرِءَ. قالَ: 'وأنا أفْعَلُ مِثْلَ ما فعلْتُما.' قالَ، فأتَي بِآخَرَ. فَمَسَحَهُ شَمْعُونُ، فَبَرِءَ. قالَ: 'بَقِيَتْ خِصْلَةٌ، إنْ أجَبْتُمانِى إلَيْها، آمَنْتُ بِإلهِكُما.' قالا: 'وَما هِيَ؟' قالَ: 'مَيِّتٌ تُحْيِيانِهِ.' قالا: 'نَعَم.' فأقبَلَ عَلَي المَلِكَ، وَقالَ: 'مَيِّتٌ يَعنيكَ أمْرُهُ؟' قالَ: 'نَعَم، ابنى.' قالَ: 'اذْهَبْ بِنا إلَي قَبْرِهِ، فإنَّهُما قَدْ أمْكَناكَ مِنْ أنْفُسِهِما.'

فَتَوَجَّهُوا إلَي قَبْرِهِ، فَبَسَطا أيْدِيَهُما، فَبَسَطَ شَمْعُونُ يَدَيْهِ. فَما كانَ بِأسْرَعَ مِنْ أنْ صُدِعَ القَبْرُ، وَقامَ الفَتَي، فأقبَلَ عَلَي أبِيهِ. فَقالَ أبُوهُ: 'ما حالُكَ؟' قالَ: 'كُنْتُ مَيِّتاً، فَفَزِعْتُ فَزْعَةً، فإذا ثَلاثَةٌ قِيامٌ بَيْنَ يَدَيِ اللهِ، باسِطُو أيْدِيهِمْ، يَدْعُونَ اللهَ أنْ يُحْيِيَنِى. وَهُما هَذانِ وَهَذا.' فَقالَ شَمْعُونُ: 'أنا لِإلهِكُما مِنَ المُؤْمِنِينَ.' فَقالَ المَلِكُ: 'أنا بِالَّذِى آمَنْتَ بِهِ، يا شَمْعُونُ، مِنَ المُؤْمِنِينَ.' وَقالَ وُزَراءُ المَلِكِ: 'وَنَحْنُ بِالَّذِى آمَنَ بِهِ سَيِّدُنا، مِنَ المُؤْمِنِينَ.' فَلَمْ يَزَلْ الضَّعِيفُ يَتْبَعُ القَوِىَّ، فَلَمْ يَبْقَ بِالأنطاكِيَّةِ أحَدٌ إلّا آمَنَ بِهِ.»

(بحار الأنوار، ١٤، ٢٥٢)

1.7.9. Abū Ḥamzah al-Thumālī said that he asked Imam Bāqir about the exegesis of the *ayah,* ﴾*And set out to them an example of the people of the town, when the messengers came to it./ When We sent to them two, the rejected both of them, then We strengthened them with a third, so they said: Surely we are messengers to you.*﴿ (36:13-14).

He said, "Allah commissioned two men to go to the people of Antioch. They brought things that were unfamiliar to those people, so the people were coarse with them, arrested them and imprisoned them in the house of idols. So, Allah commissioned a third. He entered the town, and said, 'Lead me to the gate of the king.' When he stood before the gate of the king, he said, 'I am a man who has worshiped in the deserts of the earth, and I would like to worship the God of the king.'

His speech reached the king, who said, 'Bring him into the house of the gods.' They brought him in it, and he remained there a year, with his two companions, to whom he said, 'In this way we transfer a people from one religion to another, not by bungling. Why were you not friendly?' Then he said to them, 'Do not admit to knowing me.'

Then he was brought before the king. The king said to him, 'It has reached me that you have been worshipping my god. You will always be my brother, so ask me for what you need.' He said, 'I need nothing, O king! But I saw two men there in the house of the gods, so, how is it with them?' The king said, 'Those two are men who came here, misled people from my religion, and invited them to a heavenly God.'

He said, 'O king! What a beautiful debate! If they prove right, we will follow them, and if we prove right, they will enter our religion with us. So, whatever is for us is for them, and whatever is against us is against them.' The king sent for those two. When they came before him, their companion said to them, 'What do you have for us?' They said, 'We came to invite to the worship of Allah, Who created the heavens and earth, Who creates what He wills in the wombs, Who forms as He wills, Who grows the trees and fruits and Who sends rain from the sky.'

١-٧-٩- عَنِ الحسَنِ بْنِ مَحْبُوبٍ, عَنْ مالِكِ بْنِ عَطِيَّةٍ, عَنْ أبِى حَمْزَةِ الثُّمالِيِّ, عَنْ أبِى جَعْفَرٍ عليه السلام. قالَ: «سألتُهُ, عَنْ تَفْسِيرِ هَذِهِ الآيَةِ ﴿واضْرِبْ لَهُمْ مَثَلاً أصْحابَ القَرْيَةِ إذْ جاءَها المُرْسَلُونَ.﴾ إلي قَوْلِهِ ﴿إنّا إلَيْكُمْ مُرْسَلُونَ.﴾»

فقالَ: «بَعَثَ اللهُ رَجُلَيْنِ إلَي أهْلِ مَدِينَةِ أنْطاكِيَّةَ. فَجاءاهُمْ بِما لا يَعْرِفُونَهُ. فَغَلَّظُوا عَلَيْهِما فأخَذُوهُما وَحَبَسُوهُما فِى بَيْتِ الأصْنامِ. فَبَعَثَ اللهُ الثّالِثَ، فَدَخَلَ المَدِينَةَ، فقالَ: 'أرْشِدُونِى إلَي بابِ المَلِكِ.'» قالَ: «فلَمّا وَقَفَ عَلَي بابِ المَلِكِ، قالَ: 'أنا رَجُلٌ كُنْتُ أتَعَبَّدُ فِى فَلاةٍ مِنَ الأرضِ، وَقَدْ أحْبَبْتُ أنْ أعْبُدَ إلَهَ المَلِكِ.'

فأبْلَغُوا كَلامَهُ المَلِكَ. فقالَ: 'أدْخِلُوهُ إلَي بَيْتِ الآلِهَةِ.' فأدْخَلُوهُ. فَمَكَثَ سَنَةً مَعَ صاحِبَيْهِ. فَقالَ لَهُما: 'بِهَذا نَنْقُلُ قَوْماً مِنْ دِينٍ إلَي دِينٍ، لا بِالخُرْقِ. أفَلا رَفَقْتُما؟' ثُمَّ قالَ لَهُما: 'لا تُقِرّانِ بِمَعْرِفَتِى.'

ثُمَّ أُدْخِلَ عَلَي المَلِكِ فَقالَ لَهُ المَلِكُ: 'بَلَغَنِى أنَّكَ كُنْتَ تَعْبُدُ إلَهِي. فَلَمْ أزَلْ وأنْتَ أخِي، فَسَلْنِى حاجَتَكَ.' قالَ: 'ما لِى حاجَةٌ أيُّها المَلِكُ، ولَكِنْ رَجُلَيْنِ رأيْتُهُما فِى بَيْتِ الآلِهَةِ فَما حالُهُما؟' قالَ المَلِكُ: 'هَذانِ رَجُلانِ أتَيانِى، يُضِلّانِى عَنْ دِينِى وَيَدْعُوانِى إلَي إلَهٍ سَماوِىٍّ.'

فَقالَ: 'أيُّها المَلِكُ، فَمُناظَرَةٌ جَمِيلَةٌ. فإنْ يَكُنِ الحَقُّ لَهُما اتَّبَعْناهُما، وإنْ يَكُنِ الحَقُّ لَنا دَخَلا مَعَنا فِى دِيْنِنا؛ فَكانَ لَهُما ما لَنا وَعَلَيْهِما ما عَلَيْنا. قالَ: 'فَبَعَثَ المَلِكُ إلَيْهِما. فَلَمّا دَخَلا إلَيْهِ، قالَ لَهُما صاحِبُهُما: 'ما الذى جِئْتُمانِى بِهِ؟' قالا: 'جِئْنا نَدْعُو إلَي عِبادَةِ اللهِ الذى خَلَقَ السَماواتِ والأرضَ، وَيَخْلُقُ فِى الأرْحامِ ما يَشاءُ وَيُصَوِّرُ كَيْفَ يَشاءُ، وأنْبَتَ الأشْجارَ والثِّمارَ، وأنْزَلَ القَطْرَ مِنَ السَماءِ.'»

He said to them, ‘This God of yours, to Whom and to Whose worship you invite, if we bring to you a blind person, can He restore him to health?’ They said, ‘If we ask Him to do it, He will do it, if He wants.’ He said, ‘O king! Bring a blind person who has never seen.’ One such person was brought. He said to them, ‘Supplicate your God to restore his sight.’ They stood up and prayed two prostrations (*raq‘atayn*). All at once, the eyes of the blind man opened, and he looked to the sky. Simon said, ‘O king! Bring another blind person to me.’ One was brought. Simon prayed one prostration (*sajdah*), then he lifted his head and all at once the blind person was seeing. He said, ‘O king! A proof for a proof! Bring a cripple.’ One was brought. He said the same [sort of thing as was previously mentioned to them about the blind person]. They prayed and supplicated Allah. All at once the cripple straightened his legs, stood and walked. He said, ‘O king! Bring another cripple to me.’ One was brought. He did the same [thing that he did in the case of the blind person]. The cripple got up. He said, ‘O king! They brought two proofs, and we have brought the like of both of them. One thing remains. If they do this, I will enter their religion with them.’

Then he said, ‘O king! Word has reached me that the king had an only son, and that he died. If their God revives him, I will enter their religion with them.’ The king said to him, ‘And I with you, too.’ Then Simon said to them, ‘One thing remains. The son of the king has died, so, supplicate your God to revive him.’ They fell to prostrate themselves to Allah. They lengthened their prostration (*sajdah*). Then they raised their heads and said to the kind, ‘Send someone to the grave of your son, and you will find that he has been raised from his grave, God willing.’

The people went out to look. They found him to have come out of his grave, wiping the dust from his head. They brought him to the king. He recognized his son and said to him, ‘How are you, my son?’ He said, ‘I was dead. Then I saw two men before my Lord, in prostration, supplicating Him that I be revived. Then He revived me.’ He said, ‘O my son! Would you recognize them if you saw them?’ He said, ‘Yes.’

قالَ: «فقالَ لَهُما: 'إِلَهُكُما هَذا الذى تَدْعُوانِ إِليه وإِلي عِبادَتِهِ، إنْ جِئْناكُما بِأعْمَي يَقْدِرُ أنْ يَرُدَّهُ صَحِيحاً؟' قالا: 'إنْ سألْناهُ أنْ يَفْعَلَ، فَعَلَ إنْ شاءَ.' قالَ: 'أيُّها المَلِكُ! عَلَيَّ بِأعْمَي، لا يَبْصُرُ قَطُّ.' قالَ؛ فأتِيَ بِهِ. فقالَ لَهُما: 'أدْعُوا إِلَهَكُما أنْ يَرُدَّ بَصرَ هَذا.' فقاما وَصَلَّيا رَكْعَتَيْنِ، فإذا عَيْناهُ مَفْتُوحَتانِ، وَهُوَ يَنْظُرُ إلي السَماءِ. فقالَ: 'أيُّها المَلِكُ! عَلَيَّ بِأعْمَي آخَرَ.' فأتِيَ بِهِ.» قالَ: «فَسَجَدَ سَجْدَةً، ثُمَّ رَفَعَ رأسَهُ؛ فإذا الأعمَي بَصِيرٌ. فقالَ: 'أيُّها المَلِكُ! حُجَّةٌ بِحُجَّةٍ. عَلَيَّ بِمُقْعِدٍ. فأتِيَ بِهِ. فقالَ لَهُما مِثْلَ ذَلِكَ. فَصَلَّيا وَدَعَوا اللهَ، فإذا المُقْعِدُ قَدْ أطْلَقَتْ رِجْلاهُ، وَقامَ يَمْشِي. فقالَ: 'أيُّها المَلِكُ عَلَيَّ بِمُقْعِدٍ آخَرَ.' فأتِيَ بِهِ؛ فَصَنَعَ بِهِ كَما صَنَعَ أوَّلَ مَرَّةٍ. فانْطَلَقَ المُقْعِدُ فقالَ: 'أيُّها المَلِكُ! قَدْ أتَيا بِحُجَّتَيْنِ وأتَيْنا بِمِثْلِهِما، ولَكِنْ بَقِيَ شَيْءٌ واحِدٌ؛ فانْ كانَ هُما فَعَلاهُ، دَخَلْتُ مَعَهُما فِي دِينِهِما.'

ثُمَّ قالَ: 'أيُّها المَلِكُ! بَلَغَنِي أنَّهُ كانَ لِلْمَلِكِ ابن واحِدٌ وَماتَ. فإنْ أحْياهُ إِلَهُهُما، دَخَلْتُ مَعَهُما فِي دِينِهِما.' فقالَ لَهُ المَلِكُ: 'وأنا أيْضاً مَعَكَ.' ثُمَّ قالَ لَهُما: 'قَدْ بَقِيَتْ هَذِهِ الخِصْلَةُ الواحِدَةُ. قَدْ ماتَ ابن المَلِكِ، فادْعُوا إِلَهَكُما أنْ يُحْيِيَهُ.' قالَ: 'فَخَرّا ساجِدَيْنِ لِلهِ, وأطالا السُّجُودَ, ثُمَّ رَفَعا رأسَيْهِما وَقالا لِلْمَلِكِ: 'ابْعَثْ إلي قَبْرِ ابنكَ, تَجِدْهُ قَدْ قامَ مِنْ قَبْرِهِ, إنْ شاءَ اللهُ.'

قالَ: 'فَخَرَجَ الناسُ يَنْظُرُونَ, فَوَجَدُوهُ قَدْ خَرَجَ مِنْ قَبْرِهِ, يَنْفُضُ رأسَهُ مِنَ التُّرابِ.'» قالَ: «فاتِي بِهِ إلي المَلِكِ, فَعَرَفَ أنَّهُ ابنهُ. فقالَ لَهُ: 'ما حالُكَ؟ يا بُنَيَّ!' قالَ: 'كُنْتُ مَيِّتاً, فَرأيْتُ رَجُلَيْنِ بَيْنَ يَدَيْ رَبِّي, السّاعَةَ, ساجِدَيْنِ, يَسْألانِهِ أنْ يُحْيِيَنِي, فأحْيانِي.' قالَ: 'يا بُنَيَّ! فَتَعْرِفُهُما إذا رأيْتَهُما؟' قالَ: 'نَعَم.'»

He brought the people out to a field. One by one they passed him, and the father told his son, 'Look.' The son said, 'No. No.' Then, after many had passed, the king had one of them pass, and the son said, 'This is one of them,' and he pointed to him. Then many passed by, until he saw the companion of the other. The son said, 'This is the other one.'

The prophet who was the companion of those two men said, 'As for me, I believe in your God. I know that what you have brought is the truth.' The king said, 'I, also, believe in your God.' Then all the people of his kingdom believed.

(*Biḥār* 14, 240-242, 20)

1.7.10. It is reported that Abū 'Abd Allah said, "Between David and Jesus there were four hundred eighty years. There descended to Jesus admonitions, parables and sanctions in the Gospel. There was no retaliation nor commands for punishments, nor obligatory inheritance.

There descended upon him a lightening of what was descended upon Moses in the Torah, and this is what He said, reporting the words of Jesus to the Children of Israel, ﴾*Likewise confirming the truth of the Torah that is before me, and to make lawful to you certain things that were forbidden unto you.*﴿ (3:50).

And Jesus ordered those who were with him, who followed him and who were believers to believe in the law of the Torah and the laws of all the prophets and the Gospel." And he [Abū 'Abd Allah] said, "Jesus waited for seven or eight years, then he informed them [the people] of what they ate and what they stored in their houses. And he stood up among them, and made the dead to live, and cured the born blind and the leper, and he taught them the Torah. Then Allah descended the Gospel upon him when He wanted to bring an authority for them.

And he [Jesus] sent a man to Rome. All he treated were cured of their illnesses, and he cured the born blind and the leper, until it was mentioned to the king there. So, he was brought to him. He [the king] said, 'Do you make well the born blind and the leper?' He said,

قالَ: «فأخْرَجَ الناسَ جُمْلَةً إلي الصَحْراءِ, فكانَ يَمُرُّ عَلَيْهِ رَجُلٌ رَجُلٌ, فَيقُولُ لَهُ أبُوهُ: 'اُنْظُرْ.' فَيَقُولُ: 'لا, لا.' ثُمَّ مَرَّ عَلَيْهِ بِأحَدِهِما بَعْدَ جَمْعٍ كَثِيرٍ, فَقالَ: 'هذا أحَدُهُما.' وأشارَ بِيَدِهِ إلَيْهِ. ثُمَّ مَرَّ أيْضاً بِقَوْمٍ كَثِيرِينَ, حَتَّي رأي صاحِبَهُ الآخَرَ, فَقالَ: 'وَهذا, الآخَرُ.'»

قالَ: «فَقالَ النَبِيُّ, صاحِبُ الرجُلَيْنِ: 'أمّا أنا, فَقَدْ آمَنْتُ بِإلهِكُما وعَلِمْتُ أنَّ ما جِئْتُما بِهِ هُوَ الحَقُّ.' فَقالَ المَلِكُ: 'وأنا أيْضاً آمَنْتُ بِإلهِكُما.' وآمَنَ أهْلُ مَمْلِكَتِهِ كُلُّهُمْ.»

(بحار الأنوار، ١٤، ٢٤٠-٢٤٢، ٢٠)

١-٧-١٠- الصَدُوقُ بِإسْنادِهِ, عَنْ ابن عِيسَي, عَنِ البَزَنْطِيِّ, عَنْ أبانِ بْنِ عُثْمانَ, عَنْ مُحَمَّدٍ الحَلَبِيِّ, عَنْ أبِي عَبْدِ اللهِ عليه السلام, قالَ: «كانَ بَيْنَ داوُدَ وَعِيسَي عليه السلام أرْبَعُ مِائَةِ سَنَةٍ وَثَمانُونَ سَنَةً, وأنْزَلَ عَلَي عِيسَي فِي الإنجيلِ مَواعِظَ وأمْثالٌ وَحُدُودٌ. لَيْسَ فِيها قِصاصٌ, وَلا أحْكامُ حُدُودٍ وَلا فَرْضُ مَوارِيثَ. وأنْزَلَ عَلَيْهِ تَخْفِيفُ ما كان نُزِّلَ عَلَي مُوسَي عليه السلام فِي التَوْراةِ, وَهُوَ قَوْلُهُ تَعالَي حِكايَةَ عَنْ عِيسَي, أنَّهُ قالَ لِبَنِي إسرائيلَ: ﴿وَلِأُحِلَّ لَكُم بَعْضَ الذى حُرِّمَ عَلَيْكُم﴾

وأمَرَ عِيسَي مَنْ مَعَهُ مِمَّنْ تَبِعَهُ مِنَ المُؤْمِنِينَ أنْ يُؤْمِنُوا بِشَرِيعَةِ التَوْراةِ وَشَرائِعِ جَمِيعِ النَبِيِّينَ والإنجيلِ.» قالَ: «وَمَكَثَ عِيسَي عليه السلام حَتَّي بَلَغَ سَبْعَ سِنِينَ أوْ ثَمانِياً, فَجَعَلَ يُخْبِرُهُمْ بِما يأكُلُونَ وَما يَدَّخِرُونَ فِي بُيُوتِهِم. فأقامَ بَيْنَ أظْهُرِهِمْ, يُحيِي المَوْتَي وَيُبْرِئُ الأكْمَهَ والأبرصَ, وَيُعَلِّمُهُمُ التَوْراةَ. وأنْزَلَ اللهُ عَلَيْهِ الإنجيلَ, لَمّا أرادَ أنْ يَتَّخِذَ عَلَيْهِمْ حُجَّةً.

وَكانَ يَبْعَثَ إلَي الرومِ رَجُلاً لا يُداوِي أحداً إلّا بُرِئَ مِنْ مَرَضِهِ, وَيُبْرِئُ الأكْمَهَ والأبرصَ؛ حَتَّي ذُكِرَ ذَلِكَ لِمَلِكِهِمْ. فأدْخَلَ عَلَيْهِ, فَقالَ: 'أتُبْرِئُ الأكْمَهَ والأبرصَ؟' قالَ: 'نَعَم.' قالَ: 'أتِيَ بِغُلامٍ مُنْخَسِفِ الحَدَقَةِ, لَمْ يَرَ شَيْئاً قَطُّ. فأخَذَ بُنْدُقَتَيْنِ,

'Yes.' He said, 'Bring a youth who has no eyes and has never seen anything.' He took two hazelnuts and looked at them sharply, then he put them in his eye sockets, and prayed. At once he became seeing. The king sat him next to himself, and said, 'Be with me, and do not leave my city.' He conferred upon him the best positions.

Then the Messiah sent another, and taught him something for reviving the dead. He entered Rome, and said, 'I am more knowledgeable than the physician of the king.' This was mentioned to the king. He said, 'Kill him.' The [first] physician said, 'Do not do it. Bring him. If you find him to be in error, you will kill him. In that case, you would have authority to do so.'

He was brought to him. He said, 'I revive the dead.' The king mounted and so did the people and they went to the grave of the son of the king who had recently died. The apostle of the Messiah prayed, and the first apostle who was the physician of the king said, 'Amen.' The grave split open and the son of the king emerged. Then he came walking until he sat in the lap of his father.

Then he said, 'O my son! Who revived you?' Then he looked and said, 'This one and that one.' Then they stood and said, 'We are messengers to you from the Messiah. You had not listened to his messengers. You even ordered them to be killed when they came to you.' Then he obeyed and glorified the affair of the Messiah until the enemies of Allah said what they said about him and the Jews belied him and wanted to kill him.

(*Biḥār,* 14, 251, 43)

1.7.11. It is reported that Jesus the son of Mary raised John the son of Zachariah among twelve apostles to teach the people and to prohibit them from marrying their sisters' daughters. The king of those people was attracted to the daughter of his sister and he wanted to marry her. When her mother was informed that John had prohibited this kind of marriage, she brought her daughter adorned to

فَبَنَدَقَهُما, ثُمَّ جَعَلَهُما فِي عَيْنَيْهِ وَدَعا, فإذا هُوَ بَصِيرٌ. فأقْعَدَهُ المَلِكُ مَعَهُ وَقالَ: 'كُنْ مَعِيَ وَلا تَخْرُجْ مِنْ مِصْرِى.' فأنْزَلَهُ مَعَهُ بِأفْضَلِ المَنازِلِ.

ثُمَّ إنَّ المَسِيحَ عليه السلام بَعَثَ آخَرَ وَعَلَّمَهُ ما بِهِ يُحيِى المَوْتَي. فَدَخَلَ الرومَ وَقالَ: 'أنا أعْلَمُ مِنْ طَبِيبِ المَلِكِ.' فَقالُوا لِلْمَلِكِ ذَلِكَ. قالَ: 'اُقْتُلُوهُ.' فَقالَ الطَّبِيبُ: 'لا تَفْعَلْهُ؛ أدْخِلْهُ, فإنْ عَرَفْتَ خَطاهُ قَتَلْتَهُ, وَلَكَ الحُجَّةُ.' فأدْخَلَ عَلَيْهِ, فَقالَ: 'أنا أُحْيِى المَوْتَي.' فَرَكِبَ المَلِكُ والناسُ إلَي قَبْرِ ابنِ المَلِكِ, وَكانَ قَدْ ماتَ فِي تِلْكَ الأيّامِ. فَدَعا رَسُولُ المَسِيحِ, وأمَّنَ طَبِيبُ المَلِكِ الذى هُوَ رَسُولُ المَسِيحِ أيْضاً الأوَّلُ. فانْشَقَّ القَبْرُ, فَخَرَجَ ابنِ المَلِكِ, ثُمَّ جاءَ يَمْشِي حَتَّي جَلَسَ فِي حِجْرِ أبِيهِ, فَقالَ: 'يا بُنَيَّ مَنْ أحْياكَ؟'» قالَ: «فَنَظَرَ, فَقالَ: 'هَذا وَهَذا.' فَقاما, فَقالا: 'أنا رَسُولُ المَسِيحِ إلَيكَ؛ وإنَّكَ كُنْتَ لا تَسْمَعُ مِنْ رُسُلِهِ, إنَّما تأمُرُ بِقَتْلِهِمْ إذا أتَوْكَ.' فَتابَعَ وأعْظَمُوا أمْرَ المَسِيحِ عليه السلام, حَتَّي قالَ فِيهِ أعْداءُ اللهِ ما قالُوا, واليَهُودُ يُكَذِّبُونَهُ وَيُرِيدُونَ قَتْلَهُ.»

(بحار الأنوار، ١٤، ٢٥١، ٤٣)

١-٧-١١- فِي خَبَرٍ آخَرَ, «إنَّ عِيسَي بْنَ مَرْيَمَ عليه السلام بَعَثَ يَحْيَي بْنَ زَكَرِيّا عليه السلام, فِي اثْنَي عَشَرَ مِنَ الحَوارِيِّينَ, يُعَلِّمُونَ الناسَ وَيَنْهاهُمْ, عَنْ نِكاحِ ابنةِ الأخْتِ.» قالَ: «وَكانَ لِمَلِكِهِمْ بِنْتُ أخْتٍ تُعْجِبُهُ, وَكانَ يُرِيدُ أنْ يَتَزَوَّجَها. فَلَمّا بَلَغَ أمَّها أنَّ يَحْيَي عليه السلام نَهي عَنْ مِثْلِ هَذا النكاحِ, أدْخَلَتْ بِنْتَها عَلَي المَلِكِ مُزَيَّنَةً.

the king. When the king saw her, he asked her what she desired. She said, "I want you to slaughter John the son of Zachariah." He said, "Ask me for something else." She said, "I will not ask you for anything but this."

When she refused him, he sent for a basin and sent for Johan. Then he slaughtered him. A drop of his blood fell at once to the earth and the stain of it remained until Bukht Naṣṣar reigned over them. Then an old man of the children of Israel came to him and guided him to that blood. Bukht Naṣṣar decided to kill the children of Israel because of that blood until the stain would be obliterated. So he killed seventy thousand for this in one year until it was obliterated.

(*Biḥār*, 14, 182, 24)

1.7.12. Abū Ja'far said, "The foremost[1] are four: the murdered son of Adam, the foremost of the community of Moses, who was a believer among the Pharaoh's people, the foremost of the community of Jesus, who was Ḥabīb the carpenter, and the foremost of the community of Muḥammad, who was 'Alī ibn Abī Ṭālib."

(*Biḥār,* 66, 156)

1.8. BELL

1.8.1. It is reported that al-Ḥārith al-A'war said, "I was travelling with the Commander of the Faithful, 'Alī ibn Abū Ṭālib in Ḥīrah when we came upon a monk who was ringing a church bell.

'Alī ibn Abū Ṭālib said, 'O Ḥārith! Do you know what this church bell is saying?' I said, 'Allah, His Apostle and the son of the uncle of His Apostle know better.' He said, 'It strikes the metaphore of this world and its destruction and it says, "There is no god but Allah, really, really, truly, truly. Surly this world has beguiled us, has occupied us, has made itself alluring to us. O son of this world! Take your time! Take your time! Ring, ring. O son of this world! Gather,

[1] See (56:10).

فَلَمّا رَآها سَأَلَها, عَنْ حاجَتِها. قالَتْ: 'حاجَتِى أنْ تَذْبَحَ يَحْيَي بْنَ زَكَرِيّا.' فَقالَ: 'سَلِى غَيْرَ هٰذا.' فَقالَتْ: 'لا أسْألُكَ غَيْرَ هٰذا.'

فَلَمّا أبَتْ عَلَيْهِ, دَعا بِطَشْتٍ وَدَعا بِيَحْيَي ﷺ, فَذَبَحَهُ. فَبَدَرَتْ قَطْرَةٌ مِنْ دَمِهِ, فَوَقَعَتْ عَلَي الأرْضِ, فَلَمْ تَزَلْ تَغْلُو حَتَّي بَعَثَ اللهُ بُخْتَ نَصَّرَ عَلَيْهِم. فَجاءَتْهُ عَجُوزٌ مِنْ بَنِى إسْرائِيلَ, فَدَلَّتْهُ عَلَي ذٰلِكَ الدَمِ. فَألْقَي فِى نَفْسِهِ أنْ يَقْتُلَ عَلَي ذٰلِكَ الدَمِ مِنْهُمْ, حَتَّي يَسْكُنَ. فَقَتَلَ عَلَيْها سَبْعِينَ ألْفاً فِى سَنَةٍ واحِدَةٍ, حَتَّي سَكَنَ.»

(بحار الأنوار، ١٤، ١٨٢، ٢٤)

١-٧-١٢- عَنْ أبِى جَعْفَرٍ ﷺ, قالَ: «السّابِقُونَ أرْبَعَةٌ: ابن آدَمَ المَقْتُولُ، والسّابِقُ فِى أُمَّةِ مُوسَي وَهُوَ مُؤْمِنُ آلِ فِرْعَوْنَ، والسّابِقُ فِى أُمَّةِ عِيسَي وَهُوَ حَبِيبُ النَجّارِ، والسّابِقُ فِى أُمَّةِ مُحَمَّدٍ ﷺ، وَهُوَ عَلِيُّ بْنُ أبِى طالِبٍ ﷺ.»

(بحار الأنوار، ٦٦، ١٥٦)

١-٨- النّاقُوس

١-٨-١- صالِحُ بْنُ عِيسَي العِجْلِىُّ, عَنْ مُحَمَّدِ بْنِ عَلِىٍّ الفَقِيهِ, عَنْ أبِى نَصْرٍ الشَعْرانِىٍّ, عَنْ سَلَمَةِ بْنِ الوَضّاحِ, عَنْ أبِيهِ, عَنْ أبِى إسْرائِيلَ, عَنْ أبِى إسْحاقَ, عَنْ عاصِمِ بْنِ ضَمْرَةَ, عَنِ الحارِثِ الأعْوَرِ, قالَ: «بَيْنا أنا أسِيرُ مَعَ أمِيرِ المُؤْمِنِينَ, عَلِىِّ بْنِ أبِى طالِبٍ ﷺ, فِى الحِيرَةِ؛ إذا نَحْنُ بِدَيْرانِىٍّ يَضْرِبُ بِالنّاقُوس.»

قالَ: «فَقالَ عَلِىُّ بْنُ أبِى طالِبٍ ﷺ: 'يا حارِثُ, أتَدْرى ما يَقُولُ هٰذا النّاقُوسُ؟' قُلْتُ: 'اللهُ وَرَسُولُهُ وابْنُ عَمِّ رَسُولِهِ أعْلَمُ.' قالَ: 'إنَّهُ يَضْرِبُ مَثَلَ الدُنْيا وَخَرابِها, وَيَقُولُ: 'لا إلٰهَ إلّا اللهُ, حَقّاً حَقّاً صِدْقاً صِدْقاً. إنَّ

gather. The world is annihilated moment by moment. No day passes us without a pillar falling. We have ruined the everlasting house and we made our homes in a transitory realm. We do not know how much we have fallen short in it until we die.'(1)

Ḥārith said, 'O Commander of the Faithful! Do the Christians know this?' He said, 'If they knew it, they would not have taken Christ as a god other than Allah, the Mighty and Magnificent.'

Ḥārith said, 'Then I went to the monk and said to him, "By the right of Christ over you! Ring the church bell in the way that you do."

Then he started ringing it, and I said word for word [what Imam 'Alī had told him] to 'until we die.' Then the monk said, 'By the right of your Prophet over you! Who informed you of this?' I said, 'That man who was with me yesterday.' He said, 'Is that man kin to the Prophet?' I said, 'He is the son of his uncle.' He said, 'By the right of your Prophet! Did he hear this from your prophet?' I said, 'Yes.' Then he became a Muslim. Then he said to me, 'By Allah! I found in the Torah that at the end of the prophets there is a prophet who interprets what the church bell says.'"

(*Biḥār*, 14, 334, 1)

1.9. THE CHILDREN OF ISRAEL

1.9.1. Their Food

1.9.1.1. The Prophet said, "Verily, Allah sent down a spread to Jesus and blessed him with a flat loaf of bread and fishes, so four thousand seven hundred people ate of it and were sated."

(*Biḥār,* 14, 249, 37).

---

[1] This interpretation of the sound of the church bell is in a rhymed sing-song rhythm.

الدنْيا قَدْ غرَّتْنا, وَشَغَلَتْنا واستَهْوَتْنا. يا ابن الدنْيا مَهْلاً مَهْلاً, يا ابن الدنْيا دَقاً دَقاً. يا ابن الدنْيا جَمْعاً جَمْعاً, تَفْنَي الدنْيا قَرْناً قَرْناً. ما مِنْ يَوْمٍ يَمْضِي عنّا, إلّا أوْهَي مِنّا رُكْناً. قَدْ ضَيَّعْنا داراً تَبْقَي, واستَوْطَنّا داراً تَفْنَي. لَسْنا نَدْرِي ما فَرَّطْنا فِيها، إلّا لَوْ قَدْ مِتْنا.'

قالَ الحارِثُ: 'يا أمِيرَ المُؤْمِنِينَ! النَصارَي يَعْلَمُونَ ذلِكَ؟' قالَ: 'لَوْ عَلِمُوا ذلِكَ, لما اتَّخَذُوا المَسِيحَ إلهاً مِنْ دُونِ اللهِ, عَزَّ وَجَلَّ.'»

قالَ: «فَذَهَبْتُ إلَي الدَيْرانِيِّ, فَقُلْتُ لَهُ: 'بِحَقِّ المَسِيحِ عَلَيْكَ, لَمّا ضَرَبْتَ بِالناقُوسِ عَلَي الجِهَةِ الّتِي تَضْرِبُها.»

قالَ: «فأخَذَ يَضْرِبُ, وأنا أقُولُ حَرْفاً حَرْفاً, حَتَّي بَلَغَ إلَي قَوْلِهِ: 'إلّا لَوْ قَدْ مِتْنا.' فَقالَ: 'بِحَقِّ نَبِيِّكُمْ, مَنْ أخْبَرَكَ بِهَذا؟' قُلْتُ: 'هَذا الرجُلُ الذى كانَ مَعِيَ أمْسِ.' قالَ: 'وَهَلْ بَيْنَهُ وَبَيْنَ النَبِيِّ مِنْ قَرابَةٍ؟' قُلْتُ: 'هُوَ ابن عَمِّهِ.' قالَ: 'بِحَقِّ نَبِيِّكُمْ, أسَمِعَ هذا مِنْ نَبِيِّكُمْ؟'» قالَ: « قُلْتُ: 'نَعَم.' فأسْلَمَ, ثُمَّ قالَ لِي عليه السلام ' واللهِ, إنِّي وَجَدْتُ فِي التَوْراةِ أنَّهُ يَكُونُ فِي آخِرِ الأنبياءِ نَبِيٌّ, وَهُوَ يُفَسِّرُ ما يَقُولُ الناقُوسُ.'»

(بحار الأنوار، ١٤، ٣٣٤، ١)

١-٩- بَنُو إسْرائِيل

١-٩-١- مائِدَتُهُم

١-٩-١-١- قالَ النَبِيُّ صلى الله عليه وآله: «إنَّ اللهَ أنْزَلَ مائِدَةً عَلَي عِيسَي عليه السلام وَبارَكَ لَهُ فِي أرْغِفَةٍ وَسَمِيكاتٍ، حَتَّي أكَلَ وَشَبِعَ مِنْها أرْبَعَةُ آلافٍ وَسَبْعُ مِائَةٍ.»

(بحار الأنوار، ١٤، ٢٤٩، ٣٧)

1.9.1.2. The Messenger of Allah said, "O servants of Allah! Verily, when the people of Jesus asked him to have Allah bring down a spread from heaven, Allah said, ﴾I will send it down to you, then whoever of you disbelieves after that, I will punish as I will not punish any other being.﴿ (5:115) Then He sent it down to them, and all of them who disbelieved after that, Allah transformed into a pig, monkey, bear, cat, or in the form of some birds, animals of the land or sea. So, they were transformed into four hundred forms."

(*Biḥār,* 14, 235, 8)

1.9.1.3. It is reported that Abū al-Ḥasan said, "Verily, the swine among the people of Jesus asked for a table spread to come down. Then they did not believe. So, Allah transformed them into swine."

(*Biḥār*, 14, 236, 10)

1.9.2. Their Denial

1.9.2.1. 'Anas ibn Mālik said, "The Apostle of Allah said, 'Verily the children of Israel split into seventy-one sects after Jesus. Seventy sects perished and one sect was saved. My community will split into seventy-two sects. Seventy-one sects will perish and one of them will be saved.' They said, 'O Apostle of Allah! What is that sect?' He said, 'The community, the community, the community.'"

(*Al-Khiṣāl*, 2, 584)

1.9.2.2 Muḥammad ibn Ja'far said, "Abū 'Abd Allah narrated to us from his fathers, peace be with them, 'I heard from 'Alī that he said to the cfief of the Jews, 'How many sects did you split into?' He said, 'So and so many sects.' 'Alī said, 'You lie.'

١-٩-١-٢- قالَ رَسُولُ اللهِ صلى الله عليه وآله وسلم: «يا عِبادَ اللهِ إنَّ قَوْمَ عِيسَي لَمّا سألوهُ أنْ يُنَزِّلَ علَيْهِم مائِدَةً مِنَ السَماءِ، قالَ اللهُ: ﴿إنِّي مُنَزِّلُها عَلَيْكُمْ. فَمَنْ يَكْفُرْ بَعْدُ مِنْكُمْ، فإنِّي أُعَذِّبُهُ عَذاباً لا أُعَذِّبُهُ أحَداً مِنَ العالَمِينَ.﴾ فأنْزَلَها عَلَيْهِم، فَمَنْ كَفَرَ مِنْهُمْ بَعْدُ، مَسَخَهُ اللهُ، إمّا خِنْزِيراً وإمّا قِرَداً وإمّا دُبّاً وإمّا هِرّاً وإمّا عَلَي صُورَةِ بَعْضِ الطُّيُورِ والدوابِّ الّتِي فِي البَرِّ والبَحْرِ، حَتَّي مَسَخُوا عَلَي أرْبَعِ مِائة نَوْعٍ مِنَ المَسْخِ.»

(بحار الأنوار، ١٤، ٢٣٥، ٨)

١-٩-١-٣- عَنِ الفُضَيْلِ بْنِ يَسارٍ، عَنْ أبِي الحَسَنِ عليه السلام، قالَ: «إنَّ الخَنازِيرَ مِنْ قَوْمِ عِيسَي عليه السلام سألُوا نُزُولَ المائِدَةِ، فَلَمْ يُؤْمِنُوا، فَمَسَخَهُمُ اللهُ خَنازِيرَ.»

(بحار الأنوار، ١٤، ٢٣٦، ١٠)

١-٩-٢- إنْكارُهُم

١-٩-٢-١- عَنْ أنَسِ بْنِ مالِكٍ، قالَ: «قالَ رَسُولُ اللهِ صلى الله عليه وآله وسلم: 'إنَّ بَنِي إسْرائِيلَ تَفَرَّقَتْ عَلَي عِيسَي، إحْدَي وَسَبْعِينَ فِرْقَةً؛ فَهَلَكَ سَبْعُونَ فِرْقَةً وَتَخَلَّصَ فِرْقَةٌ. وإنَّ أُمَّتِي سَتَفْتَرِقُ عَلَي اثْنَتَيْنِ وَسَبْعِينَ فِرْقَةً، يَهْلِكُ إحْدَي وَسَبْعُونَ، وَيَتَخَلَّصُ فِرْقَةٌ.' قالُوا: 'يا رَسُولَ اللهِ صلى الله عليه وآله وسلم، مَنْ تِلْكَ الفِرْقَةُ؟' قالَ: 'الجَماعَةُ، الجَماعَةُ، الجَماعَةُ.'»

(الخصال، ٢، ٥٨٤)

١-٩-٢-٢- حَدَّثَنا مُحَمَّدُ بْنُ جَعْفَرِ بْنِ مُحَمَّدٍ، قالَ: «حَدَّثَنا أبُو عَبْدِ اللهِ عليه السلام.» قالَ المَجاشِعِي: «وَحَدَّثَنا الرضا عليه السلام، عَنْ أبِيهِ مُوسَي، عَنْ أبِيهِ أبِي عَبْدِ اللهِ، جَعْفَرٍ، عَنْ آبائِهِ عليهم السلام، قالَ: 'سَمِعْتُ عَلِيّاً يَقُولُ لِرَأسِ اليَهُودِ: 'عَلَي كَمْ افْتَرَقْتُمْ؟' فَقالَ: 'عَلَي كَذا وكَذا فِرقَة.' فَقالَ عَلِيٌّ عليه السلام:

Then he faced the people and said, 'By Allah! If the seat [of government] is returned to me, I will judge among the people of the Torah by their Torah, among the people of the Gosple by their Gosple and between the people of the Qur'ān by their Qur'ān.

The Jews split into seventy-one sects, seventy of them will be in the Fire. One of them will be saved and will be in heaven and it is the sect that followed Yūsha' ibn Nūn, the executor of Moses. The Christians split into seventy-two sects. Seventy-one of them will be in the Fire and one of them will be in heaven, and it is the sect that followed Simon, the executor of Jesus. And this community will split into seventy-three sects. Seventy-two of them will be in the Fire. One of them will be in heaven, and it is the sect that follows the executor of Muḥammad.'

Then he beat his breast with his hand and said, 'Thirteen sects, among the seventy-three sects, will accept my kindness and love, but one of them will be in heaven. It is the middle rite, and the twelve sects will be in the Fire.'"

(*Biḥār*, 28, 4, 5)

1.9.2.3. 'Alī said, "O Kumayl! Nither the Christians denied Allah, the Exalted, nor the Jews, and they did not refuse Moses or Jesus, but they increased, decreased, perverted and misled. So they were cursed and hated, and did not repent or accept. O Kumayl! Our father Adam was born nither as a Jew nor a Christian, and he was not His son, but he was *ḥanīf* (upright) and Muslim. He did not do something that was obligatory, so what happened happened, until Allah accepted a sacrifice for him."

(*Bishārah al-Muṣṭafā li Shī'ah al-Murtaḍā*, 29)

1.9.2.4. Mughayrah narrated from Abū 'Abd Allah, and he from his father, and he from his grandfather, peace be with them, that he said, "The transformed among the children of Adam are thirteen kinds: monkey, swine and... As for the monkeys, they were a group that came down to a town near the beach of the sea, acted unlawfully on

'كَذِبْتَ.' ثُمَّ أقبلَ علِيٌّ عَلَي الناسِ، فقالَ: 'واللهِ لَوْ ثُنِّيَتْ لِي الوَسادَةُ، لَقَضَيْتُ بَيْنَ أهْلِ التَوْراةِ بِتَوْراتِهِمْ وبَيْنَ أهْلِ الإنجيلِ بِإنْجِيلِهِمْ وبَيْنَ أهْلِ القرآنِ بِقُرْآنِهِمْ.

افْتَرَقَتِ اليَهُودُ عَلَي إحْدَي وَسَبْعِينَ فِرْقَةً، سَبْعُونَ مِنْها فِي النارِ، وَواحِدَةٌ ناجِيَةٌ فِي الجَنَّةِ، وَهِيَ الَّتِي اتَّبَعَتْ يُوشَعَ بْنَ نُونَ وَصِيَّ مُوسَي. وافْتَرَقَتِ النَصارَي عَلَي اثْنَتَيْنِ وَسَبْعِينَ فِرْقَةً، احْدَي وَسَبْعُونَ فِرْقَةً فِي النارِ، وَواحِدَةٌ فِي الجَنَّةِ، وَهِيَ الَّتِي اتَّبَعَتْ شَمْعُونَ وَصِيَّ عِيسَي. وَتَفْتَرِقُ هذِهِ الأمَّةُ عَلَي ثَلاثٍ وَسَبْعِينَ فِرْقَةً، اثْنَتانِ وَسَبْعُونَ فِي النارِ، وَواحِدَةٌ فِي الجَنَّةِ، وَهِيَ الَّتِي إتَّبَعَتْ وَصِيَّ مُحَمَّدٍ.'

وَضَرَبَ بِيَدِهِ عَلَي صَدْرِهِ، ثُمَّ قالَ: 'ثَلاثَةَ عَشَرَ فِرْقَةً مِنَ الثَلاثِ والسَبْعِينَ فِرْقَةً، كُلُّها تَنْتَحِلُ مَوَدَّتِي وَحُبِّي. واحِدَةٌ مِنْها فِي الجَنَّةِ، وَهُمُ النَمَطُ الأوْسَطُ، واثْنَتا عَشْرَةَ فِي النارِ.''»

(بحار الأنوار، ٢٨، ٤، ٥)

١-٩-٢-٣- قالَ عَلِيٌّ عليه السلام: «يا كُمَيْلُ، إنَّ النَصارَي لَمْ تُعَطِّلِ اللهَ، تعالَي، وَلا اليَهُودَ، وَلا جَحَدَتْ مُوسَي وَلا عِيسَي؛ وَلَكِنَّهُم زادُوا وَنَقَصُوا وَحَرَّفُوا وألْحَدُوا. فَلُعِنُوا وَمُقِتُوا وَلَمْ يَتُوبُوا وَلَمْ يَقْبَلُوا. يا كُمَيْلُ، إنَّ أبانا آدَمَ عليه السلام لَمْ يَلِدْ يَهُودِيّاً وَلا نَصْرانِيّاً، وَلا كانَ ابنهُ إلّا حَنِيفاً مُسْلِماً؛ فَلَمْ يَقُمْ بِالواجِبِ عَلَيْهِ، فأدّاهُ ذَلِكَ إلَي أنْ يَقْبَلَ اللهُ لَهُ قُرْباناً.»

(بشارة المصطفَي لِشيعة المرتضَي، ٢٩)

١-٩-٢-٤- حَدَّثَنا مُحَمَّدُ بْنُ عَلِيٍّ ماجِيلَوَيْه، رَضِيَ اللهُ عَنْهُ، قالَ: «حَدَّثَنا مُحَمَّدُ بْنُ يَحْيَي العَطّارِ, ... عَنْ أبِي عَبْدِ اللهِ, عَنْ أبِيهِ, عَنْ جَدِّهِ عليه السلام، قالَ: 'المُسُوخُ مِنْ بَنِي آدَمَ ثَلاثَةَ عَشَرَ صِنْفاً، مِنْهُم القِرَدَةُ والخَنازِيرُ... فأمّا القِرَدَةُ، فكانُوا قَوْماً يَنْزِلُونَ بَلْدَةً عَلَي شاطِئِ البَحْرِ، اعْتَدُّوا فِي السَبْتِ فَصادُوا الحِيْتانِ،

Saturday and fished. So Allah, the Exalted, transformed them into monkeys. As for the swine, they were a group among the children of Israel that Jesus the son of Mary cursed. So Allah, the Exalted, transformed them into swine."

(*'Ilal al-Sharā'i'*, 2, 487)

1.9.2.5. It is reported that Abū 'Abd Allah said, "Moses told his people something that they could not bear, so they exiled him to Egypt. They fought with Moses, and he with them, and he killed them. Jesus told his people something that they could not bear, so they exiled him to Takrīt. They fought with Jesus, and he with them, and he killed them. This is the saying of Allah, the mighty and magnificent, ﴾*So a party of the children of Israel believed and another party disbelieved; then We aided those who believed against their enemy, and they triumphed over them.*﴿" (61:14).

(*Biḥār* 14, 279, 11)

1.9.2.6 It is reported that when this verse decended, ﴾*And there is not one of the followers of the Book but most certainly believes in this before his death, and on the day of resurrection he (Jesus) shall be a witness against them.*﴿ (4:159), Abū 'Abd Allah al-Ṣādiq said, "There are none who remain in rejection of what has descended about Jesus the son of Mary but disbelievers."

(*Tafsīr Furāt al-Kūfī*, 115)

1.9.2.7. Ja'far ibn Muḥammad reported from his father that the Apostle of Allah said, "O 'Alī! There is a likeness between Jesus the son of Mary and you. Allah [the Exalted] said, ﴾*And there is not one of the followers of the Book but most certainly believes in this before his death, and on the day of resurrection he (Jesus) shall be a witness against them.*﴿ (4:159). O, 'Alī! Nobody who slanders Jesus dies unless he believes in him before his death and tells the truth about him, when it is no use for him at all. And you are like him. Your enemy does not die until he sees you near his death. When he

فَمَسَخَهُمُ اللهُ، تعالي، قِرَدَةً. وأمّا الخَنازِيرُ، فكانُوا قَوْماً مِنْ بَنِى إسْرائِيلَ، دَعا عَلَيْهِمْ عِيسَي بْنُ مَرْيَمَ عليه السلام، فَمَسَخَهُمُ اللهُ، تعالَي، خَنازِيرَ.'»

(علل الشرائع، ٢، ٤٨٧)

١-٩-٢-٥- أبُو الحَسَنِ بْنُ عَبْدِ اللهِ، عَنْ ابن أبِى يَعْفُورٍ، عَنْ أبِى عَبْدِ اللهِ عليه السلام، قالَ: «إنَّ مُوسَي عليه السلام حَدَّثَ قَوْمَهُ بِحَدِيثٍ لَمْ يَحْتَمِلُوهُ عَنْهُ، فَخَرَجُوا عَلَيْهِ بِمِصْرَ، فَقاتَلُوهُ فَقاتَلَهُمْ، فَقَتَلَهُمْ. وإنَّ عِيسَي عليه السلام حَدَّثَ قَوْمَهُ بِحَدِيثٍ، فَلَمْ يَحْتَمِلُوهُ عَنْهُ، فَخَرَجُوا عَلَيْهِ بِتَكْرِيتٍ، فَقاتَلُوهُ فَقاتَلَهُمْ، فَقَتَلَهُمْ؛ وَهُوَ قَوْلُ اللهِ، عَزَّ وَجَلَّ: ﴿فَآمَنَتْ طائِفَةٌ مِنْ بَنِى إسْرائِيلَ، وَكَفَرَتْ طائِفَةٌ؛ فأيَّدْنا الذينَ آمَنُوا عَلَي عَدُوِّهِمْ فأصْبَحُوا ظاهِرِينَ.﴾

(بحار الأنوار، ١٤، ٢٧٩، ١١)

١-٩-٢-٦- عَنْ أبِى عَبْدِ اللهِ جَعْفَرِ [بْنِ مُحَمَّدٍ] الصادِقِ عليه السلام، قالَ: «لَمّا نُزِّلَتْ هَذِهِ الآيَةُ، ﴿وإنْ مِنْ أهْلِ الكِتابِ إلّا لَيُؤْمِنَنَّ بِه﴾ [الآيةَ]» قالَ: «لا يَبْقَي أحَدٌ يَرُدُّ عَلَي عِيسَي بْنِ مَرْيَمَ عليه السلام ما جاءَ بِهِ فِيْهِ، إلّا كانَ كافِراً.»

(تفسير فرات الكوفي، ١١٥)

١-٩-٢-٧- فُرات قالَ حَدَّثَنِى عُبَيْدُ بْنُ كَثِيرٍ مُعَنْعَناً، عَنْ جَعْفَرِ بْنِ مُحَمَّدٍ، عَنْ أبِيهِ عليه السلام، قالَ: «قالَ رَسُولُ اللهِ صلى الله عليه وآله وسلم: 'يا عَلِيُّ إنَّ فِيكَ مَثَلٌ مِنْ عِيسَي بْنِ مَرْيَمَ؛ قالَ اللهُ: ﴿وإنْ مِنْ أهْلِ الكِتابِ إلّا لَيُؤْمِنَنَّ بِهِ قَبْلَ مَوْتِهِ، وَيَوْمَ القِيامَةِ يَكُونُ عَلَيْهِمْ شَهِيداً.﴾ يا عَلِيُّ، إنَّهُ لا يَمُوتُ رَجُلٌ يَفْتَرِى عَلَي عِيسَي [بْنِ مَرْيَمَ عليه السلام] حَتَّي يُؤْمِنَ بِهِ قَبْلَ مَوْتِهِ، وَيَقُولُ فِيْهِ الحَقَّ حَيْثُ لا يَنْفَعُهُ ذَلِكَ شَيْئًا. وانَّكَ عَلَي مِثْلِهِ، لا يَمُوتُ عَدُوُّكَ حَتَّي يَراكَ عِنْدَ المَوْتِ، فَتَكُونُ عَلَيْهِ غَيْظاً وَحُزْناً، حَتَّي يُقِرَّ

sees you, you will be angry and sad for him. Then he will confess the truth about you, will say the truth about you and will confess your *walāyah,*[1] while it is no use for him at all."

(*Tafsīr Furāt al-Kūfī*, 116)

1.9.2.8. Al-Imām al-'Askarī said, "Allah, the Exalted, blamed the Jews and faulted their disbelieveing in Muhammad... He said, ﴿*Evil is that for which they have sold their souls—that they should deny what Allah has revealed, and there is a disgraceful punishment for the unbelievers, so they have made themselves deserving of wrath upon wrath.*﴾ (2:90) That is, they came back while the wrath of Allah was upon them after another wrath. The first wrath, when they falsified Jesus the son of Mary and the second, when they falsified Muḥammad..."

(*Tafsīr al-Imām al-'Askarī*, 402)

1.9.3. Their Extremism

1.9.3.1. 'Alī said, "Verily Jesus the son of Mary is a servant and a creature. They took him as a Lord, ﴿*but they forgot a portion of what they were reminded of*﴾" (5:14).

(*Tafsīr al-Qumī*, 1 164)

1.9.3.2. Some of our companions have reported that Ja'far ibn Wāqid and some of the companions of Abū al-Khaṭṭāb were mentioned, and someone that he had often seen ibn Wāqid, who said, "﴿*He it is who is God in the heavens and the earth*﴾ (43:84), He is the Imam." Abū 'Abd Allah said, "No, by Allah! May I never be under one roof with him. They are worse than the Jews, the Christians, the Magians, and the pagans! By Allah! Their belittling Allah never belittles His greatness a bit. What the Jews said about him was on Ezra's mind,

---

[1] The term *wilāyah* means "authority" or "guardianship"; and *walāyah* is used for love of the Ahl al-Bayt, devotion to them, obedience to their commands and holding them as models in morals and practice. See the explanation of Asaf A. A. Fyzee in his *A Shī'ite Creed* (Tehran: WOFIS, 1982), 149.

بِالحَقِّ مِنْ أمْرِكَ وَيَقُولَ فِيكَ الحَقَّ وَيُقِرَّ بِوِلايَتِكَ حَيْثُ لا يَنْفَعُهُ ذَلِكَ شَيْئاً.'»

(تفسير فرات الكوفى، ١١٦)

١-٩-٢-٨- قالَ الإمامُ عليه السلام: «ذَمَّ اللهُ، تَعالَي، اليَهُودَ، وَعابَ فِعْلَهُمْ فِي كُفْرِهِمْ بِمُحَمَّدٍ صلى الله عليه وآله وسلم، فَقالَ: ﴿بِئْسَما اشْتَرَوْا بِهِ أنْفُسَهُمْ ... ﴾ ثُمَّ قالَ: ﴿فَباؤوا بِغَضَبٍ عَلَي غَضَبٍ.﴾ يَعنِي رَجَعُوا وَعَلَيْهِمُ الغَضَبُ مِنَ اللهِ عَلَي غَضَبٍ فِي إثْرِ غَضَبٍ. والغَضَبُ الأوَّلُ حِينَ كَذَّبُوا بِعِيسَي بْنِ مَرْيَمَ، والغَضَبُ الثّانِيَ حينَ كَذَّبُوا بِمُحَمَّدٍ صلى الله عليه وآله وسلم. »

(تفسيرالإمام العسكرىّ، ٤٠٢)

١-٩-٣- غُلُوُّهم

١-٩-٣-١- قالَ عَلِيٌّ عليه السلام: «إنَّ عِيسَي بْنَ مَرْيَمَ عَبْدٌ مَخْلوقٌ، فَجَعَلُوهُ رَبّاً، ﴿فَنَسُوا حَظّاً مِمّا ذُكِّرُوا بِهِ.﴾»

(تفسير القمىّ، ١، ١٦٤)

١-٩-٣-٢- كش [رجال الكشّي] مُحَمَّدُ بْنُ مَسْعُودٍ, عَنْ عَبْدِ اللهِ بْنِ مُحَمَّدِ بْنِ خالِدٍ, عَنْ عَلِيِّ بْنِ حِسانٍ, عَنْ بَعْضِ أصْحابِنا رَفَعَهُ إلَي عَبْدِ اللهِ عليه السلام، قالَ: «ذُكِرَ جَعْفَرُ بْنُ واقِدٍ وَنَفَرٌ مِنْ أصْحابِ أبِي الخَطّابِ. فَقِيلَ: 'إنَّهُ صارَ إلَيَّ يَتَرَدَّدُ.' وَقالَ فِيهِمْ: ﴿وَهُوَ الذى فِي السَماءِ إلَهٌ وَفِي الأرضِ إلَهٌ،﴾ قالَ: 'هُوَ الإمامُ.' فَقالَ أبُو عَبْدِ اللهِ عليه السلام: 'لا واللهِ، لا يُؤْوِينِي وَإيّاهُ سَقفُ بَيْتٍ أبداً. هُمْ شَرٌّ مِنَ اليَهُودِ والنَصارَي والمَجُوسِ والَّذِينَ أشْرَكُوا. واللهِ، ما صَغَّرَ عَظَمَةَ اللهِ تَصغِيرُهُمْ شَيْءٌ قَطُّ. وإنَّ عُزَيْراً جالَ فِي صَدْرِهِ ما قالَتِ اليَهُودُ، فَمُحِيَ اسْمُهُ مِنَ النبُوَّةِ. واللهِ، لَوْ

and for this his name was erased from prophethood. By Allah! If Jesus had confessed to what the Christians said about him, Allah would have left deafness to him until the Ressurection Day. By Allah! If I were to confess to what the people of Kufa say about me, the earth would swallow me. I am nothing but a servant, a slave, who has no power to harm or benefit."

(*Biḥār*, 25, 295, 53)

1.9.3.3. It is reported that 'Alī said, "The Apostle of Allah said, 'The example of you in my community is as the example of Christ Jesus the son of Mary. His people split into three sects: a sect of believers, and they were the disciples, a sect of his enemies, and they were the Jews, and a sect that exaggerated about him, and they left the faith. And verily, my community will split into three sects on account of you. One sect is your Shī'ah, and they are the believers; one sect is your enemy, they are the doubters; and one sect are those who exaggerate about you, and they are the deniers. O 'Alī! You are in heaven, and your Shī'ah, and the lovers of your Shī'ah. And your enemy and the exaggerator are in the fire.'"

(*Biḥār*, 25, 264, 4)

1.9.3.4. It is reported that Ḥasan ibn al-Juhm said, "One day, I was present at a session with Ma'mūn, and 'Alī ibn Mūsā al-Riḍā was beside him. Jurists and theologians of various sects were gathered, and some of them questioned him...

Ma'mūn said to him, 'O Abū al-Ḥasan! I have heard that there is a group that exaggerates and goes beyond the bounds about you.' Riḍā said to him, 'My father, Mūsā ibn Ja'far reported from his father Ja'far ibn Muḥammad, from his father Muḥammad ibn 'Alī, from his father, 'Alī ibn al-Ḥusayn, from his father, al-Ḥusayn ibn 'Alī, from his father, 'Alī ibn Abū Ṭālib, that the Apostle of Allah

أنَّ عِيسَي أقَرَّ بِما قالَتِ النَصارَي، لَأوْرَثَهُ اللهُ صَمَماً إلي يَوْمِ القِيامَةِ. واللهِ، لَوْ أقرَرْتُ بِما يَقُولُ فِي أهْلُ الكُوفَةِ، لَأخَذَتْنِي الأرضُ، وَما أنا إلّا عَبْدٌ مَمْلُوكٌ، لا أقدِرُ عَلي ضَرٍّ شَيْءٍ وَلا نَفْعٍ.'»

(بحار الأنوار، ٢٥، ٢٩٥، ٥٣)

١-٩-٣-٣- مُحَمَّدُ بْنُ أحْمَدَ بْنِ شاذانِ بِإسْنادِهِ إلي الصادِقِ, عَنْ آبائِهِ, عَنْ عَلِيٍّ عليه السلام، قالَ: «قالَ رَسُولُ اللهِ صلى الله عليه وآله وسلم: 'يا عَلِيُّ مَثَلُكَ فِي أُمَّتِي مَثَلُ المَسِيحِ عِيسَي بْنِ مَرْيَمَ، إفْتَرَقَ قَوْمُهُ ثَلاثَ فِرَقٍ: فِرْقَةٌ مُؤْمِنُونَ، وَهُمُ الحَوارِيُّونَ؛ وَفِرْقَةٌ عادُوهُ، وَهُمُ اليَهُودُ؛ وَفِرْقَةٌ غَلَوْا فِيهِ فَخَرَجُوا عَنِ الإيمانِ. وانَّ أُمَّتِي سَتَفْتَرِقُ فِيكَ ثَلاثَ فِرَقٍ: فَفِرْقَةٌ شِيعَتُكَ، وَهُمُ المُؤْمِنُونَ؛ وَفِرْقَةٌ عَدُوُّكَ، وَهُمُ الشاكُّونَ؛ وَفِرْقَةٌ تَغْلُو فِيكَ، وَهُمُ الجاحِدُونَ. وأنْتَ فِي الجَنَّةِ يا عَلِيُّ، وَشِيعَتُكَ وَمُحِبُّ شِيعَتِكَ؛ وَعَدُوُّكَ والغالِي فِي النارِ.'»

(بحار الأنوار، ٢٥، ٢٦٤، ٤)

١-٩-٣-٤- تَمِيمُ القُرَشِي, عَنْ أبِيهِ, عَنْ أحْمَدَ بْنِ عَلِيٍّ الأنْصارِيِّ, عَنِ الحَسَنِ بْنِ الجُهْمِ، قالَ: «حَضَرْتُ مَجْلِسَ المأمُونِ يَوْماً وَعِنْدَهُ عَلِيُّ بْنُ مُوسَي الرضا عليه السلام، وَقَدِ اجْتَمَعَ الفُقَهاءُ وأهْلُ الكَلامِ مِنَ الفِرَقِ المَخْتَلِفَةِ. فَسألَهُ بَعْضُهُمْ...

قالَ لَهُ المأمُونُ: 'يا أبا الحَسَنِ، بَلَغَنِي أنَّ قَوْماً يَغْلُونَ فِيكُمْ وَيَتَجاوَزُونَ فِيكُمُ الحَدَّ.' فَقالَ لَهُ الرضا عليه السلام: 'حَدَّثَنِي أبِي مُوسَي بْنُ جَعْفَرٍ, عَنْ أبِيهِ جَعْفَرِ بْنِ مُحَمَّدٍ, عَنْ أبِيهِ مُحَمَّدِ بْنِ عَلِيٍّ, عَنْ أبِيهِ عَلِيِّ بْنِ الحُسَيْنِ, عَنْ أبِيهِ الحُسَيْنِ بْنِ عَلِيٍّ, عَنْ أبِيهِ عَلِيِّ بْنِ أبِي طالِبٍ عليه السلام، قالَ: 'قالَ رَسُولُ اللهِ صلى الله عليه وآله وسلم: 'لا تَرْفَعُونِي فَوْقَ حَقِّي.

said, "Do not exalt me above what is my right, Allah, the blessed and exalted, took me as a servant before He took me as a prophet. Allah, the blessed and exalted, says, ﴾*It is not for a man that Allah should give him the Book and Judgment and apostleship and yet he should say to people, "Be worshippers of me besides God;" but rather, "Be lordly that you teach the Book and what you read"/ And nor would he enjoin you that your should take the Angels nad the Apostles for lords. What! Would he enjoin you with disbelief after you submitted?*﴿. (3:79-80)"

And 'Alī said, "Two will be destroyed because of me, although it is not my fault: The exorbitant lovers and the extreme haters." We absolve ourselves from those who exaggerate about us, so that they exalt us above what is our position, just as Jesus the son of Mary absolved himself from the Christians. Allah, the mighty and magnificent, said, ﴾*And when Allah will say, 'O Jesus son of Mary! Did you say to men, "Take me and my mother for two gods besides Allah?" He will say, "Glory be to You! It did not befit me that I should say what I had no right to say; if I had said it, You would indeed have known it; You know what is in my soul, and I do not know what is in your soul. Surely, You are the great Knower of the occult./ I did not say to them aught save what You did enjoin me with: to serve Allah, my Lord and your Lord, and I was a witness of them so long as I was among them, but when You caused me to die, You were the watcher over them, and You are the witness of all things.*﴿ (5:116-117).

And He, the mighty and magnificent, said, ﴾*The Messiah does by no means disdain that he should be a servant of Allah, nor do the angels who are near to Him, and whoever disdains His service and is proud, He will gather them all together to Himself.*﴿ (4:172).

And He, the mighty and magnificent, said, ﴾*The Messiah, son of Mary, is only an apostle; apostles before him have indeed passed away; and his mother was a truthful woman. They both used to eat food. See how We make the communications clear to them, then behold, how they are turned away.*﴿ (5:75).

فانَّ اللهَ، تَبارَكَ وَتعالَي، اتَّخَذَنِي عَبْداً قَبْلَ أنْ يَتَّخِذَنِي نَبِيّاً. قالَ اللهُ، تَبارَكَ وَتعالَي: ﴿ما كانَ لِبَشَرٍ أنْ يُؤْتِيَهُ اللهُ الكِتابَ والحُكْمَ والنبُوَّةَ، ثُمَّ يَقُولُ لِلنّاسِ: 'كُونُوا عِباداً لِي مِنْ دُونِ اللهِ.' وَلَكِنْ كُونُوا رَبّانِيِّينَ بِما كُنْتُمْ تُعَلِّمُونَ الكِتابَ وَبِما كُنْتُمْ تَدْرُسُونَ. وَلا يأمُرُكُمْ أنْ تَتَّخِذُوا المَلائِكَةَ والنَبِيِّينَ أرْباباً. أيأمُرُكُمْ بِالكُفْرِ بَعْدَ إذْ أنتُم مُسْلِمُونَ؟﴾'

وَقالَ عَلِيٌّ عليه السلام: 'يَهْلِكُ فِيَّ اثنانِ وَلا ذَنْبَ لِي: مُحِبٌّ مُفْرِطٌ وَمُبْغِضٌ مُفْرِطٌ.' وإنّا لَنَبْرَءُ إلَي اللهِ، عَزَّ وَجَلَّ، مِمَّنْ يَغْلُو فِينا فَيَرْفَعُنا فَوْقَ حَدِّنا، كَبَراءَةِ عِيسَي بْنِ مَرْيَمَ عليه السلام مِنَ النَصارَي. قالَ اللهُ، عَزَّ وَجَلَّ: ﴿وإذْ قالَ اللهُ: 'يا عِيسَي بْنَ مَرْيَمَ، أأنْتَ قُلْتَ لِلنّاسِ اتَّخِذُونِي وأمِّيَ إلَهَيْنِ مِنْ دُونِ اللهِ؟' قالَ: 'سُبْحانَكَ، ما يَكُونُ لِي أنْ أقُولَ ما لَيْسَ لِي بِحَقٍّ. إنْ كُنْتُ قُلْتُهُ فَقَدْ عَلِمْتَهُ، تَعْلَمُ ما فِي نَفْسِي وَلا أعْلَمُ ما فِي نَفْسِكَ، إنَّكَ أنتَ عَلاّمُ الغُيُوبِ. ما قُلْتُ لَهُمْ إلّا ما أمَرْتَنِي بِهِ، أنْ اعْبُدُوا اللهَ رَبِّي وَرَبَّكُمْ. وَكُنْتُ عَلَيْهِمْ شَهِيداً مادُمتُ فِيهِمْ، فَلَمّا تَوَفَّيْتَنِي كُنْتَ أنتَ الرقِيبَ عَلَيْهِمْ؛ وأنْتَ عَلَي كُلِّ شَيْءٍ شَهِيدٌ.﴾

وَقالَ عَزَّ وَجَلَّ: ﴿لَنْ يَسْتَنْكِفَ المَسِيحُ أنْ يَكُونَ عَبْداً لِلّهِ وَلا المَلائِكَةُ المُقَرَّبُونَ.﴾

وَقالَ، عَزَّ وَجَلَّ: ﴿ما المَسِيحُ ابن مَرْيَمَ إلّا رَسُولٌ، قَدْ خَلَتْ مِنْ قَبْلِهِ الرسُلُ، وأمُّهُ صِدِّيقَةٌ كانا يأكُلانِ الطَّعامَ.﴾

The meaning of this is that these two persons defecated, so whoever claims that the prophets were Lords, or who claims that the Imams are Lords or prophets, or who claims that those who are not Imams are Imams, we absolve ourselves from them in this world and in the other world....'"

(*Biḥār*, 25, 134, 6)

1.9.3.5. The Commander of the Faithful said, "O Allah! I absolve myself of the exaggerators, just as Jesus the son of Mary absolved himself from the Christians. O Allah! Abandon them forever and do not help any of them."

(*Biḥār*, 25, 266, 7)

1.9.3.6. It is reported that [Imam] 'Alī said, "The Messenger of Allah called me and said, 'O 'Alī! Verily, there is a similarity between you and Jesus the son of Mary. The Christians love him so much that they put him in a position that was not for him; and the Jews hate him so much that they even slandered his mother.' And [Imam] 'Alī said, 'Two [groups of] men will be ruined because of me, he who goes to extremes in love of me for what I do not have and he who hates me with a hatred that makes him slander me.'"

(*Biḥār*, 35, 319, 13)

1.9.3.7. It is reported that Abū Baṣīr said, "One day the Apostle of Allah was sitting among us when the Commander of the Faithful came. The Apostle of Allah said to him, 'Indeed, you are similar to Jesus the son of Mary. If it were not the case that some groups from my community would say about you what the Christians have said about Jesus the son of Mary, I would speak about you in a way that you would not pass by any group without them taking the dust from your footprints in hopes of a blessing.'

وَمَعْناهُ، أنَّهما كانا يَتَغَوَّطان. فَمَن ادَّعَي لِلأنْبياءِ رُبُوبيَّةً أو ادَّعَي لِلأئِمَّةِ رُبُوبيَّةً أوْ نُبُوَّةً، أوْ لِغَيْرِ الأئِمَةِ إمامَةً، فَنَحْنُ مِنْهُ بُرَآءٌ فِى الدنْيا والآخِرَةِ... .'»

(بحار الأنوار، ٢٥، ١٣٤، ٦)

١-٩-٣-٥- الحُسَيْنُ بْنُ عُبَيْدِ اللهِ, ... عَنِ ابن نُباتَةٍ، قالَ: «قالَ أمِيرُ المُؤْمِنِينَ عليه السلام: 'اللهُمَّ إنِّى بَرِيءٌ مِنَ الغُلاةِ، كَبَراءَةِ عِيسَي بْنِ مَرْيَمَ مِنَ النَصارَي. اللهُمَّ اخْذُلْهُمْ أبَداً وَلا تَنْصُرْ مِنْهُمْ أحَداً.'»

(بحار الأنوار، ٢٥، ٢٦٦، ٧)

١-٩-٣-٦- أبُو عَمْرٍو, عَنِ ابن عُقْدَةٍ, عَنِ الحُسَيْنِ بْنِ عَبْدِ الرحْمَنِ, عَنْ أبيهِ وَعُثْمانِ بْنِ سَعِيدٍ مَعاً, عَنْ عَمْرِو بْنِ ثابِتٍ, عَنْ صَباحِ المُزَنِي, عَنِ الحارِثِ بْنِ حَصِيرَةٍ, عَنْ أبِى صادِقٍ, عَنْ رَبِيعَةِ بْنِ ناجِدٍ, عَنْ عَلِيٍّ عليه السلام، قالَ: «دَعانِى رَسُولُ اللهِ صلى الله عليه وآله وسلم، فَقالَ: 'يا عَلِيُّ، إنَّ فِيكَ شَبَهاً مِنْ عِيسَي بْنِ مَرْيَمَ، أحَبَّتْهُ النَصارَي حَتَّي أنْزَلُوهُ بِمَنْزِلَةٍ لَيْسَ بِها؛ وأبْغَضَهُ اليَهُودُ حَتَّي بَهَتُوا أمَّهُ.'» قالَ: «وَقالَ عَلِيٌّ عليه السلام: 'يَهْلِكُ فِيَّ رَجُلانِ: مُحِبٌّ مُفْرِطٌ بِما لَيْسَ فِيَّ، وَمُبْغِضٌ يَحْمِلُهُ شَنَئانِى عَلَي أنْ يَبْهَتَنِى.'»

(بحار الأنوار، ٣٥، ٣١٩، ١٣)

١-٩-٣-٧- عِدَّةٌ مِنْ أصْحابِنا، عَنْ سَهْلِ بْنِ زِيادٍ، عَنْ مُحَمَّدِ بْنِ سُلَيْمانَ، عَنْ أبِيهِ، عَنْ أبِى بَصِيرٍ، قالَ: «بَيْنا رَسُولُ اللهِ صلى الله عليه وآله وسلم ذاتَ يَوْمٍ جالِساً، إذْ أقْبَلَ أمِيرُ المُؤْمِنِينَ عليه السلام. فَقالَ لَه رَسُولُ اللهِ صلى الله عليه وآله وسلم: 'إنَّ فِيكَ شَبَهاً مِنْ عيسَي بن مَريَمَ، وَلَوْ لا أنْ تَقُولَ فِيكَ طَوائِفُ مِنْ أُمَّتِى ما قالَتِ النَصارَي فِى عيسَي بن مَرْيَمَ، لَقُلْتُ فِيكَ قَوْلاً لا تَمُرُّ بِمَلاٍ مِنَ الناسِ إلّا أخَذُوا التَرابَ مِنْ تَحْتِ قَدَمَيْكَ، يَلْتَمِسُونَ بِذَلِكَ البَرَكَةَ. »

Two Arabs, al-Mughīrah ibn Shu'bah and a group from the Quraysh that was with them became angry. They said, 'He was not satisfied to make a comparison for his cousin with anyone but Jesus the son of Mary.' Then Allah sent down to His prophet, ﴾*And when a comparison is made with the son of Mary, your people raise a clamor at it/ And they say, 'Are our gods better or is he? They do not set it forth to you save by way of disputations; nay, they are a contentious people./ He was naught but a servant on whom We bestowed favor, and We made him an example for the children of Israel./ And if We please, We could make among you angels to be successors in the land.*﴿ (43:57-60)

Then Ḥārith ibn 'Amr al-Fahrī became angry and said, 'O Allah! If this is the truth from You, that the Banī Hāshim will be successors like one Caesar after another, then rain stones down upon us or chastise us with a painful torment. Then Allah sent down to the Prophet what they had said (8:32), and this verse was sent down, ﴾*But Allah was not going to chastise them while you were among them, nor is Allah going to chastise them while yet they ask for forgiveness.*﴿ (8:33).

Then the Prophet said to him, 'O son of 'Amr! Either repent or get out of here!' He said, 'O Muḥammad! Give something from what you have for those who are not of the Quraysh. The Banū Hāshim have taken the nobility of the Arabs and non-Arabs.' The Prophet said to him, 'It is not up to me. It is up to Allah, the blessed and exalted.'..."

(*Kāfī* 8, 57, 18)

1.9.4. Their Monasticism

1.9.4.1. It is reported that the Apostle of Allah ﷺ said, "...O Abū Dhar! Allah sent Jesus with monasticism but I was sent with simple uprightness, and women and perfume are beloved by me, and prayer was made the delight of my eyes...."

(*Biḥar*, 79, 233, 58)

قالَ: «فَغَضِبَ الأعْرابيّانِ والمُغِيرَةُ بْنُ شُعْبَةَ وَعِدَّةٌ مِنْ قُرَيْشٍ مَعَهُمْ. فَقالُوا: 'ما رَضِيَ أنْ يَضْرِبَ لابْنِ عَمِّهِ مَثَلاً إلّا عيسَي بن مَريَمَ.' فأنْزَلَ الله عَلَي نَبيِّهِ صلى الله عليه وآله وسلم فَقالَ: ﴿وَلَمّا ضُرِبَ ابن مَرْيَمَ مَثَلاً إذا قَوْمُكَ مِنْهُ يَصُدُّونَ. وَقالُوا: 'آلِهَتُنا خَيْرٌ أمْ هُوَ؟' ما ضَرَبُوهُ لَكَ إلّا جَدَلاً، بَلْ هُمْ قَوْمٌ خَصِمُونَ. إنْ هُوَ إلّا عَبْدٌ أنْعَمْنا عَلَيْهِ وَجَعَلْناهُ مَثَلاً لِبَنِي إسْرائِيلَ، وَلَوْ نَشاءُ لَجَعَلْنا مِنْكُمْ [يَعْنَي مِنْ بَنِي هاشِمٍ] مَلائِكَةً فِي الأرضِ يَخْلُفُونَ.﴾»

قالَ: «فَغَضِبَ الحارِثُ بْنُ عَمْرٍو الفِهْرِيُّ، فَقالَ: 'اللهُمَّ إنْ كانَ هذا هُوَ الحَقَّ مِنْ عِنْدِكَ، أنَّ بَنِي هاشِمٍ يَتَوارَثُونَ هِرَقْلاً بَعْدَ هِرَقْلٍ، فَأمْطِرْ عَلَينا حِجارَةً مِنَ السَماءِ أوِ ائْتِنا بِعَذابٍ ألِيمٍ.' فأنْزَلَ الله عَلَيْهِ مَقالَةَ الحارِثِ، وَنَزَلَتْ هَذِهِ الآيةُ: ﴿وَما كانَ الله لِيُعَذِّبَهُمْ وأنْتَ فِيهِمْ، وَما كانَ الله مُعَذِّبَهُمْ وَهُمْ يَسْتَغْفِرُونَ.﴾

ثُمَّ قالَ لَه: 'يا ابن عَمْرٍو، إمّا تُبْتَ وإمّا رَحَلْتَ.' فَقالَ: 'يا مُحَمَّدُ بَلْ تَجْعَلُ لِسائِرِ قُرَيْشٍ شَيْئًا مِمّا فِي يَدَيْكَ! فَقَدْ ذَهَبَتْ بَنُو هاشِمٍ بِمَكْرُمَةِ العَرَبِ والعَجَمِ.' فَقالَ لَه النَبِيُّ صلى الله عليه وآله وسلم: 'لَيْسَ ذَلِكَ إلَيَّ، ذَلِكَ إلَي اللهِ تَبارَكَ وَتَعالَي.' ...»

(الكافی، ٨، ٥٧، ١٨)

١-٩-٤- رَهْبانِيَّتُهُم

١-٩-٤-١- ... عَنْ أبِي حَرْبِ بْنِ أبِي الأسوَدِ الدؤلِيِّ, عَنْ أبِيهِ, عَنْ أبِيذَرٍ رَحِمَهُ الله، قالَ: «قالَ رَسُولُ اللهِ صلى الله عليه وآله وسلم فِي ما أوْصَي إلَيهِ: '... يا أبا ذَرٍ، إنَّ الله بَعَثَ عِيسَي بْنَ مَرْيَمَ عليه السلام بِالرهْبانِيَّةِ، وَبُعِثْتُ بِالحَنِيفِيَّةِ السَمْحَةِ، وَحَبَّبَ إلَيَّ النساءَ والطيبَ؛ جُعِلَتْ فِي الصَلاةِ قُرَّةُ عَيْنِي.'»

(بحار الأنوار، ٧٩، ٢٣٣، ٥٨)

1.9.4.2. Ibn Mas'ūd said, "I was behind the Apostle of Allah on a donkey when he said, 'O son of Umm 'Abd! Do you know how the Children of Israel established monasticism?' I said, 'Allah and His Apostle know better.' He said, 'Tyrants dominated them after Jesus who rebelled against Allah. Then they became enraged at the people of faith and fought with them. They defeated the people of faith three times. Only a few of them remained.

They said, "If we appear, they will annihilate us, and no one will remain for the religion to invite people to it. So, come. Let us scatter over the earth until Allah commissions the prophet promised by Jesus (that is, Muḥammad)."

So they scattered into the mountains and initiated monasticism. Some of them clung to their religion and some disbelieved.' Then he recited this verse, *﴾As for monasticism, they invented it themselves; We did not prescribe for them anything but seeking the pleasure of Allah, and this they observed not as they ought to have observed it. And we gave to those of them who believed their due recompense; but many of them are transgressors.﴿* (57:27).

Then he said, 'O son of Umm'abd! Do you know what the monasticism of my community is?' I said, 'Allah and His Apostle know better.' He said, 'Hijrah (migration), jihad, prayer, fasting, hajj and 'umrah (the major and minor pilgrimages).'"

(*Biḥār*, 65, 320)

1.10. HIS ASCENSION

1.10.1. Jābir al-Anṣāri reported that the Prophet taught 'Alī and Fāṭimah this prayer, and said to them, "When a misfortune descends upon you or you are afraid of a king's injustice or something is lost, you should perform a good ablution, say a prayer with two *rak'at*, raise your hands to heaven and say,

١-٩-٤-٢- عَن ابن مَسْعُودٍ، قالَ: «كُنْتُ رَدِيفَ رَسُولِ اللهِ صلى الله عليه وآله وسلم علَي حِمارٍ، فَقالَ: 'يا ابن أمِّ عَبْدٍ، هَلْ تَدْرى مِنْ أيْنَ أحْدَثَتْ بَنُو إسْرائِيلَ الرهْبانِيَّةَ؟' فقُلْتُ: 'اللهُ وَرَسُولُهُ أعْلَمُ.' فقالَ: 'ظَهَرَتْ علَيْهِمُ الجَبابِرَةُ بَعْدَ عِيسَي عليه السلام، يَعْمَلُونَ بِمَعاصِي اللهِ؛ فَغَضِبَ أهْلُ الإيمانِ، فَقاتَلُوهُمْ، فَهُزِمَ أهْلُ الإيْمانِ ثَلاثَ مَرّاتٍ. فَلَمْ يَبْقَ مِنْهُمْ إلّا القَلِيلُ.

فَقالُوا: 'إنْ ظَهَرْنا هَؤُلاءِ أفْنُونا، ولَمْ يَبْقَ لِلدِّينِ أحَدٌ يَدْعُو إلَيْهِ. فَتَعالَوْا نَتَفَرَّقْ فِى الأرضِ، إلَي أنْ يَبْعَثَ اللهُ النَبِىَّ الذى وَعَدَنا بِهِ عِيسَي عليه السلام.' يَعْنُونَ مُحَمَّداً صلى الله عليه وآله وسلم. فَتَفَرَّقُوا فِى غِيْرانِ الجِبالِ، وأحْدَثُوا رَهْبانِيَّةً. فَمِنْهُمْ مَنْ تَمَسَّكَ بِدِينِهِ، وَمِنْهُمْ مَنْ كَفَرَ.' ثُمَّ تَلا هَذِهِ الآيَةَ: ﴿وَرَهْبانِيَّةً ابْتَدَعُوها، ما كَتَبْناها عَلَيْهِمْ.﴾ إلَي آخِرِها. ثُمَّ قالَ: 'يا ابن أمِّ عَبْدٍ، أتَدْرى ما رَهْبانِيَّةُ أمَّتِي؟' قُلْتُ: 'اللهُ وَرَسُولُهُ أعْلَمُ.' قالَ: 'الهِجْرَةُ والجِهادُ والصلاةُ والصومُ والحَجُّ والعُمْرَةُ.'»

(بحار الأنوار، ٦٥، ٣٢٠)

١-١٠- رَفْعُهُ إلَى السَماء

١-١٠-١- الحَسَنُ بْنُ فَضْلِ الطَّبْرِسِىُّ فِى مَكارِمِ الأخْلاقِ، عَنْ جابِرِ الأنْصارِيِّ: «إنَّ النَبِىَّ صلى الله عليه وآله وسلم عَلَّمَ عَلِيّاً وَفاطِمَةَ عليهما السلام هَذا الدعاءَ، وَقالَ لَهما: 'إنْ نَزَلَتْ بِكُما مُصِيبَةٌ، أوْ خِفْتُما جَوْرَ السُّلْطانِ، أوْ ضَلَّتْ لَكُما ضالَّةٌ، فأحْسِنا الوُضُوءَ وَصَلِّيا رَكْعَتَيْنِ وارْفَعا أيْدِيَكُما إلَي السَماءِ وَقُولا:

'O Knower of the hidden and the secrets! O Obeyed One! O Most Knowing! O Allah! O Allah! O Allah! O Vanquisher of the parties against Muḥammad ! O Outwitter of Pharaoh for Moses! O Savior of Jesus from the hands of the unjust! O, Deliverer of the people of Noah from drowning! O, Compassionate for the tears of Ya'qūb! O Remover of the Difficulties of Job! O Savior of Jonah from the darkness! O Doer of every good! O Guider to every good! O Shower of every good! O Commander to every good! O Creator of the good! O Good-doer! You are Allah. I want from You what you know I want, and You are Omniscient of all that is hidden. I ask you to bless Muḥammad and his descendants.' Then ask your need, both of you. It will be answered, God willing."

(*Mustadrak al-Wasā'il*, 8, 214, 9286)

1.10.2. (A part of the psalm "*Mashlūl*" is:) "O He who returned Joseph to Ya'qūb! O He who removed the harm from Job! O He who forgave the sin of David! O He who raised Jesus the son of Mary and saved him from the hands of the Jews! O He who answered the calling of Yūnus in the darkness! O He who chose Moses by the Words! ..."

(*Al-Miṣbāḥ*, 262)

1.10.3. It is reported that Abū 'Abd Allah said, "... as for the occultation of Jesus, the Jews and the Christians are agreed that he was killed, so Allah, the Mighty and Magnificent, belied them by His saying, ﴾*They did not kill nor crucify him, but it appeared to them so*﴿ (4:157). Likewise, the occultation of al-Qā'im, then the community will deny it."

(*Biḥār*, 51, 220, 9)

1.10.4. I asked him [Imam] about the nights of the month of Ramaḍān in which *ghusl* [major ritual ablution] is recommended. Then he said, "The nineteenth, the twenty-first and the twenty-third." And he continued, "On the night of the nineteenth, it is written who

'يا عالِمَ الغَيْبِ والسَرائِرِ، يا مُطاعُ، يا عَليمُ، يا اللهُ يا اللهُ يا اللهُ يا اللهُ، يا هازِمَ الأحْزابِ لِمُحَمَّدٍ صلى الله عليه وآله وسلم، يا كائِدَ فِرْعَوْنَ لِمُوسَي، يا مُنَجِّىَ عِيسَي مِنْ أيْدِى الظَلَمَةِ، يا مُخَلِّصَ قَوْمِ نُوحٍ مِنَ الغَرَقِ، يا راحِمَ عَبْدِهِ يَعْقُوبَ، يا كاشِفَ ضُرِّ أيُّوبَ، يا مُنَجِّىَ ذِى النونِ، مِنَ الظُلُماتِ، يا فاعِلَ كُلِّ خَيْرٍ، يا هادِياً إلَي كُلِّ خَيْرٍ، يا دالّا عَلَي كُلِّ خَيْرٍ، يا آمِراً بِكُلِّ خَيْرٍ، يا خالِقَ الخَيْرِ، وَيا أهْلَ الخَيْرِ، أنتَ اللهُ. رَغِبْتُ إلَيكَ فِى ما قَدْ عَلِمْتَ وأنْتَ عَلّامُ الغُيُوبِ. أسألُكَ أنْ تُصَلّىَ عَلَي مُحَمَّدٍ وآلِ مُحَمَّدٍ.' ثُمَّ اسْئَلا الحاجَةَ، تُجابا إنْ شاءَ اللهُ.'»

(مستدرك الوسائل، ٨، ٢١٤، ٩٢٨٦)

١-١٠-٢- مِنْ دُعاءِ المَشْلُولِ: «...يا رادَّ يُوسُفَ عَلَي يَعْقُوبَ، يا كاشِفَ ضُرِّ أيُّوبَ، يا غافِرَ ذَنْبِ داوُدَ، يا رافِعَ عِيسَي بْنِ مَرْيَمَ وَمُنَجِّيهِ مِنْ أيْدِى اليَهُودِ، يا مُجِيبَ نِداءِ يُونُسَ فِى الظُلُماتِ، يا مُصْطَفِى مُوسَي بِالكَلِماتِ... .»

(المصباح، ٢٦٢)

١-١٠-٣- قالَ أبُو عَبْدِ اللهِ عليه السلام: «... وأمّا غَيْبَةُ عِيسَي عليه السلام، فإنَّ اليَهُودَ والنَصارَي اتَّفَقَتْ عَلَي أنَّهُ قُتِلَ، وكَذَّبَهُمُ اللهُ، عَزَّ وَجَلَّ، بِقَوْلِهِ: ﴿وَما قَتَلوهُ وَما صَلَبُوهُ، وَلَكِنْ شُبِّهَ لَهُمْ.﴾ كَذَلِكَ غَيْبَةُ القائِمِ عليه السلام، فإنَّ الأُمَّةَ تُنْكِرُها لِطُولِها.»

(بحار الأنوار، ٥١، ٢٢٠، ٩)

١-١٠-٤- الحُسَيْنُ بْنُ سَعِيدٍ، عَنِ القاسِمِ بْنِ عُرْوَةٍ، عَنْ عَبْدِ اللهِ بْنِ بُكَيْرٍ، عَنْ زُرارَةٍ، عَنْ أحَدِهِما عليهما السلام، قالَ: «سألْتُهُ، عَنِ اللَيالِىَ الّتِى يُسْتَحَبُّ فِيها الغُسْلُ فِى شَهْرِ رَمْضانَ، فَقالَ: 'لَيْلَةُ تِسْعَ عَشْرَةَ وَلَيْلَةُ إحْدَي وَعِشْرِينَ وَلَيْلَةُ ثَلاثٍ وَعِشْرِينَ.' وَقالَ: 'فِى لَيْلَةِ تِسْعَ عَشْرَةَ يُكْتَبُ فِيها وَفْدُ الحاجِّ، وَفِيها يُفْرَقُ كُلُّ أمْرٍ حَكِيمٍ.

will go on the ḥajj, and every wise affair will be distributed in it. On the night of the twenty-first, Jesus was raised and the executor of Moses was taken in it, and the Commander of the Faithful was taken in it...."

(*Tahdhīb al-Aḥkām,* 4, 196)

1.10.5. It is reported that Ḥabīb ibn 'Amr said, "When the Commander of the Faithful passed away, Ḥasan stood and spoke. He said, 'O you people! On this night Jesus the son of Mary was raised.'"

(*Biḥār*, 14, 335, 1)

1.10.6. It is reported that Abū Ja'far said, "On the night when 'Alī was murdered no stone was lifted from the face of the earth unless beneath it was found pure fresh blood, until the first break of dawn. It was the same on the night Yūsha' ibn Nūn, and it was the same on the night when Jesus the son of Mary was raised, and it was the same on the night when Ḥusayn was murdered."

(*Biḥār*, 14, 336, 4)

1.10.7. 'Amr ibn Sa'īd said, "A man who was from al-Madīnah came on the night of 'al-Furqān', [the night in which right and wrong were distinguished] when Muslims and polytheists were ready to fight each [at Badr] and said, 'This night is the night of the seventeenth of Ramaḍān.' Then I came to Abū 'Abd Allah and said to him what he had said. He said, 'He who was from al-Madīnah denied it. You want the night that the Commander of the Faithful received a blow. He received a blow on the night of the nineteenth of Ramaḍān nineteen, and it is the night in which Jesus the son of Mary was raised.'"

(*Tafsīr al-'Ayyāshī*, 2, 64, 68)

1.10.8. It is reported that in response to questions put to him by his son, Zayd, Imam Ṣajjād said,"O my boy! Certainly the Ka'abah is the house of Allah, and whoever makes the pilgrimage to the house of Allah, intends to come before Allah, and the mosques are the houses of Allah, and whoever tries to get to them, tries to get to and

وَلَيْلَةُ إِحْدَي وَعِشْرِينَ، رُفِعَ فِيها عِيسَي عليه السلام، وَفِيها قُبِضَ وَصِيُّ مُوسَي عليه السلام وَفِيها قُبِضَ أَمِيرُ المُؤْمِنِينَ عليه السلام... .'»

(تهذيب الأحكام، ٤، ١٩٦)

١-١٠-٥- عَنْ حَبِيبِ بْنِ عَمْرٍو قالَ: 'لَمّا تُوُفِّيَ أَمِيرُ المُؤْمِنِينَ عليه السلام، قام الحَسَنُ عليه السلام خَطِيباً، فقالَ: «أَيُّها الناسُ، فِي هٰذِهِ اللَيْلَةِ رُفِعَ عِيسَي بْنُ مَرْيَمَ.»

(بحار الأنوار، ١٤، ٣٣٥، ١)

١-١٠-٦- بِإِسْنادِهِ, عَنْ أَبِي بَصِيرٍ, عَنْ أَبِي عَبْدِ اللهِ عليه السلام، قالَ: «قالَ أَبُو جَعْفَرٍ عليه السلام: 'لَمّا كانَتْ اللَيْلَةُ الَّتِي قُتِلَ فِيها عَلِيٌّ عليه السلام، لَمْ يُرْفَعْ, عَنْ وَجْهِ الأَرضِ حَجَرٌ إِلّا وُجِدَ تَحْتَهُ دَمٌ عَبِيطٌ حَتَّي طَلَعَ الفَجْرُ؛ وَكَذٰلِكَ كانَتْ اللَيْلَةُ الَّتِي قُتِلَ فِيها يُوشَعُ بْنُ نُونٍ عليه السلام؛ وَكَذٰلِكَ كانَتْ اللَيْلَةُ الَّتِي رُفِعَ فِيها عِيسَي بْنُ مَرْيَمَ عليه السلام؛ وَكَذٰلِكَ اللَيْلَةُ الَّتِي قُتِلَ فِيها الحُسَيْنُ عليه السلام.'»

(بحار الأنوار، ١٤، ٣٣٦, ٤)

١-١٠-٧- عَنْ عَمْرِو بْنِ سَعِيدٍ قالَ: «جاءَ رَجُلٌ مِنْ أَهْلِ المَدِينَةِ فِي لَيْلَةِ الفُرْقانِ، حِينَ التَقَي الجَمْعانِ، فَقالَ المَدَنِيُّ: 'هِيَ لَيْلَةُ سَبْعَ عَشْرَةَ مِنْ رَمَضانَ.'» قالَ: «فَدَخَلْتُ عَلَي أَبِي عَبْدِ اللهِ عليه السلام، فَقُلْتُ لَهُ وأَخْبَرْتُهُ. فَقالَ لِي: 'جَحَدَ المَدَنِيُّ، أَنتَ تُرِيدُ مُصابَ أَمِيرِ المُؤْمِنِينَ. إِنَّهُ أُصِيبَ لَيْلَةُ تِسْعَةَ عَشَرَ مِنْ رَمَضانَ، وَهِيَ اللَيْلَةُ الَّتِي رُفِعَ فِيها عِيسَي بْنُ مَرْيَمَ عليه السلام.'»

(تفسير العيّاشيّ، ٢، ٦٤، ٦٨)

١-١٠-٨- رُوِيَ عَنْ زَيْدِ بْنِ عَلِيِّ بْنِ الحُسَيْنِ عليه السلام، أَنَّهُ قالَ: «سأَلْتُ أَبِي سَيِّدَ العابِدِينَ عليه السلام، فَقُلْتُ لَهُ: 'يا أَبَهِ، أَخْبِرْنِي عَنْ... مَعْنَي قَوْلِهِ، عَزَّ وَجَلَّ: ﴿فَفِرُّوا إِلَي اللهِ.﴾' 'يَعْنِي حُجُّوا إِلَي بَيْتِ اللهِ. يا بُنَيَّ، إِنَّ الكَعْبَةَ بَيْتُ اللهِ، فَمَنْ حَجَّ بَيْتَ اللهِ

intends to come before Allah, and one who prays, as long as he is praying, stands before Allah, the mighty and magnificent. Verily, Allah, the blessed and exalted, has spots in the heavens, so whoever is elevated to one of these spots is elevated to Him. Have you not heard that Allah, the mighty and magnificent, says that the angels and the spirit are elevated to Him. And Allah, the mighty and magnificent, says, in the story of Jesus the son of Mary, ﴾*Nay, Allah took him up to Himself.*﴿ (4:158), and Allah, the mighty and magnificent, says, ﴾*To Him the good words ascend, and He elevates the good deeds to Himself.*﴿ (35:10).

(*Faqīh*, 1, 198, 603)

1.10.9. Abū Baṣīr said, "I heard from Abū Ja'far al-Bāqir, 'The Sāḥib hadha al-'amr [the twelfth Imam] is similar to four prophets. He is similar to Moses, Jesus, Joseph and Muḥammad.' I said, 'What is his similarity to Moses?' He said, 'Fearing and waiting.'[1] I said, 'What is his similarity to Jesus?' He said, 'It was said of him what was said of Jesus.'[2] I said, 'What is his similarity to Joseph?' He said, 'Prison and absence.'[3] I said, 'What is his similarity to Muḥammad?' He said, 'When he takes his stand, he will follow the way of the Apostle of Allah, except that he will explain the legacy of Muḥammad, and for eight months his sword will flash while there is disorder until he satisfies Allah.' I said, 'How will he know when Allah is satisfied?' He said, 'Allah will cast mercy into his heart.'"

(*Biḥār*, 52, 347, 97)

1.10.10. It is reported that Abū 'Abdullah said, "Nine thousand three hundred thirteen angels will descend to the Qā'im, and they are the ones who were with Jesus when Allah raised him to Himself."

(*Biḥār*, 14, 339, 15)

---

[1] See (28:21).

[2] That is, that he had been killed.

[3] There is in another narration: "As for Jesus, it that is said that he died, but he did not die. As for Joseph, it is absence from his people so that he does not know them and they do not know him." *Taqrīb al-Ma'ārif*, 190

فقدْ قصدَ إلي اللهِ؛ والمَساجِدُ بُيُوتُ اللهِ، فمَنْ سَعَي إليها فقدْ سَعَي إلي اللهِ وقَصدَ إليهِ، والمُصلّى مادامَ فِي صَلاتِهِ فهُوَ واقِفٌ بيْنَ يدَى اللهِ، عزَّ وَجلَّ. فإنَّ لِلّهِ، تَباركَ وتَعالي، بُقاعاً فِي سَماواتِهِ. فمَنْ عُرِجَ بِهِ إلي بُقْعَةٍ مِنْها فقدْ عُرِجَ بِهِ إليهِ. ألا تَسْمَعُ اللهَ، عَزَّ وَجلَّ، يقُولُ: ﴿تَعْرُجُ المَلائِكَةُ والروحُ إليهِ.﴾ ويَقُولُ اللهُ، عَزَّ وَجلَّ، فِي قِصَّةِ عيسَي بن مَريَمَ عليه السلام: ﴿بَلْ رَفَعهُ اللهُ إليهِ.﴾ ويَقُولُ اللهُ، عَزَّ وَجلَّ: ﴿إليهِ يَصْعَدُ الكَلِمُ الطيِّبُ والعَمَلُ الصالِحُ يَرْفَعُهُ.﴾'»

(كتاب من لايحضره الفقيه، ١، ١٩٨، ٦٠٣)

١-١٠-٩- عَلِيُّ بْنُ أحْمَدَ, عَنْ عُبَيْدِ اللهِ بْنِ مُوسَي, عَنْ عَبْدِ اللهِ بْنِ جبَلَةٍ, عَنْ ابن البَطائِنِيّ, عَنْ أبيهِ, عَنْ أبِي بَصيرٍ، قالَ: «سَمِعْتُ أبا جَعْفرٍ الباقِرَ عليه السلام يقُولُ: 'فِي صاحِبِ هَذا الأمْرِ شَبَهٌ مِنْ أرْبَعَةِ أنْبياءٍ: شَبَهٌ مِنْ مُوسَي وَشَبَهٌ مِنْ عِيسَي وَشَبَهٌ مَنْ يُوسُفَ وَشَبَهٌ مِنْ مُحَمَّدٍ صلى الله عليه وآله وسلم.' فقُلْتُ: 'وَما شَبَهُ مُوسَي؟' قالَ: 'خائِفٌ يَتَرَقَّبُ.' قُلْتُ: 'وَما شَبَهُ عِيسَي؟' فقالَ: 'قِيلَ فِيهِ ما قِيلَ فِي عِيسَي.' قُلْتُ: 'فما شَبَهُ يُوسُفَ؟' قالَ: 'السِّجْنُ والغيبَةُ.' قُلْتُ: 'وَما شَبَهُ مُحَمَّدٍ صلى الله عليه وآله وسلم؟' قالَ: 'إذا قامَ سارَ بِسِيرَةِ رَسُولِ اللهِ صلى الله عليه وآله وسلم، إلّا أنَّهُ يُبَيِّنُ آثارَ مُحَمَّدٍ وَيَضَعُ السيْفَ ثَمانِيَةَ أشْهُرٍ، هَرْجاً هَرْجاً، حتَّي يُرْضِى اللهَ.' قُلْتُ: 'فكَيْفَ يَعْلَمُ رِضا اللهِ؟' قالَ: 'يُلْقِى اللهُ فِي قلْبِهِ الرحْمَةَ.'»

(بحار الأنوار، ٥٢، ٣٤٧، ٩٧)

١-١٠-١٠- عَنْ أبِي عَبْدِ اللهِ عليه السلام، أنَّهُ قالَ: «يَنْزِلُ عَلي القائِمِ عليه السلام تِسْعَةُ آلافِ مَلَكٍ وَثَلاثُ مِائة وَثَلاثَ عَشَرَ مَلَكاً، وَهُمُ الذينَ كانُوا مَعَ عِيسَي لمّا رَفعَهُ اللهُ إليْهِ.»

(بحار الأنوار، ١٤، ٣٣٩، ١٥)

1.10.11. It is reported that al-Riḍā said, "When the Jews wanted to kill Jesus, he called upon Allah by our truth,[1] then He saved him from being murdered and raised him."

(*Biḥār*, 14, 339, 14)

1.10.12. It is related in the *tafsīr* attributed to Imam Ḥasan 'Askarī that regarding the verse, ﴿*and We strengthened him with the holy spirit*﴾ (2:87) he said, "He is Gabriel, and this was when Allah raised him through a hole in his house to heaven, and He cast his likeness on the one who had desired to kill him, so he was killed instead of him."

(*Biḥār*, 14, 338, 10)

1.10.13. Abū 'Abdullah said, "It is as if I were looking at al-Qā'im outside of Najaf mounted on a horse... When he raises the flag of the Apostle of Allah thirteen thousand and thirteen angels come down to him each of whom looks to him, and they are those who were with Noah on the ark, and they were with Abraham when he was cast into the fire, and they were with Jesus at his ascension....

(*Biḥār*, 19, 305, 47)

1.10.14. It is reported that Abū 'Abdullah said, "It is as though I were looking at the Qā'im outside Najaf. He is mounted on a black and white horse with a white forehead. Then he hastens his horse, so there will be no one in any city who will not think that he is with them in their city. When he unfurls the standard of the Apostle of Allah thirteen thousand thirteen angels will descend, all waiting for the Qā'im, and they are the angels who were with Noah in the ark, and they were with Abraham, the friend of God, when he was cast into the fire, and they were with Jesus when he was raised, and four thousand three hundred thirteen distinguished of these angels in ranks were present on the day of the battle of Badr, and four thousand came down wanting to fight with Ḥusayn ibn

---

[1] That is, Jesus swore by the truth of the Imams, seeking intercession through them.

١-١٠-١١- عَنِ الرضا عليه السلام: «إنَّ عِيسَي، لَمّا أرادَ اليَهُودُ قتْلَهُ، دَعا اللهَ بِحقِّنا؛ فَنَجّاهُ مِنَ القَتْلِ وَرَفَعَهُ إلَيْهِ.»

(بحار الأنوار، ١٤، ٣٣٩، ١٤)

١-١٠-١٢- «قَوْلُهُ عَزَّ وَجَلَّ: ﴿وأيَّدْناهُ بِرُوحِ القُدُسِ﴾ هُوَ جَبْرَئِيلُ، وَذلِكَ حِينَ رَفَعَهُ مِنْ رَوْزَنَةِ بَيْتِهِ إلَي السَماءِ، وألْقَي شَبَهَهُ عَلَي مَنْ رامَ قتْلَهُ، فَقُتِلَ بَدَلاً مِنْهُ.»

(بحار الأنوار، ١٤، ٣٣٨، ١٠)

١-١٠-١٣- ابن الوَلِيدِ, عَنْ الصَفّارِ, عَنْ ابن يَزِيدٍ, عَنْ ابن أبِي عُمَيْرٍ, عَنْ أبانِ بْنِ عُثْمانَ, عَنْ ابن تَغْلِبٍ, قالَ: «قالَ أبُو عَبْدِ اللهِ عليه السلام: 'كأنِّي أنْظُرُ إلَي القائِمِ عليه السلام عَلَي ظَهْرِ النَجَفِ، رَكِبَ فَرَساً... فإذا نَشَرَ رايَةَ رَسُولِ اللهِ صلى الله عليه وآله وسلم، انْحَطَّ عَلَيْهِ ثَلاثَةُ عَشَرَ ألفَ مَلَكٍ وَثَلاثَةُ عَشَرَ مَلَكاً، كُلُّهُمْ يَنْظُرُونَ القائِمَ عليه السلام، وَهُمُ الذينَ كانُوا مَعَ نُوحٍ عليه السلام فِي السَفِينَةِ، والَّذِينَ كانُوا مَعَ إبْراهِيمَ عليه السلام حَيْثُ اُلقِيَ فِي النارِ، وكانُوا مَعَ عِيسَي عليه السلام حِينَ رُفِعَ.'»

(بحار الأنوار، ١٩، ٣٠٥، ٤٧)

١-١٠-١٤- بهذا الإسنادِ, عَنْ ابن تَغْلِبٍ قالَ: «قالَ أبُو عَبْدِ اللهِ عليه السلام: 'كأنِّي أنْظُرُ إلَي القائِمِ عَلَي ظَهْرِ نَجَفٍ، فإذا اسْتَوَي عَلَي ظَهْرِ النَجَفِ، رَكِبَ فَرَساً أدْهَمَ، أبْلَقَ، بَيْنَ عَيْنَيْهِ شِمْراخٌ. ثُمَّ يَنْتَفِضُ بِهِ فَرَسُهُ، فَلا يَبْقَي أهْلُ بَلْدَةٍ إلّا وَهُمْ يَظُنُّونَ أنَّهُ مَعَهُمْ فِي بِلادِهِمْ. فإذا نَشَرَ رايَةَ رَسُولِ اللهِ صلى الله عليه وآله وسلم، انْحَطَّ عَلَيْهِ ثَلاثَةُ عَشَرَ الفَ مَلَكٍ وَثَلاثَةُ عَشَرَ مَلَكاً، كُلُّهُمْ يَنْتَظِرُونَ القائِمَ عليه السلام، وَهُمُ الذينَ كانُوا مَعَ نُوحٍ عليه السلام فِي السَفِينَةِ، والَّذِينَ كانُوا مَعَ إبْراهِيمَ الخَلِيلِ عليه السلام حَيْثُ اُلقِيَ فِي النارِ، وكانُوا مَعَ عِيسَي عليه السلام حِينَ رُفِعَ؛ وأرْبَعَةُ آلافٍ مُسَوِّمِينَ وَمُرْدِفِينَ وَثَلاثُ مِائَةٍ وَثَلاثَةُ عَشَرَ مَلَكاً يَوْمَ بَدْرٍ، وأرْبَعَةُ آلافِ مَلَكٍ الذينَ هَبَطُوا يُرِيدُونَ

'Ali, but he did not allow them, so they ascended to ask permission, after receiving which they came back down, but Ḥusayn had been killed. So they remain seperated, dust covered and weeping by the grave of Ḥusayn until the Ressurection Day. Between the grave of Ḥusayn and heaven is a passage of angels."

(*Biḥār*, 52, 325, 40)

1.10.15. It is reported that Abū al-Ḥasan al-Riḍā said: "...And all of the [eleven] Imams after the prophet were killed, some by the sword, the Commander of the Faithful and Ḥusayn, peace be with them, and the rest by poison. The tyrants of their times killed every one of them, and indeed this was done to them, truly, not like anything the extremists (*ghulāh*) or the delegators (*mufawiḍah*), may Allah curse them. They say, 'They (the Imams) were not really killed, and it was only a likeness of their affair that appeared to them.' So, they lied, may the wrath of Allah be upon them. Indeed, the affair of none of the prophets of Allah and His authorities, peace be with them, appeared doubtful to the people, except the affair of Jesus the son of Mary alone, for he was raised from the earth alive and his soul was taken between heaven and earth, then he was raised to heaven and his soul was returned to him, and that is what the saying of Allah, the Mighty and Magnificent, is about: ﴾*When Allah said: "O Jesus! I will take you to Me, and I will raise you to Me*﴿ (3:55), and Allah, the Mighty and Magnificent, said, narrating the speech of Jesus on the Resurrection Day, ﴾*And I was a witness over them, so long as I was among them, but when You took me to Yourself, You were Yourself the watcher over them. You Yourself are witness over everything.*﴿ (5:117)... And since it is permitted that all of the prophets and His messengers and authorities after Adam were born of fathers and mothers, but among them Jesus was born without any father, it will be permitted that his affair appeared doubtful to the people, but not the affairs of the other prophets and authorities, peace be with them. Likewise, it was permitted for him

القِتالَ مَعَ الحُسَيْنِ بْنِ عَلِيٍّ عليه السلام فَلَمْ يُؤْذَنْ لَهُمْ، فَصَعَدُوا فِي الاسْتِئذانِ وَهَبَطُوا وَقَدْ قُتِلَ الحُسَيْنُ عليه السلام. فَهُمْ شُعُثٌ، غُبْرٌ، يَبْكُونَ عِنْدَ قَبْرِ الحُسَيْنِ إلَي يَوْمِ القِيامَةِ. وَما بَيْنَ قَبْرِ الحُسَيْنِ إلَي السَماءِ مُخْتَلَفُ المَلائِكَةِ.'»

(بحار الأنوار، ٥٢، ٣٢٥، ٤٠)

١-١٠-١٥- قالَ أبُوالحَسَنِ الرضا عليه السلام: «... وَجَمِيعُ الأئمَّةِ [الأحَدَ عَشَرَ] بَعْدَ النَبيِّ صلى الله عليه وآله وسلم قُتِلُوا. مِنْهُمْ بِالسَيْفِ وَهُوَ أميرُ المُؤْمِنِينَ بَعْدَ النَبيِّ صلى الله عليه وآله وسلم والحُسَيْنُ عليه السلام, والباقُونَ قُتِلُوا بِالسَمِّ. قَتَلَ كُلٌّ واحِدٍ مِنْهُمْ طاغُوتَ زَمانِهِ وَجَرَي ذَلِكَ عَلَيْهِمْ عَلَي الحَقِيقَةِ والصحَّةِ, لا كَما تَقُولُهُ الغُلاةُ والمُفَوِّضَةُ, لَعَنَهُمُ اللهُ. فإنَّهُمْ يَقُولُونَ: 'إنَّهُمْ عليهم السلام لَمْ يُقْتَلُوا عَلَي الحَقِيقَةِ وانَّهُ شُبِّهَ لِلنّاسِ أمْرُهُمْ. وَكَذَبُوا, عَلَيْهِمْ غَضَبُ اللهِ, فإنَّهُ ما شُبِّهَ أمْرُ أحَدٍ مِنْ أنْبِياءِ اللهِ وحُجَجِهِ عَلَيْهِمُ السَلامُ لِلنّاسِ إلّا أمْرُ عِيسَي بْنِ مَرْيَمَ عليه السلام وَحْدَهُ. لأنَّهُ رُفِعَ مِنَ الأرضِ حَيّاً, وَقُبِضَ رُوحُهُ بَيْنَ السَماءِ والأرضِ, ثُمَّ رُفِعَ إلَي السَماءِ وَرُدَّ عَلَيْهِ رُوحُهُ. وَذَلِكَ قَوْلُ اللهِ, عَزَّ وَجَلَّ: ﴿إذْ قالَ اللهُ: 'يا عِيسَي إنِّي مُتَوَفِّيكَ وَرافِعُكَ إلَيَّ.﴾ وَقالَ اللهُ، عَزَّ وَجَلَّ، حِكايَةً لِقَوْلِ عِيسَي يَوْمَ القِيامَةِ: ﴿وَكُنْتُ عَلَيْهِم شَهِيداً مادُمتُ فِيهِمْ. فَلَمّا تَوَفَّيْتَنِي كُنْتَ أنتَ الرقِيبَ عَلَيْهِمْ وأنْتَ عَلَي كُلِّ شَيْءٍ شَهِيدٌ.﴾ وَيَقُولُ المُتَجاوِزُونَ لِلحَدِّ فِي أمْرِ الأئمَّةِ عليهم السلام: 'إنَّهُ إنْ جازَ أنْ يُشَبَّهَ أمْرُ عِيسَي لِلنّاسِ فَلِمَ لا يَجُوزُ أنْ يُشَبَّهَ أمْرُهُمْ أيْضاً؟' والَّذِي يَجِبُ أنْ يُقالَ لَهُمْ: 'إنَّ عِيسَي, عليه السلام, هُوَ مَوْلُودٌ مِنْ غَيْرِ أبٍ. فَلِمَ لا يَجُوزُ أنْ يَكُونُوا مَوْلُودِينَ مِنْ غَيْرِ آباءٍ؟' فإنَّهُمْ لا يَجْسَرُونَ عَلَي إظْهارِ مَذْهَبِهِمْ. لَعَنَهُمُ اللهُ فِي ذَلِكَ. وَمَتَي جازَ أنْ يَكُونَ جَمِيعُ أنْبِياءِ اللهِ وَرُسُلِهِ وَحُجَجِهِ بَعْدَ آدَمَ عليه السلام مَوْلُودِينَ مِنَ الآباءَ والأمَّهاتِ, وَكانَ عِيسَي مِنْ بَيْنِهِمْ مَوْلُوداً مِنْ غَيْرِ أبٍ, جازَ أنْ يُشَبَّهَ لِلنّاسِ أمْرُهُ دُونَ أمْرِ غَيْرِهِ مِنَ الأنبياءِ والحُجَجِ

to be born without a father, but not the others. Allah, the mighty and magnificent, only wanted to make his affair as a sign and mark for it to be known by this that He has power over all things.'"

(*Biḥār*, 25, 117)

1.10.16. It is reported that during his final pilgrimage, the Apostle of Allah said, "...And Jesus the son of Mary remained among his people for forty years."

(*Biḥār*, 37, 184, 69)

1.10.17. It is reported, "Ḥujjat ibn al-Ḥasan ﷺ in his *qunūt*[1] prayed, '...And I supplicate You with the supplication of Jesus Your spirit when he supplicated You and You saved him from his enemies and You raised him to Yourself....'"

(*Biḥār*, 82, 233)

1.10.18. Abū Ja'far ﷺ said, "Verily, Jesus ﷺ invited his companions [to come] the night when Allah would raise him to Himself. So, they were gathered before him at evening, and they were twelve men. He brought them into a house, then he came out to them from a fountain in a corner of the house while the water was flowing from his head, and he said, 'Verily, Allah revealed to me that He will raise me to Him now, and He will free me from the Jews. Which of you will bear my semblance, then be killed and crucified and be with me at my level?' A youth among them said, 'I, O Spirit of Allah!' He said, 'So, you are he.' Then Jesus said to them, 'Beware! Among you there is one who will disbelieve in me before twelve men become disbelievers.' A man among them said, 'I am he. O prophet of Allah!' Jesus said to him, 'If you feel it in yourself, you are he.' Then Jesus ﷺ said to them, 'Beware! After me you will divide into three sects. Two sects will blaspheme Allah and they will be in the Fire, and one sect will follow Sham'ūn, be true to Allah, and they will be in the Garden. Then Allah raised Jesus from the corner of the house, while they were looking at him." Then Abū Ja'far ﷺ

---

[1] A part of the formal prayer of Islam in which personal supplications are made.

عليه السلام, كَما جازَ أنْ يُولَدَ مِنْ غَيْرِ أبٍ دُونَهُمْ. وإنَّما أرادَ اللهُ، عَزَّ وَجَلَّ، أنْ يَجْعَلَ أمْرَهُ عليه السلام آيَةً وَعَلامَةً لِيُعْلَمَ بِذَلِكَ أنَّهُ عَلَي كُلِّ شَيْءٍ قَدِيرٌ.'»

(بحار الأنوار، ٢٥، ١١٧)

١-١٠-١٦- مِنْ مَناقِبِ الفَقِيهِ ...، عَنْ ابن امْرأةٍ، زَيْدِ بْنِ أرْقَمَ قالَ: «أقبَلَ نَبِيُّ اللهِ مِنْ مَكَّةَ فِي حَجَّةِ الوداعِ حَتَّي نَزَلَ بِغَدِيرِ الجُحْفَةِ ... فَقالَ: '... وإنَّ عِيسَي بْنَ مَرْيَمَ لَبِثَ فِي قَوْمِهِ أرْبَعِينَ سَنَةً.'»

(بحار الأنوار، ٣٧، ١٨٤، ٦٩)

١-١٠-١٧- قُنُوتُ مَوْلانا الحُجَّةِ بْنِ الحَسَنِ عليه السلام: «... وأدْعُوكَ بِما دَعاكَ بِهِ عِيسَي عليه السلام رُوحُكَ، حِينَ ناداكَ فَنَجَّيْتَهُ مِنْ أعْدائِهِ وإلَيْكَ رَفَعْتَهُ... .»

(بحار الأنوار، ٨٢، ٢٣٣)

١-١٠-١٨- أبِي، عَنْ ابن أبِي عُمَيْرٍ، عَنْ جَمِيلِ بْنِ صالِحٍ، عَنْ حَمْرانَ بْنِ أعْيَنَ، عَنْ أبِي جَعْفَرٍ عليه السلام، قالَ: «إنَّ عِيسَي عليه السلام وَعَدَ أصْحابَهُ لَيْلَةَ رَفَعَهُ اللهُ إلَيْهِ، فاجْتَمَعُوا إلَيْهِ عِنْدَ المَساءِ، وَهُمْ اثنا عَشَرَ رَجُلاً؛ فَأدْخَلَهُمْ بَيْتاً ثُمَّ خَرَجَ عَلَيْهِمْ مِنْ عَيْنٍ فِي زاوِيَةِ البَيْتِ وَيَنْفُضُ رأسَهُ مِنَ الماءِ، فَقالَ: 'إنَّ اللهَ أوْحَي إلَيَّ، أنَّهُ رافِعِي إلَيْهِ السّاعَةَ وَمُطَهِّرِي مِنَ اليَهُودِ. فأيُّكُمْ يُلْقَي عَلَيْهِ شَبَحِي فَيُقْتَلُ وَيُصْلَبُ وَيَكُونُ مَعِي فِي دَرَجَتِي؟' فَقالَ شابٌّ مِنْهُمْ: 'أنا يا رُوحَ اللهِ.' قالَ: 'فَأنْتَ هُوَ ذا.' فَقالَ لَهُمْ عِيسَي: 'أما إنَّ مِنْكُمْ لَمَنْ يَكْفُرُ بِي قَبْلَ أنْ يُصْبِحَ اثْنَتَي عَشْرَةَ كَفْرَةً.' فَقالَ لَهُ رَجُلٌ منهم: 'أنا هُوَ يا نَبِيَّ اللهِ.' فَقالَ لَهُ عِيسَي: 'أتُحِسُّ بِذَلِكَ فِي نَفْسِكَ فَلْتَكُنْ هُوَ.' ثُمَّ قالَ لَهُمْ عِيسَي عليه السلام: 'أما إنَّكُمْ سَتَفْتَرِقُونَ بَعْدِي عَلَي ثَلاثِ فِرَقٍ: فِرْقَتَيْنِ مُفْتَرِيَتَيْنِ عَلَي اللهِ فِي النارِ، وَفِرْقَةٌ تَتْبَعُ شَمْعُونَ صادِقَةً عَلَي اللهِ فِي الجَنَّةِ.' ثُمَّ رَفَعَ اللهُ عِيسَي إلَيْهِ مِنْ زاوِيَةِ البَيْتِ وَهُمْ يَنْظُرُونَ إلَيهِ.»

continued, "Verily, the Jews came seeking Jesus that night, and took the man about whom Jesus had said that he would disbelieve in him before twelve men became disbelievers. And they took the youth upon whom the semblance of Jesus had been cast. Then he was killed and crucified. And the one about whom Jesus had said that he would disbelieve in him before twelve men became disbelievers disbelieved."

(*Biḥār* 14, 336, 6)

1.10.19. Abū Ja'far al-Bāqir said, "When the Apostle of Allah ascended to heaven, he ascended on a ruby red couch crowned by green emeralds borne by angels... When he ascended to the seventh heaven Jesus met him, offered him greetings of peace, and asked him about 'Alī. He said to him, I appointed him as a successor in my community (*ummah*). He said, "You appointed a good successor. Know that verily Allah made the angels obey him." Then Moses and the prophets, one by one, met him and he spoke with them. They told him the same thing that Jesus said...."

(*Biḥār*, 18, 303, 7)

1.10.20. Hishām ibn Sālim reported that Abū 'Abd Allah said, "Gabriel, Mīkā'il and Isrāfīl brought al-Burāq to the Apostle of Allah. The Apostle of Allah [about his ascension to the Heaven] said, '... Gabriel brought me down [from al-Burāq] and said, 'Recite the prayer.' I prayed. He said, 'Do you know where you prayed?' I said, 'No.' He said, 'You prayed at a pure [town] and your pilgrimage will be to it.' Then I rode [on al-Burāq] and we went [to] where Allah willed. Then he said to me, 'Come down and recite the prayer.' I came down and prayed. He said, 'Do you know where you prayed?' I said, 'No.' He said, 'You prayed at Ṭūr Saynā, where Moses spoke with Allah.' Then I rode and we went where Allah willed. Then he said to me, 'Come down and recite the prayer.' I came down and prayed. He said, 'Do you know where you prayed?' I

ثُمَّ قالَ أبُو جَعْفَرٍ عليه السلام: «إنَّ اليَهُودَ جاءَتْ فِى طَلَبِ عِيسَي مِنْ لَيْلَتِهِمْ، فأخَذُوا الرجُلَ الذى قالَ لَهُ عِيسَي عليه السلام: 'إنْ مِنْكُمْ لمَنْ يَكْفُرُ بِى قبْلَ أنْ يُصبِحَ اثْنَتَي عَشْرَةَ كَفرَةً.' وأخَذُوا الشابَّ الذى القِىَ عَلَيْهِ شَبَحُ عِيسَي، فقُتِلَ وَصُلِبَ. وكَفَرَ الذى قالَ لَهُ عِيسَي: 'تَكْفُرُ قَبْلَ أنْ تُصبِحَ اثْنَتَي عَشْرَةَ كَفرَةً.'»

(بحار الأنوار، ١٤، ٣٣٦، ٦)

١-١٠-١٩- الشيْخُ الصالِحُ أبومُحَمَّدٍ الحَسَن، رَضِىَ اللهُ، عَنْهُ بِإسنادِهِ عَنِ الصدُوق, عَنْ أبيهِ, عَنْ مُحَمَّدِ بْنِ أبِى القاسِمِ, عَنْ مُحَمَّدِ بْنِ عَلِىٍّ, عَنْ مُحَمَّدِ بْنِ عَبْدِ اللهِ بْنِ مِهْرانَ, عَنْ صالِحِ بْنِ عُقْبَةَ, عَنْ يَزِيدِ بْنِ عَبْدِ المَلِكِ, عَنْ أبِى جَعْفَرٍ الباقِرِ عليه السلام، قالَ: «لمّا صَعَدَ رَسُولُ اللهِ صلى الله عليه وآله وسلم إلَي السَماءِ، صَعَدَ عَلَي سَرِيرٍ مِنْ ياقُوتَةٍ حَمْراءَ، مُكَلَّلةٍ مِنْ زبَرْجَدَةٍ خَضْراءَ، تَحْمِلُهُ المَلائِكَةُ... فلَمّا صُعِدَ بِهِ إلَي السَماءِ السّابِعَةِ، لَقِيَهُ عِيسَي عليه السلام، فسَلَّمَ عَلَيْهِ، وَسألَه, عَنْ عَلِيٍّ. فقالَ لَهُ: 'خَلَّفْتُهُ فِى أُمَّتِى.' قالَ: 'نِعْمَ الخَلِيفَةُ خَلَّفْتَ. أما إنَّ اللهَ فَرَضَ عَلَي المَلائِكَةِ طاعَتَهُ.' ثُمَّ لَقِيَهُ مُوسَي عليه السلام والنَبِيُّونَ، نَبِىٌّ، نَبِىٌّ. فكُلُّهُمْ يَقُولُ لَهُ مَقالَةَ عِيسَي عليه السلام... .»

(بحار الأنوار، ١٨، ٣٠٣، ٧)

١-١٠-٢٠- حَكَي أبِي, عَنْ مُحَمَّدِ بْنِ أبِى عُمَيْرٍ, عَنْ هِشامِ بْنِ سالِمٍ, عَنْ أبِى عَبْدِ اللهِ عليه السلام، قالَ: «جاءَ جَبْرَئِيلُ، مِيكائِيلُ وإسْرافِيلُ بِالبُراقِ إلَي رَسُولُ اللهِ صلى الله عليه وآله وسلم [قالَ(ص): '] ... فَنَزَلَ بِى جَبْرَئِيلُ، فقالَ: 'صَلِّ.' فَصَلَّيْتُ فقالَ: 'أتَدْرِي أيْنَ صَلَّيْتَ؟' فقُلْتُ: 'لا.' فقالَ: 'صَلَّيْت بِطَيِّبَةٍ، وإلَيها مُهاجَرَتُكَ.' ثُمَّ رَكِبْتُ، فَمَضَيْنا ما شاءَ اللهُ. ثُمَّ قالَ لِى: 'انْزِلْ وَصَلِّ.' فَنَزَلْتُ وَصَلَّيْتُ. فقالَ لِى: 'أتَدْرى أيْنَ صَلَّيْتَ؟'

said, 'No.' He said, 'You prayed at Bethlehem, in the district of Jerusalem (Bayt al-Muqaddas), where Jesus the son of Mary was born.' Then I rode and we went until we arrived at Jerusalem (Bayt al-Muqaddas.) Then I tied al-Burāq by the link by which the prophets tied it, and entered the Mosque while Gabiel was with me. We found Abraham, Moses and Jesus, among the prophets gathered by the permission of Allah... Then I was raised to the second heaven. There were two men, like each other in it. I said, 'O Gabriel! Who are these?' He said to me, 'The cousins John and Jesus the son of Mary.' Then I greeted them and they greeted me. I asked God's forgiveness for them. They asked God's forgiveness for me too, and said, 'Welcome righteous brother and righteous prophet!' The angels in that heaven were similar to the angels in the first heaven and they were humble. Allah created their faces as He wanted. All of them glorified and praised Him with different voices."

(*Tafsīr al-Qumī*, 2, 3-8)

1.11. HIS SECOND COMING

1.11.1. Shahr ibn Ḥawshab said, "Al-Ḥajjāj said to me, 'There is a verse in the Book of Allah that has wearied me.' I said, 'O Commander! Which verse is it?' He said, 'His saying, '﴾*And there is not one of the followers of the Book but most certainly believes in this before his death, and on the day of resurrection he (Jesus) shall be a witness against them.*﴿ (4:159)' By Allah! I command a Jew and a Christian to be beheaded, then I look at them with my own eyes, but I do not see them moving their lips when they die.' I said, 'May Allah reform the Commander! It is not as you have interpreted it.' He said, 'How is it?' I said, 'Verily, Jesus will descend to the world

فَقُلْتُ: 'لا.' فقالَ: 'صَلَّيْتَ بطور سَيْناءَ، حَيْثُ كَلَّمَ اللهُ مُوسَي تَكْلِيماً.' ثُمَّ رَكِبْتُ، فَمَضَيْنا ما شاءَ اللهُ. ثُمَّ قالَ لِي: 'انْزِلْ، فَصَلِّ.' فَنَزَلْتُ وَصَلَّيْتُ. قالَ لِي: 'أَتَدْرى أَيْنَ صَلَّيْتَ؟' فَقُلْتُ: 'لا.' قالَ: 'صَلَّيْتَ فِى بَيْتِ لَحْم بِناحِيَةِ بَيْتِ المَقْدِس، حَيْثُ وُلِدَ عِيسَي بْنُ مَرْيَمَ ﷺ.' ثُمَّ رَكِبْتُ، فَمَضَيْنا حَتَّي انْتَهَيْنا إِلِي بَيْتِ المَقْدِس. فَرَبَطْتُ البُراقَ بِالحَلْقَةِ الَّتِى كانَتْ الأنْبِياءُ تَرْبِطُ بِها، فَدَخَلْتُ المَسْجِدَ، وَمَعِىَ جَبْرَئِيلُ إِلِي جَنْبِى، فَوَجَدْنا إِبْراهِيمَ وَمُوسَي وَعِيسَي، فِى مَنْ شاءَ اللهُ مِنْ أَنْبِياء اللهِ، قَدْ جُمِعُوا...' قالَ: 'ثُمَّ صَعَدَ بِى إِلِي السَّماءِ الثَّانِيَةِ، فَإِذا فِيها رَجُلانِ مُتَشابِهانِ. فَقُلْتُ: 'مَنْ هَذانِ يا جَبْرَئِيلُ؟' فقالَ لِي: 'أَبْناءُ الخالَةِ، يَحْيَي وَعِيسَي بْنُ مَرْيَمَ.' فَسَلَّمْتُ عَلَيْهِما وَسَلَّما عَلَيَّ، واسْتَغْفَرْتُ لَهُما واسْتَغْفَرا لِي، وَقالا: 'مَرْحَباً بِالأخ الصالِح والنَّبِيِّ الصالِحِ.' وَإِذا فِيها مِنَ المَلائِكَةِ مِثْلُ ما فِى السَّماءِ الأُولِي، وَعَلَيْهِمُ الخُشُوعُ، قَدْ وَضَعَ اللهُ وُجُوهَهُمْ كَيْفَ شاءَ، لَيْسَ مِنْهُمْ مَلَكٌ إِلّا يُسَبِّحُ اللهَ وَيَحْمَدُهُ بِأَصْواتٍ مُخْتَلِفَةٍ.'»

(تفسير القمىّ، ٢، ٣–٨)

١–١١– نُزُولُهُ إِلِي الأرض

١–١١–١– حَدَّثَنِى أَبِى, عَنِ القاسِمِ بْنِ مُحَمَّدٍ, عَنْ سُلَيْمانَ بْنِ داوُدَ المِنْقَرِيِّ، عَنْ أَبِى حَمْزَةٍ، عَنْ شَهْرِ بْنِ حَوْشَبٍ، قالَ: «قالَ لِى الحَجّاجُ بِأَنَّ آيَةً فِى كِتابِ اللهِ قَدْ أَعْيَتْنِى. فَقُلْتُ: 'أَيُّها الأمِيرُ، أَيَّةُ آيَةٍ هِيَ؟' فَقالَ: 'قَوْلُهُ: ﴿وإِنْ مِنْ أَهْلِ الكِتابِ إِلّا لَيُؤْمِنَنَّ بِهِ قَبْلَ مَوْتِهِ.﴾ واللهِ إِنِّى لآمُرُ بِاليَهُودِيِّ والنَّصْرانِيِّ، فَيُضْرَبُ عُنُقُهُ، ثُمَّ أَرْمُقُهُ بِعَيْنِى، فَما أَراهُ يُحَرِّكُ شَفَتَيْهِ حَتَّي يَخْمُدَ.' فَقُلْتُ: 'أَصْلَحَ اللهُ الأمِيرَ، لَيْسَ عَلَي ما تَأَوَّلْتَ.' قالَ: 'كَيْفَ هُوَ؟' قُلْتُ: 'إِنَّ عِيسَي يَنْزِلُ قَبْلَ يَوْمِ القِيامَةِ إِلِي الدُّنْيا،

before the Resurrection Day, then the people of the Jewish nation or Christian nation will not remain [on the earth] unless they believe in him before their death and will pray behind al-Mahdī.' He said, 'Woe unto you! Where did you bring it from?' I said, 'Muḥammad ibn 'Alī ibn al-Ḥusayn ibn 'Alī ibn Abū Ṭālib narrated it to me.' He said, 'By Allah! You brought it from a pure spring.'"

(*Tafsīr al-Qumī*, 1, 158)

1.11.2. The Apostle of Allah said, "Good news for you. [He repeated it three times.] ... How can the community of which I am the first perish? There are twelve persons after me who are felicitous and possess understanding and Christ Jesus the son of Mary is at the end of them. But between them, the children of confusion will perish. They are not from me and I am not from them."

(*Khiṣāl*, 2, 476)

1.11.3. The Apostle of Allah said, "How can a community perish when I am at the beginning of it, Jesus the son of Mary will be at the end of it and al-Mahdī will be in the middle of it."

(*Dalā'il al-Imāmah*, 234)

1.11.4. Ḥudhayfah ibn 'Usayd al-Ghifārī said, "We sat in the shadow of a wall in al-Madīnah and the Apostle of Allah was in a room. Then he appeared over us and said, 'What are you doing?' We said, 'We are talking.' He said, 'About what?' We said, 'About the Resurrection Day (*al-Sā'ah*).' He said, 'You will not see the Resurrection Day

فَلَا يَبْقَى أَهْلُ مِلَّةٍ يَهُودِيٍّ وَلَا نَصْرَانِيٍّ إِلَّا آمَنَ بِهِ قَبْلَ مَوْتِهِ، وَيُصَلِّي خَلْفَ الْمَهْدِيِّ.' قَالَ: 'وَيْحَكَ، أَنَّى لَكَ هَذَا وَمِنْ أَيْنَ جِئْتَ بِهِ؟' فَقُلْتُ: 'حَدَّثَنِي بِهِ مُحَمَّدُ بْنُ عَلِيِّ بْنِ الْحُسَيْنِ بْنِ عَلِيِّ بْنِ أَبِي طَالِبٍ ﷺ.' فَقَالَ: 'جِئْتَ بِهَا وَاللهِ مِنْ عَيْنٍ صَافِيَةٍ.'»

(تفسير القمي، ١، ١٥٨)

١-١١-٢- حَدَّثَنَا حَمْزَةُ بْنُ مُحَمَّدِ بْنِ أَحْمَدَ بْنِ جَعْفَرِ بْنِ مُحَمَّدِ بْنِ زَيْدِ بْنِ عَلِيِّ بْنِ الْحُسَيْنِ ﷺ، ... عَنْ جَعْفَرِ بْنِ مُحَمَّدٍ، عَنْ أَبِيهِ، عَنْ آبَائِهِ، عَنْ عَلِيٍّ ﷺ، قَالَ: «قَالَ رَسُولُ اللهِ ﷺ: 'أَبْشِرُوا، ثُمَّ أَبْشِرُوا،' ثَلَاثَ مَرَّاتٍ ... 'كَيْفَ تَهْلِكُ أُمَّةٌ أَنَا أَوَّلُهَا وَاثْنَا عَشَرَ مِنْ بَعْدِي مِنَ السُّعَدَاءِ وَأُولِى الْأَلْبَابِ، وَالْمَسِيحُ عِيسَى بْنُ مَرْيَمَ آخِرُهَا! وَلَكِنْ يَهْلِكُ بَيْنَ ذَلِكَ نَتْجُ الْهَرْجِ، لَيْسُوا مِنِّي وَلَسْتُ مِنْهُمْ.'»

(الخصال، ٢، ٤٧٦)

١-١١-٣- حَدَّثَنَا أَبُو إِسْحَاقَ إِبْرَاهِيمُ بْنُ أَحْمَدَ الطَّبَرِيُّ، قَالَ: «... حَدَّثَنَا مُحَمَّدُ بْنُ إِبْرَاهِيمَ الْهَاشِمِيُّ، عَنْ أَبِي جَعْفَرٍ أَمِيرِ الْمُؤْمِنِينَ عَبْدِ اللهِ بْنِ مُحَمَّدٍ، عَنْ أَبِيهِ، عَنِ ابْنِ عَبَّاسٍ، قَالَ: 'قَالَ رَسُولُ اللهِ: 'كَيْفَ تَهْلِكُ أُمَّةٌ أَنَا أَوَّلُهَا وَعِيسَى بْنُ مَرْيَمَ فِى آخِرِهَا وَالْمَهْدِيُّ فِى وَسَطِهَا!'»

(دلائل الإمامة، ٢٣٤)

١-١١-٤- حَدَّثَنَا مُحَمَّدُ بْنُ أَحْمَدَ بْنِ إِبْرَاهِيمَ قَالَ: «... حَدَّثَنَا فُرَاتُ الْقَزَّازِ، عَنْ أَبِي الطُّفَيْلِ عَامِرِ بْنِ وَاثِلَةٍ، عَنْ حُذَيْفَةَ بْنِ أُسَيْدِ الْغِفَارِيِّ، قَالَ: 'كُنَّا جُلُوسًا فِى الْمَدِينَةِ فِى ظِلِّ حَائِطٍ.' قَالَ: 'وَكَانَ رَسُولُ اللهِ ﷺ فِى غُرْفَةٍ، فَاطَّلَعَ عَلَيْنَا، فَقَالَ: 'فِيمَ أَنْتُمْ؟' فَقُلْنَا: 'نَتَحَدَّثُ.' قَالَ: 'عَنْ

until you see ten signs before it, sunrise from the West, al-Dajjāl and the beast of the earth, three lunar eclipses on the earth, one in the East, one in the West and one in the Arabian Peninsula and the emergence of Jesus the son of Mary ..."

(*Biḥār*, 6, 304, 3)

1.11.5. Abū al-Qāsim al-Ṭā'ī said, "I asked 'Alī ibn Mūsā al-Riḍā about he who will fight with us. He said, "He who will fight with the companian of Jesus the son of Mary."

(*Ṣaḥīfah al-Riḍā*, 89)

1.11.6. It is reported that Abū 'Abd Allah said, "Jesus the son of Mary is the Spirit of Allah and His Word. He was thirty-three years old in the world. Then Allah raised him to heaven. He will descend to the earth and it is he who will kill the Antichrist (Dajjāl.)"

(*Tafsīr al-Qumī*, 2, 271)

1.11.7. Abū Ja'far about the verse ﴿*O you who believe! Be helpers of Allah, as Jesus the son of Mary said to his disciples, 'Who will be my helpers in the cause of Allah?' The disciples said, We are the helpers of Allah. So, a party of the children of Israel believed and another party disbelieved. Then We aided those who believed against their enemy, and they became uppermost*﴾ (61:14) said, "The group that became disbelievers was the group that killed and crucified one who was similar to Jesus. The group that became believers was the group [one of whose members] accepted the one who was like Jesus so that he would not be killed. Then the group that killed and crucified him was killed. This is [the explanation of] His saying, ﴿*Then We aided those who believed against their enemy, and they became uppermost*﴾."(61:14)

(*Tafsīr al-Qumī*, 2, 366)

1.11.8. It is reported that Jesus will say to al-Mahdī, "I was raised as a minister not as a commander."

(*Ṣirāṭ al-Mustaqīm*, 2, 220)

ماذا؟' قُلْنا: 'عَنِ السّاعَةِ؟' فَقالَ: 'إِنَّكُمْ لا تَرَوْنَ السّاعَةَ حَتَّي تَرَوْنَ قَبْلَها عَشْرَ آياتٍ: طُلُوعَ الشمْسِ مِنْ مَغْرِبِها، والدجالَ، وَدابَّةَ الأرضِ، وثَلاثَةَ خُسُوفٍ فِي الأرضِ، خَسَفٌ بِالمَشْرِقِ وَخَسَفٌ بِالمَغْرِبِ وَخَسَفٌ بِجَزِيرَةِ العَرَبِ، وَخُرُوجَ عِيسَي بْنِ مَرْيَمَ عليه السلام... .'»

(بحار الأنوار، ٦، ٣٠٤، ٣)

١-١١-٥- الشيْخُ أبُو القاسِمِ الطائِيُّ، قالَ: «إِنِّي سألتُ عَلِيَّ بْنَ مُوسَي الرضا عليه السلام, عَنْ مَنْ قاتَلَنا فِي آخِرِ الزَّمانِ. قالَ: 'مَنْ قاتَلَ صاحِبَ عِيسَي بْنِ مَرْيَمَ.'»

(صحيفة الرضا عليه السلام، ٨٩)

١-١١-٦- عَنْ أبِي عَبْدِ اللهِ عليه السلام: «...عِيسَي بْنُ مَرْيَمَ، رُوحُ اللهِ وَكَلِمَتُهُ؛ وَكانَ عُمْرُهُ فِي الدنْيا ثَلاثَةً وَثَلاثِينَ سَنَةً. ثُمَّ رَفَعَهُ اللهُ إلَي السَماءِ، وَيَهْبِطُ إلَي الأرضِ، بِدِمَشْقٍ وَهُوَ الذي يَقْتُلُ الدجّالَ.»

(تفسير القمیّ، ٢، ٢٧١)

١-١١-٧- قَوْلُهُ: ﴿يا أيُّها الذينَ آمَنُوا كُونُوا أنْصارَ اللهِ.﴾ إلَي قَوْلِهِ: ﴿فآمَنَتْ طائِفَةٌ مِنْ بَنِي إسْرائِيلَ وَكَفَرَتْ طائِفَةٌ.﴾ قالَ أبُوجَعْفَرٍ عليه السلام: «الَّتِي كَفَرَتْ، هِيَ الَّتِي قَتَلَتْ شَبِيهَ عِيسَي عليه السلام وَصَلَبَتْهُ؛ والَّتِي آمَنَتْ، هِيَ الَّتِي قَبِلَتْ شَبِيهَ عِيسَي حَتَّي لا يُقْتَلُ. فَقَتَلَتْ الطائِفَةَ الَّتِي قَتَلَتْهُ وَصَلَبَتْهُ وَهُوَ قَوْلُهُ: ﴿فأيَّدْنا الذينَ آمَنُوا عَلَي عَدُوِّهِمْ فأصْبَحُوا ظاهِرِينَ.﴾»

(تفسير القمیّ، ٢، ٣٦٦)

١-١١-٨- قَوْلُ عِيسَي لِلْمَهْدِيِّ: «إنَّما بُعِثْتُ وَزِيراً، وَلَمْ أُبْعَثْ أمِيراً.»

(الصراط المستقيم، ٢، ٢٢٠)

1.11.9. Ḥudhayfah reported that the Prophet said, "Al-Mahdī will turn his face to Jesus when he descends as if water were dropping from his hair, and will say to him, 'Go ahead and say the prayer.' Jesus will say, 'The prayer has been set up only for you.' So, Jesus will pray behind a man who is among my sons."

(*Ṣirāṭ al-Mustaqīm*, 2, 257)

1.11.10. It is reported that Ka'b said, "Jesus will descend from heaven. Then the Jews and Christians will come to him and say, 'We are your people.' He will say, 'You lie. The emigrants, the rest of the people of battles, are my people.' Then Jesus will come to the place that the Muslims are gathered and find their Caliph[1] is praying with them, who will say to him, 'O Christ! Pray in front of us.' He will say, 'But you pray with your people. I have been raised as a minister, not as a commander.'

(*Ṣirāṭ al-Mustaqīm*, 3, 92)

1.11.11. The Apostle of Allah said, "...The leader of the people on that day will be a righteous man. It will be said that he prays the morning prayer. When he says "Allah Akbar" and begins to pray, Jesus the son of Mary will descend. When the righteous man sees him, he will know him, return and walk back. Then Jesus will come, put his hand between his shoulders and say, 'Pray. The prayer has been set up for you.' Then Jesus will pray behind him and say, 'Open the door.' Then they will open the door."

('*Umdah*, 429)

1.11.12. It is reported that, "Jesus will descend, wearing two saffron colored robes." According to another tradition, "Jesus the son of Mary will descend to a hill of the Sacred Earth that is named Ithbanī [or Ithbayt]. Two yellow dresses are on him and the hair of his head is anointed and there is a lance (arm) in his hand by which he kills Dajjāl. He comes to Jerusalem while the people pray the afternoon prayer and Imām is in front of them. Imām comes back, but Jesus prefers him and prays behind him according the revealed

---

[1] In the literal meaning of successor to the Prophet .

١-١١-٩- عَنْ حُذَيْفَةٍ، قالَ النَبِيُّ صلى الله عليه وآله وسلم: «يَلْتَفِتُ المَهْدِيُّ، وَقَدْ نَزَلَ عِيسَي بْنُ مَرْيَمَ كأنَّما يَقْطُرُ مِنْ شَعْرِهِ الماءُ، يَقُولُ لَهُ المَهْدِيُّ: 'تَقَدَّمْ، فَصَلِّ.' فَيَقُولُ: 'إنَمّا أُقِيمَتْ الصَلاةُ لَكَ.' فَيُصَلِّي عِيسَي خَلْفَ رَجُلٍ مِنْ وُلْدِي.»

(الصراط المستقيم، ٢، ٢٥٧)

١-١١-١٠- فِي كِتابِ الفِتَنِ, عَنْ كَعْبٍ: «يَنْزِلُ عِيسَي مِنَ السَماءِ، فَتأتِيهِ اليَهُودُ والنَصارَي، وَيَقُولُونَ: 'نَحْنُ أصْحابُكَ.' فَيَقُولُ: 'كَذِبْتُمْ! أصْحابِي، المُهاجِرُونَ، بَقِيَّةُ أصْحابِ المَلْحَمَةِ.' فَياتِي مَجْمَعُ المُسْلِمِينَ، فَيَجِدُ خَلِيفَتَهُمْ يُصَلِّي بِهِمْ. فَيَقُولُ: 'يا مَسِيحُ، صَلِّ بِنا.' فَيَقُولُ: 'بَلْ صَلِّ أنتَ بِأصْحابِكَ. إنَّما بُعِثْتُ وَزِيراً وَلَمْ أبْعَثْ أمِيراً.'»

(الصراط المستقيم، ٣، ٩٢)

١-١١-١١- قالَ رَسُولُ اللهِ صلى الله عليه وآله وسلم: «...إمامُ الناسِ يَوْمَئِذٍ رَجُلٌ صالِحٌ. فَيُقالُ: 'صَلِّي الصبْحَ.' فإذا كَبَّرَ وَدَخَلَ فِي الصَلاةِ، نَزَلَ عِيسَي بْنُ مَرْيَمَ عليه السلام. فإذا رَآهُ ذَلِكَ الرجُلُ، عَرَفَهُ، فَرَجَعَ يَمْشِي القَهْقَرَي، فَيَتَقَدَّمُ عِيسَي عليه السلام، فَيَضَعُ يَدَهُ بَيْنَ كِتْفَيْهِ وَيَقُولُ: 'صَلِّ، فإنَّما أُقِيمَتْ لَكَ الصَلاةُ.' فَيُصَلِّي عِيسَي وَراءَهُ، ثُمَّ يَقُولُ: 'افْتَحُوا البابَ.' فَيَفْتَحُونَ البابَ.»

(العمدة، ٤٢٩)

١-١١-١٢- فِي الحَدِيثِ «إنَّ عِيسَي عليه السلام يَنْزِلُ فِي ثَوْبَيْنِ مَهْرُودَيْنِ.»- أيْ مَصْبُوغَيْنِ بِالهَرْدِ وَهُوَ الزَّعْفَرانُ.- قالَ: «وَفِي الحَدِيثِ: 'يَنْزِلُ عِيسَي بْنُ مَرْيَمَ عليه السلام عَلَي ثَنِيَّةٍ مِنَ الأرضِ المُقَدَّسَةِ، يُقالُ لَها: 'أثْبَنِي.' وَعَلَيْهِ مُمَصَرَتانِ، وَشَعْرُ راسِهِ دَهِينٌ، وَبِيَدِهِ حَرْبَةٌ، وَهِيَ الَّتِي يَقْتُلُ بِها الدجالَ. فَيأتِي بَيْتَ المَقْدِسِ والناسُ فِي صَلاةِ العَصْرِ، والإمامُ يَؤُمُّ بِهِمْ. فَيَتأخَّرُ الإمامُ، فَيُقَدِّمُهُ عِيسَي، وَيُصَلِّي

law of Muḥammad. Then he will kill the swine, break the crosses, destroy the churches and temples and kill the Christians unless they believe in him."

(*'Umdah*, 430)

1.11.13. Tha'labī mentioned in his *Tafsīr* with its own chain of transmission regarding "*Ḥā mīm 'ayn sīn qāf,*"[1] "*Al-sīn* is the gleam of Mahdī and *al-qāf* is the power of Jesus when he descends, kills the Christians[2] and ruins the churches."

(*Ṭarā'if*, 1, 176)

1.11.14. It is reported that the Prophet said, "Among my progeny is the Mahdi. When he emerges, Jesus the son of Mary will descend to help him, then Jesus will send him ahead and pray behind him."

(*Biḥār,* 14, 349)

1.11.15. It is reported from Abū 'Abd Allah from his fathers that Ḥasan the son of 'Alī said when disputing with the king of Byzantium, "The life of Jesus in the world was thirty-three years. Then Allah raised him to heaven and he will descend to the earth in Damascus, and it is he who will kill the Antichrist (Dajjāl)."

(*Biḥār*, 14, 247, 27)

1.11.16. Khaythama reported that Abū Ja'far said, "...O Khaythama! There will come a time for the people when they will not know who is Allah and His unity until Dajjāl appears and Jesus the son of Mary, may peace and blessings be with both of them, descends from the sky, and Allah will kill Dajjāl by his hands and a man that is from our House will pray with the people. Do you not know that Jesus will pray behind us, although he is a prophet? Beware that we are better than him."

(*Biḥār*, 24, 328, 46)

---

(1) Letters with which some of the *suwar* of the Qur'ān begin.

(2) That is, given the previous *ḥadīth*, those who refuse to believe in him.

خَلْفَهُ عَلَي شَرِيعَةِ مُحَمَّدٍ صلى الله عليه وآله وسلم. ثُمَّ يَقْتُلُ الخَنازِيرَ وَيَكْسِرُ الصَلِيبَ وَيَخْرِبُ البِيَعَ والكَنائِسَ وَيَقْتُلُ النَصارَي إلّا مَنْ آمَنَ بِهِ.'»
(العمدة، ٤٣٠)

١-١١-١٣- ذَكَرَ الثَّعْلَبِيُّ فِي تَفْسِيرِهِ حمعسق، بِإسْنادِهِ، قالَ: «السِّينُ سَناءُ المَهْدِيِّ عليه السلام، والقافُ قُوَّةُ عِيسَي عليه السلام حِينَ يَنْزِلُ فَيَقْتُلُ النَصارَي وَيَخْرِبُ البِيَعَ.»
(الطرائف، ١، ١٧٦)

١-١١-١٤- ل [الخصال] ماجِيلَوَيْهِ, عَنْ عَمِّهِ, عَنْ أحْمَدَ بْنِ هِلالٍ, عَنْ الفَضْلِ بْنِ دكِينٍ, عَنْ مُعَمَّرِ بْنِ راشِدٍ, عَنْ النَبِيِّ صلى الله عليه وآله وسلم، قالَ: «مِنْ ذُرِّيَّتِي، المَهْدِيُّ. إذا خَرَجَ نَزَلَ عِيسَي بْنُ مَرْيَمَ لِنُصْرَتِهِ، فَقَدَّمَهُ وَصَلَّي خَلْفَهُ.»
(بحار الأنوار، ١٤، ٣٤٩)

١-١١-١٥- الحُسَيْنُ بْنُ عَبْدِ اللهِ السكِّينِيّ, عَنْ أبِي سَعِيدِ البَجَلِيِّ, عَنْ عَبْدِ المَلِكِ بْنِ هارُونِ, عَنْ أبِي عَبْدِ اللهِ, عَنْ آبائِهِ عليهم السلام، قالَ: «قالَ الحَسَنُ بْنُ عَلِيٍّ عليه السلام، فِي ما ناظَرَ بِهِ مَلِكَ الرومِ: 'كانَ عُمْرُ عِيسَي عليه السلام فِي الدنْيا ثَلاثَةَ وَثَلاثِينَ سَنَةً، ثُمَّ رَفَعَهُ اللهُ إلَي السَماءِ؛ وَيَهْبِطُ إلَي الأرضِ بِدِمَشْقٍ، وَهُوَ الذي يَقْتُلُ الدجّالَ.'»
(بحار الأنوار، ١٤، ٢٤٧، ٢٧)

١-١١-١٦- جَعْفَرُ بْنُ مُحَمَّدٍ الفَزارِيّ بِإسْنادِهِ, عَنْ خَيْثَمَةٍ, عَنْ أبِي جَعْفَرٍ عليه السلام، «... يا خَيْثَمَةُ، سَياتِي عَلَي الناسِ زَمانٌ لا يَعْرِفُونَ اللهَ ما هُوَ والتوْحِيدَ، حَتَّي يَكُونَ خُرُوجُ الدجّالِ، وَحَتَّي يَنْزِلَ عِيسَي بْنُ مَرْيَمَ, عَلَيْهِما الصَلاةُ والسَلامُ, مِنَ السَماءِ، وَيَقْتُلَ اللهُ الدجّالَ عَلَي يَدَيْهِ، وَيُصَلَّي بِهِمْ رَجُلٌ مِنّا أهْلَ البَيْتِ. ألا تَرَي أنَّ عِيسَي يُصَلِّي خَلْفَنا وَهُوَ نَبِيٌّ؟ ألا وَنَحْنُ أفْضَلُ مِنْهُ.»
(بحار الأنوار، ٢٤، ٣٢٨، ٤٦)

1.12. ON THE RESURRECTION

1.12.1. Regarding the Garden, the Prophet said, "...then a man will come out with a group and the angels will be around him with wings outspread and the light will be in front of them. Then the people of the Garden will crane their necks toward him and say, 'Who is this who is thus allowed by Allah?' The angels will say, 'This is the spirit of Allah and His word! This is Jesus the son of Mary!'"

(*Ikhtiṣāṣ*, 1, 355)

1.12.2. It is reported that Samā'ah asked Abū 'Abd Allah about the intercession of the Prophet on the Resurrection Day. He answered, "The people will be [as it were] bridled by perspiration on the Resurrection Day and say, 'Bring us to Adam, he will intercede for us before our Lord.' Then they will come to Adam and say, 'O Adam! Intercede for us before your Lord.' He will say, 'I have done a sin and a mistake. So Noah is the one you must have.' They will come to Noah, but he will send them to the next prophet, and every prophet will send them to the next until they will terminate at Jesus. He will say, 'Muḥammad the Apostle of Allah is the one you must have.' They will present themselves to him and will ask him.' He will say, 'Be free.' Then he will bring them to the door of heaven and will go to meet them from the Door of Mercy and he will fall to the ground in prostration and remain as long as Allah wills. Then Allah will say, 'Raise your head and intercede, you will be answered and ask, you will be given.' It is His saying, '﴾*Maybe your Lord will raise you to a position of glory*﴿.' (17:79)

(*Tafsīr al-Qumī*, 2, 25)

1.12.3. It is reported that Abū al-Ḥasan Mūsā said, "...On the Resurrection Day there will be four of the first and four of the last on the throne of the Merciful. As for the four of the first, they will be Noah, Abraham, Moses and Jesus. As for the four of the last, they will be Muḥammad, 'Alī, Ḥasan and Ḥusayn, may Allah bless them."

(*Kāfī,* 4, 585, 4)

١-١٢- فِي القِيامَةِ

١-١٢-١- قالَ النبِيُّ صلى الله عليه وآله وسلم: «... ثُمَّ يَخْرُجُ رَجُلٌ، فِي مَوْكَبٍ حَوْلَهُ المَلائِكَةُ قَدْ صَفَّتْ أجْنِحَتَها، والنورُ أمامَهُمْ، فَيَمُدُّ إلَيْهِ أهْلُ الجَنَّةِ أعْناقَهُمْ، فَيَقُولُونَ: 'مَنْ هَذا الذى قَدْ أذِنَ لَهُ عَلَي اللهِ؟' فَتَقُولُ المَلائِكَةُ: 'هَذا رُوحُ اللهِ وكَلِمَتُهُ، هَذا عِيسَي بْنُ مَرْيَمَ.'»

(الاختصاص، ١، ٣٥٥).

١-١٢-٢- حَدَّثَنِي أبِي, عَنِ الحَسَنِ بْنِ مَحْبُوبٍ, عَنْ زَراعَةٍ [زرْعَةٍ], عَنْ سَماعَةٍ, عَنْ أبِي عَبْدِ اللهِ عليه السلام، قالَ: «سألْتُهُ, عَنْ شَفاعَةِ النَبِيِّ صلى الله عليه وآله وسلم يَوْمَ القِيامَةِ. فَقالَ: 'يُلْجِمُ الناسَ يَوْمَ القِيامَةِ العَرَقُ. فَيَقُولُونَ: 'انْطَلِقُوا بِنا إلَي آدَمَ يَشْفَعْ لَنا عِنْدَ رَبِّنا.' فَيأتُونَ آدَمَ، فَيَقُولُونَ: 'يا آدَمُ اشْفَعْ لَنا عِنْدَ رَبِّكَ.' فَيَقُولُ: 'إنَّ لِي ذَنْباً وَخَطِيئَةً، فَعَلَيْكُمْ بِنُوحٍ.' فَيأتُونَ نُوحاً، فَيَرُدُّهُمْ إلَي مَنْ يَلِيهِ، وَيَرُدُّهُمْ كُلُّ نَبِيٍّ إلَي مَنْ يَلِيهِ، حَتَّي يَنْتَهُوا إلَي عِيسَي، فَيَقُولُ: 'عَلَيْكُمْ بِمُحَمَّدٍ، رَسُولِ اللهِ.' فَيَعْرِضُونَ أنْفُسَهُمْ عَلَيْهِ وَيَسْألُونَهُ. فَيَقُولُ: 'انْطَلِقُوا.' فَيَنْطَلِقُ بِهِمْ إلَي بابِ الجَنَّةِ، وَيَسْتَقْبِلُ بابَ الرحْمَةِ، وَيَخِرُّ ساجِداً، فَيَمْكُثُ ما شاءَ اللهُ، فَيَقُولُ اللهُ: 'ارْفَعْ راسَكَ واشْفَعْ تُشَفَعْ واسْألْ تُعْطَ.' وَذَلِكَ هُوَ قَوْلُهُ: ﴿ عَسَى أنْ يَبْعَثَكَ رَبُّكَ مَقاماً مَحْمُوداً' »﴾.

(تفسير القمىّ، ٢، ٢٥)

١-١٢-٣- مُحَمَّدُ بْنُ يَحْيَي، ...، عَنْ أبِي الحَسَنِ مُوسَي عليه السلام، قالَ: «...إذا كانَ يَوْمُ القِيامَةِ، كانَ عَلَي عَرْشِ الرحْمَنِ أرْبَعَةٌ مِنَ الأوَّلِينَ وأرْبَعَةٌ مِنَ الآخِرِينَ. فأمّا الأربَعَةُ الذينَ هُمْ مِنَ الأوَّلِينَ، فَنُوحٌ وإبْراهِيمُ وَمُوسَي وَعِيسَي عليه السلام، وأمّا الأربَعَةُ مِنَ الآخِرِينَ، فَمُحَمَّدٌ وَعَلِيٌّ والحَسَنُ والحُسَيْنُ، صَلَواتُ اللهِ عَلَيْهِم...»

(الكافى، ٤، ٥٨٥، ٤)

1.12.4. It is reported that al-Ṣādiq said, "Whoever reads Sūrah Maryam frequently will receive something that helps him in his soul, property and children before his death. He will be from the people of Jesus and will be given the kingdom of Solomon the son of David on the Last Day."

(*Miṣbāḥ*, 1, 441)

1.12.5. Abū Ja'far said, "Whoever reads *Sūrah Maryam*, he will receive something that helps him in his soul, his property and children before his death. He will be from the people of Jesus the son of Mary and will be given the like of the kingdom of Solomon the son of David in this world on the Last Day."

(*A'lām al-Dīn*, 371)

١-١٢-٤- عَنِ الصادِقِ عليه السلام: «مَنْ أدْمَنَ قِرائتَها [سُورَةَ مَرْيَمَ]، لَمْ يَمُتْ مِنَ الدنْيا حَتَّي يُصيبَهُ مِنْها ما يُعِينُهُ فِي نَفْسِهِ وَمالِهِ وَوَلَدِهِ، وَكانَ فِي الآخِرَةِ مِنْ أصْحابِ عِيسَي عليه السلام، وأعْطِيَ مُلْكُ سُلَيْمانَ بْنِ داوُدَ فِي الآخِرَةِ.»

(المصباح، ١، ٤٤١)

١-١٢-٥- قالَ أبُو جَعْفَرٍ عليه السلام: «مَنْ قَرءَ سُورَةَ مَرْيَمَ، لَمْ يَمُتْ حَتَّي يُصيبَ ما يُعِينُهُ فِي نَفْسِهِ وَمالِهِ وَوَلَدِهِ، وَكانَ فِي الآخِرَةِ مِنْ أصْحابِ عِيسَي بْنِ مَرْيَمَ، وأعْطِيَ فِيها مِثْلَ مُلْكِ سُلَيْمانَ بْنِ داوُدَ فِي الدنْيا.»

(أعلام الدين، ٣٧١)

2

JESUS IN HIS OWN WORDS

2.1. Yazīd al-Kunāsī said, "I asked Abū Ja'far [Imam Bāqir], 'Was Jesus the son of Mary the authority from Allah for the people of his time when he spoke from the cradle?' He said, 'He was on that day a prophet, an authority from Allah, but not a messenger. Did you not hear his saying when he said, ❴*Verily, I am a servant of Allah. He has given me the Book, and has made me a prophet, and has made me blessed wherever I may be. And He has enjoined on me prayer and charity (zakāh) as long as I live.*❵" (19:30-31) I said, "Then was he an authority of Allah for Zachariah on that day in those circumstances while he was in the cradle?" He said, "Jesus was a sign for the people in those circumstances and mercy from Allah for Mary when he spoke, and he spoke up for her, and he was a prophet and an authority from Allah for those who heard his speech in those circumstances. Then he was quiet, and he did not speak until two years had passed. And Zachariah was the authority from Allah after the silence of Jesus for two years. Then Zachariah died. John, his son, inherited the Book and wisdom from him, while he was a small child. Have you not heard what He, the Mighty and Majestic, has said, ❴*O John! Hold the Book fast, and We granted him wisdom while yet a child.*❵ (19:12)? When Jesus reached seven years he spoke as a prophet and messenger, while he received revelation from Allah, the Exalted. So, Jesus was the authority for John and all the people. O Abū Khālid [Yazīd]! The earth cannot endure even for a single day without an authority from Allah for all people, from the day that Allah created Adam and settled him on earth."

(*Kāfī*, 1, 382, 1)

٢

عِيسَى عليه السلام بِلِسانِه

٢-١- عِدّةٌ مِن أصحابِنا, عَن أحمدَ بنَ محمّدٍ بنِ عِيسَي, عَن ابن مَحبوبٍ, عَن هشامِ بنِ سالِمٍ, عَن يَزيدٍ الكُناسِي، قالَ: «سألتُ أبا جَعْفَرٍ عليه السلام: 'أكانَ عيسَي بن مَريَمَ عليه السلام حِينَ تَكلَّمَ فِي المَهْدِ، حُجَّةَ اللهِ عَلَي أهْلِ زَمانِهِ؟' فقالَ: 'كانَ يَوْمَئِذٍ نَبِيّاً، حُجَّةَ اللهِ، غَيْرَ مُرْسَلٍ. أما تَسْمَعُ لِقَوْلِهِ، حِينَ قالَ: ﴿إنِّي عَبْدُ اللهِ آتانِيَ الكِتابَ، وَجعَلَنِي نَبِيّاً، وَجعَلَنِي مُبارَكاً أيْنَ ما كُنْتُ، وأوْصانِي بالصلاةِ والزَّكاةِ مادُمْتُ حَيّاً.﴾' قُلْتُ: 'فكانَ يَوْمَئِذٍ حُجَّةً لِلَّهِ عَلَي زَكَرِيّا فِي تِلْكَ الحالِ وَهُوَ فِي المَهْدِ؟' فَقالَ: 'كانَ عِيسَي فِي تِلْكَ الحالِ آيَةً لِلنّاسِ وَرَحْمَةً مِنَ اللهِ لِمَرْيَمَ حِينَ تَكلَّمَ، فعَبَّرَ عَنْها، وكانَ نَبِيّاً، حُجَّةً عَلَي مَنْ سَمِعَ كَلامَهُ فِي تِلْكَ الحالِ. ثُمَّ صَمَتَ، فلَمْ يَتَكَلَّمْ حَتَّي مَضَتْ لَهُ سَنَتانِ. وكانَ زَكَرِيّا الحُجَّةَ لِلَّهِ، عَزَّ وَجَلَّ، عَلَي الناسِ بَعْدَ صَمْتِ عِيسَي بِسَنَتَيْنِ. ثُمَّ ماتَ زَكَرِيّا، فَوَرِثَهُ ابنهُ يَحْيَي، الكِتابَ والحِكْمَةَ، وَهُوَ صَبِيٌّ صَغِيرٌ. أما تَسْمَعُ لِقَوْلِهِ، عَزَّ وَجلَّ: ﴿يا يَحْيَي خُذْ الكِتابَ بِقُوَّةٍ وَآتَيْناهُ الحُكْمَ صَبِيّاً.﴾ فلَمّا بَلَغَ عِيسَي عليه السلام سَبْعَ سِنِينَ، تَكلَّمَ بالنبُوَّةِ والرسالَةِ حِينَ أوْحَي اللهُ، تَعالَي، إلَيْهِ. فكانَ عِيسَي الحُجَّةَ عَلَي يَحْيَي وَعَلَي الناسِ أجْمَعِينَ. ولَيْسَ تَبْقَي الأرضُ يا أبا خالِدٍ يَوْماً واحِداً بِغَيْرِ حُجَّةٍ لِلَّهِ عَلَي الناسِ، مُنْذُ يَوْمَ خَلَقَ اللهُ آدَمَ عليه السلام وأسْكَنَهُ الأرضَ.'»

(الكافى، ١، ٣٨٢، ١)

2.2. Jesus ﷺ said, "O group of apostles! I have thrown the world down on its face for you. So, after me, do not pick it up again, for among the vile things of this world is that Allah is rebelled against in it, and among the vile things of this world is that the roots of all evil are in the love of this world."

(*Majmū'ah Warrām*, 1, 129)

2.3. Jesus ﷺ said, "Verily, I threw this world on its face for you and you sat on its back. Then none contend with you but kings and women. As for kings, do not contend with them for this world, then they will not bother you when you abandon their world. As for women, then beware of them by fasting and praying."

(*Biḥār*, 14, 327)

2.4. Jesus ﷺ said, "I am the one who threw the world on its face and sat on its back. There is no child for me to die, and no house to be destroyed."

(*Majmū'ah Warrām*, 2, 16)

2.5. Regarding [the ayah of the Qur'ān]: ﴿*And I inform you of what you eat and of what you store in your houses*﴾ (3:49), Imam Bāqir said, "Surely, Jesus ﷺ used to say to the children of Israel, 'Indeed I am the Apostle of Allah to you, and I create something like the form of a bird for you out of clay, and I blow into it, then it becomes a bird by the permission of Allah, and I cure the born blind and the leper.' They said, 'We see what you do as nothing but sorcery. So, show us a sign that we may know that you are true.' He said, 'Tell me, if I inform you of what you eat and of what you store in your houses, of what you have eaten in your houses before you left them and of what you stored for night, will you know that I am true?' They said, 'Yes.' Then he said to some of the men, 'You ate this and that, and you drank this and that, and you put up this and that.' Then

٢-٢- قالَ عِيسَي عليه السلام: «يا مَعْشَرَ الحَوارِيِّينَ، إنِّى قَدْ أكْبَبْتُ لَكُمُ الدنيا عَلَي وَجْهِها، فَلا تَنْعَشُوها بَعْدِى. فإنَّ مِنْ خُبْثِ الدنيا أنْ عُصِىَ اللهُ فِيها، وإنَّ مِنْ خُبْثِ الدنيا أنَّ الآخِرَةَ لا تُنالُ وَلا تُدْرَكُ إلّا بِتَرْكِها. فاعْبُرُوا الدنيا وَلا تَعْمُرُوها واعْلَمُوا أنَّ أصْلَ كُلِّ خَطِيئَةٍ حُبُّ الدنْيا. وَرُبَّ شَهْوَةٍ أوْرَثَتْ أهْلَها حُزْناً طَويلاً.»

(مجموعة ورّام، ١، ١٢٩)

٢-٣- قالَ عِيسَي عليه السلام: «إنِّى بَطَحْتُ لَكُمُ الدنْيا وَجَلَسْتُمْ عَلَي ظَهْرِها. فَلا يُنازِعَنَّكُمْ فيها إلّا المُلُوكُ والنساءُ: فأمّا المُلُوكُ، فَلا تُنازِعُوهُمُ الدنيا، فإنَّهُمْ لَمْ يَتَعَرَّضُوا لكُم ما تَرَكْتُمْ دُنْياهُمْ؛ وأمّا النساءُ، فاتَّقُوهُنَّ بِالصومِ والصلاةِ.»

(بحار الأنوار، ١٤، ٣٢٧)

٢-٤- قالَ عِيسَي عليه السلام: «أنا الذى أكْبَبْتُ الدنْيا لِوَجْهِها، وَجَلَسْتُ عَلَي ظَهْرِها؛ لَيْسَ لِى وَلَدٌ يَمُوتُ وَلا بَيْتٌ يَخْرَبُ.»

(مجموعة ورّام، ٢، ١٦)

٢-٥- حَدَّثَنا أحْمَدُ بْنُ مُحَمَّدٍ الهَمَدانِىُّ, عَنْ جَعْفَرِ بْنِ عَبْدِ اللهِ, عَنْ كَثِيرِ بْنِ عَيّاشٍ, عَنْ أبِى الجارُودِ, عَنْ أبِى جَعْفَرٍ عليه السلام، فِى قَوْلِهِ: ﴿وأنَبِّئُكُمْ بِما تأكُلُونَ وَما تَدَّخِرُونَ فِى بُيُوتِكُمْ.﴾ فانَّ عِيسَي كانَ يَقُولُ لِبَنِى إسْرائِيلَ: 'إنِّى رَسُولُ اللهِ إلَيْكُمْ، وإنِّى أخْلُقُ لَكُمْ مِنَ الطِّينِ كَهَيْأةِ الطَّيْرِ، فأنْفُخُ فِيهِ، فَيَكُونُ طَيْراً بِإذْنِ اللهِ؛ وابْرِءُ الأكْمَهَ والأبرصَ.' الأكْمَهُ، هُوَ الأعمَي. قالُوا: 'ما نَرَي الذى تَصْنَعُ إلّا سِحْراً، فأرِنا آيَةً نَعْلَمُ أنَّكَ صادِقٌ.' قالَ: 'أرايْتُمْ إنْ أخْبَرْتُكُمْ بِما تأكُلُونَ وَما تَدَّخِرُونَ فِى بُيُوتِكُمْ. يَقُولُ ما أكَلْتُمْ فِى بُيُوتِكُمْ قَبْلَ أنْ تَخْرُجُوا، وَما ادَّخَرْتُمْ إلَي الليْلِ، تَعْلَمُونَ إنِّى صادِقٌ.' قالُوا: 'نَعَمْ.' فكانَ يَقُولُ
لِلرَّجُلِ: 'أكَلْتَ كَذا وكَذا، وَشَرِبْتَ كَذا وكَذا، وَرَفَعْتَ كَذا وكَذا.' فَمِنْهُمْ مَنْ يَقْبَلُ

some accepted him and believed, and some disbelieved. That was a sign for them if they were believers."

(*Biḥār* 14, 246, 25)

2.6. Jesus said, "My servant is my hands and my mount is my feet; my bed is the earth and my pillow, a stone; my blanket in the winter is the east of the earth and my lamp in the night is the moon; my stew is hunger and my motto is fear; my clothing is wool and my fruit and my basil is what grows from the earth for the wild beasts and cattle. I sleep while I have nothing and I rise while I have nothing, and yet there is no one on earth more wealthy than I."

(*Biḥār,* 14, 239, 17)

2.7. It is reported that Abū 'Abd Allah said, "Jesus the son of Mary among his sayings to the children of Israel said, 'I entered into the morning among you while my stew has been hunger, my food has been something that grows from the earth for the wild animals and beasts, my lamp has been the moon, my carpet has been the earth and my pillow has been stone. There is no house for me that may be ruined, no property which may be destroyed, no child who may die and no wife who may become sad. I enter into the morning while there is nothing for me and enter into the night while there is nothing for me, and I am the most wealthy person among the children of Adam."

(*Biḥār*, 14, 321, 29)

2.8. One of the Imams is reported to have said, "It was said to Jesus the son of Mary, 'How did you begin the morning, O Spirit of Allah?' He said, 'I began the morning with my Lord, the Blessed and Supreme, above me and the fire (of hell) before me and death in pursuit of me. I have not obtained that for which I wished and I cannot keep away the things I hate. So who of the poor is more poor than I?'"

(*Biḥār*, 14, 322, 31)

مِنْهُ فَيُؤْمِنُ، وَمِنْهُمْ مَنْ يَكْفُرُ. وَكانَ لَهُمْ فِي ذَلِكَ آيَةٌ، إنْ كانُوا مُؤْمِنِينَ.'»

(بحار الأنوار، ١٤، ٢٤٦، ٢٥)

٢-٦- إرْشادُ القُلوبِ, قالَ عِيسَي عليه السلام: «خادِمِي يَداىَ، وَدابَّتِي رِجْلاىَ، وَفَراشِي الأرضُ، وَوِسادِي الحَجَرُ، وَدِفْئِي فِي الشِتاءِ مَشارِقُ الأرضِ، وَسِراجِي بِاللَيْلِ القَمَرُ، وإدامِي الجُوعُ، وَشِعارِي الخَوْفُ، وَلِباسِي الصوفُ، وَفاكِهَتِي وَرَيْحانَتِي ما أنْبَتَتِ الأرضُ لِلْوُحُوشِ والأنْعامِ. أبِيتُ وَلَيْسَ لِي شَيْءٌ، وأُصْبِحُ وَلَيْسَ لِي شَيْءٌ. وَلَيْسَ عَلَي وَجْهِ الأرضِ أحَدٌ أغْنَي مِنِّي.»

(بحار الأنوار، ١٤، ٢٣٩، ١٧)

٢-٧- عَنْ سَعْدٍ, عَنِ البَرْقِي, عَنْ عَلِيِّ بْنِ حَدِيدٍ عَمَّنْ ذَكَرَهُ, عَنْ أبِي عَبْدِ اللهِ عليه السلام، قالَ: «قالَ عِيسَي بْنُ مَرْيَمَ عليه السلام فِي خُطْبَتِهِ، قامَ لَها فِي بَنِي إسْرائِيلَ: 'أصْبَحْتُ فِيكُمْ وإدامِي الجُوعُ، وَطَعامِي ما تُنْبِتُ الأرضُ لِلْوُحُوشِ والأنْعامِ، وَسِراجِي القَمَرُ، وَفَراشِي التَرابُ، وَوِسادَتِي الحَجَرُ. لَيْسَ لِي بَيْتٌ يَخْرَبُ، وَلا مالٌ يَتْلَفُ، وَلا وَلَدٌ يَمُوتُ، وَلا امْرأةٌ تَحْزَنُ. أصْبَحْتُ وَلَيْسَ لِي شَيْءٌ، وأمْسَيْتُ وَلَيْسَ لِي شَيْءٌ. وأنا أغْنَي وُلْدِ آدَمَ.'»

(بحار الأنوار، ١٤، ٣٢١، ٢٩)

٢-٨- جَماعَةٌ, عَنْ أبِي المُفَضَّلِ بِإسْنادِهِ, عَنْ شَقِيقِ البَلْخِيِّ عَمَّنْ أخْبَرَهُ مِنْ أهْلِ العِلْمِ، قالَ: «قِيلَ لِعِيسَي بْنِ مَرْيَمَ عليه السلام: 'كَيْفَ أصْبَحْتَ يا رُوحَ اللهِ؟' قالَ: 'أصْبَحْتُ وَرَبِّي، تَبارَكَ وَتَعالَي، مِنْ فَوْقِي، والنارُ أمامِي، والمَوْتُ فِي طَلَبِي. لا أمْلِكُ ما أرْجُو، وَلا أُطِيقُ دَفْعَ ما أكْرَهُ. فأيُّ فَقِيرٍ أفْقَرُ مِنِّي؟'»

(بحار الأنوار، ١٤، ٣٢٢، ٣١)

3

THE SUPPLICATIONS OF JESUS

3.1. It is reported that one was imprisoned by the Banū 'Umayya. He saw Jesus in a dream. Jesus taught him some words. So Allah, the Exalted, released him from it the rest of his day. Here are those words: “There is no god but Allah, the King, the Plain Truth.”

(*Miṣbāḥ*, 179)

3.2. ‘Abd Allah ibn al-Mughīra said, “The righteous servant Ibrāhīm Mūsā ibn Ja‘far al-Kāẓim passed by a crying woman at Minā and her children were around her crying. A cow of theirs died before. Al-Kāẓim came near to her and said, ‘O servant woman of Allah! What makes you cry?’ She said, ‘O servant of Allah! I have a young girl, [and] orphans. We had a cow that was my livelihood and that of my household. It died and I remaind with my children and we have no remedy.’ He said, ‘O servant woman of Allah! Do you want me to make it alive?’ She was inspired, then she said, ‘Yes.’ Al-Kāẓim went aside and prayed two *rak‘a*, then he raised his hands, turned his right hand and moved his two lips. Then he stood, passed by the cow and kicked the cow or hit it with his foot. Then it stood up on the ground. When the woman looked at the cow and saw that it stood, she shouted and said, ‘Jesus the son of Mary! By the Lord of al-Ka‘ba! Then he mixed with the people and left.”

(*Da‘avāt*, 70)

3.3. It is reported that (for hardship with labor,) it should be written for her what is reported from Jesus, “O Creater of the soul from the soul, Director of the soul from the soul and Savior of the soul from the soul! Save her.”

(*Miṣbāḥ*, 159)

٣

دعاء عيسى عليه السلام

٣-١- رُوِىَ مِنْ كِتابِ المُسْتَغيثِينَ: «إنَّ شَخْصاً حَبَسَهُ بَنُو أُمَيَّة. فَرَأي عِيسَي عليه السلام فِي مَنامِهِ، فَعَلَّمَهُ هَذِهِ الكَلَماتِ. فَفَرَّجَ اللهُ، تَعالَي، عَنْهُ باقِيَ يَوْمِهِ. وَهِيَ: 'لا إلَهَ إلّا اللهُ المَلِكُ الحَقُّ المُبِينُ.'»

(المصباح، ١٧٩)

٣-٢- عَنْ عَبْدِ اللهِ بْنِ المُغِيْرَةِ، قالَ: «مَرَّ العَبْدُ الصالِحُ، أَبُو إبْراهِيمَ، مُوسَي بْنُ جَعْفَرٍ الكاظِمُ عليه السلام بِامْرأةٍ بِمِنَي، وَهِيَ تَبْكِي، وَصِبْيانُها حَوْلَها يَبْكُونَ، قَدْ ماتَتْ بَقَرَةٌ لَها، فَدَنا مِنْها، فَقالَ لَها: 'ما يُبْكِيكِ يا أَمَةَ اللهِ؟' قالَتْ: 'يا عَبْدَ اللهِ، إنَّ لِي صِبْيَةً أَيْتاماً، وَكانَتْ لَنا بَقَرَةٌ، وَكانَتْ مَعِيشَتِي وَمَعِيشَةَ عِيالِي، قَدْ ماتَتْ، وَبَقِيْتُ مُنْقَطِعاً بِي وَبِوُلْدِي، وَلا حِيلَةَ لَنا.' فَقالَ لَها: 'يا أَمَةَ اللهِ، فَهَلْ لَكَ أنْ أُحْيِيَها لَكَ؟' فَأُلْهِمَتْ أنْ قالَتْ: 'نَعَمْ.' فَتَنَحَّي عليه السلام وَصَلَّي رَكْعَتَيْنِ، ثُمَّ رَفَعَ يَدَيْهِ وَقَلَّبَ بِيَمِينِهِ وَحَرَّكَ شَفَتَيْهِ. ثُمَّ قامَ، فَمَرَّ بِالبَقَرَةِ، فَنَخَسَها أوْ ضَرَبَها بِرِجْلِهِ، فاسْتَوَتْ عَلَي الأرْضِ قائِمَةً، فَلَمّا نَظَرَتْ المَرْأةُ إلَي البَقَرَةِ قَدْ قامَتْ، صاحَتْ وَقالَتْ: 'عِيسَي بْنُ مَرْيَمَ وَرَبِّ الكَعْبَةِ!' فَخالَطَ الناسَ وَمَضَي عليه السلام.»

(الدعوات، ٧٠)

٣-٣- [لِتَعَسُّرِ الوِلادَةِ] يُكْتَبُ لَها ما رُوِىَ، عَنِ [النَبِيِّ]، عِيسَي عليه السلام: «يا خالِقَ النَفْسِ مِنَ النَفْسِ، وَمُخْرِجَ النَفْسِ مِنَ النَفْسِ، وَمُخَلِّصَ النَفْسِ مِنَ النَفْسِ، خَلِّصْها.»

(المصباح، ١٥٩)

3.4. It is reported that the Prophet said, "Whoever reads *Sūra Ṣaff*, Jesus ﷺ will pray for him and ask God's forgiveness for him in the world and he will be his companion on the Resurrection Day."

(*Miṣbāḥ*, 447)

3.5. It is reported that when Jesus ﷺ called Him by this psalm, Allah, the Exalted, raised him to Him and saved him from the Jews. It is: "O Allah! I call You by Your name, the Majestic (*al-'Aẓīm*), the One (*al-Wāḥid*) and Most Mighty (*al-A'azz*). I call you by Your name, the Everlasting Refuge (*al-Ṣamad*). I call You, O Allah! By Your name, the Majestic (*al-'Aẓīm*) and single (*al-Watr*). I call You, O Allah! By Your name, the Great (*al-Kabīr*) and Exalted (*al-Muta'āl*), by which all Your pillars were firmly set, may peace be with Muḥammad and his progeny and remove the troubles I have morning and night."

(*Miṣbāḥ*, 299)

3.6. Among the supplications narrated from Jesus the son of Mary ﷺ is: "O Allah! You are the deity of all who are in heaven and the deity of all on the earth. There is no deity in them other than You, and You are the All-wise for all in heaven and the All-wise for all on the earth. There is no All-wise in them other than You. And you are the King of all in heaven and all on the earth. There is no King in them other than You. Your power in heaven is like Your power on the earth. And Your sovereignty in heaven is like Your sovereignty on the earth. I ask you by Your All-generous Name and Your radiant face and Your eternal kingdom, do such and such for me."

(*Sharḥ Nahj al-Balāghah*, 6, 187)

3.7. Imam Ṣādiq ﷺ said, "In the Gospel Jesus ﷺ says, 'O Allah! Bestow upon me a flat loaf of barley bread in the morning and a flat loaf of barley bread in the evening, and do not bestow more than this upon me that I become rebellious.'"

(*Biḥār*, 14, 326, 39)

٣-٤- عنه صلى الله عليه وآله وسلم: «مَنْ قرأها [سُورَةَ صَفٍّ] كانَ عِيسَي عليه السلام مُصلّياً، مُسْتَغْفِراً لَهُ، مادامَ فِي الدنْيا؛ وَهُوَ يَوْمَ القِيامَةِ رَفِيقُهُ.»
(المصباح، ٤٤٧)

٣-٥- رُوِىَ أنَّهُ [عِيسَي عليه السلام] لَمّا دَعا بِهَذا الدعاءِ رَفَعَهُ اللهُ، تَعالَي، إلَيْهِ وَنَجاهُ اللهُ سُبْحانَهُ مِنَ اليَهُودِ؛ وَهُوَ: «اللهُمَّ، إنِّى أدْعُوكَ بِاسْمِكَ العَظِيمِ الواحِدِ الأعَزِّ، وأدْعُوكَ اللهُمَّ، بِاسْمِكَ الصمَدِ، وأدْعُوكَ اللهُمَّ، بِاسْمِكَ العَظِيمِ الوَتْرِ، وادْعُوكَ اللهُمَّ، بِاسْمِكَ الكَبِيرِ المُتَعالِ الذى هُوَ أثبَتَ أرْكانَكَ كُلَّها، أنْ تُصَلّىَ عَلَي مُحَمَّدٍ وَآلِهِ، وأنْ تَكْشِفَ عَنِّى ما أصْبَحْتُ فِيهِ وأمْسَيْتُ.»
(المصباح، ٢٩٩)

٣-٦- مِنَ الأدْعِيَةِ المَرْوِيَّةِ عَنْ عِيسَي بْنِ مَرْيَمَ عليه السلام: «اللهُمَّ، أنتَ إلهُ مَنْ فِى السَماءِ وإلَهُ مَنْ فِى الأرضِ، لا إلَهَ فِيهِما غَيْرُكَ، وأنْتَ حَكِيمُ مَنْ فِى السَماءِ وَحَكِيمُ مَنْ فِى الأرضِ، لا حَكِيمَ فِيهِما غَيْرُكَ، وأنْتَ مَلِكُ مَنْ فِى السَماءِ وَمَلِكُ مَنْ فِى الأرضِ، لا مَلِكَ فِيهِما غَيْرُكَ؛ قُدْرَتُكَ فِى السَماءِ كَقُدْرَتِكَ فِى الأرضِ، وَسُلْطانُكَ فِى السَماءِ كَسُلْطانِكَ فِى الأرضِ، أسْألُكَ بِاسْمِكَ الكَرِيمِ وَوَجْهِكَ المُنِيرِ وَمُلْكِكَ القَدِيمِ، أنْ تَفْعَلَ بِى كَذا وكَذا.»
(شرح نهج البلاغة، ٦، ١٨٧)

٣-٧- عَنِ الصادِقِ عليه السلام، قالَ: «فِى الإنجيلِ: 'إنَّ عِيسَي عليه السلام قالَ: 'اللهُمَّ، ارْزُقْنِى غُدْوَةً رَغِيفاً مِنْ شَعِيرٍ، وَعَشِيَّةً رَغِيفاً مِنْ شَعِيرٍ، وَلا تَرْزُقْنِى فَوقَ ذَلِكَ فأطْغَي.''»
(بحار الأنوار، ١٤، ٣٢٦، ٣٩)

3.8. Among the supplications mentioned are those of Jesus that we reported with our chain of narrators to Sa'īd ibn Hibah Allah al-Rāwandī, may Allah have mercy on him, from the book, *Qiṣaṣ al-Anbiya'* (Stories of the Prophets), with a chain of narrators to al-Ṣādiq from his fathers, peace be with them, that the Prophet said, "When the Jews gathered before Jesus to kill him, as they imagined, Gabriel came to him and covered him with his wing. Then Jesus looked at him carefully. There was writing within Gabriel and it was: 'O Allah! I call You by Your most mighty name, *al-Wāḥid* (the One), and I call You, O Allah, by Your name, *al-Ṣamad* (the Everlasting Refuge), and I call You, O Allah, by Your single name, *al-'Aẓīm* (the Majestic), and I call You, O Allah, by Your exalted name, *al-Kabīr* (the Great), by which all Your pillars stand firm, remove the troubles I have morning and night.'

When Jesus called him by this, Allah revealed to Gabriel, 'Raise him to me.'" Then the Messenger of Allah, may the blessing of Allah be with him, said, "O Children of 'Abd al-Muṭṭalib! Beseech your Lord by these words. By Allah, in Whose hand is my soul! No servant has called upon Him by them without the throne being moved, and without Allah saying to the angels, 'Bear witness that I, verily, answered him by these words and gave him what he asked in the transient world and in the term of the hereafter.'" Then he said to his companions, "Beseech by it and do not postpone the answering."

(*Biḥār* 92, 175)

3.9. This is the psalm of Jesus by another narration, "The prophet saw this psalm within Gabriel, then he taught it to 'Alī and al-'Abbās and said, 'O 'Alī! O the best one among Banū Hāshim! O the children of 'Abd al-Muṭṭalib! Ask your Lord by these words. By One, that my soul is in His hand, every believer calls [Him] by these words sincerely, the Throne, the seven heavens and the earths will tremble for it and Allah, the Exalted, says to His angels, 'Testify. I answered the caller by these words and gave him his request in this world and the other world.'" Some [of the narrators] thought that this psalm is the psalm by which Jesus the son of Mary calld Him.

٣-٨- مِنْ ذَلِكَ دُعاءُ عِيسَي عليه السلام، رَوَيْناهُ بِإسْنادِنا إلَي سَعِيدِ بْنِ هِبَةِ اللهِ الراوَنْدِيّ، رَحِمَهُ اللهُ، مِنْ كِتابِ قِصَصِ الأنبياءِ، بِإسْنادِهِ إلَي الصادِقِ عليه السلام، عَنْ آبائِهِ عليهم السلام، عَنِ النَبِي صلى الله عليه وآله وسلم، قالَ: «لَمّا اجْتَمَعَتْ اليَهُودُ إلَي عِيسَي عليه السلام لِيَقْتُلُوهُ بِزَعْمِهِمْ، أتاهُ جَبْرَئِيلُ عليه السلام، فَغَشّاهُ بِجِناحِهِ، فَطَمَحَ عِيسَي بِبَصَرِهِ، فإذا هُوَ بِكِتابٍ فِي باطِنِ جَناحِ جَبْرَئِيلَ عليه السلام، وَهُوَ: ’اللهُمَّ، إنِّي أدْعُوكَ بِاسْمِكَ الواحِدِ الأعَزِّ، وأدْعُوكَ اللهُمَّ، بِاسْمِكَ الصَمَدِ، وأدْعُوكَ اللهُمَّ، بِاسْمِكَ العَظِيمِ الوَتْرِ، وأدْعُوكَ اللهُمَّ، بِاسْمِكَ الكَبِيرِ المَتَعالِ الذي ثَبَتَتْ بِهِ أرْكانُكَ كُلُّها، أنْ تَكْشِفَ عَنِّي ما أصْبَحْتُ وامْسَيْتُ فِيهِ.‘ فَلَمّا دَعا بِهِ عليه السلام أوْحَي اللهُ، تَعالَي، إلَي جَبْرَئِيلَ، أنْ ارْفَعْهُ إلَي عِنْدِي.» ثُمَّ قالَ رَسُولُ اللهِ صلى الله عليه وآله وسلم: «يا بَنِي عَبْدِ المُطَّلِبِ، سَلُوا رَبَّكُمْ بِهَذِهِ الكَلِماتِ، فَوَاللهِ الذي نَفْسِي بِيَدِهِ، ما دَعا بِهِنَّ عَبْدٌ بِإخْلاصِ نِيَّةٍ إلّا اهْتَزَّ لَهُنَّ العَرْشُ، وَقالَ اللهُ لِلْمَلائِكَةِ: ’اشْهَدُوا، أنِّي قَدْ اسْتَجَبْتُ لَهُ بِهِنَّ وأعْطَيْتُهُ سُؤْلَهُ فِي عاجِلِ دُنْياهُ وآجِلِ آخِرَتِهِ.‘» ثُمَّ قالَ لأصحابِهِ: «سَلُوها، وَلا تَسْتَبْطِئُوا الإجابَةَ.»

(بحار الأنوار، ٩٢، ١٧٥)

٣-٩- دُعاءُ عِيسَي عليه السلام بِرِوايَةٍ غَيْرِ هَذِهِ، وَهِيَ: «إنَّ النَبِيَّ صلى الله عليه وآله وسلم رَأي فِي باطِنِ جَبْرَئِيلَ الدعاءَ، فَعَلَّمَهُ عَلِيّاً والعَبّاسَ، وَقالَ: ’يا عَلِيُّ، يا خَيْرَ بَنِي هاشِمَ، يا بَنِي عَبْدِ المُطَّلِبْ، سَلُوا رَبَّكُمْ بِهَؤُلاءِ الكَلِماتِ، فَوَالَّذِي نَفْسِي بِيَدِهِ، ما دَعا بِهِنَّ مُؤْمِنٌ بِإخْلاصٍ إلّا إهْتَزَّ لَهُنَّ العَرْشُ والسَماواتُ السَبْعُ والأرضُونَ؛ وَقالَ اللهُ تَعالَي لِمَلائِكَتِهِ: ’اشْهَدُوا أنِّي قَدْ اسْتَجَبْتُ لِلدّاعِي بِهِنَّ، وأعْطَيْتُهُ سُؤْلَهُ فِي عاجِلِ دُنْياهُ وآجِلِ آخِرَتِهِ.‘‘» وَزَعَمُوا أنَّهُ الدعاءُ الذي دَعا بِهِ عِيسَي بْنُ مَرْيَمَ، فَرَفَعَهُ اللهُ.

It is this psalm: 'O Allah! I take refuge in your name, the Unique (*al-Wāḥid*), the One (*al-Aḥad*) and Most Mighty (*al-A'azz*). I take refuge in your name, the One (*al-Aḥad*), the Everlasting Refuge (*al-Ṣamad*). I take refuge in Your name, O Allah, the Majestic (*al-'Aẓīm*) and Single (*al-Watr*). I take refuge, O Allah, in Your name, the Great (*al-Kabīr*) and Exalted (*al-Muta'āl*), by which all Your pillars have been set firm, remove the troubles I have morning and night.'"

(*Biḥār*, 92, 176)

3.10. This is one of the psalms of Jesus the son of Mary by another narration: "O Creater of the soul from the soul, Director of the soul from the soul and Deliverer of the soul from the soul! Release us and deliver us from our trouble."

(*Biḥār*, 92, 176)

3.11. Among these supplications is the supplication of Aṣif, the minister of Solomon son of David, about which it is narrated that by it he brought the throne of Bilqīs,[1] and that by it Jesus revived the dead. It is, "O Allah! I beseech You by this that You are Allah; there is no god but You, the Alive, the Self-subsisting, the Pure, the Purifying, the Light of the heavens and the earths (and according to some narrations, this last phrase is 'the Lord of the heavens and the earths'), Knower of the invisible and visible, the Great and Exalted, the Compassionate, the Beneficent, Lord of Majesty and Honor, I beseech You [by these words] to do (this or that) for me."

(*Biḥār*, 92, 175)

3.12. The Commander of the Faithful sought refuge in Allah every day through this prayer, known as *khiṣlah,* "I seek refuge in Allah, the Hearing and Knowing from Satan the cursed... O Allah! Verily I beseech You by the *ayah* by which You commanded your servant Jesus the son of Mary to call You, then you answered him, and he revived the dead, cured the blind and the leper with Your permission,

[1] The Queen of Sheba.

وَهُوَ هَذا الدعاءُ: «اللهُمَّ، إنِّى أعُوذُ بِاسْمِكَ الواحِدِ الأحَدِ، وأعُوذُ بِاسْمِكَ الأحَدِ الصمَدِ، وأعُوذُ بِكَ بِاسْمِكَ، اللهُمَّ، العَظِيمِ الوِتْرِ، وأعُوذُ اللهُمَّ، بِاسْمِكَ الكَبِيرِ المُتَعالِ الذى مَلأَ الأركانَ كُلَّها، أنْ تَكْشِفَ عَنِّى غَمَّ ما أصْبَحْتُ فِيهِ وأمْسَيْتُ.»

(بحار الأنوار، ٩٢، ١٧٦)

٣-١٠- دُعاءٌ لِعِيسَي بْنِ مَرْيَمَ عليه السلام بِرِوايَةٍ أُخْرَي، وَهُوَ: «اللهُمَّ، خالِقَ النَفْسِ مِنَ النَفْسِ وَمُخْرِجَ النَفْسِ مِنَ النَفْسِ وَمُخَلِّصَ النَفْسِ مِنَ النَفْسِ، فَرِّجْ عَنّا وَخَلِّصْنا مِنْ شِدَّتِنا.»

(بحارالانوار، ٩٢، ١٧٦)

٣-١١- مِنْ ذَلِكَ دُعاءُ آصَفَ وَزِيرِ سُلَيْمانَ بْنِ داوُدَ عليه السلام، رُوِىَ أنَّهُ أتَي بِهِ عَرْشَ بِلْقِيسَ، وأنَّهُ الدعاءُ الذى كانَ عِيسَي عليه السلام يُحيِى بِهِ المَوْتَي، وَهُوَ: «اللهُمَّ، إنِّى أسْألُكَ بِأنَّكَ أنتَ اللهُ لا إلَهَ إلّا أنتَ الحَىُّ القَيُّومُ الطّاهِرُ المُطَهَّرُ نُورُ السَماواتِ والأرَضِينَ. (وَفِى رِوايَةٍ أُخْرَي: 'رَبُّ السَماواتِ والأرَضِينَ') عالِمُ الغَيْبِ والشهادَةِ، الكَبِيرُ المُتَعالُ الحَنّانُ المَنّانُ ذُو الجَلالِ والإكْرامِ (أنْ تَفْعَلَ بِى كَذا وكَذا.)»

(بحارالأنوار، ٩٢، ١٧٥)

٣-١٢- كانَ أمِيرُ المُؤْمِنِينَ عليه السلام إذا فَرَغَ مِنَ الاسْتِغْفارِ تَعَوَّذَ بِها فِى كُلِّ يَوْمٍ وتُعْرَفُ بِالخَصْلَةِ: «أعُوذُ بِاللهِ السَمِيعِ العَلِيمِ مِنَ الشيْطانِ الرجِيمِ ... اللهُمَّ، إنِّى أسْألُكَ بِالآيَةِ الّتِى أمَرْتَ عَبْدَكَ عِيسَي بْنَ مَرْيَمَ أنْ يَدْعُوَ بِها فاسْتَجَبْتَ لَهُ، وأحْيَي المَوْتَي وأبْرَءَ الأكْمَهَ والأبرصَ بِإذْنِكَ، وَنَبَّأ بِالغَيْبِ مِنْ إلهامِكَ، وَبِفَضْلِكَ

and by Your revelation he told of mysteries with Your grace, kindness and mercy. Praise be to You, Lord of the heavens and the earth, Lord of the worlds. His is the dominion in the heavens and the earth. He is the Magnificent, the Wise. Come between us and our enemies and help us against them, O our Master and Lord."

(*Biḥār*, 84, 17)

3.13. It is reported that a man complained to Jesus عليه السلام about his debts. Jesus عليه السلام said to him, "Say: 'O God, Who takes away grief, removes sadness, disposes of sorrow, answers the prayers of the needy! O Merciful of this world and the other world and the Compassionate of them! You are Merciful to me and Merciful to all things! So, be Merciful to me, with a mercy that will make me needless of the mercy of others than You, and by that mercy let my debts be paid."

(*Mustadrak al-Wasā'il,* 13, 289, 15379)

3.14. It is reported that Gabriel brought these five psalms to Jesus the son of Mary عليه السلام as a gift of Allah, the Exalted, to supplicate by them during the first ten days of Dhu al-Ḥajja: "[1] I witness that there is no god but Allah alone, there is no partner for Him, the kingdom is for Him, praise be to Him, the good is in His hand and He is Almighty over everything. [2] I witness that there is no god but Allah Alone and Everlasting; there is no partner for Him. He did not take any wife or child. [3] I witness that there is no god but Allah Alone and Everlasting, there is no partner for Him, who did not beget and was not begotten and no one is equal to Him.[4] I witness that there is no god but Allah alone, there is no partner for Him, the kingdom is for Him, praise be to Him, He makes alive and makes dead, He is alive and does not die, the good is in His hand and He is Almighty over everything. [5] Allah is sufficient and enough for me. Allah hears whoever calls him. After Allah there is no end. I bear witness to Allah by what He claimed for Himself. He is exempt from those who disassociate from Him. The Last and the First is for Him."

(*Mafātīḥ al-Jinān,* 251)

وَرأفتِكَ وَرَحْمَتِكَ؛ فلَكَ الحَمْدُ، رَبُّ السَماواتِ والأرضِ، رَبُّ العالَمِينَ، وَلَهُ الكِبْرِياءُ فِي السَماواتِ والأرضِ وَهُوَ العَزيزُ الحَكِيمُ، حُلَّ بَيْنَنا وَبَيْنَ أعْدائِنا وانْصُرْنا عَلَيْهِمْ، يا سَيِّدَنا وَمَوْلانا.»

(بحارالأنوار، ٨٤، ١٧)

٣-١٣- إنَّ رَجُلاً شَكا إلَي عِيسَي عليه السلام دَيْناً عَلَيْهِ، فقالَ لَهُ: «قُل: 'اللهُمَّ، يا فارِجَ الهَمِّ وَمُنَفِّسَ الغَمِّ وَمُذْهِبَ الأحْزانِ وَمُجِيبَ دَعْوَةِ المُضْطَرِّينَ وَرَحْمانَ الدنْيا والآخِرَةِ وَرَحِيمَهُما، أنتَ رَحْمانِي وَرَحْمانُ كُلِّ شَيْءٍ، فارْحَمْنِي رَحْمَةً تُغْنِينِي بِها عَنْ رَحْمَةِ مَنْ سِواكَ وَتَقْضِي بِها عَنِّي الدَيْنَ.' فلَوْ كانَ عَلَيْكَ مِلْءُ الأرضِ ذَهَباً لأدّاهُ اللهُ عَنْكَ بِمَنِّهِ.'»

(مستدرك الوسائل، ١٣، ٢٨٩، ١٥٣٧٩)

٣-١٤- جاءَ جَبْرَئِيلُ بِهَذِهِ الدعَواتِ الخَمْسِ إلَي عِيسَي بْنِ مَرْيَمَ، هَدِيَّةً مِنَ اللهِ، تَعالَي، لِيَدْعُوَ بِها فِي أيّامِ العَشْرِ الأوَّلِ مِنْ ذِي الحِجَّةِ: «[١] أشْهَدُ أنْ لا إلَهَ إلّا اللهُ وَحْدَهُ لا شَرِيكَ لَهُ، لَهُ المُلْكُ وَلَهُ الحَمْدُ، بِيَدِهِ الخَيْرُ وَهُوَ عَلَي كُلِّ شَيْءٍ قَدِيرٌ. [٢] أشْهَدُ أنْ لا إلَهَ إلّا اللهُ وَحْدَهُ لا شَرِيكَ لَهُ، أحَداً صَمَداً لَمْ يَتَّخِذْ صاحِبَةً وَلا وَلَداً. [٣] أشْهَدُ أنْ لا إلَهَ إلّا اللهُ وَحْدَهُ لا شَرِيكَ لَه، أحَداً صَمَداً، لَمْ يَلِدْ وَلَمْ يُولَدْ وَلَمْ يَكُنْ لَهُ كُفُواً أحَدٌ. [٤] أشْهَدُ أنْ لا إلَهَ إلّا اللهُ وَحْدَهُ لا شَرِيكَ لَهُ، لَهُ المُلْكُ وَلَهُ الحَمْدُ، يُحيِي وَيُمِيتُ وَهُوَ حَيٌّ لا يَمُوتُ، بِيَدِهِ الخَيْرُ وَهُوَ عَلَي كُلِّ شَيْءٍ قَدِيرٌ. [٥] حَسْبِيَ اللهُ وَكَفَي، سَمِعَ اللهُ لِمَنْ دَعا، لَيْسَ وَراءَ اللهِ مُنْتَهَي، أشْهَدُ لِلهِ بِما دَعا وأنَّهُ بَرِيءٌ مِمَّنْ تَبَرَّءَ، وأنَّ لِلهِ الآخِرَةَ والأولَي.»

(مفاتيح الجنان المعرّب، ٢٥١)

4

THE CONDUCT OF JESUS

4.1. Imam 'Alī said, "John the son of Zachariah cried and did not laugh, and Jesus the son of Mary laughed and cried; and what Jesus did was more excellent than what John did."

(*Kāfī*, 2 665 20)

4.2. Abū Ja'far said, "Jesus the son of Mary and John the son of Zakarīyyā, peace be with our prophet, his progeny and them, went out to the desert. They heared the sound of a wild animal. Jesus the son of Mary said, 'O how wonderful! What is this sound?' John said, 'This is the sound of a wild animal who is giving birth.' Jesus the son of Mary said, 'Come down easily, easily, by the permission of Allah, the Exalted.'"

(*Ṭibb al-A'imma*, 98)

4.3. It is said that a man accompanied Jesus the son of Mary and said that he would go with him. They continued along until they came to a river. They sat and started to eat. They had three loaves of bread. They ate two of them and one remained. Jesus went to the river, drank some water and returned. He did not find the third loaf. He asked the man who had taken that loaf. He said that he did not know. They continued until they came to a doe followed by two fawns. Jesus beckoned one of the fawns, killed it, roasted it and they ate it. Then Jesus addressed the fawn [that had been eaten,] saying, "Live!" It came to life and went. Then Jesus said to the other man, "By the God Who has shown you this miracle, who took that loaf of bread?" He said that he did not know. They continued until they reached a lake. Jesus took the hand of the man and led him over the water. When they reached the other side, Jesus said, "By the One Who has shown you this miracle, who took that loaf of bread?" He said that he did not know. They continued until they reached a desert. They sat down.

٤

فعل عيسى عليه السلام

٤-١- عَن ابن فضّالٍ، عَنِ الحَسَنِ بْنِ الجَهْمِ، عَنْ إبْراهِيمَ بْنِ مِهْزَمٍ عَمَّنْ ذَكَرَهُ، عَنْ أبِي الحَسَنِ الأوّلِ عليه السلام، «قالَ: كانَ يَحْيَي بْنُ زَكَرِيّا عليه السلام يَبْكِي وَلا يَضْحَكُ، وكانَ عيسَي بن مَريَمَ عليه السلام يَضْحَكُ وَيَبْكِي، وكانَ الذى يَصْنَعُ عِيسَي عليه السلام أفْضَلَ مِنَ الذى كانَ يَصْنَعُ يَحْيَي عليه السلام.»

(الكافى، ٢، ٦٦٥، ٢٠)

٤-٢- عَنْ أبِي جَعْفَرٍ عليه السلام: «خَرَجَ عِيسَي بْنُ مَرْيَمَ وَيَحْيَي بْنُ زَكَرِيّا، عَلَي نَبِيِّنا وآلِهِ وَعَلَيْهِمُ السَلامُ، إلي البَرِيَّةِ. فَسَمِعا صَوْتَ وَحْشِيَّةٍ، فَقالَ المَسِيحُ، عِيسَي بْنُ مَرْيَمَ عليه السلام: 'يا عَجَباً! ما هَذا الصَوْتُ؟' قالَ يَحْيَي: 'هَذا صَوْتُ وَحْشِيَّةٍ تَلِدُ.' فَقالَ عِيسَي بْنُ مَرْيَمَ عليه السلام: 'انْزِلْ سَرْحاً، سَرْحاً، بِإذْنِ اللهِ، تَعالَي.'»

(طبّ الأئمة عليهم السلام، ٩٨)

٤-٣- قِيلَ: «صَحِبَ رَجُلٌ عِيسَي بْنَ مَرْيَمَ عليه السلام، فَقالَ: 'أكُونُ مَعَكَ وأصْحَبُكَ.' فانْطَلَقا، فانْتَهَيا إلي شَطِّ نَهْرٍ، فَجَلَسا يَتَغَدَّيانِ، وَمَعَهُما ثَلاثَةُ أرْغِفَةٍ، فأكَلا رَغِيفَيْنِ وبَقِيَ رَغِيفٌ. فَقامَ عِيسَي عليه السلام إلَي النَهْرِ فَشَرِبَ ماءً، ثُمَّ رَجَعَ فَلَمْ يَجِدْ الرغِيفَ. فَقالَ لِلرَّجُلِ: 'مَنْ أخَذَ الرغِيفَ؟' قالَ: 'لا أدْرِى.' قالَ: 'فانْطَلَقَ وَمَعَهُ صاحِبُهُ، فَرأي ظَبْيَةَ مَعَها خَشْفانِ لَها، فَدَعا أحَدَهُما، فأتاهُ، فَذَبَحَهُ، فأشْوَي مِنْهُ، فأكَلَ هُوَ وَذَلِكَ الرجُلُ.' ثُمَّ قالَ لِلْخَشْفِ: 'قُمْ بِإذْنِ اللهِ.' فَقامَ، فَذَهَبَ. فَقالَ لِلرَّجُلِ: 'أسْألُكَ بِالَّذِى أراكَ هَذِهِ الآيَة، مَنْ أخَذَ الرغِيفَ؟' قالَ: 'لا أدْرِى.' ثُمَّ انْتَهَيا إلَي

Jesus gathered some sand or dust and said, "By the permission of Allah, be gold!" It became gold. He divided it into three portions. He said, "One third is for me, one third for you, and one third for whoever took that loaf of bread." The man said, "Alright, I took that loaf of bread." Jesus said, "Then all of this gold is yours." Then he left him. The man encountered two other men in the desert. They wanted to take his gold and kill him. He said, "Let us divide the gold into three portions." They sent one of them to the village to buy food. The one who went said to himself, "Why should I let them have portions of this wealth? I shall put some poison into the food, and kill them." So, he poisoned the food. The other two said, "Why should we give a third of this wealth to him. When he comes back, let us kill him, and divide the rest of the wealth between us." When he returned, they attacked him and killed him. Then they ate the food and died. The wealth remained in the desert with the three dead men beside it. Jesus passed them and saw the situation. He said to his disciples, "This is the world, so beware of it!"

(*Majmū'ah Warrām*, 1, 179)

4.4. It is reported that Ṣādiq Ja'far ibn Muḥammad عليه السلام reported that Jesus the son of Mary عليه السلام turned to some needs, and three of his companions were with him. He passed by three golden bricks on the road. Jesus عليه السلام said to his companions, "Verily, these kill people." Then he went. One of them said, "I have a need." So, he returned. Then another of them said, "I have a need." So, he returned. Then the other one said, "I have a need." So, he returned. All three persons gathered around the gold. Two of them said to the other, "Buy some food for us." He went to buy food for them; then he put some poison in it to kill them, so that he would not have to share the gold with them. And the other two said,

وادِى ماءٍ، فأخَذَ عِيسَيعليه السلام بِيَدِ الرجُلِ فمَشَيا عَلَي الماءِ. فلَمّا جاوَزاهُ، قالَ: 'أسألُكَ بِالّذِى أراكَ هَذِهِ الآيَة، مَنْ أخَذَ الرغِيفَ؟' قالَ: 'لا أدْرِى.'» قالَ: «فانْتَهَيا إلَي مَفازَةٍ، فَجَلَسا. فَجَمَعَ عِيسَيصلى الله عليه وآله وسلم تُراباً أوْ كَثِيباً، فقالَ: 'كُنْ ذهباً بِإذْنِ اللهِ.' فَصارَ ذَهَباً. فَقَسَّمَهُ ثَلاثَة أثْلاثٍ. فَقالَ: 'ثُلْثٌ لِي وَثُلْثٌ لَكَ وَثُلْثٌ لِمَنْ أخَذَ الرغِيفَ.' قالَ: 'فأنا أخَذْتُ الرغِيفَ.' فقالَ: 'فَكُلُّهُ لَكَ.'» قالَ: «وَفارَقَهُ عِيسَيعليه السلام، فانْتَهَي إلَيْهِ رَجُلانِ فِي المَفازَةِ، وَمَعَهُ المالُ. فأرادا أنْ يأخُذاهُ مِنْهُ وَيَقْتُلاهُ. فَقالَ: 'هُوَ بَيْنَنا أثلاثٌ.' قالَ: 'فابْعَثُوا أحدَكُم إلَي القَرْيَةِ حَتّي يَشْتَرِىَ طَعاماً.' فَبَعَثُوا أحَدَهُمْ، فَقالَ الذى بُعِثَ: 'لِأىِّ شَىْءٍ أُقاسِمُ هَؤُلاءِ هَذا المالَ؟ لَكِنِّى أضَعُ فِي هَذا الطعامِ سَمّاً فأقْتُلُهُما، فَفَعَلَ. وَقالَ أولَئِكَ: 'لِأىِّ شَىْءٍ نَجْعَلُ لِهَذا ثُلْثَ المالِ، وَلَكِنْ إذا رَجَعَ قَتَلْناهُ واقتَسَمْنا المالَ بَيْنَنا.'» قالَ: «فَلَمّا رَجَعَ إلَيْهِما، قَتَلاهُ وأكَلا الطَّعامَ، فَماتا. فَبَقِيَ ذَلِكَ المالُ فِي المَفازَةِ، وأولَئِكَ الثَّلاثَةُ قَتْلَي عِنْدَهُ. فَمَرَّ بِهِمْ عِيسَيعليه السلام، وَهُمْ عَلَي تِلْكَ الحالِ. فَقالَ لِأصحابِهِ: 'هَذِهِ الدنْيا فاحْذَرُوها.'»

(مجموعة ورّام، ١، ١٧٩)

٤-٤- ابن البَرْقِي، عَنْ أبيهِ، عَنْ جَدِّهِ، عَنْ مُحَمَّدِ بْنِ عَلِيٍّ القُرَشِيِّ، عَنْ مُحَمَّدِ بْنِ سَنانٍ، عَنْ عَبْدِ اللهِ بْنِ طَلْحَةٍ وإسْماعِيلَ بْنِ جابِرٍ وَعَمّارِ بْنِ مَرْوانٍ، عَنِ الصادِقِ، جَعْفَرِ بْنِ مُحَمَّدٍعليه السلام: «أنَّ عِيسَي بْنَ مَرْيَمَعليه السلام تَوَجَّهَ فِي بَعْضِ حَوائِجِهِ، وَمَعَهُ ثَلاثَةُ نَفَرٍ مِنْ أصْحابِهِ. فَمَرَّ بِلَبِناتٍ ثَلاثٍ مِنْ ذَهَبٍ عَلَي ظَهْرِ الطَّرِيقِ. فَقالَ عِيسَيعليه السلام لِأصحابِهِ: 'إنَّ هَذا يَقْتُلُ الناسَ.' ثُمَّ مَضَي. فَقالَ أحَدُهُمْ: 'إنَّ لِي حاجَةً.'» قالَ: «فانْصَرَفَ. ثُمَّ قالَ الآخَرُ: 'إنَّ لِي حاجَةً.' فانْصَرَفَ. ثُمَّ قالَ الآخَرُ: 'لِي حاجَةٌ.' فانْصَرَفَ. فَوافَوْا عِنْدَ الذَّهَبِ ثَلاثَتُهُمْ. فَقالَ اثْنانِ لِواحِدٍ: 'اشْتَرِ لَنا طَعاماً.' فَذَهَبَ يَشْتَرِى لَهُما طَعاماً. فَجَعَلَ فِيهِ سَمّاً، لِيَقْتُلَهُما، كَيْلا

"When he comes we will kill him so that we do not have to share the gold with him." So, when he came, they stood up to him and killed him. Then they ate the food. So, they died. Then Jesus returned to them while they were lifeless around [the gold]. He lent life to them by the permission of Allah, may His remembrance be exalted, and said, "Did I not tell you that this kills people?!"

(*Biḥār* 14, 284, 5)

4.5. Jābir ibn 'Abdullah al-Anṣārī said, "'Alī prayed with us as a leader at Burāthā after his coming from faighting with Shurāt [al-Khawarij] and we were about one hundred thousand men. Then a Christian came down from his monestary and said, 'Who is the chief of this army? We said, 'He is.' He came to him, greeted to him and said, 'O my master, you are a prophet?' He said, 'No, my master, the Prophet died.' He said, 'Are you the executor of the prophet?' He said, 'Yes. Why did you ask about this?' He said, 'I established this monastery here for the sake of this place, Barāthā. I read the revealed books and found that no one prays at this place with this community but a prophet or the executer of a prophet. I came to become a Muslim.' Then he accepted Islam, and with us he left for Kūfa. 'Alī asked him, 'So, who prayed there?' He said, 'Jesus the son of Mary and his mother prayed there.' 'Alī said to him, 'Should I tell you who prayed there?' He said, 'Yes.' He said, 'Al-Khalīl [Abraham].'"

(*Faqīh*, 1, 232, 698)

4.6. Jesus said, "I saw a stone upon which was written, 'Turn me over,' then I turned it over, then I saw written on it, 'He who does not act according to what he knows will not be blessed in his search for what he does not know and what he knows will come back against him.'"

(*Biḥār*, 2, 32, 24)

يُشارِكاهُ فِي الذَّهَبِ. وَقالَ الاثنان: 'إذا جاءَ قَتَلْناهُ، كَيْ لا يُشارِكَنا.' فَلَمّا جاءَ، قاما إلَيْهِ، فَقَتَلاهُ، ثُمَّ تَغَدَّيا، فَماتا. فَرَجَعَ إلَيْهِمْ عِيسَي عليه السلام، وَهُمْ مَوْتَي، حَوْلَهُ. فَأحْياهُمْ بِإذْنِ اللهِ، تَعالَي ذِكْرُهُ. ثُمَّ قالَ: 'ألَمْ أقُلْ لَكُمْ: 'إنَّ هَذا يَقْتُلُ النّاسَ.'»

(بحارالأنوار، ١٤، ٢٨٤، ٥)

٤-٥- رُوِيَ عَنْ جابِرِ بْنِ عَبْدِ اللهِ الأنْصارِيِّ، أنَّهُ قالَ: «صَلَّي بِنا عَلِيٌّ عليه السلام بِبُراثا بَعْدَ رُجُوعِهِ مِنْ قِتالِ الشُّراةِ، وَنَحْنُ زُهاءُ مِائَةِ الفِ رَجُلٍ. فَنَزَلَ نَصْرانِيٌّ مِنْ صَوْمَعَتِهِ، فَقالَ: 'مَنْ عَمِيدُ هَذا الجَيْشِ؟' فَقُلْنا: 'هَذا.' فَأقْبَلَ إلَيْهِ، فَسَلَّمَ عَلَيْهِ، فَقالَ: 'يا سَيِّدِي، أنتَ نَبِيٌّ؟' فَقالَ: 'لا، النَّبِيُّ سَيِّدِي قَدْ ماتَ.' قالَ: 'فَأنْتَ وَصِيُّ نَبِيٍّ؟' قالَ: 'نَعَمْ.' ثُمَّ قالَ لَهُ: 'اجْلِسْ. كَيْفَ سَألتَ عَنْ هَذا؟' قالَ: 'أنا بَنَيْتُ هَذِهِ الصَّوْمَعَةَ مِنْ أجْلِ هَذا المَوْضِعِ، وَهُوَ بُراثا؛ وَقَرَأتُ فِي الكُتُبِ المُنْزَلَةِ، أنَّهُ لا يُصَلِّي فِي هَذا المَوْضِعِ بِهَذا الجَمْعِ إلّا نَبِيٌّ أوْ وَصِيُّ نَبِيٍّ. وَقَدْ جِئْتُ اُسْلِمُ.' فَأسْلَمَ وَخَرَجَ مَعَنا إلَي الكُوفَةِ. فَقالَ لَهُ عَلِيٌّ عليه السلام: 'فَمَنْ صَلَّي هاهُنا؟' قالَ: 'صَلَّي عِيسَي بن مَرْيَمَ عليه السلام وَاُمُّهُ.' فَقالَ لَهُ عَلِيٌّ عليه السلام: 'أفَاُخْبِرُكَ مَنْ صَلَّي هاهُنا؟' قالَ: 'نَعَمْ.' قالَ: 'الخَلِيلُ عليه السلام.'»

(كتاب من لايحضره الفقيه، ١، ٢٣٢، ٦٩٨)

٤-٦- قالَ عِيسَي عليه السلام: «رَأيْتُ حَجَراً مَكْتُوباً عَلَيْهِ: 'قَلِّبْنِي.' فَقَلَّبْتُهُ، فَإذا عَلَي باطِنِهِ: 'مَنْ لا يَعْمَلُ بِما يَعْلَمُ، مَشْؤُومٌ عَلَيْهِ طَلَبُ ما لا يَعْلَمُ، وَمَرْدُودٌ عَلَيْهِ ما عَلِمَ.'»

(بحارالانوار، ٢، ٣٢، ٢٤)

4.7. I heard Imam Ṣādiq say, "Fear Allah and do not envy each other. Roving through the countries was a sacred law prescribed for Jesus the son of Mary عليه السلام. So, he went out to do some roving and with him among his companions was a short man and he was very much attached to Jesus عليه السلام. So, when Jesus wound up at the sea, he said, "In the Name of Allah", with a level of certainty in him to walk on the surface of the water. Then, when he looked at Jesus عليه السلام, the short man said, "In the Name of Allah", with a level of certainty in him to walk on the water. And he caught up with Jesus عليه السلام. Then he became conceited and said, 'This is Jesus, the Spirit of Allah who goes on the water and I go on the water, too, so what is his excellence over me?"

Imam Ṣādiq عليه السلام said, "Then he was immersed in the water and he called for help. Then he [Jesus] brought him out and said to him, 'What did you say, O short man?' He said, 'I said, "This is the Spirit of Allah who goes on the water and I go on the water, and a pride with this entered into me."' Jesus عليه السلام said to him, "Verily you placed yourself in the position in which Allah should be placed, so Allah became angry with you for what you said. So turn to Allah, the Almighty and Glorious, in repentance for what you said." Imam Ṣādiq عليه السلام said, "The man returned and came back to the position in which Allah had placed him. So fear Allah and do not envy others."

(*Kāfī*, 2, 306, 3)

4.8. Ibn al-Sikkīt said to Abū al-Ḥasan عليه السلام, "Why did Allah raise Moses ibn 'Imrān عليه السلام as a prophet by his staff and his white hand and the magicians, and He raised Jesus عليه السلام by healing, and He raised Muḥammad (peace and blessings be with him and his progeny and all the prophets) by speech and the sermon?" Abū al-Ḥasan said, "Verily, when Allah raised Moses عليه السلام sorcery dominated the people of that time, so he brought to them from Allah the like of which they could not bring, and that by which he invalidated their sorcery, and by this he proved his authority over them. And verily, Allah raised Jesus عليه السلام in a time when chronic illness appeared and the people

٤-٧- عِدَّةٌ مِنْ أصْحابِنا، عَنْ أحْمَدَ بْنِ مُحَمَّدِ بْنِ خالِدٍ، عَنِ ابن مَحْبُوبٍ، عَنْ داوُدَ الرقّيِّ، قالَ: «سَمِعْتُ أبا عَبْدِ اللهِ عليه السلام يَقُولُ: 'اتَّقُوا اللهَ وَلا يَحْسُدْ بَعْضُكُمْ بَعْضاً. إنَّ عيسَي بن مَرْيَمَ كانَ مِنْ شَرائِعِهِ السَيْحُ فِي البِلادِ؛ فَخَرَجَ فِي بَعْضِ سَيْحِهِ، وَمَعَهُ رَجُلٌ مِنْ أصْحابِهِ قَصِيرٌ، وَكانَ كَثِيرَ اللزُومِ لِعِيسَي عليه السلام. فَلَمّا انْتَهَي عِيسَي إلَي البَحْرِ، قالَ: 'بِسْمِ اللهِ بِصِحَّةِ يَقِينٍ مِنْهُ.' فَمَشَي عَلَي ظَهْرِ الماءِ. فَقالَ الرجُلُ القَصِيرُ حِينَ نَظَرَ إلَي عِيسَي عليه السلام جازَهُ: 'بِسْمِ اللهِ بِصِحَّةِ يَقِينٍ مِنْهُ.' فَمَشَي عَلَي الماءِ وَلَحِقَ بِعِيسَي عليه السلام؛ فَدَخَلَهُ العُجْبُ بِنَفْسِهِ، فَقالَ: 'هَذا عِيسَى رُوحُ اللهِ يَمْشِي عَلَي الماءِ، وأنا أمْشِي عَلَي الماءِ! فَما فَضْلُهُ عَلَيَّ؟'' قالَ: 'فَرُمِسَ فِي الماءِ، فاسْتَغاثَ بِعِيسَي، فَتَناوَلَهُ مِنَ الماءِ، فأخْرَجَهُ. ثُمَّ قالَ لَهُ: 'ما قُلْتَ يا قَصِيرُ؟' قالَ: 'قُلْتُ: 'هَذا رُوحُ اللهِ يَمْشِي عَلَى الماءِ، وأنا أمْشِي عَلَي الماءِ!' فَدَخَلَنِي مِنْ ذَلِكَ عُجْبٌ.' فَقالَ لَهُ عِيسَي: 'لَقَدْ وَضَعْتَ نَفْسَكَ فِي غَيْرِ المَوْضِعِ الذي وَضَعَكَ اللهُ فِيهِ؛ فَمَقَتَكَ اللهُ عَلَى ما قُلْتَ. فَتُبْ إلَي اللهِ، عَزَّ وَجَلَّ، مِمّا قُلْتَ.'' قالَ: 'فَتابَ الرجُلُ وَعادَ إلَي مَرْتَبَتِهِ الَّتِي وَضَعَهُ اللهُ فِيها. فاتَّقُوا اللهَ وَلا يَحْسُدَنَّ بَعْضُكُمْ بَعْضاً.'»

(الكافي، ٢، ٣٠٦، ٣)

٤-٨- الحُسَيْنُ بْنُ مُحَمَّدٍ، عَنْ أحْمَدَ بْنِ مُحَمَّدٍ السَيّارِيِّ، عَنْ أبِي يَعْقُوبَ البَغْدادِيِّ، قالَ: «قالَ ابن السكِّيتِ لِأبِي الحَسَنِ عليه السلام: 'لِما ذا بَعَثَ اللهُ مُوسَي بْنَ عِمْرانَ عليه السلام بِالعَصا وَيَدِهِ البَيْضاءِ وآلَةِ السِّحْرِ، وَبَعَثَ عِيسَي بِآلَةِ الطِّبِّ، وبَعَثَ مُحَمَّداً، صَلَّي اللهُ عَلَيْهِ وآلِهِ وَعلَى جَمِيعِ الأنبياءِ، بالكَلامِ والخُطَبِ؟' فَقالَ أبُو الحَسَنِ عليه السلام: 'إنَّ اللهَ لَمّا بَعَثَ مُوسَي عليه السلام، كانَ الغالِبُ عَلَى أهْلِ عَصْرِهِ السِّحْرَ؛ فأتاهُمْ مِنْ عِنْدِ اللهِ بِما لَمْ يَكُنْ فِي وُسْعِهِمْ مِثْلُهُ، وَما أبْطَلَ بِهِ سِحْرَهُمْ، وأثْبَتَ بِهِ

were in need of medicine, so he brought from Allah the like of which they did not have, and that by which he lent life to the dead, and he cured the born blind and the leper by the permission of Allah, and by this he proved his authority over them. And verily Allah raised Muḥammad during a time when the sermon and the word[1] dominated among the people of that time so he brought them from Allah advice and precepts which refuted their sayings, and by this he proved his authority over them." Then Ibn Sikkīt said, "By Allah, I have never seen anyone like you!"

(*Kāfī*, 1, 24, 20)

4.9. It is said that Jesus was sitting with his companions when a man passed him. He said either, "He is dead," or "He will die." They lingered until he returned carrying a bundle of firewood. One of the companions said, "O Spirit of Allah! You told us that he was dead! We see him alive." Jesus said, "Put down your bundle." He put it down and opened it. All of a sudden [they saw that] there was a large black snake with a rock in its mouth. Jesus said to him, "What did you do today?" He said, "O Spirit of Allah and His Word! I had two loaves of bread, when a beggar passed me, so, I gave him one."

(*Biḥār*, 93, 135)

4.10. Abū Baṣīr said, "I heard from Imam Ṣādiq, 'Jesus, the Spirit of Allah, passed by a noisy group. He said, "What is the matter with them?" It was said, "O Spirit of Allah! This is the night for so-and-so daughter of so-and-so to go to so-and-so son of so-and-so [for the wedding night]." He said, "Today they make noise, but tomorrow they will cry." A speaker from among them said, "Why, O Apostle of Allah?" He said, "This is the night for [her] their friend to die." Then said those who accepted what he said, "Allah is true and

---

[1] Ibn Sikkīt inserts the parenthetical remark here, "and I think he said, 'poetry'".

الحُجَّةَ عَلَيْهِمْ. وإنَّ اللهَ بَعَثَ عِيسَي عليه السلام فِي وَقْتٍ قَدْ ظَهَرَتْ فِيهِ الزَّمانَاتُ واحْتاجَ النّاسُ إلَي الطبِّ، فأتاهُمْ مِنْ عِنْدِ اللهِ بِما لَمْ يَكُنْ عِنْدَهُمْ مِثْلُهُ، وَبِما أحْيا لَهُمُ المَوْتَي وأبْرءَ الأكْمَهَ والأبرصَ بِإذْنِ اللهِ، وأثْبَتَ بِهِ الحُجَّةَ عَلَيْهِمْ. وأنَّ اللهَ بَعَثَ مُحَمَّداً صلى الله عليه وآله وسلم فِي وَقْتٍ كانَ الغالِبُ عَلَي أهْلِ عَصْرِهِ الخُطَبَ والكَلامَ،' وأظُنُّهُ قالَ: 'الشِعْرَ'، فأتاهُمْ مِنْ عِنْدِ اللهِ مِنْ مَواعِظِهِ وَحِكَمِهِ ما أبْطَلَ بِهِ قَوْلَهُمْ، وأثْبَتَ بِهِ الحُجَّةَ عَلَيْهِمْ.'» قالَ: «فَقالَ ابن السِكّيتِ: 'تاللهِ ما رأيْتُ مِثْلَكَ قَطُّ... .'»

(الكافى، ١، ٢٤، ٢٠)

٤-٩- قِيلَ: «بَيْنا عِيسَي عليه السلام، مَعَ أصْحابِهِ جالِساً، إذْ مَرَّ بِهِ رَجُلٌ، فَقالَ: 'هَذا مَيِّتٌ.' أوْ 'يَمُوتُ.' لَمْ يَلْبَثُوا أنْ رَجَعَ إلَيْهِمْ، وَهُوَ يَحْمِلُ حَزْمَةَ حَطَبٍ، فَقالُوا يا رُوحَ اللهِ! أخْبَرْتَنا أنَّهُ مَيِّتٌ، وَهُوَ ذا، نَراهُ حَيّاً!' فَقالَ عليه السلام: 'ضَعْ حَزْمَتَكَ.' فَوَضَعَها، فَفَتَحَها، فإذا فِيهِ أسْوَدُ، قَدْ ألْقَمَ حَجَراً. فَقالَ لَهُ عِيسَي عليه السلام: 'أيُّ شَيْءٍ صَنَعْتَ اليَوْمَ؟' فَقالَ: 'يا رُوحَ اللهِ وَكَلِمَتَهُ، كانَ مَعِي رَغِيفانِ، فَمَرَّ بِي سائِلٌ، فأعْطَيْتُهُ واحِداً.'»

(بحار الأنوار، ٩٣، ١٣٥)

٤-١٠- عَلِيُّ بْنُ عِيسَي، عَنْ عَلِيِّ بْنِ مُحَمَّدٍ ماجِيلَوَيْهِ، عَنِ البَرْقِيِّ، عَنْ أبِيهِ، عَنْ مُحَمَّدِ بْنِ سِنانٍ، عَنْ أحْمَدَ بْنِ النَصْرِ الطحّانِ، عَنْ أبِي بَصِيرٍ، قالَ: «سَمِعْتُ أبا عَبْدِ اللهِ الصادِقَ، جَعْفَرَ بْنَ مُحَمَّدٍ عليه السلام: 'إنَّ عِيسَي رُوحَ اللهِ، مَرَّ بِقَوْمٍ مُجْلِبِينَ. فَقالَ: 'ما لِهَؤُلاءِ؟' قِيلَ: 'يا رُوحَ اللهِ، إنَّ فُلانَةَ بِنْتَ فُلانٍ، تُهْدَي إلَي فُلانِ بْنِ فُلانٍ فِي لَيْلَتِها هَذِهِ.' قالَ: 'يَجْلِبُونَ اليَوْمَ، وَيَبْكُونَ غَداً.' فَقالَ قائِلٌ مِنْهُمْ: 'وَلِمَ يا رَسُولَ اللهِ؟' قالَ: 'لِأنَّ صاحِبَتَهُمْ مَيِّتَةٌ فِي لَيْلَتِها هَذِهِ.'

His Apostle is true." The hypocrites said, "How much closer tomorrow is!" Then when they entered into the morning, they came and they found her in her condition that nothing had happened to her. Then they said, "O Spirit of Allah! She about whom you informed us yesterday that she would die has not died." Then Jesus, peace be with our Prophet and with his folk and with him [i.e. Jesus], said, "Allah does what He wants, so bring us to her." They went racing each other until they knocked on the door. Then her husband came out. Then Jesus عليه السلام said to him, "Ask permission for me to enter before your wife." Then he [her husband] entered before her and informed her that the Spirit of Allah and His Word was at the door and a group with him. He [her husband] said [to Jesus عليه السلام], "She is stupefied." Then he [Jesus] entered before her and said to her, "What did you do on this night of yours?" She said, "I did not do anything, except what I was doing in the past. There was a beggar who came to us every Thursday night and we were giving him what supported him until the next Thursday night, and he came to me last night and I was busy with something and my family was busy. Then he called out and no one answered him. Then he called out but no one answered until he called out repeatedly. Then when I heard what he said I stood concealed to give to him what we had been giving to him." He [Jesus عليه السلام] said to her, "Step aside from your seat." All at once there was a viper like the trunk of a tree beneath her dress which had clenched its tail in its teeth. He [Jesus عليه السلام] said, "Because of what you did, this turned away from you.""

(*Biḥār*, 14, 245, 22)

4.11. Abū al-Layth said in his interpretation of the Qur'ān, "The people asked Jesusعليه السلام in ridicule, 'Create a bat for us, and put a spirit in it, if you are one of the truthful.' Then he took some clay and made a bat and breathed into it. Then it suddenly flew between the sky and the earth. The clay was put in order and breathed into by Jesus, but the creation was by Allah, the Supreme. And it is said that they asked for the creation of a bat because it is more wonderful than the rest of creation."

(*Biḥār*, 61, 322)

فقالَ القائلُونَ بِمقالَتِهِ: 'صدَقَ اللهُ وَصدَقَ رَسُولُهُ.' وَقالَ أهلُ النفاقِ: 'ما أقْرَبَ غداً!' فلمّا أصبَحُوا، جاؤوا، فوَجَدُوها علَي حالِها، لَمْ يَحْدُثْ بِها شَيْءٌ. فقالُوا: 'يا رُوحَ اللهِ! إنَّ الّتِي أخبَرْتَنا أمْسِ، أنَّها مَيِّتَةٌ، لَمْ تَمُتْ.' فقالَ عِيسَي عليه السلام: 'يَفْعَلُ اللهُ ما يَشاءُ، فاذْهَبُوا بِنا إلَيْها.' فذَهَبُوا يَتَسابَقُونَ، حتَّي قرَعُوا البابَ. فخَرَجَ زَوْجُها. فقالَ لَهُ عِيسَي عليه السلام: 'اسْتاذِنْ لِي عَلَي صاحِبَتِكَ.'' قالَ: 'فدَخَلَ علَيْها، فأخْبَرَها أنَّ رُوحَ اللهِ وَكَلِمَتَهُ بِالبابِ، مَعَ عِدَّةٍ.' قالَ: 'فتَخَدَّرَتْ؛ فدَخَلَ علَيْها، فقالَ لَها: 'ما صَنَعْتِ لَيْلَتَكِ هَذِهِ؟' قالَتْ: 'لَمْ أصْنَعْ شَيْئًا، إلّا وَقَدْ كُنْتُ أصْنَعُهُ فِي ما مَضَي. إنَّهُ كانَ يَعْتَرِينا سائِلٌ فِي كُلِّ لَيْلَةِ جُمُعَةٍ، فنُنِيلُهُ ما يَقُوتُهُ إلَي مِثْلِها. وأنَّهُ جاءَنِي فِي لَيْلَتِي هَذِهِ، وأنا مَشْغُولَةٌ بِأمْرِي وأهْلِي فِي مَشاغِيلَ. فهَتَفَ فلَمْ يُجِبْهُ أحَدٌ، ثُمَّ هَتَفَ فلَمْ يُجَبْ، حتَّي هَتَفَ مِراراً. فلَمّا سَمِعْتُ مَقالَتَهُ، قُمْتُ مُتَنَكِّرَةً، حتَّي أنَلْتُهُ كَما كُنّا نُنِيلُهُ.' فقالَ لَها: 'تَنَحِّي عَنْ مَجْلِسِكِ.' فإذا تَحْتَ ثِيابِها أفْعَي، مِثْلَ جِذْعَةٍ، عاضٌّ عَلَي ذَنَبِهِ. فقالَ عليه السلام: 'بِما صَنَعْتِ صُرِفَ عَنْكِ هَذا.''»

(بحارالأنوار، ١٤، ٢٤٥، ٢٢)

٤-١١- قالَ أبُو اللَّيْثِ فِي تَفْسِيرِهِ: «إنَّ النّاسَ سألُوا عِيسَي، علَي وَجْهِ التَعَنُّتِ؛ فقالُوا لَهُ: 'اُخْلُقْ لَنا خُفّاشاً، واجْعَلْ فِيهِ رُوحاً، إنْ كُنْتَ مِنَ الصادِقِينَ.' فأخَذَ طِيناً وَجَعَلَ خُفّاشاً وَنَفَخَ فِيهِ، فإذا هُوَ يَطِيرُ بَيْنَ السَماءِ والأرضِ. وَكانَ تَسْوِيَةُ الطِّينِ والنَفْخُ مِنْ عِيسَي عليه السلام، والخَلْقُ مِنَ اللهِ، تَعالَي. وَيُقالُ: 'إنَّما طَلَبُوا مِنْهُ خَلْقَ خُفّاشٍ، لِأنَّهُ أعْجَبُ مِنْ سائِرِ الخَلْقِ.'»

(بحارالأنوار، ٦١، ٣٢٢)

4.12. Imam Ṣādiq was asked, "Did Jesus the son of Mary enliven someone after his death, so that he was eating and had a daily living, continued his life for a term and had a child?" He said, "Yes, he had a friend who was a brother in Allah to him. And when Jesus passed by he would go down to him. And Jesus would spend a while with him. Then he would leave with salutations of Peace unto him. Then his mother came out to him [Jesus]. Then she said to him, 'He died, O Apostle of Allah!' He said to her, 'Would you like to see him?' She said, 'Yes.' He said to her, 'I will come to you tomorrow to enliven him, with the permission of Allah.' When the morrow arrived he came and said to her, 'Accompany me to his grave.' So they went to his grave. Jesus stopped, then called on Allah. Then the grave opened and her son came out alive. Then when his mother saw him and he saw her, they cried. Jesus had mercy on them and said to him, 'Would you like to remain with your mother in the world?'

He said, 'O Apostle of Allah! With eating and a daily living and a term, or without a term and no daily living and no eating?' Then Jesus said to him, 'But with a daily living and eating and a term you will ive for twenty years, marry and father a child.' He said, 'Yes, in that case.'" [Imam Sādiq]said, "Then Jesus returned him to his mother and he lived for twenty years, married and fathered a child."

(*Biḥār*, 14, 234, 3)

4.13. It is reported that Jesus passed by a man who was blind, leprous and paralytic, and Jesus heard him giving thanks and saying, "Praise be to Allah Who has protected me from the trials with which He afflicts the majority of men." Jesus said, "What trial remains which has not been visited upon you?" He said, "He protected me from a trial which is the greatest of trials, and that is disbelief." Then Jesus touched him, and Allah cured him from his illnesses and beautified his face. Then he became a companion of Jesus andworshipped with him.

(*Biḥār*, 68, 33)

٤-١٢- عَنْ أبان بْن تَغْلِبٍ، قالَ: «سُئِلَ أبو عَبْدِ اللهِ عليه السلام: 'هَلْ كانَ عِيسَي بْنُ مَرْيَمَ أحْيا أحَداً بَعْدَ مَوْتِهِ، حَتَّي كانَ لَهُ أكْلٌ وَرِزْقٌ وَمُدَّةٌ وَوَلَدٌ؟'» قالَ: «فقالَ: 'نَعَمْ، إنَّهُ كانَ لَهُ صَدِيقٌ، مُؤاخٍ لَهُ فِي اللهِ، وكانَ عِيسَي يَمُرُّ بِهِ، فَيَنْزِلُ عَلَيْهِ. وإنَّ عِيسَي عليه السلام غابَ عَنْهُ حِيناً، ثُمَّ مَرَّ بِهِ لِيُسلِّمَ عَلَيْهِ؛ فَخَرَجَتْ إلَيْهِ اُمُّهُ، فَسألها عَنْهُ، فقالَتْ اُمُّهُ: 'ماتَ، يا رَسُولَ اللهِ!' فقالَ لَها: 'أتُحِبِّينَ أنْ تَراهُ؟' قالَتْ: 'نَعَمْ.' قالَ لَها: 'إذا كانَ غَداً، أتَيْتُكِ حَتَّي اُحْيِيَهِ لَكِ، بِإذْنِ اللهِ.' فَلَمّا كانَ مِنَ الغَدِ، أتاها. فقالَ لَها: 'انْطَلِقِي مَعِي إلَي قَبْرِهِ.' فانْطَلَقا، حَتَّي أتَيا قَبْرَهُ. فَوَقَفَ عِيسَي عليه السلام، ثُمَّ دَعا اللهَ، فانْفَرَجَ القَبْرُ وَخَرَجَ ابنها حَيّاً. فَلَمّا رأتْهُ اُمُّهُ وَرَءاها، بَكَيا. فَرَحِمَهُما عِيسَي عليه السلام، فقالَ لَهُ: 'أتُحِبُّ أنْ تَبْقَي مَعَ اُمِّكَ فِي الدنْيا؟' قالَ: 'يا رَسُولَ اللهِ! بِأكْلٍ وَبِرِزْقٍ وَمُدَّةٍ، أوْ بِغَيْرِ مُدَّةٍ وَلا رِزْقٍ وَلا أكْلٍ؟' فقالَ لَهُ عِيسَي عليه السلام: 'بَلْ بِرِزْقٍ وأكْلٍ وَمُدَّةٍ؛ تَعْمُرُ عِشْرِينَ سَنَةً وَتَزَوَّجُ وَيُولَدُ لَكَ.' قالَ: 'فَنَعَمْ.' إذا قالَ، فَدَفَعَهُ عِيسَي إلَي اُمِّهِ، فَعاشَ عِشْرِينَ سَنَةً وَتَزَوَّجَ وَوُلِدَ لَهُ.'»

(بحارالأنوار، ١٤، ٢٣٤، ٣)

٤-١٣- قَدْ نُقِلَ: «أنَّ عِيسَي عليه السلام مَرَّ عَلَي رَجُلٍ أعْمَي مَجْذُومٍ مَبْرُوصٍ مَفْلُوجٍ، فَسَمِعَ مِنْهُ يَشْكُرُ وَيَقُولُ: 'الحَمْدُ لِلهِ الذى عافانِى مِن بَلاءٍ ابْتَلَي بِهِ أكْثَرَ الخَلْقِ.' فقالَ عليه السلام: 'ما بَقِيَ مِنْ بَلاءٍ لَمْ يُصِبْكَ؟' قالَ: 'عافانِى مِنْ بَلاءٍ هُوَ أعْظَمُ البَلايا، وَهُوَ الكُفْرُ.' فَمَسَّهُ عليه السلام، فَشَفاهُ اللهُ مِنْ تِلْكَ الأمْراضِ وَحَسُنَ وَجْهُهُ. فَصاحَبَهُ، وَهُوَ يَعْبُدُ مَعَهُ.»

(بحارالأنوار، ٦٨، ٣٣)

4.14. It is reported that Jesus passed by a man who was blind, a leper, paralytic, both of whose sides were paralyzed, and whose flesh had fallen off from leprosy, and he was saying, "Praise be to Allah Who has preserved me from that with which He has tried many of His creatures." Jesus said to him, "O you! From what calamity have you been preserved?" He said, "O Spirit of Allah! I am better than one who has not been given what Allah has placed in my heart of His knowledge." Jesus said to him, "You speak truly. Reach out your hand." Then, when he took his hand, he came to have the most beautiful face of any of the people, and his form became better than the others. Allah took away all that had been [wrong] with him. Then he became the companion of Jesus and he worshipped with him.

(*Biḥār*, 79, 153)

4.15. It is reported that Abū 'Abdu-Allah [Imam Ṣādiq] said, "Jesus the son of Mary passed by a village whose inhabitants, birds and animals had died. Then he said, 'They died not but by His wrath, and had they died individually, they would have buried each other.' The disciples said, 'O Spirit of Allah and His Word! Call upon Allah to give them life for us, so they may inform us about their deeds, so we may avoid them.' Jesus called upon his Lord. Then it was proclaimed from the sky, 'Call them!' Then Jesus stood in the night near the earth and said, 'O dwellers of this village!' Then an answerer from among them answered him, 'Here I am, O Spirit of Allah and His Word!' He said, 'Woe unto you! What were your deeds?' He said, 'Worshipping the idol (al-Ṭāghūt) and loving the world with little fear and much desire, and negligence, trifling and playing.' He said, 'How was your love for the world?' He said, 'Like the loving of the baby for its mother. When it approached us we would be glad and would be made happy, and when it turned away from us, we would cry and it would make us sad.' He said, 'How was your worshipping of the idol?' He said, 'The obedience of the insubordinate.'

٤-١٤- رُوِيَ: «أنَّ عِيسَي عليه السلام مَرَّ بِرَجُلٍ أعْمَي، أبْرَصٍ، مُقْعَدٍ، مَضْرُوبِ الجَنْبَيْنِ بِالفالِجِ، وقَدْ تَناثَرَ لَحْمُهُ مِنَ الجُذامِ، وَهُوَ يَقُولُ: 'الحَمْدُ لِلّهِ الذى عافانِى مِمّا ابْتَلَي بِهِ كَثِيراً مِنْ خَلْقِهِ.' فَقالَ لَهُ عِيسَي عليه السلام: 'يا هَذا! وأىُّ شَىْءٍ مِنَ البَلاءِ أراهُ مَصْرُوفاً عَنْكَ؟' فَقالَ: 'يا رُوحَ اللهِ! أنا خَيْرٌ مِمَّنْ لَمْ يَجْعَلْ اللهُ فِى قَلْبِهِ ما جَعَلَ فِى قَلْبِى مِنْ مَعْرِفَتِهِ.' فَقالَ لَهُ: 'صَدَقْتَ. هاتِ يَدَكَ.' فَناوَلَهُ يَدَهُ، فإذا هُوَ أحْسَنُ النّاسِ وَجْهاً، وأفْضَلُهُمْ هَيْأةً. قَدْ أذْهَبَ اللهُ عَنْهُ ما كانَ بِهِ. فَصَحِبَ عِيسَي عليه السلام، وَتَعَبَّدَ مَعَهُ.»
(بحارالأنوار، ٧٩، ١٥٣)

٤-١٥- عِدَّةٌ مِنْ أصْحابِنا، عَنْ أحْمَدَ بْنِ مُحَمَّدِ بْنِ خالِدٍ، عَنْ مَنْصُورِ بْنِ العَباسِ، عَنْ سَعِيدِ بْنِ جَناحٍ، عَنْ عُثْمانَ بْنِ سَعِيدٍ، عَنْ عَبْدِ الحَمِيدِ بْنِ عَلِيٍّ الكُوفِيِّ، عَنْ مُهاجِرِ الأسدِيِّ، عَنْ أبِى عَبْدِ اللهِ عليه السلام، قالَ: «مَرَّ عِيسَي بن مَرْيَمَ عليه السلام عَلَي قَرْيَةٍ، قَدْ ماتَ أهْلُها وَطَيْرُها وَدَوابُّها. فَقالَ: 'أما إنَّهُمْ لَمْ يَمُوتُوا إلّا بِسَخْطَةٍ، وَلَوْ ماتُوا مُتَفَرِّقِينَ لَتَدافَنُوا.' فَقالَ الحَوارِيُّونَ: 'يا رُوحَ اللهِ وَكَلِمَتَهُ! ادْعُ اللهَ أنْ يُحْيِيَهُمْ لَنا، فَيُخْبِرُونا ما كانَتْ أعْمالُهُمْ، فَنَجْتَنِبَها.' فَدَعا عِيسَي عليه السلام رَبَّهُ. فَنُودِىَ مِنَ الجَوِّ أنْ: 'نادِهِمْ.' فَقامَ عِيسَي عليه السلام بِاللَّيْلِ عَلَي شَرَفٍ مِنَ الأرضِ، فَقالَ: 'يا أهْلَ هَذِهِ القَرْيَةِ!' فَأجابَهُ مِنْهُمْ مُجِيبٌ: 'لَبَّيْكَ، يا رُوحَ اللهِ وَكَلِمَتَهُ.' فَقالَ: 'وَيْحَكُمْ ما كانَتْ أعْمالُكُمْ؟' قالَ: 'عِبادَةُ الطّاغُوتِ وَحُبُّ الدنْيا، مَعَ خَوْفٍ قَلِيلٍ وأمَلٍ بَعِيدٍ وَغَفْلَةٍ فِى لَهْوٍ وَلَعِبٍ.' فَقالَ: 'كَيْفَ كانَ حُبُّكُمْ لِلدُّنْيا؟' قالَ: 'كَحُبِّ الصَبِى لِأُمِّهِ؛ إذا أقْبَلَتْ عَلَيْنا فَرِحْنا وَسُرِرْنا، وإذا أدْبَرَتْ عَنّا بَكَيْنا وَحَزِنّا.' قالَ: 'كَيْفَ كانَتْ عِبادَتُكُمْ لِلطّاغُوتِ؟' قالَ: 'الطّاعَةُ لِأهْلِ المَعاصِى.'

He said, 'How was the end of your work?' He said, 'We slept at night healthy and entered into the morning in al-hāw?ah (a burning abyss).' He said, 'And what is al-hāw?ah?' He said, 'Sijjin (a prison).' He said, 'And what is sijjin?' He said, 'Mountains of burning stones upon us until the Day of Resurrection.' He said, 'What did you say and what was said to you?' He said, 'We said, "Return us to the world so we may abstain from it." It was said to us, "You lie."' He [Jesus ﷺ] 'Woe unto you! How is it that one from among them did not speak to me except for you.' He said, 'O Spirit of Allah! They are bridled by rough strong angels with a bit made from fire, while although I was among them, I was not one of them. Then when the chastisement came down, it extended to me along with them. So, I am hanging by a hair at the brink of hell. I do not know whether I will fall headlong into it or I will be saved from it.' Then Jesus ﷺ turned to the Apostles and said, 'O Friends of Allah (Awliyā Allah)! Eating dry bread with crushed salt and sleeping on a dunghill is a great good with health in this world and in the next.'"

(*Kāfī*, 2, 318, 11)

4.16. It is reported that Abū 'Abdullah [Imam Ṣādiqﷺ] said, "Verily, Jesus the son of Maryﷺ came to the tomb of John the son of Zachariahﷺ and he asked his Lord to revive him. Then he called him, and he answered him and he came out from the grave and said to him, 'What do you want from me?' And he said to him, 'I want you to be friends with me as you were in this world.' Then he said to him, 'O Jesus! The heat of death has not yet subsided, and you want me to return to the world and the heat of death would return to me.' So he [Jesus] left him, and he returned to his grave."

(*Kāfī*, 3, 260, 37)

4.17. It is reported that a woman from Canaan brought her invalid son to Jesusﷺ. She said, "O Prophet of Allah! This my son is an invalid. Call on Allah for him." He said, "That which I have been commanded is only the healing of the invalids of the Children of Israel." She said, "O Spirit of Allah! Verily the dogs receive the remnants from the tables of their masters after the meal, so, avail us

قالَ: 'كَيْفَ كانَ عاقِبَةُ أمْرِكُمْ؟' قالَ: 'بِتْنا لَيْلَةً فِي عافِيَةٍ وأصْبَحْنا فِي الهاوِيَةِ.' فَقالَ: 'وَما الهاوِيَةُ؟' فَقالَ: 'سِجِّينٌ.' قالَ: 'وَما سِجِّينٌ؟' قالَ: 'جِبالٌ مِنْ جَمْرٍ تُوقَدُ عَلَيْنا إلَي يَوْمِ القِيامَةِ.' قالَ: 'فَما قُلْتُمْ وَما قِيلَ لَكُمْ؟' قالَ: 'قُلْنا: 'رُدَّنا إلَي الدنْيا فَنَزْهَدَ فِيها.' قِيلَ لَنا: 'كَذَبْتُمْ.' قالَ: 'وَيْحَكَ، كَيْفَ لَمْ يُكَلِّمْنِي غَيْرُكَ مِنْ بَيْنِهِمْ؟' قالَ: 'يا رُوحَ اللهِ، إنَّهُمْ مُلْجَمُونَ بِلِجامٍ مِنْ نارٍ بِأيْدِي مَلائِكَةٍ غِلاظٍ شِدادٍ. وإنِّي كُنْتُ فِيهِمْ وَلَمْ أكُنْ مِنْهُمْ. فَلَمّا نَزَلَ العَذابُ عَمَّنِي مَعَهُمْ. فَأنا مُعَلَّقٌ بِشَعْرَةٍ عَلَي شَفِيرِ جَهَنَّمَ، لا أدْرِي أكُبْكِبُ فِيها أمْ أنْجُو مِنْها.' فَالتَفَتَ عِيسَي عليه السلام إلَي الحَوارِيِّينَ، فَقالَ: 'يا أوْلِياءَ اللهِ، أكْلُ الخُبْزِ اليابِسِ بِالمِلْحِ الجَرِيشِ والنَوْمُ عَلَي المَزابِلِ، خَيْرٌ كَثِيرٌ، مَعَ عافِيَةِ الدنْيا والآخِرَةِ.'»

(الكافی، ٢، ٣١٨، ١١)

٤-١٦- عَلِيٌّ بْنُ مُحَمَّدٍ، عَنْ بَعْضِ أصْحابِنا، عَنْ عَلِيِّ بْنِ الحَكَمِ، عَنْ رَبِيعِ بْنِ مُحَمَّدٍ، عَنْ عَبْدِ اللهِ بْنِ سُلَيْمٍ العامِرِيِّ، عَنْ أبِي عَبْدِ اللهِ عليه السلام، قالَ: «إنَّ عيسَي بن مَريَمَ جاءَ إلَي قَبْرِ يَحْيَي بْنِ زَكَرِيّا عليه السلام، وكانَ سألَ رَبَّهُ أنْ يُحْيِيَهُ لَهُ. فَدَعاهُ، فأجابَهُ وَخَرَجَ إلَيْهِ مِنَ القَبْرِ. فَقالَ لَهُ: 'ما تُرِيدُ مِنِّي؟' فَقالَ لَهُ: 'أُرِيدُ أنْ تُؤْنِسَنِي كَما كُنْتَ فِي الدنْيا.' فَقالَ لَهُ: 'يا عِيسَي، ما سَكَنَتْ عَنِّي حَرارَةُ المَوْتِ، وأنْتَ تُرِيدُ أنْ تُعِيدَنِي إلَي الدنْيا وَتَعُودَ عَلَيَّ حَرارَةُ المَوْتِ!' فَتَرَكَهُ، فَعادَ إلَي قَبْرِهِ.»

(الكافی، ٣، ٢٦٠، ٣٧)

٤-١٧- فِي رِوايَةٍ: «أتَتْ عِيسَي امْرَأةٌ مِنْ كَنْعانَ بِابْنٍ لَها مُزْمِنٍ. فَقالَتْ: 'يا نَبِي اللهِ، ابني، هَذا، زَمِنٌ. ادْعُ اللهَ لَهُ.' قالَ: 'إنَّما اُمِرْتُ أنْ اُبْرِئَ زَمْنَيْ بَنِي إسْرائِيلَ.' قالَتْ: 'يا رُوحَ اللهِ! إنَّ الكِلابَ تَنالُ مِنْ فُضُولِ مَوائِدِ أرْبابِها، إذا رَفَعُوا مَوائِدَهُمْ.

of that which may benefit us of your wisdom." Then he supplicated Allah, the Supreme, asking for permission. Then He gave His permission, and he made him well.
(*Biḥār*, 14, 253, 45)

4.18. Al-Imām al-'Askarī said, "Jesus revived the dead. Was it not a miracle? Was it a miracle for the dead or for Jesus? Did he not create [something] like a bird from clay and it became a bird by the permission of Allah? Was it a miracle for the bird or for Jesus? Some people became monkeys. Was it not a miracle? Was it a miracle for monkeys or for the prorhet of that time? ..."
(*Tafsīr al-Imām al-'Askarī*, 319)

4.19. Imam Ṣādiq said: "Verily, when Jesus the son of Mary passed along the shore of a sea, he threw a piece of his bread into the water. Then some of the disciples said: 'O Spirit of Allah and HisWord! Why did you do this when that was your food.' He said, 'I did this in order that some animal among the animals of the sea may eat it, and the reward of Allah for this is great.'"
(*Kāfī*, 4, 9, 3)

4.20. [Imam] al-Ṣādiq said, "Verily, a man came to Jesus the son of Mary, and said to him, 'O Spirit of Allah! I have committed fornication, [or adultery, sex between a man and woman not married to eachother, in Arabic: *zinā'*] so purify me.' Then Jesus ordered the people to be called so that none should be left behind for the purification of so-and-so. Then when the people had been gathered together and the man had entered into a hole, so as to be stoned, the man called out, 'Anyone for whom Allah has a punishment should not punish me.' Then all the people left except for John and Jesus, peace be with them. Then John approached him and said to him, 'O sinner! Advise me!' Then he said to him, 'Do not remove the distance between your self and your desires or you will fall.' John said, 'Say more.' He said, 'Verily, do not humiliate the wrong-doer for a fault.' John said, 'Say more.' He said, 'Do not become angry.' John said, 'That is enough for me.'"
(*Faqīh*, 4, 33, 5019)

فأنزِلنا مِنْ حِكْمَتِكَ ما نَنْتَفِعُ بِهِ.' فاستَأذَنَ اللهَ، تَعالَي، فِي الدعاءِ، فأذِنَ لَهُ، فأبْرءَهُ.»

(بحارالأنوار، ١٤، ٢٥٣، ٤٥)

٤-١٨- قالَ الإمامُ العَسْكَرِيُّ عليه السلام: «... ألَيْسَ إحْياءُ عِيسَي عليه السلام المَيِّتَ مُعْجِزَةً؟ أهِيَ لِلْمَيِّتِ أمْ لِعِيسَي؟ أوَلَيْسَ خَلْقٌ مِنَ الطِّينِ كَهَيْئَةِ الطَّيْرِ فَصارَ طَيْراً بِإذْنِ اللهِ [مُعْجِزَةً]؟ أهِيَ لِلطّائِرِ أوْ لِعِيسَي؟ أوَلَيْسَ الذينَ جُعِلُوا قِرَدَةً خاسِئِينَ مُعْجِزَةً؟ أهِيَ لِلْقِرَدَةِ أوْ لِنَبِي ذَلِكَ الزَّمانِ؟...»

(تفسير الإمام العسكرىّ، ٣١٩)

٤-١٩- قالَ ابُو عَبدِ اللهِ عليه السلام: «إنَّ عِيسَي بن مَرْيَمَ عليه السلام، لَمّا أنْ مَرَّ عَلَي شاطِئِ البَحْرِ، رَمَي بِقُرْصٍ مِنْ قُوتِهِ فِي الماءِ. فَقالَ لَهُ بَعْضُ الحَوارِيِّينَ: 'يا رُوحَ اللهِ وكَلِمَتَهُ، لِمَ فَعَلْتَ هَذا وانَّما هُوَ مِنْ قُوتِكَ؟'» قالَ: «فَقالَ: 'فَعَلْتُ هَذا لِدابَّةٍ تأكُلُهُ مِنْ دَوابِّ الماءِ، وثَوابُهُ عِنْدَ اللهِ عَظِيمٌ.'»

(الكافى، ٤، ٩، ٣)

٤-٢٠- قالَ الصادِقُ عليه السلام: «إنَّ رَجُلاً جاءَ إلَي عيسَي بن مَريَمَ عليه السلام، فَقالَ لَهُ: 'يا رُوحَ اللهِ، إنِّي زَنَيْتُ، فَطَهِّرْنِي.' فأمَرَ عِيسَي عليه السلام أنْ يُنادَي فِي الناسِ، لا يَبْقَي أحَدٌ إلّا خَرَجَ لِتَطْهِيرِ فُلانٍ.' فَلَمّا اجْتَمَعَ واجْتَمَعُوا وَصارَ الرجُلُ فِي الحُفْرَةِ، نادَي الرجُلُ: 'لا يَحُدَّنِي مَنْ لِلَّهِ فِي جَنْبِهِ حَدٌّ.' فانْصَرَفَ الناسُ كُلُّهُمْ إلّا يَحْيَي وَعِيسَي عليه السلام. فَدَنا مِنْهُ يَحْيَي عليه السلام، فَقالَ لَهُ: 'يا مُذْنِبُ، عِظْنِي.' فَقالَ لَهُ: 'لا تُخَلِّيَنَّ بَيْنَ نَفْسِكَ وَبَيْنَ هَواها، فَتُرْدِيكَ.' قالَ: 'زِدْنِي.' قالَ: 'لا تُعَيِّرَنَّ خاطِئًا بِخَطِيئَةٍ.' قالَ: 'زِدْنِي.' قالَ: 'لا تَغْضَبْ.' قالَ: 'حَسْبِي.'»

(كتاب من لا يحضره الفقيه، ٤، ٣٣، ٥٠١٩)

4.21. It is reported that one day the rain and thunder became severe for Jesus so that he sought some place of shelter. Then a tent was set up for him in the distance, so he came to it. All at once, (he saw) there was a woman in it, so he turned from it. Suddenly, he saw a cave in a mountain, then he came to it. Then, all at at once (he saw) there was a lion in it. So he rested his hand against it (the cave), and said, "My God! For everything there is a shelter, but You put no shelter for me." Then Allah, the Supreme, revealed to him, "Your shelter is in the abode of My Mercy. By My Greatness, on the Resurrection Day, verily, I will marry you to a hundred houris created by My hand, and verily for your wedding I will provide food for four thousand years, each day of which is like the lifetime of the entire world. And Iwill command a crier to cry out, 'Where are the ascetics of the world? Be present at the wedding of the ascetic Jesus the son of Mary.'"
(*Biḥār*, 14, 328, 52)

4.22. It is reported that Imam Ali said in one of his sermons: "If you like, I will tell you about Jesus the son of Mary. He used a stone as his pillow, wore course clothing and ate rough food. His stew was hunger and his lamp in the night was the moon. His shade in the winter was the east of the earth and its west. His fruit and his basil is that which grows from the earth for the cattle. He had no wife to try him, and no son to grieve him. He had no wealth to distract him, nor greed to abase him. His mount was his feet and his servant was his hands."
(*Nahj al-Balāgha*, 1, 227)

4.23. Jesus served a meal to the Apostles, and when they had eaten it, he himself washed them. They said, "O Spirit of Allah! It would have been more proper for us to wash you!" He said, "I did this only that you would do this for those whom you teach."
(*Biḥār*, 14, 326, 42)

4.24. Jesus the son of Mary said, "O assembly of Apostles! I have a request of you. Fulfill it for me." They said, "Your request is fulfilled, O Spirit of Allah!" Then he stood up and washed their feet.

٤-٢١- رُوِىَ: «أنَّ عِيسَي عليه السلام اشْتَدَّ بِهِ المَطَرُ والرعْدُ يَوْماً. فَجَعَلَ يَطْلُبُ شَيْئاً، يَلْجأ إِلَيْهِ. فَرُفِعَتْ لَهُ خَيْمَةٌ مِنْ بَعِيدٍ. فأتاها، فإذا فِيها امْرأةٌ، فَحادَ عَنْها. فإذا هُوَ بِكَهْفٍ فِى جَبَلٍ، فأتاهُ، فإذا فِيهِ أسَدٌ، فَوَضَعَ يَدَهُ عَلَيْهِ، وقالَ: 'إلهى، لِكُلِّ شَىْء مأويً، ولَمْ تَجْعَلْ لِى مأويً!' فأوْحَي اللهُ، تَعالَي، إلَيْهِ: 'مأواكَ فِى مُسْتَقَرِّ رَحْمَتِي. وَعِزَّتِي، لأزَوِّجَنَّكَ يَوْمَ القِيامَةِ مِائة حُورِيَةٍ، خَلَقْتُها بِيَدِى؛ وَلأطْعَمَنَّ فِى عُرْسِكَ أرْبَعَةَ آلافِ عامٍ، يَوْمٌ مِنْها كَعُمْرِ الدنْيا؛ وَلآمُرَنَّ مُنادِياً يُنادِى: 'أيْنَ الزُهادُ فِى الدنْيا؟ أحْضُرُوا عُرْسَ الزّاهِدِ عِيسَي بْنِ مَرْيَمَ.'»

(بحارالأنوار، ١٤، ٣٢٨، ٥٢)

٤-٢٢- قالَ عَلِيٌّ عليه السلام: «... إنْ شِئْتَ قُلْتُ فِى عِيسَي بن مَرْيَمَ عليه السلام: 'فَلَقَدْ كانَ يَتَوَسَّدُ الحَجَرَ وَيَلْبَسُ الخَشِنَ وَيأكُلُ الجَشِبَ، وَكانَ إدامُهُ الجُوعَ وَسِراجُهُ باللَيْلِ القَمَرَ وَظِلالُهُ فِى الشِتاءِ مَشارِقَ الأرضِ وَمَغارِبَها وَفاكِهَتُهُ وَرَيْحانُهُ ما تُنْبِتُ الأرضُ لِلْبَهائِمِ. وَلَمْ تَكُنْ لَهُ زَوْجَةٌ تَفْتِنُهُ وَلا وَلَدٌ يَحْزُنُهُ وَلا مالٌ يَلْفِتُهُ وَلا طَمَعٌ يُذِلُّهُ. دابَّتُهُ رِجْلاهُ وَخادِمُهُ يَداهُ.'»

(نهج البلاغة، ١، ٢٢٧)

٤-٢٣- «صَنَعَ عِيسَي عليه السلام لِلْحَوارِيِّينَ طَعاماً، فَلَمّا أكَلُوا، وَضَّأهُمْ بِنَفْسِهِ. قالُوا: 'يا رُوحَ اللهِ! نَحْنُ أوْلَي أنْ نَفْعَلَهُ مِنْكَ!' قالَ: 'إنَّما فَعَلْتُ هَذا، لِتَفْعَلُوهُ بِمَنْ تُعَلِّمُونَ.'»

(بحارالأنوار، ١٤، ٣٢٦، ٤٢)

٤-٢٤- عَنْ مُحَمَّدِ بْنِ خالِدٍ، عَنْ مُحَمَّدِ بْنِ سِنانٍ رَفَعَهُ، قالَ: «قالَ عيسَي بن مَرْيَمَ عليه السلام: 'يا مَعْشَرَ الحَوارِيِّينَ! لِى إلَيْكُمْ حاجَةٌ، اقْضُوها لِى.' قالُوا: 'قُضِيَتْ حاجَتُكَ، يا رُوحَ اللهِ.' فَقامَ، فَغَسَلَ أقْدامَهُمْ. فَقالُوا:

They said, "It would have been more proper for us to have done this, O Spirit of Allah!" Then he said, "Verily, it is more fitting for one with knowledge to serve the people. Indeed, I humbled myself only so that you may humble yourselves among the people after me, even as I have humbled myself among you." Then Jesus said, "Wisdom is developed by humility, not by pride, and likewise plants only grow in soft soil, not in stone."
(*Kāfī*, 1, 37, 6)

4.25. Among the miracles of the Prophet is that when he went to the battle of Tabuk, twenty-five thousand Muslims, not counting servants, accompanied him. On their way they passed a mountain along the length of which there was a trickle of water, not flowing water. They said, 'How strange, that this mountain has such a trickle of water!' He told them that the mountain was weeping. They said, 'A mountain that cries?' He said, 'Would you like to know about it.' They said, 'Yes.' He said, 'O mountain! Why are you weeping?' The mountain answered in eloquent (*faṣīḥ*) language that the crowd heard, 'O Apostle of Allah! Jesus the son of Mary passed me while reciting this verse, "A fire whose fuel is men and stones." From that day I have been weeping in fear that I may be among those stones.' He said, 'Stop crying. You are not of them. They are stones of sulpher.' Suddenly, the trickle of the mountain dried up until nothing of it or its wetness was visible.

(*Biḥār* 17, 364, 5)

4.26. Mufaḍḍal ibn 'Umar said, "I said to Abū 'Abdullah, 'Who washed Faṭimah's [corpse], peace be with her?' He said, 'That was the Commander of the Faithful.' This, which he said, was shocking to me. Then he said to me, 'It seems that you are vexed by what I have informed you.' Then I said, 'It is so, may I be your sacrifice!' He said to me, 'Do not be vexed, for she was a righteous woman (*ṣiddīqah*) who could not be washed by any but a righteous man. Do you not know that no one washed [the corpse of] Mary but Jesus...'"
(*Kāfī*, 3, 159, 13)

'كُنّا نَحْنُ أحَقَّ بِهذا، يا رُوحَ اللهِ!' فقالَ: 'إنَّ أحَقَّ الناسِ بالخِدْمَةِ، العالِمُ. إنَّما تَواضَعْتُ هكَذا، لِكَيْما تَتَواضَعُوا بَعْدِى فِى الناسِ، كَتَواضُعِى لَكُمْ.' ثُمَّ قالَ عِيسَي عليه السلام: 'بِالتواضُعِ تُعْمَرُ الحِكْمَةُ، لا بِالتكَبُّرِ؛ وَكَذَلِكَ فِى السَهْلِ يَنْبُتُ الزَّرْعُ، لا فِى الجَبَلِ.'»
(الكافى، ١، ٣٧، ٦)

٤-٢٥- مِنْ مُعْجِزاتِهِ صلى الله عليه وآله وسلم، لَمّا غَزا بِتَبُوكٍ، كانَ مَعَهُ مِنَ المُسْلِمِينَ خَمْسَةٌ وَعِشْرُونَ ألفاً، سِوَي خَدَمِهِمْ. فَمَرَّ صلى الله عليه وآله وسلم فِى مَسِيرِهِ بِجَبَلٍ يَرْشَحُ الماءُ مِنْ أعْلاهُ إلِي أسفَلِهِ، مِنْ غَيْرِ سَيَلانٍ. فقالُوا: 'ما أعْجَبَ رَشْحَ هَذا الجَبَلِ!' فقالَ: 'إنَّهُ يَبْكِى.' قالُوا: 'والجَبَلُ يَبْكِى؟' قالَ: 'أتُحِبُّونَ أنْ تَعْلَمُوا ذَلِكَ؟' قالُوا: 'نَعَمْ.' قالَ: 'أيُّها الجَبَلُ! مِمَّ بُكاؤُكَ؟' فأجابَهُ الجَبَلُ، وقَدْ سَمِعَهُ الجَماعَةُ، بِلِسانٍ فَصِيحٍ: 'يا رَسُولَ اللهِ! مَرَّ بِى عِيسَي بْنُ مَرْيَمَ، وَهُوَ يَتْلُو: 'ناراً وَقُودُها الناسُ والحِجارَةُ.' فأنا أبْكِى مُنْذُ ذَلِكَ اليَوْمِ، خَوْفاً مِنْ أنْ أكُونَ مِنْ تِلْكَ الحِجارَةِ.' فقالَ: 'أسْكُنْ مَكانَكَ، فَلَسْتَ مِنْها. إنَّما تِلْكَ، حِجارَةُ الكِبْرِيتِ.' فَجَفَّ ذَلِكَ الرشْحُ مِنَ الجَبَلِ فِى الوَقْتِ، حَتَّي لَمْ يُرَ شَىْءٌ مِنْ ذَلِكَ الرشْحِ وَمِنْ تِلْكَ الرطُوبَةِ الَّتِى كانَتْ.
(بحارالأنوار، ١٧، ٣٦٤، ٥)

٤-٢٦- مُحَمَّدُ بْنُ يَحْيَي، عَنْ أحْمَدَ بْنِ مُحَمَّدِ بْنِ عِيسَي، عَنْ عَبْدِ الرحْمَنِ بْنِ سالِمٍ، عَنْ مُفَضَّلِ بْنِ عُمَرَ، قالَ: «قُلْتُ لأبِى عَبْدِ اللهِ عليه السلام: 'مَنْ غَسَّلَ فاطِمَةَ عليها السلام؟' قالَ: 'ذاكَ أمِيرُ المُؤْمِنِينَ عليه السلام.'» كَأنَّكَ اسْتَفْظَعْتَ ذَلِكَ مِنْ قَوْلِهِ. «فقالَ لِي: 'كَأنَّكَ ضِقْتَ مِمّا أخْبَرْتُكَ؟' فَقُلْتُ: 'قَدْ كانَ ذَلِكَ، جُعِلْتُ فِداكَ.' فقالَ لِي: 'لا تَضِيقَنَّ، فإنَّها صِدِّيقَةٌ لَمْ يَكُنْ يُغَسِّلُها إلّا صِدِّيقٌ. أما عَلِمْتَ أنَّ مَرْيَمَ عليها السلام لَمْ يُغَسِّلْها إلّا عِيسَي عليه السلام...'»
(الكافى، ٣، ١٥٩، ١٣)

4.27. Anas reported that the Prophet said, "The food of Jesus was broad beans, until his ascension. Jesus never ate anything changed by fire, until his ascension."

(*Biḥār*, 63, 266, 5)

4.28. It is reported that Jesus placed his head on a stone when going to sleep, then he threw it away after Iblīs (the devil) appeared to him and said, "You have come to desire the world!"

(*Majmū'a Warrām*, 1, 152)

4.29. Abū 'Abdullah said, "Verily Allah, the Mighty and Magnificent, made His greatest name from seventy-three letters. Then He gave Adam twenty-five letters of them, and He gave Noah twenty-five letters of them, and He gave Abraham eight letters of them, and He gave Moses four letters of them, and He gave Jesus two letters of them. So, he revived the dead by them, and cured the born blind and the leper. And He gave Muḥammad seventy-two letters and He kept a letter, so that it would not be known what is in Himself, and He knows what is in the souls of the servants."

(*Biḥār*, 4, 211, 5)

٤-٢٧- عَنْ أنَسٍ، قالَ النَبِيُّ (صلى الله عليه وآله وسلم): «كانَ طَعامُ عِيسَي الباقِلا، حتَّي رُفِعَ؛ ولَمْ يأكُلْ عِيسَي (عليه السلام) شَيْئًا غَيَّرَتْهُ النارُ، حتَّي رُفِعَ.»

(بحارالأنوار، ٦٣، ٢٦٦، ٥)

٤-٢٨- رُوِيَ: «أنَّ عِيسَي (عليه السلام) وَضَعَ راسَهُ عَلَي حَجَرٍ لَمّا نامَ، ثُمَّ رَماها، إذْ تَمَثَّلَ لَهُ إبْلِيسُ، وقالَ: 'رَغِبْتَ فِي الدنْيا.'»

(مجموعة ورّام، ١، ١٥٢)

٤-٢٩- أحْمَدُ بْنُ مُحَمَّدٍ، عَنْ أبِي عَبْدِ اللهِ البَرْقِي يَرْفَعُهُ إلَي أبِي عَبْدِ اللهِ (عليه السلام)، قالَ: «إنَّ اللهَ، عَزَّ وَجَلَّ، جَعَلَ اسْمَهُ الأعْظَمَ عَلَي ثَلاثَةٍ وَسَبْعِينَ حَرْفاً، فأعْطَي آدَمَ مِنْها خَمْسَةً وَعِشْرِينَ حَرْفاً، وأعْطَي نُوحاً مِنْها خَمْسَةً وَعِشْرِينَ حَرْفاً، وأعْطَي مِنْها إبْراهِيمَ ثَمانِيَةَ أحْرُفٍ، وأعْطَي مُوسَي مِنْها أرْبَعَةَ أحْرُفٍ، وأعْطَي عِيسَي مِنْها حَرْفَيْنِ، وكانَ يُحيِي بِهِما المَوْتَي وَيُبْرِئُ بِهِما الأكْمَهَ والأبرصَ، وأعْطَي مُحَمَّداً إثْنَيْنِ وَسَبْعِينَ حَرْفاً، واحتَجَبَ حَرْفاً، لِئَلاَّ يُعْلَمَ ما فِي نَفْسِهِ وَيَعْلَمَ ما فِي نَفْسِ العِبادِ.»

(بحارالأنوار، ٤، ٢١١، ٥)

5

THE CONVERSATIONS OF JESUSﷺ

5.1. Jesusﷺ said to the disciples, "Be satisfied with a little of the world, while your religion is safe, likewise the people of this world are satisfied with a little of the religion, while their world is safe; love Allah by being far from them, and make Allah satisfiedby being angry with them."

The disciples said, "O spirit of Allah, so with whom should we keep company?" He said, "He the sight of whom reminds you of Allah, his speech increases your knowledge and his action makes you desirous of the other world."

(*'Udda al-Dā'ī*, 121)

5.2. It is reported that Abu Abdullah [Imam Ṣādiqﷺ] said, "The Apostle of Allah, may the Peace and Blessings of Allah be with him and with his progeny, said, 'The Apostles said to Jesusﷺ 'O Spirit of Allah! With whom should we keep company?' He said, 'He the sight of whom reminds you of Allah, the speech of whom increases your knowledge, and the works of whom make you desirous of the other world.'"

(*Kāfī*, 1, 39, 3)

5.3. The disciples complained to Jesus the son of Mary about the disrespect of the people for them and their hating them. He said, "Be patient. Likewise the believers are hated among the people. The example of them is like the example of wheat. How sweet is its taste and how numerous are its enemies."

(*Majmū'a Warrām*, 2, 114)

٥

محادثة عيسى عليه السلام

٥-١- قالَ عِيسَي عليه السلام لِلْحَوارِيِّينَ: «ارْضَوْا بِدَنِيِّ الدنيا مَعَ سَلامَةِ دِينِكُمْ، كَما رَضِيَ أهْلُ الدنيا بِدَنِيِّ الدين مَعَ سَلامَةِ دُنْياهُمْ. وتَحَبَّبُوا إلَي اللهِ بِالبُعْدِ مِنْهُمْ، وارْضُوا اللهَ فِي سَخَطِهِمْ.» فقالُوا: «فَمَنْ نُجالِسُ؟ يا رُوحَ اللهِ!» فقالَ: «مَنْ يُذَكِّرُكُم اللهَ رُؤْيَتُهُ، وَيَزِيدُ فِي عِلْمِكُمْ مَنْطِقُهُ، وَيُرَغِّبُكُمْ فِي الآخِرَةِ عَمَلُهُ.»

(عدّةالداعى، ١٢١)

٥-٢- عِدَّةٌ مِنْ أصْحابِنا، عَنْ أحْمَدَ بْنِ مُحَمَّدٍ البَرْقِيِّ، عَنْ شَرِيفِ بْنِ سابِقٍ، عَنِ الفَضْلِ بْنِ أبِي قُرَّةَ، عَنْ أبِي عَبْدِ اللهِ عليه السلام، قالَ: «قالَ رَسُولُ اللهِ صلى الله عليه وآله وسلم: 'قالَتِ الحَوارِيُّونَ لِعِيسَي: 'يا رُوحَ اللهِ، مَنْ نُجالِسُ؟' قالَ: 'مَنْ يُذَكِّرُكُمُ اللهَ رُؤْيَتُهُ، وَيَزِيدُ فِي عِلْمِكُمْ مَنْطِقُهُ، وَيُرَغِّبُكُمْ فِي الآخِرَةِ عَمَلُهُ.''»

(الكافى، ١، ٣٩، ٣)

٥-٣- شَكا الحَوارِيُّونَ إلَي عِيسَي بْنِ مَرْيَمَ تَهاوُنَ الناسِ بِهِمْ وَبُغْضَهُمْ لَهُمْ. فقالَ: «اصْبِرُوا. كَذلِكَ، المُؤْمِنُونَ مُبْغَضُونَ فِي الناسِ. مَثَلُهُمْ كَمَثَلِ القَمْحِ، ما أحْلَي مَذاقَها! واكْثَرَ أعْداءَها!»

(مجموعة ورّام، ٢، ١١٤)

5.4. It is reported that the disciples were the followers of Jesus. Whenever they were hungry they said, "O Spirit of Allah! We are hungry." Then Jesus would hit his hands on the ground, whether smooth or hilly, and he would bring out two loaves of bread for each of them. Whenever they were thirsty they said, "O Spirit of Allah! We are thirsty." Then Jesus would hit his hands on the ground, and brought out water and they drank from it. They asked, "O Spirit of Allah! Who is better than we? Whenever we want we are given food, and whenever we want water is given to us. We have faith in you and follow you." Jesus said, "Better than you are those who work with their hands and eat from what they earn." After that the disciples washed clothes by the stream and ate from their wages for it."
(*Biḥār*, 70, 11)

5.5. Jesus was asked about the best of people. He said, "One whose speech is the mention of Allah, whose silence is contemplation, and whose vision is admonition."(1)

(*Majmu'ah Warrām*, 1, 250)

5.6. A man asked Jesus the son of Mary, "Which people is the best?" He took two handfuls of earth and said, "Which of these is the best? The people are created from earth, so the most honorable of them is the most God-wary."
(*Majmū'ah al-Akhbār fī Nafā'is al-Athār,* 106)

5.7. Al-Ṣādiq said, "It was said to Jesus son of Mary, 'What is the matter with you that you do not get married?' Then he said, 'What have I to do with getting married?' They said, '[A child] will be born for you.' He said, 'What have I to do with children? If they live, they will be a trial for us, and if they die, they will grieve us.'"
(*Faqīh*, 3, 558, 4916)

5.8. It has been reported that Abū Abdullah [Imam Ṣadiq] said, "Verily, Jesus the son of Mary said, 'I treated the sick, then I healed them by the permission of Allah, and I cured those born blind and the lepers by the permission of Allah, and I treated the dead and revived them by the permission of Allah, and I treated the fool, but I

(1) That is, he takes a lesson from what he sees.

٥-٤- قِيلَ: «إنَّهُمْ [الحَوارِيِّينَ] اتَّبَعُوا عِيسَى عليه السلام؛ فكانُوا إذا جاءُوا، قالُوا: 'يا رُوحَ اللهِ، جِئْنا.' فَيَضْرِبُ عليه السلام بِيَدِهِ الأَرْضَ، سَهْلاً كانَ أَوْ جَبَلاً، وَيُخْرِجُ لِكُلٍّ مِنْهُمْ رَغِيفَيْنِ. وإذا عَطَشُوا، قالُوا: 'يا رُوحَ اللهِ، عَطَشْنا.' فَيَضْرِبُ بِيَدِهِ الأَرْضَ، فَيَخْرُجُ ماءٌ وَيَشْرَبُونَ. فَقالُوا: 'يا رُوحَ اللهِ! مَنْ أَفْضَلُ مِنّا؟ إذا شِئْنا أُطْعِمْنا وإذا شِئْنا سُقِينا، وَقَدْ آمَنّا بِكَ واتَّبَعْناكَ.' فَقالَ عِيسَى عليه السلام: 'أَفْضَلُ مِنْكُمْ مَنْ يَعْمَلُ بِيَدِهِ، وَيأْكُلُ مِنْ كَسْبِهِ.' فَصارُوا يَغْسِلُونَ الثِّيابَ بِالكِرَي، بَعْدَ ذلِكَ، وَيأْكُلُونَ مِنْ أُجْرَتِهِ.»

(بحارالأنوار، ٧٠، ١١)

٥-٥- سُئِلَ عِيسَى عليه السلام: «مَنْ أَفْضَلُ النّاسِ؟» قالَ: «مَنْ كانَ مَنْطِقُهُ ذِكْراً، وَصَمْتُهُ فِكْراً، وَنَظَرُهُ عِبْرَةً.»

(مجموعة ورّام، ١، ٢٥٠)

٥-٦- إنَّ رَجُلاً سأل عِيسَى بْنَ مَرْيَمَ عليه السلام: «أيُّ النّاسِ أَفْضَلُ ؟» فاخَذَ قَبْضَتَيْنِ مِنْ تُرابٍ، فَقالَ: «أيُّ هاتَيْنِ أَفْضَلُ؟ النّاسُ خُلِقُوا مِن تُرابٍ، فأكْرَمُهُمْ أتْقاهُمْ.»

(مجموعة الأخبار في نفائس الآثار، ١٠٦)

٥-٧- قالَ الصّادِقُ عليه السلام: «قِيلَ لِعِيسَي بن مَرْيَمَ عليه السلام: 'ما لَكَ لا تَتَزَوَّجُ؟' فَقالَ: 'وَما أَصْنَعُ بالتَزْوِيجِ؟' قالُوا: 'يُولَدُ لَكَ.' قالَ: 'وَما أَصْنَعُ بالأَوْلادِ؟ إنْ عاشُوا فَتَنُوا، وإنْ ماتُوا أَحْزَنُوا.'»

(كتاب من لا يحضره الفقيه، ٣، ٥٥٨، ٤٩١٦)

٥-٨- الصَدُوقُ، عَنْ ابن المُتَوَكِّلِ، عَنْ عَلِيٍّ، عَنْ أبِيهِ، عَنِ البَزَنْطِي، عَنْ عَبْدِ الكَرِيمِ بْنِ عَمْرٍو، عَنْ أبي الرّبيعِ الشامِيِّ، عَنْ أبي عَبْدِ اللهِ عليه السلام، قالَ: «إنَّ عِيسَي بْنَ مَرْيَمَ عليه السلام قالَ: 'داوَيْتُ المَرْضَي فَشَفَيْتُهُمْ بِإذْنِ اللهِ، وأَبْرَأْتُ الأَكْمَهَ والأَبرصَ بِإذْنِ اللهِ، وَعالَجْتُ المَوْتَي فأَحْيَيْتُهُمْ بِإذْنِ اللهِ، وَعالَجْتُ الأَحْمَقَ،

could not correct him.' Then it was said, 'O Spirit of Allah! What is a fool?' He said, 'He is one who is admirable in his own view to himself, he who considers all of merit to be for him and not against him, and who finds all rights to be for himself and does not find against himself any right. Such is the fool for whom there is no trick to cure him.'"

(*Biḥār*, 14, 323)

5.9. Muḥammad ibn Muslim narrated from either Imam Bāqir or Imam Ṣādiq that when he was asked, "We see one with whom there is worship, endeavor and humility, but he does not speak the truth. Does it benefit him at all?" He said, "O Abū Muḥammad! The example of the Ahl al-Bayt is like that of a family that lived among the Children of Israel. None of them ever prayed for forty nights without his prayer being answered. But a man of that family prayed for forty nights, then he supplicated and his prayer was not answered. Then he came before Jesus and complained about what had happened, and he asked Jesus to pray for him. Jesus made ablutions and prayed. Then he supplicated Allah, the Mighty and Magnificent. Allah revealed to him, 'O Jesus! Verily, My servant came to Me from a door other than that by which he should approach Me. Verily he supplicated Me and in his heart there was doubt about you. If he supplicated Me until his neck broke and his fingers were bruised, I would not answer him.' Jesus turned to him and said, 'When you supplicate your Lord, do you have doubt about His prophet?' He said, 'O Spirit of Allah and His Word! By Allah, it was as you say. Supplicate Allah that He remove the doubt.' So, Jesus supplicated for him, and Allah turned to him and accepted it from him, and he became like one of his family."

(*Kāfī*, 2, 400, 9)

5.10. Verily, Jesus passed by three people. Their bodies had become thin and their colors had changed. Then he said, "What has brought you to what I see?" They said, "Fear of the Fire." He said,

فَلَمْ أقدِرْ عَلَي إصْلاحِهِ.' فقِيلَ: 'يا رُوحَ اللهِ! وَما الأحْمَقُ؟' قالَ: 'المُعْجِبُ بِرأيِهِ وَنَفْسِهِ، الذى يَرَي الفَضْلَ كُلَّهُ لَهُ، لا عَلَيْهِ، وَيُوجِبُ الحَقَّ كُلَّهُ لِنَفْسِهِ، وَلا يُوجِبُ عَلَيْها حَقاً. فَذلِكَ الأحْمَقُ الذى لا حِيلَةَ فِى مُداواتِهِ.'»

(بحارالأنوار، ١٤، ٣٢٣)

٥-٩- عن ابن أسْباطٍ، عَنِ العَلاءِ بْنِ رَزِينٍ، عَنْ مُحَمَّدِ بْنِ مُسْلِمٍ، عَنْ أحَدِهِما عليه السلام، قالَ: «قُلْتُ: 'إنّا لَنَرَي الرجُلَ لَهُ عِبادَةٌ واجْتِهادٌ وَخُشُوعٌ، وَلا يَقُولُ بِالحَقِّ. فَهَلْ يَنْفَعُهُ ذلِكَ شَيْئًا؟' فَقالَ: 'يا أبا مُحَمَّدٍ، إنَّما مَثَلُ أهْلِ البَيْتِ مَثَلُ أهْلِ بَيْتٍ كانُوا فِى بَنِى إسْرائِيلَ، كانَ لا يَجْتَهِدُ أحَدٌ مِنْهُمْ أرْبَعِينَ لَيْلَةً إلّا دَعا فَأُجِيبَ، وإنَّ رَجُلاً مِنْهُمُ اجْتَهَدَ أرْبَعِينَ لَيْلَةً ثُمَّ دَعا فَلَمْ يُسْتَجَبْ لَهُ. فَأتَي عِيسَي بن مَرْيَمَ عليه السلام، يَشْكُو إلَيْهِ ما هُوَ فِيهِ وَيَسْألُهُ الدعاءَ.' قالَ: 'فَتَطَهَّرَ عِيسَي وَصَلَّي، ثُمَّ دَعا اللهَ، عَزَّ وَجَلَّ. فَأوْحَي اللهُ، عَزَّ وَجَلَّ، إلَيْهِ: 'يا عِيسَي، إنَّ عَبْدِى أتانِى مِنْ غَيْرِ البابِ الذى أُوتِيَ مِنْهُ. إنَّهُ دَعانِى وَفِى قَلْبِهِ شَكٌّ مِنْكَ. فَلَوْ دَعانِى حَتَّى يَنْقَطِعَ عُنُقُهُ وَتَنْتَثِرَ أنامِلُهُ ما اسْتَجَبْتُ لَهُ.'' قالَ: 'فَالتَفَتَ إلَيْهِ عِيسَي عليه السلام، فَقالَ: 'تَدْعُو رَبَّكَ وأنْتَ فِى شَكٍّ مِنْ نَبِيِّهِ؟!' فَقالَ: 'يا رُوحَ اللهِ وَكَلِمَتَهُ، قَدْ كانَ واللهِ ما قُلْتَ. فادْعُ اللهَ لِى أنْ يَذْهَبَ بِهِ عَنِّي.'' قالَ: 'فَدَعا لَهُ عِيسَي عليه السلام، فَتابَ اللهُ عَلَيْهِ وَقَبِلَ مِنْهُ وَصارَ فِى حَدِّ أهْلِ بَيْتِهِ.'»

(الكافى، ٢، ٤٠٠، ٩)

٥-١٠- يُقالُ: «إنَّ عِيسَي عليه السلام مَرَّ بِثَلاثَةِ نَفَرٍ، قَدْ نَحِلَتْ أبْدانُهُمْ وَتَغَيَّرَتْ الوانُهُمْ. فَقالَ: 'ما الذى بَلَغَ بِكُمْ ما أرَي؟' قالُوا: 'الخَوْفُ مِنَ النارِ.' قالَ: 'حَقٌّ عَلَي اللهِ

"It is the duty of Allah to give security to those who fear Him." Then he passed from them to three other men. He was surprised to find them even thinner and more changed. Then he said, "What has brought you to what I see?" They said, "Yearning for the Garden." He said, "It is the duty of Allah to give to him who has hope in Him." Then he passed to three others. He was surprised to find them even thinner and their faces were shining like mirrors. Then he said, "What has brought you to what I see?" They said, "Love of Allah, the Mighty and Magnificent." Three times, he said, "You are those who are close to Allah."

(*Sharḥ Nahj al-Balāgha*, 10, 156)

5.11. The disciples asked Jesus, "Indicate to us a work by which we may enter the Garden." He said, "Do not speak at all." They said, "We cannot do that." He said, "So, do not speak except what is good."

(*Sharḥ Nahj al-Balāgha*, 10, 137)

5.12. A man said to Jesus the son of Mary, "O good teacher, indicate to me a work by which I may enter the Garden." Then he said to him, "Beware of Allah secretly and openly, and do good to your parents."

(*Mustadrak al-Wasā'il*, 15, 175, 17911)

5.13. Imām Ṣādiq said, "The disciples of Jesus complained to him about what was meeted to them by the people. Then he said, verily, in the world the believers are always disturbed."

(*Biḥār*, 78, 194)

5.14. It is reported that Abū 'Abdullah said, "The disciples complained to Jesus the son of Mary about what was thrown at them by the people. He said, 'Verily the believers always are hated among the people, like the wheat, how sweet is its taste and how many its enemies are!'"

(*Mishkāt al-Anwār*, 286)

أنْ يُؤَمِّنَ مَنْ يَخافُهُ.' ثُمَّ جاوَزَهُمْ إلَي ثَلاثَةٍ آخَرينَ، فإذا هُمْ أشَدُّ نُحُولاً وَتَغَيُّراً. فَقالَ: 'ما الذى بَلَغَ بِكُمْ ما أرَي؟' قالُوا: 'الشَوْقُ إلَي الجَنَّةِ.' فَقالَ: 'حَقٌّ عَلَي اللهِ أنْ يُعْطِىَ مَنْ رَجاهُ.' ثُمَّ مَرَّ إلَي ثَلاثَةٍ آخَرينَ، فإذا هُمْ أشَدُّ نُحُولاً، وَعَلَي وُجُوهِهِمْ مِثْلُ المَرائِىَ مِنَ النور. فَقالَ: 'ما الذى بَلَغَ بِكُمْ ما أرَي؟' قالُوا: 'حُبُّ اللهِ، عَزَّ وَجَلَّ.' فَقالَ: 'أنتُم المُقَرَّبُونَ،' ثَلاثاً.»

(شرح نهج البلاغة، ١٠، ١٥٦)

٥-١١- قالَتِ التَلامِذَةُ لِعِيسَي عليه السلام: «دُلَّنا عَلَي عَمَلٍ نَدْخُلُ بِهِ الجَنَّةَ.» قالَ: «لا تَنْطِقُوا أبَداً.» قالُوا: «لا نَسْتَطِيعُ ذَلِكَ.» قالَ: «فَلا تَنْطِقُوا إلّا بِخَيْرٍ.»

(شرح نهج البلاغة، ١٠، ١٣٧)

٥-١٢- قالَ رَجُلٌ لِعِيسَى ابن مَرْيَمَ عليه السلام: «يا مُعَلِّمَ الخَيْرِ، دُلَّنِى عَلَي عَمَلٍ أدْخُلُ بِهِ الجَنَّةَ.» فَقالَ لَهُ: «اتَّقِ اللهَ فِى سِرِّكَ وَعَلانِيَتِكَ، وَبَرَّ والِدَيْكَ.»

(مستدرك الوسائل، ١٥، ١٧٥، ١٧٩١١)

٥-١٣- إنَّ حَوارِيِّى عِيسَي عليه السلام شَكَوْا إلَيْهِ، ما يَلْقَوْنَ مِنَ الناسِ. فَقالَ: «إنَّ المُؤْمِنِينَ لا يَزالُونَ فِى الدنْيا مُنَغَّصِينَ.»

(بحارالأنوار، ٧٨، ١٩٤)

٥-١٤- عَنْ أبِى عَبْدِ اللهِ عليه السلام، قالَ: «إنَّ الحَوارِيِّينَ شَكَوْا إلَي عِيسَي بْنِ مَرْيَمَ، ما يَلْقَوْنَ مِنَ الناسِ.» فَقالَ: «إنَّ المُؤْمِنِينَ لَمْ يَزالُوا مُبْغَضِينَ فِى الناسِ، كَحَبَّةِ القَمْحِ، ما أحْلَي مَذاقَها واكْثَرَ أعْداءَها!»

(مشكاة الأنوار، ٢٨٦)

5.15. It is said that Jesus the son of Mary was sitting and an old man was working with a small shovel tilling the earth. Jesus said, "O Allah! Extract his desire from him." The old man put down the small shovel and slept for an hour. Then Jesus said, "O Allah! Return the desire to him." Then he stood up and began to work. Jesus asked him about it. He said, "When I was working I said to myself, 'How long will you work, being that you are an old man?' Then I put down the small shovel and slept. Then I said to myself, 'By Allah! You have no alternative but to live as long as you remain.' Then I stood up with my small shovel."
(*Biḥār*, 14, 329, 57)

5.16. It was said to Jesus, "[Would it not be better] if you got a house?" He said: "The remains which are left from those before us are enough for us."
(*Biḥār*, 14, 327, 51)

5.17. It is reported that Abu 'Abdullah [Imam Ṣādiq] said, "Jesus the son of Mary sent two of his companions on an errand. Then one of them returned thin and afflicted and the other like iron and fat. He said to the one who was thin, 'What did this to you, that I see you this way?' He said, 'The fear of Allah.' And he said to the other who was fat, 'What did this to you, that I see you this way?' He said, 'A good opinion of Allah.'"
(*Biḥār*, 67, 400)

5.18. Jesus said to his companions, "Accord great regard for the thing which is not eaten by the fire." They said, "What is that?" He said, "That which is good."
(*Biḥār*, 14, 330, 65)

5.19. It is reported that Jesus found fault with property and said, "It has three characteristics." It was said, "And what are they, O Spirit of Allah!" He said, "One acquires it illegitimately, and if it is acquired legitimately, it keeps one from one's duties, and if one performs one's duties, its improvement busies one rather than worship of one's Lord."
(*Biḥār*, 14, 329, 59)

٥-١٥- قِيلَ: «بَيْنَما عِيسَي بْنُ مَرْيَمَ عليه السلام جالِسٌ، وَشَيْخٌ يَعْمَلُ بِمِسْحاةٍ وَيُثِيرُ الأرضَ. فَقالَ عِيسَي عليه السلام: ‹اللهُمَّ، أنْزِعْ مِنْهُ الأمَلَ.› فَوَضَعَ الشَيْخُ المِسْحاةَ واضْطَجَعَ، فَلَبِثَ ساعَةً. فَقالَ عِيسَي: ‹اللهُمَّ، أرْدُدْ إلَيْهِ الأمَلَ.› فَقامَ، فَجَعَلَ يَعْمَلُ. فَسألَهُ عِيسَي عَنْ ذَلِكَ. فَقالَ: ‹بَيْنَما أنا أعْمَلُ، إذْ قالَتْ لِي نَفْسِي: ‹إلَي مَتَي تَعْمَلُ وأنْتَ شَيْخٌ كَبِيرٌ؟› فَألْقَيْتُ المِسْحاةَ واضْطَجَعْتُ. ثُمَّ قالَتْ لِي نَفْسِي: ‹واللهِ، لا بُدَّ لَكَ مِنْ عَيْشٍ ما بَقِيتَ.› فَقُمْتُ إلَي مِسْحاتِي.›»

(بحارالأنوار، ١٤، ٣٢٩، ٥٧)

٥-١٦- قِيلَ لِعِيسَي عليه السلام: «لَوِ اتَّخَذْتَ بَيْتاً!» قالَ: «يَكْفِينا خُلْقانُ مَنْ كانَ قَبْلَنا.»

(بحارالأنوار، ١٤، ٣٢٧، ٥١)

٥-١٧- عَنْ أبِي عَبْدِ اللهِ عليه السلام، قالَ: «بَعَثَ عِيسَي بْنُ مَرْيَمَ رَجُلَيْنِ مِنْ أصْحابِهِ فِي حاجَةٍ. فَرَجَعَ أحَدُهُما، مِثْلَ الشَنِّ البالِي؛ والآخَرُ شَحِماً وَسَمِيناً. فَقالَ لِلَّذِي مِثْلُ الشَنِّ: ‹ما بَلَغَ مِنْكَ ما أرَي؟› قالَ: ‹الخَوْفُ مِنَ اللهِ.› وَقالَ لِلآخَرِ السَمِينِ: ‹ما بَلَغَ بِكَ ما أرَي؟› فَقالَ: ‹حُسْنُ الظَنِّ بِاللهِ.›»

(بحارالأنوار، ٦٧، ٤٠٠)

٥-١٨- قالَ عِيسَي عليه السلام لِأصحابِهِ: «اسْتَكْثِرُوا مِنَ الشَيْءِ الذي لا تَأكُلُهُ النارُ.» قالُوا: «وَما هُوَ؟» قالَ: «المَعْرُوفُ.»

(بحارالأنوار، ١٤، ٣٣٠، ٦٥)

٥-١٩- رُوِيَ «أنَّ عِيسَي عليه السلام ذَمَّ المالَ، وَقالَ: ‹فِيهِ ثَلاثُ خِصالٍ.› فَقِيلَ: ‹وَما هُنَّ؟ يا رُوحَ اللهِ.› قالَ: ‹يَكْسِبُهُ المَرْءُ مِنْ غَيْرِ حِلِّهِ، وإنْ هُوَ كَسَبَهُ مِنْ حِلِّهِ مَنَعَهُ مِنْ حَقِّهِ، وإنْ هُوَ وَضَعَهُ فِي حَقِّهِ شَغَلَهُ إصْلاحُهُ عَنْ عِبادَةِ رَبِّهِ.›»

(بحارالأنوار، ١٤، ٣٢٩، ٥٩)

5.20. It is reported that Abū 'Abdullah [Imam Ṣādiq] said, "Iblis[1] said to Jesus the son of Mary, 'Does your Lord have the power to put the earth into an egg without reducing the size of the earth or enlarging the egg?' Then Jesus said, 'Woe unto you, for weakness is not attributed to Allah. Who is more powerful than He Who makes the earth subtle and makes the egg great?'

(*Biḥār*, 4, 142, 9)

5.21. It is reported that Imam Ṣadiq said, "Iblis came to Jesus, then he said, 'Do you not claim that you can revive the dead?' Jesus said, 'Yes.' Iblis said, 'Then throw yourself down from the top of the wall.' Then Jesus said, 'Woe unto you! Verily the servant does not try his Lord.' And Iblis said, 'O Jesus! Can your Lord put the earth in an egg while the egg remains in its form?' Then he said, 'Verily Allah, the Supreme, is not proscribed by impotence, but what you said cannot be.'" (i.e., it is imposible in itself, like the gathering of two opposites.)[2]

(*Biḥār*, 14, 271, 3)

5.22. It is reported that Abū 'Abdullah [Imam Ṣādiq] said, "The disciples said to Jesus the son of Mary, 'O teacher of the good! Teach us what is the most severe of things.' Then he said, 'The most severe of things is the wrath of Allah.' They said, 'Then what prevents the wrath of Allah?' He said, 'That you not be wrathful.' They said, 'What is the source of wrath?' He said, 'Pride, haughtiness and contempt for the people.'"

(*Biḥār*, 14, 287, 9)

---

[1] The devil who tempted Adam and Eve. Cf. Qur'ān 2:34; 7:11; 15:31; 38:74.

[2] The parenthetical comment is Majlisī's.

٥-٢٠- العَطارُ، عَنْ سَعْدٍ، عَنْ ابن يَزِيدٍ، عَنْ ابن أبِى عُمَيْرٍ، عَمَّنْ ذَكَرَهُ، عَنْ أبِى عَبْدِ اللهِ عليه السلام، قالَ: «إنَّ إبْلِيسَ قالَ لِعِيسَي بْنِ مَرْيَمَ: 'أيَقدِرُ رَبُّكَ عَلَي أنْ يُدْخِلَ الأرضَ بَيْضَةً، لا تَصْغُرُ الأرضُ وَلا تَكْبُرُ البَيْضَةُ؟' فَقالَ عِيسَي، عَلَي نَبِيِّنا وَآلِهِ وَعليه السلام: 'وَيْلَكَ، إنَّ اللهَ لا يُوصَفُ بِعَجْزٍ؛ وَمَنْ أقدَرُ مِمَّنْ يُلَطِّفُ الأرضَ وَيُعَظِّمُ البَيْضَةَ.'»

(بحار الأنوار، ٤، ١٤٢، ٩)

٥-٢١- الصَدُوقُ، عَنْ ابن الوَلِيدِ، عَنِ الصَفارِ، عَنْ مُحَمَّدِ بْنِ خالِدٍ، عَنْ ابن أبِى عُمَيْرٍ، عَنْ هِشامِ بْنِ سالِمٍ، عَنِ الصادِقِ عليه السلام، قالَ: «جاءَ إبْلِيسُ إلَي عِيسَي عليه السلام، فَقالَ: 'ألَيسَ تَزْعَمُ أنَّكَ تُحْيِى المَوْتَي؟' قالَ عِيسَي: 'بَلَي.' قالَ إبْلِيسُ: 'فاطْرَحْ نَفْسَكَ مِنْ فَوْقِ الحائِطِ.' فَقالَ عِيسَي: 'وَيْلَكَ، إنَّ العَبْدَ لا يُجَرِّبُ رَبَّهُ.' وَقالَ إبْلِيسُ: 'يا عِيسَي، هَلْ يَقدِرُ رَبُّكَ عَلَي أنْ يُدْخِلَ الأرضَ فِى بَيْضَةٍ، والبَيْضَةُ كَهَيْأتِها؟' فَقالَ: 'إنَّ اللهَ، تَعالَي، لا يُوصَفُ بِعَجْزٍ، والَّذِى قُلْتَ لا يَكُونُ.' (يَعْنِي، هُوَ مُسْتَحِيلٌ فِى نَفْسِهِ، كَجَمْعِ الضِّدَّيْنِ.)»

(بحار الأنوار، ١٤، ٢٧١، ٣)

٥-٢٢- عَنْ عَبْدِ اللهِ بْنِ سِنانٍ، عَنْ أبِى عَبْدِ اللهِ عليه السلام، قالَ: «قالَ الحَوارِيُّونَ لِعِيسَي بْنِ مَرْيَمَ عليه السلام: 'يا مُعَلِّمَ الخَيْرِ عَلِّمْنا، أيُّ الأشياءِ أشَدُّ؟' فَقالَ: 'أشَدُّ الأشياءِ غَضَبُ اللهِ، عَزَّ وَجَلَّ.' قالُوا: 'فَبِمَ يُتَّقَي غَضَبُ اللهِ؟' قالَ: 'بِأنْ لا تَغْضَبُوا.' قالُوا: 'وَما بَدْءُ الغَضَبِ؟' قالَ: 'الكِبْرُ والتجَبُّرُ وَمَحْقَرَةُ الناسِ.'»

(بحار الأنوار، ١٤، ٩، ٢٨٧)

5.23. Jesus met Iblis who was driving five donkeys. Loads were upon them. Jesus asked him about the loads. Iblis said, "They are for trade, and I am looking for buyers." Jesus said, "What is the trade?" Iblis said, "One of them is injustice?" He asked, "Who buys it?" He said, "Rulers. And the second is pride." He asked, "Who buys it?" He said, "Village chiefs. And the third is envy." He asked, "Who buys it?" He said, "The scholars. And the fourth is treason." He asked, "Who buys it?" He said, "Those who work for merchants. And the fifth is trickery." He said, "Who buys it?" He said, "Women."
(*Biḥār*, 61, 196)

5.24. It is reported that Imam Ṣādiq said, "Jesus the son of Mary passed by a group of people who were crying. He asked why they were crying. It was said to him that they were crying for their sins. He said, 'They should pray about them and they will be forgiven.'"
(*Biḥār*, 6, 20, 7)

5.25. Jesus passed by a group crying. He said, "What is the matter with them crying?" To him it was said, "For their sins." He said, "They should abandon them, so their sins will be forgiven."
(*Majmū'a Warrām*, 2, 114)

5.26. The Messenger of Allah said, "Jesus the son of Mary said to John the son of Zachariah, 'If what is said of you that which is true of you, then know that it was a sin which you committed, so ask the forgiveness of Allah for it, and if what is said of you is not true of you, then know that for this a good deed will be recorded for you, so do not weary yourself over it.'"
(*Biḥār*, 14, 287)

5.27. Jesus said to a worshipper, "What do you do?" He answered, "I worship." He said, "Then who provides for you?" He said, "My brother." He said, "Your brother is more of a worshipper than you are!"
(*Majmū'a Warrām*, 1, 65)

٥-٢٣- «إنَّ عِيسَي عليه السلام لَقِيَ إبْلِيسَ وَهُوَ يَسُوقُ خَمْسَةَ أحْمِرَةٍ، عَلَيْها أحْمالٌ. فَسألهُ عَنْ الأحْمالِ. فقالَ: 'تِجارَةٌ أطْلُبُ لها مُشْتَرِينَ.' فقالَ: 'وَما هِيَ التِّجارَةُ؟' قالَ: 'أحَدُها، الجَوْرُ.' قالَ: 'وَمَنْ يَشْتَرِيهِ؟' قالَ: 'السَلاطِينُ. والثّانِي، الكِبْرُ.' قالَ: 'وَمَنْ يَشْتَرِيهِ؟' قالَ: 'الدهاقِينَ. والثّالِثُ، الحَسَدُ.' قالَ: 'وَمَنْ يَشْتَرِيهِ؟' قالَ: 'العُلَماءُ. والرابِعُ، الخِيانَةُ.' قالَ: 'وَمَنْ يَشْتَرِيها؟' قالَ: 'عُمّالُ التَّجّارِ. والخامِسُ، الكَيْدُ.' قالَ: 'وَمَنْ يَشْتَرِيهِ؟' قالَ: 'النساءُ.'»

(بحارالأنوار، ٦١، ١٩٦)

٥-٢٤- أبِي، عَنْ سَعْدٍ، عَنْ ابن عِيسَي، عَنْ ابن المُغِيْرَةِ، عَنْ طَلْحَةِ بْنِ زَيْدٍ، عَنْ أبِي عَبْدِ اللهِ عليه السلام، قالَ: «مَرَّ عِيسَي بْنُ مَرْيَمَ عليه السلام عَلَي قَوْمٍ يَبْكُونَ. فقالَ: 'عَلَي ما يُبْكِي هَؤُلاءِ؟' فَقِيلَ: 'يَبْكُونَ عَلَي ذُنُوبِهِمْ.' قالَ: 'فَلْيَدْعُوها، يُغْفَرْ لَهُمْ.'»

(بحارالأنوار، ٦، ٢٠، ٧)

٥-٢٥- مَرَّ عِيسَي عليه السلام بِقَوْمٍ يَبْكُونَ. فقالَ: «ما لِهَؤُلاءِ يَبْكُونَ؟» فَقِيلَ: «لِذُنُوبِهِمْ.» فقالَ: «فَلْيَتْرُكُوها، يُغْفَرْ لَهُمْ.»

(مجموعة ورّام، ٢، ١١٤)

٥-٢٦- قالَ عِيسَي بْنُ مَرْيَمَ عليه السلام لِيَحْيَي بْنِ زَكَرِيّا عليه السلام: «إذا قِيلَ فِيكَ ما فِيكَ، فاعْلَمْ أنَّهُ ذَنْبٌ ذَكَرْتَهُ؛ فاسْتَغْفِرْ اللهَ مِنْهُ. وإنْ قِيلَ فِيكَ ما لَيْسَ فِيكَ، فاعْلَمْ أنَّها حَسَنَةٌ كُتِبَتْ لَكَ، لَمْ تَتْعَبْ فِيها.»

(بحارالأنوار، ١٤، ٢٨٧)

٥-٢٧- قالَ عِيسَي عليه السلام لِرَجُلٍ: «ما تَصْنَعُ؟» قالَ: «أتَعَبَّدُ.» قالَ: «فَمَنْ يَعُودُ عَلَيْكَ؟» قالَ: «أخِي.» قالَ: «أخُوكَ أعْبَدُ مِنْكَ.»

(مجموعة ورّام، ١، ٦٥)

5.28. It was said to Jesus, "Who trained you?" He said, "No one trained me. I saw the ugliness of ignorance and, so, I avoided it."

(*Biḥār*, 14, 326, 44)

5.29. It is reported that Jesus passed by a carcass with his disciples. Then the disciples said, "How putrid the smell of this dog is!" Then Jesus said, "How intense is the whiteness of his teeth!"

(*Biḥār*, 14, 327, 46)

5.30. Jesus passed by a grave whose occupant was being chastised. Then he passed it the following year when he was not being chastised. He said, "O Lord! I passed through this town last year and he was being chastised, and I passed through it this year while he is not being chastised." Then Allah revealed to him, "O Spirit of Allah! Verily one of his children matured and cleared some way and sheltered an orphan. Then I forgave him for the deeds of his child."

(*Kāfī*, 6, 3, 12)

5.31. The Messenger of Allah said, "My brother Jesus passed through a city when the teeth of its inhabitants were falling out and their faces were swollen. Then they complained to him. He said, 'When you sleep, you close your mouths; then the air that is in your chests boils up until it reaches the mouth; then there is no place for it to exit and it comes back to the roots of the teeth and contaminates the face. So when you sleep, you should open your lips, and make this a habit for yourselves. They did this and the (sickness) left them.'"

(*Biḥār*, 14, 321, 28)

5.32. The Apostle of Allah said, "My brother Jesus passed through a city [whose inhabitants] had yellow faces and blue eyes.(1) They cried out to him and complained of their illness. He said, 'It's treatment is with you. When you want to eat meat, you cook it without

---

(1) A blue tinge to the eyes was a sign of blindness (cataracts?). Cf. Qur'ān 20:102.

٥-٢٨- قِيلَ لِعِيسَي عليه السلام: «مَنْ أدَّبَكَ؟» قالَ: «ما أدَّبَنِى أحَدٌ. رأيْتُ قُبْحَ الجَهْلِ، فَجانَبْتُهُ.»

(بحارالأنوار، ١٤، ٣٢٦، ٤٤)

٥-٢٩- رُوِىَ «أنَّ عِيسَي عليه السلام مَرَّ مَعَ الحَوارِيِّينَ عَلَي جِيفَةٍ. فَقالَ الحَوارِيُّونَ: 'ما أنْتَنَ رِيحَ هَذا الكَلْبِ!' فَقالَ عِيسَي عليه السلام: 'ما أشَدَّ بَياضَ أسْنانِهِ!'»

(بحارالأنوار، ١٤، ٣٢٧، ٤٦)

٥-٣٠- عِدَّةٌ مِنْ أصْحابِنا، عَنْ أحْمَدَ بْنِ مُحَمَّدِ بْنِ خالِدٍ، عَنْ شَرِيفِ بْنِ سابِقٍ، عَنِ الفَضْلِ بْنِ أبِى قُرَّةَ، عَنْ أبِى عَبْدِ اللهِ عليه السلام، قالَ: «قالَ رَسُولُ اللهِ صلى الله عليه وآله وسلم: 'مَرَّ عِيسَي بن مَرْيَمَ عليه السلام بِقَبْرٍ يُعَذَّبُ صاحِبُهُ؛ ثُمَّ مَرَّ بِهِ مِنْ قابِلٍ، فَإذا هُوَ لا يُعَذَّبُ. فَقالَ: 'يا رَبِّ! مَرَرْتُ بِهَذا القَبْرِ عامَ أوَّلٍ، فَكانَ يُعَذَّبُ، وَمَرَرْتُ بِهِ العامَ، فَإذا هُوَ لَيْسَ يُعَذَّبُ.' فَأوْحَى اللهُ إلَيْهِ: 'أنَّهُ أدْرَكَ لَهُ وَلَدٌ صالِحٌ، فَأصْلَحَ طَرِيقاً وَآوَي يَتِيماً. فَلِهَذا غَفَرْتُ لَهُ بِما فَعَلَ ابنهُ.'»

(الكافى، ٦، ٣، ١٢)

٥-٣١- قالَ النَبِى صلى الله عليه وآله وسلم: «مَرَّ أخِى عِيسَي عليه السلام بِمَدِينَةٍ، وإذا أهْلُها، أسْنانُهُمْ مُنْتَثِرَةٌ وَوُجُوهُهُمْ مُنْتَفِخَةٌ. فَشَكَوْا إلَيْهِ. فَقالَ: 'أنتُم إذا نِمْتُمْ، تُطْبِقُونَ أفْواهَكُمْ، فَتَغْلِى الرِيحُ فِى الصدُورِ حَتَّي تَبْلُغَ إلَي الفَمِ، فَلا يَكُونُ لَها مَخْرَجٌ، فَتَرِدُ إلَي أُصُولِ الأسنانِ، فَيَفْسُدُ الوَجْهُ. فَإذا نِمْتُمْ، فَافْتَحُوا شَفاهَكُمْ وَصَيِّرُوهُ لَكُمْ خُلُقاً.' فَفَعَلُوا، فَذَهَبَ ذَلِكَ عَنْهُمْ.»

(بحارالأنوار، ١٤، ٣٢١، ٢٨)

٥-٣٢- قالَ النَبِىُّ صلى الله عليه وآله وسلم: «مَرَّ أخِى عِيسَي عليه السلام بِمَدِينَةٍ, وإذا وُجُوهُهُمْ صُفْرٌ وَعُيُونُهُمْ زُرْقٌ. فَصاحُوا إلَيْهِ وَشَكَوْا ما بِهِمْ مِنَ العِلَلِ. فَقالَ: 'دَواؤُهُ مَعَكُمْ. أنتُم إذا

washing it. Nothing leaves this world without having an impurity. Then they washed their meat and their illness went away.'"
(*Biḥār*, 14, 321, 27)

5.33. The Prophet said, "Jesus, my brother, passed through a city when [he suddenly realized that] worms were in its fruits. [The people of the city] complained to him about this problem. He said, 'You have the cure for this [problem], but you do not know it. You are a folk who when you plant trees you pour soil on them then you pour the water, but this is not proper. It is proper that you pour the water on the roots of the trees, then pour the soil so that the worm does not infect it.' Then they started doing as he described and [the problem] went away."

(*Biḥār*, 14, 321, 26)

5.34. It is narrated that 'Alī said: "My brother Jesus passed through a city in which a man and a woman were shouting at one another. He said, 'What's the matter with you?' The man said, 'O Prophet of Allah! This is my wife, and she is not bad, she is good, but I would like to separate from her. He said, 'Inform me, anyway, what is the matter with her.' He said, 'Her face is aged while she is not old.' He said to her, 'O woman! Would you like to regain the freshness of your face?' She said, 'Yes.' He said to her, 'When you eat, take care not to eat your fill, because when the food fills you to your chest and is greater than the amount [proper], the freshness of the face is lost.' Then she did it, and the freshness of her face came back.

(*Biḥār*, 14, 320, 25)

5.35. It has been reported that Abū Add Allah [Imam Ṣādiq] said, "The world took the form, for Jesus, of a woman whose eyes were blue. Then he said to her, 'How many have you married?' She said, 'Very many.' He said, 'Then did they all divorce you?' She said, 'No, but I killed all of them.' He said, 'Then woe be to the rest of your husbands! How they fail to learn from the example of the past ones!'"

(*Biḥār*, 14, 330, 66)

أكَلْتُمُ اللحْمَ, طَبَخْتُمُوهُ غَيْرَ مَغْسُولٍ؛ وَلَيْسَ يَخْرُجُ شَيْءٌ مِنَ الدنْيا إلّا بِجِنابَةٍ.' فَغسَلُوا بَعْدَ ذلِكَ لُحُومَهُمْ, فَذَهَبَتْ أمْراضُهُمْ.»

(بحار الأنوار، ١٤، ٣٢١، ٢٧)

٥-٣٣- قالَ النَبِيُّ صلى الله عليه وآله وسلم: «مَرَّ أخِي عِيسَي عليه السلام بِمَدِينَةٍ، وإذا فِي ثِمارِها الدودُ. فَشَكَوْا إلَيْهِ ما بِهِمْ. فَقالَ: 'دَواءُ هَذا مَعَكُمْ، وَلَيْسَ تَعْلَمُونَ. أنتُم قَوْمٌ إذا غَرَسْتُمُ الأشْجارَ، صَبَبْتُمُ التَرابَ ثُمَّ صَبَبْتُمُ الماءَ؛ وَلَيْسَ هَكَذا يَجِبُ. بَلْ يَنْبَغِي أنْ تَصُبُّوا الماءَ فِي أُصُولِ الشجَرِ، ثُمَّ تَصُبُّوا التَرابَ، لِكَيلا يَقَعَ فِيهِ الدودُ.' فاسْتَأنَفُوا كَما وَصَفَ، فَذَهَبَ ذَلِكَ عَنْهُمْ.»

(بحار الأنوار، ١٤، ٣٢١، ٢٦)

٥-٣٤- بِإسْنادِ العُمَرِي، عَنْ آبائِهِ، عَنْ عَلِيٍّ عليه السلام، أنَّ النَبِيَّ صلى الله عليه وآله وسلم قالَ: «مَرَّ أخِي عِيسَي عليه السلام بِمَدِينَةٍ، وَفِيها رَجُلٌ وامْرأةٌ يَتَصايَحانِ. فَقالَ: 'ما شأنُكُما؟' قالَ: 'يا نَبِي اللهِ! هَذِهِ امْرأتِي، وَلَيْسَ بِها بَأسٌ، صالِحَةٌ؛ وَلَكِنِّي أُحِبُّ فِراقَها.' قالَ: 'فَأخْبِرْنِي عَلَي كُلِّ حالٍ ما شأنُها.' قالَ: 'هِيَ خَلِقَةُ الوَجْهِ، مِنْ غَيْرِ كِبَرٍ.' قالَ لَها: 'يا إمْرأةُ، أتُحِبِّينَ أنْ يَعُودَ ماءُ وَجْهِكِ طَرِيّاً؟' قالَتْ: 'نَعَمْ.' قالَ لَها: 'إذا أكَلْتِ، فَإيّاكِ أنْ تَشْبَعِي؛ لأنَّ الطَّعامَ إذا تَكاثَرَ عَلَي الصدْرِ فَزادَ فِي القِدْرِ، ذَهَبَ ماءُ الوَجْهِ.' فَفَعَلَتْ ذَلِكَ، فَعادَ وَجْهُها طَرِيّاً.»

(بحار الأنوار، ١٤، ٣٢٠، ٢٥)

٥-٣٥- ابن المُغَيْرَةِ، عَنْ طَلْحَةِ بْنِ زَيْدٍ، عَنْ أبِي عَبْدِ اللهِ عليه السلام، قالَ: «تَمَثَّلَتِ الدنْيا لِعِيسَي عليه السلام، فِي صُورَةِ امْرأةٍ زَرْقاءَ. فَقالَ لَها: 'كَمْ تَزَوَّجْتِ؟' قالَتْ: 'كَثِيراً.' قالَ: 'فَكُلٌّ طَلَّقَكِ؟' قالَتْ: 'كَلاَّ، بَلْ قَتَلْتُ.' قالَ: 'فَوَيْحَ أزْواجِكِ الباقِينَ! كَيْفَ لا يَعْتَبِرُونَ بِالماضِينَ؟'»

(بحار الأنوار، ١٤، ٣٣٠، ٦٦)

5.36. It is reported that Abu Abdullah [Imam Ṣādiq] said, "The Apostle of Allah, may the Peace and Blessings of Allah be with him and with his progeny, said, 'The Apostles said to Jesus, "O Spirit of Allah! With whom should we keep company?" He said, "He the sight of whom reminds you of Allah, the speech of whom increases your knowledge, and the works of whom make you desirous of the other world."'"

(*Kāfī*, 1, 39, 3)

5.37. It has been reported by Mujahid from Ibn 'Abbās from the Apostle of Allah, "Verily, Jesus passed a city which had come to ruin and whose foundations had collapsed. He said to some of his disciples, 'Do you know what it is saying?' One said, 'No.' Jesus said, 'It says, "Verily, the true promise of my Lord has come. My rivers have dried up, though once they were full; my trees have withered, though once they were in bloom; my castles are in ruins and my residents have died. Then, oh, these are their bones within me, and their property that was gained lawfully along with their ill-gotten gains are in my belly, and the inheritance of the heavens and the earth is only for Allah."'"

(*Ādāb al-Nafs*, 1, 122)

5.38. Imam Ṣādiq said, "The Apostles met with Jesus and said to him, 'O teacher of the good! Guide us!' He said to them, 'Verily Moses the interlocutor of Allah commanded you not to swear by Allah, the Blessed and Exalted, falsely, and I command you not to swear by Allah falsely or truly.' They said, 'O Spirit of Allah! Guide us more!' Then he said, 'Verily Moses the prophet of Allah commanded you not to commit adultery, and I command you not to talk to yourselves about adultery, let alone to commit adultery. Verily one who talks to himself about adultery is like one who sets fire to a room that is decorated so the smoke damages the decor, even though the room is not burnt.'"

(*Kāfī*, 5, 542, 7)

٥-٣٦- عِدَّةٌ مِنْ أصْحابِنا، عَنْ أحْمَدَ بْنِ مُحَمَّدٍ البَرْقِيِّ، عَنْ شَرِيفِ بْنِ سابِقٍ، عَنِ الفَضْلِ بْنِ أبِى قُرَّةَ، عَنْ أبِى عَبْدِ اللهِ عليه السلام، قالَ: «قالَ رَسُولُ اللهِ صلى الله عليه وآله وسلم: 'قالَتِ الحَوارِيُّونَ لِعِيسَي: 'يا رُوحَ اللهِ، مَنْ نُجالِسُ؟' قالَ: 'مَنْ يُذَكِّرُكُمُ اللهَ رُؤْيَتُهُ، وَيَزِيدُ فِى عِلْمِكُمْ مَنْطِقُهُ، وَيُرَغِّبُكُمْ فِى الآخِرَةِ عَمَلُهُ.''»

(الكافى، ١، ٣٩، ٣)

٥-٣٧- عَنْ ابن عَبّاسٍ، عَنْ رَسُولِ اللهِ صلى الله عليه وآله وسلم: «إنَّ عِيسَي مَرَّ بِمَدِينَةٍ خَرِبَتْ عُمْرانُها، وَسَقَطَتْ بُنْيانُها؛ وَقالَ لِبَعْضِ حَوارِيِّهِ: 'أتَدْرِى ما تَقُولُ هَذِهِ القَرْيَةُ؟' قالَ: 'لا.' قالَ: 'إنَّها تَقُولُ: 'إنَّها جاء وَعْدُ رَبِّىَ الحَقُّ، فَيَبِسَتْ أنْهارِى بَعْدَ غَزارَتِها، وَجَفَّتْ أشْجارِى بَعْدَ نَضارَتِها، وَخَرِبَتْ قُصُورِي، وَماتَ سُكّانِى. فَها هِىِ عِظامُهُمْ فِى جَوْفِى، وأمْوالُهُمُ المَجْمُوعَةُ مِنْ حَلالٍ وَحَرامٍ فِى بَطْنِى؛ وَلِلهِ مِيراثُ السَمَواتِ والأرضِ.''»

(آداب النفس، ١، ١٢٢)

٥-٣٨- عَلِيُّ بْنُ إبْراهِيمَ، عَنْ أبِيهِ؛ وَعِدَّةٌ مِنْ أصْحابِنا، عَنْ أحْمَدَ بْنِ مُحَمَّدٍ، عَنْ أبِى العَباسِ الكُوفِىِّ، جَمِيعاً عَنْ عَمْرِو بْنِ عُثْمانَ، عَنْ عَبْدِ اللهِ بْنِ سَنانٍ، عَنْ أبِى عَبْدِ اللهِ عليه السلام، قالَ: «اجْتَمَعَ الحَوارِيُّونَ إلَي عِيسَي عليه السلام، فَقالُوا لَهُ: 'يا مُعَلِّمَ الخَيْرِ أرْشِدْنا.' فَقالَ لَهُمْ: 'إنَّ مُوسَي كَلِيمَ اللهِ عليه السلام أمَرَكُمْ أنْ لا تَحْلِفُوا بِاللهِ، تَبارَكَ وَتَعالَي، كاذِبِينَ، وأنا آمُرُكُمْ أنْ لا تَحْلِفُوا بِاللهِ كاذِبِينَ وَلا صادِقِينَ.' قالُوا: 'يا رُوحَ اللهِ، زِدْنا.' فَقالَ: 'إنَّ مُوسَي نَبِى اللهِ عليه السلام أمَرَكُمْ أنْ لا تَزْنُوا، وأنا آمُرُكُمْ أنْ لا تُحَدِّثُوا أنْفُسَكُمْ بِالزِّنا، فَضْلاً عَنْ أنْ تَزْنُوا. فإنَّ مَنْ حَدَّثَ نَفْسَهُ بِالزِّنا كانَ كَمَنْ أوْقَدَ فِى بَيْتٍ مُزَوَّقٍ، فأفْسَدَ التَزاوِيقَ الدخانُ، وإنْ لَمْ يَحْتَرِقِ البَيْتُ.'»

(الكافى، ٥، ٥٤٢، ٧)

5.39. It was said to Jesus, "Teach us a deed for which Allah will love us." He said, "Detest the world and Allah will love you." (*Majmū'a Warrām*, 1, 134)

5.40. 'Abdullah ibn Maghfal said, "The Apostle of Allah said, 'Verily, Jesus the son of Mary said, "O group of disciples! The congregational prayer!" Then the disciples came out ready for worship, and their stomachs were empty, their eyes sunken and their color yellow. Jesus brought them to an open ground and he went on top of a hill and praised Allah and lauded Him. Then he started to recite signs of Allah and His wisdom for them. He said, "O group of disciples! Listen to what I tell you! I find in the book sent down of Allah evident things that have been sent down by Allah in the Gospel, so act according to them!" They said, "O Spirit of Allah! What are they?" He said, "He created the night for three qualities, and He created the day for seven qualities. Whoever passes the night and day without having these qualities, the night and day will be against him on the day of resurrection. He created the night for you to rest your tired tendons that have toiled during the day, and for you to ask forgiveness for the sins you have committed during the day, and not to return to them, and to stand obedient with the obedience of the patient. So, in one third you sleep, in one third you stand and in one third you are humble before your Lord. It is for this that the night was created. He created the day for the performance of the obligatory ritual prayer about which you will be asked and for which you are answerable, and for being nice to your parents, and for toiling to earn a living for the day, and for visiting the friends of Allah so that Allah will spread His mercy for you, and for participating in funeral processions so that you will change and Allah will forgive you, and to command doing what is good and to prohibit doing what is bad, which is the apex of faith and the establishing of religion, and to struggle in the way of Allah so that you may visit Abraham the friend of the Merciful in his own place, and whoever passes the night and day without having these qualities, the night and day will be against him on the day of resurrection before the Almighty King."'"

(*Biḥār*, 55, 207, 38)

٥-٣٩- قِيلَ لِعِيسَي عليه السلام: «عَلِّمْنا عَمَلاً واحِداً، يُحِبُّنا اللهُ عَلَيْهِ.» قالَ: «أبْغِضُوا الدنْيا، يُحْبِبْكُمُ اللهُ.»
(مجموعة ورام، ١، ١٣٤)

٥-٤٠- الدرُّ المَنْثُورُ، عَنْ عَبْدِ اللهِ بْنِ مَغْفَلٍ، قالَ: «قالَ رَسُولُ اللهِ صلى الله عليه وآله وسلم: 'إنَّ عِيسَي بْنَ مَرْيَمَ عليه السلام قالَ: 'يا مَعْشَرَ الحَوارِيِّينَ، الصَلاةُ جامِعَةٌ.' فَخَرَجَ الحَوارِيُّونَ فِي هَيْأةِ العِبادَةِ، قَدْ تَضَمَّرَتِ البُطُونُ وَغارَتِ العُيُونُ واصْفَرَّتِ الألْوانُ. فَسارَ بِهِمْ عِيسَي عليه السلام إلَي فَلاةٍ مِنَ الأرضِ، فَقامَ عَلَي رأسِ جُرْثُومَةٍ؛ فَحَمِدَ اللهَ وأثْنَي عَلَيْهِ، ثُمَّ أنْشا يَتْلُو عَلَيْهِمْ مِنْ آياتِ اللهِ وَحِكْمَتِهِ. فَقالَ: 'يا مَعْشَرَ الحَوارِيِّينَ، اسْمَعُوا ما أقُولُ لَكُمْ: 'إنِّي لأجِدُ فِي كِتابِ اللهِ المُنْزَلِ الذي أنْزَلَهُ اللهُ فِي الإنجيلِ، أشْياءَ مَعْلُومَةً، فاعْمَلُوا بِها.' قالُوا: 'يا رُوحَ اللهِ، وَما هِيَ؟' قالَ: 'خَلَقَ اللَيْلَ لِثَلاثِ خِصالٍ، وَخَلَقَ النَهارُ لِسَبْعِ خِصالٍ؛ فَمَنْ مَضَي عَلَيْهِ اللَيْلُ والنَهارُ وَهُوَ فِي غَيْرِ هَذِهِ الخِصالِ، خاصَمَهُ اللَيْلُ والنَهارُ يَوْمَ القِيامَةِ، فَخَصَماهُ. خُلِقَ اللَيْلُ لِتَسْكُنَ فِيهِ العُرُوقُ الفاتِرَةُ الَّتِي أتْعَبْتَها فِي نَهارِكَ، وَتَسْتَغْفِرَ لِذَنْبِكَ الذي كَسَبْتَهُ بِالنَهارِ، ثُمَّ لا تَعُودُ فِيهِ، وَتَقْنُتَ فِيهِ قُنُوتَ الصابِرِينَ. فَثُلْثٌ تَنامُ، وَثُلْثٌ تَقُومُ، وَثُلْثٌ تَضَرَّعُ إلَي رَبِّكَ؛ فَهَذا ما خُلِقَ لَهُ اللَيْلُ. وَخُلِقَ النَهارُ لِتُؤَدِّيَ فِيهِ الصَلاةَ المَفْرُوضَةَ الَّتِي عَنْها تُسْألُ وَبِها تُخاطَبُ، وَتَبِرَّ والِدَيْكَ، وأنْ تَضْرِبَ فِي الأرضِ تَبْتَغِي المَعِيشَةَ، مَعِيشَةَ يَوْمِكَ، وأنْ تَعُودُوا فِيهِ وَلِيّاً للهِ، كَيْما يَتَغَمَّدَكُمُ اللهُ بِرَحْمَتِهِ، وأنْ تُشَيِّعُوا فِيهِ جَنازَةً، كَيْما تَنْقَلِبُوا مَغْفُوراً لَكُمْ، وأنْ تَأمُرُوا بِمَعْرُوفٍ وأنْ تَنْهَوْا عَنْ مُنْكَرٍ، فَهُوَ ذُرْوَةُ الإيمانِ وَقِوامُ الدينِ، وأنْ تُجاهِدُوا فِي سَبِيلِ اللهِ، تُزاحِمُوا إبْراهِيمَ، خَلِيلَ الرحْمَنِ فِي قُبَّتِهِ. ومَنْ مَضَي عَلَيْهِ اللَيْلُ والنَهارُ، وَهُوَ فِي غَيْرِ هَذِهِ الخِصالِ، خاصَمَهُ اللَيْلُ والنَهارُ يَوْمَ القِيامَةِ، فَخَصَماهُ عِنْدَ مَلِيكٍ مُقْتَدِرٍ.''»
(بحارالأنوار، ٥٥، ٢٠٧، ٣٨)

5.41. Fayḍ ibn al-Mukhtār said, "I heard Abū 'Abdullah [Imām Ṣādiq] say, 'When *al-mā'idah* [the table spread] was sent down to Jesus he said to the Apostles, "Do not eat from it until I give you permission." Then one of them ate from it. Then some of the Apostles said, "O Spirit of Allah! So-and-so ate from it!" Then Jesus said to him, "Did you eat from it?" He said to him, "No." Then the Apostles said, "Yes! By Allah! O Spirit of Allah! He ate from it!" Then Jesus said to him [who had thus spoken], "Affirm your brother and deny your eye."'

(*Biḥār*, 14, 235, 7)

5.42. Abū 'Alī Muḥammad ibn Hammām said, "On the ring of Abū Ja'far al-Samān, may Allah be pleased with him, [were the words]: 'There is no god but Allah, the King, the Evident Truth.' I asked him about it. He said, 'Abū Muḥammad, I mean, Imam Ḥasan al-'Askari?, reported to me from his fathers that they said, "Fāṭimah, peace be with her, had a ring of silver and agate. Before she died she gave it to al-Ḥasan, and before he died he gave it to al-Ḥusayn. Al-Ḥusayn said, 'I wanted to engrave something on it. Then I dreamed of the Messiah Jesus the son of Mary, peace be with our Prophet and his descendents and him [Jesus].' I said to him, 'O Spirit of Allah! What should I engrave on this my ring?' He said, 'Engrave on it, "There is no god but Allah, the King, the Evident Truth," for this is at the beginning of the Torah and and at the end of the Gospel.'"'"

(*Ghayba*, 297)

5.43. Aḥmad ibn Sahl said, "I heard from Abū Farwah al-Anṣārī, who was a traveler, 'Jesus said, "O company of disciples! In truth I say to you, verily the people say that a building is based on its foundation, and I do not say such things to you." They said, "Then, what do you say, O Spirit of Allah?" He said, "In truth I say to you, verily the final stone the worker sets is the foundation." Abū Farwah said, "Surely he meant the end of a task."'"

(*Biḥār*, 68, 364, 54)

٥-٤١- عَنِ الفَيْضِ بْنِ المُخْتار، قالَ: «سَمِعْتُ أبا عَبْدِ اللهِ عليه السلام، يَقُولُ: 'لَمّا أُنْزِلَتْ المائِدَةُ عَلَي عِيسَي عليه السلام، قالَ لِلْحَوارِيِّينَ: 'لا تَأكُلُوا مِنْها، حَتَّي آذَنَ لَكُمْ.' فأكَلَ مِنْها رَجُلٌ مِنْهُمْ. فَقالَ بَعْضُ الحَوارِيِّينَ: 'يا رُوحَ اللهِ، أكَلَ مِنْها فُلانٌ.' فَقالَ لَهُ عِيسَي عليه السلام: 'أكَلْتَ مِنْها؟' قالَ لَهُ: 'لا.' فَقالَ الحَوارِيُّونَ: 'بَلَي واللهِ، يا رُوحَ اللهِ! لَقَدْ أكَلَ مِنْها.' فَقالَ لَهُ عِيسَي: 'صَدِّقْ أخاكَ وكَذِّبْ بَصَرَكَ.''»

(بحارالأنوار، ١٤، ٢٣٥، ٧)

٥-٤٢- قالَ أبُو عَلِيٍّ، مُحَمَّدُ بْنُ هَمّامٍ: «وَعَلَي خاتَمِ أبِي جَعْفَرٍ السَمّانِ، رَضِيَ اللهُ عَنْهُ: 'لا إلَهَ إلّا اللهُ المَلِكُ الحَقُّ المُبِينُ.' فَسألْتُهُ عَنْهُ، فَقالَ: 'حَدَّثَنِي أبُو مُحَمَّدٍ، يَعْنِي صاحِبُ العَسْكَرِ عليه السلام، عَنْ آبائِهِ عليهم السلام، أنَّهُمْ قالُوا: 'كانَ لِفاطِمَةَ عليها السلام خاتَمٌ فَصُّهُ عَقِيقٌ، فَلَمّا حَضَرَتْها الوَفاةُ، دَفَعَتْهُ إلَي الحَسَنِ عليه السلام، فَلَمّا حَضَرَتْهُ الوَفاةُ، دَفَعَهُ إلَي الحُسَيْنِ عليه السلام. قالَ الحُسَيْنُ عليه السلام: 'فاشْتَهَيْتُ أنْ أنْقُشَ عَلَيْهِ شَيْئاً. فَرَأيْتُ فِي النَوْمِ المَسِيحَ، عِيسَي بْنَ مَرْيَمَ، عَلَي نَبِيِّنا وآلِهِ وَعليه السلام. فَقُلْتُ لَهُ: 'يا رُوحَ اللهِ، ما أنْقُشُ عَلَي خاتَمِي، هَذا؟' قالَ: 'اُنْقُشْ عَلَيْهِ: 'لا إلَهَ إلّا اللهُ المَلِكُ الحَقُّ المُبِينُ.' فإنَّهُ أوَّلُ التَوْراةِ وآخِرُ الإنْجِيلِ.''''»

(الغيبة، ٢٩٧)

٥-٤٣- أبِي، عَنْ مُحَمَّدٍ العَطّارِ، عَنْ مُحَمَّدِ بْنِ الحُسَيْنِ، عَنْ أحْمَدَ بْنِ سَهْلٍ، قالَ: «سَمِعْتُ أبا فَرْوَةَ الأنْصارِيَّ، وكانَ مِنَ السّائِحِينَ، يَقُولُ: 'قالَ عِيسَي بْنُ مَرْيَمَ: 'يا مَعْشَرَ الحَوارِيِّينَ، بِحَقٍّ أقُولُ لَكُمْ، إنَّ النّاسَ يَقُولُونَ: 'إنَّ البِناءَ بِأساسِهِ.' وإنِّي لا أقُولُ لَكُمْ كَذَلِكَ.' قالُوا: 'فَما ذا تَقُولُ يا رُوحَ اللهِ؟' قالَ: 'بِحَقٍّ أقُولُ لَكُمْ، إنَّ آخِرَ حَجَرٍ يَضَعُهُ العامِلُ، هُوَ الأساسُ.'' قالَ أبُو فَرْوَةَ: 'إنَّما أرادَ خاتِمَةَ الأمْرِ.'»

(بحارالأنوار، ٦٨، ٣٦٤، ٥٤)

5.44. Muḥammad ibn 'Alī ibn Ḥātim al-Nūfilī reported, "...Abū al-Ḥusayn Muḥammad ibn Baḥr al-Shaybāni reported that... [Malīkah] said: 'O you incapable ignorant person with regard to the children of the prophets! Listen to me, and empty your heart [to accept what I say]. I am Malīkah, the daughter of Yashū'ā the son of Ceasar, the king of Rūm, and my mother is of the descendants of the Apostles, reaching to the successor of Christ, Sham'ūn (Simon, Peter). I will tell you something very strange. Verily, my grandfather, Ceasar wanted to marry me to the son of his brother when I was a thirteen year old girl... Then I dreamt, during that night, as if Christ and Sham'ūn and a few of the Apostles gathered in the castle of my grandfather, and they erected a pulpit that was so tall as to reach into the sky, on which my grandfather placed his throne. Muḥammad entered before them with a youth and a few of his descendents. Christ rose and embraced him. Then he [Muḥammad] said, "O Spirit of Allah! I have come to you to ask your successor, Sham'ūn, for the hand of his daughter, Malīkah, for my boy there." He then indicated Abū Muḥammad with his hand, who wrote this letter [instructing the servant to purchase Malīkah, who had been taken captive]. Then Christ looked at Sham'ūn and said to him, "It is a blessing [literally, nobility has come to you]. Become family with the family of the Apostle of Allah." Sham'ūn said, "It is done!" Then Muḥammad ascended the pulpit, read a sermon and married me [to the youth, Imam 'Askarī], and Christ, the children of Muḥammad and the Apostles were witnesses to it. When I woke up from my sleep, I was afraid to tell this dream to my father and grandfather, for fear they might kill me. So, I kept it to myself, a secret, and did not reveal it to them. My breast was struck with love for Abū Muḥammad, until I could neither eat nor drink. I became weak, thin, and very sick....' Then Abū al-Ḥasan said, 'Then she became the wife of Abū Muḥammad and the mother of the Qā'im [the twelfth Imam].'"

Kamāl al-Dīn, 2, 417-424.

٥-٤٤- حَدَّثَنا مُحَمَّدُ بْنُ عَلِيِّ بْنِ حاتَمِ النَوْفِلِي، قالَ: «... حَدَّثَنا أبُو الحُسَيْنِ مُحَمَّدُ بْنُ بَحْرِ الشَيْبانِي، ...قالَتْ [مَلِيكَةُ]: 'أيُّها العاجِزُ الضَّعِيفُ المَعْرِفَةُ بِمَحَلِّ أوْلادِ الأنبياءِ، أعِرْنِى سَمْعَكَ وَفَرِّغْ لِي قَلْبَكَ. أنا مَلِيكَةُ، بِنْتُ يَشُوعا بْنِ قَيْصَرَ مَلِكِ الرومِ، وأمِّى مِنْ وُلْدِ الحَوارِيِّينَ تُنْسَبُ إلِي وَصِيِّ المَسِيحِ شَمْعُونَ. أنَبِّئُكَ العَجَبَ العَجِيبَ، إنَّ جَدِّى قَيْصَرَ أرادَ أنْ يُزَوِّجَنِى مِنْ ابن أخِيهِ وأنا مِنْ بَناتِ ثَلاثَةَ عَشَرَةَ سَنَةً ... فَأرَيْتُ فِى تِلْكَ اللَيْلَةِ كانَّ المَسِيحَ والشَمْعُونَ وَعِدَّةً مِنَ الحَوارِيِّينَ قَدْ اجْتَمَعُوا فِى قَصْرِ جَدِّى، وَنَصَبُوا فِيهِ مِنْبَراً يُبارِى السَماءَ عُلُوّاً وارْتِفاعاً فِى المَوْضِعِ الذى كانَ جَدِّى نَصَبَ فِيهِ عَرْشَهُ. فَدَخَلَ عَلَيْهِمْ مُحَمَّدٌ صلى الله عليه وآله وسلم مَعَ فِتْيَةٍ وَعِدَّةٍ مِنْ بَنِيهِ. فَيَقُومُ إلَيْهِ المَسِيحُ فَيَعْتَنِقُهُ. فَيَقُولُ: 'يا رُوحَ اللهِ، إنِّى جِئْتُكَ خاطِباً مِنْ وَصِيِّكَ شَمْعُونَ فَتاتَهُ مَلِيكَةَ لِابْنِى هَذا.' وأوْمأ بِيَدِهِ إلِي أبِى مُحَمَّدٍ، صاحِبِ هَذا الكِتابِ. فَنَظَرَ المَسِيحُ إلِي شَمْعُونَ، فَقالَ لَهُ: 'قَدْ أتاكَ الشرَفُ، فَصِلْ رَحِمَكَ بِرَحِمِ رَسُولِ اللهِ صلى الله عليه وآله وسلم.' قالَ: 'قَدْ فَعَلْتُ.' فَصَعَدَ ذَلِكَ المِنْبَرُ وَخَطَبَ مُحَمَّدٌ صلى الله عليه وآله وسلم وَزَوَّجَنِى، وَشَهِدَ المَسِيحُ عليه السلام وَشَهِدَ بَنُو مُحَمَّدٍ صلى الله عليه وآله وسلم والحَوارِيُّونَ. فَلَمّا اسْتَيْقَظْتُ مِنْ نَوْمِى، أشْفَقْتُ أنْ أقُصَّ هَذِهِ الرُؤْيا عَلَي أبِى وَجَدِّى مَخافَةَ القَتْلِ. فَكُنْتُ أسِرُّها فِى نَفْسِى وَلا أبْدِيها لَهُمْ؛ وَضُرِبَ صَدْرِى بِمَحَبَّةِ أبِى مُحَمَّدٍ حَتَّي إمْتَنَعْتُ مِنَ الطَّعامِ والشرابِ، وَضَعُفَتْ نَفْسِي وَدَقَّ شَخْصِى وَمَرِضْتُ مَرَضاً شَدِيداً ...'

فَقالَ أبُو الحَسَنِ عليه السلام: 'فَإنَّها زَوْجَةُ أبِى مُحَمَّدٍ وأمُّ القائِمِ عليه السلام'»

(كمال الدين، ٢، ٤١٧- ٤٢٤)

6

GOD'S WORDS TO JESUS

6.1. Allah revealed to Jesus the son of Mary, "O Jesus! I do not forget those who forget Me, so how could I forget those who remember Me! I am not stingy with those who disobey Me, so how could I be stingy with those who obey Me."

(*Jāmi' al-Akhbār*, 1, 180)

6.2. Allah, the Exalted, revealed to Jesus, "O Jesus the son of the virgin, al-Batūl! Cry over yourselves, like one who says his last good-bye to his family, loathes the world, abandons it to its people, and who has come to desire what is near his God."

(*'Udda al-Dā'ī*, 169)

6.3. It is reported that among what was revealed to Jesus is: "Do not be deceived by those who are disobedient to Me, who eat what I provide for them, but woship other than Me, then they call Me when they are worried, so I answer them, then they go back to what they did. Do they disobey Me or want to anger Me? [I swear] by Myself! I will take them in such a way that there is no deliverance from it and there is no refuge but Me. Where can they flee from My sky and My earth?"

(*'Udda al-Dā'ī*, 212)

6.4. 'Abdullah ibn al-Walīd said, "Abū 'Abdullah said to me, 'What do the followers say about Jesus, Moses and the Commander of the Faithful, peace be with them?' I said, 'They say, "Verily Jesus and Moses are better than the Commander of the Faithful."' He said, 'Do they think that he knew every thing that the Apostle of Allah

٦

ما أَوْحَى اللـــهُ إلى عيسى عليه السلام

٦-١- أوْحَي اللهُ، تَعالَي، إلَي عِيسَي بْنِ مَرْيَمَ عليه السلام: «يا عِيسَي، إنِّي لا أنْسَي مَنْ يَنْسانِي، فَكَيْفَ أنْسَي مَنْ يَذْكُرُنِي! أنا لا أبْخَلُ عَلَي مَنْ عَصانِي، فَكَيْفَ أبْخَلُ عَلَي مَنْ يُطِيعُنِي!»

(جامع الأخبار، ١، ١٨٠)

٦-٢- فِي ما أوْحَي اللهُ إلَي عِيسَي عليه السلام: «يا عِيسَي، ابن البِكْرِ البَتُولِ، إبْكِ عَلَي نَفْسِكَ بُكاءَ مَنْ قَدْ وَدَّعَ الأهْلَ وَقَلَي الدنْيا وَتَرَكَها لأهلِها وَصارَتْ رَغْبَتُهُ فِي ما عِنْدَ إلَهِهِ.»

(عدة الداعي، ١٦٩)

٦-٣- فِي ما أوْحِيَ إلَي عِيسَي عليه السلام: «وَلا يَغُرَّنَّكَ المُتَمَرِّدُ عَلَيَّ بِالعِصْيانِ: يأكُلُ رِزْقِي، وَيَعْبُدُ غَيْرِي، ثُمَّ يَدْعُونِي عِنْدَ الكَرْبِ فأجِيبُهُ، ثُمَّ يَرْجِعُ إلَي ما كانَ عَلَيْهِ. فَعَلَيَّ يَتَمَرَّدُ أمْ لِسَخَطِي يَتَعَرَّضُ؟ فَبِي حَلَفْتُ لآخُذَنَّهُ أخْذَةً لَيْسَ مِنْها مَنْجَي وَلا دُونِي مَلْجأ. أيْنَ يَهْرُبُ مِنْ سَمائِي وأرْضِي؟»

(عدة الداعي، ٢١٢)

٦-٤- حَدَّثَنا مُحَمَّدُ بْنُ إسْماعِيلَ، عَنْ مُحَمَّدِ بْنِ عَمْرِو الزَّيّاتِ، عَنْ عَبْدِ اللهِ بْنِ الوَلِيدِ، قالَ: «قالَ لِي أبُو عَبْدِ اللهِ عليه السلام: 'أيُّ شَيْءٍ يَقُولُ الشيعَةُ فِي عِيسَي وَمُوسَي وأمِيرِ المُؤْمِنِينَ عليه السلام؟' قُلْتُ: 'يَقُولُونَ: 'إنَّ عِيسَي

knew?' I said, 'Yes, but they do not prefer anyone over the possessors of determination (Ulū al-'Azm) among the apostles.' Abū 'Abdullah said, 'Argue with them by the Book of Allah.' I said, 'From which place of it?' He said, 'Allah, the Exalted, said to Moses, ﴾*We wrote in the tablets some knowledge of everything for him.*﴿ (7:145) He did not write everything for Moses. Allah, the Blessed and Exalted, said to Jesus, ﴾*I will explain for you something that you differ about.*﴿ (43:63) And Allah, the Exalted, said to Muḥammad, ﴾*We brought you as a witness over them and revealed the Book to you explaining clearly everything.*﴿ (16:89).

(*Baṣā'ir al-Darajāt*, 227)

6.5. It is reported that Sayyid said that among the hadiths from the Imams he saw, "Allah, the Exalted, ordered Adam to pray toward the West, and Noah to pray toward the East, and Abraham to gather them, and this is the Ka'abah. When Moses was commissioned, He ordered him to revive the religion of Adam. When Jesus was commissioned, He ordered him to revive the religion of Noah. When Muhammad was commissioned, He ordered him to revive the religion of Abraham."

(*Biḥār*, 81, 57, 9)

6.6. It is reported that Allah, the mighty and magnificent, revealed to Jesus the son of Mary, "Let him who considers Me slow in providence beware of My wrath, so that I open a door to this world against him."

(*Biḥār*, 100, 21, 16)

6.7. It is reported that one of the Imams, peace be with them, said, "The Messiah said: 'Allah, the blessed and exalted says, "My believing servant is saddened if I turn the world away from him, and that is what is most loved by Me, and that is what is most near to Me; and he is gladdened if I am open handed with him in this world, and that is what is most hated by Me, and that is what is furthest from Me.'"

(*Tuḥaf al-'Uqūl*, 1, 513)

وَمُوسَي أفْضَلُ مِنْ أميرِ المُؤمِنِينَ (ع).'» قالَ: «فقالَ: 'أيَزعَمُونَ أنَّ أمِيرَ المُؤْمِنِينَ عليه السلام قَدْ عَلِمَ ما عَلِمَ رَسُولُ اللهِ؟' قُلْتُ: 'نَعَمْ، ولَكِنْ لا يَقدِمُونَ عَلَي أولِي العَزْمِ مِنَ الرسُلِ أحَداً.' قالَ أبُو عَبْدِ اللهِ عليه السلام: 'فَخاصِمْهُمْ بِكِتابِ اللهِ.'» قالَ: «قُلْتُ: 'وَفِي أيِّ مَوْضِعٍ مِنْهُ أخاصِمُهُمْ؟' قالَ: 'قالَ اللهُ، تَعالَي، لِمُوسَي: ﴿كَتَبْنا لَهُ فِي الألْواحِ مِنْ كُلِّ شَيْءٍ عِلْماً﴾ إنَّهُ لَمْ يَكْتُبْ لِمُوسَي كُلَّ شَيْء. وَقالَ اللهُ، تَبارَكَ وَتَعالَي، لِعِيسَي: ﴿وَلِأُبَيِّنَ لَكُمْ بَعْضَ الذى تَخْتَلِفُونَ فِيهِ.﴾ وَقالَ اللهُ، تَعالَي، لِمُحَمَّدٍ صلى الله عليه وآله وسلم: ﴿وَجِئْنا بِكَ شَهِيداً عَلَي هَؤُلاءِ، وَنَزَّلْنا عَلَيْكَ الكِتابَ تِبْياناً لِكُلِّ شَيْء.﴾'»

(بصائر الدرجات، ٢٢٧)

٦-٥- فَلاحُ السّائِلِ، قالَ السَيِّدُ، ره: «رأيْتُ فِي الأحادِيثِ المأثُورَةِ: 'أنَّ اللهَ، تَعالَي، أمَرَ آدَمَ أنْ يُصَلِّي إلَي المَغْرِبِ، وَنُوحاً أنْ يُصَلِّي إلَي المَشْرِقِ، وإبْراهِيمَ عليه السلام يَجْمَعَهُما وَهِيَ الكَعْبَةُ. فَلَمّا بَعَثَ مُوسَي عليه السلام، أمَرَهُ أنْ يُحيِيَ دِينَ آدَمَ، وَلَمّا بَعَثَ عِيسَي عليه السلام، أمَرَهُ أنْ يُحيِيَ دِينَ نُوحٍ، وَلَمّا بَعَثَ مُحَمَّداً صلى الله عليه وآله وسلم، أمَرَهُ أنْ يُحيِيَ دِينَ إبْراهِيمَ.'»

(بحار الأنوار، ٨١، ٥٧، ٩)

٦-٦- رُوِيَ أنَّ اللهَ، عَزَّ وَجَلَّ، أوْحَي إلَي عِيسَي بْنِ مَرْيَمَ: «لِيَحْذَرْ الذى يَسْتَبْطِئُنِي فِي الرزْقِ أنْ أغْضَبَ، فَأفْتَحَ عَلَيْهِ باباً مِنَ الدنْيا.»

(بحار الأنوار، ١٠٠، ٢١، ١٦)

٦-٧- قالَ المَسِيحُ: «يَقُولُ اللهُ، تَبارَكَ وَتَعالَي: 'يَحْزَنُ عَبْدِيَ المُؤْمِنُ أنْ أصْرِفَ عَنْهُ الدنْيا، وَذَلِكَ أحَبُّ ما يَكُونُ إلَيَّ وأقْرَبُ ما يَكُونُ مِنِّي؛ وَيَفْرَحُ أنْ أوَسِّعَ عَلَيْهِ فِي الدنْيا، وَذَلِكَ أبْغَضُ ما يَكُونُ إلَيَّ وَأبْعَدُ ما يَكُونُ مِنِّي.'»

(تحف العقول، ١، ٥١٣)

6.8. The Apostle of Allah said, "...O Abū Dhar! Verily, Allah revealed to my brother Jesus, 'O Jesus! Do not love the world! Verily I do not love it. And love the otherworld, for it alone is the realm of the Ressurection.'"

(*Mustadrak al-Wasā'il*, 12, 39, 13456)

6.9. It is reported that Abū 'Abdullah [Imam Ṣādiq] said, "Jesus the son of Mary ascended clad in wool spun by Mary, woven by Mary and sewn by Mary. When he was brought up to heaven it was called, 'O Jesus! Cast off from yourself the finery of the world.'"

(*Biḥār*, 14, 338, 9)

6.10. I asked Abū 'Abdullah [Imam Ṣādiq] about the best thing by which the servant may draw near to his Lord and what is most beloved by Allah, the Almighty and Glorious. He said, "I know of nothing, after knowledge (*ma'rifah*), better than the ritual prayer (*ṣalah*). Do you not see that the good servant Jesus the son of Mary said: ﴾*And He enjoined on me the ritual prayer (ṣalāh) and the alms tax (zakāh) for as long as I live.*﴿" (19,31)

(*Kāfī*, 3, 264, 1)

6.11. Allah revealed to Jesus, "O Jesus! Humble your heart for me ... let me hear from you a sad sound."

(*Biḥār*, 90, 341)

٦-٨- عَنْ أبِي ذَرٍ، قالَ: «قالَ رَسُولُ اللهِ صلى الله عليه وآله وسلم: '... يا أبا ذَرٍ، إنَّ اللهَ، تَعالَي، أوْحَي إلَي أخِي عِيسَي: 'يا عِيسَي، لا تُحِبَّ الدنْيا، فإنِّي لَسْتُ أُحِبُّها؛ وأحِبَّ الآخِرَةَ، فإنَّما هِيَ دارُ المَعادِ.''»

(مستدرك الوسائل، ١٢، ٣٩، ١٣٤٥٦)

٦-٩- عَنْ ابن عُمَرَ، عَنْ بَعْضِ أصْحابِنا، عَنْ رَجُلٍ حَدَّثَهُ عَنْ أبِي عَبْدِ اللهِ عليه السلام, قالَ: «رُفِعَ عِيسَي بْنُ مَرْيَمَ عليه السلام بِمِدْرَعَةِ صُوفٍ مِنْ غَزْلِ مَرْيَمَ وَمِنْ نَسْجِ مَرْيَمَ وَمِنْ خِياطَةِ مَرْيَمَ. فَلمّا انْتَهَي إلَي السَماءِ, نُودِيَ: 'يا عِيسَي، ألْقِ عَنْكَ زِينَةَ الدنْيا.'»

(بحارالأنوار، ١٤، ٣٣٨، ٩)

٦-١٠- قالَ مُحَمَّدُ بْنُ يَعْقُوبَ الكُلَيْنِيُّ، رَحِمَهُ اللهُ: «حَدَّثَنِي مُحَمَّدُ بْنُ يَحْيَي، عَنْ أحْمَدَ بْنِ مُحَمَّدِ بْنِ عِيسَي، عَنِ الحَسَنِ بْنِ مَحْبُوبٍ، عَنْ مُعاوِيَةَ بْنِ وَهْبٍ، قالَ: 'سألتُ أبا عَبْدِ اللهِ عليه السلام عَنْ أفْضَلِ ما يَتَقَرَّبُ بِهِ العِبادُ إلَي رَبِّهِمْ، وأحَبِّ ذَلِكَ إلَي اللهِ، عَزَّ وَجَلَّ، ما هُوَ؟' فَقالَ: 'ما أعْلَمُ شَيْئًا، بَعْدَ المَعْرِفَةِ، أفْضَلَ مِنْ هَذِهِ الصَلاةِ. ألا تَرَى أنَّ العَبْدَ الصالِحَ، عِيسَي بن مَرْيَمَ عليه السلام، قالَ: ﴿وأوْصانِي بالصلاةِ والزَّكاةِ مادُمتُ حَيّاً.﴾'»

(الكافى، ٣، ٢٦٤، ١)

٦-١١- فِي ما أوْحَي اللهُ إلَي عِيسَي عليه السلام: «يا عِيسَي، أذِلَّ لِي قَلْبَكَ,... وأسْمِعْنِي مِنْكَ صَوْتاً حَزِيناً.»

(بحارالأنوار، ٩٠، ٣٤١)

6.12. Allah revealed to Jesus, "Be to the people like the earth below in meakness, like the flowing water in generosity, and like the sun and the moon in mercy, which shine on the good and sinner alike."

(*Biḥār*, 14, 3)

6.13. Allah revealed to Jesus, "O Jesus! Grant me the tears ofyour eyes, and the humility of your heart, and stand beside the tombs of the dead, and call to them aloud that you may be advised by them, and say, 'I will join you with those who join you.'"

(*Biḥār*, 79, 178)

6.14. A Christian catholicos (*jāthilīq*) met with Masab ibn Zubayr (an amir) and spoke words that angered him. He [Masab] raised a cane against him, then left him until his anger subsided. He [the catholicos] said, "If the amir permits me, I would report to him something revealed by Allah to Christ." He (Masab) turned his attention to him, and he (the catholicos) said, "Verily, Allah revealed to Christ, 'It is not fitting for a sultan to become angry, for he commands and is obeyed, and it is not fitting for him to be hastey, for nothing eludes him, and it is not fitting for him to be unjust, for injustice is repulsed by him.'" Then Masab became embarassed and was pleased with him.

(*Ādāb al-Nafs*, 2, 69)

6.15. Allah said to Jesus, "O Jesus! Verily I have granted unto you the poor and mercy upon them. You love them and they love you. They are satisfied with you as a leader and guide and you are satisfied with them as companions and followers. These are two of My characteristics. Whoever meets Me with these [characteristics] meets Me with the most pure of deeds which are most beloved by Me."

(*Biḥār*, 69, 55)

٦-١٢- أوْحَي اللهُ إلَي عِيسَيﷺ, أنْ: «كُنْ لِلنّاسِ فِي الحِلْمِ كالأرضِ تَحْتِهِمْ, وَفِي السَخاءِ كالماءِ الجارِي, وَفِي الرحْمَةِ كالشمْسِ والقمَرِ, فانَّهُما يَطّلعانِ عَلَي البَرِّ والفاجِرِ.»

(بحار الأنوار، ١٤، ٣)

٦-١٣- عَنْ أبِي بَصِيرٍ، عَنْ أبِي عَبْدِ اللهِ, جَعْفَرِ بْنِ مُحَمَّدٍﷺ, قالَ: «أوْحَي اللهُ تَعالَي إلَي عِيسَي بْنِ مَرْيَمَﷺ: 'يا عِيسَي، هَبْ لِي مِنْ عَيْنِكَ الدمُوعَ, وَمِنْ قَلْبِكَ الخُشُوعَ, واكْحُلْ عَيْنَكَ بِمِيلِ الحُزْنِ إذا ضَحِكَ البَطّالونَ, وَقُمْ عَلَي قُبُورِ الأمواتِ, فَنادِهِمْ بالصوْتِ الرفِيعِ, لَعَلّكَ تأخُذُ مَوْعِظَتَكَ مِنْهُمْ, وَقُلْ: 'إنِّي لاحِقٌ بهِمْ فِي اللاحِقِينَ.''»

(بحار الأنوار، ٧٩، ١٧٨)

٦-١٤- دَخَلَ جاثَلِيقُ النَصارَي عَلَي مَصْعَبِ بْنِ الزُّبَيْرِ, فَكَلَّمَهُ لِكَلامٍ أغْضَبَهُ, فَعَلاهُ بِقَضِيبٍ؛ فَتَرَكَهُ حَتَّي سَكَنَ غَضَبُهُ, ثُمَّ قالَ: «إنْ أذِنَ الأمِيرُ, أخْبَرْتُهُ بِما أنْزَلَ اللهُ عَلَي المَسِيحِ.» فأصْغَي إلَيْهِ. فَقالَ: «إنَّ اللهَ أنْزَلَ عَلَي المَسِيحِ: 'إنَّهُ لا يَنْبَغِي لِلسُّلْطانِ أنْ يَغْضَبَ, فانَّهُ إنَّما يأمُرُ فَيُطاعُ؛ وَلايَنْبَغِي أنْ يَعْجَلَ, فَلَنْ يَفُوتَهُ شَيءٌ؛ وَلا يَنْبَغِي أنْ يَظْلِمَ, فإنّما بِهِ يُدْفَعُ الظُلْمُ.'» فاسْتَحْيا مَصْعَبٌ وَتَرَضاهُ.

(آداب النفس، ٢، ٦٩)

٦-١٥- قالَ اللهُ، عَزَّ وَجَلَّ، لِعِيسَيﷺ: «إنِّي وَهَبْتُ لَكَ المَساكِينَ وَرَحْمَتَهُمْ, تُحِبُّهُمْ وَيُحِبُّونَكَ, يَرْضَوْنَ بِكَ إماماً وَقائِداً, وَتَرْضَي بِهِمْ صَحابَةً وَتَبعاً؛ وَهُما خُلُقانِ, مَنْ لَقِيَنِي بِهِما لَقِيَنِي بِأزْكَي الأعْمالِ وأحَبِّها إلَيَّ.»

(بحار الأنوار، ٦٩، ٥٥)

6.16. Verily Allah revealed to Jesus, "Then indeed be warned! Otherwise you should be ashamed before Me to warn [preach to] the people."

(*Irshād al-Qulūb*, 1, 112)

6.17. It is reported that Nūf al-Bukālī said, "I spent a night with the Commander of the Faithful, 'Alī ibn Abū Ṭālib. I saw that he often left his room to go outside and look at the sky. Once when he came back in, as usual, he said to me, 'Are you asleep or awake?' I said, 'I am indeed awake, O Commander of the Faithful! From the beginning of the night I have been watching you to see what you are doing.' He said, 'O Nūf! Blessed are the ascetics in this world, those who yearn for the other world, the people who spread Allah's earth beneath them [to sleep on], who lean against its dust, whose motto is His book, whose maxim is supplicating Him, whose perfume is water, and who take the world on loan in the way of Christ. Verily, Allah, the Exalted, revealed to Jesus, "O Jesus! Keep to the first way, keep to the manner of the messengers, say to your people, O brother of the warners, 'Do not enter any of My houses except with pure hearts, clean hands and lowered eyes. I will not hear the prayer of any who supplicate Me if any of My servants is oppressed by him. And I will not answer the prayer of any who has not fulfilled any of My rights over him.'"'"

(*Biḥār*, 67, 316)

6.18. Allah revealed to Jesus, "Say to the Children of Israel, 'Do not enter any of my houses unless with lowered eyes and clean hands.' And inform them that verily, I will not answer the prayer of any of them while any of my creation is oppressed by them..."

(*Biḥār*, 90, 373)

٦-١٦- رُوِىَ أنَّ اللهَ أوْحَي إلَي عِيسَي عليه السلام: «فإنِ اتَّعظْتَ, وإلّا, فاستَحْىِ مِنِّى أنْ تَعِظَ الناسَ.»
(إرشاد القلوب، ١، ١١٢)

٦-١٧- المَراغِي، عَنِ الحُسَيْنِ بْنِ مُحَمَّدٍ، عَنْ جعْفَرِ بْنِ عَبْدِ اللهِ العَلَوِىِّ، عَنْ يَحْيَي بْنِ هاشِمٍ الغَسّانِىِّ، عَنْ أبِى عاصِمٍ النَبِيلِ، عَنْ سُفْيانِ، عَنْ أبِى إسْحاقَ، عَنْ عَلْقَمَةِ بْنِ قَيْسٍ، عَنْ نَوْفِ البُكالِى, قالَ: «بُتُّ لَيْلَةً عِنْدَ أمِيرِ المُؤْمِنِينَ, عَلِىِّ بْنِ أبِى طالِبٍ عليه السلام, فرأيْتُهُ يَكْثُرُ الاخْتِلافُ مِنْ مَنْزِلِهِ, ويَنْظُرُ إلَي السماءِ.» قالَ: «فدَخَلَ كبَعْضِ ما كانَ يَدْخُلُ, قالَ: 'أنائِمٌ أنتَ أمْ رامِقٌ؟' فقُلْتُ: 'بَلْ رامِقٌ, يا أمِيرَ المُؤْمِنِينَ. ما زِلْتُ أرْمُقُكَ مُنْذُ اللَيْلَةِ بِعَيْنِي, وانْظُرُ ما تَصْنَعُ.' فقالَ: 'يا نَوْفُ, طُوبَي لِلزّاهِدِينَ فِى الدنْيا, الراغِبِينَ فِى الآخِرَةِ, قَوْمٌ يَتَّخِذُونَ أرْضَ اللهِ بِساطاً, وتُرابَهُ وِساداً, وكِتابَهُ شِعاراً, ودُعاءَهُ دِثاراً, ومَاءَهُ طِيْباً, يَقْرِضُونَ الدنْيا قَرْضاً عَلَي مِنْهاجِ المَسِيحِ عليه السلام. إنَّ اللهَ تَعالَي أوْحَي إلَي عِيسَي عليه السلام: 'يا عِيسَي، عَلَيْكَ بِالمِنْهاجِ الأوَّلِ, تَلْحَقُ مَلاحِقَ المُرْسَلِينَ. قُلْ لِقَوْمِكَ, يا أخا المُنْذِرِينَ: 'أنْ لا تَدْخُلُوا بَيْتاً مِنْ بُيُوتِى إلّا بِقُلُوبٍ طاهِرَةٍ, وأيْدٍ نَقِيَّةٍ, وأبْصارٍ خاشِعَةٍ. فإنِّى لا أسْمَعُ مِنْ داعٍ دُعاءَهُ, ولِأحد مِنْ عِبادِى عِنْدَهُ مَظْلِمَةٌ, ولا أسْتَجِيبُ لَهُ دَعْوَةً, ولِىَ قِبَلَهُ حَقٌّ لَمْ يَرُدُّهُ إلَىَّ.'''»
(بحارالأنوار، ٦٧، ٣١٦)

٦-١٨- عَنْ أمِيرِ المُؤْمِنِينَ عليه السلام قالَ: «أوْحَي اللهُ إلَي عِيسَي عليه السلام: 'قُلْ لِبَنِى إسْرائِيلَ: 'لا تَدْخُلُوا بَيْتاً مِنْ بُيُوتِى إلّا بِأبْصارٍ خاشِعَةٍ, وقُلُوبٍ طاهِرَةٍ, وأيْدٍ نَقِيَّةٍ. وأخْبِرْهُمْ إنِّى لا أسْتَجِيبُ لِأحد مِنْهُمْ دَعْوَةً, ولِأحَدٍ مِنْ خَلْقِى عَلَيْهِ مَظْلِمَةٌ.'' وفِى الوَحْىِ القَدِيمِ: 'لا تَمَلَّ مِنَ الدعاءِ, فإنِّى لا أمِلُّ مِنَ الإجابَةِ.'»
(بحارالأنوار، ٩٠، ٣٧٣)

6.19. Allah said to Jesus, "O Jesus! Your tongue must be a single tongue in secret and in public, and likewise your heart. Verily, I warn you of your self, and I suffice as the All-aware.[1] It is not proper for there to be two tongues in a single mouth, nor two swords in a single scabbard, nor two hearts in a single breast, and likewise two minds."

(*Kāfī*, 2, 343, 3)

6.20. Allah, the Great and Almighty, said to Jesus, "O Jesus! Remember me within yourself and I will remember you within myself, and remember me publicly and I will remember you publicly in a public better than that of the people. O Jesus! Soften your heart for me and remember me much in solitude, and know that my pleasure is in your shuddering [literally wagging the tail, taken as an indication of fear or being driven in an animal] for me, and be alive in that and be not dead."

(*Kāfī*, 2, 502, 3)

6.21. Allah the Supreme revealed to Jesus, "When I give you a blessing, receive it with humility, [and] I will complete it for you."

(*Biḥār*, 14, 328, 56)

6.22. Among the words revealed to Jesus is, "O Jesus! Humble yourself to those who do good, participate with them in it, be witness over them and say to the unjust of the children of Israel, 'O companians of evil and participants in it! If you do not accept the prohibition, I will transform you into monkeys and swine.'"
(*Kāfī*, 8, 138, 103)

6.23. It is reported in a long tradition that Muḥammad al-Munkadir narrated from his father that he said, "When al-Sayyid and al-'Āqib, the two bishops of Najrān, with seventy persons arrived mounted [at Madina], they came to the Prophet and I was with them... Al-'Āqib said [to his companion,]'Did you not read the fourth al-Miṣbāḥ from which were revealed to Christ, 'Say to the children of Jerusalem, 'How

---

[1] Cf. Qur'ān 17:17; 25:58.

٦-١٩- عَلِيُّ بْنُ إبْراهِيمَ، عَنْ أبِيهِ، عَنْ عَلِيِّ بْنِ أسْباطٍ، عَنْ عَبْدِ الرحْمَنِ بْنِ حمّادٍ، رَفَعَهُ، قالَ: «قالَ اللهُ، تَبارَكَ وَتَعالَي، لِعيسَي بن مَريَمَ عليه السلام: 'يا عِيسَي، لِيَكُنْ لِسانُكَ فِى السرِّ والعَلانِيَةِ لِساناً واحِداً، وَكَذلِكَ قَلْبُكَ. إنّى أحَذِّرُكَ نَفْسكَ، وَكَفَي بى خَبيراً. لا يَصْلُحُ لِسانانِ فِى فَمٍ واحِدٍ، وَلا سَيْفانِ فِى غِمْدٍ واحِدٍ، وَلا قَلْبانِ فِى صَدْرٍ واحِدٍ، وَكَذَلِكَ الأذْهانُ.'»

(الكافى، ٢، ٣٤٣، ٣)

٦-٢٠- عِدَّةٌ مِنْ أصْحابِنا، عَنْ أحْمَدَ بْنِ مُحَمَّدِ بْنِ خالِدٍ، عَنِ ابن فَضّالٍ، رَفَعَهُ، قالَ: «قالَ اللهُ، عَزَّ وَجَلَّ، لِعِيسَي عليه السلام: 'يا عِيسَي، اذْكُرْنِى فِى نَفْسِكَ، أذْكُرْكَ فِى نَفْسِي؛ واذْكُرْنِى فِى مَلَئِكَ، أذْكُرْكَ فِى مَلاٍ خَيْرٍ مِنْ مَلاٍ الآدَمِيِّينَ. يا عِيسَي، ألِنْ لِى قَلْبَكَ، وأكْثِرْ ذِكْرى فِى الخَلَواتِ، واعْلَمْ أنَّ سُرُورى أنْ تُبَصْبِصَ إلَيَّ، وَكُنْ فِى ذَلِكَ حَيّاً وَلا تَكُنْ مَيِّتاً.'»

(الكافى، ٢، ٥٠٢، ٣)

٦-٢١- أوْحَي اللهُ تَعالَي إلَي عِيسَي: «إذا أنْعَمْتُ عَلَيْكَ بِنِعْمَةٍ, فاسْتَقْبِلْها بِالاِسْتِكانَةِ, أتَمِّمْها عَلَيْكَ.»

(بحارالأنوار، ١٤، ٣٢٨، ٥٦)

٦-٢٢- «يا عِيسَى، ذِلَّ لأهْلِ الحَسَنَةِ، وَشارِكْهُمْ فِيها، وَكُنْ عَلَيْهِمْ شَهيداً. وَقُلْ لِظَلَمَةِ بَنِى إسْرائِيلَ: 'يا أخْدانَ السوْءِ والجُلَساءَ عَلَيْهِ، إنْ لَمْ تَنْتَهُوا أمْسَخُكُمْ قِرَدَةً وَخَنازِيرَ.'»

(الكافى، ٨، ١٣٨، ١٠٣)

٦-٢٣- مُحَمَّدُ بْنُ المُنْكَدِرِ، عَنْ أبِيهِ, قالَ: «لَمّا قَدِمَ السَيِّدُ والعاقِبُ, أسْقُفا نَجْرانَ, فِى سَبْعِينَ, راكِباً, وَفْداً عَلَي النَبِيِّ صلى الله عليه وآله وسلم, كُنْتُ مَعَهُمْ.... قالَ

ignorant you are! You perfume yourselves with perfume, to be perfumed with the people of this world and with your people, but your interiors are dead corpses to Me...'"

(*Biḥār*, 21, 350, 20)

6.24. [Imam] Ja'far reported that his father said, "Najashi the king of Habashah [Ethiopia] sent for Ja'far the son of Abī Ṭālib and his companions. Then they arrived before him while he was sitting in the dust in his house with worn garments.... Ja'far ibn Abī Ṭālib said to him, "O pious king! What is the matter with me, that I see you sitting in the dust in these worn garments?" He said, "O Ja'far! We find among that which has been revealed by Allah, the Supreme, to Jesus is, 'Verily, among the rights of Allah over His servants is that they should make themselves humble before Allah when He makes them blessed.'[1] So, when Allah showed favor by His prophet Muhammad, I showed this humility to Allah." He [Imam Ja'far] said, "When that news reached the Prophet, he said to his companions, 'Verily, giving alms increases abundance, so give alms and Allah will have mercy on you, and humility increases one's elevation, so be humble and Allah will elevate, and forgiveness increases glory, so forgive and Allah will grant you glory.'"

(*Biḥār*, 18, 418)

6.25. Verily Jesus passed by a grave, and he saw the angels of punishment chastise a dead person. When Jesus had finished his business and passed by the grave [again], he saw the angels of mercy. Levels of light were with them. He was surprised at that, and called upon Allah about this. Allah revealed to him, "O Jesus! This servant was a sinner, and left his wife when she was pregnant. Then

---

[1] According to another report by the same narrator: "Verily Jesus the son of Mary became more humble whenever God's blessings were granted him."

[العاقِبُ]: 'أما تَقرا المِصْباحَ الرابعَ مِنَ الوَحْىِ إلي المَسِيحِ, أنْ: 'قُلْ لِبَنِى إسْرائِيلَ: 'ما أجْهَلَكُمْ! تُطَيِّبُونَ بِالطِّيبِ, لِتُطَيِّبُوا بِهِ فِى الدنْيا عِنْدَ أهْلِها وأهْلِكُمْ، وأجْوافُكُمْ عِنْدِى جِيَفُ المَيْتَةِ...'''»

(بحار الأنوار، ٢١، ٣٥٠، ٢٠)

٦-٢٤- المُفِيدُ، عَنْ أحْمَدَ بْنِ الحُسَيْنِ بْنِ أُسامَةٍ، عَنْ عُبَيْدِ اللهِ بْنِ مُحَمَّدٍ الواسِطِي، عَنْ أبِى جَعْفَرِ مُحَمَّدِ بْنِ يَحْيَي، عَنْ هارُونِ بْنِ مُسْلِمٍ، عَنْ مَسْعَدَةِ بْنِ صَدَقَةٍ، عَنْ جَعْفَرٍ، عَنْ أبِيهِ عليه السلام, أنَّهُ قالَ: «أرْسَلَ النَجاشِيُّ, مَلِكُ الحَبَشَةِ إلي جَعْفَرِ بْنِ أبِى طالِبٍ وأصحابِهِ, فَدَخَلُوا عَلَيْهِ, وَهُوَ فِى بَيْتٍ لَهُ, جالِسٌ عَلي التَرابِ, وَعَلَيْهِ خُلُقانُ الثِّيابِ.... فَقالَ لَهُ جَعْفَرٌ: 'أيُّها المَلِكُ الصالِحُ! ما لِى أراكَ جالِساً عَلي التَرابِ, وَعَلَيْكَ هَذِهِ الخُلُقانُ؟' فَقالَ: 'يا جَعْفَرُ, إنّا نَجِدُ فِى ما أُنْزِلَ عَلي عِيسَي, صَلَّي اللهُ عَلَيْهِ, 'أنَّ مِنْ حَقِّ اللهِ عَلي عِبادِهِ, أنْ يُحْدِثُوا لِلهِ تَواضُعاً, عِنْدَ ما يُحْدِثُ لَهُمْ مِن نِعْمَةٍ.'[1] فَلَمّا أحْدَثَ اللهُ تَعالي لِى نِعْمَةَ بِنَبِيِّهِ مُحَمَّدٍ صلى الله عليه وآله وسلم, أحْدَثْتُ لِلهِ هَذا التَواضُعَ.'» قالَ: «فَلَمّا بَلَغَ النَبِىَّ صلى الله عليه وآله وسلم ذَلِكَ, قالَ لِأصحابِهِ: 'إنَّ الصَدَقَةَ تَزِيدُ صاحِبَها كِثْرَةً, فَتَصَدَّقُوا, يَرْحَمْكُمُ اللهُ؛ وإنَّ التَواضُعَ يَزِيدُ صاحِبَهُ رِفْعَةً, فَتَواضَعُوا, يَرْفَعْكُمُ اللهُ؛ وإنَّ العَفْوَ يَزِيدُ صاحِبَهُ عِزاً, فاعْفُوا, يُعِزُّكُمُ اللهُ.'»

(بحارالأنوار، ١٨، ٤١٨)

٦-٢٥- «إنَّ عِيسَي عليه السلام مَرَّ بِقَبْرٍ، فَرأي مَلائِكَةَ العَذابِ، يُعَذِّبُونَ مَيِّتاً؛ فَلَمّا انْصَرَفَ مِنْ حاجَتِهِ وَمَرَّ بِالقَبْرِ، فَرأي مَلائِكَةَ الرحْمَةِ، مَعَهُمْ أطْباقٌ مِنْ نُورٍ. فَتَعَجَّبَ مِنْ ذَلِكَ وَدَعا اللهَ مِنْ هَذِهِ، فأوْحَي اللهُ إلَيْهِ: 'يا عِيسَي،

---

[1] فَقالَ: 'إنَّ عيسَي بْنَ مَرْيَمَ كانَ إذا حَدَثَتْ لَهُ نِعْمَةٌ, ازْدادَ بِها تَواضُعاً.' (شرح نهج البلاغة، ١٤، ١٥١)

she bore and raised his child. When the child got older, she gave him to the charge of the scribes. They instructed him to say, 'In the Name of Allah, the Merciful, the Compassionate,' so I was ashamed to chastise My servant with My fire in the bowels of the earth while his child was remembering my name on the surface of the earth."

(*Majmū'ah al-Akhbār fī Nafā'is al-Āthār,* 146)

6.26. The Apostle of Allah said, "Allah, the Exalted, may His greatness be glorified, revealed to Jesus, 'Make a serious effort regarding My affairs, and do not give up. I made you without a male as a sign for the worlds. Tell the people to believe in Me and in My Apostle, the unlettered, whose ancestors are blessed, and she is with your mother in heaven. Ṭūbā[1] is for he who hears his word is contemporary with him.' Jesus said, 'O my Lord! What is Ṭūbā?' He said, 'It is a tree in heaven under which is a fountain from which those who drink will never again thirst.' Jesus said, 'Quench me with a drink of it.' He said, 'No, Jesus. It is forbidden to the prophets until that prophet drinks from it. And that heaven is forbidden to all communities until the community of that prophet enters it.'"

(*Biḥār*, 14, 323, 33)

6.27. Imam Ja'far Ṣādiq said, "Among the things which Allah, theBlessed and Supreme, exhorted Jesus was, 'O Jesus! I am your Lord, and the Lord of your fathers. My Name is the One, and I am unique and alone in the creation of all things. All things are my work, and all My creations shall return to Me.'"

(*Biḥār*, 14, 289, 13)

[1] The phrase *ṭūba 'alay* is translated as "Blessed are those," or "Happy are those," in the Arabic version of the beatitudes.

كانَ هَذا العَبْدُ عاصِياً، وكانَ قدْ تَرَكَ امْرأتَهُ حُبْلي، فوَلَدتْ وَرَبَتْ وَلَدَهُ حتَّي كَبُرَ؛ فَسَلَّمَتْهُ إلي الكُتّابِ، فلَقَّنَهُ المُعلِّمُ: 'بِسمِ اللهِ الرحمنِ الرحيمِ،' فاستَحْيَيْتُ مِنْ عَبْدِى أنْ أعذِّبَهُ بِنارِى فِى بَطْنِ الأرضِ، ووَلَدُهُ يَذكُرُ اسْمِى عَلي ظَهْرِ الأرضِ.'»

(مجموعة الأخبار في نفائس الآثار، ١٤٦)

٦-٢٦- بِالإسنادِ إلي الصدُوقِ، بِإسْنادِهِ إلي ابن أورمةَ، عَنْ عِيسَي بْنِ العبّاسِ، عَنْ مُحمَّدِ بْنِ عَبْدِ الكَرِيمِ التَقْلِيسِيِّ، عَنْ عَبْدِ المُؤْمِنِ بْنِ مَحُمَّدٍ، رَفَعهُ، قالَ: «قالَ رَسُولُ اللهِ صلى الله عليه وآله وسلم: 'أوْحَي اللهُ، تَعالي، جَلَّتْ عَظمَتُهُ، إلي عِيسَي عليه السلام: 'جُدَّ فِى أمْرِي، وَلا تَتْرُكْ. إنِّى خَلَقتُكَ مِنْ غَيْرِ فَحْلٍ آيَةً لِلْعالَمِينَ. أخْبِرْهُمْ آمِنُوا بِى وَبِرَسُولِى النَبِىِّ الأمِّيِّ، نَسْلُهُ مِنْ مُبارَكَةٍ، وَهِيَ مَعَ أمِّكَ فِى الجَنَّةِ. طُوبَي لِمَنْ سَمِعَ كَلامَهُ وأدْرَكَ زَمانَهُ وَشَهِدَ أيّامَهُ.' قالَ عِيسَي: 'يا رَبِّ، وَماطُوبَي؟' قالَ: 'شَجَرَةٌ فِى الجَنَّةِ، تَحْتَها عَيْنٌ، مَنْ شَرِبَ مِنْها شَرْبَةً لَمْ يَظْمأ بَعْدَها أبَداً.' قالَ عِيسَي: 'يا رَبِّ، اسْقِنِى مِنْها شَرْبَةً.' قالَ: 'كَلاَّ، يا عِيسَي. إنَّ تِلْكَ العَيْنَ مُحَرَّمَةٌ عَلي الأنبياءِ، حَتَّي يَشْرَبَها ذَلِكَ النَبِىُّ؛ وَتِلْكَ الجَنَّةُ مُحَرَّمَةٌ عَلي الأمَمِ، حَتَّي يَدْخُلَها أمَّةُ ذَلِكَ النَبِىِّ.''»

(بحارالأنوار، ١٤، ٣٢٣، ٣٣)

٦-٢٧- ابن المُتَوَكِّلِ، عَنِ الحِمْيَرِىّ، عَنْ ابن أبِى الخَطّابِ، عَنْ ابن أسْباطٍ، عَنْ عَلِيِّ بْنِ أبِى حَمْزَةِ، عَنْ أبِى بَصِيرٍ، عَنْ أبِى عَبْدِ اللهِ الصادِقِ، جَعْفَرِ بْنِ مُحَمَّدٍ عليه السلام، قالَ: «كانَ فِى ما وَعَظَ اللهُ، تَبارَكَ وَتَعالَي، بِهِ عِيسَي بْنَ مَرْيَمَ عليه السلام، أنْ قالَ لَهُ: 'يا عِيسَي، أنا رَبُّكَ وَرَبُّ آبائِكَ. اسْمِى واحِدٌ، وأنا الأحد المُتَفَرِّدُ بِخَلْقِ كُلِّ شَىْء، وَكُلُّ شَىْء مِنْ صُنْعِى، وَكُلُّ خَلْقِى إلَيَّ راجِعُونَ.'»

(بحارالأنوار، ١٤، ٢٨٩، ١٣)

6.28. 'Alī ibn Asbāṭ has reported from the Household of the Prophet, peace be with them, this from among the admonitions of Allah, the Exalted and Sublime, given to Jesus:

"O Jesus! I am your Lord and the Lord of your father. My name is One and I am the One, the Unique in having created everything. All things have been made by Me and all return to Me.

O Jesus! You are the Messiah by My command, and you create from clay what has a shape like a bird by My permission, and you revive the dead by My word, so be one who beseeches Me and one who fears Me, and apart from Me seek no sanctuary except toward Me.

O Jesus! I charged you in tenderness to you though mercy until you became worthy of my friendship (wilāyah) because you sought My pleasure and so you were blessed when old and you were blessed when young wherever you were. I bear witness that you are My servant, son of my handmaid. Let Me into your soul as your foremost regard, and make the remembrance of Me the means to your return, and draw near to Me through the supererogatory deeds. And trust in Me that I may suffice for you and do not trust in any other than Me so that I abandon you.

O Jesus! Be patient with calamities and be content with the decree. Be in such a way that I will be happy with you, because what pleases Me is obedience without sin.

O Jesus! Enliven the remembrance of Me by your tongue, and let there be love for Me in your heart.

O Jesus! Wake up at the hours of neglecting and give your decisions for my sake with subtle wisdom.

O Jesus! Be one who beseeches and fears Me, and let your heart die of awe of Me.

O Jesus! Be vigilant through the night seeking My pleasure, and thirst through your day for the day when you are in need of Me.

O Jesus! Compete with others by doing good as hard as you can so that you will be well known for good wherever you go.

٦-٢٨ - عَلِيُّ بْنُ إِبْراهِيمَ، عَنْ أَبِيهِ، عَنْ عَلِيِّ بْنِ أَسْباطٍ، عَنْهُمْﵙ، قالَ: «فِى ما وَعَظَ اللهُ، عَزَّ وَجَلَّ، بِهِ عِيسَى﵇:

'يا عِيسَي، أَنا رَبُّكَ وَرَبُّ آبائِكَ، اسْمِى واحِدٌ، وانا الأَحَدُ المُتَفَرِّدُ بِخَلْقِ كُلِّ شَىْءٍ، وَكُلُّ شَىْءٍ مِنْ صُنْعِى، وَكُلٌّ إِلَىَّ راجِعُونَ.

يا عِيسَي، أَنْتَ المَسِيحُ بِأَمْرِى، وأَنْتَ تَخْلُقُ مِنَ الطِّينِ كَهَيْئَةِ الطَّيْرِ بِإِذْنِى، وأَنْتَ تُحْيى المَوْتَي بِكَلامِى؛ فَكُنْ إِلَىَّ راغِباً وَمِنِّى راهِباً، وَلَنْ تَجِدَ مِنِّى مَلْجَأً إِلّا إِلَىَّ.

يا عِيسَي، أُوصِيكَ وَصِيَّةَ المُتَحَنِّنِ عَلَيْكَ بِالرَّحْمَةِ، حَتَّي حَقَّتْ لَكَ مِنِّى الوَلايَةُ بِتَحَرِّيكَ مِنِّى المَسَرَّةَ؛ فَبُورِكْتَ كَبِيراً وَبُورِكْتَ صَغِيراً حَيْثُ ما كُنْتَ. أَشْهَدُ أَنَّكَ عَبْدِى، ابنِ أَمَتِى، أَنْزِلْنِى مِنْ نَفْسِكَ كَهَمِّكَ، واجْعَلْ ذِكْرِى لِمَعادِكَ، وَتَقَرَّبْ إِلَىَّ بِالنَّوافِلِ، وَتَوَكَّلْ عَلَىَّ أَكْفِكَ، وَلا تَوَكَّلْ عَلِي غَيْرِى، فَآخُذَ لَكَ.

يا عِيسَي، اصْبِرْ عَلِي البَلاءِ وارْضَ بِالقَضاءِ، وَكُنْ كَمَسَرَّتِى فِيكَ، فَإِنَّ مَسَرَّتِى أَنْ أُطاعَ فَلا أُعْصَي.

يا عِيسَي، أَحْىِ ذِكْرِى بِلِسانِكَ، وَلْيَكُنْ وُدِّى فِى قَلْبِكَ.

يا عِيسَي، تَيَقَّظْ فِى ساعاتِ الغَفْلَةِ، واحْكُمْ لِى لَطِيفَ الحِكْمَةِ.

يا عِيسَي، كُنْ راغِباً راهِباً، وأَمِتْ قَلْبَكَ بِالخَشْيَةِ.

يا عِيسَي، راعِ اللَّيْلَ لِتَحَرِّى مَسَرَّتِى، واظْمِئْ نَهارَكَ لِيَوْمِ حاجَتِكَ عِنْدِى.

يا عِيسَي، نافِسْ فِى الخَيْرِ جُهْدَكَ، تُعْرَفْ بِالخَيْرِ حَيْثُما تَوَجَّهْتَ.

O Jesus! Judge among my servants though My counsel and establish My justice for I have brought down to you a cure for breasts against satanic disease.

O Jesus! Do not associate with anyone infatuated [with the world].

O Jesus! Indeed I say, no creature believed in Me without becoming humble to Me nor became humble to Me without seeking My requittal; so bear witness that such a one is secure from My punishment unless he changes or alters my norm (sunnah).

O Jesus, son of the Virgin Lady! Weep for yourself with the weeping of one who bade goodbye to his home, deserted this world and left it to the worldly so that he became one beseeching what is with his God.

O Jesus! In addition to this, be someone who speaks mildly, who offers salaams vigorously, and who keeps awake while the eyes of the pious sleep in order to beware of the Day of the Return and severe earthquakes and the terrors of the Resurrection Day when neither household nor wealth nor offspring shall profit one.

O Jesus! Adorn your eyes with a touch of sadness when the vain (i.e., foolish) laugh.

O Jesus! Be one of those who humble themselves and are patient, for if you attain that of which the patient have been promised, you are most fortunate.

O Jesus! Day by day abandon this world and taste that which has lost its taste, for truly I tell you; you live to an appointed hour and an appointed day, so pass through this world by what is sufficient for your survival and be content with coarse food and rough dress after you have seen what your destiny is to be, and what you have spent and wasted is recorded.

O Jesus! You are responsible, so be merciful toward the weak, just as I am merciful toward you, and do not be cruel to the orphan.

O Jesus! Weep over yourself in seclusion; let your feet regularly make for the places where prayers are performed, and let me hear the sweetest melody of the words you say in remembrance of Me. Verily, what I have done for you is good.

يا عِيسَي، أحْكُمْ فِي عِبادِي بِنُصْحِي، وَقُمْ فِيهِمْ بِعَدْلِي، فَقَدْ أنْزَلْتُ عَلَيْكَ شِفاءً لِما فِي الصدُورِ مِنْ مَرَضِ الشيْطانِ.

يا عِيسَي، لا تَكُنْ جَلِيساً لِكُلِّ مَفْتُونٍ.

يا عِيسَي، حَقاً أقولُ: 'ما آمَنَتْ بِي خَلِيقَةٌ إلّا خَشَعَتْ لِي، وَلا خَشَعَتْ لِي إلّا رَجَتْ ثَوابِي؛ فاشْهَدُ أنَّها آمِنَةٌ مِنْ عِقابِي، ما لَمْ تُبَدِّلْ أوْ تُغَيِّرْ سُنَّتِي.'

يا عِيسَي، ابن البِكْرِ البَتُولِ ابْكِ عَلَي نَفْسِكَ بُكاءَ مَنْ وَدَّعَ الأهْلَ وَقَلي الدنْيا وَتَرَكَها لِأهْلِها، وَصارَتْ رَغْبَتُهُ فِي ما عِنْدَ إلهِهِ.

يا عِيسَي، كُنْ مَعَ ذَلِكَ تُلِينُ الكَلامَ وَتُفْشِي السَلامَ، يَقْظانَ إذا نامَتْ عُيُونُ الأبرارِ، حَذَراً لِلْمَعادِ والزَّلازِلِ الشِدادِ وأهْوالِ يَوْمِ القِيامَةِ، حَيْثُ لا يَنْفَعُ أهْلٌ وَلا وَلَدٌ وَلا مالٌ.

يا عِيسَي، أكْحُلْ عَيْنَكَ بِمِيلِ الحُزْنِ، إذا ضَحِكَ البَطّالُونَ.

يا عِيسَي، كُنْ خاشِعاً صابِراً؛ فَطُوبَي لَكَ إنْ نالَكَ ما وُعِدَ الصابِرُونَ.

يا عِيسَي، رُحْ مِنَ الدنْيا يَوْماً فَيَوْماً، وَذُقْ لِما قَدْ ذَهَبَ طَعْمُهُ. فَحَقاً أقُولُ: 'ما أنتَ إلّا بِساعَتِكَ وَيَوْمِكَ؛ فَرُحْ مِنَ الدنْيا بِبُلْغَةٍ، وَلْيَكْفِكَ الخَشِنُ الجَشِبُ؛ فَقَدْ رأيْتَ إلي ما تَصِيرُ وَمَكْتُوبٌ ما أخَذْتَ وَكَيْفَ أتْلَفْتَ.'

يا عِيسَي، إنَّكَ مَسْئُولٌ، فارْحَمِ الضَّعِيفَ كَرَحْمَتِي إيّاكَ، وَلا تَقْهَرْ اليَتِيمَ.

يا عِيسَي، ابْكِ عَلَى نَفْسِكَ فِي الخَلَواتِ، وانْقُلْ قَدَمَيْكَ إلي مَواقِيتِ الصَلَواتِ، وأسْمِعْنِي لَذاذَةَ نُطْقِكَ بِذِكْرِي، فإنَّ صَنِيعِي إلَيْكَ حَسَنٌ.

O Jesus! How many nations I have caused to perish for the sins they had committed and from which I have preserved you.

"O Jesus! Minister to the weak and turn your weary eyes toward the sky and ask your needs from Me, for I am near to you, and do not call upon Me except as one who pleads with Me and whose concern is a single concern. Then, when you call on Me in this way, I will answer you.

"O Jesus! I am not content that the world should be the reward of those who were near you nor as a chastisement for those you would punish.

O Jesus! You perish and I remain, and your provision is from Me. The term appointed for you is with Me, and to Me is your return and with Me is your reckoning. So ask from me and do not ask from any other, so that your supplication may be suitable and I will answer it.

O Jesus! How numerous are the people and how few is the number of the patient. The trees are numerous, but those that are good among them are few. Do not be deceived by the beauty of a tree until you taste its fruit.

O Jesus! Do not be deceived by he who rebels against me by sin. He eats what I have provided for him but he serves another. Then he calls on Me in his sorrow, and I answer him. Then he returns to what he had been doing. Does he rebel against Me or does he seek My wrath? By Me, I have sworn I will take him with a taking from which he cannot be delivered and other than Me he can find no shelter. Where will he escape from My heaven and earth?

O Jesus! Say to the unjust from the children of Israel, do not call upon Me while you are involved in unlawful dealings and there are idols in your houses, for I have resolved that I will respond to them who call upon Me, and my response to their calls will be curses upon them lasting until they disperse.

O Jesus! How long must I wait and hope for good from people while they are heedless and reluctant to return? The words which emitted fom their mouths do not do not correspond to what is in their hearts, they subject themselves to my loathing, while seeking the love of the believers by [feigning] drawing near to Me.

يا عِيسَى، كَمْ مِنْ أُمَّةٍ قَدْ أَهْلَكْتُها بِسالِفِ ذُنُوبٍ قَدْ عَصَمْتُكَ مِنْها.

يا عِيسَى، أُرْقُقْ بِالضَّعِيفِ، وَارْفَعْ طَرْفَكَ الكَلِيلَ إلي السَّماءِ، وَادْعُنِى فإنِّى مِنْكَ قَرِيبٌ، وَلا تَدْعُنِى إلَّا مُتَضَرِّعاً إلىَّ، وَهَمُّكَ هَمَّاً واحِداً. فَإنَّكَ مَتَى تَدْعُنِى كَذَلِكَ أُجِبْكَ.

يا عِيسَى، إنِّى لَمْ أَرْضَ بِالدُّنْيا ثَواباً لِمَنْ كانَ قَبْلَكَ، وَلا عِقاباً لِمَنِ انْتَقَمْتُ مِنْهُ.

يا عِيسَى، إنَّكَ تَفْنَى وأنا أَبْقَى، وَمِنِّى رِزْقُكَ، وَعِنْدِى مِيقاتُ أَجَلِكَ، وإلىَّ إيابُكَ، وَعَلىَّ حِسابُكَ. فَسَلْنِى، وَلا تَسْأَلْ غَيْرِى، فَيَحْسُنُ مِنْكَ الدُّعاءُ، وَمِنِّى الإجابَةُ.

يا عِيسَى، ما أَكْثَرَ البَشَرَ! وأَقَلَّ عَدَدَ مَنْ صَبَرَ! الأشجارُ كَثِيرَةٌ وطَيِّبُها قَلِيلٌ، فَلا يَغُرَّنَّكَ حُسْنُ شَجَرَةٍ حَتَّى تَذُوقَ ثَمَرَها.

يا عِيسَى، لا يَغُرَّنَّكَ المُتَمَرِّدُ عَلَىَّ بِالعِصْيانِ، يَأْكُلُ رِزْقِى وَيَعْبُدُ غَيْرِى، ثُمَّ يَدْعُونِى عِنْدَ الكَرْبِ فأُجِيبُهُ، ثُمَّ يَرْجِعُ إلي ما كانَ عَلَيْهِ. فَعَلَىَّ يَتَمَرَّدُ، أَمْ بِسَخَطِي يَتَعَرَّضُ؟ فَبِى حَلَفْتُ لَآخُذَنَّهُ أَخْذَةً لَيْسَ لَهُ مِنْها مَنْجِي، وَلا دُونِى مَلْجَأً. أَيْنَ يَهْرُبُ مِنْ سَمائِى وأرْضِى؟

يا عِيسَى، قُلْ لِظَلَمَةِ بَنِى إسْرائِيلَ: 'لا تَدْعُونِى والسُّحْتُ تَحْتَ أَحْضانِكُمْ، والأصْنامُ فِى بُيُوتِكُمْ؛ فإنِّى آلَيْتُ أَنْ أُجِيبَ مَنْ دَعانِي، وأَنْ أَجْعَلَ إجابَتِى إيّاهُمْ لَعْناً عَلَيْهِمْ حَتَّى يَتَفَرَّقُوا.'

يا عِيسَى، كَمْ أُطِيلُ النَّظَرَ وأُحْسِنُ الطَّلَبَ، والقَوْمُ فِى غَفْلَةٍ لا يَرْجِعُونَ؟ تَخْرُجُ الكَلِمَةُ مِنْ أَفْواهِهِمْ، لا تَعِيها قُلُوبُهُمْ، يَتَعَرَّضُونَ لِمَقْتِى، وَيَتَحَبَّبُونَ بِقُرْبِى إلي المُؤْمِنِينَ.

O Jesus! Let your tongue say the same in secret and in the open, and let your heart and your vision be in accord with that. Turn your heart and your tongue entirely away from the forbidden, and withhold your eyes from anything in which there is no good. How many a beholder there has been whose look planted in their hearts a lust and threw them into the pit of destruction.

O Jesus! Be merciful with great mercy, and behave in such a way that you wish others to treat you, and increase your remembrance of death, and departing from your household, and avoid wasting your time, for wasting time corrupts one, and do not be heedless, for he who is heedless of Me is far away from Me. And remember Me by doing righteous acts so that I will remember you.

O Jesus! Turn toward Me after sinning, and remind those who are penitent of Me. Believe in Me and seek nearness to the believers by Me, and bid them to call upon Me with you, and beware of the call of the wronged one, for I have resolved to open a gate in the heavens to accept it and to answer him, even if later.

O Jesus! Know that evil ones infect others and the companions of evil cause others to perish, and know those to whom you are near, and choose for yourselves brothers from the believers.

O Jesus! Turn toward Me, for no sin is too great for Me to forgive, and I am the most Merciful of the Merciful. Work for yourself in the period before your death before your heirs may fail to do it for you, and worship Me for a day that is equal to a thousand years of what you reckon in which I repay for the good many times over, and evil deeds will corrupt one who performs them, so prepare the way for yourself throughout the period appointed for you, and compete with others to do whatever is righteous, for how many an assembly there have been from which people rose and were then granted sanctuary from the Fire.

O Jesus! Restrain yourself from being involved in this mortal life which comes to an end, and follow in the footsteps of those who have lived before you. Call them and speak to them in confidence. Do you feel their presence? Take your advice from them, and know that soon you will join them.

يا عِيسَي، لِيَكُنْ لِسانُكَ فى السِّرِّ والعَلانِيَةِ واحِداً، وَكَذلِكَ فَلْيَكُنْ قَلْبُكَ وَبَصَرُكَ، واطْوِ قَلْبَكَ وَلِسانَكَ عن المَحارِمِ، وَكُفَّ بَصَرَكَ عَمّا لا خَيْرَ فِيهِ، فَكَمْ مِنْ ناظِرٍ نَظْرَةً قَدْ زَرَعَتْ فى قَلْبِهِ شَهْوَةً، وَوَرَدَتْ بِهِ مَوارِدَ حِياضِ الهَلَكَةِ.

يا عِيسَي، كُنْ رَحِيماً مُتَرَحِّماً، وَكُنْ كَما تَشاءُ أَنْ يَكُونَ العِبادُ لَكَ، وَأَكْثِرْ ذِكْرَكَ المَوْتَ وَمُفارَقَة الأَهْلِينَ، وَلا تَلْهُ، فَانَّ اللهوَ يُفْسِدُ صاحِبَهُ؛ وَلا تَغْفُلْ، فإنَّ الغافِلَ مِنّى بَعِيدٌ؛ وَاذْكُرْنِى بالصالِحاتِ حَتَّي أَذْكُرَكَ.

يا عِيسَي، تُبْ إِلَيَّ بَعْدَ الذَّنْبِ، وَذَكِّرْ بِى الأَوّابِينَ، وَآمِنْ بِى، وَتَقَرَّبْ بِى إِلَي المُؤْمِنِينَ، وَمُرْهُمْ يَدْعُونى مَعَكَ؛ وإيّاكَ وَدَعْوَةَ المَظْلُومِ، فإنّى آلَيْتُ عَلَي نَفْسى أَنْ أَفْتَحَ لها باباً مِنَ السَّماءِ بالقَبُولِ وأَنْ أُجِيبَهُ وَلَوْ بَعْدَ حِينٍ.

يا عِيسَي، اعْلَمْ أَنَّ صاحِبَ السَّوْءِ يُعْدِى وَقَرِينَ السَّوْءِ يُرْدِي، وَاعْلَمْ مَنْ تُقارِنُ، واخْتَرْ لِنَفْسِكَ إخْواناً مِنَ المُؤْمِنِينَ.

يا عِيسَي، تُبْ إِلَىَّ، فإنّى لا يَتَعاظَمُنى ذَنْبٌ أَنْ أَغْفِرَهُ، وأَنا أَرْحَمُ الراحِمِينَ. اعْمَلْ لِنَفْسِكَ فى مُهْلَةٍ مِنْ أَجَلِكَ قَبْلَ أَنْ لا يَعْمَلَ لها غَيْرُكَ، واعْبُدْنِى لِيَوْمٍ كأَلْفِ سَنَةٍ مِمّا تَعُدُّونَ؛ فِيهِ أجْزِى بالحَسَنَةِ أضْعافَها، وإنَّ السَّيِّئَةَ تُوبِقُ صاحِبَها. فامْهَدْ لِنَفْسِكَ فى مُهْلَةٍ، وَنافِسْ فى العَمَلِ الصالِحِ، فَكَمْ مِنْ مَجْلِسٍ قَدْ نَهَضَ أهْلُهُ وَهُمْ مُجارُونَ مِنَ النارِ.

يا عِيسَي، ازْهَدْ فى الفانِى المُنْقَطِع، وَطَأْ رُسُومَ مَنازِلِ مَنْ كانَ قَبْلَكَ، فادْعُهُمْ وَناجِهِمْ، هَلْ تُحِسُّ مِنْهُمْ مِنْ أَحَدٍ؟ وَخُذْ مَوْعِظَتَكَ مِنْهُمْ، واعْلَمْ أنَّكَ سَتَلْحَقُهُمْ فى اللاحِقِينَ.

O Jesus! Tell him who rebels against Me by offense and who would compromise [his religion], that he should await My punishment and expect My destruction of him, soon he will be cut off with the destroyed ones. O son of Mary! Blessed are you, that you take your manners from your God, Who shows tenderness toward you mercifully, Who first bestowed blessings from Him gernerously, and He aids you in difficulties. Do not offend, O Jesus! For offenses are not lawful for you. I have made a covenant with you as I made a covenant with those who were before you, and I am a witness of that.

O Jesus! I have honored no creature as I have My religion, and I have not blessed [any creature] with the like of My mercy [for My religion].

O Jesus! I have honored nothing in creation like My religion, and I have bestowed nothing on it like My mercy.

O Jesus! Wash your exterior by water and your interior by good deeds, for verily you are returning to Me. Get ready, for that which is coming is near; and let me hear from you a sad sound.

O Jesus! That with which I have blessed you by grace without pollution, and I sought from you a loan for your soul, then you were stingy, so you will be of those who are destroyed.

O Jesus! Adorn yourself with religion and love of the needy, and walk through the earth modestly. And perform the prayers at any place, for all of them are [ritually] clean.

O Jesus! Be prepared, for whatever is coming is near, and recite My book while you are [ritually] clean, and make Me hear from you a sad voice.

O Jesus! There is no good in pleasure that does not continue, and in a life, for the one who lives it, that fades away.

O son of Mary! If only your eyes could see that which is furnished as a reward for My righteous friends, your heart would melt and your soul would depart longing for it, for there is no abode like that of the other world, where the good live as neighbors, and the cheribum enter it among them, and they are safe from the fear of the day of resurrection. It is an abode in which blessings do not change and they are not lost.

يا عِيسَي، قُلْ لِمَنْ تَمَرَّدَ عَلَيَّ بالعِصْيانِ وَعَمِلَ بالإدْهانِ: 'لِيَتَوَقَّعْ عُقُوبَتِي وَيَنْتَظِرُ إهْلاكِي إيّاهُ، سَيُصْطَلَمُ مَعَ الهالِكِينَ.' طُوبَي لَكَ يا ابن مَرْيَمَ، ثُمَّ طُوبَي لَكَ، إنْ أخَذْتَ بِأدَبِ إلَهِكَ الذى يَتَحَنَّنُ عَلَيْكَ تَرَحُّماً، وَبَداكَ بالنعَمِ مِنْهُ تَكَرُّماً، وكانَ لَكَ فِي الشدائِدِ، لا تَعْصِهِ.

يا عِيسَي، فانَّهُ لا يَحِلُّ لَكَ عِصْيانُهُ قَدْ عَهِدْتُ إلَيْكَ كَما عَهِدْتُ إلي مَنْ كانَ قَبْلَكَ، وأنا عَلَي ذَلِكَ مِنَ الشاهِدِينَ.

يا عِيسَي، ما أكْرَمْتُ خَلِيقَةً بِمِثْلِ دِينِي، وَلا أنْعَمْتُ عَلَيْها بِمِثْلِ رَحْمَتِي.

يا عِيسَي، اغْسِلْ بِالماءِ مِنْكَ ما ظَهَرَ، وَداوِ بالحَسَناتِ مِنْكَ ما بَطَنَ، فإنَّكَ إلَيَّ راجِعٌ.

يا عِيسَي، أعْطَيْتُكَ ما أنْعَمْتُ بِهِ عَلَيْكَ فَيْضاً مِنْ غَيْرِ تَكْدِيرٍ، وَطَلَبْتُ مِنْكَ قَرْضاً لِنَفْسِكَ، فَبَخِلْتَ بِهِ عَلَيْها، لِتَكُونَ مِنَ الهالِكِينَ.

يا عِيسَي، تَزَيَّنْ بالدينِ وَحُبِّ المَساكِينِ، وامْشِ عَلَي الأرضِ هَوْناً، وَصَلِّ عَلَي البِقاعِ، فَكُلُّها طاهِرٌ.

يا عِيسَي، شَمِّرْ فَكُلُّ ما هُوَ آتٍ قَرِيبٌ، واقْرءِ كِتابِي وأنْتَ طاهِرٌ، وأسْمِعْنِي مِنْكَ صَوْتاً حَزِيناً.

يا عِيسَي، لا خَيْرَ فِي لَذاذَةٍ لا تَدُومُ، وَعَيْشٍ مِنْ صاحِبِهِ يَزُولُ.

يا ابن مَرْيَمَ لَوْ رأتْ عَيْنُكَ ما أعْدَدْتُ لأوْلِيائِيَ الصالِحِينَ، ذابَ قَلْبُكَ وَزَهَقَتْ نَفْسُكَ شَوْقاً إلَيْهِ؛ فَلَيْسَ كَدارِ الآخِرَةِ دارٌ تَجاوَرَ فِيها الطَيِّبُونَ، وَيَدْخُلُ عَلَيْهِمْ فِيها المَلائِكَةُ المُقَرَّبُونَ، وَهُمْ مِمّا يأتِي يَوْمَ القِيامَةِ مِنْ أهْوالِها آمِنُونَ، دارٌ لا يَتَغَيَّرُ فِيها النَعِيمُ وَلا يَزُولُ عن أهْلِها.

O son of Mary! Vie with others for [that abode], for it is the hope of the hopeful, being such a good sight. Blessed are you, O son of Mary, if you work for it, and you are with your fathers, Adam and Ibrahim in the Garden and bliss, you seek no alternative to it and no change in it. I do this for the God-wary.

O Jesus! Flee toward Me with those who flee from a fire having a dreadful blaze and a fire having chains and shackles into which no gentle wind enters and from which no gloom ever goes, with sectors like those of the dark night, and he who is delivered from it will have attained a great achievment, and those who perish will never be delivered from it. It is the abode of tyrants, the wrongdoing oppressors, all who are rudely obstinant and all who are proud boasters.

O Jesus! It is an evil abode for those who rely on it, and evil place to stay, the abode of the oppressors. I warn you of yourself. So, be aware of Me.

O Jesus! Wherever you are, be observant of Me, and bear witness that it is I who created you, that you are My servant and that I formed you and conveyed you to the earth.

O Jesus! It is not proper for there to be two tongues in one mouth nor two hearts in one breast, and likewise for minds.

O Jesus! Do not be awake while sinning, do not be aware while wasting time. Wean yourself from destructive lusts and put away every lust that puts you far from Me. Know that to Me you are a trusted apostle, so be careful of Me. Know that your world will give you back to Me, and I will take you knowledgably, so abase yourself when you remember Me. Humble your heart when you remember Me. Be awake beside the sleep of the negligent.

O Jesus! This is My advice to you and My admonition to you, so take it from Me and I am the Lord of the worlds.

O Jesus! When My servant is patient for My sake, the reward for his work is from Me, and I am beside him when he calls on Me, and I am sufficient in avenging those who disobey Me. Where will the oppresors go to escape from Me?

يا ابن مَرْيَمَ نافِسْ فِيها مَعَ المُتَنافِسِينَ، فإنَّها أُمْنِيَّةُ المُتَمَنِّينَ، حَسَنَةُ المَنْظَرِ، طُوبَي لكَ، يا ابن مَرْيَمَ، إنْ كُنْتَ لَها مِنَ العامِلِينَ، مَعَ آبائِكَ آدَمَ وإبْراهِيمَ فِي جَنّاتٍ وَنَعِيمٍ لا تَبْغِي بِها بَدَلاً وَلا تَحْوِيلاً. كَذلِكَ أَفْعَلُ بالمُتَّقِينَ.

يا عِيسَي، إهْرَبْ إلَيَّ مَع مَنْ يَهْرَبُ مِنْ نارِ ذاتِ لَهَبٍ وَنارِ ذاتِ أغْلالٍ وأنْكالٍ، لا يَدْخُلُها رَوْحٌ وَلا يَخْرُجُ مِنْها غَمٌّ أَبَداً، قِطَعٌ كَقِطَعِ اللَيْلِ المُظْلِمِ، مَنْ يَنْجُ مِنْها يَفُزْ، وَلَنْ يَنْجُوَ مِنْها مَنْ كانَ مِنَ الهالِكِينَ. هِيَ دارُ الجَبّارِينَ والعُتاةِ الظّالِمِينَ وَكُلِّ فَظٍّ غَلِيظٍ وَكُلِّ مُخْتالٍ فَخُورٍ.

يا عِيسَي، بِئْسَتِ الدارُ لِمَنْ رَكَنَ إلَيْها، وَبِئْسَ القَرارُ دارُ الظّالِمِينَ. إنِّي أُحَذِّرُكَ نَفْسَكَ، فَكُنْ بِي خَبِيراً.

يا عِيسَي، كُنْ، حَيْثُ ما كُنْتَ، مُراقِباً لِي؛ واشْهَدْ عَلَي إنِّي خَلَقْتُكَ وأنْتَ عَبْدِي، وإنِّي صَوَّرْتُكَ وإلَي الأرضِ أهْبَطْتُكَ.

يا عِيسَي، لا يَصْلُحُ لِسانانِ فِي فَمٍ واحِدٍ، وَلا قَلْبانِ فِي صَدْرٍ واحِدٍ، وَكَذلِكَ الأذْهانُ.

يا عِيسَي، لا تَسْتَيْقِظَنَّ عاصِياً، وَلا تَسْتَنْبِهَنَّ لاهِياً، وافْطِمْ نَفْسَكَ عن الشَهَواتِ المُوبِقاتِ؛ وَكُلُّ شَهْوَةٍ تُباعِدُكَ مِنِّي فاهْجُرْها. واعْلَمْ أنَّكَ مِنِّي بِمَكانِ الرسُولِ الأمِينِ، فَكُنْ مِنِّي عَلَي حَذَرٍ. واعْلَمْ أنَّ دُنْياكَ مُؤَدِّيَتُكَ إلَيَّ، وأنِّي آخُذُكَ بِعِلْمِي؛ فَكُنْ ذَلِيلَ النَفْسِ عِنْدَ ذِكْرِي، خاشِعَ القَلْبِ حِينَ تَذْكُرُنِي، يَقْظانَ عِنْدَ نَوْمِ الغافِلِينَ.

يا عِيسَي، هَذِهِ نَصِيحَتِي إيّاكَ وَمَوْعِظَتِي لكَ، فَخُذْها مِنِّي، وإنِّي رَبُّ العالَمِينَ.

يا عِيسَي، إذا صَبَرَ عَبْدِي فِي جَنْبِي، كانَ ثَوابُ عَمَلِهِ عَلَيَّ، وَكُنْتُ عِنْدَهُ حِينَ يَدْعُونِي، وَكَفَي بِي مُنْتَقِماً مِمَّنْ عَصانِي. أيْنَ يَهْرَبُ مِنِّي الظّالِمُونَ.

O Jesus! Make your speech wholesome, and wherever you are, be both learned and a learner.

O Jesus! Send good deeds to Me, so that they will be remembered by Me for you, and grasp My advice. Verily, in it there is a cure for hearts.

O Jesus! Do not feel safe when you devise your plans from My plans, and do not forget, when alone in the world, the remembrance of Me.

O Jesus! By returning to Me, take account of yourself, so the reward may be deserved of those who work. They are given their compensation and I am the best of the givers.

O Jesus! You were created by My word, Mary gave birth to you at My command that I sent to her by My spirit, the trusted Gabriel of My angels, until you grew up as one alive and walking, and all of this was in My foreknowledge.

O Jesus! Zacharias is in the position of a father to you and as a guardian to your mother. When he went to her in the prayer niche then he found with her provisions. John is like you among My creatures. I granted him to his mother when she was old when she did not have the strength for it. By this, I wanted My sovereignty to appear to her, and My power to appear in you. The most beloved of you by Me is the most obedient to me and the most intense of you in fear of Me.

O Jesus! Wake up and do not despair of My mercy and glorify Me with those who glorify Me and with wholesome speech hallow Me.

O Jesus! How can the servants disbelieve in Me when their forelocks are in My fist and their changes take place on My earth? They are ignorant of My blessings and they are supporters of My enemy, and so the disbelievers are perishing.

O Jesus! Indeed, this world is a foul prison, and the fair seeming in it is, as you see, that over which the tyrants slaughter one another. Beware, the world and all of its blessings will come to an end, and it has but few blessings.

يا عِيسَي، أطِبِ الكَلامَ وكُنْ، حَيْثُما كُنْتَ، عالِماً مُتَعلِّماً.

يا عِيسَي، أفِضْ بالحَسَناتِ إلَيَّ حَتَّي يَكُونَ لكَ ذِكْرُها عِنْدِي؛ وتَمَسَّكْ بِوَصِيَّتِي، فإنَّ فِيها شِفاءً لِلقُلوبِ.

يا عِيسَي، لا تأمَنْ إذا مكَرْتَ مَكْرِي، ولا تَنْسَ عِنْدَ خَلَواتِ الدنْيا ذِكْرِي.

يا عِيسَي، حاسِبْ نَفْسَكَ بالرجُوعِ إلَيَّ، حَتَّي تَتَنَجَّزَ ثوابَ ما عَمِلَهُ العامِلُونَ. أولَئِكَ يُؤْتَوْنَ أجْرَهُمْ وأنا خَيْرُ المُؤْتِينَ.

يا عِيسَي، كُنْتَ خَلْقاً بِكَلامِي ولَدَتْكَ مَرْيَمُ بِأمْرِي، المُرْسَلُ إلَيْها رُوحِي، جَبْرَئِيلُ الأمِينُ مِنْ مَلائِكَتِي، حَتَّي قُمْتَ عَلَي الأرضِ حَيّاً تَمْشِي. كُلُّ ذَلِكَ فِي سابِقِ عِلْمِي.

يا عِيسَي، زَكَرِيّا بِمَنْزِلَةِ أبِيكَ وكَفِيلُ أُمِّكَ، إذْ يَدْخُلُ عَلَيْها المِحْرابَ فَيَجِدُ عِنْدَها رِزْقاً، ونَظِيرُكَ يَحْيَي مِنْ خَلْقِي، وَهَبْتُهُ لِأمِّهِ بَعْدَ الكِبَرِ مِنْ غَيْرِ قُوَّةٍ بِها، أرَدْتُ بِذَلِكَ أنْ يَظْهَرَ لَها سُلْطانِي وَيَظْهَرَ فِيكَ قُدْرَتِي. أحَبُّكُمْ إلَيَّ أطْوَعُكُمْ لِي، وأشَدُّكُمْ خَوْفاً مِنِّي.

يا عِيسَي، تَيَقَّظْ ولا تَيْأسْ مِنْ رَوْحِي، وَسَبِّحْنِي مَعَ مَنْ يُسَبِّحُنِي، وبِطَيِّبِ الكَلامِ فَقَدِّسْنِي.

يا عِيسَي، كَيْفَ يَكْفُرُ العِبادُ بِي ونَواصِيهِمْ فِي قَبْضَتِي، وتَقَلُّبُهُمْ فِي أرْضِي؟ يَجْهَلُونَ نِعْمَتِي وَيَتَوَلَّوْنَ عَدُوِّي، وكَذَلِكَ يَهْلِكُ الكافِرُونَ.

يا عِيسَي، إنَّ الدنْيا سِجْنٌ مُنْتِنُ الريحِ، وَحَسُنَ فِيها ما قَدْ تَرَي مِمّا قَدْ تَذابَحَ عَلَيْهِ الجَبّارُونَ. وايّاكَ والدنْيا، فَكُلُّ نَعِيمِها يَزُولُ، وَما نَعِيمُها إلّا قَلِيلٌ.

O Jesus! Seek Me when you go to bed, and you will find Me; and call upon me while you love Me, and I am the most hearing of the hearers; I answer the callers when they call upon Me.

O Jesus! Fear Me and make My servants fear Me. Happily the sinners may abstain from what they do because of it, so they do not perish unless they knowingly [do it].

O Jesus! Be afraid of Me as you fear predators and death you will meet. I have created all of them, so of Me alone, be afraid.

O Jesus! Verily, Mine is the kingdom and it is in My hand, and I am the King. If you obey Me, I will make you enter My Garden in the neighborhood of the righteous.

O Jesus! If I am angry with you, the pleasure of those who are pleased with you will not benefit you, and if I am pleased with you, the anger of those who are angry with you will not harm you.

O Jesus! Remember Me to yourself, and I will remember you to Myself. Remember Me among your people, and I will remember you among a people better than the children of Adam.

O Jesus! Call upon Me with the call of one who is drowning, afflicted, for whom there is none to aid.

O Jesus! Do not swear by Me falsely, so that My Throne shakes with anger. The world is short lived, but is long on hope, and with Me is a realm better than what you gather.

O Jesus! What will you do when I take out for you a book that speaks in truth, while you witness it, of the secrets you have hidden, and the deeds you have done.

O Jesus! Say to the unjust of the Children of Israel: You wash your faces and soil your hearts. Are you deceived about me, or would you be audacious toward me. For the worldly you use perfumes, but to me your stomachs are like putrid corpse, as though you were a dead people.

يا عِيسَي، ابْغِنِى عِنْدَ وِسادِكَ، تَجِدْنِى؛ وادْعُنِى وأنْتَ لِى مُحِبٌّ، فإنِّى أسْمَعُ السّامِعِينَ، أسْتَجِيبُ لِلدّاعِينَ إذا دَعَوْنِى.

يا عِيسَي، خَفْنِى وَخَوِّفْ بِى عِبادِى، لَعَلَّ المُذْنِبِينَ أنْ يُمْسِكُوا عَمّا هُمْ عامِلُونَ بِهِ، فَلا يَهْلِكُوا إلّا وَهُمْ يَعْلَمُونَ.

يا عِيسَي، ارْهَبْنِى رَهْبَتَكَ مِنَ السَبُعِ والمَوْتِ الذى أنتَ لاقِيهِ. فَكُلٌّ هَذا أنا خَلَقْتُهُ، فإيّاىَ فارْهَبُونِ.

يا عِيسَي، إنَّ المُلْكَ لِى وَبِيَدِى، وأنا المَلِكُ؛ فإنْ تُطِعْنِى أدْخَلْتُكَ جَنَّتِى، فِى جِوارِ الصالِحِينَ.

يا عِيسَي، إنِّى إذا غَضِبْتُ عَلَيْكَ، لَمْ يَنْفَعْكَ رِضا مَنْ رَضِىَ عَنْكَ؛ وإنْ رَضِيتُ عَنْكَ، لَمْ يَضُرَّكَ غَضَبُ المُغْضِبِينَ.

يا عِيسَي، اذْكُرْنِى فِى نَفْسِكَ، أذْكُرْكَ فِى نَفْسِي؛ واذْكُرْنِى فِى مَلَإكَ، أذْكُرْكَ فِى مَلاٍ خَيْرٍ مِنْ مَلاٍ الآدَمِيِّينَ.

يا عِيسَي، أدْعُنِى دُعاءَ الغَرِيقِ الحَزِينِ الذى لَيْسَ لَهُ مُغِيثٌ.

يا عِيسَي، لا تَحْلِفْ بِى كاذِباً، فَيَهْتَزَّ عَرْشِى غَضَباً. الدنْيا قَصِيرَةُ العُمْرِ، طَوِيلَةُ الأمَلِ، وَعِنْدِى دارٌ خَيْرٌ مِمّا تَجْمَعُونَ.

يا عِيسَي، كَيْفَ أنتُم صانِعُونَ إذا أخْرَجْتُ لَكُمْ كِتاباً يَنْطِقُ بالحَقِّ، وأنتُم تَشْهَدُونَ بِسَرائِرَ قَدْ كَتَمْتُمُوها، وأعْمالٍ كُنْتُمْ بِها عامِلِينَ؟

يا عِيسَي، قُلْ لِظَلَمَةِ بَنِى إسْرائِيلَ: 'غَسَلْتُمْ وُجُوهَكُمْ وَدَنَّسْتُمْ قُلُوبَكُمْ. أبِى تَغْتَرُّونَ؟ أمْ عَلَىَّ تَجْتَرِؤُونَ؟ تَطَيَّبُونَ بالطِّيبِ لأهْلِ الدنْيا، وأجْوافُكُمْ عِنْدِى بِمَنْزِلَةِ الجِيَفِ المُنْتِنَةِ، كأنَّكُمْ أقْوامٌ مَيِّتُونَ.'

O Jesus! Say to them, "Draw back your hands[1] from illicit gain, and stop your ears from listening to curses, and come near to me by your hearts for your appearance does not appeal to me.

O Jesus! Rejoice in the good deed, for it pleases Me, and weep over the evil deed, for it is a disgrace, and that which you do not like to be done unto you, do not do unto others, and if one slaps your right cheek, offer him the left one, and draw near to Me by your efforts through love, and ignore the ignorant.

O Jesus! Be humble toward the doers of good deeds and take part with them in such deeds, and be witnesses to them, and say to the unjust of the Children of Israel, "O friends of evil, and those who keep company with it! If you do not comply with the prohibitions, I will transform you into apes and swine.

O Jesus! Say to the unjust of the Children of Israel that wisdom[2] weeps in fear of Me, while you [Children of Israel] leave laughing. Has there come to you a repreive, or is there with you a guarantee against My chastisement, or that you will not be subject to My punishment? I swear by Myself, that I will abandon you as an example for those who remain.

Thus I charge you, O son of Mary, that you bring news to the Children of Israel of the Master of the messengers and My beloved, who is Aḥmad, having a red camel and a face like the moon, who is a shining light, a pure heart, courageous, venerably modest. Verily, he is a mercy to the worlds, and master of the children of Adam on the day of his meeting Me, the most honored of the foremost,[3] and the latest of the messengers from Me, an Arab, a trustworthy person, one committed to My religion, one patient for My sake and one who struggles by his hand against the idolaters for the defense of My religion. Order them to affirm him, believe in him, follow him and help him.

---

(1) Literally, "Clip your fingernails from illicit gain."

(2) Those who are wise.

(3) The foremost are the first to have believed in God.

يا عِيسَى، قُلْ لَهُمْ قَلِّمُوا أَظْفارَكُمْ مِنْ كَسْبِ الحَرامِ، واصِمُّوا أَسْماعَكُمْ، عَن ذِكْرِ الخَنا، واقْبِلُوا عَلَيَّ بِقُلُوبِكُمْ، فَإِنِّى لَسْتُ أُرِيدُ صُوَرَكُمْ.

يا عِيسَى، إِفْرَحْ بِالحَسَنَةِ فَإِنَّها لِى رِضاً، وابْكِ عَلَى السَّيِّئَةِ فَإِنَّها شَيْنٌ، وَما لا تُحِبُّ أَنْ يُصنَعَ بِكَ فَلا تَصنَعْهُ بِغَيْرِكَ، وإِنْ لَطَمَ خَدَّكَ الأَيْمَنَ فَأَعْطِهِ الأَيْسَرَ. وَتَقَرَّبْ إِلَيَّ بِالمَوَدَّةِ جُهْدَكَ، وأَعْرِضْ عَنِ الجاهِلِينَ.

يا عِيسَى، ذِلَّ لِأَهْلِ الحَسَنَةِ، وشارِكْهُمْ فِيها، وكُنْ عَلَيْهِمْ شَهِيداً؛ وقُلْ لِظَلَمَةِ بَنِى إِسْرائِيلَ: 'يا أَخْدانَ السَّوْءِ والجُلَساءَ عَلَيْهِ، إِنْ لَمْ تَنْتَهُوا أَمْسَخْكُمْ قِرَدَةً وَخَنازِيرَ.'

يا عِيسَى، قُلْ لِظَلَمَةِ بَنِى إِسْرائِيلَ: 'الحِكْمَةُ تَبْكِى فَرَقاً مِنِّى، وأَنتُم بِالضِّحِكِ تَهْجُرُونَ. أَتَتْكُمْ بَراءَتِى؟ أَمْ لَدَيْكُمْ أَمانٌ مِنْ عَذابِى؟ أَمْ تَعَرَّضُونَ لِعُقُوبَتِى؟ فَبِى حَلَفْتُ لاتْرُكَنَّكُمْ مَثَلاً لِلْغابِرِينَ.'

ثُمَّ أُوصِيكَ، يا ابن مَرْيَمَ البِكْرِ البَتُولِ، بِسَيِّدِ المُرْسَلِينَ وَحَبِيبِى، فَهُوَ أَحْمَدُ، صاحِبُ الجَمَلِ الأَحْمَرِ والوَجْهِ الأَقْمَرِ، المُشْرِقِ بِالنورِ، الطّاهِرِ القَلْبِ، الشَّدِيدِ الباسِ، الحَيِّ المُتَكَرِّمِ، فَإِنَّهُ رَحْمَةٌ لِلْعالمِينَ، وَسَيِّدُ وُلْدِ آدَمَ يَوْمَ يَلْقانِى، أَكْرَمُ السّابِقِينَ عَلَيَّ، وأَقْرَبُ المُرْسَلِينَ مِنِّى، العَرَبِى الأَمِينُ، الدَّيّانُ بِدِينِى، الصابِرُ فِى ذاتِى، المُجاهِدُ المُشْرِكِينَ بِيَدِهِ عن دِينِى، أَنْ تُخْبِرَ بِهِ بَنِى إِسْرائِيلَ وتَأْمُرَهُمْ أَنْ يُصَدِّقُوا بِهِ وأَنْ يُؤْمِنُوا بِهِ وأَنْ يَتَّبِعُوهُ وأَنْ يَنْصُرُوهُ.

Jesus said, "Who is it that I should please? Then, pleasure is for You. He said, "He is Muḥammad the Messenger of Allah to the people, all of them. In station, he is nearer to Me than they; in intercession, he is more ready than they; blessed be he as prophet, and blessed be his community (ummah) if they meet Me on his path. The inhabitants of the earth praise him, and the inhabitants of the heavens ask for his forgiveness. He is the trustworthy, the blessed, the wholesome and salutary, better than others with Me. He will be at the end of time.

When he arrives, the spouts of the heavens are loosed, and the earth puts forth its blossoms, so that they see the benediction. I will bless them by that upon which he puts his hand. He has many wives and few children. He is an inhabitant of Bakkah [Mecca] the place of the foundations of Abraham.

O Jesus! His religion is upright (Ḥanīfiyyah), and his qiblah is Yemenite,(1) and he is of My party, and I am with him, so blessed be he, then blessed be him. The Kawthar(2) is for him, and the greatest position in the gardens of Eden. He lives most honored of all who have ever lived, taken as a martyr, for whom is a fountain greater than the distance from Bakkah to the place of the rising of the sun, full of wine untouched, in which there are dishes like the constellations of the sky, and stars like the clods of the earth, agreeable, in which is every sort of wine and the flavors of every fruit in the Garden. Whoever drinks a drink from it will never thirst.

It is apportioned for him, and I have preferred him by a period of time between you and him. His secrets agree with what is apparent from him, and his words with his actions. He does not command the people, unless he first begins to practice it. His religion is a struggle in hardship and in comfort. The cities will obey him, and the ruler of

---

(1) The portion of the Arabian penninsula including Mecca and Yemen was referred to as Yemenite.

(2) The term *kawthar* has several meanings. Literally it means 'abundant [good]', and in many hadiths it is used in reference to Ḥaḍrah Fāṭimah, peace be with her. It is also considered the name of a fountain in heaven.

قالَ عِيسَي عليه السلام: 'إلهى مَنْ هُوَ حتَّي أرْضِيَهُ، فلكَ الرضا؟' قالَ: 'هُوَ مُحَمَّدٌ، رَسُولُ اللهِ إلي الناسِ كافَّةً. أقرَبُهُمْ مِنِّى مَنْزِلَةً وأحْضَرُهُمْ شَفَاعَةً. طُوبَي لَهُ مِنْ نَبِيٍّ، وَطُوبَي لِأُمَّتِهِ إنْ هُمْ لَقُونِى عَلَي سَبِيلِهِ. يَحْمَدُهُ أهْلُ الأرضِ، وَيَسْتَغْفِرُ لَهُ أهْلُ السَماءِ. أمِينٌ مَيْمُونٌ طَيِّبٌ مُطَيَّبٌ، خَيْرُ الباقِينَ عِنْدِى، يَكُونُ فِى آخِرِ الزَّمانِ.

إذا خَرَجَ أرْخَتِ السَماءُ عَزالِيَها وأخرَجَتِ الأرضُ زَهْرَتَها حَتَّي يَرَوا البَرَكَةَ، وأبارِكُ لَهُمْ فِى ما وَضَعَ يَدَهُ عَلَيْهِ. كَثِيرُ الأزْواجِ، قَلِيلُ الأوْلادِ. يَسْكُنُ بَكَّةَ مَوْضِعَ أساسِ إبْراهِيمَ.

يا عِيسَي، دِينُهُ الحَنِيفِيَّةُ، وَقِبْلَتُهُ يَمانِيَّةٌ. وَهُوَ مِنْ حِزْبِى وأنا مَعَهُ. فَطُوبَي لَهُ، ثُمَّ طُوبَي لَهُ، لَهُ الكَوْثَرُ والمَقامُ الأكْبَرُ فِى جَنّاتِ عَدْنٍ. يَعِيشُ أكْرَمَ مَنْ عاشَ، وَيُقْبَضُ شَهِيداً. لَهُ حَوْضٌ أكْبَرُ مِنْ بَكَّةَ إلي مَطْلَعِ الشَمْسِ، مِنْ رَحِيقٍ مَخْتُومٍ، فِيهِ آنِيَةٌ مِثْلُ نُجُومِ السَماءِ، وأكْوابٌ مِثْلُ مَدَرِ الأرضِ، عَذْبٍ فِيهِ مِنْ كُلِّ شَرابٍ وَطَعْمِ كُلِّ ثِمارٍ فِى الجَنَّةِ. مَنْ شَرِبَ مِنْهُ شَرْبَةً لَمْ يَظْمأ أبَداً.

وَذَلِكَ مِنْ قَسْمِى لَهُ وَتَفْضِيلِى إيّاهُ عَلَي فَتْرَةٍ بَيْنَكَ وَبَيْنَهُ. يُوافِقُ سِرُّهُ عَلانِيَتَهُ، وَقَوْلُهُ فِعْلَهُ. لا يأمُرُ الناسَ إلّا بِما يَبْدأهُمْ بِهِ. دِينُهُ الجِهادُ فِى عُسْرٍ وَيُسْرٍ. تَنْقادُ لَهُ البِلادُ، وَيَخْضَعُ لَهُ صاحِبُ الرومِ عَلَي دِينِ إبْراهِيمَ. يُسَمِّى عِنْدَ الطَّعامِ، وَيُفْشِى

Rome will humble himself before him following the religion of Abraham. He will mention the Name of God at meals, and bid peace, and he will pray while the people sleep. For him each day there will be five prayers in succession. His call to prayer will be like the call to muster troops. He will open his prayer with 'Allahu akbar (God is the greatest)' and end it with salutations of peace. He will put his feet in line in prayer as the angels place their feet in line, and his heart and head will be humbled for Me.

Light is in his breast and truth is on his tongue. And he is in the right, wherever he is. First an orphan, wandering for a time time regarding what He wills for him, his eyes sleep but his heart does not, interceding is only for him, and his community will reach the [Final] Hour,[1] and My hand will be above their hands, whoever breaks [his pledge with the Prophet ﷺ], breaks [it] against himself, and whoever is loyal to his pledge, I will be loyal to him [awarding to him] the Garden. So command the oppressors of the Children of Israel not to obliterate his books and not to distort his tradition and to offer peace to him. Surely, there is a noble station for him.

O Jesus! Whatever brings you near to Me, I have guided you to it, and all that takes you far from Me, I have prohibited it for you. So, seek what is for your own sake.

O Jesus! Surely this world is sweet, and surely I have employed you in it, so keep aside from you all from which I have warned you, and take from it all that I have given to you in forgiveness.

O Jesus! Look into your deeds with the look of a mistaken sinful servant, and do not look into the works of others from the position of Lord. Be without attachment to [this world], and do not long for it so that it causes you hardship.

O Jesus! Reason about and contemplate and look into the regions of the earth as to what has been the outcome of the oppressors.

O Jesus! All of My attributes are counsel for you, and all of My speech to you is the Truth, and I am the plain Truth. So, in truth I say, "If you disobey me after I informed you, there is no protector nor helper for you but Me.

---

(1) This indicates that he will be the final prophet.

السَّلامَ، وَيُصَلِّى وَالنَّاسُ نِيامٌ. لَهُ كُلَّ يَوْمٍ خَمْسُ صَلَواتٍ مُتَوالِياتٍ. يُنادى إِلى الصَّلاةِ كَنِداءِ الجَيْشِ بِالشِّعارِ، وَيَفْتَتِحُ بِالتَّكْبِيرِ، وَيَخْتَتِمُ بِالتَّسْلِيمِ، وَيَصُفُّ قَدَمَيْهِ فِى الصَّلاةِ كَما تَصُفُّ المَلائِكَةُ أقدامَها، وَيَخْشَعُ لى قَلْبُهُ وَرَأسُهُ. النورُ فِى صَدْرِهِ، وَالحَقُّ عَلَى لِسانِهِ، وَهُوَ عَلَى الحَقِّ حَيْثُما كانَ. أصلُهُ يَتِيمٌ ضالٌّ بُرْهَةً مِنْ زَمانِهِ عَمّا يُرادُ بِهِ. تَنامُ عَيْناهُ، وَلا يَنامُ قَلْبُهُ. لَهُ الشَّفاعَةُ، وَعَلى أُمَّتِهِ تَقومُ السّاعَةُ، وَيَدى فَوْقَ أيْدِيهِمْ. فَمَنْ نَكَثَ فَإِنَّما يَنْكُثُ عَلَى نَفْسِهِ، وَمَنْ أَوْفى بِما عاهَدَ عَلَيْهِ أَوْفَيْتُ لَهُ بِالجَنَّةِ. فَمُرْ ظَلَمَةَ بَنى إِسْرائيلَ أَلّا يَدْرُسُوا كُتُبَهُ، وَلا يُحَرِّفُوا سُنَّتَهُ، وَأَنْ يُقْرِءوهُ السَّلامَ؛ فَإِنَّ لَهُ فِى المَقامِ شَأنًا مِنَ الشَّأنِ.

يا عِيسَى، كُلُّ ما يُقَرِّبُكَ مِنِّى فَقَدْ دَلَلْتُكَ عَلَيْهِ، وَكُلُّ ما يُباعِدُكَ مِنِّى فَقَدْ نَهَيْتُكَ عَنْهُ؛ فَارْتَدَّ لِنَفْسِكَ.

يا عِيسَى، إِنَّ الدُّنْيا حُلْوَةٌ، وَإِنَّما اسْتَعْمَلْتُكَ فِيها، فَجانِبْ مِنْها ما حَذَّرْتُكَ، وَخُذْ مِنْها ما أَعْطَيْتُكَ عَفْوًا.

يا عِيسَى، أُنْظُرْ فِى عَمَلِكَ نَظَرَ العَبْدِ المُذْنِبِ الخاطِئِ، وَلا تَنْظُرْ فِى عَمَلِ غَيْرِكَ بِمَنْزِلَةِ الرَّبِّ؛ كُنْ فِيها زاهِدًا وَلا تَرْغَبْ فِيها فَتَعْطَبَ.

يا عِيسَى، اعْقِلْ، وَتَفَكَّرْ، وَانْظُرْ فِى نَواحِى الأرضِ كَيْفَ كانَ عاقِبَةُ الظّالِمِينَ.

يا عِيسَى، كُلُّ وَصْفى لَكَ نَصِيحَةٌ، وَكُلُّ قَوْلى لَكَ حَقٌّ، وَأنا الحَقُّ المُبِينُ. فَحَقًّا أقولُ لَئِنْ أنْتَ عَصَيْتَنى، بَعْدَ أنْ أنْبَأتُكَ، ما لَكَ مِنْ دُونى وَلِىٌّ وَلا نَصِيرٌ.

O Jesus! Humble your heart in meekness and look at those who are lower than you and do not look at those who are above you. And know that at the head of every mistake and sin is the love of this world. So, do not love it, for I do not love it either.

O Jesus! Make wholesome your heart for Me and remember Me much in solitude, and know that My pleasure is in your fawning love Me, in an animated and not in a lifeless manner.

O Jesus! Do not make anything My partner, and be wary on account of Me, and do not be deceived by health, so delight in yourself. Surely, this world is like a passing shadow, and what comes from it is like what goes from it. So compete in your struggle for righteousness, and be with truth wherever it is, even if you will be cut or burned by fire. So, do not deny me after knowledge. So, do not be of the ignorant. A thing is surely with things [of its own sort].

O Jesus! Pour forth tears from your eyes for Me, and humble your heart for Me.

O Jesus! Call on Me for help in hard conditions. I am He Who helps those who are upset, and Who answers the destitute. And I am the most merciful of the merciful."

(*Kāfī*, 8, 131-141, 103)

يا عِيسَي، أذِلَّ قَلْبَكَ بالخَشْيَةِ، وانْظُرْ إلي مَنْ هُوَ أسْفَلُ مِنْكَ، وَلا تَنْظُرْ إلي مَنْ هُوَ فَوْقَكَ، واعْلَمْ أنَّ راسَ كُلِّ خَطِيئَةٍ وَذَنْبٍ هُوَ حُبُّ الدنْيا، فَلا تُحِبَّها، فإنِّى لا أحِبُّها.

يا عِيسَي، أطِبْ لِى قَلْبَكَ، وأكْثِرْ ذِكْرِى فِى الخَلَواتِ؛ واعْلَمْ أنَّ سُرُورِى أنْ تُبَصْبِصَ إلَىَّ، كُنْ فِى ذَلِكَ حَيّاً، وَلا تَكُنْ مَيِّتاً.

يا عِيسَي، لا تُشْرِكْ بى شَيْئًا، وكُنْ مِنِّى عَلَي حَذَرٍ، وَلا تَغْتَرَّ بالصحَّةِ، وَتُغَبِّطْ نَفْسَكَ؛ فإنَّ الدنْيا كَفَىء زائِلٍ، وَما أقْبَلَ مِنْها كَما أدْبَرَ؛ فَنافِسْ فِى الصالِحاتِ جُهْدَكَ، وكُنْ مَعَ الحَقِّ حَيْثُما كانَ، وإنْ قُطِعْتَ وأحْرِقْتَ بالنار فَلا تَكْفُرْ بِى بَعْدَ المَعْرِفَةِ؛ فَلا تَكُونَنَّ مِنَ الجاهِلِينَ، فإنَّ الشيْءَ يَكُونُ مَعَ الشيْءِ.

يا عِيسَي، صُبَّ لِى الدمُوعَ مِنْ عَيْنَيْكَ، واخْشَعْ لِى بِقَلْبِكَ.

يا عِيسَي، اسْتَغِثْ بى فِى حالاتِ الشدَّةِ، فإنِّى أغِيثُ المَكْرُوبِينَ، وأجِيبُ المُضْطَرِّينَ، وأنا أرْحَمُ الراحِمِينَ.'»

(الكافى، ٨، ١٣١-١٤١، ١٠٣)

7

THE PREACHING OF JESUS

7.1. Jesus said, "Whoever is content with the destiny of Allah, it is as if his works are in accord with the gospel."

(*Jāmi' al-Akhbār*, 180)

7.2. Jesus said, "Sleeping on a mat and eating barely bread for seeking paradise is expeditious."

(*Majmū'a Warrām*, 2, 230)

7.3. The Prophet said, "Jesus said, 'We bring what is revealed for you, but as for the interpretation, it will be brought by the Paraclete (*fārqilīṭ*) at the end of time.'"

(*'Awālī al-La'ālī*, 4, 124)

7.4. Ja'far ibn Muḥammad narrated from his fathers, in order, that 'Alī the son of Abū Ṭālib said, "One day, the Apostle of Allah was among us on the mountain of Tahāma, and Muslims were around him. Then an old man with a staff in his hand came. The Apostle of Allah looked at him and said, 'One with the walk, voice and pride of a jinn has come.' He greeted him and the Apostle of Allah returned the greeting and said, 'Who are you?' He said, 'I am Hāma the son of al-Hīm the son of Lāqīs the son of Iblīs.' The Apostle of Allah said, 'Glory be to Allah, glory be to Allah, there is no one between you and Iblis unless two fathers!' He said, '... And I met Moses the son of 'Imrān. He said to me, 'When you meet Jesus the son of Mary, greet him.' I met Jesus the son of Mary and greeted him. He said to me, 'When you meet Muḥammad, greet him.' So I greet you O the Apostle of Allah from Jesus the son of Mary.' The Apostle of Allah said, 'Glory be to Allah. May Allah bless Jesus as long as the world remains.'"

(*Ja'faryyāt*, 176)

٧

حديث عيسى عليه السلام

٧-١- قالَ عِيسَي عليه السلام: «مَنْ رَضِيَ بِقِسْمَةِ اللهِ, فكأنَّما عَمِلَ بِالإنجيلِ.»

(جامع الأخبار، ١٨٠)

٧-٢- قالَ عِيسَي عليه السلام: «النَوْمُ عَلَي الحَصِيرِ وأكْلُ خُبْزِ الشعِيرِ, فِي طَلَبِ الفِرْدَوْسِ يَسِيرٌ.»

(مجموعة ورّام، ٢، ٢٣٠)

٧-٣- قالَ النَبِيُّ صلى الله عليه وآله وسلم: «قالَ عِيسَي عليه السلام: 'نَحْنُ نأتِيكَ بِالتنْزِيلِ, وامّا التَّأوِيلُ, فَسَياتِي بِهِ الفارْقِلِيطُ فِي آخِرِ الزَّمانِ.'»

(عوالى اللئالى، ٤، ١٢٤)

٧-٤- بِإسْنادِهِ، عَنْ جَعْفَرِ بْنِ مُحَمَّدٍ، عَنْ أبِيهِ، عَنْ جَدِّهِ عَلِيِّ بْنِ الحُسَيْنِ، عَنْ أبِيهِ، عَنْ جَدِّهِ عَلِيِّ بْنِ أبِي طالِبٍ عليه السلام, قالَ: «بَيْنَما رَسُولُ اللهِ صلى الله عليه وآله وسلم ذاتَ يَوْمٍ عَلَي جَبَلٍ مِنْ جِبالِ تَهامَة, والمُسْلِمُونَ حَوْلَهُ, إذْ أقبَلَ شَيْخٌ وَبِيَدِهِ عَصاً. فَنَظَرَ إلَيْهِ رَسُولُ اللهِ, فقالَ: 'مِشْيَةُ الجِنِّ ونَغْمَتُهُمْ وَعَجَبُهُمْ أتَي.' فسَلَّمَ, فَرَدَّ رَسُولُ اللهِ صلى الله عليه وآله وسلم, فقالَ لَهُ: 'مَنْ أنْتَ؟' فقالَ: 'أنا هامَةُ بْنُ الهِيمِ بْنِ لاقِيسَ بْنِ إبْلِيسَ.' قالَ رَسُولُ اللهِ صلى الله عليه وآله وسلم: 'سُبْحانَ اللهِ! سُبْحانَ اللهِ! ما بَيْنَكَ وَبَيْنَ إبْلِيسَ إلّا أبَوانِ.' قالَ: '... ولَقِيتُ مُوسَي بْنَ عِمْرانَ, فقالَ لِي: 'إذا لَقِيتَ عِيسَي بْنَ مَرْيَمَ, فأقرَأهُ السَلامَ.' فَلَقِيتُ عِيسَي بْنَ مَرْيَمَ فاقرَأتُهُ السَلامَ. فقالَ لِي عِيسَي بْنُ مَرْيَمَ: 'إذا لَقِيتَ مُحَمَّداً, فأقرَأهُ السَلامَ.' فَقَدْ أقرَأتُكَ يا رَسُولَ اللهِ صلى الله عليه وآله وسلم, مِنْ عِيسَي بْنِ مَرْيَمَ.' فقالَ رَسُولُ اللهِ صلى الله عليه وآله وسلم: 'سُبْحانَ اللهِ! صَلَّي اللهُ عَلَي عِيسَي مادامَتِ الدنْيا.'»

(الجعفريّات، ١٧٦)

7.5. Imam Ali said, "Jesus the son of Mary said, 'Verily the evil doer is infectious, and the associate of the wicked is brought down. So beware of those with whom you associate.'"

(*Kāfī*, 2, 640, 4)

7.6. I heard Imam Riḍā say, "Jesus the son of Mary, may Allah bless him, said to the apostles, 'O Children of Israel! Do not grieve over what you lose of this world, just as the people of this world do not grieve over what they lose of their religion, when they gain this worldof theirs.'"

(*Kāfī*, 2, 137, 25)

7.7. Imam Ṣādiq said, "Jesus the son of Mary, peace be with our Prophet and his progeny and with him, said, 'Woe unto the evil scholars! How the fire inflames them!'"

(*Kāfī*, 1, 47, 2)

7.8. And he (Jesus) said, "How long will you be advised without taking any advice? Certainly you have become a burden to the advisors."

(*Ādāb al-Nafs*, 1, 175)

7.9. It is reported from Imam Ṣādiq from his father that he said, "Jesus used to say, 'Regarding the fright which you do not know when you will encounter [i.e. death], what prevents you from preparing for it before it comes upon you suddenly?'"

(*Biḥār*, 14, 336, 67)

7.10. Imam Ja`far said, "Jesus the son of Mary said, 'He who lies much looses his worth.'"

(*Kāfī*, 2, 341, 13)

٧-٥- عِدَّةٌ مِنْ أصْحابِنا، عَنْ سَهْلِ بْنِ زيادٍ، عَنْ عَلِيِّ بْنِ أسْباطٍ، عَنْ بَعْضِ أصْحابِهِ، عَنْ أبِي الحَسَنِ عليه السلام، قالَ: «قالَ عيسي بن مريمَ عليه السلام: 'إنَّ صاحِبَ الشرِّ يُعْدِي، وقَرِينَ السوْءِ يُرْدِي. فانْظُرْ مَنْ تُقارِنُ.'»

(الكافى، ٢، ٦٤٠، ٤)

٧-٦- الحُسَيْنُ بْنُ مُحَمَّدٍ، عَنْ مُعَلَّي بْنِ مُحَمَّدٍ، عَنِ الوَشّاءِ، قالَ: «سَمِعْتُ الرضا عليه السلام، يَقُولُ: 'قالَ عيسَي بن مَرِيَمَ، صَلَواتُ اللهِ عَلَيهِ، لِلْحَوارِيِّينَ: 'يا بَنِي إسْرائيلَ، لا تأسَوْا عَلَي ما فاتَكُمْ مِنَ الدنْيا، كَما لا يأسَي أهْلُ الدنْيا عَلَي ما فاتَهُمْ مِنْ دِينِهِمْ، إذا أصابُوا دُنْياهُمْ.''»

(الكافى، ٢، ١٣٧، ٢٥)

٧-٧- قالَ أبُو عَبْدِ اللهِ عليه السلام: «قالَ عِيسَى بن مَرْيَمَ، عَلي نَبِيِّنا وآلِهِ وَعليه السلام: 'وَيْلٌ لِلْعُلَماءِ السوْءِ! كَيْفَ تَلَظَّي عَلَيْهِمُ النارُ!'»

(الكافى، ١، ٤٧، ٢)

٧-٨- قالَ عِيسَي عليه السلام: «إلَي مَتَي تُوعَظُونَ وَلا تَتَّعِظُونَ؟ لَقَدْ كَلَّفْتُمُ الواعِظِينَ تَعِباً.»

(آداب النفس ١، ١٧٥)

٧-٩- فُضالَةُ، عَنِ السكُونِيِّ، عَنِ الصادِقِ، عَنْ أبِيهِ عليه السلام, قالَ: «كانَ عِيسَي عليه السلام يَقُولُ: 'هَوْلٌ لا تَدْرِى مَتَي يَلْقاكَ, ما يَمْنَعُكَ أنْ تَسْتَعِدَّ لَهُ قَبْلَ أنْ يَفْجأكَ؟'»

(بحارالأنوار، ١٤، ٣٣٦، ٦٧)

٧-١٠- عِدَّةٌ مِنْ أصْحابِنا، عَنْ أحْمَدَ بْنِ أبِى عَبْدِ اللهِ، عَنِ الحَسَنِ بْنِ ظَرِيفٍ، عَنْ أبِيهِ، عَمَّنْ ذَكَرَهُ، عَنْ أبِى عَبْدِ اللهِ عليه السلام، قالَ: «قالَ عيسَي بن مَرِيَمَ عليه السلام: 'مَنْ كَثُرَ كَذِبُهُ ذَهَبَ بَهاؤُهُ.'»

(الكافى، ٢، ١٣، ٣٤١)

7.11. It is reported that Abū 'Abdullah, [Imam Ṣādiq] said, "The Messiah used to say: 'He who often becomes upset, his body becomes sick; he whose character is bad, his self becomes his torment; he who often talks, often stumbles; he who often lies, he loses his worth; he who quarrels with men, he loses his manliness.'"

(*Biḥār*, 14, 318, 17)

7.12. It is reported that the Commander of the Faithful [Imam Ali] said, "Jesus the son of Mary said, 'The dinar is the illness of religion, and the scholar (*al-'ālim*) is the physician of religion. So if you see that the physician brings illness upon himself, distrust him, and know that he is not to advise others.'"

(*Biḥār*, 14, 319, 21)

7.13. It is reported that Ali ibn al-Husayn [Imam Sajjad] said, "The Messiah said to his Apostles, 'Verily, this world is merely a bridge, so cross over it, and do not become preoccupied with it.'"

(*Biḥār*, 14, 319, 20)

7.14. It is reported that Imam Ṣādiq said, "Jesus the son of Mary, peace be with them, said to some of his companions, 'That which is not loved by you for someone to do to you, do not do that to others, and if someone strikes you on the right cheek, turn to him your left cheek also.'"

(*Biḥār*, 14, 287)

٧-١١- أبي، عَنْ سَعْدٍ، عَنْ ابن هاشِمٍ، عَنِ الدهْقان، عَنْ دُرُسْتٍ، عَنْ عَبْدِ اللهِ بْنِ سَنانٍ، عَنْ أبي عَبْدِ اللهِ عليه السلام, قالَ: «كانَ المَسيحُ عليه السلام يَقُولُ: 'مَنْ كَثُرَ هَمُّهُ, سَقِمَ بَدَنُهُ؛ وَمَنْ ساءَ خُلْقُهُ, عَذَّبَ نَفْسَهَ؛ وَمَنْ كَثُرَ كَلامُهُ, كَثُرَ سَقَطُهُ؛ وَمَنْ كَثُرَ كَذِبُهُ, ذَهَبَ بَهاؤُهُ؛ وَمَنْ لاحَي الرجالَ, ذَهَبَتْ مُرُوءَتُهُ.'»

(بحارالأنوار، ١٤، ٣١٨، ١٧)

٧-١٢- ابن المُتَوَكِّلِ، عَنِ السَعْدابادِىّ، عَنِ البَرْقِىّ، عَنْ أبيهِ، عَنْ مُحَمَّدِ بْنِ سَنانٍ، عَنْ زِيادِ بْنِ المُنْذِرِ، عَنْ ابن طَرِيْفٍ، عَنْ ابن نُباتَةٍ، عَنْ أمِيرِ المُؤمِنِينَ عليه السلام, قالَ: «قالَ عِيسَي بْنُ مَرْيَمَ عليه السلام: 'الدينارُ داءُ الدينِ, والعالِمُ طَبِيبُ الدينِ, فإذا رأيْتُمْ الطَّبِيبُ يَجُرُّ الداءَ إلَي نَفْسِهِ, فاتَّهِمُوهُ, واعْلَمُوا أنَّهُ غَيْرُ ناصِحٍ لِغَيْرِهِ.'»

(بحارالأنوار، ١٤، ٣١٩، ٢١)

٧-١٣- أبي، عَنْ سَعْدٍ، عَنِ الأصْبَهانِىّ، عَنِ المِنْقَرِىّ، عَنْ سُفْيانِ بْنِ عُيَيْنَةٍ، عَنِ الزُّهَرِى، عَنْ عَلِيِّ بْنِ الحُسَيْنِ عليه السلام, قالَ: «قالَ المَسِيحُ عليه السلام لِلْحَوارِيِّينَ: 'إنَّما الدنْيا قَنْطَرَةٌ, فاعْبُرُوها, وَلا تَعْمُرُوها.'»

(بحارالأنوار، ١٤، ٣١٩، ٢٠)

٧-١٤- ابن مَسْرُورٍ، عَنْ مُحَمَّدٍ الحِمْيَرِى، عَنْ أبيهِ، عَنْ ابن أبي الخَطّابِ، عَنْ ابن أسْباطٍ، عَنْ عَمِّهِ، عَنِ الصادِقِ عليه السلام, قالَ: «قالَ عِيسَي بْنُ مَرْيَمَ عليه السلام لِبَعْضِ أصْحابِهِ: 'ما لا تُحِبُّ أنْ يُفْعَلَ بِكَ, فَلا تَفْعَلْهُ بِأحَدٍ؛ وإنْ لَطَمَ أحَدٌ خَدَّكَ الأيْمَنَ, فأعْطِ الأيْسَرَ.'»

(بحارالأنوار، ١٤، ٢٨٧)

7.15. It is reported that Abū 'Abdullah [Imam Ṣādiq] said that Jesus said, "The affairs of this world and those of the other world have gotten hard. But the affairs of this world are hard because there is nothing of this world at which you may grasp that some sinner has not grabbed first, while the affairs of the other world are hard because you do not find helpers to help you toward it."

(*Kāfī*, 8, 144, 112)

7.16. The Messiah said to the Apostles, "Verily, the eating of barley bread and the drinking of plain water today in this world is for he who would enter heaven tomorrow."

(*Ādāb al-Nafs*, 2, 225)

7.17. Jesus is reported to have said, "One of the evils of this world is that Allah, the Supreme, is disobeyed in it, andthe other world will not be reached execpt by relinquishing this one."

(*Majmū'a Warrām*, 1, 78)

7.18. Jesus is reported to have said, "How can one be of the people of knowledge if the next world is shown to him while he remains involved in this world, and what harms him is more desirable to him than what benefits him?"

(*Majmū'a Warrām*, 1, 83)

7.19. It is reported by Mufaḍḍal, one of the companions of Imam al-Ṣādiq from Imam Ja'far al-Ṣādiq in a long hadith, that he said, "Jesus the son of Mary, Peacebe with our Prophet and with him, used to spend some time with the disciples and advise them, and he used to say, 'He does not know me, who knows not his soul, and he who does not know the soul between his two sides, does not know the soul between my two sides. And he who knows his soul which is between his sides, he knows me. And he who knows me knows He Who sent me.'"

(*Ādāb al-Nafs*, 2, 213)

٧-١٥- حَفْصٌ، عَنْ أبي عَبْدِ اللهِ عليه السلام، قالَ: «قالَ عِيسَي عليه السلام: 'اشْتَدَّتْ مؤُونَةُ الدنْيا وَمؤُونَةُ الآخِرَةِ. أمّا مؤُونَةُ الدنْيا، فإنَّكَ لا تَمُدُّ يَدَكَ إلي شَيْء مِنْها إلّا وَجَدْتَ فاجِراً قَدْ سَبَقَكَ إلَيْها؛ وأمّا مؤُونَةُ الآخِرَةِ فإنَّكَ لا تَجِدُ أعْواناً يُعِينُونَكَ عَلَيْها.'»

(الكافى، ٨، ١٤٤، ١١٢)

٧-١٦- قالَ المَسِيحُ لِلْحَوارِيِّينَ: «إنَّ أكْلَ خُبْزِ الشعِيرِ وَشُرْبَ الماءِ القُراحِ, اليَوْمَ فِي الدنْيا, لِمَنْ يُرِيدُ أنْ يَدْخُلَ الفِرْدَوْسَ غَداً.»

(آداب النفس، ٢، ٢٢٥)

٧-١٧- قالَ عِيسَي عليه السلام: «مِنْ خُبْثِ الدنْيا, أنَّ اللهَ تَعالَي عُصِيَ فِيها, وأنَّ الآخِرَةَ لا تُنالُ إلّا بِتَرْكِها.»

(مجموعة ورّام، ١، ٧٨)

٧-١٨- قالَ عِيسَي عليه السلام: «كَيْفَ يَكُونُ مِنْ أهْلِ العِلْمِ مَنْ يُسارُ بِهِ إلي آخِرَتِهِ, وَهُوَ مُقْبِلٌ عَلَي دُنْياهُ, وَما يَضُرُّهُ أشْهَي إلَيْهِ مِمّا يَنْفَعُهُ؟»

(مجموعة ورّام، ١، ٨٣)

٧-١٩- رَوَي المُفَضَّلُ، عَنِ الإمامِ جَعْفَرِ الصادِقِ عليه السلام, فِي حَدِيثٍ طَوِيلٍ, قالَ: «كانَ عِيسَي بْنُ مَرْيَمَ, عَلَي نَبِيِّنا وَعليه السلام, يَقِفُ بَيْنَ الحَوارِيِّينَ, فَيَعِظُهُمْ وَيَقُولُ: 'لَيْسَ يَعْرِفُنِي مَنْ لا يَعْرِفُ نَفْسَهُ. وَمَنْ لَمْ يَعْرِفْ النَفْسَ الَّتِي بَيْنَ جَنْبَيْهِ, لَمْ يَعْرِفِ النَفْسَ الَّتِي بَيْنَ جَنْبَيَّ وَغَيْرِهِ. وَمَنْ عَرَفَ نَفْسَهُ الَّتِي بَيْنَ جَنْبَيْهِ, عَرَفَنِي. وَمَنْ عَرَفَنِي, عَرَفَ الذي أرْسَلَنِي.'»

(آداب النفس، ٢، ٢١٣)

7.20. It is reported that Abū ‘Abdullah [Imam Ṣādiq] said, “Jesus the son of Mary, may the blessings of Allah be with him, said, ‘You work for the sake of this world while it is not by work that you are provided for in it. And you do not work for the sake of the next world, while it is only by work that you will be provided for in it. Woe be unto you, evil scholars (*‘ulamā*)! You take payments and waste works. The backer[1] comes close to accepting his work, and the people come close to leaving the narrowness of this world for the darkness of the grave. How can one be knowledgable who is on the way to the next world and nevertheless is going after this world, and he likes the things that harm him more than the things that benefit him?’”

(*Kāfī*, 2, 319, 13)

7.21. It is reported that Jesus said, “Woe unto you, evil scholars (*‘ulamā*)! You take payments and waste works. The Master of the work comes close to search for his work, and you come close to leaving this wide world for the darkness of the grave and its narrowness. He prohibited you from sins, likewise He ordered you to fast and say prayers. How can one be a scholar who is angry with His livelihood and debases His Dignity, while he knows that it is from the knowledge and the power of Allah? How can one be a scholar, who accuses Allah regarding what He has destined for him, so he is not satisfied with what reaches him!? How can one be a scholar, who prefers this world to the other world, turns to this world and likes the things that harm him more than the things that benefit him!? How can one be a scholar who seeks words (*kalām*) in order to report them, but does not seek to put them into practice?’”

(*Biḥār*, 2, 39)

7.22. Jesus said, “How can some one benefit himself while he trades himself for all that is in this world, then he abandons the inheritence which he has traded to others and destroys himself? But

---

[1] *Rabb al-’amal* has been translated as ‘backer’. It refers to those who support the evil *‘ulama*, following them and giving them financial backing.

٧-٢٠- عَلِيُّ بْنُ إِبْراهِيمَ، عَنْ أَبِيهِ، عَنِ القاسِمِ بْنِ مُحَمَّدٍ، عَنِ المِنْقَرِيِّ، عَنْ حَفْصِ بْنِ غِياثٍ، عَنْ أَبِي عَبْدِ اللهِ عليه السلام، قالَ: «قالَ عيسَي بن مَرْيَمَ، صَلَواتُ اللهِ عَلَيهِ: 'تَعْمَلُونَ لِلدُّنْيا، وأنتُم تُرْزَقُونَ فِيها بِغَيْرِ عَمَلٍ؛ وَلا تَعْمَلُونَ لِلآخِرَةِ، وأنتُم لا تُرْزَقُونَ فِيها إلّا بالعَمَلِ. وَيْلَكُمْ عُلَماءَ سَوْءٍ! الأجْرَ تأخُذُونَ، والعَمَلَ تُضَيِّعُونَ. يُوشِكُ رَبُّ العَمَلِ أنْ يُقبَلَ عَمَلُهُ، وَيُوشِكُ أنْ يُخْرَجُوا مِنْ ضِيقِ الدنْيا إلَي ظُلْمَةِ القَبْرِ. كَيْفَ يَكُونُ مِنْ أهْلِ العِلْمِ مَنْ هُوَ فِي مَسِيرِهِ إلَي آخِرَتِهِ، وَهُوَ مُقبِلٌ عَلَي دُنْياهُ، وَما يَضُرُّهُ أحَبُّ إلَيْهِ مِمّا يَنْفَعُهُ؟'»

(الكافي، ٢، ٣١٩، ١٣)

٧-٢١- مِنْ كَلامِ عِيسَي عليه السلام: «وَيْلَكُمْ عُلَماءَ السَوءِ! الأجْرَ تأخُذُونَ, والعَمَلُ تُضَيِّعُونَ. يُوشِكُ رَبُّ العَمَلِ أنْ يَطْلُبَ عَمَلَهُ, وَتُوشِكُونَ أنْ تَخْرُجُوا مِنَ الدنْيا العَرِيضَةِ إلَي ظُلْمَةِ القَبْرِ وَضِيقِهِ. اللهُ نَهاكُمْ عَنِ الخَطايا, كَما أمَرَكُمْ بِالصيامِ والصلاةِ. كَيْفَ يَكُونُ مِنْ أهْلِ العِلْمِ, مَنْ سَخَطَ رِزْقَهُ, واحْتَقَرَ مَنْزِلَتَهُ, وَقَدْ عَلِمَ أنَّ ذَلِكَ مِنْ عِلْمِ اللهِ وَقُدْرَتِهِ؟ وَكَيْفَ يَكُونُ مِنْ أهْلِ العِلْمِ, مَنْ اتَّهَمَ اللهَ فِيما قَضَي لَهُ, فَلَيْسَ يَرْضَي شَيْئاً أصابَهُ؟ كَيْفَ يَكُونُ مِنْ أهْلِ العِلْمِ مَنْ دُنْياهُ عِنْدَهُ آثَرُ مِنْ آخِرَتِهِ, وَهُوَ مُقبِلٌ عَلَي دُنْياهُ, وَما يَضُرُّهُ أحَبُّ إلَيْهِ مِمّا يَنْفَعُهُ؟ كَيْفَ يَكُونُ مِنْ أهْلِ العِلْمِ مَنْ يَطْلُبُ الكَلامَ لِيُخْبِرَ بِهِ, وَلا يَطْلُبُ لِيَعْمَلَ بِهِ؟»

(بحارالأنوار، ٢، ٣٩)

٧-٢٢- قالَ عِيسَي عليه السلام: «بِما ذا نَفَعَ امْرُؤٌ نَفْسَهُ؟ باعَها بِجَمِيعِ ما فِي الدنْيا, ثُمَّ تَرَكَ ما باعَها بِهِ مِيراثاً لِغَيْرِهِ, وأهْلَكَ نَفْسَهُ. وَلَكِنْ طُوبَي لامْرَءٍ خَلَّصَ نَفْسَهُ,

blessed be the man who purifies himself and prefers his soul to everything of this world."

(*Biḥār*, 14, 329, 58)

7.23. Jesus said, "Woe to the companion of the world! How he dies and leaves it, and how he relies on it and it deceives him, and how he trusts it and it forsakes him! Woe unto those who are deceived! How that which is repugnant encompasses them and that which is beloved separates from them! And that which is promised will come to them. And woe to those whose endeavors are only for the world and error. How he will be disgraced before Allah tomorrow!"

(*Biḥār*, 14, 328, 53)

7.24. Verily, Jesus said, "Why do you come to me clothed in the clothing of monks while your hearts are those of ferocious wolves? You should be clothed in the clothing of kings, and soften your hearts with fear."

(*Biḥār*, 70, 208)

7.25. Jesus said, "Who would build a house on the waves of the sea? This world is that house, so you should not take it as a dwelling."

(*Biḥār*, 14, 326, 41)

7.26. Jesus said, "The love of this world and the next cannot be aligned in the heart of a believer, like water and fire in a single vessel."

(*Biḥār*, 14, 327, 50)

7.27. Jesus said, "Blessed is he who abandons the present desire for the absent promise."

(*Biḥār*, 14, 327, 45)

7.28. And Jesus was saying, "O assembly of Apostles, love Allah by hatred of the disobedient, and approach Allah by distancing

واخْتارَها عَلَي جَمِيعِ الدنْيا.»

(بحارالأنوار، ١٤، ٣٢٩، ٥٨)

٧-٢٣- قالَ عِيسَي: «وَيْلٌ لِصاحِبِ الدنْيا! كَيْفَ يَمُوتُ وَيَتْرُكُها, وَيأمَنُها وتَغُرُّهُ, وَيَثِقُ بِها وَتَخْذُلُهُ! وَيلٌ لِلْمُغْتَرِّينَ! كَيْفَ رَهَقَهُمْ ما يَكْرَهُونَ, وَفارَقَهُمْ ما يُحِبُّونَ, وَجاءَهُمْ ما يُوعَدُونَ! وَوَيْلٌ لِمَنْ الدنْيا هَمُّهُ, والخَطايا أمَلُهُ! كَيْفَ يَفْتَضِحُ غداً عِنْدَ اللهِ!»

(بحارالأنوار، ١٤، ٣٢٨، ٥٣)

٧-٢٤- قالَ عِيسَي عليه السلام: «ما لَكُمْ؟ تأتُونِي, وَعَلَيْكُمْ ثِيابُ الرهْبان, وَقُلُوبُكُمْ قُلوبُ الذِّئابِ الضَّوارِي! البِسُوا ثِيابَ المُلُوكِ, وألِينُوا قُلوبَكُمْ بِالخَشْيَةِ.»

(بحارالأنوار، ٧٠، ٢٠٨)

٧-٢٥- قالَ عِيسَي عليه السلام: «مَنْ ذا الذى يَبْنِى عَلَي مَوْجِ البَحْرِ داراً؟ تِلْكُمُ الدنْيا, فَلا تَتَّخِذُوها قَراراً.»

(بحارالأنوار، ١٤، ٣٢٦، ٤١)

٧-٢٦- قالَ عِيسَي عليه السلام: «لا يَسْتَقِيمُ حُبُّ الدنْيا والآخِرَةِ فِى قَلْبِ مُؤْمِنٍ؛ كَما لا يَسْتَقِيمُ الماءُ والنارُ فِى إناءٍ واحِدٍ.»

(بحارالأنوار، ١٤، ٣٢٧، ٥٠)

٧-٢٧- قالَ عِيسَي عليه السلام: «طُوبَي لِمَنْ تَرَكَ شَهْوَةً حاضِرَةً, لِمَوْعُودٍ لَمْ يَرَهُ.»

(بحارالأنوار، ١٤، ٣٢٧، ٤٥)

٧-٢٨- كانَ عِيسَي عليه السلام يَقُولُ: «يا مَعْشَرَ الحَوارِيِّينَ, تَحَبَّبُوا إلَي اللهِ

[yourselves] from them, and request His contentment by their discontentment."

(*Biḥār*, 14, 330, 64)

7.29. Jesus said, "O group of Apostles! How many lamps the wind has put out, and how many worshippers pride has corrupted!"

(*Biḥār*, 69, 322, 37)

7.30. Jesus said, "Never stare at that which is not for you. If you restrain your eyes, you will never commit adultery; and if you are able to avoid looking at the garments of women who are not permitted for you, then do so."

(*Majmū' Warrām*, 1, 62)

7.31. It is reported that Imam Ṣādiq said: "Jesus the son of Maryع said, When one of you sits in his house, he should have clothes on. Verily, Allah has allotted modesty for you, just as He has allotted your sustenance."

(*Biḥār*, 68, 334, 11)

7.32. I heard Imam Ṣādiq say: "Christ said to his disciples: 'If you are my lovers and my brothers, you must acustom yourself to the enmity and hatred of the people, otherwise you will not be my brothers. I teach you this that you may learn it; I do not teach you so that you may become proud. Verily, you will not achieve that which you desire unless you give up that which you desire, and by enduring patiently that which you detest, and guard your gaze, for it plants lust in the heart, and it is sufficient to tempt him. Happy are they who see that which they desire with their eyes, but who commit no

يبُغْض أهْلِ المَعاصِى, وتَقرَّبُوا إلي اللهِ بِالتباعُدِ مِنْهُمْ, والتَمِسُوا رضاهُ بِسَخَطِهِمْ.»

(بحارالأنوار، ١٤، ٣٣٠، ٦٤)

٧-٢٩- قالَ عيسَيعليه السلام: «يا مَعْشَرَ الحَوارِيِّينَ، كَمْ مِنْ سِراجٍ أطْفأهُ الريحُ! وكَمْ مِنْ عابِدٍ أفْسَدَهُ العُجْبُ!»

(بحار الأنوار، ٦٩، ٣٢٢، ٣٧)

٧-٣٠- قالَ عِيسَيعليه السلام: «لا تَكُونَنَّ حَدِيدَ النَظرِ إلي ما لَيْسَ لَكَ. فإنَّهُ لَنْ يَزْنِى فَرْجُكَ ما حَفِظْتَ عَيْنَكَ. فانْ قَدرْتَ أنْ لا تَنْظُرَ إلي ثَوْبِ المَرْأةِ الَّتِى لا تَحِلُّ لكَ, فافْعَلْ.»

(مجموعة ورّام، ١، ٦٢)

٧-٣١- هارُونُ، عَنْ ابن صَدَقَةٍ، عَنِ الصادِقِعليه السلام قالَ: «قالَ عِيسَي بْنُ مَرْيَمَعليه السلام: 'إذا قَعَدَ أحَدُكُمْ فِى مَنْزِلِهِ, فَلْيُرْخِ عَلَيْهِ سِتْرَهُ. فإنَّ اللهَ, تَبارَكَ وتَعالَي, قَسَّمَ الحَياءَ كَما قَسَّمَ الرزقَ.'»

(بحارالأنوار، ٦٨، ٣٣٤، ١١)

٧-٣٢- أحْمَدُ بْنُ الوَلِيدِ، عَنْ أبِيهِ، عَنِ الصَقّارِ، عَنْ ابن مَعْرُوفٍ، عَنْ ابن مَهْزِيارٍ، عَنْ رَجُلٍ، عَنْ واصِلِ بْنِ سُلَيْمانَ، عَنْ ابن سَنانٍ, قالَ: «سَمِعْتُ أبا عَبْدِ اللهِعليه السلام يَقُولُ: 'كانَ المَسِيحُعليه السلام يَقُولُ لِأصحابِهِ: 'إنْ كُنْتُمْ أحِبّائِى وإخْوانِي, فَوَطِّنُوا أنْفُسَكُمْ عَلَي العَداوَةِ والبَغْضاءِ مِنَ الناسِ؛ فإنْ لَمْ تَفْعَلُوا فَلَسْتُمْ بِإخْوانِي. إنَّما أُعَلِّمُكُمْ لِتَعَلَّمُوا, ولا أُعَلِّمُكُمْ لِتَعْجَبُوا. إنَّكُمْ لَنْ تَنالُوا ما تُرِيدُونَ, إلّا بِتَرْكِ ما تَشْتَهُونَ, وبِصَبْرِكُمْ عَلَي ما تَكْرَهُونَ. وايّاكُمْ والنَظْرَةَ, فإنَّها تَزْرَعُ فِى قَلْبِ صاحِبِها الشَهْوَةَ وكَفَي بِها لِصاحِبِها فِتْنَةً. يا طُوبَي لِمَنْ يَرَي بِعَيْنَيْهِ الشَهَواتِ

disobedience in their hearts. How far is that which is in the past, and how near is that which is to come. Woe to those who have been deluded when what they loathe approaches them, and what they love abandons them, and there comes that which they were promised. Woe to those whose efforts are for the sake of this world, and whose works are mistaken. How he will be disgraced before his Lord! And do not speak much for aught but theremembrance of Allah. Those who speak much about aught but Allah harden their hearts, but they do not know it. Do not look at the faults of others over much [the phrase used here indicates spying], but look after the purity of your own selves, for you are enslaved servants. How much water flows in a mountain without its becoming soft. And how much wisdom you are taught without your hearts becoming soft. You are bad servants, and you are not pious servants. You are not nobly free. Indeed you are like unto the oleander, all who see it wonder at its flower, but when they eat from it they die. So, peace be unto you.'"

(*Biḥār,* 14, 325, 37) 7.33.

7.33. Jesus said, "O Children of Israel! Do not be excessive in eating, for those who are excessive in eating are excessive in sleeping, and those who are excessive in sleeping are deficient in praying, and of those who are deficient in praying, it is written that they are negligent."

(*Sharḥ Nahj al-Balāgha*, 19, 188)

7.34. Jesus said to his companions, "Verily, sleeping on a dunghill and eating barley bread is a great good, with a sound religion."

(*Ādāb al-Nafs,* 1, 223)

7.35. Jesus said, "O assembly of disciples! I have thrown the world prostrate before you, so do not lift it up after me, for one of the evils of this world is that Allah was disobeyed in it and one of the evils of this world is that the next world is not attained except by leaving this one. So pass through this world without making it livable, and know that the root of all wrong is the love of this world. Many a vain desire leaves an inheritance of lasting sorrow."

(*Biḥār*, 14, 327, 48)

وَلَمْ يَعْمَلْ بِقَلْبِهِ المَعاصِيَ. ما أبْعَدَ ما قَدْ فاتَ! وأدْنَي ما هُوَ آتٍ! وَيْلٌ لِلْمُغْتَرِّينَ, لَوْ قَدْ أزِقَّهُمْ ما يَكْرَهُونَ, وَفارَقَهُمْ ما يُحِبُّونَ, وَجاءَهُمْ ما يُوعَدُونَ. (فِي خَلْقِ هَذا اللَيْلِ والنَهارِ, مُعْتَبَرٌ.) وَيْلٌ لِمَنْ كانَتِ الدنْيا هَمَّهُ, والخَطايا عَمَلَهُ؛ كَيْفَ يَفْتَضِحُ غَداً عِنْدَ رَبِّهِ! وَلا تُكْثِرُوا الكَلامَ فِي غَيْرِ ذِكْرِ اللهِ, فإنَّ الذينَ يُكْثِرُونَ الكَلامَ فِي غَيْرِ ذِكْرِ اللهِ, قاسِيَةٌ قُلُوبُهُمْ, وَلَكِنْ لا يَعْلَمُونَ. لا تَنْظُرُوا إلي عُيُوبِ الناسِ كأنَّكُمْ رِئايا عَلَيْهِمْ, وَلَكِنْ انْظُرُوا فِي خَلاصِ أنْفُسِكُمْ. فإنَّما أنتُم عَبِيدٌ مَمْلُوكُونَ. إلي كَمْ يَسِيلُ الماءُ عَلَي الجَبَلِ, لا يَلِينُ؟ إلي كَمْ تَدْرُسُونَ الحِكْمَةَ, لا يَلِينُ عَلَيْها قُلُوبُكُمْ؟ عَبِيدَ السَوْءِ! فَلا عَبِيدٌ أتْقِياءُ, وَلا أحْرارٌ كِرامٌ, إنَّما مَثَلُكُمْ كَمَثَلِ الدِفْلِي, يُعْجِبُ بِزَهْرِها مَنْ يَراها, وَيَقْتُلُ مَنْ طَعِمَها. والسَلامُ.''»

(بحارالأنوار، ١٤، ٣٢٥، ٣٧)

٧-٣٣- قالَ عِيسَي عليه السلام: «يا بَنِي إسْرائِيلَ, لا تُكْثِرُوا الأكْلَ؛ فإنَّهُ مَنْ أكْثَرَ مِنَ الأكْلِ, أكْثَرَ مِنَ النَوْمِ, وَمَنْ أكْثَرَ النَوْمَ, أقَلَّ الصَلاةَ, وَمَنْ أقَلَّ الصَلاةَ, كُتِبَ مِنَ الغافِلِينَ.»

(شرح نهج البلاغة، ١٩، ١٨٨)

٧-٣٤- قالَ عِيسَي عليه السلام لِأصحابِهِ: «إنَّ النَوْمَ عَلَي المَزابِلِ وأكْلَ خُبْزِ الشَعِيرِ, خَيْرٌ كَثِيرٌ, مَعَ سَلامَةِ الدينِ.»

(آداب النفس، ١، ٢٢٣)

٧-٣٥- قالَ عِيسَي عليه السلام: «يا مَعْشَرَ الحَوارِيِّينَ, إنِّي قَدْ أكْبَبْتُ لَكُمُ الدنْيا عَلَي وَجْهِها, فَلا تَنْعَشُوها بَعْدِي فإنَّ مِنْ خُبْثِ الدنْيا, أنْ عُصِيَ اللهُ فِيها, وإنَّ مِنْ خُبْثِ الدنْيا, أنَّ الآخِرَةَ لا تُدْرَكُ إلّا بِتَرْكِها. فاعْبُرُوا الدنْيا وَلا تَعْمُرُوها, واعْلَمُوا أنَّ أصْلَ كُلِّ خَطِيئَةٍ, حُبُّ الدنْيا. وَرُبَّ شَهْوَةٍ, أوْرَثَتْ أهْلَها حُزْناً طَوِيلاً.»

(بحارالأنوار، ١٤، ٣٢٧، ٤٨)

7.36. Jesus said, "This world and the next one are rivals. When you satisfy one of them you irritate the other, and when you irritate one of them you satisfy the other."

(*Biḥār*, 70, 122)

7.37. When Jesus passed by a house the family of which had died and was replaced by others, he said, "Woe to your owners who inherited you! How they have learned no lesson from their late brothers."

(*Biḥar*, 14, 329, 60)

7.38. Jesus said, "Do not take the world as a master, for it will take you as its servants. Keep your treasure with one who will not squander it. The owners of the treasures of this world fear for its ruin, but he who owns the treasure of Allah does not fear for its ruin."

(*Biḥār*, 14, 327)

7.39. It is reported that [Imam] 'Alī said, "Jesus the son of Mary said, 'Blessed is he whose silence is contemplation (*fikr*), whose vision is an admonition, whose house suffices him and who cries over his mistakes and from whose hand and tongue the people are safe.'"

(*Biḥār*, 14, 319, 22)

7.40. And Jesus the son of Mary said, "There is no sickness of the heart more severe than calousness, and no soul is more severely afflicted than by the deprivation of hunger, and these two are the lines to exclusion and abandonment."

(*Biḥār*, 63, 337)

7.41. Jesus the son of Mary stood up among the Children of Israel to preach. He said, "O Children of Israel! Do not eat before you become hungry and when you become hungry eat but do not eat your

٧-٣٦- قالَ المَسيحُ عليه السلام: «مَثَلُ الدنْيا والآخِرَةِ, كَمَثَلِ رَجُلٍ لَهُ ضَرَّتان؛ إنْ أرْضَي إحْداهُما, سَخِطَتِ الأخْرَي.»

(بحارالأنوار، ٧٠، ١٢٢)

٧-٣٧- كانَ عِيسَي عليه السلام, إذا مَرَّ بِدارٍ قَدْ ماتَ أهْلُها وَخَلَفَ فِيها غَيْرُهُمْ, يَقُولُ: «وَيْحاً لِأرْبابِكَ الذينَ وَرَّثُوكَ! كَيْفَ لَمْ يَعْتَبِرُوا بِإخْوانِهِمُ الماضِينَ!»

(بحارالأنوار، ١٤، ٣٢٩، ٦٠)

٧-٣٨- قالَ عِيسَي عليه السلام: «لا تَتَّخِذُوا الدنْيا رَبّاً, فَتَتَّخِذَكُمْ عَبِيداً. إكْنِزُوا كَنْزَكُمْ عِنْدَ مَنْ لا يُضِيعُهُ, فإنَّ صاحِبَ كَنْزِ الدنْيا يُخافُ عَلَيْهِ الآفَةُ, وَصاحِبُ كَنْزِ اللهِ لا يُخافُ عَلَيْهِ الآفَةُ.»

(بحارالأنوار، ١٤، ٣٢٧)

٧-٣٩- ابن المُتَوَكِّلِ، عَنِ الحِمْيَرِى، عَنْ ابن هاشِمٍ، عَنْ ابن مِيْمُونٍ، عَنْ جَعْفَرِ بْنِ مُحَمَّدٍ، عَنْ آبائِهِ، عَنْ عَلِيٍّ عليه السلام, قالَ: «قالَ عِيسَي بْنُ مَرْيَمَ عليه السلام: 'طُوبَي لِمَنْ كانَ صَمْتُهُ فِكْراً, وَنَظَرُهُ عِبَراً, وَوَسِعَهُ بَيْتُهُ, وَبَكَي عَلَي خَطِيئَتِهِ, وَسَلِمَ الناسُ مِنْ يَدِهِ ولِسانِهِ.'»

(بحارالأنوار، ١٤، ٣١٩، ٢٢)

٧-٤٠- قالَ عِيسَي بْنُ مَرْيَمَ عليه السلام: «ما مَرِضَ قَلْبٌ بِأشَدَّ مِنَ القَسْوَةِ, وَما اعْتَلَّتْ نَفْسٌ بِأصْعَبَ مِنْ نَقْصِ الجُوعِ, وَهُما زِمامانِ لِلطَّرْدِ والخِذْلانِ.»

(بحار الأنوار، ٦٣، ٣٣٧)

٧-٤١- عَنْ عَلِيِّ بْنِ حَدِيدٍ, رَفَعَهُ, قالَ: «قامَ عِيسَي بْنُ مَرْيَمَ خَطِيباً فِى بَنِى إسْرائِيلَ, فَقالَ: 'يا بَنِى إسْرائِيلَ, لا تأكُلُوا حَتَّي تَجُوعُوا, وإذا جِعْتُمْ,

fill, because when you eat your fill your necks become thick and your sides grow fat and you forget your Lord."

(*Biḥār*, 63, 337, 30)

7.42. The Apostle of Allah [Muhammad] said, "Jesus the son of Mary stood up among the Children of Israel and said, 'O Children of Israel! Do not speak with the ignorant of wisdom, for otherwise you do injustice with it, and do not keep it from its folk, for otherwise you do injustice to them, and do not help the unjust with his injustice, for otherwise your virtue becomes void. Affairs are three: the affair whose righteousness is clear to you, so follow it; the affair whose error is clear to you, so avoid it; and the affair about which there are differences, so return it to Allah, the Almighty and Glorious.'"

(*Faqīh* 4, 400, 5858)

7.43. Jesus said, "In truth I say to you, just as one who is sick looks at food and finds no pleasure in it due to the severity of the pain, the masters of this world find no pleasure in worship and do not find the sweetness of it, for what they find is the sweetness of this world. In truth I say to you, just as an animal which is not captured and tamed becomes hardened and its character is changed, so too when hearts are not softened by the remembrance of death and the effort of worship they become hard and tough, and in truth I say to you, if a skin is not torn, it may become a vessel for honey, just as hearts, if they are not torn by desires, or fouled by greed, or hardened by blessings, may become vessels for wisdom."

(*Biḥār*, 14, 325, 38)

فكُلُوا وَلا تَشْبَعُوا, فإنَّكُمْ إذا شَبِعْتُمْ, غَلَظَتْ رِقابُكُمْ, وَسَمِنَتْ جُنُوبُكُمْ, وَنَسِيتُمْ رَبَّكُمْ.'»

(بحارالأنوار، ٦٣، ٣٣٧، ٣٠)

٧-٤٢- رَوَي عَلِيُّ بْنُ مَهْزِيارَ عَنِ الحُسَيْنِ بْنِ سَعِيدٍ، عَنِ الحارِثِ بْنِ مُحَمَّدِ بْنِ النعْمانِ الأحْوَلِ، صاحِبِ الطاقِ، عَنْ جَمِيلِ بْنِ صالِحٍ، عَنْ أبِي عَبْدِ اللهِ الصادِقِ، عَنْ آبائِهِ عليهم السلام، قالَ: «قالَ رَسُولُ اللهِ صلى الله عليه وآله: '... إنَّ عيسَي بن مَريَمَ عليه السلام قامَ فِي بَنِي إسْرائِيلَ، فقالَ: 'يا بَنِي إسْرائِيلَ، لا تُحَدِّثُوا بالحِكْمَةِ الجُهّالَ، فَتَظْلِمُوها، وَلا تَمْنَعُوها أهْلَها، فَتَظْلِمُوهُمْ؛ وَلا تُعِينُوا الظالِمَ عَلَي ظُلْمِهِ، فَيَبْطُلَ فَضْلُكُمْ. الأمُورُ ثَلاثَةٌ: أمْرٌ تَبَيَّنَ لَكَ رُشْدُهُ، فاتَّبِعْهُ، وأمْرٌ تَبَيَّنَ لَكَ غَيُّهُ، فاجْتَنِبْهُ، وأمْرٌ اُخْتُلِفَ فِيهِ، فَرُدَّهُ إلَي اللهِ، عَزَّ وَجَلَّ.''»

(كتاب من لايحضره الفقيه، ٤، ٤٠٠، ٥٨٥٨)

٧-٤٣- قالَ عِيسَي عليه السلام: «بِحَقٍّ أقُولُ لَكُمْ, كَما نَظَرَ المَرِيضُ إلَي الطَّعامِ فَلا يَلْتَذُّ بِهِ مِنْ شِدَّةِ الوَجَعِ, كَذَلِكَ صاحِبُ الدنْيا, لا يَلْتَذُّ بِالعِبادَةِ وَلا يَجِدُ حَلاوَتَها, مَعَ ما يَجِدُهُ مِنْ حَلاوَةِ الدنْيا. بِحَقٍّ أقُولُ لَكُمْ, كَما أنَّ الدابَّةَ إذا لَمْ تُرْكَبْ وَتُمْتَهَنْ, تَصَعَّبَتْ وَتَغَيَّرَ خُلُقُها, كَذَلِكَ القُلُوبُ, إذا لَمْ تُرَقَّقْ بِذِكْرِ المَوْتِ وَبِنَصَبِ العِبادَةِ, تَقْسُو وَتَغْلُظُ. وَبِحَقٍّ أقُولُ لَكُمْ, إنَّ الزِّقَّ إذا لَمْ يَنْخَرِقْ, يُوشِكُ أنْ يَكُونَ وِعاءَ العَسَلِ, كَذَلِكَ القُلُوبُ, إذا لَمْ تَخْرِقْها الشَهَواتُ أوْ يُدَنِّسْها الطَّمَعُ أوْ يُقَسِّها النَعِيمُ, فَسَوْفَ تَكُونُ أوْعِيَةَ الحِكْمَةِ.»

(بحارالأنوار، ١٤، ٣٢٥، ٣٨)

7.44. Abū ‘`Abdullāh al-Ṣādiq ﷺ said: “Jesus the son of Mary ﷺ said to his companions, ‘O children of Adam! Free yourselves from this world, escaping to Allah, and take your hearts out of it [this world]. Verily, you are not suitable for it [this world] and it is not suitable for you, and you do not remain in it and it does not remain for you. It is an insatiable deceiver. He who has emigrated to it is misled. He who relies on it has been duped. He who loves it and desires it is destroyed. So repent to your Lord, and fear your Lord, and beware a day when no father can compensate for his child and no child can be the compensation for his father. Where are your fathers? Where are your mothers? Where are your brothers? Where are your sisters? Where are your children? They were called and they answered, said farewell to the earth, joined the dead, and they came among the destroyed. They exit the world and separate from their loved ones, and are in need of what they sent ahead and needless of what they left behind. How much you have been advised and how much you have been prohibited, but you are frivolous and inattentive. Your likeness in this world is the like of beasts. Your zeal is for the inside of your belly and for your private parts. Do you not answer Him Who created you, while He threatened the disobedient with the Fire, and you are not able to cope with the Fire, and He promised the obedient the Garden and being near to Him in the high heaven? So compete for it and be deserving of it, and be fair to yourselves, and be kind to the weak and needy among you. And repent to Allah sincerely, and be righteous servants, and do not be oppresive kings or inordinate Pharaohs who conquers those who rebel against him by death. [And repent to] the Almighty of the mighty, Lord of the heavens and the earth, of the first and the last, Possessor of the Day of Judgment, the Severe in punishment, Whose chastisement is painful. No oppressor is saved from Him, and nothing escapes Him. Nothing slips past Him, and nothing disappears from His sight. His knowledge encompasses all thing, and He sends down to each according to his stations the Garden or the Fire. O

٧-٤٤- ابن إدْرِيْسٍ، عَنْ أبيهِ، عَنْ مُحَمَّدِ بْنِ عَبْدِ الجبّارِ، عَنِ الحَسَنِ بْنِ عَلِيٍّ بْنِ أبي حَمْزَةٍ، عَنْ سَيْفِ بْنِ عُمَيْرَةٍ، عَنْ مَنْصُورِ بْنِ حازِمٍ، عَنْ أبي عَبْدِ اللهِ الصادِقِ عليه السلام، قالَ: «كانَ عِيسَي بْنُ مَرْيَمَ عليه السلام يَقُولُ لِأصحابِهِ: 'يا بَنِي آدَمَ، اهْرَبُوا مِنَ الدنْيا إلَي اللهِ، وأخْرِجُوا قُلوبَكُمْ عَنْها، فإنَّكُمْ لا تَصلُحُونَ لَها وَلا تَصلُحُ لَكُمْ، وَلا تَبْقُونَ فِيها وَلا تَبْقي لَكُمْ. هِيَ الخَدّاعَةُ الفَجّاعَةُ. المَغْرُورُ مَنْ اغْتَرَّ بِها، المَغْبُونُ مَنْ اطْمأنَّ إلَيْها، الهالِكُ مَنْ أحَبَّها وأرادَها. فتُوبُوا إلَي بارِئِكُمْ، واتَّقُوا رَبَّكُمْ، واخْشَوْا يَوماً لا يَجْزِي والِدٌ عَنْ وَلَدِهِ وَلا مَوْلُودٌ، هُوَ جازٍ، عَنْ والِدِهِ شَيْئًا. أيْنَ آباؤُكُمْ؟ أيْنَ أمَّهاتُكُمْ؟ أيْنَ إخْوَتُكُمْ؟ أيْنَ أخَواتُكُمْ؟ أيْنَ أوْلادُكُمْ؟ دُعُوْا فأجابُوا، واسْتُوْدِعُوا الثَّرَي، وَجاوَرُوا المَوتَي، وَصارُوا فِي الهَلْكَي، خَرَجُوا عَنِ الدنْيا، وَفارَقُوا الأحِبَّةَ، واحْتاجُوا إلَي ما قَدَّمُوا، واسْتَغْنَوْا عَمّا خَلَّفُوا. فَكَمْ تُوعَظُونَ! وَكَمْ تُزْجَرُونَ! وأنتُم لاهُونَ، ساهُونَ. مَثَلُكُم فِي الدنْيا مَثَلُ البَهائِمِ، هِمَّتُكُمْ بُطُونُكُمْ وَفُرُوجُكُمْ. أما تَسْتَحْيُونَ مِمَّنْ خَلَقَكُمْ، وَقَدْ أوْعَدَ مَنْ عَصاهُ النارَ، وَلَسْتُمْ مِمَّنْ يَقْوَي عَلَي النارِ؛ وَوَعَدَ مَنْ أطاعَهُ الجَنَّةَ وَمُجاوَرَتَهُ فِي الفِرْدَوْسِ الأعلَي؛ فَتَنافَسُوا فِيهِ، وَكُونُوا مِنْ أهْلِهِ، وأنْصِفُوا مِنْ أنْفُسِكُمْ، وَتَعَطَّفُوا عَلَي ضُعَفائِكُمْ وأهْلِ الحاجَةِ مِنْكُمْ، وَتُوبُوا إلَي اللهِ تَوْبَةً نَصُوحاً، وَكُونُوا عَبِيداً أبْراراً، وَلا تَكُونُوا مُلُوكاً جَبابِرَةً، وَلا مِنَ العُتاةِ الفَراعِنَةِ المُتَمَرِّدِينَ عَلَي مَنْ قَهَرَهُمْ بِالمَوْتِ. جَبّارُ الجَبابِرَةِ، رَبُّ السماواتِ وَرَبُّ الأرَضِينَ، وإلَهُ الأوَّلِينَ والآخِرِينَ، مالِكُ يَوْمِ الدينِ، شَدِيدُ العِقابِ، ألِيمُ العَذابِ، لا يَنْجُو مِنْهُ ظالِمٌ، وَلا يَفُوتُهُ شَيْءٌ، وَلا يَعْزُبُ عَنْهُ شَيْءٌ، وَلا يَتَوارَي مِنْهُ شَيْءٌ، أحْصَي كُلَّ شَيْءٍ عِلْمُهُ، وأنْزَلَهُ مَنْزِلَتَهُ

weak son of Adam! Where would you run from Him Who seeks you in the dark of your night and the brightness of your day, and in every state in which you may be. One who advised delivered his advice; and one who has listened to the advice is saved.'"

(*Biḥār*, 14, 288, 12)

7.45. Imam al-Ṣādiq ﵇ said: "Jesus the son of Mary said to the Apostles, 'Beware of looking at what is prohibited, for it is the seed lust and plant of depravity.'"

(*Biḥār*, 101, 41)

7.46. Jesus son of Mary ﵇ said, "The most wretched of people is he who is known by the people for his knowledge and is not known for his works."

(*Biḥār*, 2, 52, 19)

7.47. Al-Ṣādiq ﵇ said, "Jesus ﵇ said, 'Keep company with him the vision and encounter—let alone speech—of whom reminds you of Allah. And do not keep company with him who is agreeable to your exterior but to whom your interior is opposed, for, verily, such a person makes a claim for what is not due to him, if you are sincere about what is to your benefit. Make the most of the vision and encounter and company of one who has three traits, even if but for an hour, for his blessings will be effective in your religion and your heart and your worship: his speech does not go beyond his action, his action does not go beyond his truthfulness, and his truthfulness is not removed from his Lord. So, keep company with him honorably, and await mercy and blessings and beware the necessity of his proof against you and tend to his time that he does not reproach you then you would incur loss, and look at him by the eye of the grace and magnanimity granted especially to him by Allah.'"

(*Biḥār*, 97, 84)

فِي جَنَّةٍ أوْ نارٍ. ابن آدَمَ الضَّعِيفَ! أيْنَ تَهْرَبُ مِمَّنْ يَطْلُبُكَ فِي سَوادِ لَيْلِكَ وَبَياضِ نَهارِكَ، وَفِي كُلِّ حالٍ مِنْ حالاتِكَ؟ قَدْ أبْلَغَ مَنْ وَعَظَ، وأفْلَحَ مَنْ اتَّعَظَ.»

(بحارالأنوار، ١٤، ٢٨٨، ١٢)

٧-٤٥- قالَ عِيسَي بْنُ مَرْيَمَ لِلْحَوارِيِّينَ: «إيّاكُمْ والنَظَرَ إلَي المَحْذُوراتِ، فإنّها بَذْرُ الشهَواتِ وَنَباتُ الفِسْقِ.»

(بحارالأنوار، ١٠١، ٤١)

٧-٤٦- قالَ عِيسَي بْنُ مَرْيَمَ عليه السلام: «أشْقَي الناسِ مَنْ هُوَ مَعرُوفٌ عِنْدَ الناسِ بِعِلْمِهِ، مَجْهُولٌ بِعَمَلِهِ.»

(بحارالأنوار، ٢، ٥٢، ١٩)

٧-٤٧- قالَ عِيسَي عليه السلام: «جالِسُوا مَنْ تُذَكِّرُكُمُ اللهَ رُؤْيَتُهُ ولِقاؤُهُ، فَضْلاً عَنِ الكَلامِ؛ وَلا تُجالِسُوا مَنْ يُوافِقُهُ ظاهِرُكُمْ وَيُخالِفُهُ باطِنُكُمْ، فإنَّ ذَلِكَ، المُدَّعِي بِمَا لَيسَ لَهُ، إنْ كُنْتُمْ صادِقِينَ فِي استِفادَتِكُمْ. فإذا لَقِيتَ مَنْ فِيهِ ثَلاثُ خِصالٍ، فاغْتَنِمْ رؤْيَتَهُ ولِقاءَهُ وَمُجالَسَتَهُ، وَلَوْ ساعَةً. فإنَّ ذَلِكَ، يُؤَثِّرُ فِي دِينِكَ وَقَلْبِكَ وَعِبادَتِكَ بَرَكاتُهُ. قَوْلُهُ لا يُجاوِزُ فِعْلَهُ، وَفِعْلُهُ لا يُجاوِزُ صِدْقَهُ، وَصِدْقُهُ لا يُنازِعُ رَبَّهُ. فَجالِسْهُ بِالحُرْمَةِ، وانْتَظِرْ الرحْمَةَ والبَرَكَةَ، واحْذَرْ لُزُومَ الحُجَّةِ عَلَيْكَ، وَراعِ وَقْتَهُ، كَيلا تَلُومَهُ فَتَخْسَرُ، وانْظُرْ إلَيْهِ بِعَيْنِ فَضْلِ اللهِ عَلَيْهِ وَتَخْصِيصِهِ لَهُ وَكَرامَتِهِ إيّاهُ.»

(بحارالأنوار، ٩٧، ٨٤)

٧-٤٨- قالَ عِيسَي عليه السلام: «بِحَقٍّ أقُولُ لَكُمْ، إنَّ أكْنافَ السَماءِ لَخالِيَةٌ مِنَ الأغنياءِ، ولَدُخُولُ جَمَلٍ فِي سَمِّ الخِياطِ أيْسَرُ مِنْ دُخُولِ غَنِيٍّ الجَنَّةَ.»

(بحارالأنوار، ٦٩، ٥٥)

7.48. Jesus said, "In truth I say to you, the folds of heaven are empty of the rich, and the entering of a camel through the eye of a needle is easier than the entering of a rich man into heaven."

(*Biḥār*, 69, 55)

7.49. Jesus the son of Mary said, "Take the truth from the folk of falsehood, but do not take the false from the folk of truth. Be critics of speech. How much aberration is adorned by a verse of the Book of Allah, like the adornment of a copper dirham with silver plating. Looking at it is the same, but those who have vision are aware."

(*Biḥār*, 2, 96, 39)

7.50. Imām Ṣādiq said: "... Jesus the son of Mary said, 'Keep your tongue to reform your heart, and be satisfied with your house, and beware of pretentiousness and excess, and be ashamed before your Lord, and cry over your mistakes, and escape from the people as you would run from the lion or viper, [for] they were medicine but today, they have become illness. Then encounter Allah when you will.'"

(*Biḥār*, 67, 110)

7.51. Jesus the son of Mary said, "O seeker of this world for the sake of doing good, abandoning the world is better."

(*Majmū'a Warram*, 1, 134)

7.52. Jesus the son of Mary said, "Beauty of dress is pride of heart."

(*Biḥār*, 70, 207)

7.53. Among the words of Jesus, "Consider your houses as way stations, and the mosques as your residences, and eat the grains of the land and drink of pure water, and go out of the world in health. Upon my life! You have directed yourself to what is other than Allah. What has corrupted you? Are you afraid of becoming lost if you direct yourself toward Allah."

(*Sharḥ Najh al-Balāghah*, 3, 155)

٧-٤٩ - عَلِيُّ بْنُ عِيسَي القاسانِيّ، عَنِ ابْن مَسْعُودٍ المَيْسَرِيِّ رفَعَهُ، قالَ: «قالَ المَسِيحُ عليه السلام: ''خُذُوا الحَقَّ مِنْ أَهْلِ الباطِلِ، وَلا تَأْخُذُوا الباطِلَ مِنْ أَهْلِ الحَقِّ. كُونُوا نُقّادَ الكَلامِ، فَكَمْ مِنْ ضَلالةٍ زُخْرِفتْ بِآيَةٍ مِنْ كِتابِ اللهِ، كَما زُخْرِفَ الدِرْهَمُ مِنْ نُحاسٍ بِالفِضّةِ المُمَوَّهَةِ؛ النَظَرُ إِلي ذَلِكَ سَواءٌ، والبُصَراءُ بِهِ خُبَراءُ.''.»

(بحار الأنوار، ٢، ٩٦، ٣٩)

٧-٥٠ - قالَ عِيسَي بْنُ مَرْيَمَ عليه السلام: «أخْزُنْ لِسانَكَ لِعِمارَةِ قَلْبِكَ، وَلْيَسَعْكَ بَيْتُكَ، وَفِرَّ مِنَ الرِياءِ وَفُضُولِ مَعاشِكَ، وابْكِ عَلَي خَطِيئَتِكَ، وَفِرَّ مِنَ الناسِ فِرارَكَ مِنَ الأسَدِ والأفعَي ، فإِنَّهُمْ كانُوا دَواءً، فَصارُوا اليَوْمَ داءً، ثُمَّ القَ اللهَ مَتَي شِئْتَ.»

(بحار الأنوار، ٦٧، ١١٠)

٧-٥١ - قالَ عِيسَي عليه السلام: «يا طالِبَ الدنْيا لِتَبِرَّ، تَرْكُكَ الدنْيا أبَرُّ.»

(مجموعة ورّام، ١، ١٣٤)

٧-٥٢ - قالَ عِيسَي عليه السلام: «جَوْدَةُ الثِّيابِ، خُيلاءُ القَلْبِ.»

(بحار الأنوار، ٧٠، ٢٠٧)

٧-٥٣ - مِنْ كَلامِ عِيسَي عليه السلام: «اتَّخِذُوا البُيُوتَ مَنازِلَ، والمَساجِدَ مَساكِنَ، وكُلُوا مِنْ بَقْلِ البَرِّيَّةِ، واشْرَبُوا مِنَ الماءِ القِراحِ، واخْرُجُوا مِنَ الدنْيا بِسَلامٍ. لَعَمْرى، لَقَدْ انْقَطَعْتُمْ إِلي غَيْرِ اللهِ، فَما ضَيَّعَكُمْ؟ أفَتَخافُونَ الضَّيْعَةَ إِذا انْقَطَعْتُمْ إِلَيْهِ؟.»

(شرح نهج البلاغة، ٣، ١٥٥)

7.54. Imām Bāqir said, "Christ said, 'O group of disciples! The foul odor of the oil will not harm you when the light of its lamp reaches you. Take knowledge from he who has it, and do not look at his works.'"

(*Biḥar*, 2, 97, 42)

7.55. Jesus used to say, "O weak son of Adam! Beware of your Lord, and cast away your greed, and be weak in the world, and be modest in your desires. Accustom your body to patience and your heart to contemplation (*fikr*). And do not withhold sustenance for tomorrow, because it is a mistake for you. And multiply praise to Allah for poverty (*faqr*), for it is a sort of impeccability that you cannot do what you want."

(*Biḥār*, 14, 329, 62)

7.56. Among the words attributed to Jesus are, "On a day when one of you fasts, he should oil his head and beard and should wipe his lips [with oil] so that the people do not know that he is fasting. When he gives [charity] by his right hand, he should hide it from his left hand. And when he prays, he should let down the curtain over his door. Verily Allah divides praise as He divides sustenance."

(*Sharḥ Nahj al-Balāgha*, 2, 181)

7.57. It is reported that Abū 'Abdullah said, "Jesus the son of Mary, passed by Ṣafā'iḥ al-Rawḥā' and he said, 'Here I am, Your servant, the son of your bondwoman, here I am.'"

(*Faqīh*, 2, 234, 2284)

7.58. Jesus used to say, "O house! You will be destroyed, and your inhabitants will die. And O soul! Work and have sustenance. And O body! Toil, then rest."

(*Biḥār* 14, 329, 61)

7.59. Jesus said, "Worship has ten parts. Nine of them are in silence and one is in withdrawing from the people."

(*Majmū'a Warrām*, 1, 106)

٧-٥٤- ابن يَزيدٍ، عَنْ ابن أبِي عُمَيْرٍ، عَنْ ابن أُذَيْنَةٍ، عَنْ زُرارَةٍ، عَنْ أبِي جَعْفَرٍ (ع)، قالَ: «قالَ المَسِيحُ (ع): 'مَعْشَرَ الحَوارِيِّين، لَمْ يَضُرُّكُمْ مَنْ نَتَنَ القَطِرانَ، إذا أصابَتْكُمْ سِراجُهُ. خُذُوا العِلْمَ مِمَّنْ عِنْدَهُ، ولا تَنْظُرُوا إلي عَمَلِهِ.'»

(بحارالانوار، ٢، ٩٧، ٤٢)

٧-٥٥- كانَ عِيسَي (ع) يقُولُ: «يا ابن آدَمَ الضَّعِيفِ! اتَّقِ رَبَّكَ، وألْقِ طَمَعَكَ، وكُنْ فِي الدنْيا ضَعِيفاً، وعَنْ شَهْوَتِكَ عَفِيفاً. عَوِّدْ جِسْمَكَ الصبْرَ وقَلْبَكَ الفِكْرَ. ولا تَحْبِسْ لِغَدٍ رِزْقاً، فإنَّها خَطِيئَةٌ عَلَيْكَ. وأكْثِرْ حَمْدَ اللهِ عَلي الفقر، فإنَّ مِنَ العِصْمَةِ أنْ لا تَقْدِرَ عَلي ما تُرِيدُ.»

(بحارالانوار، ١٤، ٣٢٩، ٦٢)

٧-٥٦- مِنَ الكَلامِ المَعْزُوِّ إلي عِيسَي بْنِ مَرْيَمَ (ع): «إذا كانَ يَوْمُ صَوْمِ أحَدِكُمْ، فَلْيَدْهُنْ راسَهُ ولِحْيَتَهُ ولْيَمْسَحْ شَفَتَيْهِ، لِئَلا يَعْلَمَ الناسُ أنَّهُ صائِمٌ. وإذا أعْطَي بِيَمِينِهِ، فَلْيُخْفِ عَنْ شِمالِهِ. وإذا صَلَّي، فَلْيُرْخِ سِتْرَ بابِهِ، فإنَّ اللهَ يُقَسِّمُ الثَّناءَ كَما يُقَسِّمُ الرزْقَ.»

(شرح نهج البلاغة، ٢، ١٨١)

٧-٥٧- رُوِيَ فِي خَبَرٍ [عَنْ أبِي عَبْدِ اللهِ (ع)]: «... مَرَّ عِيسَى بن مَرْيَمَ (ع) بِصَفائِحِ الرَوْحاءِ، وَهُوَ يَقُولُ: 'لَبَّيْكَ، عَبْدُكَ ابن أمَتِكَ، لَبَّيْكَ.'»

(كتاب من لا يحضره الفقيه، ٢، ٢٣٤، ٢٢٨٤)

٧-٥٨- كانَ عِيسَي (ع) يقُولُ: «يا دارُ! تَخْرَبِينَ، وتَفْنَي سُكّانُكَ. ويا نَفْسُ! اعْمَلِي، تُرْزَقِي. ويا جَسَدُ! انْصَبْ، تَسْتَرِحْ.»

(بحارالانوار، ١٤، ٣٢٩، ٦١)

٧-٥٩- قالَ عِيسَي (ع): «العِبادَةُ عَشْرَةُ أجْزاءٍ. تِسْعَةٌ مِنْها فِي الصَمْتِ، وَجُزْءٌ فِي الفَرارِ مِنَ الناسِ.»

(مجموعة ورّام، ١، ١٠٦)

7.60. Jesus said, "Among the greatest of sins is that when he does not know something, a servant says, 'Verily, Allah knows it,' and even when he lies about what he has dreamed, this is a great sin."

(*Biḥār*, 69, 258)

7.61. When Allah raised Jesus as a prophet, Satan turned to him and tempted him. Jesus said, "Glory be to Allah, with a plenum of His heavens and earth and the ink of His words and the weight of His throne and His own satisfaction.". [Imam] said, "When Satan heard this, he ran away in the direction he faced, unable to control himself at all, until he fell into the green waves [of the depths of the sea]."

(*Biḥār*, 90, 181, 14)

7.62. It is reported that Abū 'Abdullah said, regarding the saying of Allah, the Mighty and Magnificent, ❬*He has made me blessed wherever I may be*❭ (19:26), "Very beneficial."

(*Biḥār*, 14, 247)

7.63. The Messenger of Allah said, "Eat lentils, for they are blessed and sacred. They soften the heart and increase tears. Seventy prophets blessed them, the last of whom was Jesus the son of Mary."

(*Biḥār*, 14, 254, 48)

7.64. Jesus the son of Mary said, "Hardening of the heart is from drying of the eyes, and drying of the eyes is from accumulating sins, and accumulating sins is from loving the world, and loving the world is at the head of all error."

(*Mustadrak al-Wasā'il*, 12, 39, 13458)

٧-٦٠- قالَ عِيسَي: «إنَّ مِنْ أعْظَمِ الذُنُوبِ عِنْدَ اللهِ، أنْ يَقُولَ العَبْدُ: 'إنَّ اللهَ يَعْلَمُ،' لِما لا يَعْلَمْ. ورُبَّما يَكْذِبُ فِي حِكايَةِ المَنامِ، والإثْمُ فِيهِ عَظِيمٌ.»

(بحارالانوار، ٦٩، ٢٥٨)

٧-٦١- ابن شاذوَيْهِ، عَنْ مُحَمَّدٍ الحِمْيَري، عَنْ أبِيهِ، عَنْ ابن يَزِيدٍ، عَنْ ابن أبِي عُمَيْرٍ، عَنْ أبانِ بْنِ عُثْمانٍ، عَنْ أبانِ بْنِ تَغْلِبٍ، عَنْ عِكْرِمَةٍ، عَنْ ابن عبّاسٍ، قالَ: «لَمّا أنْ بَعَثَ اللهُ عِيسَي عليه السلام، تَعَرَّضَ لَهُ الشيْطانُ، فوَسْوَسَهُ. فَقالَ عِيسَي عليه السلام: 'سُبْحانَ اللهِ مِلْءَ سَماواتِهِ وأرْضِهِ ومِدادَ كَلِماتِهِ وزِنَةَ عَرْشِهِ ورِضا نَفْسِهِ.'» قالَ: «فَلَمّا سَمِعَ إبْلِيسُ ذلِكَ، ذَهَبَ عَلَي وَجْهِهِ، لا يَمْلِكُ مِنْ نَفْسِهِ شَيْئًا، حَتَّي وَقَعَ فِي اللجَّةِ الخَضْراءِ.»

(بحارالانوار، ٩٠، ١٨١، ١٤)

٧-٦٢- أبِي، عَنْ سَعْدٍ، عَنْ ابن يَزِيدٍ، عَنْ يَحْيَي بْنِ المُبارَكِ، عَنْ عَبْدِ اللهِ بْنِ جِبِلَّةٍ، عَنْ رَجُلٍ، عَنْ أبِي عَبْدِ اللهِ عليه السلام، فِي قَوْلِ اللهِ، عَزَّ وَجَلَّ: ﴿وَجَعَلَنِي مُبارَكاً، أيْنَ ما كُنْتُ،﴾ قالَ: «نَفّاعاً.»

(بحارالانوار، ١٤، ٢٤٧)

٧-٦٣- عَنِ الرضا، عَنْ آبائِهِ عليهم السلام، قالَ: «قالَ رَسُولُ اللهِ صلى الله عليه وآله وسلم: 'عَلَيْكُمْ بِالعَدَسِ، فإنَّهُ مُبارَكٌ، مُقَدَّسٌ، يُرَقِّقُ القَلْبَ، ويُكَثِّرُ الدمْعَةَ، وقَدْ بارَكَ فِيهِ سَبْعُونَ نَبِيّاً، آخِرُهُمْ عِيسَي بْنُ مَرْيَمَ عليه السلام.'»

(بحارالانوار، ١٤، ٢٥٤، ٤٨)

٧-٦٤- «قالَ عِيسَى ابن مَرْيَمَ: 'قَسْوَةُ القُلُوبِ مِنْ جَفْوَةِ العُيُونِ، وَجَفْوَةُ العُيُونِ مِنْ كَثْرَةِ الذُنُوبِ، وكَثْرَةُ الذُنُوبِ مِنْ حُبِّ الدنْيا، وَحُبُّ الدنْيا رأسُ كُلِّ خَطِيئَةٍ.'»

(مستدرك الوسائل، ١٢، ٣٩، ١٣٤٥٨)

7.65. Abū Amāma said, "I said, 'O Apostle of Allah! When was the beginning of your apearance?' He said, 'The calling of my father Abraham and good news of Jesus the son of Mary and my mother saw that something went out of her that castles of Syria were lightened by it.'"

(*Biḥār*, 16, 321, 9)

7.66. Daḥya al-Kalbī said, "The Apostle of Allah sent me with a letter to the Caesar. Caesar sent [some one] to the beshop [to come]. I informed him about Muḥammad and his Book. The bishop said, 'This is the prophet whom we expected, Jesus the son of Mary announced him to us. As for me, I confirm him and follow him.' Caesar said, 'As for me, if I do this my kingdom will be lost...'"

(*Biḥār*, 20, 378)

7.67. Jesus said, "Do not worry about your livelihood for tomorrow. If tomorrow is a part of your life, your livelihood will come along with your life, and if it is not a part of your life, then do not worry about the livelihood of others."

(*Majmu'ah Warrām*, 1, 278)

7.68. Jesus said, "Blessed is he to whom Allah has taught His book, and then he does not die as a tyrant."

(*Majmu'ah Warrām*, 1, 198)

7.69. Jesus said to some of the apostles, "Your distance from the wrath of Allah is in your not being wrathful."

(*Majmu'ah Warrām*, 2, 27)

7.70. Al-Sayyid ibn Ṭāwūs, may Allah have mercy on him, said, "I read in the Gospel that Jesus said, "Who among you gives his son a stone when he asks for bread? Or who gives a snake when asked for a cloak? If depite the fact that your evil is well known you give good gifts to your sons, then it is more fitting that your Lord gives good things to one who asks."

(*Biḥār*, 14, 317)

٧-٦٥- ...حَدَّثَنا الفَرَجُ بْنُ فُضالَةٍ، عَنْ لُقمانَ بْنِ عامِرٍ، عَنْ أبِى أمامَةٍ، قالَ: «قُلْتُ: 'يا رَسُولَ اللهِ، ما كانَ بَدْءُ أمْرِكَ؟' قالَ: 'دَعْوَةُ أبِى إبْراهِيمَ، وَبُشْرَي عِيسَي بْنِ مَرْيَمَ، وَرأتْ أمِّى أنَّهُ خَرَجَ مِنْها شَئٌ أضاءَتْ مِنْهُ قُصُورُ الشامِ.'»

(بحارالانوار، ١٦، ٩،٣٢١)

٧-٦٦- دِحْيَةُ الكَلْبِي، قالَ: «بَعَثَنِى رَسُولُ اللهِ صلى الله عليه وآله وسلم بِكِتابٍ إلِي قَيْصَرَ. فأرْسَلَ إلِي الأسْقُفِ، فأخْبَرَهُ بِمُحَمَّدٍ صلى الله عليه وآله وسلم وكِتابِهِ. فَقالَ: 'هَذا النَبِىُّ الذى كُنّا نَنْتَظِرُهُ، بَشَّرَنا بِهِ عِيسَي بْنُ مَرْيَمَ.' فَقالَ الأسْقُفُ: 'أمّا أنا، فَمُصَدِّقُهُ وَمُتْبِعُهُ.' فَقالَ قَيْصَرُ: 'أمّا أنا، إنْ فَعَلْتُ ذلِكَ ذَهَبَ مُلْكِي...'»

(بحار الأنوار، ٢٠، ٣٧٨)

٧-٦٧- قالَ عِيسَي عليه السلام: «لا تَهْتَمُّوا بِرِزْقِ غَدٍ، فإنْ يَكُنْ مِنْ آجالِكُمْ، فَسَيأتِى فِيهِ أرْزاقُكُمْ مَعَ آجالِكُمْ؛ وإنْ لَمْ يَكُنْ مِنْ آجالِكُمْ، فَلا تَهْتَمُّوا لِآجالِ غَيْرِكُمْ.»

(مجموعة ورّام، ١، ٢٧٨)

٧-٦٨- قالَ عِيسَي عليه السلام: «طُوبَي لِمَنْ عَلَّمَهُ اللهُ كِتابَهُ، ثُمَّ لَمْ يَمُتْ جَبّاراً.»

(مجموعة ورّام، ١، ١٩٨)

٧-٦٩- قالَ عِيسَي عليه السلام لِرَجُلٍ مِنَ الحَوارِيِّينَ: «تَباعُدُكَ مِنْ غَضَبِ اللهِ، أنْ لا تَغْضَبَ.»

(مجموعة ورّام، ٢، ٢٧)

٧-٧٠- قالَ عِيسَي عليه السلام: «أىُّ إنْسانٍ مِنْكُمْ يَسْألُهُ ابنهُ خُبْزاً، فَيُعْطِيهِ حَجَراً؟ أوْ يَسْألُهُ شَمْلَةً، فَيُعْطِيهِ حَيَّةً؟ فإذا كُنْتُمْ أنتُم الأشْرارُ تُعْرَفُونَ، تُعْطُونَ العَطايا الصالِحَةَ لِأبْنائِكُمْ، فَكانَ بِالأحرَي رَبُّكُمْ أنْ يُعْطِيَكُمُ الخَيْراتِ لِمَنْ يَسْألُهُ.»

(بحارالأنوار، ١٤، ٣١٧)

7.71. It is reported that Abu 'Abdullah said, "Christ used to say, 'If someone abandons giving aid to one who has been injured, he is certainly a partner to the party who injured him.... Likewise, do not narrate wisdom to those who are not fit for it, for they are ignorant. And to not prevent those who are fit for it, for that would be a sin. Each of you must be like a prescribing physician if he sees that the condition is appropriate to a certain medicine, otherwise, he withholds it.'"

(*Kāfī,* 8, 345, 545)

7.72. Mūsā ibn Ja'far said, "...O Hishām! Verily, the Messiah said to the apostles, 'O evil servants! The height of the date palm frightens you, and you remember its spikes and the difficulty of climbing it, but you forget the wholesomeness and benefit of its fruit; likewise you remember the difficulty of deeds for the other world, and it seems to you to take a long time, but you forget the obtaining of the blessings, light and fruit of those deeds... In truth, I say to you, one who has no debt to the people is happier and less sad than one who has debts, even if his paying it is excellent. Likewise, one who does not make a mistake is happier and less sad than one who makes mistakes, even if his repentance is pure and he returns [to goodness.] Small sins and those considered paltry are among the deceptions of Satan. He makes them seem paltry to you and makes them small in your eyes, so they will be gathered and increased and will sorround you... O evil servants! Do not be like stealing kites, deceptive foxes, misleading wolves or vicious lions. You treat the people as you do your horses, from some you steal, some you deceive and some you mislead. In truth I say to you, it is not sufficient for a body that its exterior is sound but its interior is corrupt. Likewise it is not sufficient for you that your bodies be pleasing to you while your hearts are corrupted. It is not sufficient for you that you cleanse your skins, while your hearts are unclean.

٧-٧١- عِدَّةٌ مِنْ أصْحابِنا، عَنْ سَهْلِ بْنِ زِيادٍ، عَنْ عُبَيْدِ اللهِ الدهْقان، عَنْ عَبْدِ اللهِ بْنِ القاسِمِ، عَنِ ابن أبِي نَجْرانَ، عَنْ أبانِ بْنِ تَغْلِبَ، عَنْ أبِي عَبْدِ اللهِ عليه السلام، قالَ: «كانَ المَسِيحُ عليه السلام يَقُولُ: 'إنَّ التارِكَ شِفاءَ المَجْرُوحِ مِنْ جُرْحِهِ، شَرِيكٌ لِجارِحِهِ لا مَحالَةَ؛ وَذلِكَ أنَّ الجارِحَ أرادَ فَسادَ المَجْرُوحِ، والتارِكَ لِإشْفائِهِ لَمْ يَشأ صَلاحَهُ. فإذا لَمْ يَشأ صَلاحَهُ فَقَدْ شاءَ فَسادَهُ اضْطِراراً. فَكَذلِكَ لا تُحَدِّثُوا بالحِكْمَةِ غَيْرَ أهْلِها فَتَجْهَلُوا، وَلا تَمْنَعُوها أهْلَها فَتأثَمُوا؛ وَلْيَكُنْ أحَدُكُمْ بِمَنْزِلَةِ الطَّبِيبِ المُداوِي، إنْ رأي مَوْضِعاً لِدَوائِهِ، وإلّا أمْسَكَ.'»

(الكافى، ٨، ٣٤٥، ٥٤٥)

٧-٧٢- قالَ مُوسَي ابن جَعْفَرٍ عليه السلام لِهِشامِ بن الحَكَمْ: «يا هِشامُ، إنَّ المَسِيحَ عليه السلام قالَ لِلْحَوارِيِّينَ: 'يا عَبِيدَ السَوءِ! يَهُولُكُمْ طَولُ النَخْلَةِ، وَتَذْكُرُونَ شَوْكَها وَمَؤُونَةَ مَراقِيها، وَتَنْسَوْنَ طِيبَ ثَمَرِها وَمُرافِقَتَها. كَذلِكَ، تَذْكُرُونَ مَؤُونَةَ عَمَلِ الآخِرَةِ، فَيَطُولُ عَلَيْكُمْ أمَدُهُ، وَتَنْسَوْنَ ما تُفْضُونَ إلَيْهِ، مِنْ نَعِيمِها وَنُورِها وَثَمَرِها.... بِحَقٍّ أقُولُ لَكُمْ، إنَّ مَنْ لَيْسَ عَلَيْهِ دَيْنٌ مِنَ الناسِ أرْوَحُ، وأقَلُّ هَمّاً، مِمَّنْ عَلَيْهِ الدينُ، وإنْ أحْسَنَ القَضاءَ. وكَذلِكَ، مَنْ لَمْ يَعْمَلْ الخَطِيئَةَ، أرْوَحُ، وأقَلُّ هَمّاً مِمَّنْ عَمِلَ الخَطِيئَةَ، وإنْ أخْلَصَ التَوْبَةَ، وأنابَ. وإنَّ صِغارَ الذُنُوبِ وَمُحَقَّراتِها، مِنْ مَكائِدِ إبْلِيسَ. يُحَقِّرُها لَكُمْ وَيُصَغِّرُها فِي أعْيُنِكُمْ، فَتَجْتَمِعُ وَتَكْثُرُ، فَتُحِيطُ بِكُمْ... يا عَبِيدَ السَوءِ! لا تَكُونُوا شَبِيهاً بِالحِداءِ الخاطِفَةِ، وَلا بِالثَّعالِبِ الخادِعَةِ، وَلا بِالذِّئابِ الغادِرَةِ، وَلا بِالأسْدِ العاتِيَةِ. كَما تُفْعَلُ بِالفِراسِ، كَذلِكَ تَفْعَلُونَ بِالناسِ؛ فَرِيقاً تَخْطَفُونَ، وَفَرِيقاً تَخْدَعُونَ، وَفَرِيقاً تَغْدِرُونَ بِهِمْ. بِحَقٍّ أقُولُ لَكُمْ، لا يُغْنِى عَنِ الجَسَدِ أنْ يَكُونَ ظاهِرُهُ صَحِيحاً وَباطِنُهُ فاسِداً. كَذلِكَ، لا تُغْنِى أجْسادُكُمُ الَّتِى قَدْ أعْجَبَتْكُمْ، وَقَدْ فَسَدَتْ قُلُوبُكُمْ؛ وَما يُغْنِى عَنْكُمْ أنْ تُنَقُّوا جُلُودَكُمْ، وَقُلُوبُكُمْ

Do not be like the sieve that the pure flour goes down from it and keeps the siftings. Likewise you send out wisdom from your mouths, and hatred remains in your brests..."

(*Biḥār*, 1, 145, 146)

7.73. Al-Sayyid ibn Ṭāwūs, may Allah have mercy on him, said, "I read in the Gospel that Jesus said, 'I tell you, do not worry about what you will eat or what you will drink or with what you will clothe your bodies. Is not the soul more excellent than food, and the body more excellent than clothes? Look at the birds of the air, they neither sow nor reap nor store away, yet your heavenly Lord provides for them. Are you not more excellent than they? Who among you by worrying can add a single measure to his stature? Then why do you worry about your clothes?'"

(*Biḥār*, 14, 317, 17).[1]

---

[1] Cf. Matt 6:25-34:

25 "Therefore I tell you, do not worry about your life, what you will eat or drink; or about your body, what you will wear. Is not life more important than food, and the body more important than clothes?

26 Look at the birds of the air; they do not sow or reap or store away in barns, and yet your heavenly Father feeds them. Are you not much more valuable than they?

27 Who of you by worrying can add a single hour to his life?

28 "And why do you worry about clothes? See how the lilies of the field grow. They do not labor or spin.

29 Yet I tell you that not even Solomon in all his splendor was dressed like one of these.

30 If that is how God clothes the grass of the field, which is here today and tomorrow is thrown into the fire, will he not much more clothe you, O you of little faith?

31 So do not worry, saying, 'What shall we eat?' or 'What shall we drink?' or 'What shall we wear?'

32 For the pagans run after all these things, and your heavenly Father knows that you need them.

33 But seek first his kingdom and his righteousness, and all these things will be given to you as well.

34 Therefore do not worry about tomorrow, for tomorrow will worry about itself. Each day has enough trouble of its own.

(NIV)

دَنِسَةً. لا تَكُونُوا كالمِنْخَلِ، يَخْرُجُ مِنْهُ الدقِيقُ الطَّيِّبُ، ويُمْسِكُ النخالَةَ. كَذَلِكَ، أنتُم تُخْرِجُونَ الحِكْمَةَ مِنْ أفْواهِكُمْ، ويَبْقَي الغِلُّ فِي صُدُورِكُمْ....'»

(بحارالانوار، ١، ١٤٥- ١٤٦)

٧-٧٣- قالَ عِيسَي عليه السلام: «أقُولُ لَكُمْ: 'لا تَهْتَمُّوا ما ذا تاكُلُونَ، وَلا ما ذا تَشْرَبُونَ، وَلا لِأجسادِكُمْ ما تَلْبَسُ. ألَيْسَ النَفْسُ أفْضَلَ مِنَ المأكَلِ؟ والجَسَدُ أفْضَلَ مِنَ اللباسِ؟ أنْظُرُوا إلِي طُيُورِ السَماءِ الّتِي لا تَزْرَعُ وَلا تَحْصِدُ، وَلا تَحْزَنُ؛ وَرَبُّكُمُ السَماوِيَّ يَقُوتُها. ألَيْسَ أنتُم أفْضَلَ مِنْهُمْ؟ مَنْ مِنْكُمْ يَهْتَمُّ، فَيَقْدِرُ أنْ يَزِيدَ عَلَي قامَتِهِ ذِراعاً واحِدَةً؟ فَلِما ذا تَهْتَمُّونَ باللباسِ؟'»

(بحارالانوار، ١٤، ٣١٧)

8

A PORTION OF THE GOSPEL

8.1. It is reported that Yazīd ibn Salām asked the Apostle of Allahﷺ, "Why is the *Furqān* (*distinguisher*) so called?" He said, "Because its verses and chapters are distinguished. It was not sent down on a tablet or as a book, but the Torah, the Gospel and the Pslams were all sent down on tablets and paper."

(*Biḥār*, 14, 284, 4)

8.2. The Prophet said, "The Scripture of Abraham decended on the third day of Ramaḍān, the Torah on the sixth, the Gosple on the thirteenth, the Psalms on the eighteenth, and the Qur'ān on the twenty-fourth."

(*Majmū'a Warrām*, 2, 66)

8.3. It is reported from the Gospel, "Beware of liars who come to you in sheep's clothing while in reality they are ravenous wolves. You shall know them by their fruits. It is not possible for a good tree to bear wicked fruit, nor for a wicked tree to bear good fruit."(1)

(*Biḥār*, 74, 43)

8.4. It is narrated from Sulaymān ibn Dāwūd that it has been reported that 'Alī ibn Ḥusayn said, "It is written in the Gospel, 'Do not seek knowledge that you do not know, unless you put into practice what you already know, for if knowledge is not put into practice, nothing will be increased by Allah except distance [from Him].'"

(*Biḥār*, 14, 319, 19)

---

(1) Cf. Matt 7:15-16, 18:

15 Beware of false prophets, which come to you in sheep's clothing, but inwardly they are ravening wolves.

16 Ye shall know them by their fruits.

18 A good tree cannot bring forth evil fruit, neither can a corrupt tree bring forth good fruit.

(KJV)

٨

من الإنجيل

٨-١- عَنْ يَزِيدِ بْنِ سَلامٍ أنَّهُ سأل رَسُولَ اللهِ صلى الله عليه وآله وسلم: «لِمَ سُمِّيَ الفُرْقانُ فُرْقاناً؟» قالَ: «لأنَّهُ مُتَفَرِّقُ الآياتِ والسُّوَرِ. أنْزِلَتْ فِي غَيْرِ الألواحِ وَغَيْرِ الصحُفِ, والتوْراةُ والإنجيلُ والزَّبُورُ أنْزِلَتْ كُلُّها جُمْلَةً فِي الألواحِ والوَرَقِ.»

(بحار الأنوار، ١٤، ٢٨٤، ٤)

٨-٢- إنَّ النَبِيَّ صلى الله عليه وآله وسلم قالَ: «أنْزِلَتْ صُحُفُ إبْراهِيمَ عليه السلام لِثَلاثٍ مَضِينَ مِنْ رَمْضانَ، والتوْراةُ لِسِتٍّ مَضِينَ مِنْهُ، والإنجيلُ لِثَلاثَ عَشْرَةَ، والزَّبُورُ لِثَمانِي عَشَرَةَ، والقُرْآنُ لأرْبَعٍ وَعِشْرِيْنَ مِنْهُ.»

(مجموعة ورّام، ٢ ،٦٦)

٨-٣- مِنَ الإنجيلِ: «احْذَرُوا الكَذّابَةَ، الذينَ يأتُونَكُمْ بِلِباسِ الحُمْلانِ، فَهُمْ فِي الحَقِيقَةِ ذِئابٌ خاطِفَةٌ، مِنْ ثِمارِهِمْ تَعْرِفُونَهُمْ. لا يُمْكِنُ الشجَرَةُ الطَّيِّبَةُ، أنْ تُثمِرَ ثِماراً رَدِيَّةً؛ وَلا الشجَرَةُ الردِيَّةُ، أنْ تُثمِرَ ثِماراً صالِحَةً.»

(بحارالانوار، ٧٤، ٤٣)

٨-٤- أبي، عَنِ القاسِمِ بْنِ مُحَمَّدٍ، عَنْ سُلَيْمانَ بْنِ داوُدَ، رَفَعَهُ إلي عَلِيِّ بْنِ الحُسَيْنِ عليه السلام، قالَ: «مَكْتُوبٌ فِي الإنجيلِ:'لا تَطْلُبُوا عِلْمَ ما لا تَعْلَمُونَ، وَلَمّا عَمِلْتُمْ بِما عَلِمْتُمْ. فإنَّ العِلْمَ إذا لَمْ يُعْمَلْ بِهِ، لَمْ يَزْدَدْ مِنَ اللهِ إلّا بُعْداً.'»

(بحارالانوار، ١٤، ٣١٩، ١٩)

8.5. Advice of the Messiah ﷺ in the gospel and other places from his wisdom: “Blessed are those who love and respect one another, for they shall receive mercy on the Resurrection Day.

Blessed are the peace makers among the people, for they will be brought nigh unto Him on the Resurrection Day.

Blessed are the pure of heart, for they shall meet Allah on the Resurrection Day.

Blessed are those who humble themselves in this world, for they shall inheret the thrones of sovereignty (manābir al-mulk).

Blessed are the poor, for theirs is the kingdom of heaven.

Blessed are they who mourn, for they shall be glad.

Blessed are they who bear hunger and thirst submissively, for their thirst will be quenched.

Blessed are they who do righteous deeds, for they shall be called the chosen of Allah.

Blessed are they who are abused for their purity, for theirs is the kingdom of heaven.

Blessed are you are envied and abused, and every evil and false word is told about you, then be glad and happy, for verily, your wage is plentiful in heaven.

And he [Jesus] said: O bad servants! You blame the people on the basis of suspicion, and you do not blame yourself for what is certain!

O servants of the world! You love it when things are said about you which are not true of you, and when people point you out.

O servants of the world! You shave your heads and shorten your shirts and cast your heads down [to feign humility], but you do not pull out the hatred from your hearts.

O servants of the world! Your likeness is like that of the high tombs, their exteriors cause admiration in those who look at them, and their interiors are the bones of the dead, full of misdeeds.

٨-٥- مَواعِظُ المَسيحِ عليه السلام فِي الإنجيلِ وَغَيْرِهِ وَمِنْ حِكَمِهِ:

«طُوبَي لِلْمُتَراحِمِينَ، أُولَئِكَ هُمُ المَرْحُومُونَ يَوْمَ القِيامَةِ.

طُوبَي لِلْمُصْلِحِينَ بَيْنَ الناسِ، أُولَئِكَ هُمُ المُقَرَّبُونَ يَوْمَ القِيامَةِ.

طُوبَي لِلْمُطَهَّرَةِ قُلُوبُهُمْ، أُولَئِكَ يَزُورُونَ اللهَ يَوْمَ القِيامَةِ.

طُوبَي لِلْمُتَواضِعِينَ فِي الدنْيا، أُولَئِكَ يَرِثُونَ مَنابِرَ المُلْكِ يَوْمَ القِيامَةِ.

طُوبَي لِلْمَساكِينِ، وَلَهُمْ مَلَكُوتُ السَماءِ.

طُوبَي لِلْمَحْزُونِينَ، هُمُ الذينَ يُسَرُّونَ.

طُوبَي لِلَّذِينَ يَجُوعُونَ وَيَظْمَئُونَ، خُشُوعاً، هُمُ الذينَ يُسْقَوْنَ.

طُوبَي لِلَّذِينَ يَعْمَلُونَ الخَيْرَ، أَصْفِياءُ اللهِ يُدْعَوْنَ.

طُوبَي لِلْمَسْبُوبِينَ مِنْ أَجْلِ الطَّهارَةِ، فانَّ لَهُمْ مَلَكُوتَ السَماءِ.

طُوبَي لَكُمْ إذا حُسِدْتُمْ وَشُتِمْتُمْ، وَقِيلَ فِيكُمْ كُلُّ كَلِمَةٍ قَبِيحَةٍ كاذِبَةٍ. حِينَئِذٍ فافْرَحُوا وابْتَهِجُوا، فانَّ أَجْرَكُمْ قَدْ كَثُرَ فِي السَماءِ.»

وَقالَ: «يا عَبِيدَ السَوءِ! تَلُومُونَ الناسَ عَلَي الظَّنِّ، وَلا تَلُومُونَ أَنْفُسَكُمْ عَلَي اليَقِينِ.

يا عَبِيدَ الدنْيا! تُحِبُّونَ أنْ يُقالَ فِيكُمْ ما لَيْسَ فِيكُمْ، وانْ يُشارَ إلَيْكُمْ بِالأَصابِعِ.

يا عَبِيدَ الدنْيا! تَحْلِقُونَ رُءُوسَكُمْ، وَتُقَصِّرُونَ قُمْصَكُمْ، وَتُنَكِّسُونَ رُؤُوسَكُمْ، وَلا تَنْزِعُونَ الغِلَّ مِنْ قُلُوبِكُمْ.

يا عَبِيدَ الدنْيا! مَثَلُكُمْ كَمَثَلِ القُبُورِ المُشَيَّدَةِ، يُعْجِبُ الناظِرَ ظَهْرُها، وَداخِلُها عِظامُ المَوْتَي، مَمْلُوءَةٌ خَطاياً.

O servants of the world! Your likeness is only like that of a lamp which shines for the people and burns itself.

O Children of Israel! Fill the sessions of the scholars, even if you must go on your knees, Allah will enliven the dead hearts by the light of wisdom, as He enlivens the dead earth by the heavy downpour of rain.

O Children of Israel! Shortness of speech is a great wisdom, so you should be silent; verily it is a good meekness and a decrease of your burden and a lightening of your sins. So strengthen the door of knowledge. Verily, its door is patience. Allah hates one who laughs too much at that which is not funny, and who frequently goes to bad deeds. And He loves the governer who is like a shepherd who does not neglect his flocks. So beware of Allah in secret as you are aware of the people in public. And know the word of wisdom is that sought by the believer. So, go after it before it rises away, and its rising away is the passing away of its narrators.

O you who have knowledge! Pay homage to those of knowledge for their knowledge, and leave contention with them, and belittle the ignorant for their ignorance, but do not reject them, rather bring them near and teach them.

O you who have knowledge! Know that every blessing for which you fail to give thanks is like an evil deed for which you will be taken to task.

O you who have knowledge! Know that every sin of which you have not been able to repent, is like a punishment with which you are being punished.

O you who have knowledge! There are worries about which you do not know when they will come over you, so prepare yourselves before they suddenly arrive."

يا عَبِيدَ الدنْيا! إنَّما مَثَلُكُمْ كَمَثَلِ السِّراجِ، يُضِيءُ لِلنّاسِ وَيُحْرِقُ نَفْسَهُ.

يا بَنِى إسْرائِيلَ، زاحِمُوا العُلَماءَ فِى مَجالِسِهِمْ، وَلَوْ حَبْواً عَلَي الركَبِ. فإنَّ اللهَ يُحيى القُلوبَ المَيِّتَةَ بِنُورِ الحِكْمَةِ، كَما يُحيى الأرضَ المَيِّتَة بِوابِلِ المَطَرِ.

يا بَنِى إسْرائِيلَ، قِلَّةُ المَنْطِقِ حُكْمٌ عَظِيمٌ، فَعَلَيْكُمْ بِالصمْتِ، فإنَّهُ دِعَةٌ حَسَنَةٌ، وَقِلَّةُ وِزْرٍ، وَخِفَّةٌ مِنَ الذُّنُوبِ. فَحَصِّنُوا بابَ العِلْمِ، فإنَّ بابَهُ الصبْرُ، وإنَّ اللهَ يُبْغِضُ الضَّحّاكَ مِنْ غَيْرِ عَجَبٍ، والمَشّاءَ إلي غَيْرِ أدَبٍ. وَيُحِبُّ الوالِيَ الذى يَكُونُ كالراعِى، لا يَغْفُلُ عَنْ رَعِيَّتِهِ. فاسْتَحْيُوا اللهَ فِى سَرائِرِكُمْ، كَما تَسْتَحْيُونَ الناسَ فِى عَلانِيَتِكُمْ. واعْلَمُوا أنَّ كَلِمَةَ الحِكْمَةِ، ضالَّةُ المُؤمِنِ؛ فَعَلَيْكُمْ بِها قَبْلَ أنْ تُرْفَعَ، وَرَفْعُها أنْ تَذْهَبَ رُواتُها.

يا صاحِبَ العِلْمِ، عَظِّمْ العُلَماءَ لِعِلْمِهِمْ، وَدَعْ مُنازَعَتَهُمْ، وَصَغِّرْ الجُهّالَ لِجَهْلِهِمْ، وَلا تَطْرُدْهُمْ، وَلَكِنْ قَرِّبْهُمْ وَعَلِّمْهُمْ.

يا صاحِبَ العِلْمِ، اعْلَمْ أنَّ كُلَّ نِعْمَةٍ عَجَزْتَ عَنْ شُكْرِها، بِمَنْزِلَةِ سَيِّئَةٍ تُؤاخَذُ عَلَيْها.

يا صاحِبَ العِلْمِ، اعْلَمْ أنَّ كُلَّ مَعْصِيَةٍ عَجَزْتَ عَنْ تَوْبَتِها، بِمَنْزِلَةِ عُقُوبَةٍ تُعاقَبُ بِها.

يا صاحِبَ العِلْمِ، كَرْبٌ لا تَدْرِى مَتَي تَغْشاكَ، فاسْتَعِدَّ لَها قَبْلَ أنْ تَفْجأكَ.»

Jesus ﷺ said to his companions, "Tell me, if one passed by his brother and saw that his private parts were exposed from his clothing, would he further expose them or would he cover them again?" They said, "Yes, he would cover what had been exposed." He said, "Not at all, you would remove the covering." Then they understood that it was an allegory he has given for them. They said, "O Spirit of Allah! How is that? There is a man among you who has come to know of a private matter of his brother, but has not covered it."

"In truth I say to you: I teach you that you may learn, and I do not teach you that you may be vain. You will never reach what you want, unless you abandon that which you desire. And you will not win what you wish, unless by patience with that which you dislike. Beware of looking! It sows desire in the heart, and suffices as a temptation. Blessed are those whose vision has been placed in their hearts, and whose hearts have not been placed in the vision of their eyes. Do not look at the faults of the people as if you were their lord, but look at their faults as if you were their servant. There are two kinds of men among people: the afflicted and the healthy. So, care for the afflicted, and praise Allah for health.

O Children of Isreal! Are you not ashamed before Allah? Not one of you would drink something until you made it free of any speck of dirt, but you are not disturbed at the acquisition of something prohibited though it be the size of an elephant. Have you not heard what has been said to you in the Torah? "Visit your relations and recompense them." And I say to you: Visit those who have cut themselves off from you, and give to those who would not help you, and do good to those who have done evil to you, and offer greetings of peace to those who curse you. And be fair with those who have shown enmity to you. Forgive those who have oppressed you, as you like to be forgiven for your misdeeds.

وَقالَ عليه السلام لِأصحابِهِ «يا ابن جُنْدَبٍ إنَّ عِيسَي بْنَ مَرْيَمَ قالَ لِأصحابِهِ: 'أرأيْتُمْ لَوْ أنَّ أحداً (أحدَكُمْ) مَرَّ بِأخِيهِ، فَرأي ثَوْبَهُ قَدْ انْكَشَفَ عَنْ عَوْرَتِهِ، أكانَ كاشِفاً عَنْها؟ أمْ يَرُدُّ عَلَي ما انْكَشَفَ مِنْها؟' قالُوا: 'بَلْ يَرُدُّ عَلَي ما انْكَشَفَ مِنْها.' قالَ: 'كَلّا، بَلْ تَكْشِفُونَ عَنْها.' فَعَرَفُوا أنَّهُ مَثَلٌ، ضَرَبَهُ لَهُمْ. فقالُوا: 'يا رُوحَ اللهِ، وكَيْفَ ذاكَ؟' قالَ: 'ذاكَ، الرجُلُ مِنْكُمْ يَطَّلِعُ عَلَي العَوْرَةِ مِنْ أخِيهِ، فَلا يَسْتُرُها.'

بِحَقٍّ أقُولُ لَكُمْ، أُعَلِّمُكُمْ لِتَعلَمُوا، وَلا أُعَلِّمُكُمْ لِتُعْجَبُوا بِأنْفُسِكُمْ. إنَّكُمْ لَنْ تَنالُوا ما تُرِيدُونَ، إلّا بِتَرْكِ ما تَشْتَهُونَ. وَلَنْ تَظْفَرُوا بِما تأمَلُونَ، إلّا بِالصبْرِ عَلَي ما تَكْرَهُونَ. إيّاكُمْ والنَظْرَةَ، فإنَّها تَزْرَعُ فِي القُلُوبِ الشهْوَةَ، وَكَفَي بِها لِصاحِبِها فِتْنَةً. طُوبَي لِمَنْ جَعَلَ بَصَرَهُ فِي قَلْبِهِ، وَلَمْ يَجْعَلْ قَلْبَهُ فِي نَظَرِ عَيْنِهِ. (وَلَمْ يَجْعَلْ بَصَرَهُ فِي عَيْنِهِ.) لا تَنْظُرُوا فِي عُيُوبِ الناسِ كالأربابِ، وانْظُرُوا فِي عُيُوبِهِمْ كَهَيْأةِ عَبِيدِ الناسِ. (وانْظُرُوا فِي عُيُوبِكُمْ كَهَيْأةِ العَبِيدِ.) إنَّما الناسُ رَجُلانِ: مُبْتَلِيً وَمُعافِيً، فارْحَمُوا المُبْتَلِي، واحْمَدُوا اللهَ عَلَي العافِيَةِ.

يا بَنِي إسْرائِيلَ، أما تَسْتَحْيُونَ مِنَ اللهِ؟ إنَّ أحَدَكُمْ لا يَسُوغُ لَهُ شَرابَهُ حَتَّي يُصَفِّيهِ مِنَ القَذَي، وَلا يُبالِي أنْ يَبْلُغَ أمْثالَ الفِيلَةِ مِنَ الحَرامِ. ألَمْ تَسْمَعُوا أنَّهُ قِيلَ لَكُمْ فِي التَوْراةِ: 'صِلُوا أرْحامَكُمْ، وَكافِئُوا أرْحامَكُمْ.' وأنا أقُولُ لَكُمْ: 'صِلُوا مَنْ قَطَعَكُمْ، واعْطُوا مَنْ مَنَعَكُمْ، وأحْسِنُوا إلَي مَنْ أساءَ إلَيْكُمْ، وَسَلِّمُوا عَلَي مَنْ سَبَّكُمْ، وأنْصِفُوا مَنْ خاصَمَكُمْ، واعْفُوا عَمَّنْ ظَلَمَكُمْ، كَما أنَّكُمْ تُحِبُّونَ أنْ يُعْفَي عَنْ إساءَتِكُمْ.

So, take admonition from Allah's forgiveness of you. Do you not see that His sun shines on the good and the bad among you and His rain falls on the righteous and the evil doer among you. If you do not like any but those who like you, and you do good to none but those who do good to you, and you recompense none but those who give to you, then what distinction do you have over others? Verily, this is what fools do, with whom there is no virtue and no intelligence. However, if you want to be loved by Allah, and chosen by Allah, then do good to those who do evil to you, forgive those who have oppressed you, and greet with peace those who have turned away from you. Listen to what I say, keep my testament and observe my covenant so that you may be learned and have understanding.

In truth I say to you verily your hearts are where your treasures are—because of this the people love their wealth, and they themselves long for it—so put your treasures in the sky, where moths will not eat it and theives will not obtain it. In truth I say to you, verily a servant is incapable of serving two lords. Inevitably he will prefer one of them to the other, no matter how he tries. Likewise, you cannot join together love for Allah and love for the world. In truth I say to you, verily the worst of people is the man who is a scholar and prefers the world to his knowledge, then he loves it, pursues it and strives for it, to such an extent that, if he were able to put the people into a state of confusion, he would do it. What does the expanse of the light of the sun profit a blind man who does not see it. Likewise, the knowledge of that scholar is of no profit to him, for he does not put it into practice. How plentiful is the fruit of the tree, but not all of it is of benefit or eaten. And how plentiful are the scholars, but not all of them benefit from their knowledge. And how wide is the earth, but not all of it is inhabited. And how many speakers there are, but not all of what they say is acceptable as true. So, keep away from lying scholars, who wear woolen clothes, who bend their heads down toward the earth, and so belie their sins, they look from under their eyebrows, like wolves. Their speech is contrary to their deeds. Is the grape reaped from the thorn, or the fig from the bitter gourd? Likewise the speech of a lying scholar has no effect but vanity. Not all who speak are true.

فاعْتَبِرُوا بِعَفْوِ اللهِ عَنْكُمْ. ألا تَرَوْنَ أنَّ شَمْسَهُ أشْرَقَتْ عَلَي الأبرارِ والفُجّارِ مِنْكُمْ؟ وأنَّ مَطَرَهُ يَنْزِلُ عَلَي الصالِحِينَ والخاطِئِينَ مِنْكُمْ؟ فإنْ كُنْتُمْ لا تُحِبُّونَ إلّا مَنْ أحَبَّكُمْ، وَلا تُحْسِنُونَ إلّا إلي مَنْ أحْسَنَ إلَيْكُمْ، وَلا تُكافِئُونَ إلّا مَنْ أعْطاكُمْ، فَما فَضْلُكُمْ، إذاً عَلَي غَيْرِكُمْ؟ وَقَدْ يَصْنَعُ هَذا، السُّفَهاءُ الذينَ لَيْسَتْ عِنْدَهُمْ فُضُولٌ وَلا لَهُمْ أحْلامٌ. ولَكِنْ، إنْ أرَدْتُمْ أنْ تَكُونُوا أحِبّاءَ اللهِ وأصْفِياءَ اللهِ، فأحْسِنُوا إلي مَنْ أساءَ إلَيْكُمْ، واعْفُوا عَمَّنْ ظَلَمَكُمْ، وَسَلِّمُوا عَلَي مَنْ أعْرَضَ عَنْكُمْ. اسْمَعُوا قَوْلِي، واحْفَظُوا وَصِيَّتِي، وارْعَوْا عَهْدِي، كَيْما تَكُونُوا عُلَماءَ فُقَهاءَ.'

بِحَقٍّ أقُولُ لَكُمْ، إنَّ قُلوبَكُمْ بِحَيْثُ تَكُونُ كُنُوزُكُمْ، وَلِذَلِكَ الناسُ يُحِبُّونَ أمْوالَهُمْ، وَتَتُوقُ إلَيْها أنْفُسُهُمْ؛ فَضَعُوا كُنُوزَكُمْ فِي السَماءِ، حَيْثُ لا يأكُلُها السُّوسُ، وَلا يَنالُها اللصُوصُ. بِحَقٍّ أقُولُ لَكُمْ، إنَّ العَبْدَ لا يَقْدِرُ عَلَي أنْ يَخْدِمَ رَبَّيْنِ، وَلا مَحالَةَ، أنَّهُ يُؤْثِرُ أحَدَهُما عَلَي الآخَرِ، وإنْ جَهَدَ. كَذَلِكَ ،لا يَجْتَمِعُ لَكُمْ حُبُّ اللهِ وَحُبُّ الدنْيا. بِحَقٍّ أقُولُ لَكُمْ، إنَّ شَرَّ الناسِ لَرَجُلٌ عالِمٌ، آثَرَ دُنْياهُ عَلَي عِلْمِهِ، فأحَبَّها وَطَلَبَها وَجَهَدَ عَلَيْها، حَتَّي لَوْ اسْتَطاعَ أنْ يَجْعَلَ الناسَ فِي حَيْرَةٍ، لَفَعَلَ. وَما ذا يُغْنِي عَنِ الأعمَي سِعَةُ نُورِ الشمْسِ، وَهُوَ لا يَبْصُرُها. كَذَلِكَ، لا يُغْنِي عَنِ العالِمِ عِلْمُهُ، إذْ هُوَ لَمْ يَعْمَلْ بِهِ. ما أكْثَرَ ثِمارَ الشجَرِ! وَلَيْسَ كُلُّها يَنْفَعُ وَيُؤكَلُ، وَما أكْثَرَ العُلَماءَ! وَلَيْسَ كُلُّهُمْ يَنْتَفِعُ بِما عَلِمَ، وَما أوْسَعَ الأرضَ! وَلَيْسَ كُلُّها تُسْكَنُ، وَما أكْثَرَ المُتَكَلِّمِينَ! وَلَيْسَ كُلُّ كَلامِهِم يُصَدَّقُ. فاحْتَفِظُوا مِنَ العُلَماءِ الكَذَبَةِ، الذينَ عَلَيْهِمْ ثِيابُ الصوفِ، مُنَكِّسِي رُؤوسِهِمْ إلَي الأرضِ، يُزَوِّرُونَ بِهِ الخَطايا، يَرْمُقُونَ مِنْ تَحْتِ حَواجِبِهِمْ كَما تَرْمُقُ الذِّئابُ، وَقَوْلُهُمْ يُخالِفُ فِعْلَهُمْ. وَهَلْ يُجْتَنَي مِنَ العَوْسَجِ، العِنَبُ؟ وَمِنَ الحَنْظَلِ، التِينُ؟ وَكَذَلِكَ، لا يُؤَثِّرُ قَوْلُ العالِمِ الكاذِبِ، إلّا زُوراً. وَلَيْسَ كُلُّ مَنْ يَقُولُ يُصْدُقُ.

In truth I say to you, the plant grows in soft ground, not in rock, and likewise wisdom thrives in the heart of the humble, and it does not thrive in the heart of the arrogant oppressor. Did you not know that whoever raises his head to the ceiling breaks it, and whoever lowers his head beneath the ceiling is shaded by it and it protects him, and likewise, whoever does not humble himself to Allah, He debases him, and whoever humbles himself to Allah, He elevates him. Indeed, it is not always the case that honey will be safe in any pouch (of hide), and likewise the hearts are not always such that wisdom thrives in them. While the skin is not torn, dried out nor has become malodorous, it may be a vessel for honey, and likewise the hearts, while they are not torn by desires, fooled by greed nor hardened by pleasures, they may be vessels for wisdom.

In truth I say to you, surely fire does not occur in a single house, but it spreads from house to house, until many houses are burnt, unless the first house is reached and it is destroyed to its pillars. Then the fire finds no place to burn. Likewise the first oppressor, if his hand is stopped, no one will be found after him to be an unjust leader for others to follow, just as if the fire finds no wood or boards in the first house, it will not burn anything.

In truth I say to you, whoever looks at a snake that intends to strike his brother and does not warn him until it kills him, he will not be secure from partnership in his murder. Likewise, whoever looks at his brother doing something wrong, and does not warn him of its consequences until it encompasses him, he will not be secure from partnership in his sin. Whoever has the power to change an oppressor but does not change him, he is like an agent [of oppression]. How can the oppressor be frightened when he is safe among you and he is neither prohibited, nor changed, nor are his hands restrained? Why should the oppressors then give up? How should they not become arrogant? It is enough that one of you say, 'I shall not oppress, but whoever wants to oppress, go ahead,' and he sees oppression but does not change it. If it were as you say, why are you punished with the oppressors, though you do not commit their deeds, when the chastisement descends upon them in this world.

بِحَقٍّ أقولُ لَكُمْ، إنَّ الزَّرْعَ يَنْبُتُ فِي السَهْلِ، وَلا يَنْبُتُ فِي الصَفا؛ وَكَذَلِكَ، الحِكْمَةُ تَعْمُرُ فِي قَلْبِ المُتَواضِعِ، وَلا تَعْمُرُ فِي قَلْبِ المُتَكَبِّرِ الجَبّارِ. أَلَمْ تَعْلَمُوا أَنَّهُ مَنْ شَمَخَ بِراسِهِ إِلي السَقْفِ، شَجَّهُ؟ وَمَنْ خَفَضَ بِراسِهِ عَنْهُ، إسْتَظَلَّ تَحْتَهُ وأَكَنَّهُ؟ وَكَذَلِكَ، مَنْ لَمْ يَتَواضَعْ لِلَّهِ خَفَضَهُ، وَمَنْ تَواضَعَ لِلَّهِ رَفَعَهُ. إنَّهُ لَيْسَ، عَلَي كُلِّ حالٍ، يَصْلَحُ العَسَلُ فِي الزِّقاقِ؛ وَكَذَلِكَ، القُلُوبُ لَيْسَ، عَلَي كُلِّ حالٍ، تَعْمُرُ الحِكْمَةُ فِيها. إنَّ الزِّقَّ ما لَمْ يَنْخَرِقْ أَوْ يَقْحَلْ أَوْ يُتْفَلْ، فَسَوْفَ يَكُونُ لِلْعَسَلِ وِعاءً، وَكَذَلِكَ، القُلُوبُ، ما لَمْ تَخْرِقْها الشَهَواتُ وَيُدَنِّسْها الطَمَعُ وَيُقَسِها النَعِيمُ، فَسَوْفَ تَكُونُ أَوْعِيَةً لِلْحِكْمَةِ.

بِحَقٍّ أقولُ لَكُمْ، إنَّ الحَرِيقَ لَيَقَعُ فِي البَيْتِ الواحِدِ, فَلا يَزالُ يَنْتَقِلُ مِنْ بَيْتٍ إِلي بَيْتٍ, حَتَّي تَحْتَرِقَ بُيُوتٌ كَثِيرَةٌ, إلّا أنْ يُسْتَدْرَكَ البَيْتُ الأَوَّلُ, فَيُهْدَمُ مِنْ قَواعِدِهِ, فَلا تَجِدُ فِيهِ النارُ مَعْمَلاً. وَكَذَلِكَ الظّالِمُ الأَوَّلُ, لَوْ يُؤْخَذُ عَلَي يَدَيْهِ, لَمْ يُوجَدْ مِنْ بَعْدِهِ إمامٌ ظالِمٌ فَيَأْتَمُّونَ بِهِ, كَما لَوْ لَمْ تَجِدْ النارُ فِي البَيْتِ الأَوَّلِ خَشَباً وأَلْواحاً, لَمْ تَحْرِقْ شَيْئًا.

بِحَقٍّ أقولُ لَكُمْ, مَنْ نَظَرَ إلي الحَيَّةِ, تَؤُمُّ أخاهُ لِتَلْدَغَهُ, ولَمْ يُحَذِّرْهُ حَتَّي قَتَلَتْهُ, فَلا يأمَنُ أنْ يَكُونَ قَدْ شَرِكَ فِي دَمِهِ. وَكَذَلِكَ, مَنْ نَظَرَ إلي أَخِيهِ يَعْمَلُ الخَطِيئَةَ, ولَمْ يُحَذِّرْهُ عاقِبَتَها حَتَّي أَحاطَتْ بِهِ, فَلا يأمَنُ أنْ يَكُونَ قَدْ شَرِكَ فِي إثْمِهِ. وَمَنْ قَدَرَ عَلَي أنْ يُغَيِّرَ الظّالِمَ ثُمَّ لَمْ يُغَيِّرْهُ, فَهُوَ كَفاعِلِهِ. وَكَيْفَ يَهابُ الظّالِمُ, وَقَدْ أَمِنَ بَيْنَ أَظْهُرِكُمْ, لا يُنْهَي, وَلا يُغَيَّرُ عَلَيْهِ, وَلا يُؤْخَذُ عَلَي يَدَيْهِ؟ فَمِنْ أَيْنَ يَقْصُرُ الظّالِمُونَ؟ أَمْ كَيْفَ لا يَغْتَرُّونَ؟ فَحَسْبُ أنْ يَقُولَ أَحَدُكُمْ لا أَظْلِمُ, وَمَنْ شاءَ فَلْيَظْلِمْ, وَيَرَي الظُّلْمَ فَلا يُغَيِّرُهُ. فَلَوْ كانَ الأَمْرُ عَلَي ما تَقُولُونَ, لَمْ تُعاقَبُوا مَعَ الظّالِمِينَ, الذينَ لَمْ تَعْمَلُوا بِأَعْمالِهِمْ, حِينَ تَنْزِلُ بِهِمْ العَثْرَةُ فِي الدنْيا.

Woe unto you, O servants of evil! How can you hope that Allah may secure you from the terror of the day of resurrection, when you are afraid to obey Allah because you fear people, and you obey them in disobedience to Him, and you keep your promises to them contrary to His covenant.

In truth I say to you: Allah will not make secure from the terror of that day those who take servants as lords aside from Him.

Woe unto you, O servants of evil! For the sake of this base world and ruinous lusts you give up the realm of heaven and you forget the horror of the day of resurrection.

Woe unto you, O servants of this world! For the sake of evanescent boons and life that will be cut off, you run away from Allah, and you dislike the encounter with Him. So how is Allah to love the encounter with you while you dislike the encounter with Him? Allah only loves the encounter with those who love the encounter with Him, and He dislikes the encounter of those who dislike the encounter with Him. How can you imagine that you are the friends of Allah to the exclusion of other people, while you run away from death and you take refuge in this world. Of what benefit to the dead are the good scent of camphor and the whiteness of his shroud, and all of them are in the earth. Likewise, the joy of this world that is adorned for you is of no benefit to you, and all of that is to pass away and cease. Of what benefit to you is the purity of your bodies and the cleanliness of your complexions when you are headed for death, and in the dust you will be forgotten, and you will be immersed in the darkness of the grave.

Woe unto you, servants of this world, you carry a lamp in the light of the sun while its light is enough for you. You have given up seeking illumination by it in the darkness, and it is for the sake of this that it has been made subservient to you. Likewise you seek illumination by the light of knowledge for the affairs of the world, while these have been guaranteed for you, and you have abandoned seeking illumination for the affairs of the other world, while it has been given to you for this. You say that the other world is real, while you prepare this world [for yourselves]. You say that death is real,

وَيْلَكُمْ، يا عَبِيدَ السَوءِ! كَيْفَ تَرْجُونَ أنْ يُؤَمِّنَكُمُ اللهُ مِنْ فَزَعِ يَوْمِ القِيامَةِ, وأنتُم تَخافُونَ الناسَ فِي طاعَةِ اللهِ, وتُطِيعُونَهُمْ فِي مَعْصِيَتِهِ, وتَفُونَ لَهُمْ بِالعُهُودِ الناقِضَةِ لِعَهْدِهِ؟

بِحَقٍّ أقُولُ لَكُمْ, لا يُؤَمِّنُ اللهُ مِنْ فَزَعِ ذَلِكَ اليَوْمِ, مَنْ اتَّخَذَ العِبادَ أرْباباً مِنْ دُونِهِ.

وَيْلَكُمْ, يا عَبِيدَ السَوءِ! مِنْ أجْلِ دُنْيا دَنِيَّةٍ وَشَهْوَةٍ رَدِيَّةٍ, تَفْرُطُونَ فِي مُلْكِ الجَنَّةِ, وتَنْسَوْنَ هَوْلَ يَوْمِ القِيامَةِ.

وَيْلَكُمْ, يا عَبِيدَ الدنْيا! مِنْ أجْلِ نِعْمَةٍ زائِلَةٍ وَحَياةٍ مُنْقَطِعَةٍ, تَفِرُّونَ مِنَ اللهِ وَتَكْرَهُونَ لِقاءَهُ. فَكَيْفَ يُحِبُّ اللهُ لِقاءَكُمْ وأنتُم تَكْرَهُونَ لِقاءَهُ؟ فإنَّما يُحِبُّ اللهُ لِقاءَ مَنْ يُحِبُّ لِقاءَهُ, ويَكْرَهُ لِقاءَ مَنْ يَكْرَهُ لِقاءَهُ. وكَيْفَ تَزْعُمُونَ أنَّكُم أوْلِياءُ اللهِ مِنْ دُونِ الناسِ, وأنتُم تَفِرُّونَ مِنَ المَوْتِ, وتَعْتَصِمُونَ بِالدنْيا؟ فَما ذا يُغْنِي عَنِ المَيِّتِ طِيبَ رِيحِ حُنُوطِهِ وبَياضَ أكْفانِهِ, وكُلُّ ذَلِكَ يَكُونُ فِي التُرابِ؟ كَذَلِكَ, لا يُغْنِي عَنْكُمْ بَهْجَةُ دُنْياكُمْ, الَّتِي زُيِّنَتْ لَكُمْ, وكُلُّ ذَلِكَ إلِي سَلْبٍ وزَوالٍ. ما ذا يُغْنِي عَنْكُمْ نَقاءَ أجْسادِكُمْ وَصَفاءَ الوانِكُمْ, وإلِي المَوْتِ تَصِيرُونَ, وَفِي التُرابِ تُنْسَوْنَ, وَفِي ظُلْمَةِ القَبْرِ تُغْمَرُونَ؟

وَيْلَكُمْ, يا عَبِيدَ الدنْيا! تَحْمِلُونَ السِّراجَ فِي ضَوْءِ الشمْسِ, وَضَوْؤُها كانَ يَكْفِيكُمْ, وتَدْعُونَ أنْ تَسْتَضِيئُوا بِها فِي الظُلَمِ, وَمِنْ أجْلِ ذَلِكَ سُخِّرَتْ لَكُمْ. كَذَلِكَ, اسْتَضَائتُمْ بِنُورِ العِلْمِ لِأمْرِ الدنْيا, وقَدْ كَفَيْتُمُوهُ, وتَرَكْتُمْ أنْ تَسْتَضِيئُوا بِهِ لِأمْرِ الآخِرَةِ, وَمِنْ أجْلِ ذَلِكَ أعْطِيتُمُوهُ. تَقُولُونَ: 'إنَّ الآخِرَةَ حَقٌّ,' وأنتُم تُمَهِّدُونَ الدنْيا؛ وَتَقُولُونَ: 'إنَّ المَوْتَ حَقٌّ,' وأنتُم تَفِرُّونَ مِنْهُ؛ وَتَقُولُونَ: 'إنَّ اللهَ يَسْمَعُ وَيَرَي,'

but you run away from it. You say that Allah hears and sees, but you do not fear His reckoning of you. How can one who hears you trust you. One who unknowingly lies is more excused than one who knowingly lies, while lying is not excused at all.

In truth I say to you, just as an animal which is not captured and tamed becomes hardened and its character is changed, so too when hearts are not softened by the remembrance of death and the effort of worship they become hard and tough. Of what benefit for a dark house is a lamp placed above its roof, while its interior is dismal and dark? Likewise, it is of no benefit to you that the light of knowledge be in your mouth while your interior is dismal and destitute. So, hurry to your dark houses and illuminate them. Likewise, hurry to your hard hearts with wisdom before errors overcome it, then they will be harder than stone. How can one carry a heavy load if he does not seek help with carrying it? Or how can the burdens of sin be put down by one who does not ask the pardon of Allah for them? Or how can clothes be purified by one who does not wash them? And how can one get clear of wrongs who does not bury them? Or how can one be saved from drowning in the sea if he crosses it without a ship? And how can one be saved from the trials of this world if he does not treat them with seriousness and struggle? And how can one reach one's destination if he travels without a guide? And how can one arrive at the Garden if he does not see the signs of religion? And how can one achieve the pleasure of Allah if he does not obey Him? And how can one see the flaw of one's face if he does not look in the mirror? And how can one perfect the love of his friend if he does not grant him some of what he has. And how can one perfect the love of his Lord if he does not lend Him some of that with which he has been provided?

In truth I say to you, verily just as the sea does not become any less if a ship sinks in it and the ship does not harm the sea at all, likewise you do not lessen Allah at all by your sins, and you do not harm Him, but you harm and lessen your own self; and just as the multitude of those who go about in the light of the sun does not lessen it, but they thrive and live, likewise, the multitude of what He

وَلَا تَخَافُونَ إِحْصَاءَهُ عَلَيْكُمْ. وَكَيْفَ يُصَدِّقُكُمْ مَنْ سَمِعَكُمْ؟ فانَّ مَنْ كَذَبَ مِنْ غَيْرِ عِلْمٍ, أَعْذَرُ مِمَّنْ كَذَبَ عَلَي عِلْمٍ, وانْ كانَ لَا عُذْرَ فِى شَىْءٍ مِنَ الكِذْبِ.

بِحَقٍّ أَقُولُ لَكُمْ, إِنَّ الدابَّةَ إِذا لَمْ تُرْتَكَبْ وَلَمْ تُمْتَهَنْ وَتُسْتَعْمَلْ, لَتَصعَّبُ وَيَتَغَيَّرُ خُلْقُها. وَكَذَلِكَ, القُلُوبُ, إِذا لَمْ تُرَقَّقْ بِذِكْرِ المَوْتِ وَتُتْعِبْها دُؤُوبُ العِبادَةِ, تَقْسُو وَتَغْلُظُ. ما ذا يُغْنِى عَنِ البَيْتِ المُظْلِمِ أَنْ يُوضَعَ السِّراجُ فَوْقَ ظَهْرِهِ, وَجَوْفُهُ وَحْشٌ مُظْلِمٌ؟ كَذَلِكَ, لا يُغْنِى عَنْكُمْ أَنْ يَكُونَ نُورُ العِلْمِ بِأَفْواهِكُمْ, وَأَجْوافُكُمْ مِنْهُ وَحْشَةٌ مُعَطَّلَةٌ. فَأَسْرِعُوا إِلِي بُيُوتِكُمُ المُظْلِمَةِ, فَأَنِيرُوا فِيها. كَذَلِكَ فَأَسْرِعُوا إِلِي قُلُوبِكُمُ القاسِيَةِ بِالحِكْمَةِ, قَبْلَ أَنْ تَرِينَ عَلَيْها الخَطايا, فَتَكُونُ أَقْسَى مِنَ الحِجارَةِ. كَيْفَ يُطِيقُ حَمْلَ الأَثْقالِ مَنْ لا يَسْتَعِينُ عَلَي حَمْلِها؟ أَمْ كَيْفَ تُحَطُّ أَوْزارُ مَنْ لا يَسْتَغْفِرُ اللهَ مِنْها؟ أَمْ كَيْفَ تُنْقَى ثِيابُ مَنْ لا يَغْسِلُها؟ وَكَيْفَ يَبْرَئُ مِنَ الخَطايا, مَنْ لا يُكَفِّرُها؟ أَمْ كَيْفَ يَنْجُو مِنْ غَرَقِ البَحْرِ, مَنْ يَعْبُرُ بِغَيْرِ سَفِينَةٍ؟ وَكَيْفَ يَنْجُو مِنْ فِتَنِ الدنْيا, مَنْ لَمْ يُداوِها بِالجِدِّ والإِجْتِهادِ؟ وَكَيْفَ يَبْلُغُ مَنْ يُسافِرُ بِغَيْرِ دَلِيلٍ؟ وَكَيْفَ يَصِيرُ إِلِي الجَنَّةِ, مَنْ لا يُبْصِرُ مَعالِمَ الدِينِ؟ وَكَيْفَ يَنالُ مَرْضاةَ اللهِ, مَنْ لا يُطِيعُهُ؟ وَكَيْفَ يَبْصُرُ عَيْبَ وَجْهِهِ, مَنْ لا يَنْظُرُ فِى المِرْآةِ؟ وَكَيْفَ يَسْتَكْمِلُ حُبَّ خَلِيلِهِ، مَنْ لا يَبْذُلُ لَهُ بَعْضَ ما عِنْدَهُ؟ وَكَيْفَ يَسْتَكْمِلُ حُبَّ رَبِّهِ, مَنْ لا يُقْرِضُهُ بَعْضَ ما رَزَقَهُ؟

بِحَقٍّ أَقُولُ لَكُمْ, إِنَّهُ كَما لا يَنْقُصُ البَحْرَ أَنْ تَغْرَقَ فِيهِ السَّفِينَةُ, وَلا يَضُرُّهُ ذَلِكَ شَيْئًا, كَذَلِكَ لا تَنْقُصُونَ اللهَ بِمَعاصِيكُمْ شَيْئًا, وَلا تَضُرُّونَهُ. بَلْ أَنْفُسَكُمْ تَضُرُّونَ, وإِيَّاها تَنْقُصُونَ. وَكَما لا تَنْقُصُ نُورَ الشمْسِ كَثْرَةُ مَنْ

gives you and provides for you does not lessen Him, but you thrive by His providence and by Him you live. He increases [His providence] for those who thank Him, He is Grateful, All-knowing.[1]

Woe unto you, O evil paid laborer, you take the wage and eat what is provided for you, and you wear the clothing, and you build the houses, and you spoil the work of He who hired you. Soon the One who hired you for this work will call you, then He will look at the work that you spoiled, then He will bring down for you what humiliates you and He will order that your necks be pulled out from their roots, and He will order that your arms be cut off at their joints. Then He will order that your bodies be pulled along on your bellies to the middle of the road, so that you may be a lesson for the pious and a warning for the unjust.

Woe unto you, O evil scholars, do not tell yourselves that your appointed times will be delayed so that death will not come down upon you. Soon it will come down upon you, enter upon you and cause you to emigrate. Then, from now on put His call in your ears, and from now on grieve over yourselves, and from now on cry over your mistakes, and from now on make preparations and take your supplies[2] and hurry to the repentance of your Lord.

In truth I say to you, verily, just as the sick look at good food and are not pleased by it, due to the intensity of their pain, likewise the worldly person is not pleased with worship and he does not find its sweetness, due to his love of wealth. And just as the sick are pleased by the description of the medicine by the learned doctor in which there is hope of a cure, then when the doctor reminds them of the bitterness of the medicine and its taste, this clouds their view of the cure, likewise the worldly people are pleased with the delights of the world and the variety in it, then when they remember the suddenness of death, this clouds their view of these delights and spoils them.

---

(1) See Qur'ān (2:157).

(2) "For indeed the best of supplies is *taqwā* (God-wariness)", *Nahj al-Balāgha.*

يَتَقَلَّبُ فِيها, بَلْ بِهِ يَعِيشُ وَيَحْيَي, كَذَلِكَ, لا يَنْقُصُ اللهَ كَثْرَةُ ما يُعْطِيكُمْ وَيرْزُقُكُمْ. بَلْ بِرِزْقِهِ تَعِيشُونَ, وَبِهِ تَحْيَوْنَ؛ يَزِيدُ مَنْ شَكَرَهُ, إنَّهُ شاكِرٌ عَلِيمٌ.

وَيْلَكُمْ، يا أجَراءَ السَوْءِ! الأجْرَ تَسْتَوْفُونَ, والرزْقَ تأكُلُونَ, والكِسْوَةَ تَلْبَسُونَ, والمَنازِلُ تَبْنُونَ, وَعَمَلَ مَنِ اسْتاجَرَكُمْ تُفْسِدُونَ! يُوشِكُ رَبُّ هَذا العَمَلِ أنْ يُطالِبَكُمْ, فَيَنْظُرُ فِي عَمَلِهِ الذى أفْسَدْتُمْ, فَيُنَزِّلُ بِكُمْ ما يُخْزِيكُمْ؛ وَيأمُرُ بِرِقابِكُمْ, فَتُجَدُّ مِنْ أصُولِها؛ وَيأمُرُ بِأيْدِيكُمْ, فَتُقْطَعُ مِنْ مَفاصِلِها؛ ثُمَّ يأمُرُ بِجُثَثِكُمْ, فَتُجَرُّ عَلي بُطُونِها, حَتَّي تُوضَعَ عَلي قَوارِعِ الطَّرِيقِ, حَتَّي تَكُونُوا عِظَةً لِلْمُتَّقِينَ وَنَكالاً لِلظَّالِمِينَ.

وَيْلَكُمْ، يا عُلماءَ السَوءِ! لا تُحَدِّثُوا أنْفُسَكُمْ, أنَّ آجالَكُمْ تُسْتأخَرُ, مِنْ أجْلِ أنَّ المَوْتَ لَمْ يَنْزِلْ بِكُمْ. فَكأنَّهُ قَدْ حَلَّ بِكُمْ, فأظْعَنَكُمْ. فَمِنَ الآنَ فاجْعَلُوا الدعْوَةَ فِي آذانِكُمْ, وَمِنَ الآنَ فَنُوحُوا عَلي أنْفُسِكُمْ, وَمِنَ الآنَ فابْكُوا عَلي خَطاياكُمْ, وَمِنَ الآنَ فَتَجَهَّزُوا, وَخُذُوا أهِبَّتَكُمْ, وَبادِرُوا التَوْبَةَ إلي رَبِّكُمْ.

بِحَقٍّ أقُولُ لَكُمْ, إنَّهُ كَما يَنْظُرُ المَرِيضُ إلي طَيِّبِ الطَّعامِ, فَلا يَلْتَذُّهُ, مَعَ ما يَجِدُهُ مِنْ شِدَّةِ الوَجَعِ, كَذَلِكَ, صاحِبُ الدنْيا لا يَلْتَذُّ بِالعِبادَةِ وَلا يَجِدُ حَلاوَتَها, مَعَ ما يَجِدُ مِنْ حُبِّ المالِ. وَكَما يَلْتَذُّ المَرِيضُ نَعْتَ الطَّبِيبِ العالِمِ، بِما يَرْجُو فِيهِ مِنَ الشفاءِ, فإذا ذَكَرَ مِرارَةَ الدواءِ وَطَعْمَهُ, كَدَرَ عَلَيْهِ الشفاءُ. كَذَلِكَ, أهْلُ الدنْيا, يَلْتَذُّونَ بِبَهْجَتِها وأنْواعِ ما فِيها. فإذا ذُكِّرُوا فُجأةَ المَوْتِ, كَدَّرَها عَلَيْهِمْ وأفْسَدَها.

In truth I say to you, verily all the people see the stars but the only ones who are guided by them are those who know their courses and stations, and likewise, you learn wisdom, but only those who put it into practice are guided by it.

Woe unto you, O servants of this world! Thresh the wheat and make it good and grind it fine to savor its taste so the eating of it delights you. Likewise, purify your faith to savor its sweetness so its fruits may benefit you.

In truth I say to you, if you find a lamp that burns oil in a dark night, you seek light by it, and the smell of the oil does not prevent you from this. Likewise, it is suitable for you that you obtain wisdom from those in whom you find it, and his evil desires do not prevent you from this.

Woe unto you, O servants of this world! Your reasoning is not like that of the wise, your understanding is not like that of the patient, your knowing is not like that of the scholars; and you are not like the pious servants, and not like the noble free men. Soon this world will pull you out by your roots, and turn you on your faces, and cast you on your noses. Then your mistakes will take you by the forelocks, and your knowledge will push you from behind, until they surrender you to the King, the Reckoner, naked and alone, and He will punish you for your bad deeds.

Woe unto you, O servants of this world! You have not been given power over all people except by knowledge, then you threw it away and you did not put it into practice, and you turned toward the world, and by it you judge, and you prepare yourselves for it, and you prefer it and make it prosper, and how long will you last for this world? And for God you do not do anything in it.

In truth I say to you: you will not attain the dignity of the other world except by leaving what you love. So, do not wait until tomorrow for repentance. Before tomorrow there is a day and a night and during them the decree of Allah comes and goes.

In truth I say to you: Indeed you small wrongs and their being made to seem little are plots of Iblis. He makes them seem little to you and he makes them small in your eyes; then they accumulate and increase and surround you.

بِحَقٍّ أقُولُ لَكُمْ, إنَّ كُلَّ الناس يُبْصِرُ النجُومَ, ولَكِنْ لا يَهْتَدِي بِها إلّا مَنْ يَعْرِفُ مَجارِيَها ومَنازِلَها. وكَذَلِكَ, تَدْرُسُونَ الحِكْمَةَ, ولَكِنْ لا يَهْتَدِي لَها مِنْكُمْ إلّا مَنْ عَمِلَ بِها.

وَيْلَكُمْ, يا عَبِيدَ الدنْيا! نَقُّوا القَمْحَ وَطَيِّبُوهُ وأدِقُّوا طَحْنَهُ, تَجِدُوا طَعْمَهُ, يَهْنَئُكُمْ أكْلُهُ. كَذَلِكَ, فأخْلِصُوا الإيمانَ, تَجِدُوا حَلاوَتَهُ وَيَنْفَعْكُمْ غِبُّهُ.

بِحَقٍّ أقُولُ لَكُمْ, لَوْ وَجَدْتُمْ سِراجاً يَتَوَقَّدُ بِالقَطْرانِ فِي لَيْلَةٍ مُظْلِمَةٍ, لاسْتَضَأْتُمْ بِهِ, ولَمْ يَمْنَعْكُمْ مِنْهُ رِيحُ قَطْرانِهِ. كَذَلِكَ, يَنْبَغِي لَكُمْ أنْ تأخُذُوا الحِكْمَةَ مِمَّنْ وَجَدْتُمُوها مَعَهُ, وَلا يَمْنَعُكُمْ مِنْهُ سُوءُ رَغْبَتِهِ فِيها.

وَيْلَكُمْ, يا عَبِيدَ الدنْيا! لا كَحُكَماءَ تَعْقِلُونَ, وَلا كَحُلَماءَ تَفْقَهُونَ, وَلا كَعُلَماءَ تَعْلَمُونَ, وَلا كَعَبِيدٍ أتْقِياءَ وَلا كأحْرارٍ كِرامٍ. تُوشِكُ الدنْيا أنْ تَقْتَلِعَكُمْ مِنْ أصُولِكُمْ, فَتُقَلِّبَكُمْ عَلي وُجُوهِكُمْ, ثُمَّ تُكِبُّكُمْ عَلي مَناخِرِكُمْ, ثُمَّ تأخُذُ خَطاياكُمْ بِنَواصِيكُمْ, وَيَدْفَعُكُم العِلْمُ مِنْ خَلْفِكُمْ, حَتَّي يُسَلِّماكُمْ إلي المَلِكِ الديّانِ عُراةً, فُراديً؛ فَيَجْزِيكُمْ بِسُوءِ أعْمالِكُمْ.

وَيْلَكُمْ, يا عَبِيدَ الدنْيا! ألَيْسَ بِالعِلْمِ أعْطِيتُمُ السُّلْطانَ عَلي جَمِيعِ الخَلائِقِ, فَنَبَذْتُمُوهُ, فَلَمْ تَعْمَلُوا بِهِ, وأقْبَلْتُمْ عَلي الدنْيا؟ فَبِها تَحْكُمُونَ, وَلَها تُمَهِّدُونَ, وإيّاها تُؤْثِرُونَ وَتُعَمِّرُونَ. فَحَتَّي مَتَي أنتُم لِلدُّنْيا, لَيْسَ لِلَّهِ فِيكُمْ نَصِيبٌ؟

بِحَقٍّ أقُولُ لَكُمْ, لا تُدْرِكُونَ شَرَفَ الآخِرَةِ إلّا بِتَرْكِ ما تُحِبُّونَ. فَلا تَنْتَظِرُوا بِالتوْبَةِ غَداً, فإنَّ دُونَ غَدٍ يَوْماً وَلَيْلَةً, قَضاءُ اللهِ فِيهِما يَغْدُو وَيَرُوحُ.

بِحَقٍّ أقُولُ لَكُمْ, إنَّ صِغارَ الخَطايا وَمُحَقَّراتِها, لَمِنْ مَكائِدِ إبْلِيسَ؛ يُحَقِّرُها لَكُمْ وَيُصَغِّرُها فِي أعْيُنِكُمْ, فَتَجْتَمِعُ فَتَكْثُرُ وَتُحِيطُ بِكُمْ.

In truth I say to you: To extol by lying and to boast of the purity of one's religiosity is at the head of notorious evil, and verily, love of this world is the head of every wrong.

In truth I say to you: there is nothing that does more to bring one to nobility in the other world and does more to help one with the occurrences of the world than constant prayer, and there is nothing nearer to the Merciful than it, so do this constantly and increase it. And every righteous work draws one nigh unto Allah, so prayer is the nearest to Him, and is most preferred by Him.

In truth I say to you: Surely, every work of an oppressed one who is not helped in word, in action, or in resentment, he is a great one in the kingdom of heaven. Who of you has seen light whose name is darkness or darkness whose name is light? Likewise being a believer and being an disbeliever cannot be gathered in a servant, and he cannot prefer this world while yearning for the other world. Does the sower of barley reap wheat, or does the sower of wheat reap barley? Likewise, every servant reaps in the other world what he has sown, and he will be compensated for what he has wrought.

In truth I say to you: Surely the people are two sorts with regard to wisdom. One makes it firm by his word, and spoils it by his bad work, and one makes it firm by his word and confirms it by his work. What a difference between them! Blessed are those who are scholars in their actions, and woe to those who are scholars [merely] in their words.

In truth I say to you: He who does not purify his sowings of weeds, they multiply in it until they take over and spoil them, and likewise he who does not expel the love for this world from his heart, it takes over his heart until he does not find the taste of love for the other world.

Woe unto you, O servants of this world! Take to the mosques of your Lord as prisons for your bodies, and make your hearts houses of piety, and do not make your heart a refuge for desires.

In truth I say to you: the most impatient of you with troubles, is he who has the most intense love of this world, and the most patient of you with troubles is the most disinterested with the world.

بِحَقٍّ أَقُولُ لَكُمْ, إِنَّ المِدْحَةَ بِالكِذْبِ وَالتَّزْكِيَةَ فِى الدِين, لَمِنْ رَاسِ الشُّرُور المَعْلُومَةِ؛ وإِنَّ حُبَّ الدنْيا, لَرَاسُ كُلِّ خَطِيئَةٍ.

بِحَقٍّ أَقُولُ لَكُمْ؛ لَيْسَ شَىْءَ أَبْلَغَ فِى شَرَفِ الآخِرَةِ وَأَعْوَنَ عَلَي حَوَادِثِ الدنْيا مِنَ الصَّلاةِ الدَّائِمَةِ, وَلَيْسَ شَىْءَ أَقْرَبَ إِلَي الرحْمَنَ مِنْها, فَدُومُوا عَلَيْها واسْتَكْثِرُوا مِنْها. وَكُلُّ عَمَلٍ صالِحٍ يُقَرِّبُ إِلَي اللهِ, فالصلاةُ أَقْرَبُ إِلَيْهِ وَآثَرُ عِنْدَهُ.

بِحَقٍّ أَقُولُ لَكُمْ, إِنَّ كُلَّ عَمَلِ المَظْلُوم الذى لَمْ يُنْتَصَرْ بِقَوْلٍ وَلا فِعْلٍ وَلا حِقْدٍ, هُوَ فِى مَلَكُوتِ السَّماء عَظِيمٌ. أَيُّكُمْ رَأي نُوراً اسْمُهُ ظُلْمَةَ، أَوْ ظُلْمَةَ اسْمُها نُورٌ؟ كَذَلِكَ, لا يَجْتَمِعُ لِلْعَبْدِ أَنْ يَكُونَ مُؤمِناً كافِراً, وَلا مُؤثِراً لِلدُنْيا راغِباً فِى الآخِرَةِ. وَهَلْ زارِعُ شَعِير يَحْصُدُ قَمْحاً أَوْ زارِعُ قَمْح يَحْصُدُ شَعِيراً؟ كَذَلِكَ, يَحْصُدُ كُلُّ عَبْدٍ فِى الآخِرَةِ ما زَرَعَ, وَيُجْزَي بِما عَمِلَ.

بِحَقٍّ أَقُولُ لَكُمْ, إِنَّ النَاسَ فِى الحِكْمَةِ رَجُلانِ: فَرَجُلٌ أَتْقَنَها بِقَوْلِهِ وَضَيَّعَها بِسُوء فِعْلِهِ, وَرَجُلٌ أَتْقَنَها بِقَوْلِهِ وَصَدَّقَها بِفِعْلِهِ؛ وَشَتَّانَ بَيْنَهُما. فَطُوبَي لِلْعُلَماء بِالفِعْلِ, وَوَيْلٌ لِلْعُلَماء بِالقَوْل.

بِحَقٍّ أَقُولُ لَكُمْ, مَنْ لا يُنَقَّى مِنْ زَرْعِهِ الحَشِيشَ, يَكْثُرُ فِيهِ حَتَّي يَغْمُرَهُ, فَيُفْسِدُهُ. وَكَذَلِكَ, مَنْ لا يُخْرِجُ مِنْ قَلْبِهِ حُبَّ الدنْيا, يَغْمُرُهُ حَتَّي لا يَجِدُ لِحُبَّ الآخِرَةِ طَعْماً.

وَيْلَكُمْ يا عَبِيدَ الدنْيا! اتَّخِذُوا مَساجِدَ رَبِّكُمْ سُجُوناً لِأَجْسادِكُمْ, واجْعَلُوا قُلُوبَكُمْ بُيُوتاً لِلتَّقْوَي, وَلا تَجْعَلُوا قُلُوبَكُمْ مَأوِيً لِلشَّهَواتِ.

بِحَقٍّ أَقُولُ لَكُمْ, إِنَّ أَجْزَعَكُمْ عَلَي البَلاءِ, لَأَشَدُّكُمْ حُبّاً لِلدُنْيا. وإِنَّ أَصْبَرَكُمْ عَلَي البَلاءِ, لَأَزْهَدُكُمْ فِى الدنْيا.

Woe unto you, O evil scholars! Were you not dead, then He revived you? Then when He revived you, you died.[1] Woe unto you! Were you not unlettered, then He taught you? Then when He taught you, you forgot. Woe unto you! Were you not empty, then Allah made you understand? Then when you were made to understand, you became ignorant. Woe unto you! Were you not astray, then He guided you? Then when He guided you, you went astray. Woe unto you! Were you not blind and He made you see? Then when He made you see, you became blind. Woe unto you! Were you not deaf, then He made you hear? Then when He made you hear, you became deaf. Woe unto you! Where you not dumb, then He made you speaking? Then when He made you speaking, you became dumb. Woe unto you! Did you not seek an opening, then when the opening was made for you, you retreated to [the ways of] your forefathers? Woe unto you! Were you not humbled and He made you honored? Then when you were honored you subjugated, transgressed and disobeyed. Woe unto you! Were you not oppressed in the earth, fearing that people would snatch you away, then He helped and supported you? Then when He helped you, you became arrogant and overbearing. Then alas to you because of your humiliation on the Day of Resurrection, how it will make you negligible and small.

Alas to you, O evil scholars! You do the deeds of infidels, and you have the hope of inheritors, and you have the assurance of the secure, but the order of Allah is not as you wish and choose, rather you have children for death, and you build and make habitable for destruction, and you make preparations for your legacy.[2]

In truth I say to you: Verily Moses (a) used to command you: Do not swear by Allah truly or falsely, but say no or yes.[3]

---

[1] With respect to the spiritual life intended by God, they became like the dead.

[2] That is, you will not be able to enjoy the worldly profits yourselves, but will have to leave them to your heirs.

[3] In *Biḥār* 14, 313, this narration is reported as follows: "In truth I say to you: Verily Moses (a) used to command you: Do not swear by Allah falsely. But I say to you: Do not swear by Allah truly or falsely, but say no and yes." Majlisī narrates this from the edition he had of *Tuḥaf al-'Uqūl,* so it seems that the copiest of the present edition of *Tuḥaf al-'Uqūl* left out the part mentioned in *Biḥār.*

وَيْلَكُمْ يا عُلَماءَ السَّوءِ! أَلَمْ تَكُونُوا أَمواتاً, فأَحياكُمْ؟ فَلَمّا أَحْياكُمْ, مِتُّمْ. وَيْلَكُمْ, أَلَمْ تَكُونُوا أُمِّيِّينَ, فعَلَّمَكُمْ؟ فَلَمّا عَلَّمَكُمْ, نَسِيتُمْ. وَيْلَكُمْ, أَلَمْ تَكُونُوا جُفاةً, فَفَقَّهَكُمُ اللهُ؟ فَلَمّا فَقَّهَكُمْ جَهِلْتُمْ. وَيْلَكُمْ, أَلَمْ تَكُونُوا ضَلالاً, فَهَداكُمْ؟ فَلَمّا هَداكُمْ ضَلَلْتُمْ. وَيْلَكُمْ, أَلَمْ تَكُونُوا عُمياً, فَبَصَّرَكُمْ؟ فَلَمّا بَصَّرَكُمْ عَمِيتُمْ. وَيْلَكُمْ, أَلَمْ تَكُونُوا صُمّاً, فَأَسْمَعَكُمْ؟ فَلَمّا أَسْمَعَكُمْ صَمَمْتُمْ. وَيْلَكُمْ, أَلَمْ تَكُونُوا بُكْماً, فَأَنْطَقَكُمْ؟ فَلَمّا أَنْطَقَكُمْ بَكِمْتُمْ. وَيْلَكُمْ, أَلَمْ تَسْتَفْتِحُوا؟ فَلَمّا فَتَحَ لَكُمْ, نَكَصْتُمْ عَلَي أَعْقابِكُمْ. وَيْلَكُمْ, أَلَمْ تَكُونُوا أَذِلَّةً, فَأَعَزَّكُمْ؟ فَلَمّا عَزَزْتُمْ قَهَرْتُمْ واعْتَدَيْتُمْ وَعَصَيْتُمْ. وَيْلَكُمْ, أَلَمْ تَكُونُوا مُسْتَضْعَفِينَ فِى الأرضِ, تَخافُونَ أَنْ يَتَخَطَّفَكُمُ النّاسُ, فَنَصَرَكُمْ وأَيَّدَكُمْ؟ فَلَمّا نَصَرَكُمْ اسْتَكْبَرْتُمْ وَتَجَبَّرْتُمْ. فَيا وَيْلَكُمْ, مِنْ ذُلِّ يَوْمِ القِيامَةِ؛ كَيْفَ يُهِينُكُمْ وَيُصَغِّرُكُمْ!

وَيا وَيْلَكُمْ, يا عُلَماءَ السَّوءِ! إِنَّكُمْ لَتَعْمَلُونَ عَمَلَ المُلْحِدِينَ, وتَأْمَلُونَ أَمَلَ الوارِثِينَ, وَتَطْمَئِنُّونَ بِطُمَأْنِينَةِ الآمِنِينَ. ولَيْسَ أَمْرُ اللهِ عَلَي ما تَتَمَنَّوْنَ وَتَتَخَيَّرُونَ, بَلْ لِلْمَوْتِ تَتَوالَدُونَ, ولِلْخَرابِ تَبْنُونَ وتَعْمُرُونَ, ولِلْوارِثِينَ تُمَهِّدُونَ.

بِحَقٍّ أَقُولُ لَكُمْ, إِنَّ مُوسَى عَلَيْهِ كانَ يَأْمُرُكُمْ أَنْ لا تَحْلِفُوا بِاللهِ صادِقِينَ وَلا كاذِبِينَ, ولَكِنْ قُولُوا: 'لا وَنَعَمْ.'

O children of Israel! For you are the vegetables of the fields and barley bread, and I prohibit wheat bread for you, for I fear you will not establish thanksgiving for it.

In truth I say to you, surely the people are well off or afflicted. So, praise Allah for being well off, and have mercy on those who are troubled.

In truth I say to you, for every bad word you say, you will be given its answer on the Day of Resurrection.

O evil servants! When one of you brings close a sacrificial [animal] to slaughter, then he is reminded that his brother has something against him, then he should leave his sacrifice and go to his brother and make him satisfied, then he should return to his sacrifice and slaughter it.

O evil servants! If a shirt is taken from one of you, then give your cloak with it. And whoever is slapped on his cheek, he should let his other cheek [be slapped]. And whoever is subjected to one mile, let him go another mile with him.

In truth I say to you, of what benefit is it for the body that its exterior is sound and its interior rotten. And of what benefit is it to you that your bodies be pleasing to you, while your hearts are rotten. And of what benefit is it to you if you purify your skins but your hearts are unclean.

In truth I say to you, do not be like a sieve that expels good flour and retains the waste. Likewise, you expel wisdom from your mouths, and hatred remains in your breasts.

In truth I say to you, begin with evil and abandon it, then seek good. It will benefit you. If you gather good with evil, the good will not benefit you.

In truth I say to you, one who wades it a stream, inevitably water will reach his clothes, even if he makes an effort that it does not reach them. Likewise, he who loves the world will not be saved from wrongdoing.

يا بَنِي إسْرائِيلَ, علَيْكُمْ بِالبَقلِ البرِّىِّ وَخُبْزِ الشعِيرِ, وإيّاكُمْ وَخُبْزَ البُرِّ؛ فإنِّى أخافُ علَيْكُمْ أنْ لا تَقُومُوا بِشُكْرِهِ.

بِحَقٍّ أقُولُ لَكُمْ, إنَّ الناسَ مُعافيً وَمُبْتَليً, فاحْمِدُوا الله علَي العافِيَةِ, وارْحَمُوا أهْلَ البَلاءِ.

بِحَقٍّ أقُولُ لَكُمْ, إنَّ كُلَّ كَلِمَةٍ سَيِّئَةٍ تَقُولُونَ بِها, تُعْطَوْنَ جَوابَها يَوْمَ القِيامَةِ.

يا عَبِيدَ السَوءِ! إذا قَرَّبَ أحَدُكُم قُرْبانَهُ لِيَذْبَحَهُ, فَذَكَرَ أنَّ أخاهُ واجِدٌ علَيْهِ, فَلْيَتْرُكْ قُرْبانَهُ, وَلْيَذْهَبْ إلَي أخِيهِ, فَلْيُرْضِهِ؛ ثُمَّ لِيَرْجِعْ إلَي قُرْبانِهِ, فَلْيَذْبَحْهُ.

يا عَبِيدَ السَوءِ! إنْ أخِذَ قَمِيصُ أحَدِكُمْ, فَلْيُعْطِ رِداءَهُ مَعَهُ. وَمَنْ لُطِمَ خَدُّهُ مِنْكُمْ, فَلْيُمَكِّنْ مِنْ خَدِّهِ الآخَرَ. وَمَنْ سُخِّرَ مِنْكُمْ مِيلاً, فَلْيَذْهَبْ مِيلاً آخَرَ مَعَهُ.

بِحَقٍّ أقُولُ لَكُمْ, ما ذا يُغْنِى عَنِ الجَسَدِ, إذا كانَ ظاهِرُهُ صَحِيحاً وَباطِنُهُ فاسِداً؟ وَما تُغْنِى عَنْكُمْ أجْسادُكُمْ إذا أعْجَبَتْكُمْ, وَقَدْ فَسَدَتْ قُلُوبُكُمْ؟ وَما يُغْنِى عَنْكُمْ أنْ تَنْقُوا جُلُودَكُمْ, وَقُلُوبُكُمْ دَنِسَةٌ؟

بِحَقٍّ أقُولُ لَكُمْ, لا تَكُونُوا كالمِنْخَلِ, يُخْرِجُ الدقِيقَ الطَيِّبَ وَيُمْسِكُ النخالَةَ. كَذَلِكَ, أنتُم تُخْرِجُونَ الحِكْمَةَ مِنْ أفْواهِكُمْ, وَيَبْقَي الغِلُّ فِى صُدُورِكُمْ.

بِحَقٍّ أقُولُ لَكُمْ, ابْدَؤوا بِالشرِّ فاتْرُكُوهُ, ثُمَّ اطْلُبُوا الخَيْرَ يَنْفَعْكُمْ. فانَّكُمْ إذا جَمَعْتُمْ الخَيْرَ مَعَ الشرِّ, لَمْ يَنْفَعْكُمُ الخَيْرُ.

بِحَقٍّ أقُولُ لَكُمْ, إنَّ الذى يَخُوضُ النَهْرَ, لا بُدَّ أنْ يُصِيبَ ثَوْبَهُ الماءُ, وإنْ جَهَدَ أنْ لا يُصِيبَهُ. كَذَلِكَ, مَنْ يُحِبُّ الدنْيا لا يَنْجُو مِنَ الخَطايا.

In truth I say to you, blessed are they who spend the night in prayer, they are those who will inherit perpetual light, because they stood on their feet in the darkness of the night in their places of prayer; they implore their Lord in hope that He may save them from affliction tomorrow.

In truth I say to you, the world was created as a farm, in it the servants sow the sweet and the bitter, evil and good. The good has a beneficial outcome on the Day of Reckoning, and evil has trouble and wretchedness on the Day of Harvesting.

In truth I say to you, the wise will be compared to the ignorant, and the ignorant will be compared to his desires. I commend you to seal your mouths with silence so that nothing may go out of them that is not permitted for you.

In truth I say to you, you will not attain that for which you hope unless by being patient with what you detest, and you will not obtain what you will unless by abandoning what you desire.

In truth I say to you, O servants of this world! How can one attain the other world, who does not reduce his lust for this world and does not cut off his yearning for it?

In truth I say to you, O servants of this world! You do not love this world, and you do not hope for the other world. If you did love this world, you would honor the work by which you attain it, and if you did want the other world, you would perform the deeds of one who hopes for it.

In truth I say to you, O servants of this world! One of you hates his companion on the basis of suspicion, and does not hate himself on the basis of certainty.

In truth I say to you, one of you becomes angry when one of your faults is mentioned to you, while it is true; but you delight when you are praised for what is not in you.

بِحَقٍّ أَقُولُ لَكُمْ, طُوبَي لِلَّذِينَ يَتَهَجَّدُونَ مِنَ الليْلِ. أُولَئِكَ الذِينَ يَرِثُونَ النورَ الدائِمَ, مِنْ أَجْلِ أَنَّهُمْ قامُوا فِى ظُلْمَةِ الليْلِ عَلَي أَرْجُلِهِمْ فِى مَساجِدِهِمْ, يَتَضَرَّعُونَ إِلَي رَبِّهِمْ, رَجاءَ أَنْ يُنَجِّيَهُمْ فِى الشدَّةِ غَداً.

بِحَقٍّ أَقُولُ لَكُمْ, إِنَّ الدنْيا خُلِقَتْ مَزْرَعَةً, تَزْرَعُ فِيها العِبادُ الحُلْوَ والمُرَّ والشرَّ والخَيْرَ. والخَيْرُ لَهُ مَغْبَّةٌ نافِعَةٌ يَوْمَ الحِسابِ, والشرُّ لَهُ عَناءٌ وَشِقاءٌ يَوْمَ الحَصادِ.

بِحَقٍّ أَقُولُ لَكُمْ, إِنَّ الحَكِيمَ يَعْتَبِرُ بِالجاهِلِ, والجاهِلُ يَعْتَبِرُ بِهَواهُ. أُوصِيكُمْ أَنْ تَخْتِمُوا عَلَي أَفْواهِكُمْ بِالصمْتِ, حَتَّي لا يَخْرُجَ مِنْها ما لا يَحِلُّ لَكُمْ.

بِحَقٍّ أَقُولُ لَكُمْ, إِنَّكُمْ لا تُدْرِكُونَ ما تَأمَلُونَ, إِلَّا بِالصبْرِ عَلَي ما تَكْرَهُونَ؛ وَلا تَبْتَغُونَ ما تُرِيدُونَ, إِلَّا بِتَرْكِ ما تَشْتَهُونَ.

بِحَقٍّ أَقُولُ لَكُمْ, يا عَبِيدَ الدنْيا! كَيْفَ يُدْرِكُ الآخِرَةَ, مَنْ لا تَنْقُصُ شَهْوَتُهُ مِنَ الدنْيا, وَلا تَنْقَطِعُ مِنْها رَغْبَتُهُ؟

بِحَقٍّ أَقُولُ لَكُمْ, يا عَبِيدَ الدنْيا! ما الدنْيا تُحِبُّونَ وَلا الآخِرَةَ تَرْجُونَ. لَوْ كُنْتُمْ تُحِبُّونَ الدنْيا, أَكْرَمْتُمُ العَمَلَ الذِى بِهِ أَدْرَكْتُمُوها؛ وَلَوْ كُنْتُمْ تُرِيدُونَ الآخِرَةَ, عَمِلْتُمْ عَمَلَ مَنْ يَرْجُوها.

بِحَقٍّ أَقُولُ لَكُمْ, يا عَبِيدَ الدنْيا! إِنَّ أَحَدَكُمْ يُبْغِضُ صاحِبَهُ عَلَي الظَّنِّ, وَلا يُبْغِضُ نَفْسَهُ عَلَي اليَقِينِ.

بِحَقٍّ أَقُولُ لَكُمْ, إِنَّ أَحَدَكُمْ لَيَغْضَبُ إِذا ذُكِرَ لَهُ بَعْضُ عُيُوبِهِ, وَهِىَ حَقٌّ؛ وَيَفْرَحُ إِذا مُدِحَ بِما لَيْسَ فِيهِ.

In truth I say to you, the spirits of the satans do not live as long in anything as they live in your hearts. Allah has given you this world only that you act in it for the other world. He has not given it to you that you become too occupied in it for the other world. He has expanded it for you only that you know that He has helped you to worship by it, and He has not helped you to sin by it. He has commanded you in it only to obey Him, and He has not commanded you in it to disobey Him. He helps you in it only for what is lawful, and He does not make lawful for you what is unlawful. He has spread it for you only that you may have relations with one another, and He has not spread it that you cut off relations from one another.

In truth I say to you, wages are coveted, but none attains them but those who work for them.

In truth I say to you, a tree does not become perfect unless by good fruit; and likewise, religion does not become perfect unless by avoidance of the unlawful.

In truth I say to you, the farm does not become right except by water and soil; likewise faith does not become right except by knowledge and action.

In truth I say to you, water extinguishes fire; likewise clemency extinguishes anger.

In truth I say to you, water and fire cannot be put together in a bowl; likewise, understanding and blindness cannot be put together in one heart.

In truth I say to you, there is no rain without a cloud; likewise, there is no action pleasing to the Lord without a pure heart.

In truth I say to you, surely the sun is the light of all things, and surely wisdom is the light of every heart, and God-wariness is the head of every wisdom, and truth is the gate to every good, and the mercy of Allah is the gate to every truth, and the keys to it are prayer and supplication and action. How can a gate be opened without a key.

بِحَقٍّ أقُولُ لَكُمْ, إنَّ أرْوَاحَ الشياطِينَ ما عَمَّرَتْ فِي شَىْء ما عَمَّرَتْ فِي قُلُوبِكُمْ. فإنَّما أعْطَاكُمُ اللهُ الدنْيا, لِتَعْمَلُوا فِيها لِلآخِرَةِ, ولَمْ يُعْطِكُمُوها, لِتَشْغَلَكُمْ عَنِ الآخِرَةِ. وانَّما بَسَطَها لَكُمْ, لِتَعْلَمُوا أنَّهُ أعانَكُمْ بِها عَلَي العِبادَةِ, ولَمْ يُعِنْكُمْ بِها عَلَي الخَطايا. وإنَّما أمَرَكُمْ فَيها بِطاعَتِهِ, ولَمْ يأمُرْكُمْ فِيها بِمَعْصِيَتِهِ. وإنَّما أعانَكُمْ بِها عَلَي الحَلالِ, ولَمْ يَحِلَّ لَكُمْ بِها الحَرامَ. وإنَّما وَسَّعَها لَكُمْ لِتَواصَلُوا فِيها, ولَمْ يُوَسِّعْها لَكُمْ لِتَقاطَعُوا فِيها.

بِحَقٍّ أقُولُ لَكُمْ, إنَّ الأجْرَ مَحْرُوصٌ عَلَيْهِ, وَلا يُدْرِكُهُ إلّا مَنْ عَمِلَ لَهُ.

بِحَقٍّ أقُولُ لَكُمْ, إنَّ الشجَرَةَ لا تَكْمُلُ إلّا بِثَمَرَةٍ طَيِّبَةٍ. كَذَلِكَ, لا يَكْمُلُ الدينُ إلّا بِالتحَرُّجِ عَنِ المَحارِمِ.

بِحَقٍّ أقُولُ لَكُمْ, إنَّ الزَّرْعَ لا يَصْلُحُ إلّا بِالماءِ والترابِ. كَذَلِكَ, الإيمانُ لا يَصْلُحُ إلّا بِالعِلْمِ والعَمَلِ.

بِحَقٍّ أقُولُ لَكُمْ, إنَّ الماءَ يُطْفِئُ النارَ. كَذَلِكَ, الحِلْمُ يُطْفِئُ الغَضَبَ.

بِحَقٍّ أقُولُ لَكُمْ, لا يَجْتَمِعُ الماءُ والنارُ فِي إناءٍ واحِدٍ. كَذَلِكَ, لا يَجْتَمِعُ الفِقْهُ والعَمَي فِي قَلْبٍ واحِدٍ.

بِحَقٍّ أقُولُ لَكُمْ, إنَّهُ لا يَكُونُ مَطَرٌ بِغَيْرِ سَحابٍ. كَذَلِكَ, لا يَكُونُ عَمَلٌ فِي مَرْضاةِ الربِّ إلّا بِقَلْبٍ نَقِيٍّ.

بِحَقٍّ أقُولُ لَكُمْ, إنَّ الشمْسَ نُورُ كُلِّ شَىْء, وانَّ الحِكْمَةَ نُورُ كُلِّ قَلْبٍ, والتقْوَي رَأسُ كُلِّ حِكْمَةٍ, والحَقُّ بابُ كُلِّ خَيْرٍ, وَرَحْمَةُ اللهِ بابُ كُلِّ حَقٍّ؛ وَمَفاتِيحُ ذَلِكَ, الدعاءُ والتضَرُّعُ والعَمَلُ. وَكَيْفَ يُفْتَحُ بابٌ بِغَيْرِ مِفْتاحٍ؟

In truth I say to you, a wise man does not plant a tree unless he is pleased with it, and he does not ride on a horse unless he is pleased with it; likewise, the knowing believer does not do a deed unless it is pleasing to his Lord.

In truth I say to you, verily, polishing makes a sword right and makes it shine; likewise wisdom in the heart polishes it and makes it shine, and in the heart of the wise it is like water in the dead earth. It revives his heart like water revives the dead earth, and in the heart of the wise it is like light in the darkness, he walks by it among the people.

In truth I say to you, carrying stones from the tops of mountains is better than saying something to someone who does not understand what you say, like one who puts a stone in water to soften it, like one who prepares food for the people of the graves.

Blessed is he who refrains from excessive speech, because he fears the wrath of His Lord. And he does not narrate a narration unless he understands it, and he does not envy someone for his speech until his action becomes clear for him.

Blessed is he who learns from the learned that of which he is ignorant, and who teaches the ignorant of what he knows.

Blessed is he who honors the scholars for their knowledge, and who abandons disputing with them, and who takes lightly the ignorant for their ignorance,[1] and does not drive them away, but brings them close and teaches them.

In truth I say to you, O group of disciples, surely today, you are like the alive among the people who are dead, so do not die with the death of those alive."[2]

(*Tuḥaf al-'Uqūl,* 501-513)

---

[1] The term *jahl,* which is normally translated as *ignorance* is generally contrasted with *Ḥilm* (clemency), so that the ignorant are those who are intolerant.

[2] The disciples are told that they differ from others (in having true life) and they are warned not to become like the others (by losing the true life they have).

بِحَقٍّ أَقُولُ لَكُمْ, إِنَّ الرَّجُلَ الحَكِيمَ لا يَغْرِسُ شَجَرَةً إلَّا شَجَرَةً يَرْضاها, وَلا يَحْمِلُ عَلَي خَيْلِهِ إلَّا فَرَساً يَرْضاهُ. كَذَلِكَ, المُؤمِنُ العالِمُ لا يَعْمَلُ إلَّا عَمَلاً يَرْضاهُ رَبُّهُ.

بِحَقٍّ أَقُولُ لَكُمْ, إِنَّ الصَّقالَة نُصْلِحُ السَّيْفَ وَتَجْلُوهُ. كَذَلِكَ, الحِكْمَةُ لِلْقَلْبِ تَصْقُلُهُ وَتَجْلُوهُ؛ وَهِيَ فِى قَلْبِ الحَكِيمِ, مِثْلُ الماءِ فِى الأرضِ المَيِّتَةِ, تُحْيِى قَلْبَهُ كَما يُحيِى الماءُ الأرضَ المَيِّتَة؛ وَهِيَ فِى قَلْبِ الحَكِيمِ مِثْلُ النورِ فِى الظُّلْمَةِ, يَمْشِى بِها فِى الناسِ.

بِحَقٍّ أَقُولُ لَكُمْ, إِنَّ نَقْلَ الحِجارَةِ مِنْ رُؤُوسِ الجِبالِ, أَفْضَلُ مِنْ أَنْ تُحَدِّثَ مَنْ لا يَعْقِلُ عَنْكَ حَدِيثَكَ؛ كَمَثَلِ الذى يَنْقَعُ الحِجارَةَ لِتَلِينَ, وَكَمَثَلِ الذى يَصْنَعُ الطَّعامَ لِأَهْلِ القُبُورِ.

طُوبَي لِمَنْ حَبَسَ الفَضْلَ مِنْ قَوْلِهِ الذى يَخافُ عَلَيْهِ المَقْتَ مِنْ رَبِّهِ, وَلا يُحَدِّثُ حَدِيثًا إلَّا يَفْهَمُ, وَلا يَغْبِطُ امْرِءاً فِى قَوْلِهِ حَتَّي يَسْتَبِينَ لَهُ فِعْلُهُ.

طُوبَي لِمَنْ تَعَلَّمَ مِنَ العُلَماءِ ما جَهِلَ, وَعَلَّمَ الجاهِلَ مِمّا عَلِمَ.

طُوبَي لِمَنْ عَظَّمَ العُلَماءَ لِعِلْمِهِمْ, وَتَرَكَ مُنازَعَتَهُمْ؛ وَصَغَّرَ الجُهّالَ لِجَهْلِهِمْ, وَلا يَطْرُدُهُمْ, ولَكِنْ يُقَرِّبُهُمْ وَيُعَلِّمُهُمْ.

بِحَقٍّ أَقُولُ لَكُمْ, يا مَعْشَرَ الحَوارِيِّينَ, إنَّكُمْ اليَوْمَ فِى الناسِ, كالأحياءِ مِنَ المَوْتَي, فَلا تَمُوتُوا بِمَوْتِ الأحياءِ.»

(تحف العقول، ٥٠١-٥١٣)

8.6. Verily Allah the Supreme said to Jesus, "Glorify those of knowledge and know of their excellence, then verily their excellence over that of all my creation—except for the prophets and messengers—is like that ofthe sun over the stars, and like that of the other world over this world, and like My excellence over all things."

(*Biḥār*, 2, 2, 91)

8.7. Jesus said, "You heard what was said to the people of yore, 'Do not commit adultery.' and I tell you, he who has looked at a woman and desired her has committed adultery in his heart. If your right eye betrays you, then take it out and cast it away, for it is better for you that you destoy one of your organs than that you cast your entire body into the fire of hell. And if your right hand causes you to sin, cut it off and cast it away, for it is better for you to destroy one of your organs than that your entire body goes to hell."

(*Biḥār*, 14, 318)

8.8. Al-Sayyid ibn Ṭāwūs, may Allah have mercy on him, said, "I read in the Gospel that Jesus boarded a ship and his disciples were with him, when suddenly there was a great confusion in the sea, so that the ship came near to being covered by the waves. And it was as though [Jesus] was asleep. Then his disciples came to him and awakened him and said, 'O our master! Save us so that we do not perish.' He said to them, 'O you of little faith! What has frightened you?' Then he stood up and drove away the winds, and there was a great stillness. The people marvelled, and said, 'How is this? Verily the winds and the sea listen to him.'"

(*Biḥār*, 14, 268)

٨-٦- قالَ مُقاتِلُ بْنُ سُلَيْمانَ: «وَجَدْتُ فِي الإنجيلِ أنَّ اللهَ تَعالَي قالَ لِعِيسَي عليه السلام: 'عَظِّمِ العُلَماءَ واعْرِفْ فَضْلَهُمْ, فإنِّي فَضَّلْتُهُمْ عَلَي جَمِيعِ خَلْقِي, إلّا النَبِيِّينَ والمُرْسَلِينَ, كَفَضْلِ الشمْسِ عَلَي الكَواكِبِ, وكَفَضْلِ الآخِرَةِ عَلَي الدنْيا, وكَفَضْلِي عَلَي كُلِّ شَيْء.'»

(بحارالأنوار، ٢، ٢، ٩١)

٨-٧- قالَ السَيِّدُ بن طاوُس، رَحِمَهُ اللهُ، فِي سَعْدِ السُّعُودِ: «قَرأتُ فِي الإنجيلِ: 'قالَ عِيسَي عليه السلام: 'سَمِعْتُمْ ما قِيلَ لِلأوَّلِينَ: 'لا تَزْنُوا.' وأنا أقُولُ لَكُمْ: 'إنَّ مَنْ نَظَرَ إلِي امْرأةٍ فاشْتَهاها، فَقَدْ زَنَي بِها فِي قَلْبِهِ. إنْ خانَتْكَ عَيْنُكَ اليُمْنَي، فاقْلَعْها و.ألقِها عَنْكَ، لِأنَّهُ خَيْرٌ لَكَ أنْ تُهْلِكَ أحَدَ أعْضائِكَ، وَلا تُلْقِيَ جَسَدَكَ كُلَّهُ فِي نارِ جَهَنَّمَ. وإنْ شَكَّكَتْكَ يَدُكَ اليُمْنَي، فاقْطَعْها وألْقِها عَنْكَ، فإنَّهُ خَيْرٌ لَكَ أنْ تُهْلِكَ أحَدَ أعْضائِكَ، مِنْ أنْ يَذْهَبَ كُلُّ جَسَدِكَ فِي جَهَنَّمَ.'''»

(بحارالانوار، ١٤، ٣١٨)

٨-٨- قالَ السَيِّدُ بن طاوُس فِي سَعْدِ السُّعُودِ: «رأيْتُ فِي الإنجيلِ: 'إنَّ عِيسَي عليه السلام صَعَدَ السَفِينَةَ، وَمَعَهُ تَلامِيذُهُ، وإذا اضْطِرابٌ عَظِيمٌ فِي البَحْرِ، حَتَّي كادَتْ السَفِينَةُ تَتَغَطَّي بِالأمواجِ، وكانَ هُوَ كالنائِمِ. فَتَقَدَّمَ إلَيْهِ تَلامِيذُهُ، وأيْقَظُوهُ، وَقالُوا: 'يا سَيِّدَنا! نَجِّنا، لِكَيلا نَهْلَكُ.' فَقالَ لَهُمْ: 'يا قَلِيلِي الإيمانِ! ما أخْوَفَكُمْ!' فَعِنْدَ ذَلِكَ قامَ، وانْتَهَرَ الرياحَ، فَصارَ هَدْءاً عَظِيماً؛ فَتَعَجَّبَ الناسُ، وَقالُوا: 'كَيْفَ هَذا! إنَّ الرياحَ والبَحْرَ لَتَسْمَعانِ مِنْهُ.'»

(بحارالانوار، ١٤، ٢٦٨)

8.9. Allah the Supreme said in the seventeenth chapter of the Gospel: "Woe unto those who have heard the knowledge but have not sought it. How they will be gathered with the ignorant into the fire. And learn the knowledge and teach it, for even if knowledge does not bring you felicity, it will not bring you wretchedness, and even if it does not raise you, it will not lower you, and even if it does not enrich you, it will not impoverish you, and even if it does not benefit you, it will not harm you. And do not say, 'We fear that we may come to know but not to act', but say, 'We we hope to come to know and to act. And knowledge intercedes on behalf of one who has it, and it is the duty of Allah not to disgrace him. Indeed, on the Resurrection Day Allah will say: O assembly of the learned (ualama)! What is your opinion of your Lord? Then they will say: It is our opinion that He will have mercy upon us and forgive us. Then the Almighty will say: Indeed, I have done so. Indeed, I have entrusted you with My wisdom not because I wanted evil for you, but because I wanted good for you. So enter among My good servants into my garden (paradise) by My mercy.'"(1)

(*Biḥār*, 1, 186, 110)

---

(1) Cf. Matt 8:23-27:

23 And when he was entered into a ship, his disciples followed him.

24 And, behold, there arose a great tempest in the sea, insomuch that the ship was covered with the waves: but he was asleep.

25 And his disciples came to him, and awoke him, saying, Lord, save us: we perish.

26 And he saith unto them, Why are ye fearful, O ye of little faith? Then he arose, and rebuked the winds and the sea; and there was a great calm.

27 But the men marvelled, saying, What manner of man is this, that even the winds and the sea obey him!

(KJV)

٨-٩- فِى الإنجِيلِ، فِى السُّورَةِ السَّابِعَة عَشَرَ مِنْهُ: «وَيْلٌ لِمَنْ سَمِعَ بِالعِلْمِ، وَلَمْ يَطْلُبْهُ. كَيْفَ يُحْشَرُ مَعَ الجُهّالِ إِلِي النارِ؟ اطْلُبُوا العِلْمَ وَتَعَلَّمُوهُ، فَإِنَّ العِلْمَ إِنْ لَمْ يُسْعِدْكُمْ لَمْ يُشْقِكُمْ، وإِنْ لَمْ يَرْفَعْكُمْ لَمْ يَضَعْكُمْ، وإِنْ لَمْ يُغْنِكُمْ لَمْ يُفْقِرْكُمْ، وإِنْ لَمْ يَنْفَعْكُمْ لَمْ يَضُرُّكُمْ. وَلا تَقُولُوا: 'نَخافُ أَنْ نَعْلَمَ فَلا نَعْمَلُ،' وَلكِنْ قُولُوا: 'نَرْجُو أَنْ نَعْلَمَ وَنَعْمَلَ.' والعِلْمُ يَشْفَعُ لِصاحِبِهِ، وَحَقٌّ عَلَي اللهِ أَنْ لا يُخْزِيَهُ. إِنَّ اللهَ يَقُولُ يَوْمَ القِيامَةِ: 'يا مَعْشَرَ العُلَماءِ، ما ظَنُّكُمْ بِرَبِّكُمْ؟' فَيَقُولُونَ: 'ظَنَنّا أَنْ تَرْحَمَنا، وَتَغْفِرَ لَنا.' فَيَقُولُ، تَعالي: 'فَإِنِّى قَدْ فَعَلْتُ. إِنِّى اسْتَوْدَعْتُكُمْ حِكْمَتِى، لا لِشَرٍّ أَرَدْتُهُ بِكُمْ، بَلْ لِخَيْرٍ أَرَدْتُهُ بِكُمْ. فَادْخُلُوا فِى صالِحِ عِبادِى، إِلِي جَنَّتِى وَرَحْمَتِى.'»

(بحارالانوار، ١، ١٨٦، ١١٠)

9

RESPECT SHOWN BY CHRISTIANS TO JESUS ﷺ

9.1. It is reported that Zayn al-'Abidīn said, "When the head of al-Ḥusayn was brought to Yazīd, he convened sessions for wine drinking and had the head of al-Ḥusayn brought, placed before him and he would drink wine in front of it.

One day, a messenger from the king of Rūm was present at one such session of Yazīd, and he was one of the nobles and greats of Rūm. He said, "O King of the Arabs! Whose head is this?" Yazīd said to him, "What is this head to you?" He said, "When I return to our king, he will ask me about everything I saw. So, I would like to report to him about the story of this head and its owner so that our king may share in your joy and happiness." Yazīd said, "This is the head of al-Ḥusayn ibn 'Alī ibn Abū Ṭālib." The man from Rūm said, "Who is his mother?" He said, "Fāṭimah the daughter of the Messenger of Allah."

The Christian said, "Fie on you and on your religion! I have a religion better than yours. Verily, my father is one of the descendents of David, and there are many generations between David and my father. But the Christians honor me and take some of the earth from beneath my feet as a blessing because of my father, as one of the descendents of David. But you kill the son of the daughter of the Messenger of Allah, while between them there is only one mother! What sort of religion do you have?" Then he said to Yazīd, "Have you heard the story of the Church of the Hoof?" He said to him,

٩

احترام النصارى لعيسى عليه السلام

٩-١- رُوِىَ عَنْ زَيْنِ العابِدِينَ عليه السلام: «إنَّهُ لَمّا أُتِىَ بِراْسِ الحُسَيْنِ إلَي يَزِيدٍ، كانَ يَتَّخِذُ مَجالِسَ الشراب، وَياْتِى بِراْسِ الحُسَيْنِ، وَيَضَعُهُ بَيْنَ يَدَيْهِ، وَيَشْرَبُ عَلَيْهِ. فَحَضَرَ فِى مَجْلِسِهِ ذاتَ يَوْمٍ رَسُولُ مَلِكِ الرومِ، وَكانَ مِنْ أشْرافِ الرومِ وَعُظَمائِهِمْ. فقالَ: 'يا مَلِكَ العَرَبِ! هَذا راْسُ مَنْ؟' فقالَ لَهُ يَزِيدُ: 'ما لَكَ وَلِهَذا الراْسِ؟' فقالَ: 'إنِّى إذا رَجَعْتُ إلَي مَلِكِنا، يَسْأَلُنِى عَنْ كُلِّ شَىْءٍ رَأَيْتُهُ. فَأَحْبَبْتُ أنْ أُخْبِرَهُ بِقِصَّةِ هَذا الراْسِ وَصاحِبِهِ، حَتَّي يُشارِكَكَ فِى الفَرَحِ والسُّرُورِ.' فقالَ لَهُ يَزِيدُ: 'هَذا راْسُ الحُسَيْنِ بْنِ عَلِيٍّ بْنِ أبِى طالِبٍ.' فقالَ الرومِىُّ: 'وَمَنْ أُمُّهُ؟' فقالَ: 'فاطِمَةُ، بِنْتُ رَسُولِ اللهِ.' فقالَ النَصْرانِىُّ: 'أُفٍّ لَكَ وَلِدِينِكَ! لِى دِينٌ أحْسَنُ مِنْ دِينِكَ. إنَّ أبِى مِنْ حَوافِدِ [:أحْفاد] داوُدَ عليه السلام، وَبَيْنِى وَبَيْنَهُ آباءٌ كَثِيرَةٌ، والنَصارَي يُعَظِّمُونِى وَياخُذُونَ مِنْ تُرابِ قَدَمِى تَبَرُّكاً بِأبِى، مِنْ حَوافِدِ داوُدَ. وأنتُم تَقْتُلُونَ ابن بِنْتِ رَسُولِ اللهِ، وَما بَيْنَهُ وَبَيْنَ نَبِيِّكُمْ إلّا أُمٌّ واحِدَةٌ! فأىُّ دِينٍ دِينُكُمْ؟' ثُمَّ قالَ لِيَزِيدٍ: 'هَلْ سَمِعْتَ حَدِيثَ كَنِيسَةِ الحافِرِ؟' فقالَ لَهُ: 'قُلْ حَتَّي أسْمَعَ.' فقالَ:

"Tell it to me so I can hear it." He said, "There is a sea between Oman and China that it takes a year to cross. Along the way there is no inhabited place except one city in the middle of the water. It is eighty by eighty farsangs. There is no city on the earth bigger than it, and camphor and emeralds are brought from it. Its trees are aloes wood and ambergris. It is in the hands of the Christians. No king has sovereignty over it except them. There are many churches in that city. The biggest of them is the Church of the Hoof. There is a small golden box in its sanctuary in which is hung a hoof. They think this is the hoof of a donkey that Jesus used to ride. They decorated the area around the box with gold and silk brocade. Every year many Christians make a pilgrimage to it and walk around it, kiss it, and offer their supplications to Allah, the Exalted.

This is their manner and habit regarding the hoof of the donkey they think Jesus, their prophet, used to ride. And you kill the son of your prophet's daughter!? Then Allah does not bless you and your religion." Yazīd said, "Kill this Christian so that he cannot expose me in his cities." When the Christian realized this, he said to him, "Do you want to kill me?" He said, "Yes." He said, "Know that I saw your prophet last night in my dreams. He said to me, 'O Christian! You are of the people of heaven!' I was surprised by what he said to me. Now I bear witness that there is no god but Allah and Muḥammad is the Messenger of Allahﷺ." Then he jumped to the head of al-Ḥusayn, embraced it, began to kiss it and cried until he was killed."

(*Biḥār*, 45, 144)

'بَيْنَ عُمّانَ والصين بَحْرٌ، مَسِيرَةُ سَنَةٍ، لَيْسَ فِيها عُمْرانٌ، إلّا بَلْدَةً واحِدَةً فِي وَسَطِ الماءِ، طُولُها ثَمانُونَ فَرْسَخاً فِي ثَمانِينَ، ما عَلَي وَجْهِ الأرض بَلْدَةٌ أكْبَرُ مِنْها، وَمِنْها يُحْمَلُ الكافُورُ والياقُوتُ، أشْجارُهُمُ العُودُ والعَنْبَرُ. وَهِيَ فِي أيْدِي النَصارَي، لا مُلْكَ لِأحَدٍ مِنَ المُلُوكِ فِيها سِواهُمْ. وَفِي تِلْكَ البَلْدَةِ كَنائِسُ كَثِيرَةٌ، أعْظَمُها كَنِيسَةُ الحافِرِ، فِي مِحْرابِها حُقَّةُ ذَهَبٍ مُعَلَّقَةٌ، فِيها حافِرٌ، يَقُولُونَ: 'إنَّ هَذا حافِرُ حِمارٍ، كانَ يَرْكَبُهُ عِيسَي.' وَقَدْ زَيَّنُوا حَوْلَ الحُقَّةِ بِالذَّهَبِ والديباجِ، يَقْصُدُها فِي كُلِّ عامٍ عالَمٌ مِنَ النَصارَي، وَيَطُوفُونَ حَوْلَها وَيُقَبِّلُونَها وَيَرْفَعُونَ حَوائِجَهُمْ إلَي اللهِ، تَعالَي.

هَذا شَأنُهُمْ وَدَأبُهُمْ بِحافِرِ حِمارٍ، يَزْعُمُونَ أنَّهُ حافِرُ حِمارٍ، كانَ يَرْكَبُهُ عِيسَي نَبِيُّهُمْ؛ وأنتُم تَقْتُلُونَ ابن بِنْتِ نَبِيِّكُمْ. فَلا بارَكَ اللهُ، تَعالَي، فِيكُمْ وَلا فِي دِينِكُمْ.' فَقالَ يَزِيدُ: 'اُقْتُلُوا هَذا النَصْرانِيَّ، لِئَلّاَ يَفْضَحَنِي فِي بِلادِهِ.' فَلَمّا أحَسَّ النَصْرانِيُّ بِذَلِكَ، قالَ لَهُ: 'تُرِيدُ أنْ تَقْتُلَنِي؟' قالَ: 'نَعَمْ.' قالَ: 'اِعْلَمْ أنِّي رأيْتُ البارِحَةَ نَبِيَّكُمْ فِي المَنامِ، يَقُولُ لِي: 'يا نَصْرانِيُّ! أنتَ مِنْ أهْلِ الجَنَّةِ.' فَتَعَجَّبْتُ مِنْ كَلامِهِ. وأنا أشْهَدُ أنْ لا إلَهَ إلّا اللهُ، وأنَّ مُحَمَّداً رَسُولُ اللهِ صلى الله عليه وآله وسلم.' ثُمَّ وَثَبَ إلَي راسِ الحُسَيْنِ، فَضَمَّهُ إلَي صَدْرِهِ، وَجَعَلَ يُقَبِّلُهُ وَيَبْكِي حَتَّي قُتِلَ.»

(بحارالأنوار، ٤٥، ١٤٤)

المراجع

١- ابن طاووس، السيّد علىّ بن موسي، إقبال الأعمال، طهران، دار الكتب الإسلاميّة، ١٣٦٧ هجرى شمسى.

٢- ------، السيّد علىّ بن موسي، الطرائف، قم، الخيّام، ١٤٠٠ هجرى قمرى.

٣- ------، السيّد على بن موسي، سعد السعود، قم، دار الذخائر.

٤- ابنا بسطام، عبدالله والحسين، طبّ الأئمةعليهم السلام، قم، الشريف الرضىّ، ١٤١١ هجرى قمرى.

٥- الأحسائىّ، ابن أبى الجمهور، عوالى اللئالى، قم، سيّد الشهداءعليه السلام، ١٤٠٥ هجرى قمرى.

٦- الإمام الحسن العسكرىّ عليه السلام، تفسير الإمام العسكرىّعليه السلام، قم، مدرسة الإمام المهدىّ (عج)، ١٤٠٩ هجرى قمرى.

٧- الإمام الصادق عليه السلام، مصباح الشريعة، بيروت، مؤسّسة الأعلمى للمطبوعات، ١٤٠٠ هجرى قمرى.

٨- الإمام على بن ابى طالب عليه السلام، نهج البلاغة، قم، دار الهجرة.

٩- الإمام على بن موسي الرضا عليه السلام، صحيفة الرضا، المشهد المقدّس، المؤتمر العالميّ للإمام الرضاعليه السلام، ١٤٠٦ هجرى قمرى.

١٠- التميميّ المغربىّ، نعمان بن محمد، دعائم الإسلام، مصر، دار المعارف، ١٣٨٥ هجرى قمرى.

١١- جلالى الشاهرودىّ، محمد حسن، مجموعة الأخبار فى نفائس الآثار، النجف الأشرف، مطبعة القضاء، ١٣٩٠ هجرى قمرى.

١٢- الحرّ العاملىّ، وسائل الشيعة، قم، مؤسّسة آل البيت عليهم‌السلام، ١٤٠٩ هجرى قمرى.

١٣- الحرّانى، الحسن بن شعبة، تحف العقول، قم، جماعة المدرّسين، ١٤٠٤ هجرى قمرى.

١٤- حسين بن سعيد الأهوازىّ، كتاب الزهد، طبعة سيد ابوالفضل حسينيان، ١٤٠٢ هجرى قمرى.

١٥- الحلّىّ، ابن بطريق يحيى بن الحسن، العمدة، قم، جماعة المدرّسين، ١٤٠٧ هجرى قمرى.

١٦- الحلّىّ، ابن فهد، عدّة الداعى، قم، دارالكتاب الإسلامىّ، ١٤٠٧ هجرى قمرى.

١٧- الديلمىّ، الحسن بن ابى الحسن، إرشاد القلوب، قم، الشريف الرضيّ، ١٤١٢ هجرى قمرى.

١٨- ــــــــــــــــــــــ، أعلام الدين، قم، مؤسّسة آل البيت عليهم السلام، ١٤٠٨ هجرى قمرى.

١٩- الراوندیّ، قطب الدین، الخرائج والجرائح، قم، مؤسّسة الإمام المهدیّ (عج)، ١٤٠٩ هجری قمری.

٢٠- ـــــــــــــــ، الدعوات، قم، مدرسة الإمام المهدیّ (عج)، ١٤٠٧ هجری قمری.

٢١- الشعیریّ، تاج الدین، جامع الأخبار، قم، الشریف الرضیّ، ١٣٦٣ هجری شمسی.

٢٢- الصدوق، محمّد بن علی بن حسین بن بابویه القمیّ، الخصال، قم، جماعة المدرّسین، ١٤٠٣ هجری قمری.

٢٣- ـــــــــــــــــــــــــــــ، علل الشرائع، قم، مكتبة الداوریّ.

٢٤- ـــــــــــــــــــــــــــــ، عیون أخبار الرضا عليه السلام، جهان، ١٣٧٨ هجری قمری.

٢٥- ـــــــــــــــــــــــــــــ، كتاب من لا یحضره الفقیه، قم، جماعة المدرّسین، ١٤١٣ هجری قمری.

٢٦- ـــــــــــــــــــــــــــــ، معانی الأخبار، قم، جماعة المدرّسین، ١٣٦١ هجری شمسی.

٢٧- الصفّار، محمّد بن الحسن بن فروخ، بصائر الدرجات، قم، مكتبة آیة الله المرعشیّ، ١٤٠٤ هجری قمری.

٢٨- الطبرسیّ، ابو منصور احمد بن علیّ، الإحتجاج، قم، المرتضي، ١٤٠٣ هجری قمری.

٢٩- الطبرسیّ، ابوالفضل على بن الحسن، مشكاة الأنوار، مكتبة حيدريّة، النجف الأشرف، ١٣٨٥ هجری قمری.

٣٠- الطبریّ، عماد الدين، بشارة المصطفي لشيعة المرتضي، النجف الأشرف، المطبعة الحيدريّة، ١٣٨٣ هجری قمری.

٣١- الطبریّ، محمّد بن جرير، دلائل الإمامة، قم، دار الذخائر للمطبوعات.

٣٢- الطوسیّ، الاستبصار، طهران، دار الكتب الإسلاميّة، ١٣٩٠ هجری قمری.

٣٣- -----، التهذيب، طهران، دار الكتب الإسلاميّة، ١٣٦٥ هجری شمسی.

٣٤- -----، الغيبة، قم، مؤسّسة المعارف الإسلاميّ، ١٤١١ هجری قمری.

٣٥- العاملیّ الكفعمیّ، إبراهيم بن علیّ، المصباح، قم، الشريف الرضیّ، ١٤٠٥ هجری قمری.

٣٦- العياشیّ، محمّد بن المسعود، تفسير العياشیّ، طهران، المطبعة العلميّة، ١٣٨٠ هجری قمری.

٣٧- العيناثیّ، السيّد محمّد، آداب النفس، طهران، بين الحرمين، ١٣٨٠ هجری قمری.

٣٨- القمیّ، الشيخ عبّاس، مفاتيح الجنان المعرّب طبقاً لمتون الأحاديث ونصوص المصادر، تعريب: السيّد محمد رضا النوریّ النجفیّ، بيروت، دار إحياء التراث العربیّ.

٣٩- القميّ، على بن إبراهيم بن هاشم، تفسير القميّ، قم، مؤسّسة دارالكتاب، ١٤٠٤ هجرى قمرى.

٤٠- الكلينيّ الرازيّ، محمّد بن يعقوب، الكافى، طهران، دار الكتب الإسلاميّة، ١٣٦٥ هجرى شمسى.

٤١- الكوفيّ، فرات بن إبراهيم، تفسير فرات، بتحقيق كاظم المحموديّ، طهران، وزارة الإرشاد، ١٤١٠ هجرى قمرى.

٤٢- الكوفيّ، محمّد بن محمّد بن الأشعث، الجعفريّات (الأشعثيّات)، طهران، مكتبة نينوَي الحديثة.

٤٣- المجلسيّ، محمّد باقر بن محمّد تقيّ بن مقصود عليّ، بحار الأنوار، بيروت، مؤسّسة الوفاء، ١٤٠٤ هجرى قمرى.

٤٤- المحدّث النوريّ، مستدرك الوسائل، قم، مؤسّسة آل البيت عليهم السلام، ١٤٠٨ هجرى قمرى.

٤٥- المعتزليّ، ابن أبى الحديد، شرح نهج البلاغة، قم، مكتبة آية الله المرعشيّ، ١٤٠٤ هجرى قمرى.

٤٦- المفيد، محمّد بن محمّد بن نعمان، الاختصاص، قم، المؤتمر العالميّ للشيخ المفيد، ١٤١٣ هجرى قمرى.

٤٧- المفيد، محمّد بن محمّد بن نعمان، الأمالى، قم، المؤتمر العالميّ للشيخ المفيد، ١٤١٣ هجرى قمرى.

٤٨- النباطيّ البياضيّ، على بن يونس، الصراط المستقيم، النجف الأشرف، المطبعة الحيدريّة، ١٣٨٤ هجرى قمرى.

٤٩- ورّام بن أبى فراس، مجموعة ورّام، قم، مكتبة الفقيه.